An Introduction to Group Dynamics

An Introduction to Group Dynamics

DONELSON R. FORSYTH

VIRGINIA COMMONWEALTH UNIVERSITY

With a Chapter by Thomas V. McGovern
Virginia Commonwealth University

BROOKS/COLE PUBLISHING COMPANY
MONTEREY, CALIFORNIA

To Nancy Louise

Consulting Editor:
Lawrence S. Wrightsman
University of Kansas

Brooks/Cole Publishing Company
A Division of Wadsworth, Inc.

Printed in the United States of America
10 9 8 7 6 5 4 3 2 1

Library of Congress Cataloging in Publication Data

Forsyth, Donelson R., 1953-
  An introduction to group dynamics.

  Bibliography: p.
  Includes index.
  1. Social groups. I. Title.
HM131.F685 1983   302.3   82-12783
ISBN 0-534-01225-6

Subject Editor: *Claire Verduin*
Manuscript Editor: *Suzanne Lipsett*
Production Editor: *Jane Stanley*
Interior Design: *Katherine Minerva*
Cover Design: *Pamela J. Wilson*
Art Co-ordinator: *Rebecca Ann Tait*
Illustrations: *Brenda Booth*
Typesetting: *Graphic Typesetting Service, Inc.,*
Los Angeles, California

Preface

If I had to summarize the purpose of this book in a single statement, it would be *to review theory and research dealing with group processes while demonstrating the relevance of this work in applied settings.* Social scientists in such fields as anthropology, sociology, and psychology have long been interested in the study of groups, and their continued efforts have resulted in the generation of a substantial body of empirically based knowledge. Through the years we have discovered that groups can be many things—fascinating, frightening, complicated, frustrating, provocative, and uninvolving—but whatever their character, groups are always fundamentally relevant to a fuller understanding of social behavior.

A preface is an appropriate place to set forth assumptions and perspectives as well as to admit biases and limitations, so I will begin by explaining my general approach to group processes. *Balance* is a key word, for throughout *An Introduction to Group Dynamics* I have sought to maintain a balanced stance when presenting ideas, evidence, and viewpoints. Although a certain amount of personal bias is perhaps inevitable, from the first page to the last I worked to balance the following aspects of the material:

1. *Theory with research.* Conceptual analyses of group processes are reviewed in depth, but empirical studies that highlight important principles derived from relevant theory are cited to show how theoretical systems are revised through research.
2. *Theory with application.* Group dynamics appeals both to the theoretically-minded basic research scientist and the applications-oriented group practioner. Although a strong empirical approach is stressed, applications are introduced throughout, and the final three chapters are devoted to studies of groups in industrial, organizational, educational, judiciary, athletic, and therapeutic contexts.

3. *Traditional with contemporary topics.* Classic analyses of groups (leadership, reactions to deviancy, determinants of group performance) are integrated with contemporary topics (deindividuation, groupthink) to achieve an up-to-date yet historically grounded overview of theory and research dealing with groups.

4. *The psychological with the sociological viewpoint.* Studies of group dynamics are being conducted by researchers in a wide variety of fields, including anthropology, speech and communication, political science, business, education, and psychiatry, but the social-psychological viewpoint often predominates. Therefore, whenever possible the text integrates both psychological and sociological perspectives on social-psychological processes to achieve a comprehensive analysis of group behavior.

With respect to organizational aspects, while I tried to examine all aspects of group dynamics in the text, the phrase *an introduction to* in the title is there for a reason. Assuming that this book will be used in a basic course in groups, I was primarily concerned with surveying the major areas in sufficient depth to enable the reader to grasp the essentials. This emphasis on seminal issues sometimes meant that less central, though nonetheless interesting, topics were slighted, but in all instances I concentrated on subjects that have consistently been the focus of theory and research. Also, wherever more detailed analyses are available in major review articles or books, I have referred to these sources and have urged the reader to follow up the text's discussion with the supplementary readings.

Each chapter was written to stand as a single unit; thus, instructors who prefer a sequence of topics other than that reflected in the Contents can assign chapters in a varying order. Also, each chapter consists of a number of independent subsections that examine single aspects of the area but form an integral component of the overall chapter. These subsections were designed to be easily readable in a single sitting. Finally, examples are cited throughout the discussion to help the reader perceive the relevance of the material to everyday situations, and detailed analyses of special topics are included to heighten interest and motivation levels. Every attempt has been made to create a textbook that "teaches" group dynamics, rather than one that simply exposes the student to basic principles and research findings.

Any book, and especially one that examines groups, results from the collective efforts of many individuals who deserve special thanks. Although I alone am responsible for the final contents of the text, Professor Lawrence Wrightsman of the University of Kansas, the consulting editor on the project, vastly improved the final product by sharing his expertise, knowledge, and enthusiasm with me. Professor William Ray Pope of Mary Washington College read virtually the entire manuscript and provided both helpful comments concerning weaknesses and encouragement for strengths. Additional helpful comments were provided by Philip Brickman, of the University of Michigan at Ann Arbor, Rick Crandall, Francis Dane of the State University of New York, Oswego, Sara B. Kiesler, of Carnegie-Mellon University, Charles E. Miller, of Northern Illinois University, and John P. Wilson of Cleveland State University. I would also like to thank Richard Kishur, Nancy Forsyth, and Travis Forsyth for their valuable help, as well as the many students who read, or listened to lectures derived from, earlier drafts of the manuscript. I owe a special debt of gratitude to my technical consultant, Mrs. Elizabeth Martin, who helped with every phase of the project from preparing preliminary chapters, contacting publishers, and providing encouragement during the "slow" periods, to pointing out inaccuracies and ambiguities, suggesting relevant examples, and preparing the final copy. Judy Anderson's help with some last minute rush work also proved indispensible, as did the support of the Brooks/Cole editorial staff. Thanks also go to my colleague Tom McGovern for his contribution of Chapter 16.

I would also like to thank the many people who contributed to my intellectual development. First and foremost, I thank Barry Schlenker, my advisor throughout graduate school and beyond, for his many contributions to my training and development. Thanks also to Marv Shaw, my "groups mentor," for giving me a firm foundation in research and theory on groups, and to Russ Clark for teaching me my first lessons in social psychology. Finally, I acknowledge my debt to the many theorists and researchers whose work has been my subject matter.

Donelson R. Forsyth

Contents

Part Two: Basic Group Processes   47

3
FORMING: BECOMING A GROUP   48

4
STORMING: CONFLICT IN GROUPS   78

5

NORMING: THE DEVELOPMENT OF GROUP STRUCTURE   109

6

PERFORMING: WORKING TOGETHER IN GROUPS   140

Part Three: Social Influence Processes   171

7

POWER   172

10

THE ENVIRONMENT AND GROUP BEHAVIOR   273

Part Four: Problems in Groups   307

11

DEINDIVIDUATION   308

12

GROUPTHINK   339

Part Five: Applications   403

14
GROUPS IN ORGANIZATIONS AND INDUSTRY   404

PART
ONE

Orientation and Methods

The two chapters in this part introduce the study of groups by building a context for subsequent discussions, explorations, and understandings. In later sections of the book we will see how social scientists, intrigued by the complexities of human interaction in groups, have gained an understanding of why groups come into being, how they evolve, what factors influence their underlying processes, and how they sometimes go astray. However, before we can partake of the fruits of these theoretical and empirical efforts, we must first deal with some basic questions about groups and the methods used to study them. Therefore, in Chapter 1 we begin by clarifying the meaning of the word group and describing the various approaches taken by social scientists who investigate groups. Chapter 2 concludes this brief introduction by comparing several different kinds of research strategies that can be applied to groups.

1

An Introduction to the Study of Groups

Daniel Defoe's character Robinson Crusoe was lucky. Cast up on the shore of a tropical island, he alone had survived the wreck of his ship. The climate of the island was comfortable, the food plentiful, and the animals peaceful. He had seed for crops, tools for working, weapons to protect himself, and clothes to cover himself. But Robinson Crusoe was alone. Although he gave thanks for his good fortune in being saved from the sea, he cursed his solitary life, complaining, "I am cast upon a horrible, desolate island; void of all hope of recovery. I am singled out and separated, as it were, from all the world, to be miserable. I am divided from mankind, a solitary; one banished from human society. I have no soul to speak to or to relieve me" (Defoe, 1908, p. 51). The lucky Robinson Crusoe did not feel very lucky, for he was no longer a member of any human group.

Unlike the unfortunate Crusoe, most of us live out our lives in the midst of groups. People perform so many activities in groups—working, playing, worshiping, learning, eating, traveling, and even sleeping—that it sometimes seems as if groups are everywhere, doing just about anything. To grasp the central role that groups play in social life, imagine a list of everything you do in a typical day from the moment you wake up to the moment you fall asleep. Next, delete from your list all the activities you perform with groups of people and see what is left. Although the length of such a list varies greatly among individuals, chances are that your solitary activities are not very numerous. To rephrase a well-worn saying, human beings are group-oriented animals.

The Nature of Groups

Undeniably, groups occupy a central position in the scheme of social life, but in some respects their pervasiveness is the very factor that prevents us from fully understanding them. In living most of our lives surrounded by groups, in the midst of groups, trying to get into groups, and trying to get out of groups, we can become so accustomed to them that their influence on our behavior goes unnoticed. Therefore, to gain a fresh perspective on groups, let us begin with three examples of individuals surviving, working, and dying in groups.

Examples

THE MOUNTAIN

A Fairchild F-227 was on a chartered flight from Uruguay to Chile when it crashed in the Andes. Although the sky was clear, the pilot had miscalculated his position, and rather than descending for his final landing approach, he was actually flying into an extinct volcano, Tinguiririca. On impact, both wings and the tail section sheared off the airplane's fuselage, which plummeted down the side of the mountain at a speed exceeding 200 miles per hour. When it came to rest, it lay in the snow on the side of a 12,000-foot mountain, surrounded on three sides by other mountain peaks.

None of the plane's crew lived long after the crash; only the passengers survived. This group was composed of an amateur rugby team—the Old Christians—and the teammates' families and friends, who were accompanying them to a match in Santiago, Chile. Thirty-two of the 40 passengers survived the initial crash, only to find themselves trapped in the subzero temperatures of the Andes in winter, with some wine and candy their only supplies and the remnants of the fuselage, with a gaping hole where the tail section had been, their only shelter.

Despite the near hopelessness of their situation, in the next few days the group members began to work to improve their chances of survival. Marcelo Perez, the captain of the rugby team, divided the survivors into teams and gave them specific tasks to perform. These included melting snow for drinking water, looking after the needs of the injured, and cleaning the tiny cabin of the plane, which offered their only complete protection from the elements. Marcelo himself took charge of distributing the meager supplies. Although the survivors tried to work together as much as possible, as time wore on disagreements arose that split the group apart. The group argued constantly over the likelihood of a rescue, with some individuals insisting that searchers would soon find them while others maintained that they must try to climb down from the mountains. At night the cries of the injured were often answered with anger rather than pity, for the severely cramped sleeping arrangements created continual conflict. As the days passed without any sign of rescue, the survivors became increasingly withdrawn and irritable.

Three incidents turned the survivors into a group with the common if elusive goal of survival. First, they eventually realized they would have to begin eating meat from the frozen bodies of those who had already died. This decision was inevitable, but it took great group unity to overcome the revulsion and guilt each individual felt. Second, on the 17th day of their ordeal, an avalanche filled the cabin while the group slept, smothering with snow all those who could not extricate themselves. This further misfortune worked to intensify the interdependence of the boys within the group, who decided that escape from the mountain was the only solution. This final decision prompted them to organize a two-member team of "expeditionaries" who would go for help. Although the expeditionaries were granted special privileges, which included increased allotments of food and water, their control over the rest of the group was kept in check by a subgroup of three cousins, the only familial subgroup that still existed intact within the total group. Everyone else had lost their relatives and close friends in the crash or avalanche, and their previous leader, Marcelo, had died in the snow. The triumvirate of cousins took on much of the business of running the group's activities and planning the expedition.

By banding together, the group was able to train and provision two of their fittest members to make the trip down from the mountains. After walking for ten days and sleeping in the open at night, the two expeditionaries managed to reach a small farm on the edge of the great mountain range. Their sudden appearance after 70 days was followed by an air-rescue operation that lifted the remaining

14 from their "home" in the Andes. Those who had managed to stay alive later pointed out "that it was their combined efforts which saved their lives" (Read, 1974, p. 310).

THE DECISION

At first glance, it seemed like a straightforward question that required a straightforward answer. The year was 1961, relations between Cuba and the United States had reached a new low, and the Central Intelligence Agency of the United States had asked the obvious question: "Should the United States invade Cuba?" An ad hoc advisory committee, specially created by President John F. Kennedy to decide this question, was to consider the pros and cons and give the CIA its answer.

Unfortunately, the group gave the wrong answer. They put into effect a modified version of the CIA's plan, which involved landing a force of 1400 Cuban exiles—secretly trained by the CIA and armed with U. S. weapons—on Cuban soil. The committee members themselves chose the site for the landing: a small inlet on the southern side of Cuba called Bahía de Cochinos—the Bay of Pigs. The force was to quickly establish a beachhead and then strike at will against strategic military installations on Cuba. The general population, realizing that the time for their liberation from Castro's domination had come, would rise up in revolution. Castro would be ousted, and a leader more favorable toward the United States would be installed in his place.

But on April 17, 1961—the day of the Bay of Pigs invasion—little went according to the CIA's carefully constructed plan. The Cuban air force, which the planners had assumed to be completely ineffectual, shot down several of the disguised American bombers providing air support, sank ammunition freighters trying to reach the beachhead, and attacked the land forces. The committee had grossly underestimated the Cuban army as well, for they had assumed it to be disorganized, ill-equipped, and small. Unfortunately, by the next day 200 of the landing-force troops had been killed, and eventually the remaining 1200 were captured. The attack was a complete disaster; it probably could not have turned out any worse if the designers had deliberately planned a failure.

What had gone wrong? How could the committee have overlooked so many obvious problems? Although the group members could be accused of incompetence, their credentials were impressive (Janis, 1972; Sorensen, 1966). The committee's leader, John F. Kennedy, had a complete and unassailable position of power among the members, for he was the leader not only of this group but also of the entire country. The other committee members boasted years of experience in making careful, monumentally important governmental decisions, and various warfare specialists from the CIA and the military attended all the meetings. All in all, the group members should have combined to form a highly trained, well-informed team capable of analyzing the complexities involved and making a good decision.

Furthermore, the members of the committee seemed to work well with one another. Although the group was newly formed (Kennedy had been in office for only a few days before facing the decision on the invasion), a strong feeling of mutual respect had already welded the group into a highly cohesive unit. The CIA and military representatives were slightly removed from the inner circle, but the members of the committee were impressed by each other's competence. In fact, their highly positive perceptions of the group had led many of the members to assume that their decision-making processes would prove infallible. They further assumed that the small problems evident in the plans—such as the low morale of the invaders, a lack of secrecy that would undermine the element of surprise, the small size of the attack force, and the moral questions concerning the right of the United States to invade the small neighboring country—could be brushed aside with little debate. Later descriptions of the meetings (Schlesinger, 1965) documented the air of confidence that permeated the group and the feeling among the discussants that they should not oppose the wishes of the majority. Thus, although some members privately questioned the invasion, they never expressed their doubts publicly. The president himself promoted this false sense of agreement by continually shifting the discussion in directions favorable to the invasion, glossing over points of dissent and disagreement. The result: the committee overlooked critical details that proved fatal to its plans as it rushed headlong toward its unenviable place in history.

THE LEADER

Jim Jones was a leader. Ordained as a minister in the Christian Church (Disciples of Christ) in the early 1960s, he built his California-based church into a massive organization of completely dedicated believers. Described as a dynamic, entrancing speaker who could hold an audience in rapt attention, Jones preached an ideology based on a mixture of Christianity and Marxism. Much of his message emphasized the importance of interracial harmony, a cause Jones furthered through his own participation in the civil rights movement and his adoption of seven children, all of different races. In 1963 he formed his own church, the People's Temple Full Gospel Church. His persuasiveness influenced many, and his message reached out to the rich and poor, young and old, and educated and uneducated. The membership soon swelled to 8000, all united in their acceptance of Jones's political, religious, and social teachings.

For some time the People's Temple was accepted as a particularly civic-minded and altruistic religious organization that benefited many. With time, however, stories of the bizarre and brutal rites that characterized the church services began to surface. Ex-members claimed that at some meetings those who had displeased Jones were severely beaten before the whole congregation, with microphones being used to amplify the victims' screams. Apparently, Jones, who insisted on being called Father, demanded absolute dedication from his followers and ruled over them with an iron hand. He frequently made sexual demands of both the male and female church-goers, and required large monetary donations from even the most financially destitute. One man, for example, worked two jobs—one by day, one by night—so he could donate $2000 a month to the church. His reward was to be beaten before the congregation when he fell asleep during an all-night prayer meeting. Many members even signed over all their property to the church, and one couple—after Jones demanded it—actually turned over their 6-year-old son.

One particularly macabre story, which had far deeper implications than anyone realized at the time, concerned Jones's preoccupation with suicide. During some services, Jones would use a sacramental wine. However, after the entire congregation had finished the wine, Jones would announce that the wine had contained poison and that all would be dead within half an hour. Jones even planted confederates in the audience who simulated collapse, complete with stage blood flowing from their mouths. After watching his followers suffer, thinking that they would soon be dead, Jones announced that he had merely been testing their faith in him. Through repetition of this ceremony, the thought of suicide, so alien to most people, became commonplace and even accepted by the church members.

To escape the media's continuing "attacks" which labeled the group a cult, and also to placate his growing fear of persecution at the hands of the government, Jones moved the group to the South American country of Guyana. In the relative isolation of the jungle, Jones established Jonestown, his vision of a utopian community. Although press releases described the settlement as an ideal community, rumors once more began circulating; these suggested that Jonestown was more like a prison than a utopia. Once church members were convinced to migrate to Guyana, Jones would confiscate their passports and force them to work long hours in the fields. Armed guards were posted to prevent desertion, and meals were grossly inadequate. In addition, the mock mass suicide rituals, which Jones came to call the "White Night," were practiced repeatedly at Jonestown.

Jones's power came to an abrupt end when a delegation headed by congressional representative Leo Ryan was attacked at a small airstrip near Jonestown. Although several members of the party escaped serious harm, five people were killed, including Ryan himself. When the assassins returned to tell Jones of their attack, Jones apparently realized that the incident would spur a full investigation of his church, and so he ordered the "White Night." This night, however, was no rehearsal. Over a loud-speaker system Jones explained the need for the "revolutionary suicide of the faithful," and ordered his followers to take their own lives. Armed guards prevented all but a few from escaping, and during the ceremony Jones continued to instruct the members to accept their deaths with dignity. Large vats of grape-flavored poison were mixed, and the cyanide was administered to everyone, from infants to adults. The liquid was forced on any who resisted.

When authorities reached the settlement the next day they were met by a scene of unbelievable ghastliness. On Jones's orders, whole families had taken the poison and died side by side. Although initial counts estimated the deat at nearly 500 and fostered hopes that as many as 400 had escaped into the jungle, the team that removed the bodies for transportation back to the United States discovered that the original estimate had been too small. Many children's bodies had gone uncounted, since they lay hidden under their parents' bodies. The final count came to more than 900, and included Jones himself. His body was found near the "throne" from which he had directed the mass suicide. Over the chair remained the motto "Those who do not remember the past are condemned to repeat it." (See Krause, 1978, for a detailed description of the development and demise of this cult.)

A Definition

The groups in our three examples seem to be as different from one another as they are similar. While all the groups had leaders, among the Andes survivors the leadership role developed slowly, in the presidential committee the leader was an elected official, and in People's Temple the leader established his power through illegitimate means. Similarly, while all the groups had at least two members, the People's Temple boasted hundreds of members whereas fewer than 15 men composed the committee. Furthermore, in all the groups the interactions of group members followed a stable pattern, but in one group the norms underlying these interactions were rigidly formalized whereas in the other two they remained both informal and only implicitly recognized. Given these differences, the question arises "Can we accurately call all three of these social collectives *groups?*"

To settle this issue we must define what we mean by the term **group**—a task more complicated than it may seem. Many group dynamicists have offered what they believe to be the best definition of the concept, but the sampling of definitions shown in the box reveals that no single approach has been accepted by all. Yet, while different theorists highlight different aspects of groups in their analyses— such as relations to one another, face-to-face communication, influence, status, and roles—many theorists emphasize **social interaction** in their definitions. We understand intuitively that three people seated in separate rooms with no means of communication can hardly be considered a social group, for their isolation prevents interaction. If, however, we create the potential for interaction by letting at least one person influence, and be influenced by, the others, then these three individuals can be considered a rudimentary group. By emphasizing the importance of social interaction among people, we can define a **group** as two or more individuals who influence one another through social interaction.

Before considering the general characteristics of groups, we should emphasize several aspects of this definition. First, as with most definitions, the choice of central concepts—in this case, interaction—is a fairly arbitrary one; many other concepts

---

A SAMPLING OF DEFINITIONS OF THE TERM *GROUP*

A group is a collection of individuals who have relations to one another that make them interdependent to some significant degree [Cartwright & Zander, 1968, p. 46].

We mean by a group a number of persons who communicate with one another often over a span of time, and who are few enough so that each person is able to communicate with all the others, not at second hand, through other people, but face-to-face [Homans, 1950, p. 1].

Two or more persons who are interacting with one another in such a manner that each person influences and is influenced by each other person [Shaw, 1981, p. 454].

A group is a social unit which consists of a number of individuals who stand in (more or less) definite status and role relationships to one another and which possess a set of values or norms of its own regulating the behavior of individual members, at least in matters of consequence to the group [Sherif & Sherif, 1956, p. 144].

A group is a number of people in interaction with one another, and it is this interaction process that distinguishes the group from an aggregate [Bonner, 1959, p. 4].

For a collection of individuals to be considered a group there must be some *interaction* [Hare, 1976, p. 4].

are plausible alternatives. Second, by treating aggregates containing only two members as groups, the definition intentionally overlooks some of the uniqueness of dyads. Third, by failing to specify an upper limit in size, the definition suggests that such collectives as mobs, crowds, and such congregations as that of People's Temple are appropriate subjects of study by group dynamicists.

Characteristics

Although the definition of *cow* is "the mature female of domestic cattle, genus *Bos*" (Webster, 1976, p. 421), a person who is thirsty for milk would be better off knowing the characteristics of the cow—four legs, tail, pendant udder, cud-chewing—than the definition. Similarly, knowing the definition of a group will not be of much value without knowledge of the common characteristics of groups. Although many group features could be noted (see, for example, Bogardus, 1954; Borgatta, Cottrell, & Myer, 1956; DeLamater, 1974; Hare, 1976), we shall limit our discussion to several of the more important characteristics of groups.

INTERACTION

If you were to observe a group of people, you would probably notice first the many ways in which the members influenced each other's behavior. Depending on the group, the members might be talking among themselves, telling stories, exchanging occasional smiles, or (especially in children's groups) even pushing each other down. Regardless of the group activity, these patterns of mutual influence can usually be described as interaction. Indeed, many theorists have underscored the importance of interaction (for example, Bonner, 1959; Homans, 1950; Stogdill, 1959) to conclude that in groups the behavior of every group member can potentially affect all the other members of the group. Although interaction with other members may be discontinuous or short-lived, the interaction that does occur—physical, verbal, nonverbal, emotional, and so on—is a key feature of group life.

STRUCTURE

All but the most ephemeral groups develop structure—a stable pattern of relationships among members. Although a wide variety of terms can be used to describe such structures, three of the most useful are roles, norms, and intermember relations. **Roles,** of course, are the behaviors expected of persons who occupy given positions in the group. **Norms** are the rules that identify and describe appropriate behaviors. Lastly, **intermember relations** can be based on many factors—such as authority, attraction, and communication—but all are similar in that they link members to one another. For example, one aspect of the structure of Kennedy's advisory committee can be seen in the roles that the group members adopted during the deliberations; some individuals became "supporters," some "defenders," some "nontalkers," and very few became "critics." Additionally, norms encouraging agreement developed within the group, and these implicit rules partly explain why no one felt comfortable about challenging the faulty plan. Finally, stable relationships developed among all members, and status, communications, and attraction patterns therefore routinized the group's reactions.

GOALS

Groups usually *exist for a reason.* Although the goals of the group may be intrinsic to the group process itself—as with a party, where the goal of the gathering is simply to have fun—in many other instances people join groups in order to achieve extrinsic goals that they would be unable to achieve individually. The sharing of common goals is one of the strongest unifying factors within groups, and shared goals also motivate the individual group members to behave in ways that result in the group's successful goal completion.

GROUPNESS

Donald T. Campbell (1958a) uses the word **entitativity** to describe the extent to which something seems to be an entity—that is, a single, unified object. He points out that while most people would readily agree that certain common objects—chairs, tables, buildings, or cars—are entities, collections of human beings sometimes are but sometimes aren't perceived to be unified entities. For example, from one perspective the spectators at a football game may seem to be a disorganized mass of individuals who happen to be in the same place at the same time and not really a group at all. But at another level the tendency for the spectators to shout the same cheer, to express similar emotions, and to move together gives the fans the appearance of entitativity. According to Campbell, one of the features of all

---

PERCEIVING GROUPS

Assume for a moment that you must locate a group and record its characteristics as part of a class assignment. You go to the library and relax in a chair with a good view of four students seated at the same table. You watch these people read silently to themselves for a while, but as the minutes go by a question begins to disturb you: Are these people really a group? Perhaps they are actually just four individuals seated at the same table, an aggregate of strangers who don't really fit the definition of group.

According to Donald T. Campbell (1958a), your misgivings stem from the absence of certain cues that can be taken as evidence of groupness (or entitativity). Drawing on the work of early psychologists who wondered how the human mind decides whether something perceived is a *Gestalt*— a unified system of interrelated parts— or a random collection of unrelated elements (Kohler, 1947; Wertheimer, 1938), Campbell emphasizes the impact of three basic principles of organization on our perceptions of groups. These organizing principles are

1. *common fate*—the extent to which individuals in the aggregate seem to experience the same, or interrelated, outcomes;
2. *similarity*—the extent to which the individuals display the same behaviors or resemble one another; and
3. *proximity*—the distance among individuals in the aggregate.

Applied to the four individuals seated at the same table, the principle of common fate predicts that the degree of groupness you attribute to the cluster would increase if, for example, all the members got up and left the room together or began laughing together. Your confidence that this cluster was a "real" group would also be bolstered if you noticed that all four read from the same textbook or wore the same Greek organization shirt. Finally, if the members moved to reduce the distance among them, then you would become even more certain that you were watching a group.

groups is entitativity, or perceived groupness: people perceive groups to be single, unified wholes rather than simply clusters of people who happen to be sitting close to one another.

Although perceived groupness is an obvious feature of most groups, its importance should not be overlooked. For example, the impact of the perception of entitativity was documented in one study that compared the responses of females who thought they were members of a group to those who thought they were behaving in an individualistic situation (Zander, Stotland, & Wolfe, 1960). Because the women were required to work on an experimental task in separate testing cubicles, the researchers assumed that their perceptions of entitativity would be low—they wouldn't feel like members of a group. Half the women, however, were repeatedly told that the researchers believed they were a group rather than just an aggregate of individuals. As predicted, these women attributed groupness to their aggregate, and in consequence rated themselves more negatively after group failure rather than success. The self-evaluations of members of low-entitativity aggregates were uninfluenced by the "group's" outcome.

DYNAMIC INTERDEPENDENCY

The study of the behavior of groups is called **group dynamics** for a good reason, for groups tend to be active, energized, vibrant, and changing. This strong and pervasive emphasis on the term *dynamic* in the study of group behavior implies many things about groups and their study, including the existence of (1) interdependent group phenomena; (2) developmental processes that begin with a conglomeration of individuals but end with the formation of a group; (3) changes in groups over time; and (4) sequences of stability, disruption, and dissolution.

The Nature of Group Dynamics

A Definition

Kurt Lewin (1943, 1948, 1951) is generally given the credit for coining and popularizing the term *group dynamics*. Although Lewin used the label to refer to what happened in group situations, the more important usage of the term—at least in the present context—is in reference to the *study* of these processes. Two of the most prolific researchers in the field, Dorwin Cartwright and Alvin Zander, later supplied a much more formal definition of the area of group dynamics, calling it a *"field of inquiry dedicated to advancing knowledge about the nature of groups, the laws of their development, and their interrelations with individuals, other groups, and larger institutions"* (1968, p. 7, emphasis added).

Cartwright and Zander also pointed out what group dynamics is *not*. It is not, for example, a therapeutic perspective holding that psychological well-being can be ensured through participation in small groups guided by a skilled leader/therapist. Nor is it the communication of certain rules or guidelines concerning interpersonal relations and enabling individuals to develop the skills needed for smooth and satisfying social interactions. Finally, *group dynamics* does not refer to a loose collection of maxims concerning how groups *should* be organized—emphasizing, for example, such niceties as equal participation by all group members, democratic leadership, and high levels of intragroup communication to ensure group member

---

KURT LEWIN (1890–1947)

Kurt Lewin's empirical and theoretical efforts were instrumental in sparking widespread interest in group dynamics. Born in Poland in 1890, Lewin studied and taught in Freiberg, Munich, and Berlin before moving to the United States in 1933. For the next decade he taught at the Child Welfare Research Station at the University of Iowa and refined *field theory*, his psychological theory of human behavior. Throughout this period his emphasis on behavior in groups increased, and in 1945 he established the Research Center for Group Dynamics at Massachusetts Institute of Technology. At this center, which was later moved to the Institute for Social Research at the Uni-

versity of Michigan, Lewin continued to study the consequences of interdependence among group members. During his scientific career he and his colleagues examined leadership climates, industrial productivity, ways to reduce prejudice, and the influence of groups on attitudes, all within the general field-theory framework. Although Lewin died unexpectedly of a heart attack just as group dynamics was beginning to develop more fully, his students and colleagues continue to carry on the Lewinian tradition in their theory, research, and applications (Lippitt, 1947; Marrow, 1969; Schellenberg, 1978).

---

satisfaction. Rather, group dynamics is an attempt to subject the many aspects of groups to scientific analysis through the construction of theories concerning groups and the rigorous testing of the adequacy of these theories through empirical research.

Characteristics

Although you may have formed the impression that group dynamics is a well-formed, highly integrated framework for understanding groups, group dynamics is in reality more of an "approach" within many different branches of the social sciences rather than a unified discipline. To a large degree, this lack of unity is the result of the newness of the group-dynamics perspective relative to other sciences, such as physics and chemistry. In addition, the current status of group dynamics stems from its many unique characteristics, which, if discussed in more detail, will clarify this growing field of study.

A HOLISTIC APPROACH

Although early Gestalt psychologists (Kohler, 1947; Wertheimer, 1938) were more concerned with perception and learning than groups, Lewin was their student and applied many of their Gestalt concepts to the study of groups (Lewin, 1951). In a group context, this holistic perspective argues that a group must be examined as a *Gestalt*—that is, as a configuration that has, as a unified system, properties that cannot be fully understood by piecemeal examination. The dictum of the Gestalt approach, "the whole is greater than the sum of the parts," argues that groups cannot be understood by considering only the qualities and characteristics of each member. When individuals merge into a group something new is created and that new product itself must be the object of study.

The holistic perspective finds expression in both field theories and systems theories of group behavior. Lewin developed field theory around the idea that behavior must be considered to be a function of both the personal characteristics of the individual *and* the characteristics of the environment, an idea he summarized with the formula $B = f(P, E)$. In a group context, this formula implies that the behavior of the group member is determined by the interaction of his or her personal characteristics with environmental factors, which include features of the group, the group members, and the situation. All these factors, when considered as a totality, formed what Lewin called the **lifespace.** Lewin further postulated that group dynamicists should (1) start at the group level and work downward to the individual level, (2) focus on the variables currently present in the lifespace rather than on historical factors important in the group's past, and (3) graphically represent the forces present in a group situation.

Although few studies directly tested field theory, the approach did much to ensure the holistic nature of group dynamics. First, field theory pointed to the interrelatedness of group phenomena and the inescapable conclusion that changes in one aspect of a group will necessarily lead to changes in other group features. Second, while emphasizing the complexity of groups, field theory argued that their dynamics could be understood if researchers were careful not to forget the integrative assumption of $B = f(P, E)$. Third, Lewin's reliance upon graphs and figures to represent group forces helped clarify such concepts as cohesiveness and conflict over group goals (for example, Festinger, 1950; French, 1941).

In recent years many of the emphases of Gestalt psychology and field theory have been synthesized within general systems theory (for example, J. G. Miller, 1978). Although systems theory draws on many different sources, most definitions of **systems** are strikingly similar to the previously discussed definitions of groups. For example, one theorist (J. G. Miller, 1978) defines a system as

> a set of interacting units with relationships among them. The word "set" implies that the units have some common properties. These common properties are essential if the units are to interact or have relationships. The state of each unit is constrained by, conditioned by, or dependent on the state of other units. The units are coupled. Moreover, there is at least one measure of the sum of its units which is larger than the sum of that measure of its units [p. 16].

Thus a group—as a system—receives inputs from the environment, processes this information through internal communication, and then outputs its products. Groups are recognized as being capable of formulating goals and working towards these goals through united action, and group members are responsive to environmental feedback concerning the efficacy of their actions. The communication of information—a key concept in systems theory—similarly plays a central role in groups that must analyze inputs, convey data to members, and formulate decisions regarding group action. Indeed, larger groups may be built upon a number of smaller subsystems, all of which are integrated into an overall Gestalt. In sum, the concepts of systems theory—input, output, feedback, subsystems, and communications—all are applicable to groups.

INTERDISCIPLINARY CHARACTER

The influence of groups is widespread. For example, researchers who prefer to study individuals may find themselves wondering what impact group participation will have on the individual's cognitions, attitudes, and behavior. Those who study organizations may find that these larger social entities may actually depend upon the dynamics of small subgroups within the organization, and therefore be forced to look more closely at small-group processes. Indeed, social scientists examining such global issues as the development and maintenance of culture may find themselves turning their attention toward small groups as the unit of cultural transmission.

Although the core of group-dynamics theory and research is heavily social psychological, the relevance of groups to topics studied in many academic and applied disciplines gives group dynamics an interdisciplinary character. To convey a sense of this interdisciplinary breadth, consider the fields listed in Table 1-1. Beginning first with the more academic disciplines, we see that theory and research dealing with groups are relevant to nearly all the social sciences. To oversimplify the complexities of these various fields, psychology tends to focus on the behavior of individuals in groups. Sociology, in contrast, focuses more on the group and its relation to society. Cultural anthropology finds that group processes are relevant to understanding many of the common features of various societies; political scientists examine the principles of group relations and leadership; and speech/communication researchers focus more specifically on the communication relations in groups. Although the overall aims of these disciplines may be quite different, all must consider groups.

Groups are also relevant to many applied areas, as Table 1-1 shows. The study of groups in the work setting has long occupied business-oriented researchers concerned with the effective organization of people. Although early discussions of

TABLE 1-1. Topics in group dynamics studied in various disciplines

Discipline	Some relevant topics
Psychology	Social facilitation; problem solving; attitude change; perceptions of others; social comparison
Sociology	Coalition formation; influence of norms on behavior; role relations; deviance
Anthropology	Groups in cross-cultural contexts; societal change; groups based on sex, age, race
Political science	Leadership; intergroup relations; political influence; power
Speech and communication	Information transmission in groups; problems in communication; communication networks
Business and industry	Motivation; productivity; improving organizational effectiveness; structuring goals
Social work	Improving adjustment through group participation; family counseling
Education	Classroom groups; team teaching; class composition and educational outcomes
Clinical/counseling psychology	Therapeutic change through group counseling, sensitivity training, encounter
Criminal justice	Organization of law enforcement agencies; gangs; jury deliberations; patrol-team effectiveness
Sports and recreation	Team performance; effects of victory and failure; cohesion and performance

business administration and personnel management tended to overlook the importance of groups, the 1930s witnessed a tremendous growth in management-oriented group research (for example, Barnard, 1938; Mayo, 1933). People in organizations ranging from businesses to hospitals to the armed forces began to take notice of the critical role interpersonal relations played in their own organizations, and soon principles of group behavior became an integral part of most philosophies of effective administrative practices.

Other professions have both influenced and have been influenced by group work. Social workers frequently found themselves dealing with such groups as social clubs, gangs, neighborhoods, and family clusters, and an awareness of group processes helped crystalize their understanding of group life. Educators were also influenced by group research, as were many of the medical fields that dealt with patients on a group basis. Although this listing of disciplines is far from inclusive, it does convey the idea that the study of groups is not limited to any one field. As A. Paul Hare, the compiler of a useful handbook of group research (Hare, 1976) and his colleagues once noted, "This field of research does not 'belong' to any one of the recognized social sciences alone. It is the common property of all" (Hare, Borgatta, & Bales, 1955, p. vi).

DIVERSE METHODS OF RESEARCH

A host of empirical procedures has been used to further our understanding of group processes. In the next chapter four of the more frequently used methods—case study, observation, self-report, and experimentation—are examined in detail, but this brief list does little to suggest the varieties of methods employed. Some researchers, for example, prefer to examine closely group processes and then perform a qualitative analysis of their observations, while other researchers insist upon quantitative measurement methods and elaborate experimental controls. Some researchers prefer to conduct their studies in field situations using naturally occurring groups, while others bring groups into the laboratory or even create ad hoc groups for the research. Some exploratory studies of groups are undertaken by researchers who have no clear idea of what results to expect, while other research is designed to test hypotheses carefully derived from a specific theory. Some researchers have studied group phenomena by asking volunteers to role-play group members, while still others have simulated group interaction with computers. The use of these diverse methods has led to the investigation of many different aspects of groups, but it has also led to many disagreements among researchers who have refused to accept the methods of others.

ACTION-ORIENTED RESEARCH

In most sciences a line is drawn between basic and applied research. Basic research (sometimes called pure research) examines "basic" theoretical questions in an attempt to acquire more knowledge about a particular subject. Applied research, in contrast, argues that usefulness is the supremely important quality of research, and accruing data about esoteric, inapplicable theories is often viewed as misplaced effort. It may help to exaggerate the differences between these two perspectives: the basic scientist assumes that the best way to proceed is through attention to theory and theory-related research—that is, by seeking knowledge for its own sake. The applied scientist focuses on a specific problem and performs research aimed at providing an answer to this question—that is, by seeking knowledge as a means to an end.

Group dynamics, like many social sciences, does not easily fit either of these classifications. Although some researchers identify themselves as basic scientists, their findings can be applied to further our understanding of everyday problems of interpersonal relations. Moreover, practitioners who work with groups but have no interest in generating theoretically elegant conceptualizations nevertheless provide theoretically minded group dynamicists with much raw material for theory construction. Overall, research in group dynamics can usually be called **action research**—Lewin's term for the use of the scientific method in solving research questions that have significant social value. Lewin argued for the intertwining of basic and applied research, for he firmly believed that there "is no hope of creating a better world without a deeper scientific insight into the function of leadership and culture, and of other essentials of group life" (Lewin, 1943, p. 113). To achieve this goal, he assured practitioners that in many instances "there is nothing so practical as a good theory" (Lewin, 1951, p. 169), while charging basic researchers with the task of developing theories that can be applied to important social problems (Cartwright, 1978).

Basic Issues

Although the preceding section alludes to many of the fundamental characteristics of group dynamics, the listing only hints at the intricacies of this fascinating discipline: the divergent theoretical and empirical perspectives endorsed by its practitioners, the issues they consider important, the disagreements that enliven their communications, and the goals they seek. Of course, these aspects of the field will become clearer as we move through the book, but several critically important issues worth noting at the outset are examined below.

AN INDIVIDUAL OR GROUP FOCUS?

Ivan Steiner, in an insightful analysis of the historical roots of group dynamics, describes two contrasting approaches (Steiner, 1974). The first perspective, which Steiner labels the *individualistic orientation,* focuses on the individual in the group. In order to explain the behavior of the person, a researcher usually hypothesizes some type of internal mediating mechanism—such as an attitude, a cognition, or a personality trait—and then attempts to verify the importance of the postulated internal state. Steiner compares this perspective with what he calls a *groupy approach* that "also maintains that one must observe the individual's behavior and relate it to other events. But the individual is presumed to be an element in a larger system, a group, organization, or society. And what he does is presumed to reflect the state of the larger system and the events occurring in it" (p. 96). Although these two perspectives are not inherently incompatible, they quite frequently lead to conflicting conclusions about what aspects of groups should be studied and what methods should be used. Sociological researchers tend to take the group-oriented perspective, while psychological researchers favor the individualistic orientation.

Steiner traces the origins of this divergence in perspective back to the very beginnings of both psychology and sociology. In the late 1800s Emile Durkheim (1964, 1966) was trying to establish a science of sociology grounded in data rather than speculation by proposing that society is based on a fundamental solidarity among people. This solidarity is derived from interpersonal relations among members of **primary groups**—that is, small groups of people characterized by face-to-face interaction, interdependency, and strong group identification. Families, children's play groups, sets of emotionally close peers, and groups of business colleagues are examples of primary groups. Durkheim argued that these small groups were the building blocks of society, and worked upward from this level to an analysis of social systems in general.

Like the early crowd psychologists (for example, Le Bon, 1895), Durkheim was fascinated by the extent to which large groups of people sometimes acted with a "single mind." Durkheim felt that such groups, rather than being merely collections of individuals in a fixed pattern of relationships with one another, were linked together by some unifying force that went beyond any single individual. This force was so strong in some groups that the will of the individual could be completely dominated by the will of the group, which Durkheim called the **groupmind** or *collective conscious*.

Psychologists interested in group phenomena tended to reject the reality of such concepts as groupmind or collective conscious. Floyd A. Allport, the foremost representative of this perspective, argued that such terms as groupmind were unscientific, since they referred to phenomena that simply did not exist. In his 1924 text *Social Psychology,* he baldly stated "nervous systems are possessed by individuals; but there is no nervous system of the crowd" (p. 5), and "Only through social psychology as a science of the individual can we avoid the superficialities of the crowdmind and collective mind theories" (p. 8). Taking the individualistic perspective to the extreme, Allport also concluded that groups should never be studied by psychologists, since they did not exist as scientifically valid phenomena. Because Allport believed "the actions of all *are* nothing more than the sum of the actions of each taken separately" (p. 5), he felt that a full understanding of the behavior of individuals in groups could be achieved simply through studying the psychology of the group members. Groups, in a scientific sense, were not real entities.

Although Allport's reluctance to accept such dubious concepts as groupmind into social psychology helped to ensure the field's scientific status, his belief that groups could be completely understood from the individualistic perspective meant that—at least for psychologists—group processes and such concepts as norms, roles, leadership, and interpersonal communication were unscientific and therefore unimportant. Until the reality-of-groups question could be answered, many psychologists refused to study groups.

Fortunately for group dynamics, researchers eventually recognized that *group* was as scientific a concept as such individualistic notions as *mind, attitude,* and *value.* In addition, researchers such as Muzafer Sherif (1936) were able to demonstrate that a *social norm*—which was considered by Allport to be an unscientific reification—could be experimentally created, varied, and studied in a laboratory setting. Third, such theorists as Campbell (1958a) pointed out that groups become real when they possess the characteristics of entities. With his concept of entitativity

THE SOCIAL REALITY OF NORMS

In the late 1800s Emile Durkheim published the intriguing results of his study of differences in the suicide rates of different countries and different religious groups (1897/1966). Although he explored a range of possible explanations, his final conclusion suggested that the differential suicide rates stemmed from a relative lack of social structure in some groups. Although the idea of living in a society where few norms exist sometimes seems appealing, Durkheim concluded that normlessness, or *anomie,* causes stress, tension, and even suicide (Durkheim, 1897/1966).

Despite the exactitude of Durkheim's methods, some psychologically oriented theorists rejected his conclusions by maintaining that norms were mere fictions created by Durkheim to explain his findings, and that suicide could be better explained by considering individual characteristics and qualities. The debate over the usefulness of the concept of norms—and other group-oriented concepts—continued for a number of years, until Muzafer Sherif (1936) demonstrated that norms could be arbitrarily created in a laboratory setting. Using the autokinetic effect—the apparent movement of a stationary pinpoint of light in an otherwise completely darkened room—Sherif showed that groups of people judging how far the light moved eventually accepted a standard estimate in place of their own idiosyncratic judgments. This norm provided a frame of reference for responses in the ambiguous situation, and it continued to influence individuals' perceptions even when they later responded alone. In view of Sherif's findings, most theorists were forced to admit that the behavior of individuals in groups may be significantly influenced by unobservable, but potent, social forces such as norms.

he rejected the argument that groups must be labeled as either *real* or *unreal.* Instead, he concluded that all groups vary in amount of perceived groupness, depending upon the observer's perspective.

Although most would consider the reality-of-groups debate settled (Warriner, 1956), the different perspectives described by Steiner—the group versus the individual as the unit of analysis—have left a gap in group dynamics (Archibald, 1976; Cartwright, 1979; Newcomb, 1978; Pepitone, 1981; Stryker, 1977). Group dynamicists in psychology and sociology tend to ignore theory and research that originates in the other discipline, yet they continue to study the same basic phenomena. Unfortunately, a complete explanation of group behavior should be based on both approaches; thus such observers as Steiner (Cartwright, 1979; Pepitone, 1981; Stryker, 1977) favor the integration of these perspectives. Toward this end, throughout our discussions of groups we will try to strike a fair balance between group-oriented analyses and individualistic analyses. Although in some cases we may fall short of our goal of integration, by drawing from both perspectives we will increase the likelihood that we will achieve our primary goal: an understanding of groups.

GROUPS: GOOD OR BAD?

Divergent opinions exist concerning the value of groups. To some, membership in groups is highly rewarding, for it combines the pleasures of interpersonal relations with goal strivings. For others, however, groups are best avoided—they set the stage for interpersonal conflict while wasting time, turning out poor products, and yielding few benefits. Taking this latter view to make a point about negative biases in group research, social psychologist Christian J. Buys recently noted that groups seem to do more harm than good: for example, they make bad decisions, they refuse to help others in need, they engage in strange behavior, they riot, and they select inappropriate leaders (Buys, 1978a). Given these problems with groups, Buys whimsically suggests that all groups be eliminated since "humans would do better without groups" (p. 123).

Although Buys's suggestion is a satirical one, it does make the point that groups are neither all good nor all bad. While they are so "beneficial, if not essential, to humans" that "it seems nonsensical to search for alternatives to human groups," evidence indicates that groups sometimes have a negative effect on humans (Buys, 1978b, p. 568). Thus, while group membership leads to many positive consequences, we cannot ignore some of the more problematic aspects of groups. [As a footnote, Buys' work prompted a number of rejoinders by other group researchers. One group-produced paper suggested that Buys had misassigned responsibility for the problems; the authors argued that humans would do better without other humans rather than without any groups (Kravitz, Cohen, Martin, Sweeney, McCarty, Elliott, & Goldstein, 1978). Another paper proposed that groups would do better without humans (Anderson, 1978), while a third simply argued that groups would do better without social psychologists (Green & Mack, 1978).]

GROUPS OVER TIME: PHASES OR STAGES

Group dynamicists have long been cognizant of the capacity of groups to change over time. While some groups are so stable that their basic processes and structures remain unchanged for days, weeks, or even years, such groups are rarities. As complex systems of interdependent human beings, change is a more typically observed outcome. For example, in the weeks between crashing on the mountainside and the final rescue, the Andes group changed dramatically. Throughout the ordeal conflicts surfaced and became submerged again, questions of authority were raised before being settled through change, and aspects of group structure took one form after another. The group was never static, but instead developed continually over time.

Well over 100 theories have been advanced by group dynamicists seeking to describe the kinds of developmental changes seen in most groups, but most of these models have taken one of two basic approaches (Hill & Gruner, 1973; Shambaugh, 1978). **Recurring-phase models** suggest that certain issues tend to dominate group interaction during the various phases of group development but that these issues can recur later in the life of the group. For example, Robert Freed Bales' equilibrium model is based on the premise that group members strive to maintain a balance between task-oriented actions and emotionally expressive behaviors (Bales, 1965). The group tends to oscillate back and forth between these two concerns, sometimes achieving high solidarity but then shifting toward a more work-centered focus. Similarly, researchers dealing primarily with therapeutic groups often describe three basic themes as running through the groups at various times during their development: (1) dependency on the leader, (2) pairing among members for emotional support, and (3) fight-flight reactions (responding to a threat to the group by confronting or evading the problem). To understand the group's development, one must describe the group's shifting position with regard to these three themes (Bion, 1961; Stock & Thelen, 1958; Whitaker & Thelen, 1975).

Although most of the recurrent phase theorists would agree that group development generally follows a sequential pattern, with certain themes dominating others at various times in the group's history, these same theorists suggest that these phases follow no consistent order. For example, while one group may shift from a concern with leader dependency to pairing to conflict (fight-flight), another group may follow a reverse order. Thus, recurring-phase theories differ in this respect from **sequential-stage** theories, which seek to specify the "typical" order of the phases of group development. One exemplifying stage theory, which Bruce W. Tuckman developed after reviewing 50 studies dealing with group development, is shown in Table 1-2 (Tuckman, 1965; Tuckman & Jensen, 1977). In the first phase the group forms and members become oriented towards one another. In the second phase the group members often find themselves in conflict, and some solution is sought to improve the storming group environment. In the next phase along with roles and other structural components, norms develop that regulate behavior. In the fourth phase the group has reached a point where it can perform as a unit to achieve desired goals, while the final stage ends the sequence of development with the group's adjournment.

In sum, group dynamicists recognize that groups change over time and that conclusions based on observations taken at Time 1 may not hold for the same group at Time 2. Furthermore, two general explanations are usually advanced to account for this change: recurring-phase theories and sequential-stage theories.

TABLE 1-2. Five stages of group development

Stage	Major processes	Characteristics
Forming	Development of attraction bonds; exchange of information; orientation towards others and situation	Tentative interactions; polite discourse; concern over ambiguity; silences
Storming	Dissatisfaction with others; competition among members; disagreement over procedures; conflict	Ideas are criticized; speakers are interrupted; attendance is poor; hostility
Norming	Development of group structure; increased cohesiveness and harmony; establishment of roles and relationships	Agreement on rules; consensus-seeking; increased supportiveness; we-feeling
Performing	Focus on achievement; high task orientation; emphasis on performance and productivity	Decision making; problem solving; increased cooperation; decreased emotionality
Adjourning	Termination of duties; reduction of dependency; task completion	Regret; increased emotionality; disintegration

(Sources: Tuckman, 1965; Tuckman & Jensen, 1977).

Both of these frameworks provide useful perspectives for understanding group development, and since the disparities between the two approaches are fairly small, most recent theories recommend a synthesis of the phase and stage approaches (Caple, 1978; Shambaugh, 1978; Lacoursiere, 1980). Movement of groups through the various stages occurs as basic themes surface and are dealt with, and this movement often follows a pattern such as that shown in Table 1-2, because these themes tend to become relevant at certain times during the group's existence. However, because the issues underlying the themes are never completely resolved, the stages can recur.

Research Topics

Many topics have been investigated since early researchers first began comparing how people behaved in groups and by themselves. Although the vast number of articles and books published about group dynamics may make the task of reviewing past work on groups seem nearly insurmountable (Hare's 1976 bibliograpy lists 6037!), this introduction will selectively examine areas that have consistently been the focus of theory and research. The major topics of research in group dynamics that make up the parts of this book can be divided into five sections, as shown in Table 1-3.

PART ONE: ORIENTATION AND METHODS

This chapter and the next introduce the reader to the concepts of groups and group dynamics by emphasizing the importance of theory and research. As has been made clear, groups are multifaceted social entities that resist clear definition. Indeed, even the area of social science devoted to studying groups—group dynamics—is an intriguing mixture of many characteristics spanning several dis-

**TABLE 1-3. Topics in group dynamics
and chapters in this book in which they are covered**

Part	Topic	Chapter
One: Orientation and methods	An introduction to group dynamics	1
	Studying groups empirically	2
Two: Basic group processes	Forming: becoming a group	3
	Storming: conflict in groups	4
	Norming: the development of group structure	5
	Performing: working together in groups	6
Three: Social influence processes	Power and influence	7
	Leaders and leadership	8
	Conformity and deviancy	9
	The environment and group behavior	10
Four: Problems in groups	Deindividuation	11
	Groupthink	12
	Conflict between groups	13
Five: Applications	Groups in organizations and industry	14
	Groups in educational, judiciary and athletic contexts	15
	Interpersonal skills training in groups	16

ciplines. In Chapter 2 this brief introduction to groups and their dynamics concludes with an overview of research developments and types of methodologies employed.

PART TWO: BASIC GROUP PROCESSES

Before dealing with some specific topics in groups, such as leadership, conformity, and social influence, we must first examine the "basics"—why people join groups, the sources of conflict in groups, the nature of group structure, and the processes involved in groups as they work on problems and tasks. In order to organize our discussion of these basic processes, we will use four of the five stages from Tuckman's model of group development as chapter headings. First, in Chapter 3 we will explore *forming;* sources of attraction in groups. Next, in Chapter 4, the *storming* resulting from interpersonal conflict is examined. Chapter 5 covers the *norming* processes, and Chapter 6 considers *performing* in groups—groups working on problem-solving tasks, decision making, production tasks, and problems calling for creativity.

PART THREE: SOCIAL-INFLUENCE PROCESSES

Because many aspects of group life can be better understood once we can explain how people influence one another, a host of social-influence processes are considered in Part Three. The ability to influence the behavior of others provides the theme for Chapter 7, which reviews bases of power in groups, obedience pressures, and coalition formation. Theory and research dealing with leadership in groups are examined in Chapter 8, followed by a chapter dealing with conformity and deviancy in groups. This part concludes with a chapter that relates environmental variables—territoriality, personal space, crowding, and seating arrangements—to group dynamics.

PART FOUR: PROBLEMS IN GROUPS

As two of the examples cited in this chapter made abundantly clear, the effects of group membership are not always positive. Chapter 11 begins this section by studying the rare, but fascinating, instances of individuals engaging in atypical behavior in groups. Chapter 12 then considers groups—like President Kennedy's advisory committee—that make poor decisions even after a great deal of deliberation, and the final chapter of this section reviews research relevant to conflict between groups.

PART FIVE: APPLICATIONS

Although the practical applications of groups are noted throughout the text, more detailed integrations of research and practical problem solving are examined in this final section. First, Chapter 14 explores and confirms the relevance of group dynamics to improving productivity and employee satisfaction in business and industry. Second, Chapter 15 briefly reviews several types of groups found in everyday settings—classrooms, juries, and sports teams—and shows how these action groups can be better understood in the context of group dynamics. Finally, Chapter 16 ends this section and the book by discussing some of the therapeutic and interpersonal benefits of groups.

Summary

If we were to consider the characteristics of several groups—such as a rugby team stranded on a mountainside, a governmental committee making a monumentally important decision, or a religious movement changing over time—we would be struck as much by these groups' similarities as their differences. While many social aggregates fall under the category headed *group,* all are essentially similar in that they involve *two or more individuals who influence one another through social interaction.* Indeed, interactions, as well as group structure, goals, groupness (entitativity), and dynamic interdependency among members are primary features of groups.

The term *group dynamics* describes not only processes that take place in groups but also the "field of inquiry dedicated to advancing knowledge about the nature of groups" (Cartwright & Zander, 1968, p. 7). In this relatively young science, group dynamicists often take a holistic approach, which derives from Kurt Lewin's field theory and from general systems theory. The field also tends to be interdisciplinary, for it cuts across the boundaries of many social sciences (for example, psychology, sociology, anthropology, and political science) and several applied disciplines. In consequence, group dynamicists utilize a wide variety of research methods, and sometimes perform *action research* to solve questions dealing with significant social issues.

The study of groups is based on several assumptions that may or may not be universally endorsed by all group dynamicists. For example, while some investigators prefer to understand group behavior by focusing on the individual in the group, others take a more group-oriented approach. Second, some researchers tend to focus on either the positive or the negative features of groups, even though most agree that groups generally possess both good and bad attributes. Third, because groups are dynamic, researchers are generally sensitive to developmental changes that take place over time, and primarily describe these changes in terms of recurrent phases or sequential stages. Fourth, much of the research on groups can be organized around various topics, including (1) orientation and methods of research, (2) basic group processes (group formation, conflict, structure, and performance), (3) social-influence processes (power, leadership, conformity, deviancy, and the group environment), (4) problems in groups (deindividuation, groupthink, and intergroup conflict), and (5) applications (groups in industries, organizations, classrooms, sports, judicial contexts, and therapeutic settings).

2

Studying Groups Empirically

Suppose you found yourself suddenly elected leader of a club, committee, or organization. Although you take your duties quite seriously, you have never been a leader before, and things don't go as smoothly as you would like. Frustrated by your failures, you resolve to improve your understanding of the basic principles of leadership by careful study, but very soon you realize that you can draw your conclusions from many different sources. For example, you could turn to philosophy for answers, since great thinkers through the ages have often discussed the courses and strategies of leadership. Or you could heed the advice of expert authorities—outstanding leaders such as presidents of nations, military heroes, or executives—who have offered guidelines for effective leadership.

Alternatively, you could seek an answer through scientific research. Although many disciplines attempt to formulate general principles concerning the nature of the world, it is the scientist who attempts to test the adequacy of these ideas by studying *empirical evidence*—that is, facts based on observation and experience rather than common-sense beliefs or untested assumptions. As George Caspar Homans explains, "When the test of the truth of a relationship lies finally in the data themselves, and the data are not wholly manufactured—when nature, however stretched out on the rack, still has a chance to say 'No!'—then the subject is a science" (1967, p. 4).

In the two sections of this chapter, which are closely related, we will examine some of the scientific methods that are used to gather empirical information about groups. Our focus in the first section will be on the historical developments that helped an unexplored fledgling subarea of both psychology and sociology evolve into the science of group processes. The second section presents the basic features of several research methods that have frequently been used in groups research. This section includes, for each method, a description of a major study in group dynamics that exemplifies the application of the method (for a more detailed review, see Kidder, 1981).

The Development of Group-Research Techniques

The social sciences, including sociology and psychology, are often considered the "adolescents" of the sciences because of their relative youth when compared with such fields as physics and astronomy. Although other scientific fields had been studied for centuries, it was not until 1822 that Comte coined the term *sociology,* and the first psychological laboratory was not established until 1879, by Wundt. But while both sociology and psychology are "young" sciences, group dynamics is far younger still, for it did not emerge as a unified discipline until the 1940s. Dorwin Cartwright and Alvin Zander (1968), in their review of the origins of group dynamics, suggest that the slow development of group dynamics was due in part to several unfounded assumptions about groups. For example, many people felt that the dynamics of groups were a private affair, and not something that scientists should lay open to public scrutiny. Others felt that human behavior was too complex to be studied scientifically, and that this complexity was magnified enormously when groups of interacting individuals became the objects of interest. Still others believed that the causes of group behavior were so obvious that they were unworthy of scientific attention.

Eventually, these beliefs gave way and social scientists began turning their attention to the study of group dynamics. Yet even before these researchers could make any headway in their studies toward understanding groups, they had to overcome many obstacles. Essentially, researchers simply lacked the necessary tools for doing group research. They had no way to describe objectively the behavior of individuals in groups. The relationships linking the group members to one another could not be systematically assessed. The experimental methods needed for investigating groups were untried. Thus, real progress in group dynamics had to wait until satisfactory *research techniques* were developed. In the following sections we will trace the growth and impact of three important research tools—strategies for group observation, sociometric measurement methods, and experimental techniques—that gave group dynamics a foothold in the scientific tradition.

The Structured Observation of Groups

In the early days of group dynamics researchers attempted to use simple observational techniques to learn more about the activities of groups. After all, the approach had been used for centuries by historians, philosophers, and literary figures, and the idea of answering questions about groups by watching them seemed both reasonable and efficient (Cartwright & Zander, 1968). Unfortunately, the problem that observers of groups must necessarily face is that of objectivity. Unless it can be guaranteed that the account of the group processes offered is accurate and unbiased by the beliefs and values of the observer, the scientific status of the information contained in the observation will be highly questionable.

The problem of lack of objectivity in group observation was clearly demonstrated by Albert H. Hastorf and Hadley Cantril (1954). They asked college students to watch a film of two groups—two teams playing a football game. The game selected was played between Dartmouth and Princeton, and had been characterized by extremely rough play and many penalties. The Princeton quarterback, an all-American, left the game in the second quarter with a broken nose and a mild concussion. In the third quarter, the Dartmouth quarterback's leg was broken when he was tackled in the backfield. The entire game had been filmed, so Hastorf and Cantril were able to show the film both to Dartmouth and Princeton students, asking them to record the number and severity of the infractions committed by the two teams.

As Hastorf and Cantril expected, their student observers weren't very objective. As Figure 2-1 shows, Dartmouth students "saw" the Princeton Tigers commit about the same number of fouls as the Dartmouth players. Princeton students, however, disagreed with the Dartmouth observers; they saw the Dartmouth team commit more than twice as many fouls as the Princeton team.

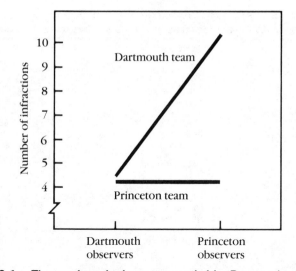

FIGURE 2-1. The number of infractions recorded by Dartmouth and Princeton students while watching the Dartmouth/Princeton game. (Source: Hastorf and Cantril, 1954).

A solution to the problem of objectivity in observations of group action was achieved by developing **structured coding systems.** Although many such systems have been used (see Hare, 1976, for a review), all are similar in that they help observers categorize group behavior. Like the biologist who classifies living organisms under such categories as phylum, subphylum, class, and order, or like the psychologist who classifies people into various personality groupings or "types," the group researcher wants to be able to classify each group behavior into an objectively definable category. Therefore, in developing the structured coding system, researchers first decide which behaviors in the group are of interest and which are not. Next, they set up the categories, or "pigeonholes," to be used in the classification system. Then, while observing the group, researchers simply note the occurrence and frequency of these targeted behaviors.

Researchers can now choose from a wide assortment of structured coding systems (Fisher, 1980; Hare, 1976; Stiles, 1978), but the system developed by Robert Freed Bales has proven to be a particularly useful observational technique (Bales, 1950, 1970, 1980). As shown in Table 2-1, the first form of Bales's **Interaction Process Analysis** (*IPA*) classified each bit of behavior performed by a group member into one of 12 categories. Six of these categories (1 to 3, 10 to 12) reflect **socioemotional activity**—behavior that focuses on interpersonal relationships in the group—and encompass both positive and negative actions. The other six categories reflect **task activity**—behavior that focuses on the problem the group is trying to solve—and encompass the giving and asking for information, opinions, and suggestions.

To use the IPA, researchers must first teach at least two observers the precise meaning of each category. These observers must become practiced at listening to a group discussion, breaking the verbal content down into the "smallest meaningful units" that can be distinguished (Bales, 1950, p. 7), and then classifying

**TABLE 2-1. The categories of the original
and the revised interaction process analysis system**

	Original IPA categories (Bales, 1950)	Revised IPA categories (Bales, 1970)
A. Positive (and mixed) actions	1. Shows solidarity 2. Shows tension release 3. Agrees	1. Seems friendly 2. Dramatizes 3. Agrees
B. Attempted answers	4. Gives suggestion 5. Gives opinion 6. Gives orientation	4. Gives suggestion 5. Gives opinion 6. Gives information
C. Questions	7. Asks for orientation 8. Asks for opinion 9. Asks for suggestion	7. Asks for information 8. Asks for opinion 9. Asks for suggestion
D. Negative (and mixed) actions	10. Disagrees 11. Shows tension 12. Shows antagonism	10. Disagrees 11. Shows tension 12. Seems unfriendly

(Source: Bales, 1970).

these units as to category. Thus, some skill is involved in this form of observation. As the group members interact, observers would record, on a profile form containing the categories listed in Table 2-1, who spoke to whom (for example, Person 1 to Person 3) and the type of statement made (say, a statement that "shows solidarity" or "seems friendly"). For example, if Subject 1 begins the group discussion by asking "Should we introduce ourselves?" and Subject 2 answers "Yes," then the observers would write 1-2 beside Category 8 (Person 1 asks for opinion) and 2-1 beside Category 5 (Person 2 gives opinion to Person 1). If later in the interaction Person 3 angrily tells the entire group "This group is a boring waste of time," then the coders would write 3-0 beside Category 12 (Person 3 seems unfriendly to entire group).

When used with well-trained observers, the IPA yields a reliable and valid record of group interaction. In addition, because the number of times a particular type of behavior occurs is recorded, the amount of interaction in the group can be represented numerically, allowing for comparison across categories, group members, and even different groups. Furthermore, in working with process analysis for more than 40 years, Bales has continually improved the IPA on the basis of available data. As Table 2-1 indicates, in 1970 Bales revised several of the categories to increase their usefulness during observation, and even more recently he proposed a further elaboration of the entire system. This newest version—*SYMLOG* (*SY*stem of *M*ultiple *L*evel *O*bservation of *G*roups)—will be examined in more detail in Chapter 5 (Bales, 1980; Bales, Cohen, & Williamson, 1979).

Sociometry

Jacob L. Moreno, in one of his earliest research studies, was confronted with a problem. He had been studying an institutionalized community of adolescent women who lived in 14 neighboring cottages. Although neighbors, the women were not very friendly. Discipline problems were rampant, and disputes continually arose among the groups and among members of the same group who shared a cottage. The simple solution that Moreno posed was to regroup the women into more compatible units and put the greatest physical distances between hostile groups. He achieved this goal by asking the women to indicate—on a confidential questionnaire—those individuals in the community they liked the most. On the basis of these responses, Moreno was able to place together individuals who had expressed a mutual attraction for one another and thereby to reduce the overall level of antagonism in the community (Moreno, 1953).

Thus, Moreno had developed **sociometry,** a technique for measuring the social relationships linking group members together. The technique itself consists of a series of relatively straightforward steps. First, the individual group members are asked to answer one or more questions about their fellow group members. Typically, the central question concerns which person in the group they like the most, but other questions have been used, such as "Who in the group would you like to work with the most?" or "Who do you like the least?" The number of choices permitted is limited by the researcher (it usually varies from one to three) and respondents are asked to refrain from nominating people who are not members of the group.

In the second phase, the researcher tries to summarize these choices by drawing a **sociogram**—a diagram of the relationships among group members. To start, the researcher graphs, in the shape of an oval, a number of circles representing all the group members. Next, he or she draws in the choices of each group member for the others, using lines capped with arrows to indicate the direction of relationships. Next, as depicted in Figure 2-2, the researcher draws the diagram again to organize it into a more meaningful pattern. For example, those individuals who are frequently chosen as most liked by others could be put in the center of the diagram while the least frequently chosen people could be placed about the periphery.

In the final stage, the researcher identifies the configurations of the group and the positions of each member. This step often includes the identification of (1) *stars,* the highly popular group members; (2) *isolates,* the infrequently chosen individuals; (3) *pairs,* two people who, by listing one another as their first choices, have reciprocal bonds; and (4) *chains,* clusters of individuals within the group who make up a subgroup or clique. The researcher may also wish to calculate several indexes that summarize sociometric choice. Some of the more popular measures that can be computed from a sociogram include (1) *choice status,* the number of times a person is chosen by the other group members; (2) *rejection status,* the number of times a person is rejected by others; (3) *group cohesion,* the relative number of mutual pairs in a group; and (4) *group integration,* the relative number of isolates. Lastly, if respondents have provided several nominations reflecting both liking and disliking, then more elaborate sociometric methods can be used to organize the choice and rejection data (see Lindzey & Borgatta, 1954; Moreno, 1960; Northway, 1967).

Sociometry proved to be an invaluable research tool. Although a simple procedure, it yielded a comprehensive picture of a group that facilitated in-depth understanding. The essence of a group can be depicted with a sociogram, and leaders, isolates, subgroups, and other informal structures of groups can be identified with the instrument. Although typically based on questionnaire results, researchers found that they could construct sociograms on the basis of observa-

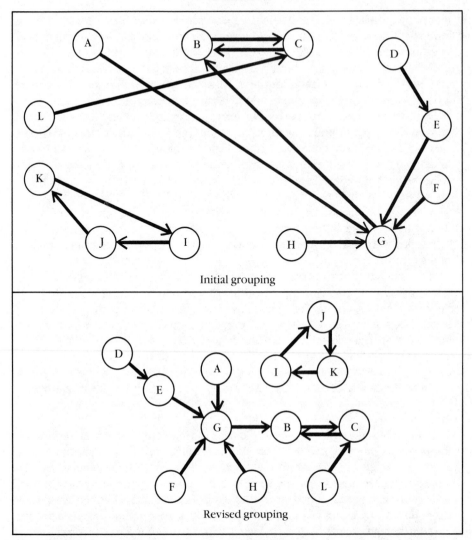

FIGURE 2-2. Sociogram of a 12-person group. *G* is a star; *L* and *D* are isolates; *B* and *C* are a pair; and *I, J,* and *K* form a chain.

tions, and that these graphs facilitated intergroup comparison when indexes of interrelationships were used to quantify choices.

Although sociometry is not used as frequently today as it was in the 1940s and 1950s, the technique still deserves a central position in the field of group dynamics. With a sociogram the researcher can summarize valuable information about the relationships that bind people together, and the pictorial representation provides a clarity that earlier researchers had considered unattainable. The value of sociometry is attested to by the quantity of research that used the approach to explore group structure, and by the fact that one of the first journals devoted to group-dynamics research—established in 1937 by Moreno—was entitled *Sociometry.*

Although this tribute to sociometry was, unfortunately, rescinded in 1979 when the journal was renamed *Social Psychology Quarterly,* the impact of the method remains.

Advances in Research Design

With structured coding systems researchers could carefully record group behavior, and sociometry made possible the measurement of group structure. However, the potential utility of these two tools was not realized until researchers had developed ways to conduct research with groups of people. Fortunately the period of 1900 to 1940 witnessed a gradual refinement of research designs applicable to groups, and the theorists and researchers of the 1940s and 1950s were therefore able to build on a foundation laid by these earlier efforts. Although space constraints limit us from describing here all the historically important advances in research design that took place in the early part of this century (see Borgatta, 1981; Hare, 1976; Pepitone, 1981; and Zander, 1979a for more detailed reviews), we can survey three general areas—the influence of groups on individuals, industrial research, and the experimental study of norms.

GROUPS AND INDIVIDUALS

In the early days of social-psychological research, questions of individual performance in group settings were favorite topics of research. For example, one of the first laboratory studies in social psychology compared the performance of school children working alone and in noninteracting groups (Triplett, 1897). The children's responses in this investigation showed signs of **social facilitation**—improved performance when working in the presence of others—and soon many other investigators began examining related topics. Furthermore, this interest in task performance soon led to a broader question: "Are individuals, when compared to groups of individuals, superior or inferior in task performance?" In time investigators came to realize that experimental studies of groups were not so difficult after all. Although in their initial studies group interaction was so elaborately restricted that the relevance of these investigations for understanding nonlaboratory groups seemed questionable, in later work these restrictions were relaxed and groups' processes were studied directly (Steiner, 1974). Thus, while the early efforts focused more closely on the individual in the group than on the group per se, researchers eventually began to consider the group as well.

INDUSTRIAL RESEARCH

While academic researchers were studying questions of group and individual performance, Elton Mayo and his associates at the Hawthorne Plant of the Western Electric Company were conducting their landmark studies of industrial behavior (Landsberger, 1958; Mayo, 1945; Roethlisberger & Dickson, 1939). In order to identify the physical features of the work setting that improved or impeded work performance, Mayo and his colleagues systematically varied a number of features while measuring worker output. For example, one group of female workers assembling components for telephones was placed in a separate room where members' performance could be carefully monitored. Next, the researcher introduced factors into the situation that were expected to hurt performance, such as reduced lighting and fewer rest periods, and factors that were assumed to help performance, such as brighter lighting and more rest periods. Surprisingly, all innovations led to improved worker output, apparently because motivation was heightened by the interest the company and research team had shown in the well-being and adjustment of the work group. To Mayo's credit, he recognized that the physical features he had manipulated were not as important as the social factors present in the work group, and he shifted his focus to the social organization of the group, supervisor/subordinate relations, group norms, and the attitudes and motives of the workers.

Although the validity of the Hawthorne studies findings has recently been questioned (Bramel & Friend, 1981; Franke, 1979), at the time Mayo's work underscored the importance of considering interpersonal factors in the work setting (for example, Barnard, 1938; McGregor, 1960). Furthermore, the work also convinced many reluctant psychologists and sociologists that potentially important benefits could be gained by studying organizational issues experimentally. Lastly, the research made salient a problem that still concerns students of group processes. Quite simply, Mayo demonstrated that group members act differently when they believe they are being observed by social scientists interested in their behavior. This change in behavior as a result of observation, known as the **Hawthorne effect,** continues to limit the generalizability of research findings based on field and laboratory situations in which group members know they are being studied.

STUDYING NORMS EXPERIMENTALLY

A final project that significantly influenced the development of experimental techniques in group dynamics research during this period was Muzafer Sherif's classic study of social norms (1936). As previously described in Chapter 1 (see box on page 18), Sherif experimentally created and manipulated a social norm in a group setting. This research did much to establish experimentation as a suitable method for group-dynamics research by demonstrating that (1) group concepts, such as norms, could be experimentally manipulated, (2) meaningful research could be conducted in a laboratory setting using ad hoc rather than naturally occurring groups, and (3) the impact of the Hawthorne effect was minimal provided the setting was carefully controlled.

Research Methods in Group Dynamics

Barriers to the scientific study of groups were overcome through the development of essential research techniques such as structured observational systems, sociometry, and experimentation, and social scientists began studying groups in earnest. The interest in group phenomena that seemed to explode upon the scientific community in the 1940s has continued unabated, and through the years researchers have utilized a number of empirical methods for testing the validity of hypotheses about groups. Although in some respects these methods overlap considerably, each approach has its own strengths and weaknesses. In studying these methods, we will focus on four basic designs: case studies, observational research, self-reports, and experiments. In addition, four research projects that have shaped the face of group dynamics will be used to exemplify each method. Thus, as we learn something about methods, we can also learn a bit more about the dynamics of groups.

Case Studies

The first, and probably least frequently used, empirical procedure is the case study. This method, which crops up from time to time in diverse areas ranging from clinical psychology to history, is appealing for its apparent simplicity. The researchers select a single group—such as a sports team, religious movement, or governmental committee—and try to find out all they can about the group and its dynamics. Although in some cases the information about the group comes from the researchers' own experiences within the group, facts about the group may also be culled from interviews with members, descriptions of the group written by journalists, or members' biographical writings. On the basis of this information, an overall picture of the group is constructed, and the extent to which the examined case supports the researchers' hypothesis can then be estimated.

An excellent example of the use of the case-study method in group dynamics is Irving Janis' study of **groupthink** (1972). Janis, well known as a social psychologist, became intrigued with the underlying causes of the poor decision-making strategies used by groups responsible for such fiascoes as the Bay of Pigs invasion, the defense of Pearl Harbor prior to its attack during World War II, and the escalation of the Vietnam War. In order to develop a theoretical explanation for these blunders, Janis sought out available information about several such bumbling groups, and then looked for their similarities. After making a thorough examination of historical documents, minutes of the meetings, diaries, letters, published memoirs of the group members, and public statements made to the press, Janis concluded that these groups were the victims of groupthink,—"a deterioration of mental efficiency, reality testing, and moral judgment that results from in-group pressures" (p. 9). As a result of this research, Janis was able to specify the major determinants and symptoms of groupthink and to suggest actions that can be taken to avoid it. Because of the importance of groupthink, we will return to the topic again in far more detail in Chapter 12.

Like any research technique, the case study has both advantages and disadvantages. The approach allows in-depth understanding of the group or groups under study, and yields descriptions of group events often unsurpassed by any other data-collection method. Second, the measures used in a case study are completely nonreactive. The events have often already transpired, so researchers need not worry about altering the phenomenon under study. Finally, and at a more pragmatic level, case studies can be relatively easy to carry out and they make for fascinating reading.

One drawback of the case-study method, on the other hand, is the possibility that the group studied is completely unique and therefore nonrepresentative of other groups. In many cases the information gathered by the investigator cannot be represented in objective, unambiguous terms, and interpretations can therefore be influenced by the assumptions and biases of the researcher. Even worse, the materials themselves may be inaccurate or unavailable to the researcher. Janis, for example, was forced to "rely mainly on the contemporary and retrospective accounts by the group members themselves, . . . many of which are likely to have been written with an eye to the author's own place in history" (p. v). Finally, case studies can rarely yield statements concerning the causal relationships among important variables in the group under study. In our example, although groupthink appears to have caused the poor decisions, some other, unnoticed variable could actually have been the prime causal agent.

Observational Research

Groups are an integral part of our daily lives. If we are alone, a group is usually ready nearby to take us in. If the group we belong to dissolves, we end up joining another. Even when we are in one group, we are surrounded by still others. Because groups seem to be virtually inescapable, the opportunities to further understand them through observation are nearly limitless. Admittedly, when applied to groups observational methods often cut across many of the other methods of research, but the goal of any observational study is always the same: *to describe systematically and record events that transpire in groups* in order to test the adequacy of some hypothesis concerning their dynamics (Kidder, 1981).

STREET-CORNER SOCIETY

William Foote Whyte used observational techniques in a study he reports in his book *Street Corner Society* (1943). Whyte wished to understand as completely as possible the groups and social structure of an Italian-American slum in the heart of Boston. He moved to the district, which he gives the fictitious name Cornerville, lived for a time with an Italian family, joined the "Nortons"—a group of young men who gathered at a particular corner on Norton Street—and also participated in a more upwardly mobile social club known as the Italian Community Club. During the three and one-half years that Whyte spent at Cornerville, he kept extensive notes of community life, and when integrated these yielded a detailed portrait of this unique community and its groups.

Whyte's study of Cornerville deserves a central place in the study of group dynamics for more than one reason. Whyte's research made it quite clear that an investigator could not achieve full understanding of a community without taking groups into account. For example, if a young man belonged to a "corner-gang" such as the Nortons, his life was dramatically influenced by this group; he became a corner-boy first, an individual second. Doc, the leader of the Nortons, pointed out that a corner-boy would be lost without his gang.

> They come home from work, hang on the corner, go up to eat, back on the corner, up to a show, and they come back to hang on the corner. If they're not on the corner, it's likely the boys there will know where you can find them. Most of them stick to one corner. It's only rarely that a fellow will change his corner [p. 256].

Whyte also succeeded in describing a group in *action*. Rather than portraying the group as a static entity, Whyte described groups as they are: as dynamic interpersonal systems that evolve over time. He was also able to clarify formerly vague concepts such as leadership, power, and cohesiveness by tying these terms to directly observable, unambiguously described group events. Finally, the book is filled with suggestive, testable hypotheses that were subsequently examined in depth by other researchers.

QUESTIONS TO ASK ABOUT OBSERVATIONAL RESEARCH

We do not pretend that all observational studies use the same methods that Whyte used; they clearly do not. The term *observational research* is quite broad, and covers many studies that seem more dissimilar than similar. The differences among observational studies can perhaps be best understood by examining three questions researchers must ask themselves before undertaking any study:

1. Should we actually *participate* in the group(s) we are observing?
2. How should we *structure* our observations of the group(s)?
3. Should we try to *compare* the group we observe to other groups?

The researchers' answers to these questions can dramatically alter the final research product. But exactly why are each of these questions so important?

Participating in the group.   Whyte decided to study the Boston slum groups from within; he actually joined these groups. This technique of group observation is called **participant observation,** which can be defined as "a process in which the observer's presence in a social situation is maintained for the purpose of scientific investigation. The observer is in a face-to-face relationship with the observed, and, by participating with them in their natural life setting, he gathers data" (Schwartz & Schwartz, 1955, p. 344).

As a member of the group, Whyte gained access to information that would have been hidden from an external observer. Unfortunately, his presence in the group may also have changed the group itself. He went bowling with the Nortons, gambled with them, and even lent money to some of the members. Undoubtedly his presence in the group modified its structure, and the group Whyte therefore describes is not a typical corner-gang, but rather a corner-gang with a sociologist in it.

In order to limit the possibilities of contamination, some researchers prefer to use *overt observation methods,* in which an external observer whose presence is known to the group members records the group's activities. Although overt observation reduces the possibility of directly changing the group, the Hawthorne effect suggests that observation can indirectly produce a change away from "typical" group behavior. As one corner-boy who realized he was being "watched" by Whyte once remarked, "You've slowed me down plenty since you've been down here. Now, when I do something, I have to think what Bill Whyte would want to know about it and how I can explain it. Before I used to do things by instinct" (p. 301).

If the researchers decide to answer no to the question "Should we actually participate in the group(s) we are observing?" then they may adopt other methods besides overt observation. For example, *covert observation* involves recording behavior from a concealed location without the observer's knowledge. Although such methods are commendable methodologically, their ethical ramifications with respect to invasion of privacy are questionable, and they considerably limit the amount of information the observer can acquire (Cook, 1981; Reynolds, 1979). The use of noninvasive methods is generally considered to be less controversial and thus preferable.

Structuring observations.   Researchers must also decide whether to begin their observations by looking for particular behaviors or simply to try to "take it all in" with no preconceptions about what to look for. Several researchers point out the importance of letting the group "speak" for itself, so that any observations made are unbiased by the a priori and possibly incorrect assumptions of the research team (Glaser & Strauss, 1967). Others argue that such openness should be avoided, since it puts too much trust in the observational powers of the researchers, who may let initial, though implicit, expectations shape their records (Kidder, 1981). This latter approach recommends the use of highly structured observation scales, such as Bales's IPA, and well-trained observers.

Finding a reasonable answer to the question of structure will probably depend upon the stage of the research and the researchers' ability to make use of structured methods. Very little research had been done on community groups before Whyte began his work, and therefore little information about these groups was available to him for use in structuring an observational system. As a result, he simply observed as much as he could each day, made extensive notes when possible, and waited for some overall guiding theme to make itself evident. Whyte was rewarded when it became clear to him after many hours and pages of observation that "an analysis of leadership would provide a means of integrating the study" (p. vii). Thus, if the research is more exploratory, designed to develop theory first and validate hypotheses second, then an unstructured observational approach would be appropriate. If, however, the researcher has a hypothesis in mind and can make use of more structured observational methods, then the rigor and objectivity of a structured approach would seem preferable.

Comparative observations.   While some observational research focuses on a single group, many more studies are comparative; that is, they involve observing two or more groups (or the same group at different times) and drawing inferences concerning the causes of their different dynamics. For example, Whyte observed two different groups: the Nortons and the Italian Community Club (ICC). The Nortons was composed primarily of corner-boys—"groups of men who center their social activities upon particular street corners, with their adjoining barbershops, lunchrooms, poolrooms, or clubrooms" (p. xviii). The ranks of the ICC, on the other hand, were dominated by upwardly mobile men who had attended college. Whyte often compared the dynamics of the two groups in hopes of learning more about how these different characteristics influenced such factors as group organization and social structure.

Comparative observation often gives the researcher a special understanding of the groups under scrutiny. If the groups are similar in many respects but still display differences in their dynamics, the researcher may be able to narrow down the list of possible causal variables to determine which is producing the differences. Unfortunately, researchers who try to make causal inferences from observations of naturally occurring groups must exercise caution; as with archival research and survey research methods, to be discussed next, without experimentation the possibility always exists that some unnoticed factor is the actual causal force.

ADVANTAGES AND DISADVANTAGES

As with the case-study method, observational research possesses both positive and negative features. Looking first at the positive side of the ledger we can point to the real-life quality of observational research. The groups investigated by observation are, in general, groups that would be interacting, functioning, and performing whether or not a study was being conducted, and this aspect lends confidence to the researchers' assumption that what they record is important. This advantage is further buttressed when the method of observation has a minimal effect on the group processes, hence ensuring that what is seen is something that is "real." Lastly, observational research yields a remarkably large amount of often intriguing information about groups.

Unfortunately, the disadvantages of observational research stem from its advantages. In observational research no attempt is made to manipulate variables, and researchers are therefore unable to make strong causal inferences. Second, the more carefully the researchers avoid disrupting the group's natural functioning, the more likely they are to be ethically condemned for invading the privacy of those studied. Finally, the amount of information obtained in an observational study can be so overwhelming that the researchers know neither where to start in making sense of the group's dynamics nor which variables should be the focus of their observations.

Self-Report Measures

Self-report research is based on the simple idea that if you want to know how group members feel about something or why they performed a particular behavior, then the obvious solution is to ask them. How one goes about asking can vary—from administering carefully constructed standardized psychological *tests* and specially designed *questionnaires* to performing face-to-face *interviews*—but the essential method always involves asking a question and recording the answer. These techniques are called self-report measures because respondents themselves are asked to describe their current feelings, attitudes, or beliefs.

One group-dynamics study that made excellent use of such methods was Theodore Newcomb's investigation of the attitudes of the women students at Bennington College (Newcomb, 1943). In this now classic "Bennington study," Newcomb was able to demonstrate that one of the central concepts of the individualistic orientation to understanding social behavior—the attitude—was in fact greatly influenced by group processes. As a new member of the Bennington faculty, Newcomb became intrigued with the divergent attitudes among the first-year students, the more advanced students, and the students' families. Most Bennington students came from upper-crust New England families whose strong conservatism was indicated by their presidential preferences. As Figure 2-3 indicates, the majority of the families of the students favored Alfred M. Landon, the conservative candidate, rather than Franklin D. Roosevelt, the liberal, and eventually victorious, candidate. First-year students shared the attitudes of their families, but the match

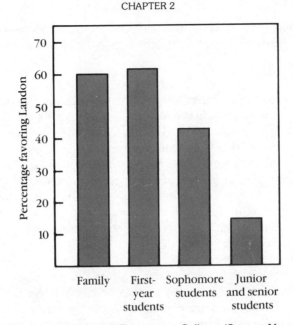

FIGURE 2-3. Attitude change at Bennington College. (Source: Newcomb, 1943).

between student and family attitude was much poorer where upper-class students were concerned.

Newcomb explained this shift by hypothesizing that the people around us who play significant roles in our lives—our **reference group**—can indirectly influence our attitudes. For new students the primary reference group was still the family, hence the close match between family attitudes and new-student attitudes. Once at Bennington, however, students' reference groups became other students and faculty members, and the longer students remained at Bennington, the more likely were their attitudes to become more similar to the attitudes of the rest of the college population. While the family group would support a conservative attitude, the college community supported only liberal attitudes, and many Bennington women shifted their attitudes in response to this reference-group pressure.

To investigate this reference-group hypothesis, Newcomb used questionnaires, sociometry, and interviews to assess the attitudes, popularity, and family back-grounds of an entire class of Bennington students over a four-year period, from their entrance in 1935 to their graduation in 1939. The results of this massive project lent strong support to the strength of reference-group influence. Newcomb found a consistent trend toward liberalism in many of the students, and reasoned that this change resulted from peer-group pressure because it was more pro-nounced among the popular students. Those who endorsed nonconservative atti-tudes were (1) "both capable and desirous of cordial relations with the fellow community members" (p. 149), (2) more frequently chosen by others as friendly, and (3) a more cohesive subgroup than the conservative students. Individuals who did not become more liberal tended to be isolated from the college's social life or to be very family-oriented. The magnitude and importance of this group experience are underscored by the consideration that the more liberal attitudes

THE IMPACT OF CHANGING REFERENCE GROUPS

From a Bennington student of 1935:

An increasing crescendo of scattered remarks of my friends mounts up in my mind and culminates in a dissonant, minor-chord. What is the matter with these dissatisfied, bewildered, cynical girls? It's a simple answer, yet dishearteningly complex. Bennington is their trouble. I can't speak for all of us, but a hell of a lot of us are in this fix. We come from fine old Tory families who believe firmly in Higher-Education—Good God knows why. So they sent us to a well-spoken-of college with an interesting-sounding scheme of education. . . . We came home, some of us, talking a new language, some cobwebs swept out, a new direction opening up ahead we were dying to travel. Liberal, we thought we were. "What the hell's happened to you? Become a parlor Pink? . . ."

The more education, the broader-minded—and the narrower the circle of kindred souls. It's closing in on us now. Soon we'll graduate, and what then? Back to the old "set" which we've outgrown? To people we can never be completely satisfied with again as friends, and who distrust us now, if we've been brave enough to show our colors [pp. 11–12].

(Source: Newcomb, 1943).

---

created by the reference group remained a part of the beliefs of many of the Bennington graduates some 25 years later (Newcomb, Koenig, Flacks, & Warwick, 1967).

The power of self-report methods is evident in the Bennington study, but the limitations of such research should not be passed over. Self-report research suffers from the same problem that case-study and observational research encounter—it limits the feasibility of making causal inferences. For example, while Newcomb's data indicate that the attitude changes he measured were related to peer-reference-group pressures, he could not conclusively rule out other possible causes. Perhaps, unknown to Newcomb, the most popular women on campus tended all to read the same books, which contained arguments that persuaded them to give up their conservative attitudes. While this explanation is unlikely, it cannot be eliminated given the methods used by Newcomb.

Other problems crop up as well. Once a survey has been designed, changes are relatively difficult to make. Self-report researchers are quite aware that finding explanations for group phenomena depends very much on knowing what questions to ask the group members. While the observer may be able to incorporate previously unnoticed variables into the research scheme once the project is launched, the self-report researcher is likely either to fail to notice unexpected variables or to experience great difficulty in adapting the survey to include them. Lastly, a maze of technical questions confronts the researcher designing questionnaires. Unless questions are worded properly, responses will be difficult to interpret. The link between the quality of the results and the quality of the survey itself is captured in the inelegant phrase "garbage in, garbage out." Questionnaires composed of poorly selected or ambiguously worded questions are always exceedingly difficult to interpret. Other technical problems include interviewer effects, respondent biases, and sampling problems (Kidder, 1981).

Despite these limitations, self-report methods are indispensable research tools for many problems in group dynamics. For example, researchers might be interested in the hypothesis that the best-liked people in groups will also be the people who have the most favorable attitudes toward the group itself. Thus, two variables—liking and attitude toward the group—must be measured. While the observer of a group may have difficulty determining whether or not a group member is well liked just by watching, the survey researcher could easily test for liking by administering a sociometric self-report questionnaire. In addition, the researcher, by asking the right kinds of questions of the right people, can zero in on the specific problem of interest. Researchers can ask questions that directly measure reports of feelings about others and the group, and the responses to such questions are relatively easy to interpret. Because questionnaire responses can be objectively coded, very specific conclusions can be drawn from questionnaire and interview responses. Thus, survey methods are of value for two basic reasons: they can be used to tap variables directly that may be difficult to assess otherwise, and they can yield very specific conclusions about the relationships among variables.

Experimentation

Between 1937 and 1940, Kurt Lewin, Ronald Lippitt, and Ralph White (1937; White & Lippitt, 1968) investigated what effects, if any, a leader's "style" might have on group members. Lewin and his colleagues arranged for 10- and 11-year-old boys to meet after school in small, five-member groups to work on hobbies such as woodworking and painting. Because the researchers believed that the style a leader adopts significantly influences a group, each of these work groups was led by an adult who assumed one of three particular styles of leadership—autocratic, democratic, and laissez-faire. The *autocratic* leader made all the decisions for the group, never asking for input from the boys. The boys rarely knew what the group would be doing next, were not permitted to decide for themselves how to approach the task at hand, and were even told who they would work with. The autocratic leader tended to give many orders, to criticize the boys unreasonably, and to remain aloof from the group.

The *democratic* leader, on the other hand, set no policies for the group; the group members themselves made all decisions while guided by the leader. The leader frequently explained long-term goals and steps to be taken to reach the goals, and members were free to choose their work partners. Democratic leaders rarely gave orders and commands, and the criticism they did give group members was always deserved. Lastly, the democratic leader did not remain apart from the group, but attempted to foster a spirit of cooperation and egalitarianism. The final type of leader was labeled *laissez-faire,* an idiomatic French expression meaning "let people do (or make) what they choose." The laissez-faire leader was, in a sense, not even a leader. He never participated in the group interactions, allowing the boys to work in whichever way they wished. Although he did make it clear that he would provide information if asked, he rarely offered information, criticism, or guidance spontaneously.

Once these three types of leaders were established in the groups, the researchers set about recording the many types of behavior they felt would be influenced by leadership style. Two of the most important variables the researchers measured

FROM THE RESPONDENT'S PERSPECTIVE

Group dynamics researchers sometimes make mistakes when they write their questionnaire measures, and these mistakes can be very trying for the respondent. To give you an idea of just how important good item writing can be, try your hand at answering the following questions.

After your group finishes work, please answer each of the following items by placing the appropriate letter in the space to the left of each question.

_____ 1. In my opinion, the group was
   a. a wonderful, tremendously fulfilling experience.
   b. horribly boring.

_____ 2. How much existentially useful information did you assimilate during the group's dialectical interplay?
   a. a great deal
   b. some
   c. very little
   d. none at all

_____ 3. Did you think that, in general, the group members' communications were not unambiguous?
   a. a great deal
   b. some
   c. very little
   d. none at all

_____ 4. Did you consider the group experience to be exciting and informative?

   a. definitely yes
   b. yes
   c. no
   d. definitely no

_____ 5. If given the chance, in my spare time I would prefer to
   a. participate in a similar group.
   b. read comic books.
   c. goof off.

Each of these items makes a mistake. The first is guilty of *response restriction*. What if you don't care one way or another? How would you answer? Questions 2 and 3 are just plain *ambiguous*—2 for using obscure terms and 3 because the wording is very confusing and the construction is a double negative. The fourth question is, in measurement terms, *"double-barreled"*; it asks for two bits of information at once. The problem arises when the respondent thinks the group interaction was information-packed but boring. (Item 4 also lacks a neutral, "undecided" response alternative between the "yes" and the "no." The item fails to account for the ambivalent response.) Finally, the first response alternative to Question 5 is clearly more *socially desirable* than the other alternatives. If the respondents are concerned with maintaining an acceptable public image, then such lopsided desirability could cloud interpretation of their responses.

---

were group productivity and aggressiveness. The autocratic groups tended to spend more time working (74%) than the democratic group (50%), which in turn spent more time working than the laissez-faire group (33%). Although these results would seem to argue in favor of an autocratic leadership style to "get the job done," the observers also noted that when the leader left the room for any lengthy period of time, the democratically led groups kept right on working, while the boys in the autocratic groups stopped working. The second variable, aggressiveness, also revealed interesting differences among the groups. In general, most of these differences appeared when the laissez-faire and democratically led groups were compared with the autocratic group. In the latter group observers noted high rates of hostility among members, more demands for attention, more destructiveness, and a greater tendency to single out one group member to serve as the target of almost continual verbal abuse. Lewin suggested that this *scapegoat* provided an outlet for pent-up hostilities that could not be acted out against the powerful group leader.

THE CHARACTERISTICS OF EXPERIMENTS

Because the Lewin, Lippitt, and White research is an experiment, it differs from the previously discussed research techniques in three important ways. First, the researchers selected a variable that they believed *caused* changes in group processes. This variable, which is called the **independent variable,** was then systematically manipulated by the researchers. In the leadership study, this meant putting together groups that were led by different types of leaders—either autocratic, democratic, or laissez-faire.

Second, the researchers systematically assessed the effects of the independent variable by measuring such factors as productivity and aggressiveness. The variables measured by the researcher are called **dependent variables,** because their magnitude will *depend* upon the strength and nature of the independent variable. Thus, in the leadership study the researchers hypothesized that group leadership style will influence productivity and aggressiveness, and tested this hypothesis by manipulating the independent variable (style) and measuring the dependent variables (productivity and aggressiveness).

Third, the experimenters tried to maintain *control* over other variables that might have hampered interpretation of the results of the research. The researchers never assumed that the only determinant of productivity and aggressiveness was leadership style. Of course, other variables, such as the personality characteristics and abilities of the group members, could influence the dependent variables. In the experiment, however, the researchers were uninterested in these other variables. Their hypotheses were specifically focused on the relationship among leadership style, productivity, and aggressiveness. Therefore, they made certain that these other variables were controlled in the experimental situation. For example, they took pains to ensure that the groups they created were "roughly equated on patterns of interpersonal relationships, intellectual, physical, and socio-economic status, and personality characteristics" (White & Lippitt, 1968, p. 318), and randomly assigned groups to experimental conditions. By controlling these other possible causal variables, the researchers could be far more confident that any differences among the groups on the dependent variables were produced by the variable that they had manipulated, and not some other variable they forgot to control.

In sum, then, the key characteristics of an experiment are the *manipulation* of the independent variable(s), the *systematic assessment* of the dependent variable(s), and the *control* of other possible contaminating factors.

ADVANTAGES AND DISADVANTAGES

As will become clear in later chapters, group dynamicists frequently rely on experimentation to test their hypotheses about groups. This preference for experimentation over the other research techniques derives, in part, from the inferential power of experimentation. Because of the way in which experiments are designed,

MISUNDERSTANDING EXPERIMENTATION

In a time in which much of our knowledge comes from scientific research, most people are well aware of scientific experiments and their values. Unfortunately, social-science research is sometimes misunderstood, particularly when the research is experimental. For example, many people believe that in order for a study to be an experiment, it must have a *control condition*—that is, people (or groups of people) who remain unexposed to the independent variable. For example, in Lewin's research on leadership style, a control would have been groups of boys who had no adult leader at all. A control condition, however, while often incorporated in an experimental study, is not an absolute necessity. What is required are two or more conditions that can be compared with one another, but none of these conditions must be a control condition.

A second area of ambiguity concerns confusion between the *random selection* of participants in a study and the *random assignment* of participants to conditions in an experiment. Random selection of participants is done to heighten the generalizability of the results. For example, many survey researchers go to great lengths to ask their questions of a *sample* that is representative of the entire population. Random selection of participants is not, however, a necessary feature of an experiment; random assignment of participants to conditions is.

For example, assume that some researchers wish to study the impact of a strong leader on group dynamics. They set up 20 groups, giving the leaders in 10 of the groups a great deal of power over the group activities and decisions and the leaders in the 10 remaining groups very little power. After the groups do their work for 30 minutes, liking for the group is measured sociometrically. It is crucially important that the assignment of each group to one of the two conditions (strong versus weak leader) be done randomly. No two groups are identical, and these variations result in some groups being more cohesive than others, some being more friendly than others, or some working harder than others. The random assignment of groups to the two conditions will help to ensure the evening out of these initial inequalities, thus making it clear that any differences found on the dependent measure are due to the independent variable, not to uncontrolled differences among the participating groups.

they allow the researcher to make inferences about the causal relationships linking variables together. As logic would suggest, if a change is recorded in some dependent variable, then that change must have been caused by something. If *every* variable except one—the independent variable—has been held constant or controlled, then the change must have been caused by the independent variable. Although survey and observation studies, if properly designed and analyzed, sometimes suggest which relationships are causal, the researcher's confidence is greater if an experiment has been conducted.

Experimentation necessarily involves manipulating the independent variable, assessing the dependent variable, and controlling other possible "confounding" variables. Unfortunately, each of these necessary steps can add to the artificiality of the experimental situation. The major problem is that, in seeking rigorous control, experimenters may end up studying closely monitored but sterile group situations. To achieve the desired degree of control, experiments are often performed in laboratories and group members are frequently volunteers who work in the groups under study for relatively short periods of time. Although an experimenter can heighten the reality of the situation for people working in a laboratory exper-iment by refraining from explaining the nature of the experiment to participants, such deception on the part of researchers can be challenged on ethical grounds. In addition, while experiments can be conducted in the field using already existing groups, such a move will almost necessarily involve the sacrifice of some degree of control and will reduce the strength of the researchers' conclusions. Hence, the major advantage of experimentation—ability to draw causal inferences—can be offset by the major disadvantage of experimentation—basing conclusions on arti-ficial, highly contrived groups that have no parallels among naturally occurring groups.

Choosing a Research Design

The student of group dynamics may, after a long and perhaps frustrating dis-cussion of research methods, their advantages, and disadvantages, be tempted to ask the inevitable question "Which of these research techniques is the best?" To this question the researcher must respond with the obvious, but probably dissat-isfying, answer "It depends!"

In this instance, however, the researcher is not being noncommittal but rather truthful. Each of the four methods discussed possesses disadvantages that limit its usefulness and unique advantages that, depending on the researchers' goals, rec-ommend its application. Case studies limit the researcher's ability to draw conclu-sions, to quantify results, and to make objective interpretations. But certainly some topics, such as groupthink, are difficult to study by any other method. As Janis himself points out, it would be difficult to examine groups that make decisions about national policies, including war and civil defense, through observation, sur-vey, or experimentation. But the real forte of the case-study approach is its power to facilitate the development of theoretical explanations. The approach provides grist for the theoretician's mill, enabling the investigator to formulate hypotheses that set the stage for other research methods.

The stimulation of theory is also frequently a consequence of an observational study. Before group dynamicists can construct adequate (and sometimes compli-cated) theories of group behavior, they must achieve a clear picture of the behav-iors displayed by the group. While in most instances observational research can provide only tentative tests of hypotheses concerning the underlying causes of this group behavior, such methods do remain the best means for adequately and accurately describing a group.

To a lesser extent, self-report methods also generate descriptions of group phe-nomena, but from the perspective of the participant rather than the observer. When the researchers' interests are turned in the direction of relating to group dynamics individualistic variables—such as group-member perceptions, feelings, or beliefs—then self-report methods may be the only means of assessing these private and unobservable variables. Such research is limited in terms of causal power, but yields excellent and quantitatively sound information concerning the relationships among variables and, when compared with observational research and experimentation, usually comes out ahead on the ethical dimension. Asking a person to answer a questionnaire is, in general, considered to be far less ethically questionable than is covert observation or the manipulation of situational factors without the participants' awareness.

Lastly, experimentation provides the firmest test of causal hypotheses predicting that variable X will cause such and such a change in variable Y. In the properly designed and well-conducted experiment, the researcher can test several hypotheses about groups, making the method both rigorous and efficient. But where an artificial setting would yield meaningless results, where the independent variable cannot be manipulated, or where too little is known about the topic even to suggest what variables are causal, some other approach would be preferable.

Summary

The growth of group dynamics as a scientific discipline ultimately depended upon the development of research techniques and designs that could be applied to the empirical study of group processes. Although the gradual progress of the field in the early part of this century was stimulated by many developments, *structured coding systems, sociometry,* and advances in *experimental design* played particularly significant roles during this period. Today these techniques have been incorporated into the varied research practices of group dynamicists, who now use many methods to study groups. For example, Irving Janis' study of *groupthink* utilized a *case-study* approach by examining the nature of historically important groups in dramatic detail. William F. Whyte, in contrast, primarily relied on *observational methods* to investigate the nature of "corner-gangs" in an urban community. At Bennington College, Theodore Newcomb's study of attitude change resulting from reference-group influence was based on *self-report measures* of political preferences and popularity, while the classic study of leadership styles by Lewin, Lippitt, and White was an *experiment.*

Although each of these four methods possesses weakness, each one possesses many strengths as well. In general, the conclusions drawn from case studies can be highly subjective, but they stimulate theory and provide detailed information about particular groups. While observation studies vary considerably in terms of a number of characteristics—such as the degree of researcher intrusion into the group, the specificity of the observation system used, and the emphasis on intergroup comparisons—such methods give researchers a clear picture of group interaction and development. Self-report measures are especially useful when individualistic variables are of interest, but many topics cannot be fruitfully studied through questionnaires, opinion surveys, or interviews. Lastly, while groups studied in experimental settings may not reflect the dynamics of naturally occurring groups, experimentation provides the clearest test of cause-effect hypotheses.

PART
TWO

Basic
Group Processes

Throughout the life cycle of a group, a host of basic social processes combine to determine the nature of the group and the behaviors of its members. This part reviews many of these basic group processes in depth, and draws upon Bruce W. Tuckman's theory of group development for an organizing theme that unifies the various chapters (Tuckman, 1965). In Chapter 3, processes that influence the earliest stage of group life are examined to explain why groups form. Next, in Chapter 4, the conflicts and interpersonal storms that sometimes occur in groups are considered, and Chapter 5 analyzes the nature of group structure—role differentiation, norm development, and the patterning of intermember relations. The part ends with a review in Chapter 6 of factors that determine how groups perform on various tasks.

3

Forming: Becoming a Group

All of us wish we were alone at times—
off in a private world where no one can bother us. Yet most want to join with
others in a group more often than we long for these times of privacy. To provide
a partial answer to the question "Why do groups form?" in this chapter we review
four theoretical perspectives on group formation along with relevant research.
Because each of these theoretical approaches emphasizes different mechanisms—
psychodynamic needs, sociobiological pressures, social-comparison processes, and
interpersonal attraction—by considering them all we will be giving comprehensive
answers to questions concerning group formation. In addition, although this chapter is primarily concerned with the many factors that explain why people voluntarily join groups, many of the processes to be examined also account for the
development of attraction bonds in arbitrarily formed, accidental aggregates of
people.

The Psychodynamic Perspective

The psychodynamic perspective traces the origin of social behaviors to the
dynamic interplay among basic psychological needs and desires. As might be
expected, the essentials of this approach were first discussed by Sigmund Freud
(1922), founder of a psychodynamic theory that emphasized deep-seated needs
that in many cases were unknown to the individual. As we will see, when applied
to group formation Freud's psychodynamic theory argues that people join groups
because membership satisfies certain basic biological and psychological needs that
would otherwise remain unfulfilled.

Freud's Replacement Theory

In *Group Psychology and the Analysis of the Ego,* Freud (1922) explained group
formation in terms of two interrelated processes: identification and transference.
Focusing first on identification, Freud suggested that individuals' emotional energy
(libido) can be directed either toward themselves or toward other people. Although
self-love tends to dominate the earliest stages of a person's life, children eventually
learn to direct their expressions of love toward their parents through the process
of *identification.* In Freud's (1922, p. 63) terms, "identification endeavors to model
a person's own ego after the fashion of the one that has been taken as a 'model.'"
Through identification, children usually select their same-sex parents as the *ego
ideal* toward which they themselves should strive. With this acceptance of the
parent as the object of affection, a strong bond is formed, and within this relationship the child finds satisfaction through a sense of belonging, dependency
upon another, protection from external threats, and enhanced self-development.

Another of Freud's concepts, *transference*, explains how the formation of the child's first group influences his or her later group behavior. During therapy, Freud often recognized that patients would sometimes accept the therapist as their ego ideals, allowing the latter to represent what their parents stood for when they were children. Freud believed that a similar type of transference is the key determinant of group formation, since individuals in groups tend to accept leaders as authority figures just as they previously perceived their parents. This transference leads to identification with the leader, who becomes the ego ideal for all the group members. The group members, recognizing their common ego ideal, develop strong solidarity and cohesiveness through the process of identification. The group becomes a "number of individuals who have substituted one and the same object for their ego ideal and have as a consequence identified themselves with one another in their ego" (Freud, 1922, p. 80). In essence, then, in Freud's theory of group formation groups are viewed as the means by which people can "replace" the original family group; group membership is an unconscious means of regaining the security of the family (Billig, 1976; Janis, 1963).

Freud's replacement theory of groups offers many insights into group formation processes. First, exploratory studies of long-term, emotionally intensive groups—such as families, therapeutic groups, and combat units—reveal processes that are consistent with Freud's hypotheses. Second, Freud was certainly partly correct in arguing that groups form in order to satisfy individuals' needs. Third, although Freud may have exaggerated the extent to which unconscious needs determine behavior, his approach usefully proposes that individuals may join groups for less-than-rational reasons. Lastly, despite an overemphasis on the influence of child-

GROUP IDENTIFICATION AND THE "OLD SERGEANT" SYNDROME

Irving Janis (1963) describes how the formation of emotional ties in combat battalions closely parallels Freud's analysis of group formation. According to Janis, soldiers seem to accept their commander as a psychological replacement for their parents, and therefore willingly accept his commands. Furthermore, as a result of the dangers facing the group, soldiers experience an intense need for psychological support, which is partly satisfied by forming strong interpersonal bonds with the other unit members. These other members become, psychologically, the individual's siblings.

Although this dependency provides the soldier with a source of psychological support, overdependence can lead to a reaction known as the "Old Sergeant" syndrome—so named because it seemed to be most prevalent among noncom-missioned officers who had experienced a long period of combat. According to Janis, the syndrome stems from a psychological inability to replace comrades lost during combat. As casualties increase, the original members of the squad restrict their interactions to "old-timers" who were part of the original group. Although the division may be reinforced with new members, the original members are reluctant to establish emotional ties with the newcomers, partly out of fear that the pain associated with losing friends in combat will recur. As a consequence, the soldier becomes more and more detached from the group and can no longer use the group as a barrier against anxiety. In such a situation the soldier can lose confidence, fail to respond in combat, and suffer intense grief, eventually requiring psychiatric treatment.

hood experiences in later life, Freud's suggestion that people join groups simply because they have been in groups since infancy is a plausible possibility.

On the negative side, Freud's theory can be criticized for many shortcomings: an overemphasis on ill-defined processes, a myopic focus on psychological variables, and an aversion to solid empirical evidence. These limitations so severely threaten the scientific status of Freud's theory that some investigators completely reject the position. Others, however, have sought to extend Freud's initial position to compensate for some of its theoretical and empirical deficiencies. One of the most successful of these latter approaches—William C. Schutz's FIRO—is discussed in the next section.

FIRO

William C. Schutz's Fundamental Interpersonal Relations Orientation, or **FIRO** (pronounced to rhyme with *Cairo*) also traces the behavior of adults back to their earliest experiences as children in family groups. Like Freud in his analysis of group formation, Schutz hypothesized that the behavior of adults in groups often (1) parallels, or covaries with, their childhood behaviors in the family group, and (2) imitates, or covaries with, their parents' behaviors in the family group. In developing the FIRO approach Schutz emphasized three areas: dimensions of interpersonal needs, types of group-member compatibility, and the measurement of interpersonal orientation (Schutz, 1958).

THE THREE DIMENSIONS OF INTERPERSONAL NEEDS

Schutz labeled his theory the Fundamental Interpersonal Relations Orientation because he assumed group behavior to be in large part determined by interactants' basic interpersonal orientations toward others. He hypothesized the existence of three basic needs satisfied through group formation: inclusion, control, and affection.

First, *the need for inclusion* is a desire to find a sense of belonging and togetherness through interaction. Inclusion needs involve one's own acceptance of others as friends and comrades as well as the acceptance of oneself by these other people. To describe this motivation Schutz uses such terms as *associate, mingle, communicate, belong,* and *join.*

Second, an individual may join a group in order to satisfy *the need for control* over other people—that is, to establish and maintain a sense of leadership in the group through the organization and maintenance of the group's processes. An individual high in the need for control wishes to dominate others; but someone who wants to be controlled will be perfectly happy obeying others' orders. Such words as *power, authority, dominance, control,* and *ruler* all imply a strong need to control the group activities, while *follower* and *submissive* suggest a need to be controlled.

Third, like Freud, Schutz suggests a need for emotional bonds that link group members. Schutz labeled this desire to establish and maintain emotional relations with others *the need for affection,* and describes it with words like *love, like, cohesiveness, friendship,* and *personal.* As with inclusion and control, affective needs include a desire to like others as well as a desire to be liked by these other people.

TYPES OF COMPATIBILITY

Although these three needs—inclusion, control, and affection—are the prime motivations for group formation, Schutz argues it is not possible to predict when a group will develop until one considers the compatibility of the interactants. For example, what if four individuals meeting for the first time all displayed a great need to control the group's processes? Because the behavior of each person would conflict with the needs of the others, it is unlikely that a group would be formed. According to Schutz, what is needed for group formation is **originator compatibility.** People in groups who wish to originate inclusion, control, and affection should be complemented by others who wish to receive inclusion, control, and affection. Hence, originator compatibility occurs when

1. people who very actively initiate group activities work with those who want to be included in such activities (inclusion),
2. those who wish to dominate and control the activities of others work with those who want to be controlled (control),
3. those who wish to give affection work with those who want to receive affection (affection) [Schutz, 1958, p. 109].

A second type of compatibility described by Schutz—**interchange compatibility**—concerns the extent to which individuals in groups agree about how much inclusion, control, and affection should exist in the group. For example, if one group member believes that members should exchange only a small amount of affection while a second member believes in exchanging a great deal of affection, these two individuals' needs will be incompatible. Writes Schutz:

1. In the area of inclusion, people must agree on how involved they like to become with other persons, varying from always with others to always alone.
2. In the area of control, people must agree on how much of an authority structure they will operate under, varying from entirely structured to entirely unstructured.
3. In the area of affection, people must agree on the same degree of closeness of personal feelings, of expression of confidences, and so forth, varying from close and intimate to very cool and distant [1958, p. 111].

Although Schutz mentions several other types of compatibility (for example, reciprocal and need compatiblities), he points out that originator and interchange compatibilities are the most basic determinants of group formation.

THE MEASUREMENT OF FIRO

Schutz devised a scale to measure the three different needs and called this personality index the FIRO-B, since it referred largely to interpersonal behavior. As the examples in Table 3-1 show, items were included to measure the three basic dimensions of interpersonal relations he emphasized: inclusion, control, and affection. Because he felt that each one of these dimensions involves a need to express the behavior toward others (for example, "I want to be included in the group" or "I want to control others") and a need to receive the behavior from others (for example, "I want others to include me in their groups" or "I want others to control me"), FIRO-B contains the six subscales shown in Table 3-1.

TABLE 3-1. Example items from FIRO-B

Dimension	Example items
Inclusion	
Expressed behavior of self	I try to be with other people.
	I join social groups.
Behavior wanted from others	I like people to invite me to things.
	I like people to include me in their activities.
Control	
Expressed behavior of self	I try to take charge of things when I am with people.
	I try to have other people do things I want done.
Behavior wanted from others	I let other people decide what to do.
	I let other people take charge of things.
Affection	
Expressed behavior of self	I try to be friendly to people.
	I try to have close relationships with people.
Behavior wanted from others	I like people to act friendly toward me.
	I like people to act close toward me.

Reprinted by permission of the author and publisher, THE INTERPERSONAL UNDERWORLD, by W. Schutz, 1958, Science and Behavior Books, Inc., Palo Alto, California, 94306.

Schutz was able to use the FIRO-B index in studying his predictions concerning the relationship between compatibility and group formation. For example, in one project Schutz (1958) constructed groups of varying compatibility by taking into account members' FIRO-B scores. For compatible groups Schutz created originator compatibility by placing in each group one member with a high need for control, one member with a high need for inclusion, and three members with lower needs for control and inclusion. In addition, interchange compatibility was established by grouping together people with similar needs for affection. Thus, while all the groups in this set were compatible, levels of affection were high in half of the groups and low in the other half.

A set of incompatible groups was also created. First, these groups were comprised of people who varied significantly in their need for affection, ranging from high to low. Second, Schutz also made certain that each group contained two members who were high in the desire to control others and two members who were high in the desire for inclusion, thereby setting up originator incompatibility. As Schutz predicted, cohesiveness was higher in the compatible groups than in the incompatible groups. In addition, the compatible groups worked on problems far more efficiently than the incompatible groups. Other research reported by Schutz (1958) has further emphasized the importance of group-member compatibility by finding that groups that form spontaneously—such as street gangs and friendship circles in fraternities—tend to be characterized by high interchange and originator compatibility.

In sum, FIRO theory is a psychodynamic approach, since it explains group formation in terms of basic psychological needs. However, unlike Freud in his transference theory, Schutz is careful to define these basic needs, and he has also developed a technique for measuring these needs. Furthermore, FIRO is particularly useful in explaining how group formation depends upon intermember compatibility. Many other approaches fail to consider the complex question of compatibility among people in a group, but FIRO clearly specifies when individuals must match one another along the three basic dimensions specified by Schutz, as well as the level of originator compatibility needed in the group as a whole.

The Sociobiological Perspective

A second approach to group formation is based on the supposition that people join groups to satisfy a biologically rooted urge to affiliate. Like psychodynamic theorists, advocates of this perspective believe that joining together with others is basic to human nature, but unlike the psychodynamic theorists they emphasize the adaptive functions of this affiliative urge. Several closely related fields of study are based on this biological approach to behavior, but here we will focus on arguments derived from **sociobiology**.

Surviving in Groups

Sociobiology is based on Charles Darwin's theory of evolution. According to Darwin, living organisms evolve over time through a process of natural selection: species members with characteristics that increase their *fitness* tend to survive longer and be more successful in passing their genes along to future generations. Although much of Darwin's work dealt with biological and anatomical fitness, sociobiology utilizes the concept when explaining the behavior of animals in social situations. To the sociobiologist, recurring patterns of behaviors among animals ultimately stem from evolutionary processes that increase the likelihood of adaptive social actions while extinguishing nonadaptive practices (Wilson, 1975). In a sense, every regularly performed social behavior can be interpreted as an attempt to increase the individual's reproductive success.

Applied to group formation, sociobiology suggests that joining together with other members of one's species is "an expression of the evolutionarily or culturally stabilized strategies of individual animals that on average enhance their reproductive success" (Crook, 1981, p. 88). Although living in groups poses some disadvantages, these limitations are far outweighed by the adaptive advantages of groups, shown in Table 3-2 (Bertram, 1978; Harvey & Greene, 1981; Scott, 1981). For example, in nearly all species subject to predation there is "safety in numbers." Although predators may be more likely to notice a group than a solitary individual, when grouped together prey is more effective in detecting approaching predators, communicating warnings, and managing a collective defense. Groups are also effective in feeding-related behaviors, and they aid in the procurement of mates and in providing care for injured and young animals. In general, group living appears to offer significant survival advantages over individual living in a wide variety of species, and joining together with others can thus be considered a highly adaptive social behavior. In fact, some sociobiologists believe that if ecological factors—such as the scattering of food over a wide area—did not force the spacing out of species members, virtually "all species subject to predation would probably be gregarious" (Crook, 1981, p. 88).

TABLE 3-2. The adaptive advantages and disadvantages of groups

Function	Advantages of groups	Disadvantages of groups
Defense	Increased protection from predation Cooperative signaling Mutual defense	Prey more noticeable when in groups
Feeding	Catching food through cooperative hunting Feeding facilitation Cultivation by group Sharing excess food	Competition for limited food
Reproduction	Access to opposite sex Enhanced variety	Competition for mates
Nurturance and Rearing	Providing care for sick, injured, young Facilitation of learning	Spread of contagious diseases more likely

(Sources: Bertram, 1978; Harvey & Greene, 1981; Scott, 1981).

The "Herd" Instinct

Given that affiliation enhances the individual's fitness, some theorists have suggested that the need to affiliate is not learned through experience, but is a manifestation of an instinctive drive that is common in many species. Although the idea of a "herd" instinct in humans is not new (Edman, 1919; McDougall, 1908), the sociobiological perspective offers a provocative explanation for the origin of this instinctive gregariousness (Lorenz, 1966; Tiger, 1969). According to theory, about 15 million years ago, when our genetic ancestors left the protection of the rain forests to become ground dwellers, environmental pressures forced them to become more gregarious. Group formation afforded a degree of protection from predation, and the hunting group offered the only efficient means of capturing prey. Affiliating increased our ancestors' fitness, so individuals who were genetically predisposed to affiliate were more likely to live to breeding age than those who isolated themselves. Thus, affiliating individuals were more likely to mate and pass on their genetic predisposition to affiliate to their offspring. After countless generations, affiliation became a part of the biological make-up of humans, since affiliating individuals were the fittest, and therefore were evolutionarily favored through natural selection.

Although this analysis of the roots of the affiliative drive is not accepted by all sociobiologists, several bits of evidence attest to the tremendous force of the need to be with others. For example, research indicates that many species, including humans, prefer to join with others when fearful (Latané & Glass, 1968; Schachter, 1959). Across a number of studies (for example, Sarnoff & Zimbardo, 1961; Schachter, 1959), individuals awaiting a negative event—such as receiving a series of painful electrical shocks—prefer to wait with other people rather than by themselves, and other evidence suggests that joining a group is an effective way to reduce fear (Kissel, 1965). Human groups also tend to become more cohesive when facing a threatening, rather than nonthreatening, situation (Kleiner, 1960; Pepitone & Kleiner, 1957), and protracted periods of social isolation can be extremely disabling for human beings (Zubek, 1973).

Other evidence, however, seems to weight against an instinctual position. Harry Harlow's research with infant monkeys, for example, indicates that early experiences during infancy can change affiliative tendencies (Harlow & Harlow, 1966). Although a genetic approach to affiliation would argue that monkeys raised in isolation should still display affiliative tendencies, since experience alone cannot alter instinctual drives, Harlow found that monkeys raised in isolation were antisocial when they reached adulthood. This dramatic impact of early experience on affiliative behavior attests to the learned, rather than genetic, determinants of group formation. Second, an intriguing—and somewhat controversial—prediction derived from the sociobiological approach seems to have been disconfirmed by recent evidence. Because a Darwinian approach suggests that present-day needs to affiliate are, in part, produced by the importance of group formation during the hunting activities of our ancestors, the perspective suggests that affiliative drives may be greater in males than females. Recent research, however, has failed to support this prediction. In addition, some advocates of the instinctivist position have been heavily criticized for their tendency to generalize from nonhuman species to humans and from agrarian, preliterate societies to industrialized cultures (see Quadagno, 1979, for a critique). Lastly, although the bulk of the empirical evidence indicates that sociobiologists are correct in ascribing many adaptive benefits to group living, the fact that groups promote the survival of their members does not necessarily mean that the desire to join with others is instinctive in origin.

In view of the many objections that have been raised against the sociobiological approach, an instinctivist explanation of affiliation should be entertained only with caution. Yet in spite of these difficulties, the approach does point out the universal nature of affiliation and the many benefits of gregariousness. Although it remains unclear whether affiliation is produced by instinctual factors that are inherent in human nature or by environmental factors, the need to gather with others in groups is undoubtedly a powerful determinant of behavior. The sociobiological approach offers an intriguing explanation for this phenomenon, and raises several interesting questions that future research efforts may someday answer.

Social-Comparison Processes

The **social-comparison perspective** agrees with sociobiologists' belief that the need to join with others is very strong, but rejects the notion that instincts are the source of this gregariousness. If individuals join a group when they are threatened, sociobiologists would argue that this reaction suggests the operation of an instinctive need to seek shelter with others. The social-comparison theorist, however, would argue that people seek the company of others in fearful situations for informational, rather than instinctual, reasons. This approach, which was first elaborated by Leon Festinger (1950, 1954), suggests that in many cases people seek out others because they require information about themselves and the environment, and that this needed information is only available from other people. Although in some instances physical reality provides an objective standard for the validation of personal opinions, beliefs, or attitudes, in other cases individuals must turn to social reality to test their validity. Individuals compare themselves with others, and will conclude that their beliefs, opinions, or attitudes are "correct," "valid," or "proper"

IS BONDING STRONGER IN MALES THAN FEMALES?

Anthropologist Lionel Tiger (1969) uses an evolutionary perspective to explain why women tend to be excluded from groups in many military, governmental, judicial, and business settings. According to Tiger, in our evolutionary past joining with others was more adaptive for men than women. Men tended to be the hunters, since pregnancy did not restrict their mobility, and this activity could be best accomplished through cooperative group effort. Although women could participate in the hunt, Tiger suggests that males who permitted females in the group would be "at a long-run disadvantage" since

> a female hunter would be less fleet, generally less strong, possibly more prone to changes in emotional *tonus* as a consequence of the estrous cycle, and less able to adapt to changes in temperature than males. Also they could interfere with the co-operative nature of the group by stimulating competition for sexual access [Tiger, 1969, p. 45].

Furthermore, because the tasks of women, such as child rearing and food gathering, could be performed by individuals alone, Tiger suggests that females who concentrated on maternal tasks were more likely to survive than females who hunted. In consequence, through a process of natural selection a strong *bonding instinct* developed in males, while a maternal instinct developed in females.

Although Tiger's thesis is consistent with a sociobiological perspective, recent evidence fails to confirm his assumption that the bonding instinct is stronger in males than in females (Booth, 1972; Latané & Bidwell, 1977). For example, one study (Booth, 1972) surveyed the frequency of group behavior reported by 800 adults. While men did indeed join more groups than females, women—and not men—were more likely to participate in same-sex groups. Furthermore, women spent more time in their groups than did men, and the all-female groups tended to be more closely knit than the all-male groups. On the basis of these findings, the investigator concluded that the desire to bond is no stronger in males than in females.

---

if they correspond with the interpretations of appropriate others. Hence, according to Festinger's viewpoint people affiliate with others *in order to gain information via social-comparison processes.*

Schachter's Studies of Social Comparison

Stanley Schachter (1959) argued that the need to achieve the cognitive clarity that Festinger described is a direct cause of group formation. Extending the basic theoretical framework, he predicted that (1) individuals will affiliate when their opinions, attitudes, or beliefs are "shaken," (2) that uninterpretable events lead to a "search for social reality information," and that (3) affiliation will successfully satisfy this need for information (p. 6). Although a preliminary study of individual reactions to social isolation provided suggestive evidence concerning the validity of these hypotheses, Schachter undertook a series of studies in which he placed subjects in an anxiety-producing situation and then assessed their desire to affiliate with other people.

In the initial investigation the college women who served as subjects "entered a room to find facing them a gentleman of serious mien, horn-rimmed glasses, dressed in a white laboratory coat" with a "stethoscope dribbling out of his pocket"

(p. 12). This experimenter, who introduced himself as Dr. Gregor Zilstein of the Medical School's Departments of Neurology and Psychiatry, announced in ominous tones that the women were to be subjects in a study of the effects of electric shock on human beings. Because Schachter assumed that the need to affiliate increases as the need for information increases, he manipulated the anxiety the women experienced while waiting to receive their shocks. The *low-anxiety* subjects were greeted in a room that contained no electrical instrumentation and were told the shock would be so mild that "what you feel will not in any way be painful. It will resemble more a tickle or a tingle than anything unpleasant" (p. 14). The unfortunate *high-anxiety* subjects, however, faced a vast collection of electronic equipment and were informed, "These shocks will hurt, they will be painful. As you can guess, if, in research of this sort, we're to learn anything at all that will really help humanity, it is necessary that our shocks be intense . . . these shocks will be quite painful, but, of course, they will do no permanent damage" (p. 13).

After listening to this information about shock intensities, subjects were told it would be a few minutes before they would be given their shocks, and that they were to wait their turn. At this point the dependent variable, desire to affiliate, was assessed by asking subjects if they wanted to wait alone, with others, or didn't really care one way or the other. As Schachter predicted, many more of the women in the high-anxiety condition (63%) than in the low-anxiety condition (33%) expressed a desire to wait with others.

Schachter admitted that these results provided only ambiguous support for his social-comparison-theory predictions. As noted earlier in this chapter, individuals often seek out others when fearful simply for the comfort of "safety in numbers." Thus, the increase in affiliation that occurred in the high-anxiety condition did not necessarily imply that these subjects were attempting to gather information. In order to check the social-comparison prediction more closely, Schachter replicated the high-anxiety condition of his original experiment, complete with the Dr. Zilstein, the shock equipment, and the measure of desire to affiliate. In this second study anxiety was held constant at a high level and instead the amount of information that could be gained by affiliating was manipulated. Half of the anxious women were assigned to the *same-state condition.* They were told that if they chose to wait in a room with other people, these others would be women waiting to take part in the experiment. In contrast, subjects assigned to the *different-state condition* were told that they could join "girls waiting to talk to their professors and advisors" (p. 22).

Schachter felt that if the women believed the others could not provide them with any social-comparison information then there would be no reason to affiliate with them. Supporting this prediction, 60% of the women in the same-state condition asked to wait with others, while no one (0%) in the different-state condition expressed affiliative desires. As Schachter concluded, these results suggest a limitation of the old saw "misery loves company." According to Schachter "Misery doesn't love just any kind of company, it loves only miserable company" (p. 24).

Social Comparison and Affiliation: Further Findings

Although Schachter's findings lent fairly strong support to Festinger's initial ideas concerning social comparison under uncertain conditions, they were only the first step in studies of social comparison and group formation. In a brief summary of the highlights of this research we will turn our attention to three questions that Schachter's studies left largely unanswered:

1. Do people affiliate to validate their beliefs or reduce their fear?
2. Why do some people wish to wait with others when anxious while others don't?
3. How does affiliation reduce cognitive uncertainty?

SOCIAL COMPARISON VERSUS FEAR REDUCTION

Although Schachter's theoretical framework primarily argued that affiliation fulfilled social-comparison needs, his research findings were far from unequivocal. For example, after reviewing his work Schachter himself concluded that the gregariousness of his distressed subjects could have resulted from a desire for information, a desire to reduce fear levels, or both of these motivations. In order to separate these competing motives, later research exposed three-woman groups to one of three independent-variable conditions: some subjects were told to expect severe electric shock, others mild electric shock, while still others were told the experimenters did not know exactly how painful the shocks might be (Darley & Aronson, 1966). After each subject stated her fears concerning the shocks, she was given false information about the other participants that indicated that one of the women was slightly more fearful than she was but that the second was considerably less fearful. The researchers predicted that if fear reduction was the critical motive for affiliation, then high-anxiety subjects would choose to affiliate with the less fearful women, but that if people affiliate for information, then these subjects would choose the more fearful women, who also would be more similar to them. In the low-anxiety conditions the experimenters felt that fear would be so minimal that the subjects would need no social-comparison information.

The results clearly indicated that women in the high-fear condition preferred to wait with others who were similarly fearful, but the affiliative preferences of women facing the ambiguous shock were less consistent with the theory. These individuals strongly preferred to wait with the less fearful female or with no one at all. Apparently when uncertainty is extremely high, individuals desire information about the situation but would prefer to discover that they have nothing to fear. Other research suggests that uncertainty creates strong pressures to affiliate (Gerard, 1963; Gerard & Rabbie, 1961) but that people seek reassuring as well as clarifying information (Wills, 1981). Apparently individuals under stress form groups both to gain information and to reduce their anxiety levels.

INDIVIDUAL DIFFERENCES IN AFFILIATION

Birth order.   In a pilot study that preceded his experiments, Schachter (1959) was startled by the significant individual differences he found in reactions to social isolation. Five student volunteers were given food, water, and $10 a day to stay in a locked windowless room for as long as they could stand it. One lasted only two hours before nearly breaking down the door to escape, three stayed for two days, and a fifth withstood eight days and even then reported no ill effects.

In explanation Schachter suggested birth order—a person's relationship to his or her siblings as determined by order of birth—as a possible cause of individual differences in affiliative needs. Schachter speculated that first-borns and only children receive greater stimulation and more protective guidance from their parents than do later borns. This increased child/parent interaction, which has been documented in recent research (Lewis & Kreitzberg, 1979; Zajonc, Markus, & Markus, 1979), causes the first-born to be more *other oriented* and stronger in the desire to seek social-comparison cues. As Table 3-3 shows, Schachter's hunch concerning birth order was confirmed. When he examined affiliation among first- and later-borns, he discovered that the tendency to join others in the high-anxiety conditions was largely produced by the first-borns' responses. Although other research failed to find birth-order effects (for example, Darley & Aronson, 1966) the effect has surfaced in many other studies and most theorists therefore accept as a fact first-borns' higher need for affiliation (Warren, 1966; compare with Cottrell & Epley, 1977).

n-affiliation.   Many theorists believe that the affiliation motive is one of many different motivations that influence human behavior (Murray, 1938). Although the need to be with others is strong in some people it can be weak in others, creating stable differences in the need to affiliate—abbreviated as *n-affiliation*. Although the strength of n-affiliation can be measured with self-reports or observations of behavior, projective techniques such as the Thematic Aperception Test (TAT) are also often used (Atkinson, 1958). With this method respondents are shown a series of pictures and asked to make up imaginative stories that describe the "who," "what," and "why" of whatever is depicted. The imagery, themes, needs, actions, goals, and other key symbols presented in these stories are then analyzed by the investigator to detect consistent trends that suggest a desire to join with others or remain apart.

The assumption that n-affiliation is positively correlated with group formation has been supported across a wide range of studies. When compared to "loners," individuals high in n-affiliation tend to join groups more frequently (Smart, 1965), communicate more with other group members (Exline, 1962), seek more social approval from others (Byrne, 1961), and accept other group members more readily (French & Chadwick, 1956). Other research indicates that first-borns and females are higher in n-affiliation than later-borns and males (Dember, 1964; Gordon, 1965). Although this generalized need to affiliate with others goes beyond the more specific social-comparison needs discussed in this section, n-affiliation should be considered a potential cause of group formation; a person's decision to join a group may depend, in part, on predispositions based on personality characteristics.

TABLE 3-3. Birth-order differences in affiliation

Birth order	High-anxiety-condition waiting preference		Low-anxiety-condition waiting preference	
	Together	Alone or don't care	Together	Alone or don't care
First-born and only children	32	16	14	31
Later born	21	39	23	33

(Source: Schachter, 1959).

THE IMPACT OF AFFILIATION

The social-comparison explanation of affiliation assumes that people in ambiguous situations get together in groups to trade information. If the subjects in Schachter's experiments, for example, had actually formed their groups, the members would have exchanged information about and analyses of the situation; questions should have been rampant concerning the identity of Zilstein, the degree of pain involved in the shocks, the possibility of refusing to finish the study, and the experimenters' reasons for inducing pain. Unfortunately, in most of the research the subjects never really formed groups; thus we have no way of knowing if the hypothesized intragroup comparisons would actually have taken place.

To fill this gap in the research, a team of investigators asked four to six strangers to meet at a room labeled with the sign "Sexual Attitudes—Please Wait Inside" (Morris, Worchel, Bois, Pearson, Rountree, Samaha, Wachtler, & Wright, 1976). No experimenter greeted the subjects as they arrived, but the contents of the room were systematically varied to create three experimental conditions. In the *fear condition* a table in the otherwise empty room supported several electronic devices and information sheets that suggested the study involved electric shock and sexual stimulation. In the *anxiety condition* the equipment was replaced by a number of contraceptive devices, books on venereal disease, and some color pictures of nude men and women. In the *ambiguity condition* subjects found only two cardboard boxes filled with computer cards on the table. Observers behind a one-way mirror watched the group for 20 minutes, recording interaction, action, withdrawal, controlled nonreaction (for example, deliberate talking about something other than the experiment), and escape behaviors.

Analysis of the group's interactions indicated that affiliating individuals do indeed engage in social comparison. Groups in the fear condition interacted more, both verbally and nonverbally, and also displayed withdrawal reactions and controlled nonreactions. In the anxiety condition—where subjects were presumably embarrassed about the situation they had gotten themselves into—interaction was low while withdrawal was high. Lastly, the completely ambiguous condition tended to fall between these two conditions.

Like many other studies of social-comparison processes (see Suls & Miller, 1977, and Wills, 1981 for more detailed reviews), the findings lend strong support to Festinger's initial hypotheses. Taken as a whole, these investigations show that in many ambiguous situations people join together with others as a means of better understanding their social reality. In sum, it seems that we can add one more general factor to our list of reasons for joining groups: the satisfaction of psychological needs, increasing adaptive fitness, *and* the need for information.

The Social-Exchange Perspective

Leon Festinger, in his theory of social comparison (1954), focused primarily on the consequences of **information dependence**: the dependence of people on others for information about social reality. However, Festinger and other theorists (for example, Deutsch & Gerard, 1955; Kelley, 1951) have also underscored the dependence of people on groups for a wide range of other positive consequences (or effects), and this **effect dependence** is another major determinant of group formation. In this final section we will consider how social-exchange theory accounts for interpersonal attraction in terms of both the positive and the negative effects of group membership.

Interpersonal Exchange

A great many theorists and researchers investigating the foundations of inter-personal attraction use **social-exchange theory** as a framework for the interpretation of their findings. Although this explanation of attraction is not necessarily more "correct" than the many alternative perspectives dealing with effect dependence, its broad orientation has proven itself useful as a general perspective for summarizing and interpreting many of the variables that influence group formation.

While many models of group attraction can be called exchange theories (for example, Adams, 1965; Altman & Taylor, 1973; Blau, 1964; Foa & Foa, 1971; Homans, 1974; Huesmann & Levinger, 1976; La Gaipa, 1977; Lerner, 1974), the basic concepts are perhaps best described by Harold Kelley and John Thibaut (1978; Thibaut & Kelley, 1959). They begin their discussion by assuming that social interaction is analogous to economic activity. That is, individuals make decisions concerning the desirability of interaction with others on the basis of the interpersonal *value* of such interaction. As in a business setting where the desirability of some economic venture—such as manufacturing a new product—is determined by the costs involved in raw materials and product development *and* projections concerning the profits to be secured once the product hits the market, individuals' willingness to embark on some new interpersonal relation, such as joining a group, depends upon their beliefs about (1) the *rewards* (the possible gratifications and satisfactions they think they will receive from group membership) and (2) the *costs* (the possible frustrations and dissatisfactions that could result). Although social-exchange theory does not clearly specify how rewards are balanced against costs (does the individual cognitively subtract possible costs from rewards? divide rewards by costs? and so on), the overall *value* of the group membership depends upon the proportion of rewards to costs. Relationships with many rewards and few costs are seen as desirable, whereas membership in groups with few rewards and many costs is viewed as undesirable. Overall, individuals' preferences for interaction will hedonistically conform to a **minimax principle:** *people will join groups that provide them with the maximum number of valued rewards while incurring the fewest number of possible costs.*

Because of the critical importance of the reward-to-cost balance, Kelley and Thibaut introduced two concepts—**comparison level** and **comparison level for alternatives**—to describe how this balance determines group formation. Comparison level (*CL*) is the standard by which the individual evaluates the desirability of group membership. The CL derives from the average of all outcomes known to the individual and is usually strongly influenced by previous relationships. If, for example, individuals have previously been members of groups that yielded very positive rewards with very few costs, then their CL should be higher than that of individuals who have experienced fewer rewards and more costs through group membership. According to Thibaut and Kelley, groups that "fall above CL would be relatively 'satisfying' and attractive to the member; those entailing outcomes that fall below CL would be relatively 'unsatisfying' and unattractive" (1959, p. 21).

Comparison level for alternatives (CL_{alt}), on the other hand, is the standard by which individuals compare groups to other available groups. For example, individuals may be able to join several groups at any point in time, all of which are above their CL and hence should be "satisfying." However, the group with the "best" reward-to-cost balance will determine individuals' CL_{alt}, making membership in that group more probable than membership in groups with a less favorable reward-to-cost ratio. Thibaut and Kelley write, "CL_{alt} can be defined informally as the lowest level of outcomes a member will accept in the light of available alternative opportunities" (p. 21).

The concepts of CL and CL_{alt} are fairly complex, but are clarified through application. Assume that Student X is considering joining a study group that has already been formed by X's classmates. According to social-exchange theory, X will first attempt to predict what positive and negative outcomes will result from membership in the group. On the plus side of the ledger, X may believe that joining the group will make learning easier, will lead to increased interaction with several attractive members of the opposite sex, and will also yield an improved course grade. On the negative side, however, X thinks that a good deal of time and energy will be wasted just trying to get the group together and working in a coordinated fashion, that several of the group members are not the sort of people X would usually want as friends, and that the group may also lead to increased interaction with several *unattractive* members of the opposite sex.

Table 3-4 summarizes how the CL and CL_{alt} are related both to satisfaction and to decision to join the group. Membership per se will be largely determined by CL_{alt}, while satisfaction with membership will be determined by CL. If X decides that the outcomes that would result from group membership are so much more positive than negative that membership will be satisfying, the group's value surpasses X's CL. On the other hand, X may believe that the group is below his or her CL, since too many costs are involved relative to the number of valued rewards. Second, the value of alternative relations must also be considered, and the suggested study group must exceed X's CL_{alt} before he or she will join. In fact, X may decide that remaining outside the study group will yield a more favorable reward-to-cost ratio; in this instance remaining alone will establish the lower limit of X's CL_{alt}.

**TABLE 3-4. The impact of comparison level
and comparison level for alternatives on satisfaction
with group membership and decision to join a group**

		Membership in the group is	
		Above X's CL	*Below X's CL*
Membership in the group is	*Above X's CL_{alt}*	Membership is satisfying, X will join	Membership is dissatisfying, but X will join
	Below X's CL_{alt}	Membership is satisfying, but X will not join	Membership is dissatisfying, and X will not join

(Source: Thibaut & Kelley, 1959.)

In sum, when the individual receives many rewards from group membership while incurring few costs, group activity should be satisfying and relatively long-lasting. Yet predicting that groups form when rewards are high and costs are low is not very risky; indeed, the social-exchange hypothesis seems so obvious that it can hardly be denied. However, the value of this emphasis on costs and rewards lies in *application*. The impact of a large number of variables on group formation has been documented by careful research, and these voluminous findings take on a certain order when incorporated within the social-exchange framework. The approach also explains the role that groups play in meeting the personal needs and goals of their individual members, but from a different perspective than that offered by the psychodynamic and sociobiological theories. Lastly, social-exchange theory can be usefully applied to explain the stability of newly formed groups, increases in the cohesiveness of existing groups, and the magnitude of liking felt by new members who are just joining a group.

The Rewards of Groups

On the first day of class most students file in a few minutes before the scheduled meeting time, pick a seat, and think about what the course will cover, how much work will be involved, and what sort of grade can be expected. Yet, by the third or fourth class meeting, a different sort of atmosphere usually pervades the class-room. Subgroups of friends have formed, and these groups buzz with discussions of extracurricular topics while waiting for the class to begin. To explain why these groups form, a social-exchange theorist would attempt to assess the consequences of group membership in terms of rewards and costs. Although generating an exhaustive listing of all the rewards and costs of groups would be a considerable task, the researcher could focus on some of the more frequently studied and better understood benefits and liabilities of group membership. Taking a similar approach, in the next two sections of this chapter we will examine first the rewards and then the costs of joining with others in groups.

SOCIAL INTERACTION

Henry W., a widower, is 78 years old and lives alone in a small apartment. His wife died some 15 years ago, and the couple never had children. Henry does not attend a church, does not belong to any clubs, and has no friends he meets with on a regular basis. Several of his nieces have settled nearby though, and two afternoons a week Henry visits them to talk, exchange news, and be entertained by the younger children of the household. Although the visits are not lengthy, he looks forward to each one with pleasure, for these small visits break up the monot-ony, isolation, and loneliness of the rest of the week.

The satisfaction Henry takes in interacting with his relatives highlights one of the most obvious rewards of groups to their members—that of social interaction itself. Indeed, simply being with other people is probably one of the most basic reasons people join together in groups. Groups make social interaction possible and this interaction is enjoyed for its own sake.

The importance of this most basic consequence of group formation is well demonstrated in a series of studies performed by J. L. Gewirtz and his colleagues (Gewirtz, 1969; Gewirtz & Baer, 1958a; 1958b; Landau & Gewirtz, 1967). Gewirtz suggests that human beings' need to affiliate with others is partially satisfied through interaction. Just as basic biological drives, such as thirst and hunger, become stronger the longer they remain unsatisfied, the need to affiliate with others becomes stronger the longer a person has been deprived of social contact. To test this prediction the investigators (Gewirtz & Baer, 1958a) gave 32 nursery-school children the opportunity to play a game that involved dropping marbles one at a time into a box. Although the children were free to drop the marbles through either of two holes in the box's lid, the teacher only reinforced the child with verbal praise when the marble was dropped through the hole that the teacher had secretly selected as the "target" hole.

Gewirtz predicted that the effectiveness of the social reinforcement (praise) would depend upon the deprivation state of the child. Therefore, for half the playing times the children were isolated from social contact for 20 minutes before playing the game, while for the remaining times the children were not deprived of social interaction. As predicted, when the children had been isolated for the brief preplay period they were more responsive to the praise than when they had not. In a second study (Gewirtz & Baer, 1958b) the researchers further demonstrated the importance of social interaction by adding a condition in which childrens' need to affiliate was "satiated." Gewirtz argued that just as learning theorists note that giving food to an organism that has just eaten is not reinforcing, social reinforcers are not rewarding for a person who has just experienced a great deal of social interaction. Therefore, a third group of children, just before playing the game, interacted extensively with their teacher. According to the reinforcement viewpoint, these children were less deprived and hence would be less responsive to praise than children who were not satiated. The results supported this hypothesis, since deprived children were more responsive to the praise than nondeprived children, who in turn were more responsive to the praise than the satiated children. Overall, then, the results of this research indicate that one source of rewards in a group is the interaction that the group activity makes possible, and that the value of such a reward increases when people have been isolated from others. The rewarding nature of group interaction may also explain why interaction alone is sometimes sufficient to produce liking.

SOCIAL SUPPORT

Songwriter Paul Simon describes the second basic reward that derives from group formation in his song "Bridge over Troubled Water." Like a bridge that aids travelers by bearing their weight during the crossing and spanning obstacles, other people can be a source of comfort, encouragement, approval, and support. Simon's song suggests that support from others is particularly important when "times get rough," but at other times as well people need the encouragement that can be gained from others. Although social support takes many forms, two group processes that have been extensively studied by researchers are social approval and belief confirmation.

Social approval. One of the most positive means of providing social support for others involves showing them that you approve of them as persons. Although researchers occasionally discover exceptions to the general *reciprocity principle—*

ATTRACTION TO OTHERS AND THE SPATIAL ECOLOGY OF GROUP FORMATION

Many years ago Leon Festinger and his colleagues (Festinger, Schachter, & Back, 1950) measured the sociometric choices of students living in two university housing projects. The researchers discovered that these choices were influenced by a host of factors, but they were particularly surprised to find that the physical distance between people was one of the most important determinants of friendship choices: people liked people who lived close by.

At least two general factors can account for these pronounced effects of "spatial ecology." First, while small distances among people are not rewarding in and of themselves, small distances may increase the amount of interaction among people while also decreasing the time and energy required for this interaction. Second, the tendency for friendships to develop between neighbors may stem from a *mere-exposure effect*: increased liking for stimuli that are repeatedly presented to individuals (Zajonc, 1968; for reviews see Grush, 1979, and Harrison, 1977). Although

mere exposure to another person may seem to be insufficient to produce liking, the impact of exposure on group formation has been demonstrated in a number of studies that have varied the number of encounters between strangers (Brockner & Swap, 1976; Insko & Wilson, 1977; Saegert, Swap, & Zajonc, 1973; Tyler & Sears, 1977). For example, in one cleverly designed experiment (Saegert et al., 1973, Experiment 1), female college students drank a series of pleasant-tasting or foul-tasting liquids. Between each trial some of the women were moved from one tasting booth to another, but their rotations were carefully controlled so that each woman spent 10, 5, 2, 1, or 0 tasting trials with another subject. Consistent with the exposure effect, the greater the exposure to another woman, the more this stimulus person was liked—irrespective of the kind of liquids being tasted. Apparently familiarity—and interaction—breeds liking rather than contempt.

people like those who admire them and dislike those who do not—most findings confirm this intuitively appealing notion (Shrauger, 1975). For example, in one study Theodore Newcomb (1960, 1961, 1963) provided 17 male college students with room and board in a dormitory for an entire year under the provision that they complete a series of questionnaires, attitude scales, and other instruments each week. Newcomb found that ratings of group members' attractiveness, particularly in the early weeks of the study, tended to be reciprocated. In other words, if person A reported a great deal of liking for Person B, he also tended to believe that B liked him back a great deal.

Although the reciprocity principle holds in most situations, several limiting conditions should be noted (Mettee & Aronson, 1974). While reciprocity may be critically important during the early stages of group formation, the importance of mutual attraction may diminish as the relationship progresses (Newcomb, 1979). In addition, while A will usually respond to B's approving statements with increased attraction to B, reciprocity is low when A's self-appraisals are clearly negative (Deutsch & Solomon, 1959; Newcomb, 1956; Regan, 1976) or B's statements of approval are interpreted as ingratiation tactics (Jones, Gergen, & Jones, 1963).

Belief confirmation. Newcomb's research also indicated that belief similarity is an important determinant of group formation. Fairly soon after moving into the dormitory the students began cloistering into several subgroups within the total group population. When Newcomb examined these subgroupings, he was struck by the subgroup members' similarity in terms of values, beliefs, and interests. One group clique, for example, contained men who endorsed liberal political and religious attitudes, were all registered in the arts college, came from the same part of the country, and shared similar aesthetic, social, theoretical, economic, political, and religious values. Members of the second subgroup, on the other hand, were all veterans, majors in engineering, emphasized practical interests, and shared similar religious, economic, and political values. A third subgroup differed from the first two cliques in that its members were all from small Midwestern towns and were all Protestants. Lastly, the four men who did not belong to any subgroup displayed unique values and interests. Other studies have replicated these results (Byrne, Ervin, & Lamberth, 1970; Griffitt & Veitch, 1974; Kandel, 1978).

Newcomb concluded that similarity in beliefs, interests, values, and attitudes is an important determinant of group formation, since this agreement assures group members that their beliefs are acceptable and accurate. Providing support for this explanation of the "similarity-attraction effect," Don Byrne and his colleagues (Byrne, 1971; Clore & Byrne, 1974) found that belief similarity leads to increased attraction only when the beliefs concern events that cannot be easily evaluated by comparison with reality. In addition, (1) similarity is an indication that future interactions will be conflict-free and rewarding (Insko & Schopler, 1972); (2) group members tend to like similar others because they will give back very positive self-evaluations (Aronson & Worchel, 1966); and (3) most cognitive-consistency theories (for example, Heider, 1958) predict that disliking others who share our beliefs leads to cognitive imbalance and is therefore avoided.

GROUP-MEMBER CHARACTERISTICS

If a group dynamicist approached you on the street and asked you to explain why you had joined a particular group, it is unlikely that you would point to the importance of the social interaction and the support you would gain by group membership. Instead, if you responded like most people queried about their friendship choices, you would tend to explain your affiliative behavior by pointing out the "good" characteristics of the people in the group. Indeed, studies of group formation indicate that people report they prefer to be with others who are physically healthy, vigorous, and sources of new experiences (Bonney, 1947); generous, enthusiastic, sociable, punctual, fairminded, and dependable (Thibaut & Kelley, 1959); authentic, accepting, helpful, and strong in character (La Gaipa, 1977); as well as considerate, happy, truthful, and intelligent (Lott, Lott, Reed, & Crow, 1970). Yet explaining group formation in terms of group-member characteristics is still consistent with the social-exchange framework. As Thibaut and Kelley are careful to note, such characteristics as authenticity, competence, and sociability increase attraction because they suggest that future interactions will be rewarding ones. Competent individuals increase our chances of achieving success, helpful people assist us with our problems, and sociable people make interaction more enjoyable. In other words, we prefer to be in groups whose membership consists of people with "good" traits because we assume they will provide us with many rewards while exacting few costs. With this clarification in mind, let us now turn to a more detailed discussion of two characteristics that research indicates are highly valued group-member traits: competence and physical attractiveness.

Competence.   Clearly competent, intelligent, task-proficient people are viewed as more desirable group members than incompetents. Take, for example, a group of elementary school children "choosing up sides" for a game of softball during recess. With surprising speed and precision the most able players are nominated captains. Next, these two begin to select their teams with an eye to ability at the sport being played. Selection progresses, with sporadic conferences among the assembled team members, until the worst (and by this time most unhappy) members are all that compose the field of possibles. After some grumbling, eventually even these low-ability children are apportioned to the two teams.

Research suggests that group formation proceeds along similar lines in adult groups as well. In one study (Gilchrist, 1952) college students worked individually and in pairs on tests of reasoning ability. After each task the experimenter gave the participants feedback that indicated whether they had done very well or very poorly. When asked who they would most like to work with on later experimental tasks, subjects invariably chose those who had demonstrated their competence by successful performance on the two tasks. Other research (Iverson, 1964) even suggests that individuals with high levels of competence are relatively insulated from the possibility of receiving negative evaluations from others. In this research subjects listened to a speech ostensibly recorded either by a competent person (an authority in the field of mental testing) or a less competent one (a high school student). In subsequent ratings the competent speaker was rated more positively than the less competent speaker even when the highly competent speaker made insulting references to the listeners' "mental and physical weaknesses," tendencies towards "irresponsible behaviors," and "mental deficiences."

There are, of course, limitations to the desirability of competent co-members. For example, when individuals experience repeated failures on a task they may prefer to be joined by people with a level of ability that matches but does not exceed their own (Shaw & Gilchrist, 1955). Also, some people seem to prefer to be with people they know well even when these friends perform the required tasks poorly (French, 1956). Lastly, Elliot Aronson (1980, p. 247) argues that people who are *too* competent are sometimes rejected as group members because their presence makes the rest of the group feel incompetent: "Although we like to be around competent people, a person who has a great deal of ability may make us uncomfortable. That person may seem unapprochable, distant, superhuman." Indeed, research has confirmed Aronson's suspicion that highly competent people who reveal their fallibility by making minor mistakes are, in some cases, better liked than unerring group members (Aronson, Willerman, & Floyd, 1966; Helmreich, Aronson, & LeFan, 1970; Mettee & Wilkins, 1972).

Physical attractiveness.   Aronson (1980) also notes that while most people would probably deny that their choices of business associates, friends, or club members are influenced by judgments of physical attractiveness, research indicates that people's good looks constitute a major asset that, like any other valued commodity, is "traded" during social interaction. Supporting this contention, in

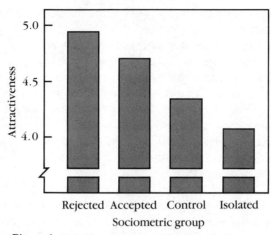

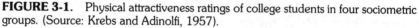

FIGURE 3-1. Physical attractiveness ratings of college students in four sociometric groups. (Source: Krebs and Adinolfi, 1957).

one study of individuals who were randomly paired together, liking for the partner was significantly correlated with the partner's physical attractiveness and virtually unrelated to other characteristics such as intelligence, personableness, self-esteem, and adjustment (Walster, Aronson, Abrahams, & Rottman, 1966). Although these results may not apply to group interactions, since only short-term, mixed-sex dyads were studied, related research conducted with first-year college students revealed a similar bias in favor of moderately attractive peers (Krebs & Adinolfi, 1975). Based on sociometric ratings by same-sex peers, this investigation identified the four "types" of students shown in Figure 3-1. Students who received the most positive sociometric nominations were placed in the *accepted* group, those who received an average number of nominations were placed in the *control* group, students who were sociometrically rejected were placed in the *rejected* group, and any students who went unnominated (in either positive terms or negative terms) were classified as *isolated*. Next, trained judges rated the physical attractiveness of the subjects using high school graduation photographs, and the average attractiveness scores of the students in the four groups were than compared. As Figure 3-1 indicates, physical attractiveness was positively related to acceptance with one important exception: extremely attractive individuals tended to be rejected by their classmates. Other evidence suggested that the highly attractive students in this study tended to be individualistic, ambitious, and achievement oriented, so they may have been rejected for failing "to demonstrate a concern for their less attractive peers" (Krebs & Adinolfi, 1975, p. 251).

THE REWARDING NATURE OF GROUP ACTIVITIES

Individuals often form groups or join already existing aggregates when the activities of the group are ones the members like. Thus an individual who enjoys playing poker might join a group of people that gets together for cards every Thursday night. A person who likes to cook might organize a gourmet supper club with three other people with a similar interest. A juvenile delinquent who finds fun in vandalism might join a street gang. These groups attract members because of the rewarding nature of the group activities.

John Thibaut (1950) experimentally verified the impact of group activities on group attraction. Groups of either 10 or 12 boys were assembled and then divided into two teams; the subjects then played a series of three games in which one team had to assist the other. For example, when the group was playing a beanbag-toss game, the favored team threw the beanbags, while the other team merely held the target and retrieved the thrown beanbags for the favored group. Thibaut arranged to have one particular team engaged at all times in the preferred behaviors, while the second team only served the first team. As anticipated, the teams that engaged in favored activities demonstrated greater increases in group cohesiveness than teams that engaged in less preferred activities.

Muzafer and Carolyn Sherif (Sherif & Sherif, 1953) also report evidence attesting to the role of group activities in group formation. In order to study the development of group structure and sources of intergroup conflict, the Sherifs broke up a single group of boys at a camp into two small groups. Because a second phase of the project (described in more detail in Chapter 13) depended upon successfully creating two highly cohesive teams, the Sherifs made certain that the two arbitrarily created groups engaged in very enjoyable activities. As soon as the assignments were made, "cars took each group separately from the camp for a hike and cook-out, activities which had first preferences with most of the boys" (p. 247). The researchers arranged for five days of softball, hiking, football, swimming, fishing, and volleyball, and soon original friendships were completely replaced by a strong sense of in-group identity and attraction. The attempt was completely successful at creating two groups simply by making certain the group activities were highly enjoyable.

GOALS

One final source of reward that becomes available through group formation exists when group membership facilitates the attainment of desired goals. As everyday experience would suggest, certain goals that individuals acting alone are unable to reach can be achieved by groups. In the Sherifs' studies, for example, many group activities could only be successfully accomplished when the entire group worked together. Indeed, in the later phases of that research the Sherifs attempted a return to the conditions that originally existed in the camp. At first, the experimenters assumed that the same technique used to form the two teams—performance of preferred activities—could be used to reunite the original group. Therefore, the groups were brought together for meals and sporting activities. Unfortunately, these methods were less successful this time around. Fights occasionally broke out between the two teams' members, and little intermixing of the two groups occurred. Instead, the introduction of tasks that could be accomplished solely through intergroup cooperation seemed to be the only method that was successful in forming a united group. For example, the Sherifs found that starting a camp-wide "superstars" baseball team that played teams from other camps proved to be a very effective means of reducing the intergroup conflicts. In addition, in later research (Sherif, Harvey, White, Hood, & Sherif, 1961) a series of emergencies that could only be dealt with successfully through cooperation among *all* the campers succeeded in dispelling hostilities and eventually led to the formation of a single fairly cohesive group.

The Costs of Group Interaction

According to social-exchange theory, an atmosphere of ambivalence pervades the initial stages of group formation. Uncertain about the rewards and costs that will stem from the group activities, individuals try (1) to test the effects of group membership while still keeping other options open and (2) to predict the future value of the relationship. Through these two processes, which Thibaut and Kelley (1959) label experience sampling and forecasting, candidates for group membership estimate the reinforcement potential of group membership by considering the rewards the group offers: social interaction with others who possess valued traits, social support, pleasant group activities, and improved chances of goal attainment. However, experience sampling and forecasting are also designed to uncover possible costs that may derive from group membership, costs that can include primary tension, personal investments, social rejection, interference, and reactance.

PRIMARY TENSION

When groups first begin to form, an element of tension is present in many of the group's interactions (Bormann, 1975; Thibaut & Kelley, 1959). Group members must deal with people they hardly know, and this initial unfamiliarity leaves them feeling uncomfortable and constrained. Often all the members of a new group are on their guard, carefully monitoring their behavior to make certain that they avoid any embarrassing lapses of social poise. Feeling as if they have been "thrown together" with a bunch of strangers, they may be reluctant to discuss their personal views and values with people they know so little about. This ambiguous situation is further complicated by the absence of any specific norms regarding the regulation of interaction and goal attainment as well as uncertainty about role differentiation and enactment. To people who believe they lack the social skills necessary to cope with this situation (Cook, 1977), this **primary tension** is so intensely punishing that group membership is actively avoided.

PERSONAL INVESTMENTS

Few business executives expect to earn something for nothing. While the attainment of high profit with no initial investment may be the dream of many corporate moguls, the most common rule of any entrepreneurial enterprise is "you have to spend money to make money." Similarly, if individuals hope to experience rewards through group membership then they must be prepared to make some personal investments in the group.

In some instances these investments will be tangible costs. For example, many voluntary groups require their members to pay an application fee prior to admittance, and, subsequently, annual dues. Other groups may require not only monetary investments, but also the provision of goods and services to the other group members (Foa & Foa, 1971). However, a greater portion of these investments will be social costs. For example, in a group individuals must devote time and effort to group processes that they had previously spent on more individually oriented activities. In order to better understand and relate to the group, individual members must gather information about their co-members by formulating attributions concerning their personality characteristics, interests, and attitudes (Heider, 1958). In addition, through self-disclosure of their own characteristics, group members must reveal enough information about themselves to enable others to get to know them better (Jourard, 1971). In time, a level of familiarity will be reached, but not before the group members have made considerable investments of personal effort and time.

Although the investment of personal resources in the group is one cost that can reduce the appeal of group membership, everyday experience suggests that people sometimes become *more* favorable toward their group the *more* they invest in it. For example, many groups—such as fraternities, sororities, and various secret societies—require new members to go through elaborate initiation rites before they can become full-fledged members because these personal investments strengthen the bond between the individual and the group. Similarly, people who join emotionally involving groups such as social movements or cults sometimes become more and more committed to the movement each time they make a personal investment in the group. Membership may cost them their jobs, their friends, their reputations, and their possessions, but each investment ties them more strongly to the group.

In explanation, the psychologists who studied such a group—one that formed around psychic Marion Keech—suggested that the increased attraction that fol-

---

THE PROPHET

The binding effects of personal investments are illustrated by a group that formed around psychic Marion Keech, who believed she was receiving messages from the "Guardians", whom she identified as the inhabitants of a planet named Clairon. Through these messages the Guardians warned Ms. Keech of the impending destruction of the world by flood, but they assured her that the small group of men and women who met regularly to discuss their messages to Ms. Keech would be rescued by flying saucer before the December 21 deadline.

Unfortunately for the group, the world did not end on that day. By the time midnight of the 21st had come and gone with no sign of unearthly intervention, the tension in the group waiting for the Guardians had become unbearable. For weeks each member had supported the group's prophecy, often at the expense of friendships, finances, and public embarrassment. Some were college students who had let their grades go, since study-

ing, they believed, was of little importance. Others had stopped paying their bills, quit their jobs, and severed relations with unbelieving family and friends. The group had changed their lives, and many felt they could never reclaim their past ways of life. In the words of one member, "I've had to go a long way. I've given up just about everything. . . . I can't afford to doubt. I have to believe" (Festinger, Riecken, & Schachter, 1956, p. 168).

Despite Ms. Keech's incorrect prediction, the group did not disband after December 21. On that day Ms. Keech received a message stating that the dedication of the group so impressed God that the Earth had been spared, and many of the members felt that they had helped save the world from a terrible flood. In the days after the disconfirmed prophecy the members seemed to become even more committed to their group, and worked to recruit new members by publicizing the group's activities.

lowed personal investments resulted from members' attempts to reduce the conflict among their cognitions (beliefs) about the group (Festinger, Riecken, & Schachter, 1956). On the one hand, they believed they had voluntarily invested time, energy, and personal resources in a group with certain positive features. However, they also believed that the group had certain negative characteristics that created costs best avoided. As cognitive dissonance theory would predict (Festinger, 1957), the two cognitions "I have invested in the group" and "the group has some cost-creating characteristics" are inconsistent with one another and cause a feeling of psychological discomfort that the person will be motivated to reduce. Although people can reduce cognitive dissonance in many ways, one frequently enacted mode of dissonance resolution involves emphasizing the rewarding features of the group while minimizing the costly characteristics. By thinking more about the positive features of the group, individuals can reduce their uncertainty about the value of the group.

To test this intriguing hypothesis, Elliot Aronson and Judson Mills (1959) manipulated group members' investments in a group by randomly assigning them to one of three experimental conditions: a severe initiation condition, a mild initiation condition, and a control condition. In the two initiation conditions female college students had to pass an "embarrassment test" before they were allowed to join the group discussing topics related to sexual behavior. In the *severe-initiation condition* the women had to read aloud to the male experimenter a series of obscene words and two "vivid descriptions of sexual activity from contemporary novels." In the *mild-initiation condition* subjects read five sex-related but nonobscene words. In the *control condition* no mention was made of the "embarrassment test."

At this point the subjects were told that the group they would be joining was already meeting but that because they were not suitably prepared for the day's discussion they could not join in. However, they were given the opportunity to listen to the group discussion via headphones in order to become familiar with the nature of the group. But rather than allowing the subjects to listen to a group, the experimenter played a tape recording of a standard group discussion that had been "deliberately designed to be as dull and banal as possible" (Aronson & Mills, 1959, p. 179). The participants discussed "dryly and haltingly" the sexual behavior of animals, mumbled frequently, uttered disjointed sentences, and lapsed into long silences.

Aronson and Mills expected that cognitive dissonance would be greatest for people who had worked hardest to join the boring group. As predicted, when participants were later asked to evaluate the quality of the group discussion, subjects from the severe-initiation condition were the most positive. Ratings of the group discussion and the group members, which could range from highly negative (0) to highly positive (255), were generally positive, but the average rating of 195.3 in the severe-initiation condition was significantly greater than the average ratings by subjects in the control condition (166.7) or the mild-initiation condition (171.1). Later researchers (Gerard & Mathewson, 1966) extended this work by finding that subjects who experienced strong electric shocks before joining a group rated the group more positively than did subjects who received only mild shocks. Although recent research suggests that the more favorable ratings that follow severe initiations may stem more from a desire to "save face" after making a faulty decision (Schlenker, 1975) than from the intrapsychic discomfort of cognitive dissonance, the effect itself remains clear: *people become more favorable toward their group after they invest in it.*

SOCIAL REJECTION

Just as acceptance by others has been found to be a very significant source of reinforcement in groups, rejection by others seems to be an equally potent source of punishment. In one study (Pepitone & Wilpinski, 1960) the researchers examined the impact of rejection on group formation by asking college students in three-person groups to discuss several controversial issues. Unknown to the true subjects in the experiment, the other two group members were actually confederates of the experimenter who either accepted or rejected the comments of the subject. Indeed, during a break between the discussion and the completion of a measure of attraction to the group, the rejecting confederates excluded the subject from their discussion by talking among themselves and giving the subject an occasional "dirty" look. Naturally, subjects were less attracted to their co-members when they had rejected them; even more interesting, the rejection also served to lower subjects' opinions of themselves.

Research also indicates that even people who *deserve* to be rejected by others because they possess negative characteristics or perform poorly on group tasks do not react favorably when rejected. In one study (Skolnick, 1971), groups of eight subjects were told they would be divided into two teams that would be competing for a prize. Before forming into teams, however, the subjects completed two performance tests and were given feedback about their work—half were randomly told that they had performed better than everyone in the group (success) and half were told that their performances were worse than everyone else's (failure). Next, subjects were given the chance to evaluate one other person in the group, supposedly so the researcher could more effectively form the teams. This evaluation was to be based on the performance on the two tests, so subjects were given information about one other person's score and then asked to write a short note to this person. When the notes were exchanged, the experimenter inserted prepared messages that contained one of two statements: "You are the person I most prefer to have on my team" or "You are the person I least prefer to have on my team."

Subjects were then asked to indicate their liking for the person who sent them the note. As anticipated, the accepting note writer was liked more frequently than the rejecting note writer. However, even when the subjects believed they had failed on the pretests and hence deserved to be rejected by their potential partners, they were especially appreciative of the acceptance and dissatisfied with rejection. This study and others (see Shrauger, 1975, for a review) suggest that rejection by others is punishing and decreases the probability of group formation, especially if the individual's self-acceptance has recently been shaken by failure or other negative experiences.

A less extreme form of group rejection occurs when individuals believe that the group is ignoring their inputs. In a study conducted some years ago, researchers (Zander & Cohen, 1955) instructed groups of seven people to role-play members of a university committee deciding how a substantial sum of money was to be spent. Before discussion commenced, two of the members were asked to leave the room. During their absence the experimenters gave the remaining members extra instructions, indicating that one of the absent subjects was to be treated as a high-status official (a dean) while the other subject was to enjoy lower status (a freshman). Although the absent members were to be treated in accordance with their roles, the group members were cautioned not to discuss the role designations with the absent members.

After the "freshmen" and "deans" had rejoined the groups and the problem had been discussed, subjects were asked to give their reactions to the groups. Although the two identified subjects in each group had been unaware of their roles, they had been treated differentially by the remaining group members and hence had much different reactions to the groups. Relative to the "deans," the "freshmen" felt the groups had given less attention to their opinions and that their influence on the group processes was small. These lower status group members were also less attracted to the group than the others and felt they had made a poorer impression. Similar effects are found when groups grow so large in size that the rank-and-file members feel left out of discussions. In one study (Bales, Strodtbeck, Mills, & Roseborough, 1951), all members of groups participated provided the groups remained small in size. However, when the number of individuals in the group exceeded four, the groups' processes tended to be dominated by certain key group members and the remaining members found few chances to interject their opinions.

INTERFERENCE

Group Leader A, a traditionalist, believes that groups should work toward their goals in as serious and logical a manner as possible. Group Member B, a frustrated comedian, believes that the monotony of the group's meeting should be punctuated by jokes, puns, and horseplay. B, therefore, characteristically performs behaviors that are detrimental to the interests of A. A, on the other hand, does things that reduce the rewards B experiences. Thibaut and Kelley label such conflict among members **interference,** and suggest that it is often experienced as a cost of group life because there are so many ways for our fellow group members to increase our costs and/or lower our rewards. For example, they can make noise when we are trying to get work done and make it impossible for us to concentrate (Chapanis, Garner, & Morgan, 1949). They can make us feel uncomfortable and crowded by watching us as we try to do our work (Greenberg & Firestone, 1977). They can get in our way when the room in which we must work is limited in size (Heller, Groff, & Solomon, 1977). They can perform poorly at the task at hand and cause the group to fail (Zander, 1968) or subject us to their second-hand cigarette smoke. A list of the ways in which group members interfere with one another would be quite long (Kelley, 1979).

REACTANCE

When individuals join groups, they often find that their individual freedom is restricted. Thibaut and Kelley note that, just to overcome the problems of interference, people in groups must eliminate those behaviors that cause conflict and

THE ATTRACTIVENESS OF GROUP MEMBERS WHO SMOKE CIGARETTES

The cigarette habits of group members can, in some instances, seriously impact other group members. While smokers are often tempted to "light up" during a group interaction, nonsmokers are sometimes very offended when exposed to smoke. Unfortunately, smokers can be equally offended when nonsmokers ask them to refrain from smoking, so the interference between smoker and nonsmoker is mutual.

To study some of the consequences of smoking habits on attraction in groups, researchers (Bleda & Sandman, 1977) arranged for males to work on a task in the presence of a male confederate who *did not smoke,* who *smoked courteously* by blowing his smoke away from the subject, or who *smoked discourteously* by blowing his smoke towards the subject. When subjects later rated the confederate on a scale that ranged from 3 (very negative) to 21 (very positive), the researchers found that reactions varied depending on the subjects' personal smoking preferences. As the figure shows, (1) subjects who did not smoke rated anyone who smoked more negatively; (2) subjects who smoked, but refrained from doing so during the experiment, rated only the discourteous smoker more negatively; and

(3) subjects who themselves smoked during the experiment did not rate anyone more negatively. Overall, this study—and others (for example, Polivy, Hackett, & Bycio, 1979)—indicate that people who smoke cigarettes in groups are not liked as much as nonsmokers.

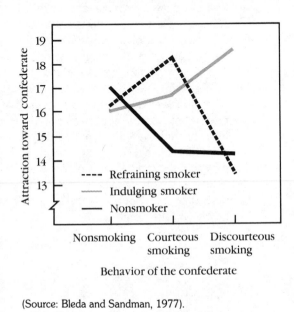

(Source: Bleda and Sandman, 1977).

---

perform only those responses that will be compatible with other individuals' actions. Certainly in many instances this demand for synchronization within the group will mean that individuals must restrict their behavior to fewer and perhaps less desirable alternatives. Even if a person is reluctant to change his or her behavior, the group as a whole may bring pressures to bear until the required modification is made. Groups tend to be remarkably intolerant of any deviation from the group norms and therefore develop implicit pressures that result in an eventual restriction of possible behaviors. Typically, individuals who deviate from the accepted pattern of behavior are directly or indirectly sanctioned by the group and suffer ostracism if they do not conform their behavior with what is considered acceptable. As we shall find repeatedly in later chapters, an often experienced consequence of group membership is a reduction in the freedom to act in ways the group would consider deviant.

Individuals must restrict their behavior not only to avoid interfering with other group members and to maintain conformity with norms, but also because they must obey any orders given them by more powerful members of higher status.

While the upper echelons of the group may enjoy the benefits of close adherence to their demands, those of lesser status who must comply with these requests suffer further losses of freedom. One consequence of this restriction in responses that occurs in groups is descirbed by **reactance** theory (Brehm, 1976; Brehm & Brehm, 1981). According to this perspective most people prefer to believe that they themselves are free to determine their own behavior. This desire to maintain a sense of freedom is so strong that, if others reduce their ability to behave as they please, they will be motivated to reassert their freedom in the situation. Thus, if joining a group means that some behavior options must be discarded, a person may experience psychological reactance and seek to reestablish his or her freedom by refusing to agree with the other group members (Brehm & Mann, 1975) or by abandoning the group altogether (Worchel & Brehm, 1971).

Summary

The four perspectives examined in this chapter to explain group formation exhibit both similarities and differences. Although these approaches contrast sharply in scope and emphasis, all note the critical importance of groups in meeting human needs—whether these needs be psychodynamic, instinctual, informational, or interpersonal in origin. First, affiliation may derive from the basic psychological needs specified by Freud in his *psychodynamic theory* of groups, or the need for inclusion, control, or affection specified in the *FIRO* model. Second, at another level groups may exist because group life is a wonderfully adaptive mechanism that enhances one's fitness. From this *sociobiological viewpoint*, evolutionary mechanisms may have created a socially oriented species whose members are genetically predisposed to live with others rather than alone. Third, the predominance of groups in human societies may stem from the fact that people rely on others for information about their social world. As Schachter's research aptly demonstrates, in ambiguous situations people turn to others to evaluate their attitudes, opinions, values, and beliefs, and this *social-comparison process* seems to be an effective method for understanding social reality. Finally, people may join with others simply because they can gain greater rewards and incur fewer costs as group members than as individuals. While on the negative side group membership leads to tension, investment, rejection, interference, and loss of freedom, these costs are often compensated for by the many rewards of groups: social interaction; social support; contact with competent, attractive others; pleasant activities; and the attainment of desired goals. The balance between these rewards and costs of group membership can be explained by *social-exchange theory,* which argues that individuals seek out membership in groups that exceed their comparison levels.

4

Storming:
Conflict in Groups

Storms are a natural — and virtually unavoidable—aspect of this planet's weather system. They range in intensity from light rainshowers to thunderstorms to hurricanes, and they seem to occur at the most inopportune times in even the most moderate of climates. Similarly, interpersonal storms are a natural—and virtually unavoidable—aspect of social interaction within groups. While these "storms" can range from minor disagreements to unresolvable disputes that destroy the group, conflicts seem to occur even in groups with very pleasant, friendly "climates."

This chapter describes the ways in which conflicts can develop in groups and the causes and value of these phenomena. Although many different kinds of conflicts could have been considered, this chapter focuses specifically on intragroup conflict, leaving the analysis of conflict between groups—intergroup conflict—to later chapters (see particularly Chapter 13). The first section traces the pattern of conflict development through five stages and describes the group mechanisms involved at each stage. The next covers a number of potential causes of group conflict, and the chapter then closes with an examination of the value of conflict for dynamic groups.

The Course of Conflict

The term *conflict*—which is derived from the Latin *conflictus,* a "striking together with force"—implies disagreement, discord, and friction among members of a group; interaction where words, emotions, and actions "strike together" to produce disruptive effects. While in previous meetings the group may have been the picture of tranquility, tension between members suddenly surfaces. Perhaps one of the more talkative, dominant members of the group is bluntly told to "let somebody else say something for a change." Perhaps the "joker" in the group, known for wisecracking and cutting up, is finally told to make a substantive contribution to the group effort. Perhaps the importance of the group and its goals are challenged by one of the more marginal members. In any event, the emergence of dissent marks the beginning of a sequential process of conflict involving a number of stages. These various stages can be examined from many perspectives (for example, Bales & Strodtbeck, 1951; Bennis & Shepard, 1956; Bion, 1961; Ellis & Fisher, 1975), but the approach presented here focuses on the five stages shown in Figure 4-1. Although groups need not move through all the components of the model, since conflict can be cut short at any stage, the course of conflict in groups generally follows this sequence: disagreement, confrontation, escalation, de-escalation, and resolution.

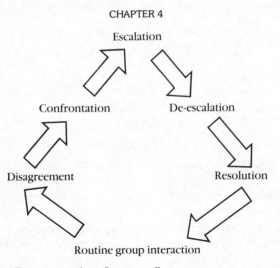

FIGURE 4-1. The course of conflict in small groups.

Disagreement

After the initial embarrassments and inhibitions that arise from interaction with unfamiliar others subside, group members typically begin exchanging information about themselves and their goals to enable members to understand better their relationships with one another. It is during this exploration of interpersonal and task realms that the group frequently discovers that disagreement exists between two or more members. The rate of interaction begins to slow, and the attention of the entire group focuses on the source of the conflict. At this stage the group members must identify the type of disagreement that separates the interactants, assess the seriousness of the conflict as a threat to group processes, and consider its implications for group unity. These needs result in a good deal of verbal exploration as the members seek to clarify the problem.

First, group members must decide if a real disagreement exists or if the disparity is actually a simple misunderstanding. Although a group member may believe that disagreement exists, further exploration of the problem may indicate that no real conflict is involved. For example, a guard on a men's basketball team may come to believe that the forward is more interested in getting glory for himself than in trying to help the team win. However, after a discussion in which the forward has the chance to explain his feelings and motivations, the possible conflict might be erased and good relations reestablished. Such conflicts, sometimes called *false conflicts* (Deutsch, 1973) or *autistic conflicts* (Holmes & Miller, 1976; Kriesberg, 1973), are more apparent than real but if left unexamined can mushroom into true conflicts.

In addition to the autistic-realistic question, the group must also decide whether the issue is of immediate concern to the group's goals or whether it can be passed over for the time being. Members can end disagreements over minor issues—as when members argue over the merits of movies, shoes, hairstyles, mouthwashes, or jokes—by asking the warring factions to consider the difficulty on their own time. In addition, the group might identify some problems that surface during discussion as potentially important but obviously unresolvable or irrelevant to the group's goals, and thus sidestep them.

Third, although some disagreements are real and of some importance to the group, they may be easily solved by changing some minor situational factor. For example, the group member who has aroused the ire of others by consistently arriving for meetings ten minutes late can be told to show up on time or be dropped from the group; the discord over who sits where at the rectangular table might be alleviated by moving to a round table; or two group members' petty squabblings over the wording of an announcement could be quelled by the leader. Such disagreements, sometimes called *contingent conflicts* since they depend upon some minor feature of the situation (Deutsch, 1973), are easily solvable without any undue increase in group tension.

Often when the source of a conflict is considered, other previously unnoticed issues of disagreement begin to arise. Thus, although the original conflict may have concerned a minor point of disagreement—such as how to control the flow of communication or when to break for lunch—it can lead to other, more basic points of contentiousness. More issues are brought out into the open, and soon the minor differences extend to many other areas. Furthermore, members who were reluctant to break the smooth preconflict interaction now realize that the damage is already done, and join in the fray by expressing the dislikes and disagreements they had previously suppressed.

Confrontation

At the disagreement stage the group has come to believe that a real difference exists between two or more group members. Furthermore, no simple solution to this discord is readily apparent, and the issues involved are perceived as important enough to warrant the seeking of a solution. It is during the confrontation phase that true **conflict** exists in the group; that is, *the actions and/or beliefs of one or more members of the group are incompatible with—and hence are resisted by— one or more of the other group members.* The two opposing factions debate the issues involved, and much of the group interaction is devoted to attempts to convert the opponent through persuasion. Each side explains its position, cites the factors that justify its stance, and points out the errors in the other's thinking. The rate of communication among disagreeing members jumps, but for now the content of the discussion focuses on substantive issues. During this confrontation, however, several interesting psychological and interpersonal mechanisms are set into motion.

COMMITMENT INTENSIFICATION

Everything seems to be going smoothly at a meeting called to decide if the company should remodel its current offices or move into new quarters. Suddenly, though, you realize that young Franklin is arguing in favor of the remodeling plan. Although you haven't really given it much thought, you feel that new quarters would be a nice change, and had assumed that Franklin would think so too. As you listen to Franklin's enumeration of the merits of remodeling, you begin to search for weaknesses in her position while organizing the points that weigh in favor of moving. Soon you begin to think that the group would be making a grave error in endorsing the remodeling plan, so you take steps to change the group's opinion. You now announce your position to the rest of the group with little qualification, begin buttressing that stance with favorable arguments, and attack several of the weaknesses in Franklin's plan. Although initially you had been uncertain as to which plan was best, your commitment to moving is now obvious as you express your opinions in very definite terms and tenaciously refuse to yield even minor concessions to those who favor the remodeling plan.

This intensification of commitment frequently results from confrontation with others and stems from a variety of sources, some of which are more rational than others. On the logical side, to persuade other participants you must emphasize the factors that favor your position, and this overattention to positive arguments results in your selective retention of position-consistent information. In a sense, you persuade yourself as you try to persuade others (Hovland, Janis, & Kelley, 1953). In addition, your own behavior during the discussion—arguing in favor of Plan A rather than Plan B, for example—tells you that you must strongly favor Plan A. This tendency to infer commitment from the observation of one's own behavior is called **self-perception** (Bem, 1972), and apparently occurs whenever people voluntarily commit themselves to a given position (Kiesler, 1971).

Two less logical processes generating the intensification of commitment are rationalization and reactance. Often when group members take a position on an issue they begin to overlook the possibility that they may have made an error and invent explanations for any disconfirmations of their beliefs. Indeed, recent research indicates that individuals who publicly commit themselves to a position tend (1) to doubt the veracity of information that conflicts with their stance and/or (2) to increase their dedication to their original position (Batson, 1975). In part, this intensification may stem from psychological *reactance*: the need to reestablish freedom whenever it is threatened. In his research, Jack Brehm (1976; Brehm & Brehm, 1981) has discovered that persuasive attempts, particularly if viewed as coercive or biased, often backfire in a "boomerang" effect as the target actually becomes more committed to the original position. For example, in one study in which two teammates had to make a choice between two alternatives marked 1-A or 1-B, 73% chose 1-A if the partner stated "I prefer 1-A," but only 40% chose 1-A if the partner demanded "I think we should both do 1-A" (Brehm & Sensenig, 1966). Similarly, in a later study (Worchel & Brehm, 1971) 83% of the members of a group refused to go along with a group participant who said "I think it's pretty obvious all of us are going to work on task A."

TENSION BUILDING

As commitment increases, anxiety and tension become more dominant. Although a confrontation may erupt when group members begin to disagree over how to solve a problem at hand or how to reach goals, conflict often spreads to more affective areas as emotions run high (Fisher, 1980). The tension rises as interactants become locked into their positions, and emotional expressions begin to replace logical discussions.

Allan Teger (1980) has studied emotionality and tension during group conflict by conducting "dollar auctions." Using both naturally occurring groups and groups formed in the laboratory, Teger tells participants he will auction off a dollar bill to the highest bidder. Interactants are instructed to offer bids, just as in an auction, but one unique rule is added: although the highest bidder gets to keep the dollar bill, the second highest bidder not only gets nothing but also must pay the amount he or she bid. In all the groups, members are at first reluctant to compete with one another under these rules, but soon the bids begin to climb over 50¢ toward the $1 mark. As the stakes increase, however, the group members realize that quitting will be very costly, and thus they become entrapped in the confrontation (Brockner, Shaw, & Rubin, 1979). To understand better the nature of this *entrapment,* consider the predicament of two hypothetical group members, Jim and Joel. All other players have dropped out, and Jim's bid of 80¢ has just been bettered by Joel's bid of 90¢. Although Jim would like to quit, he would be out 80¢ while Joel would be making 10¢. So Jim raises his bid to $1 to avoid the loss of his 80¢ investment. Joel now faces a similar dilemma, for he will lose 90¢ if he gives up. Therefore, even though he feels somewhat foolish offering more money than the bill is actually worth, Joel bids $1.10. As this example shows, entrapment can be very costly; Teger has found that the bidding nearly always exceeds $1, and on occasion has even gone as high as $20.

As the bidding approaches and then surpasses $1, Teger notes the atmosphere of the group changes dramatically. Although joking and conversation typify the low bidding stages, nervous tension grips the group as the bidding increases. Participants trapped in the exchange become emotionally involved, betraying greater unhappiness and nervousness as they risk more money. When their comments during the auction were coded by observers, indications of greater anxiety and tension—such as nervous laughter, worry, and concerns about money and time—were noted as participants' bids passed $1. These overt signs of tension were accompanied by physiological symptoms of stress, including changes in body temperature and heart rate. Apparently confrontation leads to noticeable increases in tension as well as physiological arousal (see Blascovich, Nash, & Ginsburg, 1978; Van Egeren, 1979).

COALITION FORMATION

Chapter 7 covers the factors that determine the formation of **coalitions** —subgroups within a larger group—in small groups, but these factors are worth discussing in the context of the conflict process since coalitions often develop during the final phases of confrontation (Bennis & Shepard, 1956). While the initial disagreement may involve only two group members, these persons typically marshal the forces of the group against one another, compelling previously neutral members to identify with one faction or the other. Similarly even when members initially express many different views, with time these multiple-party conflicts are reduced to two-party blocs through coalition formation (Mack & Snyder, 1957). As a result, the group becomes *schismatic*—polarized around the issues—as the once-limited dispute engulfs the entire group (Gustafson, 1978).

Escalation

The commitment, anxiety, and polarization of the group that comes about during confrontation is frequently followed by a period of conflict escalation. Rather than moving directly from confrontation to conflict resolution, many groups are caught up in a *conflict spiral*—conflict leading to more conflict leading to more conflict. The final remnants of group unity are shattered as the combatants' exchanges become increasingly hostile; persuasive influence is dropped in favor of coercion, promises are replaced by threats, and in extreme cases verbal attacks become physically violent assaults. The conflict escalates, seemingly uncontrolled, and the intensity of the dispute reaches a new high. Although this escalation is often self-defeating for both sides, a host of subsidiary factors seems to "feed the fire," including distrust, frustration, and negative reciprocity.

MISUNDERSTANDING AND DISTRUST

Imagine that you and one other person are waiting to participate in a social-psychological experiment. Before you have a chance to speak to the other individual, researchers in white laboratory coats lead each of you off to different rooms. In your small cubicle you learn that you will be given the chance to earn some money by playing a simple game. When it is your turn, all you have to do is choose between two options, labeled A and B. If you choose the "right" option, you will get anywhere from 50¢ to $1. If, however, you pick the "wrong" option, you could lose as much as $1.

To complicate things, you are also told that neither A nor B will always be the "right" solution, because you are not playing the game alone. The person you waited with (Person X) is in the next room, and X will also be choosing between A and B in the hopes of earning some money. The two of you will be making your choices at the same time, and the researchers have developed a complicated, but interesting, scheme for your payment. They explain that each turn of the game will have one of four outcomes:

1. If you choose A and X chooses A, then both of you will earn 50¢.
2. If you choose A and X chooses B, then you will lose $1, but X will earn $1.
3. If you choose B and X chooses A, then you will earn $1, and X will lose $1.
4. If you choose B and X chooses B, then you will both lose 50¢.

These instructions confuse you for a moment, but eventually you understand when the experimenter shows you a chart similar to Figure 4-2.

You begin thinking that these researchers must lose a great deal of money until suddenly you realize that the situation is more complicated than it first seemed. Certainly you would like to get the $1, but to do so you must choose B. However, X (who you must assume wants the money too) must also choose B to get the $1. Unfortunately, when you pick B and X picks B, you will both lose 50¢. So, rather than try for the whole $1, you begin thinking that both you and X should choose A, thereby earning 50¢ each. But what if X, a stranger you have no way of communicating with, "cheats" and picks B while you pick A? Then you'll lose $1 while X gains $1. But what if X is afraid of losing the money, and so picks B as a defense? Or what if you pick B but X tries to cooperate and therefore picks A? What if . . . ?

Morton Deutsch, a social psychologist who has devoted more than thirty years to the study of social conflict, suggests that the impact of distrust and misunderstanding on conflict escalation is uniquely summarized in this experimental situa-

Your choice

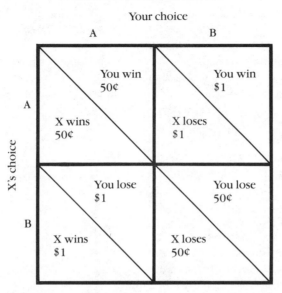

FIGURE 4-2.   The payoffs associated with Choices A and B.

tion (Deutsch, 1958, 1960, 1973). In this deceptively simple situation, players can maximize their own winnings by exploiting a partner who cooperates. In addition, if the other person attempts to maximize his or her profit by making competitive responses, then the participant will again be better off (or at least, will lose the least) if this competition is answered with competition. However, mutual competition means that both parties lose money, while mutual cooperation maximizes the group's joint winnings. Thus, the group would benefit the most from cooperation, but any shade of doubt about the trustworthiness of the partner will evoke competition and conflict. This dilemma is a form of the **Prisoner's Dilemma Game (PDG),** which derives its name from a hypothetical situation studied by mathematical game theorists.

Although the PDG is an artificial procedure that oversimplifies the complexities of conflict in groups (see Wrightsman, O'Connor, & Baker, 1972, for a review), the game nicely highlights the links among distrust, misunderstanding, and conflict escalation. First, the payoff matrix is deliberately constructed to make the exploitation of a cooperating partner a tempting alternative. Recognizing this temptation, participants sometimes feel that their partners cannot be trusted to make responses that benefit both players, and in defense of their own winnings they make competitive choices. Where players fail to trust one another, the conflict escalates (Brickman, Becker, & Castle, 1979). Second, the behaviors and motives of the other player are often completely misunderstood by participants, and this misunderstanding only adds to the conflict. For example, in many studies once two players' choices were

> out of phase—e.g., one choosing cooperatively and the other not—it was extremely difficult for them to get together again. Thus if Person I chose cooperatively and Person II chose uncooperatively, Person I might get angry and choose uncooperatively while Person II would choose cooperatively [Deutsch, 1973, p. 193].

THE PRISONER'S DILEMMA GAME (PDG)

The experimental dilemma described in the example is often called a "Prisoner's Dilemma Game" in reference to a hypothetical quandary that ensnares two prisoners (Luce & Raiffa, 1957). Once taken into custody, the two villains (here named Bonnie and Clyde) are questioned in separate rooms. Although their interrogators are certain that they are guilty of the crime, they also realize that without a confession the two criminals will have to be set free. Therefore, they present each prisoner with two alternatives: confess to the crime or remain silent. If Bonnie confesses and Clyde does not, then Bonnie will get no sentence at all but Clyde will get ten years. Conversely, if Clyde confesses but Bonnie does not, then Clyde will be set free while Bonnie is locked away for ten years. If, however, both confess, then a five-year sentence will be arranged, while if neither one confesses then both will be tried on a minor charge that carries the light sentence of one year. The dilemma for the prisoners is obvious. By confessing the prisoner will end up with either no sentence or an intermediately long sentence, but by remaining silent the prisoner will get either one year or ten years. Clearly, the situation tests the amount of trust the two prisoners have for one another.

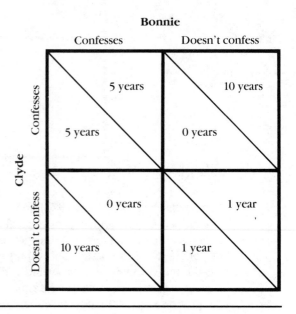

As a result of this misunderstanding and distrust, players tend to move away from cooperative responses until they become opponents locked in an escalating cycle of competition. This self-defeating competition can be very frustrating for participants, and the resulting sense of frustration can set into motion a second conflict-escalating mechanism: overt hostility.

FRUSTRATION AND OVERT HOSTILITY

One of the oldest social-psychological explanations of hostility and physical violence is based on the link between frustration and aggression. According to this view (Berkowitz, 1962, 1978) individuals who are unable to attain the goals they desire because of some environmental restraint or personal limitation sometimes experience frustration. This frustration, in turn, produces a readiness to respond in an aggressive manner that boils over into hostility and violence if situational cues that serve as "releasers" are present. Unfortunately, all these elements appear during intragroup conflict. When group members find themselves in disagreement with others, they attempt to solve the dispute. If, however, the conflict reaches the escalation stage, the disparity between the antagonists has increased rather than decreased, and the goal of conflict resolution has become frustratingly far away. Furthermore, any belligerence, argumentativeness, or hostility among the group members serves as a cue for the release of verbal, and in some cases, physical violence.

John R. P. French, in an early laboratory study of conflict in groups (1941), demonstrated the link between frustration and aggression by examining the reactions of 16 groups as they worked on a series of difficult problems. The groups' frustration derived from the fact that while subjects were instructed to finish the problems as quickly as possible, all the tasks were, in fact, insoluble. Although all groups showed signs of increased hostility, French also found systematic differences in groups' reactions to their difficulties. In groups composed of subjects who had never interacted prior to the meeting, frustration led to deep divisions in the groups. The polarization was so intense that half of these groups either split up into subgroups to work on the problems or forced one or more of their members to leave the group and sit in a corner! When the group members knew each other prior to the meeting, however, the frustration did not produce as much separation between members, but interpersonal aggression—such as overt hostility, joking hostility, scapegoating, and domination—was relatively high. Indeed, in one group of "friends" rates of aggression escalated so quickly that observers lost track of how many offensive remarks were made; they estimated that the number surpassed 600 comments during the 45-minute work period.

RECIPROCITY

Although we have seen how groups can be pushed further and further into escalating conflict by distrust and misunderstanding as well as frustration and hostility, norms of reciprocity are a third influencing factor at this stage in the conflict cycle. Conflict-ridden groups may, at first consideration, seem to be "out of control" and normless, but James Tedeschi and his colleagues (for example, Tedeschi, Gaes, & Rivera, 1977; Tedeschi, Smith, & Brown, 1974) have persuasively argued that escalating patterns of conflict are, in part, the products of norms of reciprocity and self-defense. In social interaction, reciprocity suggests that when people who help you later need help, you are obligated to return their favor. However, *negative reciprocity* implies that people who harm you are also deserving of harm themselves. The converse of "you scratch my back, I'll scratch yours" is "an eye for an eye, a tooth for a tooth."

Tedeschi points out that the norm of reciprocity increases the probability of escalation of conflict. If one group member criticizes the ideas, opinions, or characteristics of another, the victim of the attack will feel justified in counterattacking unless some situational factor legitimizes the aggression of the former. Indeed, laboratory studies involving two partners delivering electric shocks to one another typically find that partners return what they themselves received. If the opponent gives you one shock, you return one shock; if, however, the other zaps you with seven shocks, seven shocks are meted out in return (Berkowitz & Geen, 1962; Buss, 1961).

The norm of reciprocity also explains a phenomenon Harold Kelley and Anthony Stahelski have labeled *behavioral assimilation*: the eventual matching, or assimilation, of the behaviors displayed by interacting group members. This behavioral assimilation was revealed in early research (for example, Pruitt, 1968) that found that individuals who played the PDG with cooperative partners tended themselves to cooperate. Those who met competitors, however, soon became assimilated to this strategy as they themselves became more competitive. Kelley and Stahelski (1970a, 1970b, 1970c) extended this finding by suggesting that behavioral assimilation occurs primarily during competition rather than cooperation. In their research individuals played the PDG with other subjects who chose either cooperative responses or competitive responses. Kelley and Stahelski found that if individuals who began by cooperating played cooperative partners, they remained cooperative. If, on the other hand, their partners began competing with them, behavioral assimilation occurred and the previously cooperative players became competitive. In other words, when faced with competition from others, cooperators felt the norm of reciprocity justified increasingly competitive responses. Hence, conflict tends to beget conflict.

Kelley and Stahelski also suggest that negative reciprocity (competing with competitors) may be stronger than positive reciprocity (cooperating with cooperators). In their research, individuals who began by competing with others tended to continue competing even when they were faced with highly cooperative partners. The norm of positive reciprocity dictates that these competitors should have met this cooperation with reduced competition, but Kelley and Stahelski found little evidence of this. Although other research has shown that negative reciprocity is minimal if cooperatively oriented individuals have the opportunity to withdraw from the interaction or can communicate their "good" intentions to their partners (Garner & Deutsch, 1974; Miller & Holmes, 1975), other findings have confirmed the greater strength of negative reciprocity (Schlenker & Goldman, 1978).

De-escalation

If the group successfully weathers the first three stages of the conflict process—disagreement, confrontation, and escalation—then in time the conflict-reduction processes of the fourth stage, de-escalation, may begin to take effect. Just as many factors trigger the escalation of conflict, so a host of factors reverse the direction of the group's movement in the conflict spiral. While members may become strongly committed to their own viewpoints, they cannot help but recognize that time and energy are being wasted by the continuing debate. The high levels of tension cannot be maintained indefinitely, and with the drop in arousal and anxiety comes an increase in rationality and understanding. Interruptions during the escalation phase help the group members "cool off" and achieve a broader perspective concerning the issues. Also, the fear of undermining the foundations of the group prompts a return to more normal relations. Once more, several interrelated mechanisms characterize groups working to manage their conflicts. Below we discuss each of these mechanisms.

NEGOTIATION

Previous researchers (for reviews, see Druckman, 1977; Pruitt, 1981; Rubin & Brown, 1975) have pointed out that conflict is often reduced through interpersonal *negotiation*. Such negotiations always involve at least two persons (or, more generally, two "parties") and are based on the assumption that everyone would benefit by reaching a solution. Naturally, the interactants prefer certain solutions to others, but through negotiation the discussion becomes focused on specific issues and the exchange of offers and counteroffers. Also, while some negotiation situations involve *distributive issues*—one party will benefit if the other party agrees to make a concession—other negotiations involve *integrative issues*—the two parties are working together to seek a solution that will benefit all parties. The buyer/seller relationship is an example of distributive bargaining, while two group members trying to choose a solution to a problem would be engaged in integrative bargaining. Because bargaining and negotiation plays a larger, and more formalized, role in the reduction of intergroup conflict, further discussion of relevant theory and research will be postponed until Chapter 13.

BUILDING TRUST

Although **trust** may be the foundation of successful interpersonal relations, it can be difficult to believe that the "word, the promise, the verbal or written statement of another individual or group can be relied upon" (Rotter, 1980, p. 35). While continued cooperation among people over a long period of time generally increases mutual trust, for a group that has been wracked by disagreement, confrontation, and escalating conflict, mutual trust becomes much more elusive (for a general discussion of trust in groups, see Haas & Deseran, 1981).

In general, trust can be reclaimed if individuals communicate their intentions carefully and exhibit consistency between their announced activities and their actual behavior (Lindskold, 1978). However, while communication is recommended as a means of increasing trust (Deutsch, 1973), to be effective the discussion should make explicit references to trust, cooperation, and fairness (Swingle & Santi, 1972). Furthermore, if group members can demonstrate openness, respect for the needs and feelings of others, and a willingness to help others, then trustworthiness is increased. Finally, if group members respond cooperatively to a member who acts competitively—even when they know in advance that the noncooperator plans to compete—then trust should increase (Brickman et al., 1979). (A note of caution is appropriate concerning this last point: if the opposing group member interprets this cooperation as a sign of weakness, then exploitation, not trust, may result [Sermat, 1964; Solomon, 1960].)

THIRD-PARTY INTERVENTION

Although in many conflict situations the uninvolved group members may stand back and let the disputants "battle it out," impasses, unflagging conflict escalation, or the combatants' entreaties may cause other group members or outside parties to help clarify the source of the problem and thus resolve the conflict. Go-betweens, moderators, facilitators, diplomats, advisors, mediators, or judges are all types of third-party intervenors, and their effectiveness as conflict deescalators seems to be confirmed by relevant research. In one study (Pruitt & Johnson, 1970) subjects were told that they would be negotiating for the purchase of a product. On each trial of the game, they could offer as little as $4 or as much as $7.50 for the merchandise, but the seller could require more. Participants were to bargain until a mutually agreeable price was found.

All the subjects thought the "seller" was another subject, but in actuality all bargained with a simulated adversary who gave into the demands of the "buyer" in a prearranged pattern of concessions. Half the subjects were told that they had to reach a price as quickly as possible, while the remaining subjects were put under no time pressures. The subjects exchanged their offers in the presence of a third person, who served as an observer and a provider of advisory information to both buyer and seller. Although this person was supposedly also a subject, advisors were also confederates of the experimenter and deliberately offered advisory information to only half of the subjects. In these instances the third party sent the subject a note reading "On the basis of my predictions I would suggest you agree on a price of $___. A copy of this note has also been sent to your opponent" (p. 241). In the no-mediation condition the observer made no suggestions.

Figure 4-3 summarizes some of the findings of this investigation. As expected, both the presence of time pressures and an intervention by a third party influenced the concession rate. Subjects tended to reach a fair middle ground more quickly when time pressures were high and the mediator suggested they give in, while the concession rate was lowest when time pressures were low and no mediator intervened.

Jeffrey Rubin (1980) reviewed the results of a number of studies dealing with the processes and effectiveness of third-party interventions. His findings are summarized in the three assertions paraphrased below:

1. Third parties help opponents make conciliations without embarrassment and thereby promote more rapid and effective conflict resolutions (p. 380).
2. Traditional third-party intervention techniques (for example, mediation, arbitration, counseling) that are effective when conflict intensity is low may prove to be ineffectual and even exacerbating when conflict intensity is high (p. 383).
3. The parties to a conflict may view third-party intervention as an unwelcome and unwanted intrusion: disputants may wish to resolve the conflict on their own accord (p. 385).

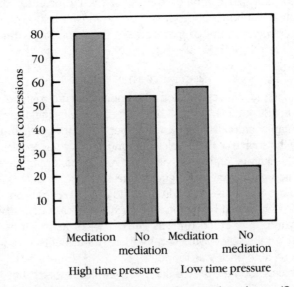

FIGURE 4-3. Concession rates in the four experimental conditions. (Source: Pruitt and Johnson, 1970)

Conflict Resolution

In one way or another, all group conflicts reach a stage of resolution. Although all group members may not be satisfied with the outcome, no group can attain its goals if the problems produced by conflict are left unsolved. Hence, the involved individuals must somehow return to the state of agreement that typified the pre-conflict group, but this termination of in-fighting can come about in a variety of different ways (Kriesberg, 1973). First, one of the disputants can withdraw his or her demands, but without really being convinced that the other side is "right." However, for the sake of group unity or in the interest of saving time, the participant may nonetheless withdraw all complaints.

Second, one faction may manage to impose its views on the other parties. For example, a group leader or similar authority may be persuaded to take one side in the issue, and may mandate a decision on the issue under consideration. Imposition can also involve a vote on the issues by all the group members with the understanding that the majority's decision will stand. Alternatively, an arbitrary decision can be made by flipping a coin or threatening punishment. A third means of achieving agreement is via compromise; group members concede points they favor until agreement is reached. Naturally, bargaining and negotiation are the means used to reach this mutual compromise.

Fourth, the group's dilemma may be solved by the conversion of one side to the point of view expressed by the other. In other words, as a result of the group discussion, persuasion, and perhaps promises, one party may eventually conclude that the other party was, after all, correct. Fifth and last, the conflict may be resolved through group dissolution. The group may, under the pressure of apparently insoluble conflict, splinter into subgroups. A less extreme form of dissolution occurs when the minority that opposes the majority is cast out of the group.

The Causes of Conflict

Many of the causes of intragroup stresses became evident in the preceding section as each phase of group conflict—disagreement, confrontation, escalation, de-escalation, and conflict resolution—was discussed. Yet the processes involved in conflict are complex, and we could consider many other factors in discussing causes. Indeed, certain factors are often highlighted as the causes of conflict, with some theorists preferring to emphasize communication difficulties, others organizational structures, and others social and psychological factors. Unfortunately, all these factors—alone and in combination with many others—interact to produce conflict, making a complete listing of potential problem areas impossible. However, once we admit that the list is incomplete, we can arrange and relate to intragroup conflict some general categories of causal variables. This section concentrates on issues that are raised by the following four questions:

1. Is conflict more likely when the interdependence among members is a consequence of competitive rather than cooperative goal structures?
2. What personal characteristics of the group members—such as their personality traits, their status, or their interpersonal style—influence their actions in conflict situations?

3. Does the power to threaten and punish other group members reduce conflict?
4. Is group conflict substantially intensified by the perceptual and attributional errors that group participants sometimes make?

Interdependence

When three people who are seated in a room working on a series of problems are unable to communicate, can solve their problems without help from one another, and will receive rewards or punishments based solely on their own performance levels, then these three people are independent of one another. If, however, the behaviors of one or more of these individuals influences the behaviors and outcomes of others, then these people are **interdependent.** In most groups this interdependence is obvious. In sports, for example, the outcomes of the team are closely tied to the outcomes of each individual player. Although one team member, such as the quarterback of a football team, may be the most important player on the team, if his teammates do not give him enough time to pass or enough protection when he runs, then his outcomes—and their outcomes—are placed in doubt. As Harold Kelley (1968, p. 399) explains it, individuals are interdependent when the "satisfaction of each person's needs is dependent in some manner upon the actions of other persons."

Theorists (for example, Deutsch, 1973; Schelling, 1960) have pointed out that conflict and interdependence often coincide but that not all types of interdependence cause conflict. Rather, most suggest that when interdependence is based on cooperation among members, then conflict is low; if, on the other hand, interdependence involves competition among group members, then conflict will be high. Take, for example, a group working on a task. If the situation is one of *pure cooperation,* then the success of any one group member will improve the chances of success for the other members. According to Deutsch (1949a), a kind of "promotive interdependence" exists because if one group member attains the desired goal, she or he helps others in the group reach theirs. The situation is one of *pure competition* when the success of any one member of the group means that someone else in the group must fail. During *"contrient interdependence"* (Deutsch, 1949a) one member of the group can reach his or her goals if, and only if, the other members of the group can't.

The extent to which a group interaction emphasizes cooperation, competition, or a mixture of these motives (see Figure 4-4) depends upon many elements in the situation, but two crucially important factors are the group's goal structures and norms. Looking first at goal structures, Deutsch documented the impact of contrient and promotive interdependence by creating a number of groups using volunteers from an introductory psychology class (Deutsch, 1949a, 1949b). In the cooperative groups students were told that the group's performance would determine their grades in the psychology course. All groups would supposedly be compared, and members of those that did well would get high grades while members of those that did more poorly would get low grades. In the competition groups, students were told that their ranking with respect to the others in their group would determine their course grades. The individual who did the best in their group would get the highest grade, while the individual who did the worst would get the

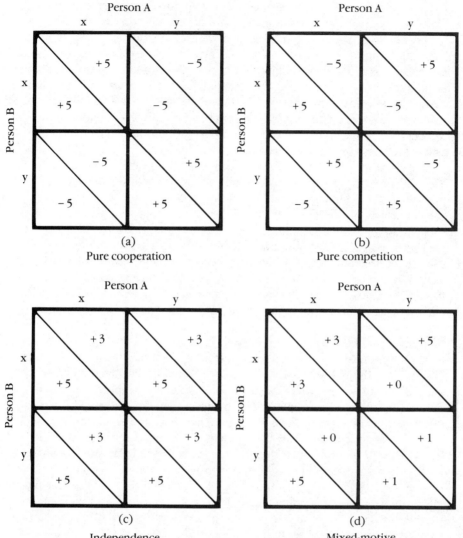

Person A

(a)
Pure cooperation

Person A

(b)
Pure competition

Person A

(c)
Independence

Person A

(d)
Mixed-motive

FIGURE 4-4. Matrix representations of four types of interdependence. Assuming that two individuals (A and B) have only two choices (x and y) in a group situation, four types of interdependence can be charted in simple matrices. As with the Prisoner's Dilemma Game matrix, the numbers in each cell of the matrix represent possible outcomes that vary in magnitude. For example, for matrix (a), if Person A chooses x while Person B chooses y, then both A and B will experience a −5 outcome. If, however, both A and B choose y, then both will experience a +5 outcome. Thus, each matrix represents a different type of interdependence. First, (a) represents pure cooperation because A's actions directed toward achieving a positive outcome also improve B's chances of achieving a similarly positive outcome: both individuals succeed and fail together. Next, (b) represents pure competition, since the success of one individual necessarily requires the failure of the other. Third, (c) represents independence, since the group members' outcomes are not influenced by the other's choice. And finally, (d), like the PDG, is a mixed-motive situation, since some aspects of the reward structure call for a competitive response but other aspects call for cooperation.

lowest grade. Hence members of cooperative groups sought promotively inter-dependent goals, while competitive groups sought contriently interdependent goals.

The results of the research confirmed Deutsch's hypotheses concerning the impact of competition on conflict. When cooperating rather than competing, groups evidenced more friendliness during the meetings, members were more encouraging toward one another, and the contributions of others were more positively evaluated. Further, members of competitive groups—relative to those in cooperative ones—reported less dependency on others, a weaker desire to win the respect of others, and greater rejection by the group (for additional information on goal structures in educational groups, see Chapter 15).

In his later research Deutsch also documented the influence on conflict of the second key factor, group norms dealing with interdependence (Deutsch, 1973, pp. 184–185). To manipulate norms of interdependence, Deutsch arranged for subjects to play the PDG under one of three different sets of instructions. Some subjects were told that cooperation was expected: "You're interested in your partner's welfare as well as in your own. . . . You want to win as much money as you can for yourself, and you do want him to win." Others, however, were told, "You want to make rather than lose money, but you also want to come out ahead of the other person. . . . His feelings don't make any difference to you." For others, a norm of individualism was emphasized: "You are to have no interest whatsoever in whether the other person wins or loses. . . . You don't care how he does, and he doesn't care how you do."

Not surprisingly, when the norms of the experimental situation emphasized cooperation, the players chose so that each would be benefited and tended to earn more money than when the norms of the situation emphasized competition or individualism. Overall, cooperation between members increased the group's effectiveness, while competition created conflict. Similar advantages of cooperation were also found in a field study of two employment agencies (Blau, 1954). In one agency, group members considered the successful placement of an applicant a team success, and thus cooperation with one another was high. In the second agency, however, personnel competed by working alone and keeping job information from one another. Naturally, conflicts, anxiety, and ineffectiveness were more pronounced in the second agency (see Schmitt, 1981, for a more detailed review of this area).

THE PERSONAL CHARACTERISTICS OF THE PARTICIPANTS

When people become members of a group, they soon become aware of the characteristics of their fellow members. Some, they discover, are kind and helpful; others, however, are obnoxious and overbearing. Some may be concerned with working effectively toward tasks at hand; others seem more interested in enjoying themselves. Others may try to dominate the group, and still others may be withdrawn and aloof.

Naturally, a good deal of research has examined the link between the personal characteristics of group members and conflict, but the complexity of the problem is enormous. For example, although the intuitively obvious prediction that groups of friends experience less conflict than groups of strangers has been confirmed, in some situations the lack of friendship seems to limit conflict; when group members don't know one another well they are often reluctant to admit that they disagree (Schachter, Ellertson, McBride, & Gregory, 1951). Similarly, although placing high-status individuals in groups with lower status participants often successfully squelches conflict, in other situations conflict can escalate under these circumstances, since the higher status person ignores the lower status person's needs (Torrance, 1954, 1957). Another example, one involving sex differences, suggests that women often display less conflict with others by maintaining friendlier intermember relations. Yet in some settings—particularly in PDG research—women are sometimes less cooperative, more aggressive, and more retaliatory (Bixenstine, Chambers, & Wilson, 1964; Hottes & Kahn, 1974).

Extensive reviews of the previous research (see, for example, Hare, 1976; Tedeschi, Schlenker, & Bonoma, 1973; Terhune, 1970) conclude that many group-member characteristics are related to conflict, but general conclusions are still difficult to formulate. As Kenneth Terhune (1970) points out in his detailed analysis of personality and conflict, researchers encounter difficulties in (1) generalizing from findings based on laboratory studies to more complex, nonlaboratory conflicts, (2) accurately assessing the critical personal characteristics of group members, (3) measuring conflict behaviors, and (4) capturing and understanding the interaction between situational and personal characteristics. As a result, about the only sweeping statement that can be accepted with confidence is that the relationship between "personality and conflict is complicated" (Terhune, 1970, p. 225).

One variable that is consistently stressed more than others focuses on the **interpersonal style** of interacting group members ("interpersonal reactivity" for Apfelbaum, 1974; "interpersonal orientation" for Blake & Mouton, 1964 and Rubin & Brown, 1975; "interpersonal sensitivity" for Hermann & Kogan, 1977). For example, Robert Blake and Jane Mouton (1964, 1970) hypothesize that group members' interpersonal style depends upon how they answer two basic questions: "How important is the production of results by the group?" and "How important are the feelings of people who are in disagreement?" To some participants, the key responsibility of the group is to clear up any conflict so that work on the problem at hand can continue. For others, positive feelings in the group seem to be critical, making greater emphasis on intragroup harmony and personal satisfaction central goals. Others may consider both of these goals—adequate problem solving and supporting others—to be critical.

Blake and Mouton summarize the effects of these differing interpersonal styles in their **conflict grid** (1964, 1970), which is presented in Figure 4-5. Both dimensions—concern for people and concern for results—are represented as nine-point scales ranging from "low concern" to "high concern." Although in theory a person's orientation could fall at any of 81 possible positions on the grid, Blake and Mouton emphasize five of these orientations; these include the four corner positions and one in the very center. Each of these positions represents a basic "style of interaction," or management in a group, and hence should be related to behavior during conflict.

According to Blake and Mouton, a 9,1 individual (high on concern for production, low on concern for people, located in the lower right corner of the grid) deals with conflict by confronting it and overwhelming it at all costs. Such a person views group disagreements as "win/lose" situations and finds satisfaction in forcing

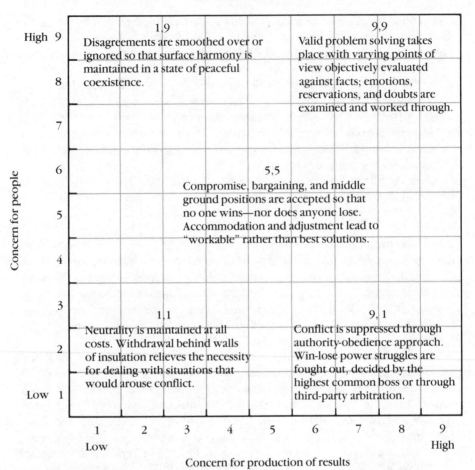

FIGURE 4-5. The conflict grid. (Reproduced by special permission from *The Journal of Applied Behavioral Science,* "The Fifth Achievement," by Robert R. Blake and Jane Syrgley Mouton, Volume 6, Number 4, p. 418, Copyright 1970, NTL Institute.)

her or his ideas on the others—concession and compromise are only for losers. The 1,9 in contrast, feels that open conflict among members reveals a failure for the group, and so tries to maintain smooth, satisfying relationships. The 1,9 is quite willing to concede to other group members in order to avoid "making waves" or "causing trouble." The "compromiser," located at 5,5, in the center of the grid, is quick to negotiate with others and serve as an arbitrator, but sometimes sacrifices both results and individuals' feelings when seeking a workable solution. At the extremes of the two dimensions we find the problem-solving 9,9 and the apathetic 1,1. These two orientations stand in opposition to each other, for the 9,9 values both people and products highly, and therefore confronts conflict in a rational but sensitive manner, whereas the 1,1 is unconcerned with his or her fellow group members or with the production of results. The latter typically denies the existence of conflicts in the group and prefers that differences be resolved outside the group context.

As you would expect, when individuals with differing interpersonal styles meet in a group, the result is often conflict. The 9,1, for example, often adopts an abrasive style of behavior, spurring more moderate members to react with criticism and requests for fairer treatment. The 9,1, however, is unconcerned with maintaining smooth interpersonal relations, and so refuses to modify his or her behavior. Unfortunately, when the 9,1 confronts a 1,9, the 9,1 usually wins. If, on the other hand, the 9,1 is paired with another 9,1, the conflict usually ends in a stalemate. When individuals in conflict both endorse a problem-solving orientation (9,9), the difficulties are quickly analyzed and resolved (Cummings, Harnett, & Stevens, 1971; Harnett, Cummings, & Hamner, 1973; Shure & Meeker, 1967).

Influence Strategies

During group interactions, participants can use many strategies to influence other group members. For example, the production-oriented 9,1 may try to overwhelm others through verbal debate, threats, personal criticisms, or other competitive power tactics. Other members may adopt more moderate methods, such as reasoned persuasion, promises of rewards, or reminders about norms and duties. Although the use of various strategies is examined in detail in Chapter 7, this topic is introduced here since the more abrasive interpersonal strategies—threats, punishments, and negative reinforcements—tend to increase group conflict. Many years ago Morton Deutsch and Robert Krauss (1960) tested the hypothesis that the use of threats during a group conflict will lead to increased hostility, counterthreats, and unwillingness to compromise by studying pairs of female subjects playing a simple "trucking game." Each participant was to imagine herself the

---

HOW TO WIN IN GROUPS

In some unfortunate instances group members approach conflicts from a win-lose perspective. They feel that group meetings serve as a proving ground for ideas and individuals, and therefore seek to promote their own viewpoints while detracting from the positions advocated by others. In such cases the group interaction can turn into a conflict-laden debate as "competitors" use unfair tactics such as the following:

1. Turning aside questions by referring the query to individuals not present at the meeting. (Example: "I realize that could be a problem, but I discussed it with Jane and she believes it can be worked out easily.")

2. Criticizing others' interpretations of your previous remarks, even if accurate. (Example: "I recall the discussion, but you seem to have completely misinterpreted my meaning.")

3. Reminding the group members of a previous failure caused by your "opponent." (Example: "I hope this new idea is nothing like your last one. That one was a big waste of our time.")

4. Asking your opponent to restate complicated arguments, preferably after 10 or 15 minutes have intervened. (Example: "Let's go back to that idea you mentioned earlier; would you mind running through that again?")

5. Deliberately misinterpreting others. (Example: "So you think we should just abandon the whole project?")

6. Saving telling criticisms until the group has almost reached a consensus. (Example: "I just thought of something; isn't there a law against this kind of intervention?")

Source: Snell, 1979.

owner of a trucking company—Acme or Bolt—that carried merchandise over the roads portrayed in Figure 4-6. Each time Acme's truck reached her designated destination, she would earn 60¢ minus any "operating costs"—1¢ for each second taken up by the trip. Bolt was rewarded on a similar contract.

Subjects soon discovered that a problem of coordination existed for members of the dyad. In order to cut operating expenses to a minimum, ideally each company would travel on the main road, labeled Route 216 on the map. Unfortunately, a stretch of this highway was only a one-lane road and the rules of the game stipulated that this section was too narrow to allow the trucks to pass each other. The only solution when trucks encountered one another along this route was for one player to back up to her starting position to let the other through. Of course, the problem could have been avoided by taking the winding alternate route, but this path was so long that the extra time taken during transit meant that operating costs would cut deeply into profits.

Although all the pairs played the same basic game, some were provided with the power to threaten their opponents but others were not. In the *unilateral-threat condition* Acme was told that a gate—which only she could open and close—was located at the fork in Route 216. When the gate was closed, neither truck could pass this point in the road, making the control of the gate a considerable benefit to Acme. For example, if Bolt attempted to use the main route, all Acme had to do was close the gate, forcing Bolt to back up and enabling Acme to reopen the gate and proceed quickly to her destination. Thus, when only Acme possessed

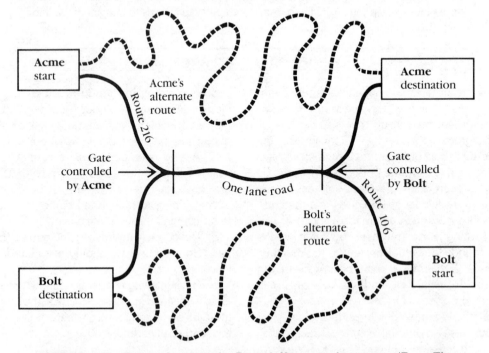

FIGURE 4-6. The road map in the Deutsch-Krauss trucking game. (From *The Resolution of Conflict: Constructive and Destructive Processes,* by M. Deutsch. Copyright 1973 by Yale University Press. Reprinted by permission.)

the gate, Bolt's profits were greatly threatened. In the *bilateral-threat condition* both sides had the use of gates located at the ends of the one-lane section of Route 216. Lastly, in the *control condition* no gates were given to the players.

Deutsch and Krauss found that subjects who could not threaten one another soon learned to resolve the conflict over the one-lane road. For the majority of these pairs, a norm of turn-taking developed such that when one player used the main route first the other waited; on the next turn the other player would then be given first priority. On the average, each subject playing the game in the control condition made $1 profit. These winnings, however, soon turned to losses when one of the players was given a gate. In the unilateral threat condition subjects lost an average of $2.03. Although Bolt's losses were twice as great as Acme's, the possession of the gate did not benefit the latter greatly, since even Acme lost more than a dollar at the game.

Conflict, however, was clearly the most intense when both Acme and Bolt possessed a gate. In the bilateral threat condition subjects consistently lost rather than made money, because both players were usually forced to take the longer route for their opponents regularly closed the gates on the main route. Losses in the bilateral threat condition averaged $4.38. On the basis of these findings Deutsch and Krauss concluded that the capacity to threaten others sets up a conflict situation, and that the actual use of threats serves to intensify conflict. Subsequent investigations have supported this conclusion (for example, Borah, 1963; Deutsch & Lewicki, 1970; Froman & Cohen, 1969; Gallo, 1966), and in general indicate that earnings are highest when neither side can threaten the other. More surprisingly, these studies also suggest that if one party can or does threaten the other party, the threatened party will fare best if he or she *cannot* respond with a counterthreat.

In sum, influencing others by using threats may cause the situation to become "dynamically competitive" as "each party employs counterthreats and counterdemands in response to the other's threats in an escalatory cycle" (Milburn, 1977, p. 131). This conclusion suggests that the common-sense rule that open communication in groups that are experiencing conflicts curbs conflict (for example, Filley, 1975; Johnson & Johnson, 1975) should be qualified: if group members are exchanging threats and demands, then communication will increase rather than decrease conflict. For example, when Deutsch and Krauss let subjects in the bilateral threat conditions communicate, messages typically emphasized threats and did little to reduce conflict (Deutsch, 1973; see Table 4-1). However, subsequent research suggests that communication will effectively deter conflict if subjects have been trained to use communication appropriately (Krauss & Deutsch, 1966) or if threats—such as those based on the gates in the trucking game—are not permitted (Smith & Anderson, 1975).

Misunderstandings and Misperceptions

Group participants' understanding of the group environment is greatly influenced by their answers to such questions as "What caused him to act that way?" or "Why did she say that?" According to **attribution theory,** a social-psychological explanation of how people make inferences about the causes of behaviors and events, people continually formulate intuitive causal hypotheses so that they

TABLE 4-1. Communication between Acme and Bolt during bilateral threat

Acme	Bolt
Trial 1	
You decide on your route?	I'm taking the main route.
I am, too.	Oh, we're stopped. What happens now?
What did you say?	Did you stop?
Yeah, the lane is blocked completely.	Well, who's going to back up?
Well, I don't know. You back up this time?	All right, I'll back up.
All right.	Your gate is locked.
I know it's locked.	That wasn't very fair.
Anything's fair.	Well, what are you going to do?
I don't have to do anything. I'm going to my destination.	This is not funny.
(laughs)	At your destination?
No!	I'll never reach mine at this point.
I've reached mine.	Well?
Sit tight.	Planned your next route?
No, have you?	I've got some ideas.
Thanks a lot.	I'm getting there slowly but surely.
Trial 7	
We're both stopped.	Are you going to open your gate?
Why should I?	I'll do the same next time.
Is that a threat?	You playing tricks?
No.	I'll lose five dollars this trip because of you.
Trial 9	
I see you've got your gate closed. What route are you on?	Why should I tell you?
Okay, if that's the way you want to play.	No, I'll tell you where I am if you tell me where you are.
I asked you first.	. . . How far are you?
I don't believe you.	Have it your way.
Trial 18	
What route are you taking?	(no answer)
I think we both are going bankrupt.	They [sic] just don't trust each other, right?
Trial 20	
	Your gate's closed again.
So is yours, so that means you must have taken the alternate route.	Why? What gives you that idea?
Well, you wouldn't be crazy enough to go the main route with my gate closed.	Well, maybe I think I can persuade you to open it.
You know better than that.	Do I? . . . I get the use of these gates all mixed up. I shut mine when I don't want to and,
If I go into the trucking business I'm not going to have gates.	oh, ...

(From *The resolution of conflict: Constructive and destructive processes*, by M. Deutsch. Copyright 1973 by Yale University Press. Reprinted by permission.)

can understand and predict events that transpire in the group (Heider, 1958). Attributions become especially important in the context of group conflict, since these causal beliefs sometimes determine group members' perceptions of their associates' motives and intentions (Steiner, 1959) and also partially mediate reactions to their behaviors (Horai, 1977; Messé, Stollak, Larson, & Michaels, 1979). For example, when group members argue, they must determine why they disagree. If members conclude that their disagreement stems merely from the group's attempts to make the right decision, then the disagreement will probably not turn into true conflict. If, however, participants attribute the disagreement to others' incompetence, belligerence, or argumentativeness, then the simple disagreement could escalate into conflict.

If group members' attributions of causes were always accurate, then they would help interactants understand one another better and thereby usually function as conflict reducers. Attributions, however, are not always accurate; indeed, research indicates that perceptual biases regularly distort individuals' attributional inferences. One bias—labeled the **fundamental attribution error** by Lee Ross (1977)—stems from attributors' tendency to believe other people's behavior to be caused by personal (dispositional) rather than situational (environmental) factors. That is, the attributor overestimates the causal importance of personality, beliefs, attitudes, and values, and underestimates that of situational pressures. Demonstrating the impact of this fundamental attribution error on group dynamics, Harold Kelley and his associates (Kelley, 1979; Orvis, Kelley, & Butler, 1976) asked 41 young couples to recall and describe any recent conflicts they may have experienced. Not surprisingly, the couples found this an easy task, and generated more than 700 examples, which typically involved one person performing a behavior that the other person reacted to in a negative way. Although the negative event alone was sufficient to cause conflict between the two, the situation was further complicated by divergent attributional interpretations. The person who initiated the conflict by performing the negative behavior felt that the act was caused by extenuating circumstances, somebody else, or a desire to do the right thing. The person who was upset by the behavior, however, rejected these explanations of the event. He or she explained the action by emphasizing negative personal characteristics of the other person—for example, poor judgment, irresponsibility, selfishness, a lack of concern, a tendency to show off, and incompetence. Naturally, each interactant considered the other person's perceptions of the situation to be unfair and unreasonable, and therefore the conflict invariably escalated.

This fundamental attribution error apparently produces systematic differences in the attributional conclusions reached both by a person who actually performs the behavior—the actor—and the person who watches the behavior—the observer. These attributional differences were summarized by Edward E. Jones and Richard Nisbett (1971) in their **actor-observer hypothesis**: an actor will explain his or her behavior in terms of situational factors, but an observer will explain the actor's behavior in terms of the latter's dispositional characteristics. This hypothesis has considerable relevance in small groups, for it implies that group members may be predisposed to misinterpret the behavior of other group members. For example, when Person A argues with Participant O, A believes that O's unreasonable stance on the issue has forced the discussion, but O believes that A is, by nature, argumentative. Although the distortion produced by actor/observer differences is minimal when the group interaction is pleasant (Rosenberg & Wolfsfeld, 1977) or interactants are careful to empathize with one another (Regan & Totten, 1975), the effect seems to grow stronger during conflict. One study (Miller & Norman, 1975) compared the attributions of *active observers*—those who not only observed others but also interacted with others—to the attributions of *passive observers*—

individuals who were not actually part of the group. During the experiment the active observers played the PDG with a partner (actually, the experimenter) who consistently chose either cooperative or competitive responses. When these two sets of observers later estimated the extent to which the behavior of the partner was a good indicant of personality, active observers made more dispositional attributions than passive observers—provided their partner had competed. In other words, the observer's bias was greatest during conflict.

These findings and others (Cunningham, Starr, & Kanouse, 1979) suggest that attributions are often biased in a negative direction, with the result that people tend to assume the worst about other group members. Supporting this conclusion, one extensive series of studies into interpersonal perception (Maki, Thorngate, & McClintock, 1979) asked subjects to play a simulation game with a partner whose behavior was (1) competitive (he or she maximized personal gains while minimizing the partner's gains), (2) cooperative (maximized joint gains), (3) individualistic (ignored the partner's gains but maximized personal gains), or (4) altruistic (ignored personal gains but maximized the partner's gains). When asked to describe their partner's motives, subjects were most accurate when playing an individualistic or competitive person, and least accurate in interpreting cooperation and altruism. Apparently group members had difficulty believing that their associates were behaving in a prosocial altruistic manner, but readily believed the suggestion that their behaviors revealed conflict.

Other investigators find that some people are stronger in attributional negativity than others. Kelley and Stahelski (1970a, 1970b), for example, draw a broad distinction between people who tend to compete with others and those who tend to cooperate. While cooperators' attributions about others are usually accurate, competitors' tend to assume that their fellow group members are also competitive. In support of this hypothesis, Kelley and Stahelski found that when cooperators play the PDG with other cooperators, their perceptions of their partner's strategy are inaccurate only 6% of the time. When competitors play the PDG with cooperators, however, they misinterpret their partner's strategy 47% of the time, mistakenly believing that the cooperators are competing. Another study (Messé, Stollak, Larson, & Michaels, 1979) distinguished between negatively biased people, who pay more attention to negative behaviors, and positively biased people, who are more attuned to positive behaviors. Although negatively biased subjects were more dominant, less submissive, and less helpful than positively biased attributors, they tended to handle intragroup conflict more effectively.

The Value of Conflict

Although its negative connotations lead many people to conclude that conflict is "bad" and "destructive," disagreeing is a natural consequence of joining a group. Observers of all types of groups—work groups, therapy groups, experimental groups, business groups—have documented clashes among members and invariably conclude that group conflict is as common as group harmony (Bales, Cohen, & Williamson, 1979; Bennis & Shepard, 1956; Fisher, 1980; Tuckman, 1965). As sociological theory suggests (see, for example, Dahrendorf, 1958, 1959), the dynamic nature of the group ensures continual change, but along with change come stresses and strains that surface in the form of conflict. Although in rare instances group members may avoid all conflict because their actions are perfectly coordinated, in most groups the push and pull of interpersonal forces inevitably exerts its influence.

Lewis Coser's theorizing (Coser, 1956; Turner, 1974) has done much to emphasize the positive value of group conflict. He concludes that while some conflicts can tear a group apart, others promote in-group unity. Although the hypothesis that conflict creates unification may, at first glance, seem paradoxical, Coser (1956, p. 80) convincingly argues that

> conflict may serve to remove dissociating elements in a relationship and to reestablish unity. Insofar as conflict is the resolution of tension between antagonists it has stabilizing functions and becomes an integrating component of the relationship. . . . Conflicts, which serve to "sew the social system together" by cancelling each other out, thus prevent disintegration along one primary line of cleavage.

Others (Bennis & Sheppard, 1956; Deutsch, 1969) have noted that interdependency among members and the stability of a group cannot deepen until intragroup hostility has surfaced, been confronted, and resolved. Low levels of conflict in a group could be an indicant of remarkably positive interpersonal relations, but more likely the group members are simply uninvolved, unmotivated, unstimulated, and bored. Indeed, Coser argues that the absence of conflict tells us little about the stability of the group, since the more cohesive the group, the more intense is the intragroup conflict.

In addition to helping unify a group, conflict also preserves a group by providing a means of venting interpersonal hostilities. During conflict escalation hostility increases, but members can reduce this stress by confronting the problem and communicating dissatisfactions honestly and openly. If hostilities are never expressed in the group, then they may build up to a point where the group can no longer continue as a unit.

The importance of expressing hostility was studied in one experiment by asking two members of a three-person group to exchange written information about their personalities (Thibaut & Coules, 1952). One of the group members, however, was a confederate of the experimenter, and he sent preplanned messages intended to create interpersonal hostility. For example, his third note stated (p. 771),

> I know I'll succeed in my profession, because I am so far above everyone else in my class. I got 98 on my last biology exam and that's pretty good. I am the best student in the lab course also.

In Note 7 he wrote,

> Since I am kind of weak, I haven't been good in any sports—but that's just kid stuff, I want to be a *man*. I am sure if I wanted to be a good athlete I would be very successful even though I don't care much for physical contact of that sort.

Note 8, however, was the strongest for it directly attacked the subject:

> You know, you're so full of bull———that I'm not going to talk about myself anymore. You're the most egotistical, deceitful *liar* I've ever seen. How anybody

can fake about his own abilities as much as you have I'll never know. I don't think you're the type of guy I'd care to associate with. Why don't you play it straight, fellow?

Naturally, the subjects were angered by this attack, and wished to respond to it. However, only half were given the opportunity to communicate with one last note; the remaining subjects had to keep silent.

After the exchange of the messages, each subject wrote a personality sketch describing his or her partner. As predicted, people who had been given the chance to respond to the interpersonal attack described their partners in friendlier terms and revealed less hostility. Apparently the opportunity to express their hostility resulted in less conflict.

One final value of conflict has been elaborated by Ernest Bormann in his **threshold theory of group tension** (1975). According to Bormann, groups experience two types of social tension—primary and secondary. *Primary tension* is similar to what Thibaut and Kelley (1959) call "strangeness," and occurs early in the life of the group. Initially group members feel awkward, are reluctant to express their views, politely take turns talking, and try to avoid arguing with one another. With time, this primary tension is dispelled as the "ice is broken" and group members become better acquainted. The group establishes a routine of interaction, which remains in effect until it is broken by *secondary tension*. This type of conflict is much more intense, and follows the pattern of intragroup conflict described earlier.

Although Bormann admits that uncontrolled secondary conflict can destroy the group, he goes on to hypothesize a *tolerance threshold* for the group. As Figure 4-7 shows, every group has a threshold for tension that represents its optimal level of conflict among members. Conflict too far below this level results in group apathy, boredom, and lack of involvement. Prolonged conflict above this level, on the other hand, causes shared disagreement, heightened hostility, and a loss of group effectiveness. What is needed, then, is a balance between too little tension and too much tension.

An application of the threshold theory of group tension to four hypothetical groups is shown in Figure 4-8. Group A, after initially reducing primary tension, experienced a large amount of uncontrolled secondary tension. The amount of tension is far above the tolerance threshold, and it remains at high levels for a prolonged period of time. Such a group would, in all likelihood, fail to exist for long unless steps were taken quickly to reduce the conflict. Group B, on the other hand, never got past the primary-tension phase. Although such groups are not very common, they sometimes occur, as when group members are perhaps forced to join the group, remain uninvolved in the group interactions, or owe commitments to other groups or activities. Membership in such a group is often very unpleasant for group members and again a short lifespan is predicted.

While Group C may seem to be a "perfect" group due to its low level of secondary tension, Bormann suggests that looks can be deceiving. Although it is possible that the low tension is the result of a perfect coordination among group members, it may stem instead from boredom and apathy. Group members may be too uninvolved to argue about the issues at hand, and thus conflicts may never

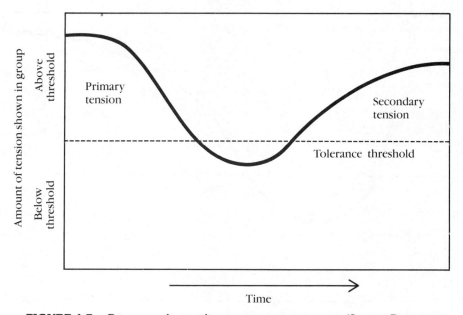

FIGURE 4-7. Primary and secondary tension areas in groups. (Source: Bormann, 1975)

arise. On the other hand, the group may be experiencing conflict but be unwilling to confront the problems.

Ideal groups, according to the threshold notion of conflict, are similar to Group D. Although D clearly experiences frequent episodes of conflict, these episodes have mostly positive consequences—the clarification of goals, an increased understanding of differences and points of contention, successful intermember discussion, stimulation of interests, and the release of hostility. The group has apparently managed to develop techniques that limit escalation, and thereby to control the magnitude and longevity of the conflict. At minimum, the group interaction will probably be lively.

Summary

In general terms, *intragroup conflict* can be said to exist whenever the actions and/or beliefs of one or more members of the group are incompatible with—and hence are resisted by—one or more group members. In tracing the development of conflict in groups, we can identify five stages in the process: disagreement, confrontation, escalation, de-escalation, and resolution. Once the members examine the nature of the *disagreement* and come to believe that the issue is important enough to require resolution, then the group members confront the problem through active discussion. During this *confrontation* period the discussants often become more intensely committed to their respective viewpoints, and tension can build as *coalitions* form in the group. These mechanisms lead to a third stage—*escalation*—which is typified by an upward *conflict spiral* fed by misunderstandings, distrust, frustration, hostility, and negative reciprocity. In time, however, *de-*

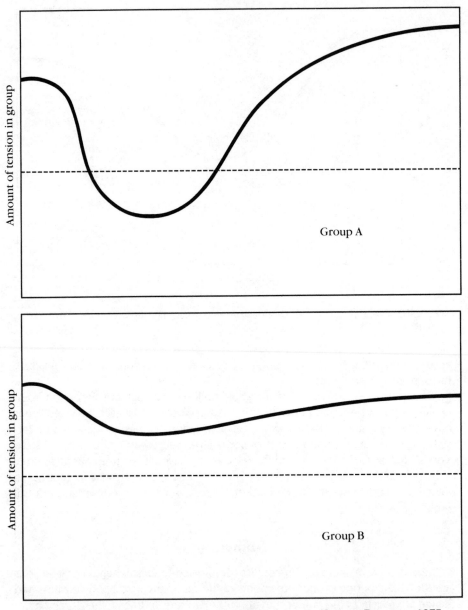

FIGURE 4-8.   Tension curves in four hypothetical groups. (Source: Bormann, 1975 and Fisher, 1980)

escalation of the conflict begins as the group strives to reach agreement on the issues under discussion, and this de-escalation often benefits from negotiation among members, the development of trust, and third-party intervention. Finally, if the efforts of the group members during the de-escalation period are successful, then the group reaches conflict *resolution*.

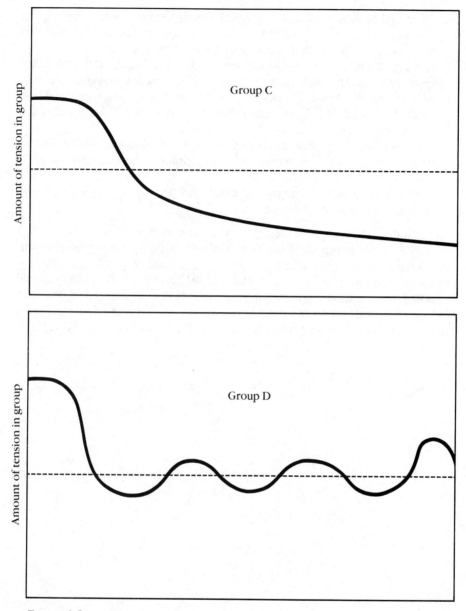

Figure 4-8 continued.

Throughout this sequence a host of factors can be working to increase conflict among members, including the interdependence among members, their personal characteristics, the types of influence strategies they employ, and the magnitude of any misunderstandings and misperceptions formulated by participants. Let us summarize these four factors:

1. All group behavior implies an element of *interdependence* among people, but evidence indicates that conflict is much more likely to occur when this interdependence is competitive, rather than cooperative, in nature.
2. Although the relationship between the personal characteristics of members and group behavior is complicated, reactions in conflict situations seem to covary with *interpersonal style*; for example, people who are highly concerned with productivity tend to behave quite differently during conflict from individuals who adopt a more interpersonally oriented style.
3. The use of abrasive *influence strategies*—such as threats and punishments—tends to heighten conflict, particularly if all parties in the confrontation have the capacity to threaten one another.
4. Conflict can be exacerbated by members' tendency to fail to understand adequately the *causes* of others' actions.

Finally, despite the negative connotations associated with the concept of conflict, research suggests that conflict is both a natural and necessary part of group dynamics. Confronting conflict not only creates strong feelings of group unity, but can also serve as an avenue for venting interpersonal hostilities. In fact, the *threshold theory* of group tension suggests that groups tend to be characterized by boredom and apathy when conflict is too far below the tolerance threshold, while groups that repeatedly confront and resolve conflicts are the more effective and enjoyable.

5

Norming: The Development of Group Structure

The heavens themselves, the planets and this center
Observe degree, priority and place,
Insisture, course, proportion, season, form,
Office, and custom, in all line of order. . . .

Shakespeare, *Troilus and Cressida*

imagine that you are an explorer of distant solar systems. Although you have encountered many strange and unique worlds in your travels, as you approach your latest discovery you look for the features you have grown to expect: a large gaseous sun that provides warmth and light, one or more planets revolving about the sun in their own orbits and at varying distances, and smaller objects revolving about the planets. Furthermore, you pay strict attention to the planetary regularities that derive from physical laws concerning velocity, mass, and gravity: the strength of forces holding the planets in their orbits, the influence of every object in the system on every other object, and the pattern of relationships within the system. Thus, as a seasoned explorer you expect to find within any solar system (1) certain types of objects (a sun, planets, moons) and (2) evidence of the operation of certain physical laws that determine (3) the relationships among these objects (gravitational attraction, repulsion, and so on).

Now imagine that you are an explorer of small groups. Although you have encountered many strange and unique groups in your studies, as you approach any group you look for the features you have grown to expect: a leader who directs the activities of the group and provides emotional warmth, along with one or more group members, each interacting with the leader and the other members in various ways. Furthermore, you pay strict attention to the regularities within the group: the strength of the forces holding members in the group, the influence of every person on every other person, and the pattern of relationships within the group. Thus, within any group you expect to find (1) certain types of group members (a leader, follower, deviate) and (2) evidence of the operation of certain group "laws" that determine (3) the relationships among these members (leader talks to the follower, follower dislikes the deviate, and so on).

This analogy between a solar system and a group is offered because it makes more meaningful what is initially a vague concept—**group structure.** Although an astronomer and a group dynamicist may be tempted to treat each system or group they observe as a unique entity, they would stand to gain more if they noted and described similarities that apply to all systems or all groups. Thus, the astronomer, confronting a new solar system, would look beyond the unique features for evidence of the system's basic structure—types of planets, operation of physical laws, and relationships among the celestial bodies. Similarly, the group dynamicist looks beyond the unique features of the group for evidence of its basic structure—types of group *roles,* existence of group *norms,* and *intermember relations.* Armed with an understanding of these three facets of the group, the observer can gain a grasp of the group's structure, the unseen framework that holds the group together and partially accounts for the regularities in group members' behaviors. Once group structures are identified, the nature of interpersonal relations in groups can be understood as clearly as the movement of planets about the sun.

Although the structure of groups can be viewed from a number of different perspectives (Scott & Scott, 1981), this chapter approaches the topic by considering uniformities in group members' behaviors, the regulatory standards of groups, and several of the ways in which members can be linked together. In later sections of the chapter we examine in detail three types of intermember relationships—authority relations, attraction relations, and communication relations. Before considering these issues, however, we explore two key concepts—roles and norms—by applying them to a particularly interesting group: the survivors of an airplane crash stranded high in the Andes.

Roles

In Chapter 1 we briefly described the adventures of the courageous group of men and women who, despite all odds, survived a violent airplane crash in the Andes. Although fortunate even to survive, the passengers soon found that they would have to cope with many more misfortunes before their rescue. The pilot and copilot, who might have provided leadership and information about wilderness survival, were killed by the force of the impact. Nearly everyone who survived suffered an injury, and several people were critically injured. The only shelter from the cold and snow was the broken hulk of the airplane, and the crowded conditions caused discomfort and pain. Food was scarce, water could be obtained only by melting snow during the daylight hours, and the only fuel for a fire came from a couple of wooden crates.

If the survivors had been rescued the day after the crash, then a group structure would never have developed. The time these people spent together on the mountainside would have been too brief and an elaborate system of internal relations would have been unnecessary. Unfortunately, the Uruguayan Air Force was unable to locate the crash site and gave up the search after eight days. Left alone in the snow-covered Andes to wrest their survival from the harsh climate, the group was forced to fend for itself. Hungry, injured, and exhausted, each member's survival became inextricably linked to that of every other as the individuals banded together to meet the challenge. This necessity for group coordination spurred the development of relatively specific roles and norms within the group.

The Nature of Roles

On the day after the crash the passengers roused themselves out of their shock and began to care for the injured, to secure food and water, and to construct a rude shelter inside the battered fuselage. Marcelo, the captain of the rugby team that had chartered the flight, took control of the overall situation and organized the efforts of those who could work. Two of the boys were medical students, and they were given the responsibility for helping the injured. One of the older women in the group agreed to work as their "nurse." Another group of boys was given the task of melting snow into drinking water, and another team arranged and kept clean the cabin of the airplane. These various positions in the group—leader, doctor, nurse, snow melter, cabin cleaner—defined the roles enacted by the group members. When a person took a particular role in the group, he or she tended to engage in a fairly standard set of behaviors—giving directions, helping the sick, melting snow, or cleaning. Furthermore, the interactions among group members fell into a pattern that was in large part determined by the roles within the group. As these new roles developed, the survivors changed from a rugby team and their relatives into members of a structured group.

The concept of *role* was borrowed by social scientists from the theater, where the term has long been used to refer to the character an actor portrays during a dramatic presentation. Indeed, the term's meaning changed very little when introduced into the area of group dynamics, and the relationship between an actor's role in a play and a member's role in a group remains close. For example, just as a role in a play determines the dialogue spoken and the actions taken by an actor, so roles in a group dictate the "part" members take as they interact, down to the contributions they make and the sorts of behaviors they perform (see box). In addition, like roles in a play, group roles are independent of the personal characteristics of specific individuals and can be filled by any person who takes them. Just as any actor can become Romeo in Shakespeare's *Romeo and Juliet* by following the script properly, any person who performs the appropriate behaviors can fill the role of leader, outcast, or questioner in a small group. In most cases, even when the person who has filled a role departs, the role itself remains and is filled by a new member.

We can note other similarities between dramatic roles and group roles. When an actor lands the role of Romeo, he memorizes the script and rehearses his actions. Although he must perform certain behaviors as part of his role (he wouldn't be Shakespeare's Romeo if he didn't fall in love with Juliet or poison himself in his mistaken grief), he can vary certain parts of his role by reciting his lines in an original way or by changing his stage behaviors. He cannot, however, diverge too far from the script, or the rest of the cast would be unable to adapt their performances to his changes. Similarly, roles in social groups are to a large extent flexible but still require certain behaviors. Interactions with the other members of the group would become chaotic if a member filling a certain role failed to meet its basic

---

BIDDLE ON THE DEFINITION OF ROLE

As leading role theorist Bruce J. Biddle notes, the word *role* surfaces frequently in social science discourse, but with subtly different shades of meaning. To some, the word *role* denotes the *behaviors* that people generally perform as group members. To others, roles provide the basis for *expectations* concerning the behavior of people in various *positions* in the group. Biddle (1979, pp. 56–57), however, suggests that both conceptions err by emphasizing "phenomena that

may cause, be associated with, or result from the performance of roles." Biddle feels that such narrow definitions are "limiting, and to examine 'the whole ball of wax' we should begin with the broadest meaningful definition of the role concept." For Biddle, a role is best defined as *"behaviors that are characteristic of persons in a context."* (For an advanced analysis of role processes, see Biddle 1979.)

requirements, and the entire group could become disorganized. Furthermore, just as the director of the play can replace the actor who presents an unsatisfactory Romeo, so the group can replace members who do not adequately fill their roles (Biddle, 1979; Sarbin & Allen, 1968).

Role Differentiation

Group roles and dramatic roles bear many similarities to each other, but they differ significantly as well. Whereas in plays the roles are created by the playwright and the actors are carefully assigned to them, in a small group roles develop over time. When the group first forms the participants typically consider themselves "members," basically similar to each other. Yet gradually, in a process called **role differentiation,** various roles emerge. Among the Andes survivors, this process proceeded very rapidly, as is consistent with past research suggesting that differentiation is greatest in groups that must cope with an emergency or deal with difficult problems (Bales, 1958). In this group, along with a leader, doctor, nurse, and cleaner emerged the role of "inventor," who created makeshift snowshoes, hammocks, and water-melting devices; "explorer," who was determined to hike down from the mountains; as well as "complainer," "pessimist," "optimist," and "goldbricker."

Much research has been performed on the process of role differentiation in small groups. In general this research has been aimed at discovering whether any regularities mark this developmental process, and at discerning the types of roles that are most likely to form. Naturally, researchers admit that many different kinds of groups exist and that certain roles within any particular group may be unique to that group, but they also suggest that some roles are more common than others and that certain roles will develop in all kinds of groups. For example, while the roles of Romeo and Juliet may be unique to Shakespeare's play, a protagonist and antagonist are found in almost any play.

TASK ROLES AND SOCIOEMOTIONAL ROLES

Early theorists suggest that the first level of group differentiation is reached when the majority of the members recognize one or more individuals as leaders and the remainder as followers (see Hare, 1976). The *leader* tends to be a person most concerned with accomplishing the task at hand, organizing the group to move toward goal attainment, and providing support for all the other group members. *Followers,* on the other hand, accept the guidance of the leader and try to fulfill the tasks required of them. Among the Andes survivors, Marcelo became recognized as leader quickly, for his position as team captain generalized to the new situation. He took responsibility for organizing the group into work squads and controlled the rationing of their meager food supplies. The rest of the members obeyed his orders, respected his opinions, and relied upon him to do what he could to maximize their chances for rescue. Like doctor and patient, teacher and student, or mother and daughter, Marcelo and his followers were *role partners* linked together in a reciprocal relationship. Because most of Marcelo's leadership activities were centered around the performance of group tasks, he filled the **task-specialist** role in the group.

Although Marcelo proved to be an admirable leader in terms of getting many necessary tasks accomplished (finding drinking water, cleaning, doctoring, and so on), he did not satisfy the emotional needs of the group. By the ninth day of the ordeal morale was sagging, and Marcelo began crying silently to himself at night. Yet, as if to offset Marcelo's inability to cheer up the survivors, several group members became more positive and friendly, actively trying to reduce conflicts and to keep morale high. For example, the only surviving female, Liliana Methol, provided a "unique source of solace" for the young men she cared for and she came to take the place of their absent mothers and sweethearts. One of the younger boys "called her his god-mother, and she responded to him and the others with comforting words and gentle optimism" (Read, 1974, p. 74).

The development of a "supportive," nurturant role in addition to the task-specialist role is consistent with laboratory studies of role differentiation (Bales, 1958; Parsons, Bales, & Shils, 1953; Slater, 1955). Although a group may require the services of a task specialist to help it work in the direction of its goals, if interpersonal strains and stresses cannot be controlled then the group may dissolve before task completion. In many instances, however, the leader cannot simultaneously fulfill both the task and emotional needs of the group. According to Robert Freed Bales (1955), when task specialists try to move groups toward their goals, they must necessarily give orders to others, restrict the behavioral options of others, complain about fellow members, and prompt others into action. Although these actions may be necessary to reach the goal, the rest of the group tends to react negatively to the task specialist's prodding, and hence tension in the group increases. Because most of the group members believe the task specialist to be the source

TABLE 5-1. The differing behaviors of task specialists and socioemotional leaders. The category number from Bales's Interaction Process Analysis is given in parentheses

		Socioemotional leaders		Task specialists
Behaviors initiated	show	solidarity (1) tension release (2) agreement (3) tension increase (11)	give	suggestions (4) opinions (5) orientation (6)
	ask for	orientation (7) opinions (8) suggestions (9)	show	disagreement (10) antagonism (12)
Behaviors received	shows of	solidarity (1) tension release (2)	shows of	agreement (3) disagreement (10) tension increase (11) antagonism (12)
	given	suggestions (4) opinions (5) orientation (6)		
	requests	for suggestions (9)	requests	for orientation (7) for opinions (8) for suggestions (9)

(Source: Slater, 1955)

of the tension, "someone other than the task leader must assume a role aimed at the reduction of interpersonal hostilities and frustrations" (Burke, 1967, p. 380). The peace keeper who intercedes and tries to maintain harmony while the task specialist leads the group toward great achievements is the **socioemotional specialist.**

The interdependence of these two roles in a group was illuminated in a classic study that made use of Bales's Interaction Process Analysis system of group observation (Slater, 1955). As noted in Chapter 2, Bales's system classifies group behavior into one of the 12 categories listed in Table 2-1. Half the categories in the system (1 to 3, 10 to 12) focus on positive (solidarity, tension release, agreement) and negative (disagrees, shows tension, shows antagonism) socioemotional behavior and thus should be more closely linked to that role. The other six categories, however, are more task oriented because they involve either direct attempts to solve specific problems in the group (4 to 6) or are concerned with information exchange via questioning (7 to 9). Using this system, the researcher recorded and compared the behaviors initiated by and received by the task specialist (labeled the *idea man* by Slater) and the socioemotional specialist (labeled the *best-liked man*). As Table 5-1 shows, the individuals in the two roles behaved very differently. The task specialist tended to dominate in the problem-solving area by giving more suggestions and opinions and by providing more orientation than the socioemotional specialist. The latter, however, dominated in the emotive areas by showing more solidarity, tension release, and greater agreement with other group members. When on the receiving end, however, the task specialist tended to elicit more questions along with more displays of tension, antagonism, and disagreement, whereas the socioemotional specialist received more demonstrations of solidarity, tension reduction, and problem-solving solutions. Bales (1958) suggests that these data demonstrate that both types of roles frequently exist simultaneously in groups, although alternative interpretations have been offered (Verba, 1961; Wilson, 1970).

In keeping with Bales's distinction between task and socioemotional roles, researchers at the National Training Laboratories (NTL), a training/research organization devoted to the improvement of group effectiveness, concluded that many roles within groups could be classified either as task roles or maintenance roles (Benne & Sheats, 1948). The NTL listing, however, elaborates on this dichotomy by breaking the two general roles up into smaller, more functionally definable ones. The result is the impressive cataloging of roles in Table 5-2.

A THREE-DIMENSIONAL THEORY OF ROLES

For a number of years Bales felt that role differentiation resulted in the two dimensions—task and socioemotional concerns—that he and his colleagues had uncovered in their earlier researches. In time, however, he came to conclude that three dimensions would be needed to describe fully the structure of roles in groups (Bales, 1970, 1980; Bales, Cohen, & Williamson, 1979). These three dimensions, which have been identified in a broad range of studies (Borgatta, Cottrell, & Mann, 1958; Carter, 1954; Schutz, 1958; Triandis, 1978; Wish, Deutsch, & Kaplan, 1976), are (1) dominance/submission, (2) friendly/unfriendly, and (3) instrumentally controlled/emotionally expressive.

TABLE 5-2. Task roles and socioemotional roles in groups

Role	Function
Task roles	
1. Initiator contributor	Recommends novel ideas about the problem at hand, new ways to approach the problem, or possible solutions not yet considered.
2. Information seeker	Emphasizes "getting the facts" by calling for background information from others.
3. Opinion seeker	Asks for more qualitative types of data, such as attitudes, values, and feelings.
4. Information giver	Provides data for forming decisions, including facts that derive from expertise.
5. Opinion giver	Provides opinions, values, and feelings.
6. Elaborator	Gives additional information—examples, rephrasings, implications—about points made by others.
7. Coordinator	Shows the relevance of each idea and its relationship to the overall problem.
8. Orienter	Refocuses discussion on the topic whenever necessary.
9. Evaluator-critic	Appraises the quality of the group's efforts in terms of logic, practicality, or method.
10. Energizer	Stimulates the group to continue working when discussion flags.
11. Procedural technician	Cares for operational details, such as the materials, machinery, and so on.
12. Recorder	Provides a secretarial function.
Socioemotional roles	
1. Encourager	Rewards others through agreement, warmth, and praise.
2. Harmonizer	Mediates conflicts among group members.
3. Compromiser	Shifts his or her own position on an issue in order to reduce conflict in the group.
4. Gatekeeper and expediter	Smooths communication by setting up procedures and ensuring equal participation from members.
5. Standard setter	Expresses, or calls for discussion of, standards for evaluating the quality of the group process.
6. Group observer and commentator	Informally points out the positive and negative aspects of the group's dynamics and calls for change if necessary.
7. Follower	Accepts the ideas offered by others and serves as an audience for the group.

(Source: Benne and Sheats, 1948)

When these three dimensions are combined, they yield the three-dimensional cube pictured in Figure 5-1. To interpret this rather imposing theoretical model, assume that behavior along each of the three dimensions can be classified as (1) upward, downward, or neutral; (2) positive, negative, or neutral; and (3) forward, backward, or neutral. Next, labels based on combinations of the letters of these reference directions can be used to describe what type of group behavior is being performed (if neutral on a particular dimension the letter is simply omitted). For example, the section on the front facet, top left-hand corner is labeled UNB, corresponding to behaviors that are upward/negative/backward (dominant, unfriendly, and emotionally expressive). Similarly, the position marked UF is upward/forward, the position marked PB is positive/backward, and so on.

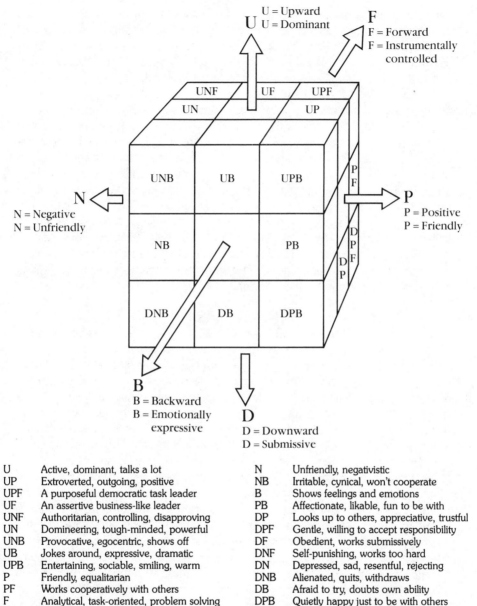

U	Active, dominant, talks a lot	N	Unfriendly, negativistic
UP	Extroverted, outgoing, positive	NB	Irritable, cynical, won't cooperate
UPF	A purposeful democratic task leader	B	Shows feelings and emotions
UF	An assertive business-like leader	PB	Affectionate, likable, fun to be with
UNF	Authoritarian, controlling, disapproving	DP	Looks up to others, appreciative, trustful
UN	Domineering, tough-minded, powerful	DPF	Gentle, willing to accept responsibility
UNB	Provocative, egocentric, shows off	DF	Obedient, works submissively
UB	Jokes around, expressive, dramatic	DNF	Self-punishing, works too hard
UPB	Entertaining, sociable, smiling, warm	DN	Depressed, sad, resentful, rejecting
P	Friendly, equalitarian	DNB	Alienated, quits, withdraws
PF	Works cooperatively with others	DB	Afraid to try, doubts own ability
F	Analytical, task-oriented, problem solving	DPB	Quietly happy just to be with others
NF	Legalistic, has to be right	D	Passive, introverted, says little

FIGURE 5-1. The SYMLOG model. (Source: Bales, 1980)

This three-dimensional system is the basis for a new measure of group inter-action named **SYMLOG,** a *System for the Multiple Level Observation of Groups* (Bales et al., 1979). SYMLOG, which replaces Bales's earlier Interaction Process Analysis as a means of coding group behavior (Bales, 1950), seems to summarize both the structure of the group and the personality characteristics of the interactants (Breiger & Ennis, 1979; Mills, 1971). Since each dimension is segmented into thirds, the model describes 3^3 "types" of roles that can be found in groups (actually, 27 types, minus the section of the cube that is neutral on all three dimensions for a total of 26 roles). These roles, identified by their letter labels, and their typical characteristics are shown in the legend to Figure 5-1.

Although SYMLOG can be used in many different ways, one approach requires rating each group member's tendency to engage in the 26 roles shown in the figure. Three summary scores (one for each dimension) can then be calculated for each of the group members, who can then be compared along the three dimensions. Such an approach was exemplified in a recent study in which subjects rated the social behavior of such notable figures as Jesus, Hitler, Groucho Marx, and Henry Ford (the automobile magnate). The investigators discovered that the three dimensions of SYMLOG neatly summarized these ratings, and that the classifications of these stimulus persons followed predictable patterns. For example, Hitler was viewed as UNF, Jesus was PF, Groucho was UPB, and Ford was UF. The investigators concluded that SYMLOG seems to measure role structures adequately, but they cautiously suggested that other roles not measured by SYMLOG may also be important (Isenberg & Ennis, 1981).

Role Conflict

The roles of Romeo and Juliet are not the only parts that must be played in Shakespeare's drama. Innumerable supporting actors are needed for the "bit parts"—such as guard, festival celebrant, and spectator—and while these actors may have only a few lines or actions, their presence helps make the play. The minor roles, however, differ from the leading roles in terms of their relative complexity. While Romeo is in many scenes, displaying many emotions, taking many actions, and reciting line after line of dialogue, the guard's actions are relatively few and limited in scope. In addition, while the role of Romeo includes subsidiary roles—lover, swordsman, devoted son, and friend—the guard is basically just a guard.

Variations in the complexity of roles also occur in groups where the occupant of one role may be expected to perform only one type of behavior, while a wide range of behaviors may be expected of another role. Furthermore, some group members may find themselves occupying several roles at the same time, with the requirements of each role making demands on his or her time and abilities. At times the multiple activities required by the many roles people occupy are completely compatible, since those required by one mesh with those required by the other. In some instances, however, individuals may experience role conflict, because the expectations that define the "proper" activities associated with a role are incompatible. Although many varieties of role conflict have been identified by theorists (Graen, 1976; Kahn, Wolfe, Quinn, Snoek, & Rosenthal, 1964; Van Sell, Brief, & Schuler, 1981), two of the more frequently mentioned types are interrole conflicts and intrarole conflicts.

Interrole conflict occurs when a person who plays two or more roles discovers that behaviors associated with Role A are incompatible with those associated with Role B. For example, consider a member of a small production crew who has developed strong friendships with several co-workers but has just been appointed to the position of supervisor. Although he or she may try to fulfill both roles, the expectations of the "buddy" role interfere with those of the "boss" role. Similarly, the woman who decides upon a career in management may discover that the expectations associated with this role clash with those associated with the traditional female sex role. She finds she cannot enact both roles simultaneously, for the manager role demands dominance and a strong task orientation, whereas the female stereotype typically emphasizes socioemotionality and passivity. For a more personal example, consider the student role, which may comprise expectations that are inconsistent with other roles, such as boyfriend/girlfriend or husband/wife. If the student role required spending every free moment in the library or studying conscientiously for exams, then such roles as lover, companion, and friend would be neglected.

Intrarole conflict results from contradictory demands within a single role as defined by the person playing the role (the role taker) and/or the other members of the group (the role senders). To use an earlier example, the role of supervisor of a production crew in a factory involves potentially inconsistent behaviors (Katz & Kahn, 1978). At one level the supervisor is the leader of the group, taking part in multiple activities such as overseeing the quality of production, training new personnel, and providing feedback or goal-orienting information. At another level, however, supervisors become the supervised as they take directions from a higher level of management. Thus, while the members of the team may expect the manager to "keep their secrets" and support them in any disputes with the management, the upper echelon expects obedience and loyalty (Miles, 1976). In addition, intrarole conflict can also stem from differences in expectations held by the role taker and role senders. For example, the newly appointed supervisor may assume that leadership means giving orders, maintaining a strict supervision, and criticizing incompetence. The work group, however, may feel that leadership entails eliciting cooperation in the group, providing support and guidance, and delivering rewards. Such contrasting expectations would invariably produce problems in the group's role relations.

Because role conflict is typically associated with unsatisfying interpersonal relations, poor group performance, low leadership endorsement, rejection of other group members, job dissatisfaction, and membership termination (see Van Sell, Brief, & Schuler, 1981, for an extensive review), small groups as well as larger organizations are often structured to insulate members from conflict. For example, roles that can create incompatibilities are often separated spatially and temporally, as in the case of the supervisor who is manager during working hours but a friend after hours or the man who is a husband at home but the boss at work. Naturally, the individual must be careful to engage in behaviors appropriate to the specific roles, since slipping into the wrong role at the wrong time can lead to considerable embarrassment (Gross & Stone, 1964). In addition, groups sometimes develop explicit rules regarding when one role should be sacrificed so that another can be enacted. Alternatively, a group member may be (1) prevented from occupying positions that can create role conflicts (as when the president of a country is required to place any business interests in a trust) or (2) permitted to withdraw from a role once conflict occurs (Sarbin & Allen, 1968).

While the concept of role serves an admirable descriptive function—it neatly describes and catalogs some regularities in behaviors found in groups—it never actually explains why the behaviors occur. Pointing to the roles in a group to account for behavior is like explaining why the earth revolves around the sun by saying that "the earth is a planet and planets always revolve around a sun." Similarly, if one asks such a question as "Why is the leader the person who organizes the group activities?" an answer such as "That's part of the role of being a leader" seems tautological. Another concept is needed to account for members' tendency to conform to group roles and for their negative reactions to out-of-role behaviors. Although the concept of a role describes which behaviors occur in a group, we need the concept of a norm to explain the why.

Norms

The survivors of the airplane crash in the Andes soon discovered that all the group members would have to adhere to certain rules if they were to endure their plight. With food, water, and shelter severely limited, the group members were forced to interact with and rely upon each other continually, and any errant action on the part of one person would disturb, and even endanger, several other people. Hence, rules were soon established concerning how the group would sleep at night, what types of duties each healthy individual was expected to perform, how food and water were to be apportioned, and where and at what times individuals would take care of their sanitary needs.

The Nature of Group Norms

The rules that describe the actions that should be taken by group members are known as **norms.** They serve as the standards by which group members regulate their own behaviors and thereby improve the coordination among interactants. Groups typically accept both *prescriptive norms,* which describe the kinds of behaviors that should be performed, and *proscriptive norms,* which describe the kinds of behaviors that are to be avoided. For example, some of the prescriptive norms of the Andes group were "Food should be shared equally," "Those who can should work to help those who are injured," and "Follow the orders of the leader," while some proscriptive norms were "Do not urinate inside the airplane," "Do not take more than your share of food and water," and "Do not move around during the night." Norms, however, not only describe what should or should not be done; they also contain an evaluative component, by which people who break the norms are considered "bad" and are open to sanction by the other group members. For instance, in the Andes group those who failed to do their fair share of work, who bothered others by moving at night, or who ate too much were verbally criticized by the others, given distasteful chores, and sometimes even denied food and water.

Although group norms can actually be written down and hence become the formal "laws" of the group, in most instances norms are adopted implicitly. Groups rarely "vote" on which norms to adopt, but rather gradually align their behaviors until they match certain standards. As a consequence, norms are often taken for granted so fully that members fail to realize their existence until a norm has been violated. For example, although the Andes survivors had been raised in a culture that condemned cannibalism, this taboo had rarely been discussed openly or evaluated explicitly. However, when they found themselves growing weak from starvation and saw that the only feasible food source was the bodies of those who had died in the crash, they realized that their only chance of survival lay in eating human flesh. The strength of society's implicit norm against cannibalism was so strong, however, that many of the group members felt physically revolted when the topic was discussed. The group leaders supported the cannibalism idea, and eventually the belief that "in this situation it is permissible to eat human flesh" became a group norm. Group pressures were brought to bear on those who refused to eat, and in the end nearly everyone accepted the inevitable. As the days went by the horror of the situation gradually wore away until cannibalism was a "normal" type of activity. Although many group members had simply been conforming to the demands of the group when they forced themselves to eat, they, along with the others, *internalized* the norm. That is, they came to eat the meat not merely because they were forced to by others, or because they wanted to please others by seeming agreeable, but because they had personally accepted the norm of cannibalism (Kelman, 1961).

Although in most instances a person who violates a norm will be sanctioned, most groups tolerate some variability so long as the deviation is not too great. For example, while the group members who were given the task of cutting up the bodies were not supposed to take any extra for themselves, some pilfering was permitted as a reward for working on this gruesome task. As author Piers Paul Read explains in his book *Alive* (1974, p. 125),

> Everyone who worked at cutting up the meat did it, even Fernandez and the Strauches, and no one said anything so long as it did not go too far. One piece in the mouth for every ten cut up for the others was more or less normal. Mangino sometimes brought the proportion down to one for every five or six and Paez to one for three, but they would not hide what they did and desisted when the others shouted at them.

Before elaborating on the nature of norms by discussing (1) their development and (2) norms of reward, it will be useful to summarize the critical characteristics of norms. First, norms are rules that describe the actions that should or should not be taken. Second, an evaluative element is involved, since norms usually suggest that certain behaviors are "better" than others. Third, in many cases norms are not formally adopted by the group, but instead result from a gradual change in behavior until most participants accept the standard as the guideline for action. Fourth, norms are often taken for granted by group members, becoming evident only when violated. Fifth, although people may obey group norms merely to avoid sanctions or to seem agreeable, when the group members internalize a norm it becomes a part of their total value system; hence, members often follow norms not because of external pressure but because normative action is personally satisfying. Sixth, while extremely counternormative behaviors are usually followed by negative sanctions, some degree of deviation from a norm is often permitted.

The Development of Norms

The changes in the Andes survivors' acceptance of cannibalism exemplify the processes through which group norms develop. To survive, the group had to replace the culture's taboo against eating human flesh with a norm that encouraged survival through cannibalism. In the days leading up to a group discussion of the issue, the members gradually revised their personal standards and, as early as the fourth day, one group member remarked that the only source of nourishment was the frozen bodies of the crash victims. Although the others took the remark to be a joke, by the tenth day "the discussion spread as these boys cautiously mentioned it to their friends or those they thought would be sympathetic" (Read, 1974, p. 76). When the question was discussed by the entire group, a small subgroup of boys argued in favor of eating the corpses, but many others in the group claimed they could not bring themselves to think of their dead friends as food. The next day, however, their hopes of rescue were crushed when they learned by radio that the Air Force had given up the search. The realization that help was not forthcoming forced most of the group members to consume a few pieces of meat, and in the end cannibalism was accepted.

According to Muzafer Sherif, this type of change reflects how people in groups over time come to develop standards that serve as frames of reference for behaviors and perceptions (M. Sherif, 1936, 1966; C. W. Sherif, 1976). Although a group facing an ambiguous problem or situation may start off with little internal consensus and great variability in behavior, members soon structure their experiences until they conform to a standard developed within the group. Although this standard could be pressed upon the group by an outside authority or a group leader, Sherif notes that in most instances group norms develop through reciprocal influence. In the Andes group, individuals did not actively try to conform to the judgments of others, but used the information contained in other's responses to revise their own opinions and beliefs. Writes Sherif (1966, pp. xii–xiii): "When the external surroundings lack stable, orderly reference points, the individuals caught in the ensuing experience of uncertainty *mutually* contribute to each other a mode of orderliness to establish their own orderly pattern."

To demonstrate reciprocal group-member influences in the development of group norms, Sherif developed the experiment described earlier based on the **autokinetic effect,** the apparent movement of a stationary pinpoint of light in an otherwise completely darkened room. Individuals, dyads, and triads were placed in the darkened room, shown the light, and then asked to make a judgment about how far the dot of light moved. By repeating this task many times, Sherif found that individuals making judgments by themselves tended to establish their own idiosyncratic average estimates, which varied from 1 to 10 inches depending upon the individual. When people made their judgments in groups, however, their personal estimates slowly blended with those of other group members until a consensus was reached. As Figure 5-2 shows, before joining the group individuals varied considerably in their distance guesses; one subject indicated the light moved an average of 7 inches on each trial, and the other two individuals' estimates averaged less than 1 inch and less than 2 inches. When these individuals were part of a group, however, their judgments converged over time in what Sherif called a funnel pattern; by the final session, a norm of just over 2 inches had been formed.

Sherif concluded that new norms develop within groups whenever the context provides for little information to guide actions or to enable members to formulate beliefs. Furthermore, while later researchers tended to use this autokinetic research

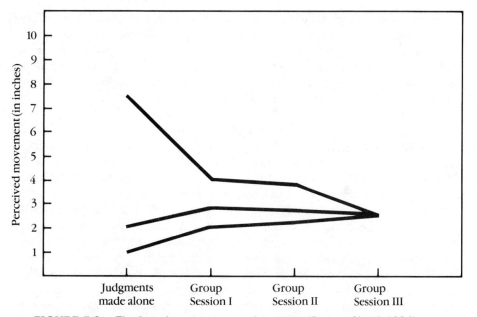

FIGURE 5-2. The funnel pattern in norm formation. (Source: Sherif, 1936)

as an example of compliance, Sherif insisted that the influence among all group members was mutual; people were not simply trying to go along with the judgments of others, but rather were actively trying to get a better estimate of the distance by considering all sources of information, including the others' judgments. Hence, the development of norms in the autokinetic situation resulted from a general tendency for groups to structure their behaviors and perceptions rather than from a demand for agreement (Pollis, Montgomery, & Smith, 1975).

Sherif later demonstrated that subjects in the situation had actually internalized the group norm by showing how, during subsequent individual sessions, subjects still relied on the previously established group norm (Sherif, 1966). In addition, other researchers (Jacobs & Campbell, 1961) were able to show how norms may eventually establish "a life of their own." These researchers placed a confederate in each three-member group and instructed this individual to make judgments along with the others but to steadfastly maintain that the dot of light was moving about 15 inches, clearly an excessive estimate given that most estimates averaged about 3 to 4 inches. Because of the funneling processes, however, this individual was able to deflect the rest of the group members' judgments upward so that a higher norm of movement was established in the group. Once this arbitrary standard had been created, the group confederate was removed from the group and replaced by a naive subject. The remaining group members, however, still retained the large distance norm, and the newest addition to the group gradually adapted to the higher standard. The researchers continued to replace group members with new subjects, but new members continued to shift their estimates in the direction of the group norm. Eventually this arbitrary group norm disappeared as judgments of distance came back down to an average of 3.5 inches, but in most cases the more reasonable norm did not develop until group membership had changed five or six times. Although these findings suggest that in some instances arbitrary norms will eventually disappear from the group, other research indicates that *degree of arbitrariness* is a key factor. A less arbitrary norm, such as a smaller amount of movement in the autokinetic situation, that is established through the use of confederates can last indefinitely (MacNeil & Sherif, 1976).

Norms of Reward

The bewildering number and variety of possible types of group norms suggest that few wide-ranging generalizations can be offered concerning the types of norms that are typically found in groups. However, nearly all groups have to deal with the problem of allocating resources, so many groups have developed norms dictating how rewards are to be distributed to group members. In the Andes group, for example, the group's resources were severely limited, and therefore a fair means of doling them out to members had to be developed. Unfortunately, if the resources are highly valued, the members of the group may desire to acquire as large a share of the payoff as possible, even if such greediness means other members will receive smaller shares. Thus, the group must discuss and agree upon the norms that will be used to allocate the group's limited resources, or else be forced into a debate about who deserves what each time the payoff is to be divided.

Although a number of possible norms could be used to allocate rewards, a good deal of theory and research focuses on the *norm of equity* (Walster, Walster, & Berscheid, 1978). According to this norm, group members should receive outcomes in proportion to their inputs. That is, if an individual has invested a good deal of time, energy, money, or other types of inputs in the group, then he or she could expect to receive a good deal of the group payoff. Similarly, individuals who contribute little should not be surprised when they receive little. However, the *norm of equality,* in contrast to the norm of equity, recommends that all group members, irrespective of their inputs, should be given an equal share of the payoff. For example, in the Andes group several of the boys, although healthy, refused to do what the others considered to be their fair share. To punish them, the leaders decided that the boys would receive no food until they worked to earn it. Fortunately for the boys, the leaders soon replaced this equity norm with an equality norm—all received food and water no matter what their contribution to the group.

Although many discussions of reward allocation emphasize the importance of equity and equality (Berkowitz & Walster, 1976), other norms may also develop within groups (Lerner, Miller, & Holmes, 1976; Leventhal, 1976). These other standards could include, for example, the following:

1. A *power norm* (to the victor goes the spoils), which allocates most to those who control the group;
2. A *Marxian norm,* which suggests that those with the greatest need should receive the most while those with the least need receive the least;
3. A *norm of social responsibility,* which requires those with the most to give up their share to those who have little; and

4. *A norm of reciprocity,* which argues that people should match the allocations they give to others with a payoff of equal size.

Because the impact of norms of allocation has been a significant focus of research in recent years, more will be said about this topic in Chapter 7.

Intermember Relations

Return for a moment, to your imaginary role as interplanetary explorer. You have charted the many features of the new solar system, being careful to note what types of planets exist (life-supporting, size, atmospheres, and so on) and the physical laws governing the movements of the system. Your analysis, however, is not yet complete, since you have failed to note what relationships link the planets together. For example, you may have described in faithful detail the characteristics of one of the system's moons, but unless you record which planet the moon orbits the description will be inadequate. Although you might depict fully each planet's size, atmosphere, and topography, you will also have to describe the planets' orbital locations, the relative distances between them, and their reciprocal influences upon one another in order to present a comprehensive picture of the solar system.

Analogously, although a great deal can be said about the arrangement of the individual members within the group once the role of each member and the norms guiding his or her behavior are identified, our understanding of a group remains incomplete until we analyze the connections among all group members. For example, our case study of the Andes survivors has shown that certain roles, such as task specialist and socioemotional specialist, developed within the group and that behaviors became organized around certain norms. However, at present our analysis of this group falls short, since we have not yet determined the overall group organization. Therefore, this section focuses on the relationships that link members together in the group. Herein we will consider three critically important forms of association: authority relations, attraction relations, and communication relations.

Authority Relations

Although the concept of equality for all human beings is a central premise of the most prominent social and political philosophies, in countless situations some people are singled out as "more equal" than others. In the microsociety represented by the small group this inequality becomes evident as the group members come to exercise varying levels of control over the group, are themselves more or less influenced by others, and play a larger or smaller part in the determination of the group's goals and decisions. Group members may all start off on an equal footing, but soon certain individuals begin to coordinate the activities of the group, providing others with guidance and relaying communications to the various group members (Bales, 1950). These variations among the group members—which have been termed differences in authority, status, prestige, or power—create a stable pattern of intermember relations that can be described as a hierarchy of authority. As depicted in Figure 5-3, the greatest authority resides in the hands of

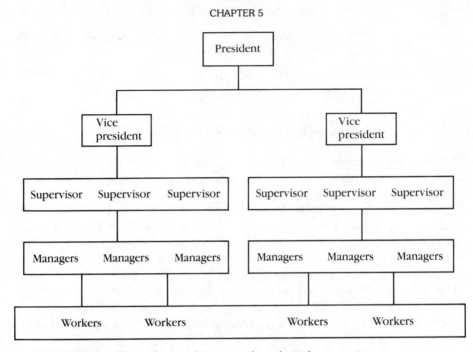

FIGURE 5-3.   The authority relations in a hypothetical organization.

a relatively small number of individuals at the "top of the heap." The president and vice presidents are the *powerholders* of the group; they make major decisions that affect the entire group, take responsibility for the group's performance, issue orders to other group members, and usually serve as foci for intragroup communications. As the diagram shows, below these individuals lies a stratum of members who have less power than the vice presidents but more than the occupants of lower echelons. As we descend the ladder of organization we find that the authority of each level diminishes while the number of occupants at each subordinate level increases. Hence, the authority structure of the group tends to be pyramid shaped.

Given that Figure 5-3 represents a small business, the authority structure of the organization is probably completely formalized, and may even be charted on the wall of the president's conference room as an ever-present reminder of the "chain of command." However, authority relations are also a part of the structure of more informally organized groups, and though they may not be as explicitly described, they still significantly influence group members' interactions. For example, among the Andes survivors a stable hierarchy of authority developed after an avalanche of snow killed several of the group members, including the leader—Marcelo. In response to this loss and the clear need to organize a party to travel down the mountain to seek help, the group gradually became structured along the lines shown in Figure 5-4.

Fito Strauch, who was the informally accepted leader, exercised the most control over the rest of the group members along with his two cousins, E. Strauch and Fernandez. The three men, the only remaining filial group, formed a coalition and

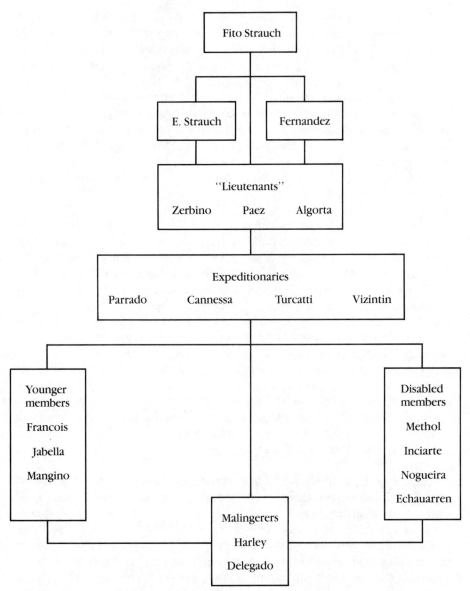

FIGURE 5-4. The authority structure among the Andes survivors.

were recognized by most of the other group members as best suited to lead the group. This triumvirate, however, was supported by its "lieutenants": a group of three younger men who made certain that the leaders' orders were enforced and who also carried out certain minor duties. Although their requests carried less force than those of, say, Fito Strauch, they still commanded a fair amount of respect, since they were the recognized emissaries of the top leaders.

Below the lieutenants we find a special class of group members called the expeditionaries. These were the individuals who had been designated by the rest of the group as the fittest and strongest, and who had therefore been chosen to hike down the mountain in search of help. In preparing for their journey they were given special privileges concerning sleeping arrangements, clothing, food, and water. Although they were not leaders in the usual sense, the expeditionaries could require lower echelon members to obey their orders. These lesser groups fell into three clusters of varying authority. The rank-and-file members included three men who, because of their youth and dispositions, were considered to be childish and unstable. Their authority was equal to that of the four men who had received disabling injuries, but somewhat greater than that of the two group members who were considered to be malingerers. As in a formally organized group, the lines of group authority formed a pyramidlike pattern.

WHY AUTHORITY RELATIONS?

Although various theories have been propounded to explain the pervasive tendency for groups to develop authority hierarchies, one of the most sophisticated and well-validated formulations is **expectation-states theory.** Developed by Joseph Berger and his colleagues (Berger, Cohen, & Zelditch, 1972; Berger, Conner, & Fisek, 1974; Berger, Fisek, Norman, & Zelditch, 1977), this theory traces differences in status back to group members' expectations. To begin, Berger notes that status hierarchies are likely to exist in groups that are working collectively on a task members deem to be fairly important. Because the group hopes it can successfully complete the project, the possibility that certain members of the group may possess skills and abilities that will facilitate goal attainment begins to dominate the thoughts of the members. At this point, the status-organizing process begins in the group as those people who are expected to contribute most are implicitly identified. These individuals are permitted (and encouraged) to perform more numerous and varied group actions, provide greater input and guidance for the group, influence others by evaluating their ideas, and reject the influence attempts of others.

The theory also describes how the characteristics of the group members can be used to formulate expectations. Some characteristics, which Berger labels **specific-status characteristics,** define expectations because they are relevant to the skills and abilities necessary in the given situation. For example, in the Andes group the higher status expeditionaries were chosen on the basis of several specific qualities—strength, determination, health, and maturity. In the selection of an expeditionary, the "state" (position) of each group member on each of these specific skills was evaluated, and those who possessed the best combination were chosen.

In the absence of specific-status information, groups may still formulate expectations by considering **diffuse-status characteristics**—any quality of the person that the members think is relevant to ability and evaluation. Sex, age, wealth, ethnicity, status in other groups, or cultural background can serve as diffuse-status characteristics if group members associate these qualities with certain skills, as did the members of the Andes group. Among the survivors age was considered to be an important characteristic, with youth being negatively valued.

Empirical investigations of the expectation-state approach have, for the most part, supported the theory's predictions (see Webster & Driskell, 1978, for a summary and review). First, a host of studies have verified the assumption that a positively evaluated "state" on a specific-status characteristic such as ability or knowledge causes increases in authority (Greenstein & Knottnerus, 1980). Second, the theory explains why characteristics that are irrelevant in the group situation—such as military rank (Torrance, 1954) or sex (Strodtbeck, James, & Hawkins, 1957; Nemeth, Endicott, & Wachtler, 1976)—sometimes influence status rankings. Last, the theory has recently been expressed mathematically (Berger et al., 1977) and its prediction formulas appear to be quite accurate. When researchers reanalyzed 14 separate experimental studies of status development in small groups, they found that "Berger et al.'s linear model fits the data from these experiments remarkably well. We conclude that these results demonstrate the utility and apparent validity of the central concepts and assumptions of this theory of status-organizing processes" (Fox & Moore, 1979, p. 126; for a critical analysis, see Greenstein, 1981; Ofshe & Lee, 1981).

STATUS INCONGRUENCY

The assumption that group members consider a number of characteristics in determining authority rankings hints at a possible problem. What occurs when an individual's various status characteristics yield conflicting conclusions about authority? If multiple characteristics are a part of the process, then it seems highly likely that while some of an individual's characteristics may be valued positively, these may be offset by other characteristic states valued negatively. For example, in the Andes group Algorta possessed several characteristics that could have disqualified him for any high-status position. He was not part of the rugby team, had few friends in the group, and came from a background that differed from that of the others. However, he was healthy, strong, and put his abilities to use to help everyone in the group. Although his diffuse-status characteristics initially separated him from the others, in time his willingness and ability to work earned him a position as one of the group's "lieutenants."

Inconsistency in the rankings of an individual's status characteristics—**status incongruency**—has been identified as a possible impediment to the group's status-organizing process. Consider as an example a decision-making group with 12 members that includes the following individuals:

1. Mr. Black, a 35-year-old black executive with outstanding credentials and long experience in a leadership position;
2. Mr. White, a 58-year-old white high school teacher who is very outspoken on the issues being discussed; and
3. Dr. Prof, a 40-year-old white female college professor who teaches in the college of business administration and who has written several books on organizational development.

Speaking hypothetically, let us say that although Dr. Prof seems to be the most highly qualified for the role of leader, the rest of the group, in a decidedly sexist reaction, feel that Prof, being a woman, would be ineffective in that role. Similarly, Mr. Black seems to possess the experience that should earn him high status, but the group, being equally biased against racial minorities, feels that being black is a negative characteristic and thus disqualifies Mr. Black. Mr. White, on the other hand, poses little incongruency for the group, since the group members consider advanced age, white skin, and vocality to be positive features. Hence, White ends up as the group leader.

Although the group puts Mr. White ahead of Dr. Prof and Mr. Black, most theories of status incongruency go on to predict that our hypothetical group will be characterized by individual stress and group strain. Those with the inconsistent characteristics, Prof and Black, are assumed to experience psychological discomfort since they are not sure what the others expect of them and may also feel that the group's authority rankings are unfair. In addition, the rest of the group is uncertain about the status of these two problematic members, and interactions are thus uncomfortable and awkward. When dealing with Mr. Black, for example, another group member would not know if Black is an equal-status peer, of inferior status, or a superior group member, and in part Black may not know either.

While several studies have found evidence of the negative effects of status incongruency (Brandon, 1965; McCranie & Kimberly, 1973), Paul Crosbie (1979) suggests that these findings may stem from a failure to consider original status rankings. According to Crosbie, previous researchers frequently confounded incongruency with original status ranking since they forgot that a status-incongruent individual must, by definition, possess at least one low-status quality whereas a status-congruent person could have all high-status qualities. Hence, when incongruent status individuals report dissatisfaction, it is difficult to tell if their reaction is due to the incongruency or their dissatisfyingly low original status ranking. To investigate this possibility, Crosbie studied 19 groups of college students playing a simulation game that created differences in status based on money earned and political position (SIMSOC, Gamson, 1972). After several hours of play, he measured ten different characteristics that the group members could be using to establish authority rankings—sex, helpfulness, attractiveness, cooperativeness, money earned, leadership, power, prestige, position, and class standing—and also measured members' satisfaction with the group. Initially he found that incongruencies in some of these status characteristics tended to be associated with dissatisfaction and a desire to withdraw. For example, people who possessed inconsistent status characteristics such as low leadership status but high prestige status were more dissatisfied than those with consistent status characteristics. However, when Crosbie statistically controlled for differences in original rankings this relationship disappeared. That is, the actual source of the dissatisfaction was not the inconsistency between leadership status and prestige status, but the simple fact that the individual was low in leadership status.

On the basis of these findings Crosbie rejected what most previous theorists had considered to be a well-established group phenomenon. He concluded that "knowledge of status inconsistency in these groups, irrespective of the theoretical genesis of the inconsistency, does not significantly enhance the ability to explain behavior above and beyond the explanatory power provided by knowledge of the original status rankings" (1979, p. 122). Although this conclusion seems reasonable based on his carefully performed study, additional data are needed to close the case against status-incongruency effects.

Attraction Relations

As part of the series of industrial studies conducted at the Western Electric Company's Hawthorne Works in Chicago, a small group of men were observed while they worked at wiring equipment to be used in telephone switches (Roethlisberger & Dickson, 1939). Nine of the men in the group were "wirers," connecting wires to the banks of terminals in each piece of equipment—and three of the men were "solderers," soldering the wires into permanent positions. Lastly, their work was checked by one of two "inspectors." Each piece of equipment required some 3000 connections, and each wirer usually turned out about two finished products per day.

During the six months of the Bank Wiring Observation Room Study, the men continued to wire, solder, and inspect the equipment, just as they had before the start of the project. However, because they had been isolated from the rest of the plant and sequestered in a small observation room, group formation and interaction was almost inevitable. Indeed, after a time, roles and norms for the group developed along with a clear hierarchy of authority and status. A certain rate of production was considered appropriate, and anyone who worked too far above or below this norm was sanctioned. One person was given the role of "lunch boy"—the conveyor of food orders from the plant restaurant to the work room—and nicknames such as Cyclone, the Shrimp, and Chiseler became popular forms of address.

However, to describe the group in just these terms would be to miss a vital part of the social structure. The individuals were not just workers in a factory or members of a work group; they were also *friends*. The close association necessary for their jobs created nearly continuous interaction, and with this interaction came the development of **attraction relations**: stable patterns of liking and disliking linking each of the group members. Although these relations were rarely discussed by the group members, the researchers had no difficulty discerning these affective patterns, and by observing group interaction they developed the graph of attraction relations, both negative and positive, pictured in Figure 5-5. As the graph indicates, in one cluster workers were linked by bonds of friendship (I_1, W_1, W_2, W_3 and S_1), while dislike predominated in the other cluster (I_3, W_4 to W_9, S_2, and S_4). Overall, Inspector 3 (I_3) was the most disliked member of the group, while Solderer 1 (S_1) was the best liked member.

MEASURING ATTRACTION RELATIONS

Any pictorial representation of the attraction relations of a group, whether based on the actual choices reported by group members or the conclusions of some outside observer, is called a **sociogram.** As noted in Chapter 2, the concept and method of sociometry are credited to Jacob L. Moreno, who believed human groups to be unique social entities owing to the tendency for members to react to one another on a spontaneous affective level. According to Moreno, group relations can take on many different colors—hate, condemnation, liking, friendship, sorrow, love, and so on—but only rarely do group members react neutrally to one another. The sociogram was developed to capture the essence of these affective relationships, and in its original usage applied only to graphs based on

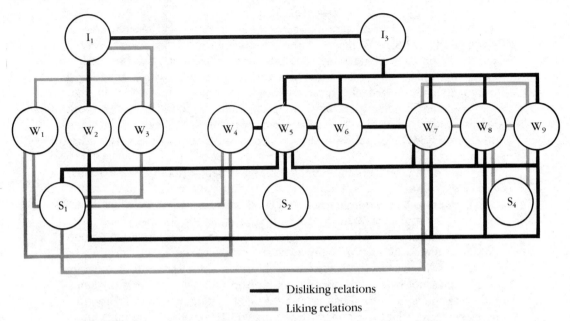

FIGURE 5-5. Patterns of liking and disliking in the Bank Wiring Observation Room group. (Source: Roethlisberger and Dickson, 1939)

choices group members reported to the researcher. In time, however, the terms *sociogram* and *sociometry* took on more general meanings, referring to any method that is used to assess the pattern of likes and dislikes in the group situation (Moreno, 1960).

Although the early sociometric studies demonstrated that attraction relations could be fairly easily recorded, they also hinted at a possible problem. While respondents could readily provide the researcher with information about their favorite choice of partner in the group, they typically wanted to know what activities would be involved. For example, one study asked the residents of a state institution for women to indicate with whom they preferred to spend leisure time and with whom they preferred to live or work (Jennings, 1950). Unexpectedly, the women's choices varied considerably depending on the criteria; one woman might be preferred for recreation, but another was the choice as partner at work. Apparently, the statement "An attraction relationship exists between Member X and Member Y" is vague, because the basis of the attraction—affection, friendship, respect, love, or hate—is unspecified (Blau, 1962; Triandis, 1977).

Mady W. Segal (1979) addressed the problem of the multiple meaning of attraction when applied to group structures by comparing three kinds of interpersonal choices: friendship, liking, and respect. Overall, Segal felt that the three measures would be similar but that each tapped a different type of attraction. In contrasting friendship and liking, Segal points out that friends will in all probability like one another, but that nonfriends may be both liked and disliked; that is, liking is a necessary but insufficient condition for friendship. Furthermore, the concept of friendship implies a relationship between two people, whereas liking connotes feeling rather than stable patterns of behavior. Respect, on the other hand, is based more on perceived status than an affective reaction, and so should be less closely linked to friendship and liking.

To examine this proposition Segal asked the members of two college football teams to rate one another on scales that assessed friendship, liking, and respect. As she had predicted, friendship choices tended to be more mutual than either liking or respect choices; the players' choices of friends were reciprocal, whereas other choices tended to be scattered throughout the group. In addition, friendship ratings, on the average, were lower than the ratings of liking and respect, suggesting that many people can be liked and respected, but that fewer can be named as close friends. Lastly, ratings of friendship were most closely associated with recreational activities (such as watching television together, "hanging around" together, and so on), followed by liking and respect. The implications of this suggestive research are clear: (1) researchers should be careful to word their queries appropriately concerning intragroup sentiment in order to tap the specific variety of attraction of interest; (2) generalizations from one kind of relationship to another (for example, friendship to liking) should be made with caution; and (3) future researchers could profitably turn their attention to the study of the antecedents and consequences of each type of attraction in a group.

MAINTAINING STRUCTURAL BALANCE

Several theories have been developed to explain why some intermember attraction patterns seem to occur only rarely while other patterns are more frequently observed (Cartwright & Harary, 1956, 1970; Heider, 1958; Newcomb, 1963). For example, consider a subgroup of the wiring room workers composed of a solderer, a wirer, and an inspector. Although most would agree that the triad would be very cohesive and stable if everyone in this group liked everyone else, what would happen if (1) the wirer disliked the inspector and liked the solderer, but (2) the solderer liked both the inspector and the wirer? Would the wirer's and solderer's discrepant reactions to the inspector create discomfort for the members, and possibly cause the group's attraction relations to change?

Fritz Heider believed that the key to understanding the relationship between the stability of the group and attraction patterns lay in the **balance** between liking and disliking in the group. In the simple case of a two-person group, balance could be achieved only if attraction (or repulsion) was mutual. For example, in the diagrams of the Bank Wiring Observation Room workers in Figure 5-5 we can see that all the choices of friends and foes are reciprocal ones. W_1 is attracted to W_4, and W_4 seems to like W_1 in return. Disliking is also symmetrical, for just as I_1 dislikes W_2, W_2 dislikes I_1. According to Heider, these simple dyadic relations are balanced because the pairwise relationships between X and Y are the same— both like or both dislike one another. The dyad would become imbalanced if one of the individuals, say W_1, liked W_4 but W_4 disliked W_1. Heider's idea of balance provides an explanation for the reciprocity principle that typically holds at the dyadic level.

Heider's concept of balance also applies to larger groups. Assuming all liking (positive) and disliking (negative) relationships in the group are mutual (that is, if Fritz likes Grace, then Grace likes Fritz), Heider's balance theory postulates that the group's structure will be balanced if (1) all relationships between members are positive or (2) an even number of negative relationships occurs in the group. Consider the small subgroup of W_8, W_9, and S_4 in Figure 5-5. Because all three members of this triad like one another, the clique is balanced. However, if one of the members—say, W_8—disliked W_9, then the group would be imbalanced because the number of negative relationships in the group would be uneven. However, if S_4 also disliked W_9, then the group would be balanced, since the number of negative relationships would then be even. Hence, a triad will be balanced if all pairwise relationships are positive, or if one of the pairwise relationships is positive and the remaining two are negative.

The balance of a still larger group can also be calculated by isolating "cycles" within the group, where a cycle is defined as a series of relationships that starts with Person X and eventually ends up back at Person X (Cartwright & Harary, 1956, 1970). For example, in Figure 5-5 the path from $W_7 \rightarrow W_8 \rightarrow S_4 \rightarrow W_9 \rightarrow W_7$ would be a four-person cycle that begins and ends with W_7. As with triads, the cycle is imbalanced if it contains an odd number of negative relations, but is balanced if all relations are positive or the number of negative is even. For example, the W_7 cycle we just examined is balanced because all the relations are positive. However, in the cycle $I_1 \rightarrow W_3 \rightarrow S_1 \rightarrow W_5 \rightarrow I_3 \rightarrow I_1$, three relationships are negative, so it is imbalanced. Because the occurrence of a single unbalanced cycle within a group can cause the entire group to become imbalanced, this approach would argue that the Bank Wiring Observation Room work group was somewhat unstable. (See Cartwright & Harary, 1956 and Mayer, 1975, for overviews of this and other approaches to the calculation of stability in larger group structures.)

Before closing this discussion of attraction relations, it is important to stress the impact of balance on group stability. Balance theory predicts that imbalanced groups are unpleasant for participants and that the latter will be motivated to correct the imbalance and restore the group's equilibrium. Heider notes, however, that this restoration of balance can be achieved through either interpersonal changes in the group or intrapsychic changes in the individual. In the first case, an individual who is disliked by the other group members may be ostracized (Taylor, 1970) or forced to change his or her behavior. In addition, the group may break up into smaller, better balanced cliques that lessen the chances for hostility and stress (Newcomb, 1981). (This clique-formation process apparently took place in the Bank Wiring Observation Room group.) Alternatively, group members may reduce imbalance by changing their attitudes about the other members of the group.

Communication Relations

In the early 1950s researchers at the Group Networks Laboratory at Massachusetts Institute of Technology embarked on a program of experimental studies of a third way in which group members can be interconnected (Bavelas, 1948, 1950; Bavelas & Barrett, 1951; Leavitt, 1951). In addition to authority and attraction relations, group members are also linked in a **communication network,** and the patterns of this network can be significantly related to other aspects of the group's overall structure. In the Andes group, for example, the three leaders stayed in close communication, discussing among themselves any problems before relaying their interpretations to the other group members. In contrast, the injured members were virtually cut off from communicating with the others during the daylight hours, and occasionally complained that they were the last to know of any significant developments. Hence, the other group members tended to route all information through the leaders, who saw to it that the rest of the group was subsequently informed.

Although many different methods have been used to study communication networks in groups, one standard technique controls the channels of communication used by members. For example, in one often cited study, Harold J. Leavitt (1951) seated five males at a circular table (each chair, however, was separated from the other chairs by means of a tall partition) and gave them a simple task to solve. Each individual was given a card on which were printed five of the following symbols: $\bigcirc \ \triangle \ \ast \ \square \ + \ \diamond$. Although everyone was given a different card, one symbol out of the six possible was common to all the group members' cards. The problem assigned to the group was to identify the common symbol. Naturally, subjects could easily solve the problem by comparing all the cards, but Leavitt controlled the group's communication processes by allowing the exchange of messages among some members but not among others. This manipulation was easily accomplished by simply opening particular slots in the walls of the partitions separating the participants.

Some of the many networks that have been used in this type of study are illustrated in Figure 5-6, but Leavitt only used four—the wheel, chain, Y, and circle. When in a wheel, one person in the group could communicate with everyone, while the other four individuals were connected only to this individual. In the circle everyone interacted with two other individuals, while in the chain and Y interactions the number of links varied from one to three persons. Leavitt found that in all networks save the circle, peripheral group members tended to send information to the more central member(s), who integrated the data and sent back a solution. Naturally, this information summarization was most easily accomplished in the wheel, as all members could interact directly with the central member, while in the Y and chain the pooling process took longer, since some members had to act as go-betweens. The circle network, unlike the others, never adopted a centralized organizational structure.

In the years since the MIT researchers first published their findings, the number of experiments reported in this area has grown considerably (Collins & Raven, 1968; Shaw, 1964, 1978), with the overall findings showing that communication structures in groups significantly influence such aspects of the group as problem-solving efficiency, leadership, and member satisfaction. The final sections of this chapter provide an overview of this important area, including (1) centralization and group efficiency, (2) positional effects, and (3) hierarchical networks.

THE EFFICIENCY OF COMMUNICATION NETWORKS

Marvin E. Shaw, after reviewing the bulk of the research examining communication networks in small groups, concluded that one of the most important features of a network—at least when predicting efficiency—is *degree of centralization* (Shaw, 1964, 1978). Although this variable can be assessed mathematically by considering the relative number of links joining the positions in the network (Bavelas, 1948, 1950; Freeman, 1977; Moxley & Moxley, 1974), for our purposes

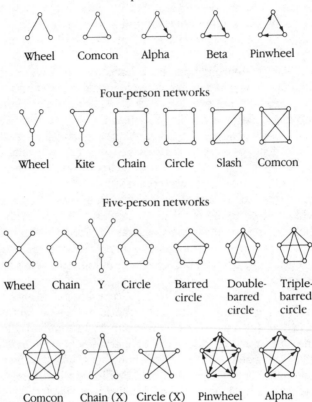

FIGURE 5-6. Some common communication networks in small groups. (Source: Shaw, 1964)

a broad distinction between centralized and decentralized patterns will suffice. With centralized networks, one of the positions is located at the "crossroads" of communications, as in the wheel and Y of Figure 5-6. As Leavitt's findings suggested, groups with this type of structure tend to use the hub position as the data-processing center and its occupant typically collects information, synthesizes it, and then sends it back to others. In decentralized structures, like the circle or comcon, the number of channels at each position is essentially equal, so no one position is more central than another. These groups tend to use a variety of organizational structures when solving their problems, including an "each-to-all" pattern, where everyone sends messages in all directions until someone gets the correct answer.

The early MIT studies tended to recommend centralized nets over decentralized nets where optimal efficiency was desired. For example, Leavitt's findings suggested that individual and group error rates are lower in the centralized Y and wheel than in the more decentralized chain and circle. Other studies tended to support this conclusion, as centralized groups out-scored decentralized groups in time taken in finding a solution, number of messages sent, finding and correcting errors, and improvement with practice (Shaw, 1964, 1978). However, most of the studies that found evidence of the centralized-network superiority used fairly simple tasks modeled after the problem used by Leavitt. When these tasks were replaced with more complicated ones—arithmetic, sentence construction, problem solving, and discussion—the findings tended to be reversed, as the decentralized networks out-performed the centralized ones.

These seemingly paradoxical findings led Shaw to propose that network efficiency is related to **information saturation.** When a group is working on a problem, exchanging information, and making a decision, the central position in the network can best manage the inputs and interactions of the group. However, as work progresses and the number of communications being routed through the central member increases, a saturation point can be reached where the individual can no longer efficiently monitor, collate, or route incoming and outgoing messages. Although saturation can occur in a decentralized network, it is more likely in a centralized one working on complex problems where the hub position receives a large number of communications on many different channels. Because the "greater the saturation the less efficient the group's performance" (Shaw, 1964, p. 126), the most adequate generalization about type of network and efficiency predicts that *when the task is simple, centralized networks are more efficient than decentralized networks; when the task is complex, then decentralized networks are superior to centralized networks.*

POSITIONAL EFFECTS

When Mr. Stuart Dent enrolls in college, he finds himself in many different types of courses with many different types of organizational structures. In one seminar class the group sits in a circle, discussing topics suggested by the teacher or the other students. When Stu leaves that class he goes to one of his more typical courses, where 40 to 50 students sit in rows listening to a lecturer. Naturally, he can ask a question if he wants to, but he must first raise his hand before the teacher will permit him to speak. Lastly, one of his night courses is a large class of 500 students in which the instructor must use a microphone to be heard. Stu hardly ever gets a chance to ask a question in that class, but when he does the instructor must repeat (and sometimes reword) the question over the microphone. Stu dislikes the large class because he feels "left out" of the educational process, since the instructor controls all the communication in the classroom.

Mr. Dent's reactions to his classes are in many ways similar to the reactions of people in centralized versus decentralized communication networks. For most people, a decentralized network is preferable, since it encourages independence of action, autonomy, and self-direction (Shaw, 1964). In centralized networks, most of the group's actions are controlled by whoever is in the central position and that person—like the teacher in a lecture-style classroom—can arbitrarily open and close channels of communication. While central-position occupants typically report that they are very much satisfied with the group structure, the more peripheral members emphasize their dissatisfaction. That is, position is linked to satisfaction such that the more removed the position from the center of the network, the less satisfied is the occupant. This effect logically suggests that, because the number of peripheral positions in a centralized network exceeds the number of central positions, the overall level of satisfaction in a centralized group is low.

Position is linked not only to satisfaction and enjoyment, but also to leadership development. In Leavitt's study, for example, participants completed a questionnaire at the close of the session that included the item "Did your group have a leader? If so, who?" The responses to this query concerning leadership indicated that the individual in the most central position of the network was chosen to be the leader by 100% of the group members in the wheel, by 85% of the group members in the Y, and by 67% of the group members in the chain. In contrast, leadership choices in the egalitarian circle were approximately equally divided across all the different positions.

COMMUNICATIONS IN HIERARCHICAL NETWORKS

Although some groups may use one of the communication patterns depicted in Figure 5-6, groups that form their own communication network often develop a hierarchically structured network (Goetsch & McFarland, 1980). In such networks, information can pass horizontally to members on the same "rung" of the communication "ladder," but researchers tend to focus more heavily on communications that move vertically, upward and downward through the hierarchy (Jablin, 1979). Furthermore, because the communication hierarchy generally follows the same pattern as the lines of group authority, the content of the upward and downward communications tends to be somewhat different (Browning, 1978; Katz & Kahn, 1978). Information passed downward from superior to subordinate can explain which actions are to be taken, provide reasons for actions, pressure the receiver to act in a certain manner, or provide feedback concerning performance. Upward communications from subordinates to superiors can contain data concerning performance, insinuations about a peer's performance, requests for information, expressions of distrust, strictly factual information, or grievances concerning the group's policies. These upward communications, however, tend to be fewer in number, briefer, and more guarded than downward communications. Indeed, in larger organizations the upward flow of information may be much impeded by the mechanics of the transferral process (Manis, Cornell, & Moore, 1974) and by

---

MUM'S THE WORD

The two young men among the Andes survivors who had been assigned the job of monitoring the newscasts on a small transistor radio were shocked to hear that, after only eight days of searching, the Uruguayan Air Force had canceled the search. Of the two who heard the broadcast, one flatly refused to tell the others about the cancellation, since it would destroy their hopes. The other insisted that they be told the truth, and when he dutifully relayed the information they reacted with anger and bitterness.

This reluctance to tell the others bad news is one form of the **MUM effect**—keeping Mum about Undesirable Messages (Tesser & Rosen, 1975). According to research, individuals are not only reluctant messengers when the information describes personal inabilities or shortcomings, but also when they are not at fault for the problems described in the negative information. Apparently, people avoid the role of "bearer of bad tidings," since they fear that the negative feelings the bad news creates will generalize from the message to the messenger.

the lower status members' reluctance to send information that might reflect unfavorably on their performance, abilities, and skills (Bradley, 1978; Browning, 1978). In fact, the research described in the box suggests that the low-status members' selective reticence may mean that good news will travel quickly up the hierarchy, whereas the top of the ladder will be the last to learn bad news (see Jablin, 1979, for a detailed review of communication in hierarchical organizations).

Summary

Although we may be tempted to treat each of the many and varied groups we commonly observe as a unique social aggregate with unique features, in this chapter we saw how all groups possess a basic underlying *structure*—an unseen framework that holds the group members together and partially accounts for regularities in their behaviors. Focusing first on *roles*—behaviors characteristic of persons in a context—we saw that individuals who occupy certain positions in the group generally perform certain types of behaviors. The follower, the socioemotional specialist, and the task specialist are all typical roles that can evolve in groups through *role differentiation*, although group members can still experience role conflict if they occupy incompatible roles (*interrole conflict*) or the demands of a single role are contradictory (*intrarole conflict*).

A second aspect of group structure, norms, describes the "rules" in a group that explain what actions should, and shouldn't, be performed by group members. Although these rules are sometimes explicitly adopted by the group, they are more often implicit guidelines that if violated lead to negative sanctioning. Like roles, norms take time to develop within a group and can take many different forms, but most groups will adopt norms that dictate how resources are distributed among members.

The final component of group structure concerns the relationships that link members to one another, and includes *authority, attraction,* and *communication* relations. Even in informal groups some members command more authority than others, for as one theoretical perspective (*expectation-states theory*) explains, differences in authority derive from specific and diffuse status characteristics. Furthermore, if these status-earning characteristics are *incongruent* with one another— that is, members have some characteristics that earn high status but others that disqualify them from authority—then the group's *status-organizing processes* can be disrupted. Similarly, incongruencies in attraction relations—patterns of liking and disliking in the group that are generally measured sociometrically—can create imbalances that are unpleasant for members. Lastly, communications in a group often follow a stable, predictable pattern, and these *networks* can influence group efficiency, satisfaction, and information exchange. For example, evidence indicates that *centralized networks* are efficient only for simple tasks, and that peripheral members are often dissatisfied in such networks. Also, more information generally flows downward rather than upward in *hierarchical networks,* and the information that is sent upward is often unrealistically positive.

6

Performing:
Working Together in Groups

Across the gamut of human experience we find example after example of *group performance:* people making decisions, solving problems, increasing their productivity, completing tasks, and attaining valued goals by working with others in groups. In office buildings executives hold conferences to solve problems of management and production; in courthouses juries weigh evidence to determine guilt and innocence; in factories production lines turn out finished products; in schools teachers work with their pupils in small learning groups; on mountainsides climbers team up to reach the highest summit. In these, and in all the thousands of other varieties of group performance, interdependent individuals are pooling their personal efforts to reach more or less specifiable goals.

Yet despite this widespread use of groups in government, industry, education, and the private sector, groups are often the object of surprisingly consistent criticisms. While people use groups to pursue goals, discuss problems, concoct plans, forge products, and perform tasks, they often grumble about the time they "waste" in groups, and swap jokes such as "an elephant is a mouse designed by a committee," "trying to solve a problem through group discussion is like trying to clear up a traffic jam by honking your horn," and "committees consist of the unfit, appointed by the unwilling, to do the unnecessary." It is as if all agree with the philosopher Nietzsche that "madness is the exception in individuals but the rule in groups."

Of course, the critics of groups are sometimes right: people can work very ineffectively when they are members of groups. Yet groups can work effectively as well, and it is possible to cite as many examples of efficient groups as of inefficient groups. From a balanced perspective, arguing that groups are *always* bad makes little sense; nor can we claim that they *always* work well. Thus, the key question to ask is not "Are groups effective?" but the more complicated query "*When* are groups effective?"

This second question serves as the underlying theme for this chapter. In the three chapters that led up to this issue we dealt with a number of basic group processes—group formation, interpersonal conflict, and the development of structure—but now we are ready to apply these processes to groups working to achieve a particular outcome. In our discussion we will focus on three major topics: (1) the performance of individuals when other people are present, (2) task performance in groups where interaction is possible, and (3) ways to improve group performance. Still, throughout we will continually return to the question "When are groups effective?" Although the answer to the question may be unclear at times, by the end of this chapter we will be better able to decide if groups fulfill a useful performance function or if Carl Jung was right when he suggested that whenever "a hundred clever heads join a group, one big nincompoop is the result."

Before beginning, however, we should note that all too often the topic "working together in groups" summons up images of strictly task-oriented groups: staid executives debating across a conference-room table, workers adding to a product as it passes along an assembly line, or laborers pooling their efforts to move a heavy object. Undeniably, for these kinds of groups performance is nearly everything, virtually the group's raison d'être. However, even in groups that are not generally considered task oriented, performance processes can still be identified. Although group members may gather for purely social reasons, as is the case at parties, social events, rap sessions, and other "recreational" activities, the group may nonetheless face problems needing solution (rearranging the furniture in the room, discovering why the record player isn't working), decisions (choosing a restaurant for dinner, selecting a game to play), goal definition (having fun, relaxing), and so on. Therefore, though many of the examples and illustrations in this chapter feature task-oriented groups, issues of group performance are also relevant to many other kinds of groups.

Performance When Others Are Present

When you worked out the problem at home the answer seemed simple, but when you did the calculations in front of the class you made all sorts of errors. You tried as hard as you could during practice to beat your best time, but you didn't manage to do it until the day of the race. You rehearsed the lines to yourself for days on end, but on opening night you forgot your part. You spent months practicing by yourself, and they paid off when your flawless execution before the big crowd enabled you to win the gymnastics meet.

The tasks described in these examples lie at the interface of individual performance and group performance; such activities can be performed by individuals working in isolation *or* in the presence of others. While such tasks do not require "true" group activity, since they can be accomplished without direct interaction with others, these situations are of considerable interest because they signify the first step away from a nonsocial, purely individualistic orientation and toward a social, group-dynamics focus. Recognizing this importance, researchers who hoped to better their understanding of some of the most basic consequences of joining groups in performance situations began their investigations by asking "Do individuals perform better, or worse, in the presence of others?"

Social Facilitation

Interest in the influence of others on individuals' performance dates back to 1897 and the classic analyses performed by an early social scientist named Norman Triplett. A bicycling enthusiast, Triplett became curious about the differences in speeds achieved by cyclists during competitive races, when paced by motor-driven cycles, and when racing against the clock. He observed that the records established in these three categories were hardly equal; invariably better times were reported for races, while the slowest times occurred in unpaced, individual events.

Intrigued by these differences, Triplett went on to conduct what is generally recognized as the first social-psychological laboratory experiment. To test the hypothesis that people worked more effectively when others were present, he arranged for 40 children to play a game, in pairs or alone, that involved moving a silk band around a 4-meter course by turning a fishing reel. As he had anticipated, the subjects' times were better when they played the game in pairs, so Triplett concluded that *presence of others enhances individuals' performances.* In time, this phenomenon would become known as **social facilitation** (Allport, 1920; Dashiell, 1930; Travis, 1925).

In Triplett's work the children worked on the same task while in the same room, but they did not interact with one another. Later researchers labeled this type of situation the *coaction paradigm,* and compared it with situations requiring performance before a *passive audience.* These two approaches to the study of social facilitation are examined in the next two sections.

COACTION PARADIGMS

Coaction occurs whenever we are performing a task while others around us are engaged in a similar activity. Eating a meal with your family, taking a test in a classroom, riding a bicycle with a friend, driving along a crowded highway, or studying in the reading room of the library are all everyday instances of coaction. Triplett's experiment used a coaction paradigm, since the children worked on the same type of task.

Floyd H. Allport's early studies of what he called "co-working" or "co-feeling" groups are prime examples of the coaction paradigm (Allport, 1920, p. 159). In all these investigations Allport arranged for his subjects to complete certain tasks twice: once while alone in a small testing cubicle and once with others at a common table. In an attempt to reduce pressures toward competition he cautioned his subjects not to compare their scores with one another, and he also told participants that he himself would not be drawing interindividual comparisons. However, despite the absence of competition between coactors, Allport found a slight but consistent improvement in the coacting condition as compared to the isolation condition. For example, when given a word and asked to free associate by writing down as many of their thoughts as possible, 14 of the 15 subjects generated more associates in coaction condition. Similar effects were found when participants crossed out vowels in newspaper articles, performed multiplications, and generated arguments designed to disprove points made in passages taken from philosophical works. However, on these more complex tasks Allport also found evidence of detrimental effects of coaction. Subjects still produced more in the group setting, but their products tended to be lower in quality.

Thus, while Allport's studies provided partial support for the facilitating effects of coaction, his data also raise the possibility that coaction may worsen performance. Indeed, Allport's findings served as a warning of what was to come in subsequent research conducted over the next 45 years; in some instances investigators reported gains in performance through coaction (for example, Carment, 1970; Dashiell, 1930; Weston & English, 1926), but evidence of performance decrements during coaction were also discovered (as in Burwitz & Newell, 1972; Martens & Landers, 1972; Travis, 1928). Clearly, coaction is not always facilitating.

AUDIENCE PARADIGMS

One of the first scientific demonstrations of social facilitation in the presence of a passive spectator occurred in, of all places, an exercise laboratory (Meumann, 1904). By around the turn of the century, studies of muscular exertion and exercise had become feasible through the development of the ergograph, a device that precisely recorded how far an individual, working at the upper limit of his or her capacity, could move a weight. People who worked the ergograph typically reached a uniform level of performance that remained fairly constant across time, but one researcher noticed that this rate improved when an observer was present in the room. When he unexpectedly returned to his lab one night a subject whose performance had been constant for several days of testing changed. Although the ergograph did not detect any increase in the amount of effort being expended, the subject was still able to move the weight a greater distance. The investigator concluded that the presence of a spectator was facilitating.

Naturally this "discovery" sparked a number of investigations of the effects of a passive audience on individual performance and, as with the coaction paradigm, the results of these researches tended to be inconsistent. For example, in one experiment 22 college students were asked to hold a pointer over a small target that was attached to a rotating disk (the pursuit-rotor task). When they performed the task before an audience of advanced undergraduates their tracking of the target was better than when they performed alone (Travis, 1925). Yet in another study of 60 subjects trying to learn lists of nonsense syllables, subjects required fewer repetitions of the list when they were working alone than when they were working before an audience (Pessin, 1933). As was the case for coaction studies and research utilizing nonhuman species, working with an audience is sometimes but not always facilitating. Hence, the major question becomes "When does the presence of others help and when does it hurt?"

When Facilitation Occurs: The Zajonc Explanation

The contradictory findings from the coaction and audience paradigms puzzled group dynamicists for many years, so much so that interest in social facilitation dwindled in the 1940s and 1950s. Then, in an article published in 1965, Robert B. Zajonc integrated the divergent results by drawing a distinction between **dom-**

OF MICE, MEN, AND COCKROACHES

Social facilitation is not limited to *Homo sapiens*; rather, the effects of the presence of other members of one's own species appear in all sorts of organisms, including mice, rats, ants, bees, chickens, grasshoppers, and even cockroaches. For example, in one study performed by Robert Zajonc and his colleagues 32 female cockroaches (*Blatta orientalis*) learned a maze or a simple runway task while alone, with coacting pairs, or while being watched by other cockroaches (the cockroach spectators watched from their side of a plastic barrier). As with human studies, both facilitating and inhibiting effects were obtained: for the simple runway task the presence of an audience or coactor improved performance; for the more complicated maze task the presence of an audience or coactor impaired performance (Zajonc, Heingartner, & Herman, 1969).

inant and **nondominant responses.** Relying heavily on psychological learning theories (for example, Spence, 1956), Zajonc pointed out that the behavior most likely to occur in any learning or performance situation is dominant; it stands at the top of the response hierarchy, "dominating" all other potential responses. Other behaviors, although present in the organism's behavioral repertoire, are less likely to be observed, and these are nondominant (or subordinate) responses.

With the dominant/nondominant-response distinction in mind, Zajonc turned to the other pieces of the puzzle. First, he pointed out that extensive studies of many different kinds of organisms repeatedly demonstrated that increases in arousal, activation, motivation, or drive level enhance the emission of dominant responses while impeding the performance of nondominant responses. Second, he reexamined previously reported social facilitation studies and found that the presence of others nearly always facilitates certain kinds of behaviors, well-learned or instinctual responses in particular. Third, he noted that when inhibiting effects of coaction or observation are reported, they almost always occur for novel, complicated, or unpracticed tasks. Putting these facts together, Zajonc came to the following conclusions:

1. The presence of others creates a state of arousal (or increased drive) in the organism.
2. This arousal "enhances the emission of dominant responses" (Zajonc, 1965, p. 273).
3. If dominant responses are "correct" or "appropriate," the presence of an audience will increase the likelihood that correct responses occur.
4. If dominant responses are "incorrect" or "inappropriate," the presence of an audience will increase the likelihood that incorrect responses occur.

The bulk of the experimental studies of social facilitation fall easily into place when viewed from the parsimonious perspective suggested by Zajonc. For example, one of the replications of Allport's initial studies with the free-association task failed to find improvement in the coaction condition (Travis, 1928). However, while the procedures utilized in the two studies were practically identical, the participants in the later study were all stutterers. Because verbal production is not an easily performed, dominant response for these individuals, the presence of an audience impeded their performance.

A more recently conducted study is another clear example of the importance of taking the type of task into account (Markus, 1978). Supposedly to create uniformity in participants' appearances, the researcher asked subjects to (1) take off their shoes, (2) don a pair of large socks and shoes, and (3) put on a lab coat that tied in the back. Later, subjects (4) removed the coat, shoes, and socks, and (5) put on their own shoes. Because Tasks 1 and 5 were both highly familiar activities and Tasks 2, 3, and 4 were novel actions, the investigator predicted that the presence of others would speed up the performance of 1 and 5 while slowing down the performance of 2 through 4. Therefore, the investigator unobtrusively timed and recorded the time taken on each activity and had the subjects perform the tasks while alone, in the presence of an attentive observer, or in the presence of an incidental observer (who sat with his back to the subject working on a piece of equipment).

When the two categories of tasks—dominant and nondominant—were compared, the results presented in Table 6-1 were obtained: the presence of others facilitated well-learned responses but inhibited unfamiliar responses.

Why Facilitation Occurs

Few researchers would challenge Zajonc's basic prediction concerning the facilitation of dominant responses. Indeed, most of the reviews of research literature that have appeared since 1965 emphasize the importance of the dominant/non-dominant-response distinction in explaining facilitation (see, for example, Cottrell, 1972; Geen, 1980; Geen & Gange, 1977; Zajonc, 1980), and formal definitions of social facilitation typically limit the process to tasks involving only dominant responses. As one theorist writes, "social facilitation refers to the enhancement of an organism's dominant responses by the simple physical presence of species-mates, independent of any informational or interactional influences the others may exert" (Sanders, 1981a, p. 227). Nevertheless, while the *when* of social facilitation is now fairly well understood, considerable debate still rages over the *why* of social facilitation. The field has progressed, however, since Triplett first offered a range of possible causes back in 1897 (see the box), but three general explanations are still considered viable: increased arousal, apprehension over evaluation, and distraction.

AROUSAL

When Zajonc first outlined his predictions concerning **compresence** (his term for the "state of responding in the presence of others"), he hypothesized that the "mere presence" of a member of the same species raises the performer's arousal level by touching off a basic alertness response (1965, 1980). Given the primary importance of social stimuli in the life of many organisms, Zajonc believes that compresence arouses the individual "simply because one never knows, so to speak, what sorts of responses—perhaps even novel and unique—may be required in the next few seconds" (1980, p. 50). Although other theorists have sometimes suggested that the typical concomitants of compresence—heightened competitiveness, fear of evaluation, distraction, imitation, and so on—actually mediate social facilitation, Zajonc considers these processes to be ancillary effects of only incidental relevance to the basic phenomenon. Hence he uses the phrase "mere presence" to reinforce the idea that social facilitation refers only to the directly arousing effects of compresence.

TABLE 6-1. Mean time in seconds to complete tasks requiring dominant and nondominant responses

	Condition		
Type of Responses	*Alone*	*Incidental audience*	*Audience*
Dominant	16.46	13.49	11.70
Nondominant	28.85	32.73	33.94

(Source: Markus, 1978)

TRIPLETT'S INSIGHTS

Triplett personally felt that the improved performance of cyclists during races or when paced by a motorized cycle was caused by a psychological stimulation produced by the presence of others (Shaw, 1981). Nevertheless, he felt that other factors may also be important, and some of his hypotheses are listed below.

1. Because the pacing machine or lead rider creates a partial vacuum, followers are pulled along with less effort.
2. The lead rider or the pacing machine breaks down the wind resistance and makes the followers' job easier.
3. The presence of other riders buoys up the spirits of the competitors, encouraging them to expend greater effort.
4. The front runner, concerned about having to set the pace for the rest of the field, loses energy through worrying.
5. Riders become hypnotized by watching the revolving spokes of the pacing machine or the bicycles of those around them; left in a mild hypnotic trance, they are able to expend more effort while ignoring feelings of physical exhaustion.
6. Because the followers can simply "follow the leader," all their cognitive and physical energy can be devoted to pedaling their bicylces.

(Source: Triplett, 1897)

APPREHENSION OVER EVALUATION

Zajonc's mere-presence hypothesis was later modified by Nickolas B. Cottrell in his learned-drive theory of social facilitation (Cottrell, 1972). While Zajonc argued that the alertness response is a reflexive and perhaps innately determined reaction, Cottrell argued that the drivelike properties of compresence come about through learning. In the young organism the mere presence of another organism is motivationally neutral, for it neither increases nor decreases alertness, arousal, or drive. However, through experience with an audience or coactors, the individual learns that the receipt of rewards and punishments often covaries with the presence of others. Eventually, the

> individual learns to anticipate subsequent positive or negative outcomes whenever others are merely present and not overtly doing anything that has motivational significance for him. It is these anticipations, elicited by the presence of others, that increase the individual's drive level [Cottrell, 1972, p. 277].

Although other theorists have suggested variations on the basic **evaluation apprehension** theme (Henchy & Glass, 1968; Weiss & Miller, 1971), Cottrell's perspective—with its subtle emphasis on the increase in arousal brought about by the link between the presence of others and the receipt of positive and negative outcomes—remains the most viable model in this category.

DISTRACTION

In contrast to both of these drive theories of social facilitation, Glenn S. Sanders and his colleagues (Sanders, 1981a; Sanders & Baron, 1975; Sanders, Baron, & Moore, 1978) have proposed that the presence of others during task performance distracts the performer. However, while on the one hand this distraction interferes with attention given to the task, on the other hand it creates response conflicts in the organism that can be overcome with greater effort. Therefore, on simple tasks the interference effects are inconsequential relative to the improvement brought about by the conflict, and performance is thus facilitated. On more complex tasks the increase in drive is insufficient to offset the effects of distraction, and performance is therefore impaired. Sanders labels this explanation **distraction/conflict theory.**

Conclusions

The three social-facilitation theories discussed in this section all emphasize different variables when predicting performance—mere presence, apprehension over outcomes, or distraction. Yet all three approaches have been at least partially supported empirically; thus, none can be recommended as "best" or dismissed altogether (Geen, 1980, 1981; Sanders, 1981a). At this point, it will be useful to summarize briefly some of the relevant findings.

1. The mere-presence hypothesis has been supported on three counts. First, while one may wonder if any task is completely neutral, activities that involve little threat of evaluation—eating, drinking, getting dressed, or offering opinions—still show social facilitation effects (Markus, 1978). Second, even when the companion refrains from attending to the individual in any way—as was the case in the incidental-observer condition of the dressing/undressing study (Markus, 1978)— social facilitation still occurs. Third, one has difficulty applying the concept of apprehension or distraction to certain organisms, such as cockroaches or chickens, that have shown effects of compresence.

2. The primary hypothesis that derives uniquely from Cottrell's theory—that any stimulus increasing the organism's apprehension over future rewards or punishments should increase drive levels—has also been confirmed. Studies have shown that little facilitation occurs if the audience can't see the subjects perform (Cottrell et al., 1968), if the subjects respond covertly (Martens & Landers, 1972; Sasfy & Okun, 1974), or if subjects realize the audience will not be evaluating their performance (Henchy & Glass, 1968).

3. While studies of the distracting effects of others on performance are less numerous, the available data support the chain of logic underlying the theory. First, research indicates that individuals working in the presence of others do indeed report feeling distracted (Baron, Moore, & Sanders, 1978). Second, when subjects are frequently interrupted or allowed to work without distraction, interruptions improve simple task performance slightly while significantly interfering with performance on complex tasks (Sanders & Baron, 1975)—perhaps because the presence of others inhibits the cognitive rehearsal needed for higher-level learning (Berger et al., 1981). Lastly, social facilitation effects have been found to be strongest when participants' attention is drawn away from the task and focused on the other coactors (Sanders, Baron, & Moore, 1978).

In sum, the experts still disagree about the ultimate cause of the social-facilitation effect: some favor the mere-presence perspective (Markus, 1981; Zajonc, 1980), others the evaluation-apprehension notion (Geen, 1981; Shaw, 1981), and still others advocate the distraction/conflict hypothesis (Sanders, 1981a, 1981b).

However, given the amount of research testifying to the impact of each factor, researchers have begun to reject the idea that any one approach is better than the others. Instead of trying to discover which theory is "right" or more adequately subsumes the others, these investigators have realized that in any given situation variables deriving from arousal, evaluation apprehension, *and* distraction may be equally important, making it necessary to take them all into consideration when making predictions. In consequence, researchers have begun refocusing their efforts in an attempt (1) to clarify when each variable is particularly important and (2) to synthesize these and other variables into a more generally applicable model of social facilitation.

Furthermore, despite these theoretical uncertainties, the conclusions of social facilitation research may still be fruitfully applied to better our understanding of performance in many everyday situations. For example, Zajonc's distinction between dominant and nondominant tasks suggests that the presence of others interferes with learning—since learning implies that the dominant responses are not the correct ones—but will facilitate performance once the behavior becomes routine. This hypothesis applies to all sorts of behaviors, including learning new athletic skills, acquiring a second language, memorizing and reciting a speech, or even studying for a test. Indeed, Zajonc goes so far as to advise students to avoid trying to learn difficult materials in study groups, since such an arrangement may interfere with the acquisition of information. Instead he recommends that the student should

> study all alone, preferably in an isolated cubicle, and arrange to take his exami-
> nations in the company of many other students, on stage, and in the presence of
> a large audience. The results of his examination would be beyond his wildest
> expectations, provided, of course, he had learned his material quite thoroughly
> [Zajonc, 1965, p. 274].

Performance in Interacting Groups

As we move from a situation that involves only coaction or a passive audience to one that features interaction among group members, we find ourselves making a sizeable jump along the continuum of complexity. When we studied social facilitation, we were able to ignore many aspects of group process, since the participants did not actually interact. When we turn our attention to interacting groups, however, the list of factors that influence performance grows far longer, for it includes all the relevant background variables concerning the group, its members, and the interaction process (see, for example, Hackman & Morris, 1975; McGrath, 1964; Tubbs, 1978).

As a first step in coping with this matrix of causal factors, we begin our analysis of performance in interacting groups by considering the kind of **task** that the group is trying to accomplish. Although limited generalizations about the effectiveness of groups can be offered even when task variables are ignored, most theorists agree that we can achieve far greater precision by taking into account the "task environment" (for example, Davis, 1969; Laughlin, 1980; Shaw, 1981). In essence, though a group of people may be extremely effective when working on one type of task, their effectiveness might dissolve when they attempt some other problem or activity. Since the transfer of effectiveness across tasks cannot be guaranteed, we must begin our analysis by describing the link between performance and the type of task at hand.

In focusing on tasks, however, we must also deal with the basic issue of how to classify the many performance situations—solving problems, creating products, making decisions, generating ideas, learning facts, achieving goals—that groups encounter. For example, one approach to classification suggests that a broad distinction can be made between intellectual and judgmental tasks (Laughlin, 1980). An alternative approach emphasizes three different categories: production, discussion, and problem-solving tasks (Hackman & Morris, 1975). Still a third approach suggests that six basic task dimensions must be considered: (1) the difficulty of the problem, (2) the number of acceptable solutions, (3) the intrinsic interest level of the task, (4) the amount of cooperation required among members, (5) the task's intellectual and/or manipulative requirements, and (6) the participants' familiarity with the task (Shaw, 1963, 1981).

While these approaches, as well as the many other perspectives on the problem of task classification (for example, Davis, 1969; Hare, 1976), are useful and valid, in this chapter we will rely on the classification scheme suggested by group dynamicist Ivan Steiner (1972, 1976). His *typology of tasks*—which is based on the divisibility of the task, the type of product desired, and the procedures used when individual members' inputs are combined—is examined in the next section.

Steiner's Typology of Tasks

Steiner's approach to task classification is based on the three questions in Table 6-2. Beginning with the first question—Can the task be broken down into subcomponents or is division of the task inappropriate?—Steiner notes that some tasks are divisible while others are unitary. For example, building a house, planting a garden, or working a series of math problems by assigning one to each group member are all *divisible* tasks, since the entire task can be split into parts. Other tasks, however, are *unitary,* since splitting makes little sense: only one painter is needed for a small closet in a house, only one gardener can plant a single seed, and only one person need solve a simple math problem.

The second question—Which is more important: quantity produced or quality of performance?—compares maximizing and optimizing tasks. According to Steiner, when groups work on *maximizing* tasks, the more they produce the better. For example, in a relay race, a tug-of-war, or a wooden-block-stacking problem, the ultimate judgment of task performance rests on the sheer quantity; the emphasis is on maximal production. In contrast, performance on optimizing tasks is dependent upon a predetermined set of criteria; a good performance is one that most closely approximates the optimum performance. Examples of optimizing tasks include estimating the number of beans in a jar or coming up with the best solution to a problem.

The third question—How are individual inputs related to the group's product?—is the most complex, for many answers are possible. First, *additive* tasks are those that involve adding or summing individual inputs to yield a group product. Second, *compensatory* tasks (Steiner, 1976) require a "statisticized" group decision derived from the average of individual members' solutions (Lorge, Fox, Davitz, & Brenner,

TABLE 6-2. A summary of Steiner's typology of tasks

Question	Answer	Task type	Examples
Can the task be broken down into subcomponents or is division of the task inappropriate?	Subtasks can be identified	Divisible	Playing a football game, building a house, preparing a six-course meal
	No subtasks exist	Unitary	Pulling on a rope, reading a book, solving a math problem
Which is more important: quantity produced or quality of performance?	Quantity	Maximizing	Generating many ideas, lifting the greatest weight, scoring the most runs
	Quality	Optimizing	Generating the best idea, getting the right answer, solving a math problem
How are individual inputs related to the group's product?	Individual inputs are added together	Additive	Pulling a rope, stuffing envelopes, shoveling snow
	Group product is average of individual judgments	Compensatory	Averaging individuals' estimates of the number of beans in a jar, weight of an object, room temperature
	Group selects the product from pool of individual members' judgments	Disjunctive	Questions involving "yes-no, either-or" answers such as math problems, puzzles, and choices between options
	All group members must contribute to the product	Conjunctive	Climbing a mountain, eating a meal, relay races, soldiers marching in file
	Group can decide how individual inputs relate to group product	Discretionary	Deciding to shovel snow together, opting to vote on the best answer to a math problem, letting leader answer question

(Source: Steiner, 1972, 1976)

1958). Third, when the group must come up with a single specific answer to an "either/or," "yes/no" type problem, the task is *disjunctive*. Fourth, if all the group members must perform some specific action before the task is completed, then the task is *conjunctive*. Finally, if group members are free to choose the method by which they will combine their inputs, the task is *discretionary*.

When these three basic questions are all taken into account, any particular task can be specified as to type. For example, a tug-of-war contest is unitary, maximizing, and additive. Assembling a motor in a production line is divisible, optimizing, and, in some instances, conjunctive. Playing softball is unitary, maximizing, and additive for the team at bat, but divisible and optimizing for the team in the field. Making a complex decision (such as choosing to invade Cuba at the Bay of Pigs or designing a new social-welfare program) would most likely be divisible, optimizing, and discretionary. In addition, some combinations of task characteristics are rare. For example, on most divisible tasks the question of how to combine inputs is often completely irrelevant—as with the team in the field during a softball game. Similarly, maximizing tasks are very rarely discretionary, since it rarely makes sense to use any procedure other than an additive process when the goal is maximizing the amount produced.

More importantly, Steiner's taxonomy helps us to formulate precise predictions about performance because group effectiveness often covaries closely with the type of task being attempted. The application of Steiner's taxonomy of tasks to situations calling for group performance is examined in the next section.

Predicting Group Performance

In Steiner's theory, task classification is important because different types of tasks require different sorts of *resources*: skills, abilities, tools, materials, equipment, time, and so on. If the group members possess these resources, then the group *may* be successful. If, in contrast, the group members lack the requisite resources, then failure is likely. From Steiner's perspective, the potential productivity of any group can thus be calculated by determining the type of task at hand, using this information to deduce the resources needed by the group members, and then observing the group to determine if the members in fact possess these resources. In the following subsections this basic approach to group performance is applied to groups performing additive, compensatory, disjunctive, conjunctive, and discretionary tasks.

ADDITIVE TASKS

Table 6-2 indicates that additive tasks require the summing together of individual group members' inputs to maximize the group product. In consequence, so long as each group member can perform the simple individualistic task required—such as pulling on a rope, cheering at a football game, clapping after a concert, or raking leaves in a yard—then the productivity of the group will probably exceed the productivity of the single individual. The old saw "Many hands make light the work" seems accurate in reference to additive tasks (Latané, Williams, & Harkins, 1979).

However, while additive tasks generally find groups outperforming even the most proficient group member, this effect does not mean that groups will work with complete efficiency. Even though group processes are very simple for most additive tasks (just add each group member's input together to yield the group product) losses owing to faulty group process can still keep the group from reaching its potential productivity level. Such process losses were documented many years ago by a German psychologist named Ringelmann, who studied additive tasks by asking individuals and groups to pull on a rope attached to a pressure gauge (reported in Moede, 1927). Naturally, he found that groups were "stronger" than individuals; as Table 6-3 indicates, individuals, on the average, exerted 63 kg of pressure, dyads about 118 kg, triads 160 kg, and groups with eight members mustered 248 kg of pressure. Yet while these figures generally confirmed the idea that more people contributing to an additive task resulted in improved performance, Ringelmann's data also reveal a disturbing inhibition of individual productivity. Group "strength" rose with each additional member, but individual effort seemed to decline. Dyads only managed to pull about 1.9 times as much as one

TABLE 6-3. Evidence of the Ringelmann effect

	Group Size			
	1	2	3	8
Actual productivity	63	118	160	248
Potential productivity	63	126	189	504
Process loss	——	8	29	256

(Source: Steiner, 1972)

person, triads only 2.5 times as much, while eight-person groups performed at only 3.9 times the individual level. This intriguing inverse relationship between the number of people in a group and the quality and/or magnitude of individual performance has been dubbed the **Ringelmann effect.**

Why might a group of people working on an additive task fail to be as productive as they could be? According to Steiner, the answer to this question lies in the concept of **process losses.** While his model assumes that the nature of the task and the resources of the group members determine potential productivity, he argues that the processes that unfold within the group as the members work on the task can detract from the group's proficiency. Accordingly, Steiner's "law" of group productivity predicts

$$\begin{matrix} \text{Actual} \\ \text{productivity} \end{matrix} = \begin{matrix} \text{Potential} \\ \text{productivity} \end{matrix} - \begin{matrix} \text{Losses owing to} \\ \text{faulty process} \end{matrix}$$

In support of Steiner's process-loss explanation, recent researchers have found that the Ringelmann effect appears to be caused by two types of problems: **coordination losses** and **social loafing** (Latané et al., 1979). First, individuals have difficulty combining their inputs in a maximally effective fashion; on a task such as rope pulling, they tend to pull and pause at different times, resulting in a failure to reach full productivity potentials (Ingham, Levinger, Graves, & Peckham, 1974). Second, people simply don't work as hard on additive tasks when their individual efforts will remain unknown. This "reduction of individual effort exerted when people work in groups compared to when they work alone" has been labeled social loafing (Williams, Harkins, & Latané, 1981, p. 303), and has been found to apply to cognitive tasks as well as physical tasks (Petty, Harkins, & Williams, 1980).

The impact of these two factors was clarified in one recent study that measured blindfolded subjects' production of noise as they shouted (Latané, et al., 1979, Experiment 2). Through a system of earphones, tape recordings, and sound-level meters, Bibb Latané and his colleagues were able carefully to measure the noise produced (in dynes/cm^2) by subjects working in one-, two-, or six-person groups. As expected, "even though total output increased with group size, the output of each member decreased, with six-person groups performing at only 36% of capacity" (Latané, 1981, p. 353; see Figure 6-1, "actual groups"). Latané notes that part of this loss in productivity stemmed from subjects' canceling out of one anothers' noise—a form of faulty coordination—but that social loafing was probably also to blame. In order to assess more directly the effects of loafing, a *pseudo-group condition* was also run in which subjects only *thought* they were shouting with

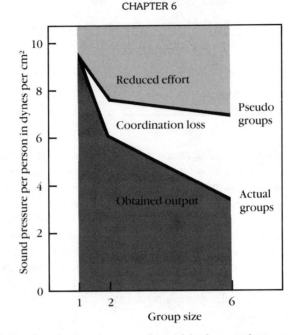

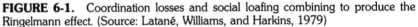

FIGURE 6-1. Coordination losses and social loafing combining to produce the Ringelmann effect. (Source: Latané, Williams, and Harkins, 1979)

one or five other people (the earphones and a background tape recording of shouts prevented subjects from detecting the deception). The loss of productivity brought about by social loafing, independent of faulty coordination, is apparent in Figure 6-1, which suggests that both factors combine to produce the Ringelmann effect. (A suggested third factor—that individuals working in groups "save up" energy for situations in which they must perform alone—does not appear to be valid; Harkins, Latané, & Williams, 1980; Kerr & Bruun, 1981.) Supporting this view, other evidence indicates that the Ringelmann effect can be significantly reduced if steps are taken to prevent coordination problems and social loafing (Kerr & Bruun, 1981; Williams, Harkins, & Latané, 1981. For a further discussion of social loafing, interpreted in the context of social-impact theory, see Latané, 1981. See the box.)

COMPENSATORY TASKS

Referring back to Steiner's typology in Table 6-2, we find that compensatory tasks are those that require the averaging together of individual judgments to yield the group's product. Although very few tasks are strictly compensatory, in the sense that they can only be performed by the averaging of individual inputs, groups will often choose to use compensatory methods to solve problems. For example, if a finance committee must decide how much money to allocate for Project X, the chairperson can simply telephone members and ask for their personal estimates. In taking the average of each member's suggestion, the chair would be using a compensatory approach.

Marvin E. Shaw, after reviewing a number of studies that compared the quality of group judgments reached through compensatory methods and individual judg-

"HOW MANY PICKLES COULD A PICKLE PACKER PACK IF . . . ?"

Studies indicate that social loafing can be significantly reduced if individual outputs are made more identifiable. In other words, if an additive group task is changed into a coaction task, then effort reductions are minimized (Kerr & Bruun, 1981; Williams et al., 1981). A tentative explanation of this phenomenon is the possibility that apprehension over outcomes, which theorists think plays a significant role in producing social facilitation effects, may also be related to the Ringelmann effect. When coactors or an audience know an individual's outcomes, the latter experiences apprehension that facilitates his or her performance. But when the presence of others reduces evaluative pressures by masking individual outcomes, then social loafing becomes more likely (Jackson & Latané, 1981; Williams et al., 1981). This analysis can be applied to the problem of the pickle packer:

A key job [in a pickle factory] is stuffing dill pickle halves into jars. Only dill halves of a certain length can be used. Those that are too

long will not fit and those that are too short will float and dance inside and look cheap and crummy. The dill halves and the jars are carried on separate high-speed conveyor belts past the contingent of pickle stuffers. If the stuffers don't stuff quickly enough the jars pile up at the workers' stations while they look for pickles of the appropriate length, so stuffers have a great temptation to stuff whatever pickles come readily to hand. The individual outputs of stuffers are unidentifiable, since all jars go into a common hopper before they reach the quality control section. Responsibility for the output cannot be focused on any one worker. This combination of factors leads to poor performance and improper packing. The present research suggests making individual production identifiable and raises the question, "How many pickles could a pickle packer pack if pickle packers were only paid for properly packed pickles?"

(Source: Williams, Harkins, and Latané, 1981)

---

ments, concludes that the bulk of the evidence indicates that judgments yielded by the averaging process are more accurate than those of individuals (Shaw, 1981). For example, in one of the earliest studies in this area (Knight, 1921), college students estimated the temperature of their classroom. Naturally, some people overestimated the temperature, but others underestimated; thus, the "group" judgment, which was an average of those offered, was more accurate than the judgments made by 80 percent of the individuals.

DISJUNCTIVE TASKS

Interest in disjunctive tasks—problems that require an either/or answer—is often traced back to a study conducted in the early 1930s (Shaw, 1932). Four-person same-sex groups worked on tasks like those shown in the box on page 156. All were unitary, optimizing, and disjunctive, since they could not be profitably broken down into subtasks; a "best answer" was sought; and only one answer could be turned in as the group's solution. Across all these tasks, groups out-performed individuals, although time costs were greater in groups.

These findings were initially explained in terms of the enhanced opportunity for detecting errors and rejecting incorrect suggestions when working in groups, but later researchers proposed an alternative explanation (for example, Marquart, 1955). This reinterpretation, which can be termed the **truth-wins rule,** proposes

EXAMPLES OF DISJUNCTIVE TASKS

1. *The chain puzzle.*

Isaac is staying at a motel when he runs short on cash. Checking his finances, he discovers that in 23 days he will have plenty of money but until then he will be broke. The motel owner refuses to let Isaac stay without paying his bill each day, but since Isaac owns a heavy gold chain with 23 links, the owner decides that it will be okay if Isaac pays for each of the 23 days with one gold link. Then when Isaac receives his money, the motel owner will return the chain.

Isaac is very anxious to keep the chain as intact as possible, so he doesn't want to cut off any more of the links than absolutely necessary. The motel owner, however, insists on payment each day, and will accept no advance payment. *Question*: How many links must Isaac cut while still paying the owner one link for each successive day? (Source: Marquart, 1955)

2. *The missionary/cannibal problem.*

Three missionaries and three cannibals are on one side of the river, and want to cross to the other side by means of a boat that can only hold two persons at a time. All the missionaries but only one cannibal can row. For obvious reasons, the missionaries must never be outnumbered by the cannibals, under any circumstances or at any time, except where no missionaries are present at all. *Question*: How many crossings will be necessary to transport the six people across the river? (Source: Shaw, 1932)

3. *The horse-trading problem.*

A man bought a horse for $60 and sold it for $70. Then he bought it back for $80 and again sold it for $90. *Question*: How much money did he make in the horse-trading business? (Source: Maier & Solem, 1952)

(The solutions are revealed in the box on page 161)

---

that the group will successfully solve any disjunctive problem if and only if one of the members of the group can solve the problem when working alone. A major assumption of several models of rational group decision making (Davis, 1973; Lorge & Solomon, 1955; Smoke & Zajonc, 1962; Thomas & Fink, 1961), the truth-wins rule assumes that the correct answer, once presented to the group members, will be so obvious that the group will readily adopt it. Hence, truth always wins. In addition, because larger groups are more likely to contain that one individual who knows the right answer, group size is correlated with disjunctive task performance. Thus, the truth-wins rule not only accounts for the results of the 1932 study, but also explains why larger groups out-perform smaller groups when tasks are disjunctive (Bray, Kerr, & Atkin, 1978).

Unfortunately, researchers soon discovered instances when truth lost. For example, in one study 67 groups discussed the horse-trading problem described in the box (Maier & Solem, 1952, p. 280). Although many of the groups contained at least one person who knew that the correct answer was $20, fewer than 80% of these groups actually solved this disjunctive task. Apparently, those members who originally knew the right answer had a difficult time persuading their fellow group members to adopt their solutions. In fact, some people later changed their answers to match the incorrect solution advocated by their groups. Only when a significant proportion of the group knew the correct answer was the group likely to select the right response. For the horse-trading problem, truth wins only if supported by other group members; this is the **truth-supported wins rule** (Laughlin, 1980).

We can untangle these contradictory findings by considering the two essential steps involved in solving disjunctive problems. First, someone in the group must suggest the correct answer. Second, the members of the group must adopt the answer as the group solution. If both these steps fail to occur, the group will be unable to answer the problem correctly. For some tasks, the second step occurs almost automatically; the solution, once proposed, is so satisfyingly correct that the group immediately endorses it. Therefore, truth wins. (Such problems are typically called **Eureka tasks**; examples include the missionary/cannibal problem and the chain puzzle.) For other tasks, such as the horse-trading problem, the correctness of the answer is less obvious, so Step 2 is much more difficult. For these kinds of problems, the truth-supported wins rule seems to apply best (Laughlin, 1980; Laughlin & Adamopoulos, 1980; Stasser, Kerr, & Davis, 1980). To generalize, groups working on disjunctive tasks sometimes but not always outperform individuals. If the group is working on a Eureka disjunctive task, the group should succeed more frequently than individuals. If, in contrast, the group is working on a non-Eureka-type task, group effectiveness is less predictable. People working together will out-perform only a subset of the individual members.

CONJUNCTIVE TASKS

Fairly clear predictions can be made about the performance of groups working on unitary conjunctive tasks. Because all group members must complete (or at least contribute) to conjunctive tasks, groups invariably perform at the level of the group member with the poorest performance! The speed of a group of mountain climbers moving up the slope is determined by the slowest member. The trucks in a convoy can move no faster than the slowest vehicle. Mourners at a funeral procession can walk only as quickly as the pallbearers. Research has confirmed this logical consequence of conjunctive tasks (Frank & Anderson, 1971; Steiner, 1972).

Often, however, conjunctive tasks are divisible; they can be broken down into subcomponents that can be performed by individual members. For example, building an automobile can be construed as the creation of many subproducts that, once combined, yield the final product. Once tasks are divided, groups can function more effectively under conjunctive processes, provided members can be *matched* to tasks that coincide with their ability levels and interests. If the least competent member is matched with the easiest task, then a more satisfying level of performance may be obtainable. If, of course, the least competent member is matched with a difficult subtask, then performance will decline still further (see Steiner, 1972, Chapter 3, for a detailed review of group performance on divisible tasks).

DISCRETIONARY TASKS

The final category of tasks in our overview comprises any task that group members can perform using their own preferred combination procedures. For example, a group working on the problem "Estimate the temperature of the room," could arrive at an answer through a variety of means. One simple method would involve averaging together individual judgments. Alternatively, members could determine whether anyone in the group was particularly good at such judgments, and then use this "expert's" answer as the group solution. In any case, the temperature-judging task is discretionary, because members themselves can choose the method for combining individual inputs.

Naturally, in order to make predictions about groups' performance on discretionary tasks we must first consider which procedure is being used to deal with the task. Although space limitations prevent us from reviewing all the social combination procedures studied by researchers, in the following subsections we discuss several of the more frequently used decision rules (see Davis, 1969; Laughlin, 1980; Shiflett, 1979; Stasser, Kerr, & Davis, 1980 for reviews).

Delegating decisions.   The group could transfer responsibility for making the decision to some other person or group. The chairperson, for example, may have the authority to resolve this issue on his or her own, but in doing so the chair would not be using the group's resources effectively. While simple routine matters ("How many paper clips should we order?") or issues that the members know very little about ("What is the best type of photocopying equipment now on the market?") can be solved without recourse to group input (Vroom & Yetton, 1973; see Chapter 8), a more group-centered approach is often a better strategy when issues are complicated and members have a stake in the outcomes. Other forms of delegation include (1) having a higher authority listen to members' ideas on the issue before formulating a decision, (2) asking an expert to provide an answer, or (3) forming a subcommittee made up of a few members to study the issue and form a conclusion. All these methods are similar in that they take some of the decision-making power away from the members, who may feel that their inputs have been ignored. However, the amount of time saved sometimes justifies delegated decisions, particularly when tasks are routine or extremely technical, or group commitment to the decision is of little importance.

Averaging individual inputs.   If the group treated the issue at hand as a compensatory task, then each member could make his or her decision privately (either before or after a group discussion), and these private recommendations could then be averaged together to yield an overall conclusion. For example, to choose among five possible projects, each member could rank all the options from 1 (the best) to 5 (the least important), and the group could then average these rankings together. The project with the smallest average ranking would "win." Averaging ensures that all group members have input into the decision, and individual errors or extreme opinions are canceled out during the averaging process. If, however, this procedure is used without discussion, the decision may be an arbitrary one that fails to satisfy any of the group members, all of whom may end up feeling little responsibility for implementing it.

Balloting.   In a similar fashion, members can vote for the project of their choice, after first deciding whether a simple majority (more than 50%), a two-thirds majority (at least 66%), or some other margin of preference will be used. Like an averaging procedure, voting closes discussion on the issue, providing the mechanism for making a clearcut decision. Unfortunately, it can also leave a significant proportion of the group feeling alienated, contributing to members' refusals to help implement the solution and a decline in the group's future effectiveness (Castore & Murnighan, 1978). Furthermore, using a voting procedure can also "politicize" the group, as members get together before the session to apply pressures, form coalitions, and trade favors to ensure passage of the proposals they favor. Thus, while balloting seems to be a natural group technique, since it incorporates parliamentary procedure and is based on democratic ideals, it is not without certain liabilities.

Consensus. In the abstract, discussion to consensus—the unanimous agreement of all group members—seems to be an ideal procedure. The decision is given detailed consideration, all the group's resources are fully utilized, and the in-depth discussion binds members both to the group and the decision itself. No one in the group occupies a position of "minority," whose ideas lose out in the final ballot, and the high levels of communication among members lead to improved effectiveness in the future.

Unfortunately, consensus carries many prerequisites that are not necessarily met in all group situations. Reaching consensus invariably takes a good deal of time, and if rushed the strategy can misfire. If members are not "in touch" with the group's dynamics, then pressures to conform, manipulative maneuverings, and leader domination can result in decisions being "railroaded" through the group. Lastly, if members are not interested in reaching the best decision through consensus, then they might make uninformed suggestions, raise irrelevant issues, keep silent to avoid prolonging the discussion, or stubbornly argue for their own viewpoint. In consequence, seeking consensus can in some instances become a "terribly misused and abused approach to problem solving and decision making" (Napier & Gershenfeld, 1981, p. 401).

In sum, the many strategies for solving discretionary tasks possess both advantages and disadvantages. Selection of a particular method requires that many factors be considered, including the importance of the quality and originality of the solution, the importance of its acceptance by others, and the expertise of the group members (Stumpf, Freedman, & Zand, 1979; Stumpf, Zand, & Freedman, 1979). However, as one researcher notes, perhaps the most important determinant of performance on such tasks is a willingness to search for and use the most appropriate—rather than the easiest or most often used—decisional procedure (Shiflett, 1972).

Limitations and Conclusions

Ivan Steiner's approach to the complex question of performance in interacting groups begins with a focus on the type of task being attempted. If we gauge the adequacy of the group by comparing it with the performance of individuals working alone, we see that groups clearly out-perform the most skilled individual only when the task is an additive one (See Table 6-4). Groups do, however, generally perform better than the average group member on many other kinds of tasks (compensatory, disjunctive-Eureka, divisible conjunctive with matching, and discretionary), but some tasks seem to bring about poorer performances (disjunctive-non-Eureka, conjunctive-unitary).

TABLE 6-4. A summary of the potential productivity of groups working on various types of tasks

Type of Task	Productivity Effect	Description
Additive	"Better than the best"	Group out-performs even the best individual member
Compensatory	"Better than most"	Group out-performs a substantial number of the individual members
Disjunctive (Eureka)	"Equal to the best"	Group performance matches the performance of the "best" member
Disjunctive (non-Eureka)	"Less than the best"	Group performance can match that of the "best" member, but often falls short
Conjunctive (unitary)	"Equal to the worst"	Group performance matches the performance of the "worst" member
Conjunctive (divisible with matching)	"Better than the worst"	If subtasks properly matched to ability of members, group performance can reach high levels
Discretionary	"Variable"	Group performance is substantially dependent on the performance process adopted by the group

(Source: Steiner, 1972, 1976)

Before moving on to the final section of this chapter—improving group performance—we should note some limitations of our analysis. First, by focusing on productivity in interacting groups, we have virtually ignored many other variables, such as member satisfaction, changes in goals, and increases or decreases in group cohesiveness (some of these topics are, however, addressed in Chapter 14). Second, to reach general conclusions about group performance, we have implicitly assumed that potential productivity is solely determined by two factors: the nature of the task and the resources of the group. In consequence, as other variables become important in a group performance setting, the generalizations in Table 6-4 may become less accurate. Lastly, by implicitly accepting Steiner's "law" of group productivity, we have assumed that group process rarely leads to increases in potential productivity; in other words, process always involves either losses or no gain, but never boosts productivity. As several theorists have noted, however, it may sometimes be the case that process can improve productivity beyond the limits set by task demands and group resources (Hackman & Morris, 1975; Shaw, 1976). Marvin E. Shaw suggests the more appropriate "law" might be

$$
\begin{array}{ccc}
\text{Actual} & & \text{Potential} & & \text{Losses due to} & & \text{Gains from} \\
\text{productivity} & = & \text{productivity} & - & \text{faulty process} & + & \text{group process}
\end{array}
$$

This possibility, while not well confirmed by research (Kelley & Thibaut, 1969), has prompted many group dynamicists to suggest ways to push actual productivity beyond the limits specified in Steiner's law. Some of their ideas are described in the concluding section of this chapter.

Improving Group Performance

This final section of the chapter examines several possible factors that can work to "hold groups back" from realizing their potential and some possible solutions

SOLUTIONS TO THE PROBLEMS SHOWN IN THE BOX ON PAGE 156

1. *The chain puzzle.* Although many groups answer 11, since that would involve cutting only every other link, the actual answer is 2! If the 4th and 11th links are cut, all the values from 1 to 23 can be obtained by getting "change" back from the motel owner. Separate links (the 4th and the 11th) are given on Days 1 and 2, but on Day 3 the 3-link unit is given to the owner, who returns the separate links. These links are then used to pay on Days 4 and 5, but on Day 6 the 6-link unit is used and the owner returns the others as change. This process can be continued for 23 days.

2. *The missionary/cannibal problem.* The entire process requires 13 crossings. (In the table below,

M1, M2, and M3 are the three missionaries, C1 and C2 are the two cannibals, and RC is the cannibal who can row).

1. M1 and C1 cross
2. M1 returns
3. RC and C2 cross
4. RC returns
5. M1 and M2 cross
6. M1 and C1 return
7. RC and M1 cross
8. M1 and C2 return
9. M1 and M3 cross
10. RC returns
11. RC and C1 cross
12. RC returns
13. RC and C2 cross

3. *The horse-trading problem.* $20.

to these problems. Although a number of solutions are offered, we focus primarily on the communication process, process planning, and the use of special performance procedures.

The Communication Process

Communication within groups is a multifaceted phenomenon. When examined in its essential form it can be said to involve simply the channeling of a "message" from a "sender" to a "receiver," but in actual interpersonal relations the process is rarely this straightforward. Communication involves a host of interrelated variables—the semantic and symbolic content of the message; the channels used for conveying information; the receiver's decoding of the information; the amount of "noise" in the system (extraneous sounds, misstatements made by the sender, distracting comments); clarifying feedback sequences; and the nonverbal messages conveyed through tone of voice, posturing, gestures, interpersonal distancing, and facial expressions—all of which make the task of defining *communication* an exercise in futility (see Dance, 1970; Fisher, 1980; Phillips, 1973 for reviews).

Yet despite the inherent difficulties in studying communication, we can draw certain limited conclusions by focusing specifically on the link between communication and task performance. Fundamentally, this link seems quite transparent, for common sense tells us that in groups blessed with successfully communicating members problems are fewer, decision making is easier, misunderstandings have less importance, and pleasures are more abundant. In contrast, poor communication in groups seems to set the stage for apathy, inefficiency, animosity, and group dysfunction.

Unfortunately, empirical studies of communication and group performance do not completely support this intuitively appealing notion; it seems, in fact, that the ability to communicate with others is a mixed blessing. While we can exchange information by communicating, we can also create gross misunderstandings and deceptions. While we can reduce conflict by communicating, we can also fan the flames of group dispute by verbalizing feelings of hatred, disgust, or annoyance (see Chapter 4). And while we can often find novel approaches to problems as well as heightening our creativity by communicating, we can also pressure others to conform to our wishes and sanction individual variations (see Chapters 9 and 11).

We can develop more refined analyses of the impact of communication on group process once we consider other factors, such as the content of the communication and how the message is received by others. To focus first on content, if members spend their time communicating threats, as was the case in the trucking-game experiments reviewed in Chapter 4 (Deutsch & Krauss, 1960), or discussing irrelevancies (Harper & Askling, 1980), then communication can have disastrous effects on productivity. If, on the other hand, the group keeps to task-relevant issues while maintaining objectivity, then communication plays a more beneficial role in group performance. For example, in one early study researchers carefully monitored group members' communications while working on a problem that could only be solved by properly sequencing individuals' responses (Lanzetta & Roby, 1960). Although subjects varied in their knowledge of the task and the extent of training to perform it, their utilization of essential resources through effective communication proved to be the best predictor of success. More recently, a detailed case study of groups working on projects for a college class found that the groups that eventually succeeded used communication to their benefit, while the poorly performing groups did not (Harper & Askling, 1980). In summarizing, the researchers suggest that the successful groups, relative to those that failed, boasted more active, highly involved leaders who stimulated open communication by focusing members' attention on the tasks at hand. Furthermore, the overall rate of communication seemed to be higher in the successful groups, as indicated by a significant correlation between participation rates and product quality (rs ranged from .67 to .83). A similarly strong relationship between communication and problem-solving performance was evidenced in an entirely different setting— research teams working in industry ($r = .50$; Katz & Tushman, 1979)—and in other studies communication has been found to limit the extent to which groups unwittingly fall into **social traps** (see box). Thus, communication often, but not always, facilitates performance.

Regarding the question of misinterpretation, most experts on group communication agree that misunderstanding seems to be the rule in groups, with accurate understanding being the exception. At the encoding level, senders may simply lack the skills needed to communicate successfully; they fail to make certain that their verbal and nonverbal messages are accurate and easily decipherable, and thereby unintentionally mislead, confuse, or even insult other members (Gulley & Leathers, 1977). Failure in encoding can, in some instances, also be strategic, as when a gatekeeper illicitly blocks the transmission of critical information or a group member, following a "hidden agenda," leads the group away from task-relevant issues in the hope of achieving secret personal goals (Seaman, 1981).

At the decoding level, inaccuracies arise from both the simple information-processing limitations of human beings (Collins & Guetzkow, 1964) and their faulty listening habits (see Chapter 16). When one researcher sifted through the research literature dealing with inadequacies in information processing, he found consistent evidence pointing to the existence of no fewer than ten different errors that are relevant in group situations (Campbell, 1958b). These biases include *leveling* (decoded messages "if imperfect will on the average be shorter, simpler, and less detailed" than the original message [p. 342]); *order effects* (the "middle portion of the message will be least well retained" [p. 343]); *sharpening* (the message will be reinterpreted "in the direction of dividing the content into clear-cut 'entities,' reducing gradations both by exaggerating some differences and losing others" [p. 344]); and *assimilation* (a shifting in the meaning of the message so that it matches "important past messages" [p. 350] or personal expectations and beliefs). With so many interference-generating mechanisms at work, it is no small wonder that members often complain "Isn't anybody listening to what I am saying?"

Lastly, miscommunication can arise when the group's interaction falls into a pattern of **defensive communication.** In his classic analysis of this problem, Jack Gibb (1961, 1973) suggested that whenever members of a group feel personally threatened, they begin to behave defensively. Effort is shifted from the group tasks to defensive tactics, and individual efficiency drops as concern over evaluations, worry about others' intentions, counterattack planning, and "defen-

---

SOCIAL TRAPS AND COMMUNICATION

Groups sometimes find themselves enmeshed in social traps—situations that tempt individual members to act in their own self-interest to the detriment of the group's overall needs (Platt, 1973). For example, consider a group of sheepherders who must all use the same common grazing land. Although at first the land can easily support many sheep, the individuals wish to maximize their personal profit, and therefore add more animals to their own flocks. These additional sheep earn the individuals extra profit, but in the long run—if all the group members act in a similar fashion—increasing the size of the flocks will exhaust the available resources. Thus, the sheepherders must choose between short-term gains leading to long-term losses and short-term losses followed by long-term gains (Hardin, 1968).

Many laboratory studies have examined social traps by simulating the so-called *commons dilemma.* A group of four or five people are given the chance to draw as many tokens as they want from a pool of available tokens, but all are informed that after each round of "harvesting" the pool regenerates in direct proportion to the number of tokens remaining in the pool. If members quickly draw out all the tokens, the pool is permanently exhausted; cautious removal of only a small number of tokens ensures replenishment of the resource. Nonetheless, group members often act in their own self-interest by drawing out all the tokens, even when they understand the nature of social traps and realize the pool is quite small (Brechner, 1977; Edney, 1980). If, however, members are encouraged to communicate freely with one another, groups are much more likely to solve the dilemma and efficiently manage their resources. For example, in one study subjects either (1) faced the situation unprepared, (2) were given information about the nature of social traps, (3) were provided with a trap-avoiding strategy, or (4) were allowed free communication (Edney, 1980). Overall, the communication condition proved superior to the other three conditions, suggesting that groups can avoid traps if their members can plan a strategy for dealing with the situation through direct face-to-face communication.

sive listening" escalate. Through content analyzing tape recordings of groups working in a wide range of contexts, Gibb was able to conclude that defensiveness nearly always works to undermine communication effectiveness, whereas reducing defensiveness often leads to increases in efficiency.

Gibb's defensive-communication theory also comprises a set of six factors that, when present in a group, tend to put people on the defensive. For example, if you were a member of a group, you might slip into a defensive communication mode if you felt that the group climate was characterized by several of the factors shown in Table 6-5. Gibb suggests that a defensive climate can be made more supportive if members don't evaluate, but merely describe; if control over others is treated as an unimportant issue relative to solving the problem at hand; if group behavior seems spontaneous rather than strategic; and if empathy, equality, and provisionalism replace gestures of neutrality, superiority, and certainty. (Other suggestions for improving your group communication skills can be found in Chapter 14.)

PROCESS PLANNING

You are a member of the University Planning Committee. Today's task is deciding what to do with the $3 million left in the University Improvement Fund. The chairperson of the panel outlines the options open to the group, explaining that members must decide on one of the following: (1) building a new gymnasium, (2) adding to the existing library, (3) refurbishing the student union, (4) updating the school's computer system, and (5) constructing a new administration building.

Such a meeting would probably begin with a roar of discussion over the merits of each project, but notice that it is important to consider another, more fundamental issue before raising the question "Which project should we select?" Unless the organizational rules of the committee specify the strategies that the group must use to perform tasks, members should first settle some process-related questions.

TABLE 6-5. Characteristics of defensive and supportive group climates

Characteristic	Defensive climate	Supportive climate
1. Evaluation versus description	1. People in the group seem to be judging your actions.	1. People in the group are seen as trying to describe outcomes and information.
2. Control versus problem oriented	2. Others are seen as manipulative, attempting influence.	2. Others seem to be focused on the problem at hand.
3. Strategy versus spontaneity	3. Members seem to plan out their "moves," interactions, and comments.	3. Interaction seems to flow smoothly with little strategic control.
4. Neutrality versus empathy	4. People in the group seem to react to you with aloofness and disinterest.	4. People in the group seem to identify with your ideas and interests.
5. Superiority versus equality	5. Others seem condescending, acting as if they are better than you are.	5. Group members treat one another as equals.
6. Certainty versus provisionalism	6. Some people in the group seem to feel that their own ideas are undoubtedly correct.	6. People in the group are not committed to any one viewpoint, for they are keeping an open mind.

(Source: Gibb, 1961, 1973)

For example, members may want to "brainstorm" for a few minutes to generate ideas on the five options. They may wish to set up the ground rules for discussion and select the methods to be used to make the final decision. They may wish to examine the criteria to be used in selecting among the possible projects, call in experts to add to the discussion, or better define the role of the chairperson. Rather than simply blundering ahead on the task, the group could actually control the group's processes by devising a performance strategy.

Unfortunately, group members rarely show much interest in *process planning*. For example, in one study of 100 recorded discussions that occurred in task-oriented groups, fewer than 1.5 comments about process were made per group. In fact, many groups never even discussed strategies, and when someone did raise the issue additional comments from other group members were unlikely to follow (Hackman & Morris, 1975). Other studies have found that group members (1) when first presented with a task tend to start working on the problem immediately rather than considering process-related issues (Varela, 1971); (2) often believe that planning activities are a low-priority item relative to actual task activities, even when they are cautioned that proper advance planning is critical (Shure, Rogers, Larsen, & Tassone, 1962); and (3) assume that discussing process is a waste of time, typically holding whatever procedure was previously used to be the most appropriate (Hackman & Morris, 1975).

Yet controlling process by good planning generally has positive effects. In the study of 100 recorded discussions mentioned above, investigators found that strategy comments, while rarely in evidence, were significantly correlated with improvements in performance (Hackman & Morris, 1975). Similarly, in a study of groups working on a role-play problem involving survival on the moon, the only factor that distinguished successful from failing groups was the number of strategy-planning remarks made during the group discussion (Hirokawa, 1980). Lastly, in a project that experimentally manipulated the use of process planning, groups were more productive when they were encouraged to discuss their performance strategies before working on a task requiring intermember coordination (Hackman, Brousseau, & Weiss, 1976). Process planning also led to more positive ratings of group atmosphere, increments in verbal interaction, greater satisfaction with leadership, and task-performance flexibility. Overall, these studies suggest that groups can enhance their effectiveness by planning performance strategies rather than simply letting the process unfold.

Special Performance Procedures

In some instances a period of process planning may convince the group members that the methods used in the past are no longer adequate, since a fresh solution is needed, antagonism among members is so great the communications are misleading, too little is known about the situation, or the group meetings are becoming too predictable. Fortunately, over the past few decades practitioners who work with groups have developed a number of special performance procedures designed to overcome each of these problems; thus, groups may find solutions through their application. Four of these novel group process techniques—brainstorming, NGT, Delphi, and synectics—are discussed below.

BRAINSTORMING

Groups often work on problems that can be solved through convergent thinking and discussion. Members pool, discuss, and clarify their varied ideas and bits of information on a topic, and eventually the discussion converges on an acceptable solution. However, when innovative, original, or novel answers are needed, then divergent processes facilitate idea generation. Divergent thinking and discussion call for increasing the originality and quantity of ideas, cognitive flexibility, and associative skills (joining previously unliked ideas together to yield new solutions), and are most closely associated with creativity.

One of the best-known group creativity procedures, **brainstorming,** was developed by Alex F. Osborn in an attempt to stimulate divergent thinking. An advertising executive, Osborn found himself continually scrambling for fresh ideas to use in marketing campaigns, so he developed a systematic approach to idea generation that utilized group discussion. Although variations on the basic method are numerous, Osborn's method includes the following rules for each member (Osborn, 1957):

1. *Expressiveness*:   express any idea that comes to mind, no matter how strange, wild, or fanciful. Freewheeling is encouraged, and constraint is avoided.
2. *Nonevaluative*:   ideas are not to be evaluated in any way during the generation phase. All ideas are valuable, and criticizing another's viewpoint is not allowed.
3. *Quantity*:   the more ideas the better. Quantity is desired, for it increases the possibility of generating an excellent solution.
4. *Building*:   modifying and extending others' ideas is recommended. Brainstorming is conducted in a group so that participants can draw from one another.

Osborn also recommends the recording of all ideas in full view of participants, stimulating ideas by asking open-ended questions, utilizing a turn-taking procedure if interaction becomes unequal, and evaluating ideas at a later session. Warm-up exercises can also be used to "break the ice" and get discussion rolling (Rickards, 1974).

Brainstorming remains a popular creativity technique (Coon, 1976; Rickards, 1974; Ulschak, Nathanson, & Gillan, 1981) despite the fact that the bulk of the empirical evidence weighs against Osborn's method (see Lamm & Trommsdorff, 1973, for a review). Although initial studies conducted in the late 1950s found positive effects of brainstorming, these investigations "stacked the deck" against individuals; while subjects in groups had been instructed to follow the four basic brainstorming rules suggested by Osborn, individuals weren't given any special rules concerning creativity (Cohen, Whitmyre, & Funk, 1960; Meadow, Parnes, & Reese, 1959). When individuals working alone were better informed about the purposes of the study and the need for highly creative responses, they tended to generate more solutions than individuals working in groups (Dunnette, Campbell, & Jaastad, 1963; Taylor, Berry, & Block, 1958). Similarly, when interacting groups were compared with "nominal" groups (groups composed of individuals working alone whose efforts are added together to yield the group's score), nominal groups out-performed brainstorming groups provided the individuals were aware of Osborn's rules (Bouchard & Hare, 1970; Bouchard, Barsaloux, & Drauden, 1974; Bouchard, Drauden, & Barsaloux, 1974). While training in brainstorming procedures, practice (Bouchard, 1972a), and allowing subjects to record their ideas *after* the brainstorming session (Philipsen, Mulac, & Dietrich, 1979) improve the group's proficiency, if members are not skilled brainstormers this technique is no better than allowing individuals instructed in brainstorming to generate ideas separately.

NGT: NOMINAL-GROUP TECHNIQUE

Researchers interested in the effects of group interaction on performance often include *nominal groups* in their studies for control purposes. The members of these groups don't actually interact, but when their products are summed or averaged their performance can then be compared with those of the interacting groups. Thus, these aggregates are groups "in name only" (hence the designation *nominal*), but, as we found in our review of brainstorming, such minimal groups often perform quite well when the task involves idea generation or problem solution. The major drawback to their use, of course, is that feedback, resolution of disagreements, and commitment to the final decision are less likely if members never have the opportunity to interact with one another.

Recognizing the benefits of both nominal groups and interacting groups, André L. Delbecq and Andrew H. Van de Ven developed an approach to organizational decision making that includes elements of both nominal and interacting groups (Delbecq & Van de Ven, 1971; Van de Ven & Delbecq, 1971; Delbecq, Van de Ven, & Gustafson, 1975). This special procedure, which they have named the **nominal-group technique (NGT),** involves four basic phases. During Step 1 the group discussion leader introduces the problem or issue in a short, straightforward statement that is written on a blackboard or flipchart. Once they understand the statement, the members silently generate ideas concerning the issue in writing, usually working for from 10 to 15 minutes. During Step 2, the members share their ideas with one another in a round-robin fashion; each person states an idea, which is given an identification letter and written beneath the issue statement, before the next individual adds his or her contribution. Step 3 requires discussion of each item, focusing primarily on clarification. At Step 4, members simply rank the five solutions they most prefer, writing their choices on an index card. The leader then collects the cards, averages the rankings to yield a group decision, and informs the group of the outcome. Delbecq and Van de Ven suggest that at this point the group leader may wish to add two additional steps to further improve the procedure: a short discussion of the vote (optional Step 5) and a revoting (optional Step 6; Delbecq, Van de Ven, & Gustafson, 1975).

Although investigations of the effectiveness of NGT have been few, available data attest to the procedure's usefulness (Gustafson, Shukla, Delbecq, & Walster, 1973; Van de Ven, 1974). For example, Van de Ven (1974) arranged for groups to work on difficult tasks that tended to elicit highly emotional arguments. He found that members of NGT groups, as compared with unstructured interacting groups, generated more ideas and also reported feeling more satisfied with the process. In explanation, Van de Ven suggested that NGT succeeds in optimally balancing task concerns with socioemotional forces. By working alone during Step 1, members can generate many ideas without fear of sanctions by their fellow conferees. Then, in the interaction phase, the group is able to hash out differences and misunderstandings, all the while becoming committed to the final decision. Lastly, the ranking/voting procedures provide for an explicit mathematical solution that fairly weights all members' inputs. However, the developers of NGT do note several drawbacks to the approach: certain materials are needed, NGT meetings typically can focus on only one topic, and members sometimes feel uncomfortable following the highly structured NGT format.

THE DELPHI TECHNIQUE

Unlike the procedures discussed thus far, the **Delphi technique** requires no face-to-face interaction whatsoever. Originally developed by decision makers at the Rand Corporation (Dalkey, 1968; Delbecq et al., 1975), the procedure is named for the famed Delphic oracle of Greek mythology. Supposedly, those who wondered about their future could consult the oracle for guidance, and in some instances receive accurate, though somewhat ambiguous, prophecies of what lay in store for them. (One Greek king of legend was reportedly told that attacking a neighboring territory would bring about the "fall of a great empire." He attacked and lost, realizing too late that the prophecy referred to his own empire.) Similarly, the Delphi technique was first used for forecasting technological developments, although now it is used for selecting from alternative problem solutions, making decisions, generating information, and relaying information.

The Delphi process involves the repeated assessment of members' opinions via questionnaires. First, the project planners design a questionnaire containing clearly written, open-ended questions relevant to the topic. Only a few items are developed at this point, but these must be centrally important in the opinion of the planners. For example, if the issue concerned increasing group-performance efficiency, a single item asking respondents to list factors that facilitate or impede the group's effectiveness would suffice. Next, project planners identify and contact respondents and ask them to complete the questionnaire. These persons are selected from the group as a whole on the basis of the depth of their involvement with the issue, and if generalizability is desired then proper sampling procedures are followed. For the efficiency issue, individuals in all types of positions within the group should be contacted. Once the questionnaires are returned, the project planners develop and distribute a new instrument based on the initial responses. The repeated revision of the questionnaire is known as *iteration*, and is carried out again and again until specific solutions to the problem are obtained from group members. In some instances two iterations may be sufficient, but for complex, unclear problems many more iterations may be necessary.

As a performance technique, Delphi can be very usefully applied when issues need clarification, when the opinions of a wide range of people are important, and when it is impossible for the people whose input is required to meet face to face. However, Delphi requires considerable time and effort. A staff must write and send out the questionnaires, and the average duration of the Delphi process is 45 days (Delbecq et al., 1975). Furthermore, if respondents are not motivated to complete and return the questionnaire, then the process breaks down completely. Like the NGT, relatively few investigations of the utility of Delphi have been conducted, but the limited evidence suggests that the technique is more effective than an unstructured problem-solving session (Dalkey, 1968, 1969; Van de Ven, 1974), but less effective than NGT (Gustafson et al., 1973; see Sackman, 1975 for a critical review of Delphi).

SYNECTICS

William Gordon (1961) and George Prince (1970, 1975) have together developed a special form of brainstorming that they believe more adequately harnesses the creativity of group members than the conventional approach. Based on the idea that groups habitually try to solve problems through convergent thinking, Gordon and Prince suggest several ways to energize divergent thought processes by forcing members to look at the elements of the problem from new perspectives. Hence, they use the word **synectics** to describe their approach: "*synectics,* from the Greek, means the joining together of different and apparently irrelevant elements. Synectics theory applies to the integration of diverse individuals into a problem-stating, problem-solving group" (Gordon, 1961, p. 1).

In some respects synectics follows the usual group discussion pattern of problem statement, discussion, solution generation, and decision. However, certain creative features are added to these more typical stages to try to stimulate divergent thinking. For example, during the initial exploration of the issues a *spectrum policy* is adopted. This discussion norm explicitly recognizes that few ideas are all good or all bad, and calls for the analysis of all sides of the issue. This spectrum policy is reiterated throughout the meeting. A period for the expression of *wishes and goals* is also often included in synectics, providing members with an opportunity to vent their frustrations ("I wish that we could work together more efficiently"), agree on goals ("I feel that we should be striving toward greater productivity with less friction"), and stimulate creative thinking ("I wish that I were William Gordon"). *Excursions* are also a major element in synectics. These "vacations" from the problem deliberately distract the group from the issue, providing a chance for creative thought. Excursions are recommended whenever the group "runs dry" or seems stagnated, and often involve metaphors, analogies, and fantasy. For example, a personal analogy requires personal involvement with the problem, as when group members trying to design aids for wheelchair-bound disabled people actually navigate around the building in wheelchairs. Direct analogies involve comparing parallel events, as when conflict between groups is likened to war between nations. Symbolic analogies—comparing notably dissimilar objects or events—are more fanciful, as when a group is said to function like a computer. Lastly, fantasy analogies represent the peak of the creative process, for at this stage elements of the problem are compared with make-believe events or objects; another group may be likened to the many-headed Hydra of mythology, the inefficiency of the group may be blamed on invisible gremlins who undo each day's efforts, or the group members may describe themselves as the characters in a famous book or movie. Group leaders can plan to use one or more of these kinds of analogies in advance, but in any case they should attempt to integrate the material generated during the excursion with the other discussion results (see Ulschak et al., 1981, for a more detailed description of synectics).

Analyses of the effectiveness of synectics are quick to point out that certain features must be present in the group situation before this approach will work

(Rickards, 1974). A fairly open, cooperative group member provides a starting base, but a skilled group leader or facilitator is also an important feature. Members must be willing to follow the sometimes unusual suggestions of the leader, and a refusal to allow creative forces to surface often disables the process. The spectrum policy is a critical feature of synectics, and seems to be difficult for some individuals to accept, as is the synectic emphasis on making statements rather than asking questions. However, studies of groups that employ synectics-like techniques—for example, using analogies to increase creativity—have found that such groups are superior to traditional brainstorming groups (Bouchard, 1972b; Bouchard et al., 1974a).

Summary

In this chapter we began our study of *group performance* with respect to problem solving, decision making, and task-oriented settings by focusing on deceptively simple *coaction* and *audience* situations. Although early researchers were uncertain of the effects of such *compresence*—responding when others are present—Robert Zajonc's *social facilitation* hypothesis predicts that compresence facilitates the performance of simple tasks requiring dominant responses, but interferes with the performance of complex tasks requiring nondominant responses. Social facilitation can be accounted for in terms of a general, unlearned *arousal* mechanism, a feeling of *apprehension* during evaluation, or a *distraction/conflict* process, but available evidence suggests that these three processes, as well as others, probably combine to determine task performance when others are present.

Moving to the more complex situation in which individuals interact with one another during the performance process, we examined the five types of tasks specified in Ivan Steiner's taxonomy: *additive, compensatory, disjunctive, conjunctive,* and *discretionary* tasks. Although the group's ability to perform all these tasks successfully depends upon members' *resources* and the *processes* utilized to combine individuals' inputs, in general groups do well on additive tasks, even though the *Ringelmann effect* results in decreased individual effort. Compensatory and disjunctive tasks also find the group out-performing most of the individual members, although performance on disjunctive tasks can be undermined if the solution, once suggested, is not so obviously correct that the group readily accepts it. Conjunctive tasks, because they require inputs from all members, may be poorly performed by groups, while the effectiveness of groups working on discretionary tasks depends on the method chosen to combine individuals' inputs (for example, delegating decisions, averaging inputs, balloting, and consensus). Furthermore, performance on all these various types of tasks can be further improved if the group members (1) pay close attention to the content of the group *communication* and how these messages are being perceived by others, (2) plan group problem-solving *processes,* and (3) utilize *special performance procedures* (for example, brainstorming, NGT, Delphi, synectics) when appropriate.

PART
THREE

Social-Influence Processes

Social influence lies at the heart of group dynamics, for group membership necessarily implies that members can influence each others' behaviors and outcomes. In the following four chapters we analyze social influence, beginning in Chapter 7 with the concept of power: effecting behavioral and/or psychological change in another person through the process of social influence. Bases of power, power tactics, obedience, coalition formation, and the consequences of power are all reviewed in Chapter 7, but a special form of power—leadership—is examined separately, in Chapter 8. There we consider the factors that determine the emergence, behaviors, and effectiveness of leaders in various kinds of groups, and in Chapter 9 we present an analysis of social influence that results in conformity in the group. Finally, because social influence always occurs in an environmental context, in Chapter 10 we study how territoriality, interpersonal distancing, and seating arrangements affect and are affected by social-influence mechanisms.

7

Power

When the world first heard that more than 900 members of a religious group known as the People's Temple had committed mass suicide in a small village hidden away in a South American jungle, it reacted with shock and disbelief. To most, the idea that so many people could commit suicide for so little reason was appalling, and as journalists elaborated the gruesome details this incredulity grew into bafflement. Why would the group's leader, Jim Jones, formerly noted for his humanitarian acts of social reform, command his followers to take poison? Why did the group members obey his order when refusal could have had no worse consequences than obedience? Even more perplexing, what force could move parents to willingly give poison to their children?

Such an amazing and unexpected series of events could not for long go unexplained, and soon a myriad of suggestions appeared that sought to account for the tragedy of Jonestown. To many analysts, the explanation lay with Jim Jones himself—his childhood, his persuasiveness, his irrational fears of persecution. Others emphasized the kind of people who were members of the "cult"—their psychological instability, their willingness to identify with the cause, and their religious fervor. Still others suggested more fantastic explanations, proposing that the Jonestown colonists had been systematically eradicated by government agents, that the colonists—as native Californians—were mentally unstable from the very start, or that some divine power had intervened to punish Jones for his sacrilege. Despite the plausibility, and in many cases, ingeniousness, of some of these possibilities, this chapter uses a different frame of reference in investigating the chain of events that led up to the Guyana suicides. Focusing on Jones, on the isolation of the village, on the kind of people in the cult, on the group norms, and so on, provides pieces of the Jonestown puzzle, but an additional concept—one essential variable—must be considered before these pieces can all be fit into place. This key is the concept of **power.**

Social Power in Groups

Dorwin Cartwright, a leading researcher and theorist in group dynamics, believes that few interactions advance very far before elements of power and influence come into play. Leaders who demand obedience from their followers, the person who agrees to help another provided the other reciprocates the favor, the boss who offers employees a bonus if they work overtime, the female who tries to "pick up" a male in a bar, and the teacher who warns students to sit silently at their desks are all experiencing the dynamics of social power as they influence and are in turn influenced by others. Indeed, Cartwright concluded many years ago (1959, p. 183) that "such concepts as influence, power, and authority (or their equivalents) must be employed in any adequate treatment of social interaction wherever it may take place." Bertrand Russell (1938, p. 10) stressed even more heavily the importance of power when he wrote "The fundamental concept in social science is Power, in the same sense in which Energy is the fundamental concept in physics."

Defining Power

Like *love, power* is an ambiguous term. As power theorist David Kipnis (1974) notes when comparing the two terms, the meaning of *love* can differ considerably from person to person. To some, *love* refers to a special state of attraction between two people. To others, the word refers to sexual and physical pleasure. To still others, *love* can imply irrational, emotion-laden behavior, or commitment and caring about others. In a similar manner, the meaning of *power* varies among people. Some theorists believe that the term should be reserved for coercive, illegitimate forms of social influence such as threats and punishments (Bachrach & Baratz, 1963). Others reserve the term for group authorities and leaders, suggesting that power lies in the hands of those who control important resources (Shaw, 1981). Still others suggest that *power* has so many different meanings (Pollard & Mitchell, 1973) that it may not mean anything!

Despite this ambiguity, most definitions of *power* make reference to *behavioral or psychological change through the process of social influence.* For example, John R. P. French and Bertram Raven (1959) suggest that an act of power necessarily involves one person causing another person to perform a behavior that is contrary to the latter's desire. Max Weber defines power as "the probability that one actor within a social relationship will be in a position to carry out his own will despite resistance" (1947, p. 27). Other definitions cite similar themes: power is variously defined as "control or influence over the actions of others to promote one's goals without their consent, against their will, or without their knowledge or understanding" (Buckley, 1967, p. 186); "the capacity to produce intended and foreseen effects on others" (Wrong, 1979, p. 21); and "the interaction between two parties, the powerholder and the target person, in which the target person's behavior is given new direction by the powerholder" (Kipnis, 1974, p. 9).

This theme of forces operating in opposition to one another is made even more salient in the equational definitions of power offered by Kurt Lewin (1951) and French and Raven (1959). According to Lewin's definition (1951, p. 336), the amount of power Person A holds over Person B depends upon the force that A brings to bear on B, and B's ability to resist A's pressure, or

$$\text{the power of A/B} = \frac{(\text{maximum force A can induce on B})}{(\text{maximum resistance B can offer against A})}$$

French and Raven modified this formula slightly by proposing that

$$\text{the power of A/B} = \left(\begin{array}{c}\text{maximum force A}\\\text{can induce on B}\end{array}\right) - \left(\begin{array}{c}\text{maximum resistance B}\\\text{can offer against A}\end{array}\right)$$

Although these definitions may seem excessively formal in the abstract, when applied to a specific group interaction, such as that at the Guyana colony, they help us to define more precisely the meaning of social power. For example, Jim

Jones was the clear powerholder in the People's Temple. All accounts of the group agree that he was the hub of the entire organization, and that he exerted a strong influence over the group even before the move to Guyana. His church was apparently well organized, for Jones surrounded himself with loyal followers who would support his sometimes eccentric decisions. Jones's influence was so strong that he could mobilize large numbers of people in support of any political rally he endorsed, and he managed to convince many of his followers to join him in his utopian Jonestown. In contrast, the members of the People's Temple offered little resistance to Jones's pressures, for they never rebelled in spite of his demands for large tithes, his threats of death, the marathon "conditioning" sessions he set up, and his use of corporal punishment. In terms of the French and Raven equation, the amount of resistance to subtract from Jones's forceful influence was zero; Jones was the all-powerful figure in the group.

Bases of Power

Even if we accept the fact that according to definitions proffered by many theorists Jones was the primary powerholder in his group, we are still left with the task of explaining the *source* of his power. Jones was able to extract a deadly degree of obedience from his followers, but we have explained little if we are unable to describe the bases of this power—the interpersonal sources of Jones's control over the members of the People's Temple. Where exactly did Jones's power come from?

John R. P. French and Bertram Raven (1959), in a brilliant analysis of power that has since become a standard work in the field of small groups, explained the origin of power by focusing on five critical **power bases.** Although they pointed out that these bases typically overlap and that other bases could also contribute to increases in power, French and Raven emphasized the five sources listed in Table 7-1; reward, coercive, legitimate, referent, and expert power. Each of these bases is examined below.

REWARD POWER

Many of the initiates of the People's Temple joined because Jones offered them things they wanted but could not obtain for themselves. Jones's congregation drew from all sectors of society, but he was adept in offering each member what he or

TABLE 7-1. Five bases of power

Label	Definition
1. Reward power	The powerholder's control over the positive and negative reinforcements desired by the target person.
2. Coercive power	The powerholder's ability to threaten and punish the target person.
3. Legitimate power	Power that stems from the target person's belief that the powerholder has a justifiable right to require and demand the performance of certain behaviors.
4. Referent power	Power that derives from the target person's identification with, attraction to, or respect for the powerholder.
5. Expert power	Power that exists when the target person believes that the powerholder possesses superior skills and abilities.

(Source: French & Raven, 1959)

she needed most. To the poor and elderly Jones provided security, economic support, and companionship. To those interested in progressive political reform he offered the means of effecting valued changes. To the gullible he provided miracles and faith healings, convincing many that he could cure cancer with the touch of his hand. His philosophy was an appealing mixture of socialism, humanism, and mysticism that promised a peaceful, happy future in Jonestown.

All these actions involved an element of reward—or at least the promise of a valued reward. Jones's **reward power** drew from his followers' belief that he controlled resources that they valued, and that he would make rewards available to them provided they performed the appropriate behaviors. This conception of reward power is generally consistent with behaviorism's emphasis on control through reinforcement. However, reward power is only feasible in a group where the following three conditions are met: (1) the resource offered as a reward must be valued, (2) the group members must depend on the powerholder for the reward, and (3) the powerholder's promises of reward must be credible. Although a wide range of rewards can function as reinforcers—gold stars for students, salaries for workers, social approval for insecure friends, food for the starving poor, freedom for prisoners, or even suicide for those who are leading tortured lives—an effective reinforcer in one situation may fail in another. Only if the group members value the resource—perhaps because it is limited or because they expect high levels of reinforcement—will delivering rewards lead to power. Reward power can also be reduced if alternative means of need satisfaction, such as joining another group or making a deal with another powerful group member, are open to the group members. Where such avenues are blocked, giving the powerholder sole control of distributing the valued commodities, then the latter's position becomes more secure. Furthermore, credibility in promises implies that members will trust the powerholder to make good on the promise of rewards.

For example, when middle-class individuals approached Jones in the early stages of the group's development, he promised them happiness and social reform; if he had told them that joining the church would earn them three square meals a day and freedom from harsh beatings they would have been uninfluenced, since they already had these things. Yet later, after the move to Jonestown, these same individuals would work long hours in exchange for meals of rice and beans and the suspension of punishment. In addition, by isolating the settlement Jones ensured that these needs could not be fulfilled by others, guaranteeing his followers' complete dependence upon him alone. Lastly, many members apparently believed Jones's idealistic promises, and when disbelief came it was already too late. By this time he had managed to strengthen his position in the group by building his coercive power.

COERCIVE POWER

Accounts of the development of the People's Temple vividly describe Jones's growing reliance on physical and psychological punishment as a means of exacting obedience from his followers. Public beatings were a fairly common method of punishing wrongdoers, and Jones sometimes conducted all-night prayer sessions designed to "break the will" of his congregation. He also threatened group members with death if they failed to obey him, and warned them of the horrible consequences (arrest and execution) that would overtake those who refused to join him in Jonestown. Once in Guyana Jones continued to use physical beatings as punishment, as well as solitary confinement, denials of food and water, and long hours of labor in the fields.

Jones's use of **coercive power**—threats, warnings of danger, and punishment—to influence others was hardly without precedent. Countries threaten other countries with attacks and economic sanctions. Employers threaten employees with loss of pay, transferral to undesirable jobs, or even firing. Teachers punish mischievous students with an arsenal ranging from extra assignments to detentions and suspension. Disagreeing friends insult and humiliate one another, gang members coerce other members through acts of physical violence, and religious leaders threaten members with loss of grace or ostracism. However, while the use of coercive power seems to be both pervasive and efficient, this method of influence is not without certain negative side-effects. French and Raven note that strong coercion typically leads to compliance with the powerholder's demands, but not to any private internal acceptance of the rule or order. Hence, coercive powerholders must maintain close surveillance over the group if they wish to be effective. They also point out that rewarding powerholders are usually better liked than coercive powerholders, and that the target person may respond to coercion by escaping from the powerholder's region of control. Norms of reciprocity also weigh against the unprovoked use of coercion, for when these norms are in operation target persons may return threat for threat. As recent research indicates, when people are rewarded by a powerholder, they tend to reciprocate with cooperation; if, in contrast, powerholders employ coercion, they are met with malevolence and animosity (Schlenker, Nacci, Helm, & Tedeschi, 1976). Pressures toward the formation of revolutionary coalitions—subgroups formed in opposition to the powerholder—are also strongest when the powerholder chooses to use coercive influence methods that the group feels are unfair (Lawler & Thompson, 1978, 1979).

Unfortunately, it seems that Jones was able to prevent these reactions to his coercive measures. He was forced to use very strict surveillance to prevent escapes from the Jonestown colony, but the vast majority of the members complied with his final orders.

LEGITIMATE POWER

When the police officer tells the bystander to move along, she hurries off down the street. When the lieutenant enters the room, the sergeant snaps to attention. The classroom quiets down when the professor reaches the podium. The office workers feign a tremendous outburst of activity when their boss enters the work area. The congregation contributes willingly under the watchful eye of the minister.

Although several bases of power are involved in these examples, the influence of **legitimate power** is particularly striking in each instance. According to French and Raven, legitimate power is unlike the other bases, because it emphasizes the powerholder's right to command the target and the target person's duty to obey the powerholder. Legitimate power may be achieved by any one of a variety of means—appointment by a legitimizing agent, election by members of the group, qualification through possession of specified characteristics, and so on—provided that the method is supported by group norms as the appropriate means of gaining this position of authority. As a base, legitimate power is particularly potent because it springs from the group structure itself—roles, norms, and intermember relations—rather than from the delivery or withholding of valued resources. When individuals obey the commands of another because they hope to earn a reward or avoid a punishment, the reason for the obedience is transparently obvious. Take away the powerholder's control over the resources, and the base of power is gone. If, however, the powerholder is a legitimate authority in the group, members obey because they personally accept the norms of the group; they voluntarily obey from an internalized sense of duty, loyalty, or moral obligation. As one power theorist (Wrong, 1979, p. 52) notes,

> Legitimate authority is more efficient than coercive or induced authority in that it minimizes the need for maintaining means of coercion in constant readiness, continual surveillance of the power subjects, and regular supplies of economic or non-economic rewards. For these reasons, naked (that is, coercive) power always seeks to clothe itself in the garments of legitimacy.

(See the box for some research into the "garments of legitimacy.")

Jones's legitimate power emanated from his successful retention of prominent political and religious offices. He managed to ally himself with powerful political forces in the San Francisco area, and he soon won a series of accolades: "Humanitarian of the Year," San Francisco Housing Authority Chairpersonship, and the Martin Luther King, Jr., Humanitarian Award. More importantly, however, he established himself and his church as a legitimate religious force. His credentials as an ordained minister legalized his right to lecture and preach, and a decision to join his congregation was tantamount to an agreement to follow his dictates. In time his persuasive oratory convinced many that he was truly the supreme religious

---

DO CLOTHES MAKE THE AUTHORITY?

Doctors have their white coats and black bags; police officers their crisp uniforms, shiny badges, and guns; firefighters their hats and boots. Do these uniforms serve as signs of authority, suggesting that the orders of the wearer should be obeyed even if he or she is acting outside the normal limits of authority? To find out, Leonard Bickman compared subjects' obedience to a male dressed in a sports coat and tie with obedience to a uniformed guard who resembled a police officer in all respects except that he carried no gun. These two types of authorities wandered about Brooklyn, New York, ordering people to do such things as pick up litter ("Pick up this bag for me!") and donate money to a motorist ("This

fellow is overparked at the meter but doesn't have any change. Give him a dime!"). Bickman found that far more people obeyed the guard than the civilian.

The use of a uniform to increase authority has its limits, however. When Bickman tested people's reactions to a different sort of uniform—an experimenter dressed up as a milk-delivery person—obedience equaled that found in the civilian condition. Apparently not all uniforms elicit equal amounts of respect, perhaps because only police uniforms imply that the wearer can back up her or his threats with coercive power.

(Source: Bickman, 1974)

authority—that he had the God-given right to demand their obedience in all aspects of their lives and that they, as his disciples, were morally compelled to obey.

French and Raven derived the label *referent power* from the concept of reference group. As noted in Chapter 2, a reference group provides its members with standards by which they can evaluate their own attitudes, beliefs, and behaviors. For example, Newcomb's Bennington study documented the strong influence of a reference group (college students' peers and professors) by finding a shift in student attitude from conservative to liberal during the college years (Newcomb, 1943). Although this conformity in attitude may have been partly due to the student's desire to secure rewards and avoid punishment, referent power undoubtedly played a role, since the women gained a sense of intrinsic personal satisfaction from their identification with the reference group. These students were "Bennington women," and therefore they had to act like and think like Bennington women.

Just as a reference group provides others with social-comparison information, so an individual who possesses **referent power** serves as a model for others' self-evaluations. Identification with the powerholder is the key factor involved in this type of power, for the target admires, respects, and hopes to resemble the powerholder as much as possible. Typically, attraction is also involved—one rarely tries to emulate those one dislikes—and the target person can become excessively concerned with pleasing and satisfying the referent powerholder. Some examples of referent power at work include a boy mimicking his older brother; the youngster who, in standing up to the neighborhood bully, earns the respect of his or her buddies; soldiers going into battle willingly following the example of courage and bravery set by their leaders; athletes who put forth tremendous effort in hopes of pleasing their hard-driving but beloved coach; the 13-year-old girl who smokes cigarettes because her best friend does; young lovers who "would do anything" to win the hearts of their beloveds; and the unknown author who works long hours to emulate the style of his favorite novelist.

Applying the concept of referent power to Jonestown, we see that the People's Temple exerted a strong social influence over its members, with the bulk of this referent power residing in the hands of Jones himself. He offered the devoted a clear path to salvation, and they needed only to study his teachings and obey his orders to be saved. The strength of his personality, the simplicity of his ideology, and his willingness to act on his beliefs inspired a sincere trust among his followers, who eventually accepted him as the final source of truth and knowledge. Many group members came to love their leader fervently and made tremendous financial and emotional sacrifices in the hopes of pleasing him. As one observer commented, "To his followers, Jones was a god whose power they could take into themselves merely by obeying him" (Allen, 1978, p. 121). Jones was truly a **charismatic leader** (see the box on page 180).

An extremely successful real estate broker, tired of being repeatedly cheated out of his commission by owners and buyers who arranged property closings

CHARISMA: MORE THAN A NICE SMILE

The noted sociologist Max Weber, intrigued by the sheer magnitude of the power wielded by leaders such as Hitler, Lenin, and Mussolini, introduced the term **charisma** to account for the almost irrational devotion followers exhibited for their leaders (1947). Although the term is sometimes incorrectly used to refer to a charming, pleasant leader (for example, "Kennedy's good looks and warm smile made him a charismatic leader"), charisma actually refers to the great referent power of the "savior-leader." Charismatic leaders such as Jim Jones usually appear on the scene when a large group of people are dissatisfied or faced with a distressful situation. They offer these people a way to escape their prob-

lems, and the masses react with "intense loyalty and enthusiastic willingness to take the path the leader is pointing out" (Tucker, 1977, p. 388). In the vivid words of social critic Eric Hoffer (1951, p. 105), the charismatic leader

> personifies the certitude of the creed and justifies the resentment dammed up in the souls of the frustrated. He kindles the vision of a breathtaking future so as to justify the sacrifice of a transitory present. He stages the world of make-believe so indispensable for the realization of self-sacrifice and united action. He evokes the enthusiasm of communion—the sense of liberation from a petty and meaningless individual existence.

behind his back, decided early in his career to increase his power in such transactions by becoming an "expert from afar" (Ringer, 1973). He would fly to a prospective client's city in his jet, bringing his own office equipment (calculators, typewriters, supplies), several secretarial assistants, reference manuals, contracts, and reports. He always dressed impeccably, feigned an interest in the quality of the building construction, and seemed to know more about the real estate than the owners themselves. Eventually the buyer and seller would be so intimidated by the power of this expert that they wouldn't consider shortchanging him on his commission.

The broker's remarkable success with these tactics (he now earns nearly a million dollars a year from his commissions) speaks of the impact of **expert power.** The buyers and sellers attributed special skills, abilities, and knowledge to the broker, and were therefore likely to rely on his judgments and decisions. So long as he could convince his clients that he knew more about the facts than they did, and that he was not trying to misrepresent these facts to swindle them, he managed to maintain a strong position of power. Like the physician interpreting a patient's symptoms, a local resident giving directions to an out-of-towner, a teacher dictating the correct spelling of a word for a student, or an automobile mechanic explaining the source of an engine problem to a mechanically inept driver, the broker was able to transform his special knowledge into power.

The broker, as it turns out, was an expert in the area of real estate sales, but according to French and Raven this fact was almost irrelevant; the key was his clients' belief in his special expertise. Similarly, Jones's actual skills, abilities, and knowledge were less important than his followers' perceptions of their leader. Although uninvolved analysts found it difficult to think of Jones as a religious or political expert, his followers apparently felt that he was the most knowledgeable religious figure of modern times. Through artful persuasion, he convinced them that he had a special insight into social and religious questions, giving his predictions a ring of truth. He also claimed to have a network of spies in government and law-enforcement agencies, and based many of his warnings on these "reliable" sources of information. Of all the bases specified by French and Raven, Jones's expert power was probably the weakest, but he still managed to convince some members of his special expertise.

Using Power Tactics

Although the power an individual enjoys in a group may derive from the various power bases specified by French and Raven, during group interaction people can rely on additional, and much more specific, means of social influence. For example, what would you do if members of your group were steadfastly arguing a position that was contrary to your own preferred viewpoint? Would you threaten them with harm? offer them rewards if they would change their beliefs? warn them of the dire consequences of their actions? try to persuade them to abandon their misguided arguments? physically attack them? Exactly what would you do to "get your way"?

While many theorists have offered good descriptions of the basic types of strategies available in commonplace settings (Dion & Stein, 1978; Donohue, 1978; Parsons, 1962; Tedeschi, Schlenker, & Bonoma, 1973; Wrong, 1979), Toni Falbo has recently concluded that influence tactics vary along two basic dimensions: (1) rationality versus nonrationality and (2) directness versus indirectness (1977). First, some tactics—such as bargaining with people or trying to persuade them—are *rational* modes of influence, since they emphasize reasoning, logic, and rational behaviors. Others, in contrast, are *nonrational* strategies of influence, because they rely on emotionality and misinformation rather than careful analysis. Examples of nonrational strategies are a simple evasion of the issue or an attempt to deceive those who disagree with you. Second, such tactics as threatening another person or simply going ahead and doing what you want to do despite objections (a method known as *fait accompli*) are *direct* paths to getting your way. Other tactics, such as hinting or ingratiating oneself, are more *indirect* modes of influence.

Falbo derived these two dimensions of social-influence strategies by analyzing the content of college students' essays on "How I Get My Way" when dealing with other people. The students alluded to more than 340 tactics of influence, but Falbo found that 91% of these strategies could be classified into one of the 16 categories listed in Table 7-2. Subsequent analysis (using a statistical procedure known as multidimensional scaling) then revealed that these 16 power strategies differed in terms of rationality and directness. Tactics such as bargaining, compromise, and persuasion were all rated as highly rational power tactics, but others— evasion, threat,and deceit—were judged to be nonrational; threats, persistence, and fait accompli were more direct strategies, but others like hinting and thought manipulation were indirect methods.

Although these two dimensions seem to summarize adequately the differences among the 16 strategies Falbo reports, she was also interested in exploring the impact of these power tactics on actual group behavior. For example, how are people who report using deceit to influence others received by others? Would they be evaluated differently if they had reported using persuasion or bargaining? threats

TABLE 7-2. Examples and definitions of sixteen power tactics

Strategy	Definition	Example
Reason	Any statement about using reason or rational argument to influence others.	I argue logically. I tell all the reasons why my plan is best.
Expertise	Claiming to have superior knowledge or skills.	I tell them I have a lot of experience with such matters.
Compromise	Both agent and target give up part of their desired goals in order to obtain some of them.	More often than not we come to some sort of compromise, if there is a disagreement.
Bargaining	Explicit statement about reciprocating favors and making other two-way exchanges.	I tell her that I'll do something for her if she'll do something for me.
Persuasion	Simple statements about using persuasion, convincing, or coaxing.	I get my way by convincing others that my way is best.
Simple statement	Without supporting evidence or threats, a matter-of-fact statement of one's desires.	I simply tell him what I want.
Persistence	Continuing in one's influence attempts or repeating one's point.	I reiterate my point. I keep going despite all obstacles.
Assertion	Forcefully asserting one's way.	I voice my wishes loudly.
Thought manipulation	Making the target think that the agent's way is the target's own idea.	I usually try to get my way by making the other person feel that it is his idea.
Fait accompli	Openly doing what one wants without avoiding the target.	I do what I want anyway.
Hinting	Not openly stating what one wants; indirect attempts at influencing others.	I drop hints. I subtly bring up a point.
Emotion-target	Agent attempts to alter emotions of target.	I try to put him in a good mood.
Threat	Stating that negative consequences will occur if the agent's plan is not accepted.	I'll tell him I will never speak to him again if he doesn't do what I want.
Deceit	Attempts to fool the target into agreeing by the use of flattering or lies.	I get my way by doing a good amount of fast talking and sometimes by telling some white lies.
Emotion-agent	Agent alters own facial expression.	I put on a sweet face. I try to look sincere.
Evasion	Doing what one wants by avoiding the person who would disapprove.	I got to read novels at work as long as the boss never saw me doing it.

(Source: Falbo, 1977)

or fait accompli? To examine these questions, Falbo arranged for the essay writers to meet in same-sex groups of three to five persons to discuss the topic "What I plan to get out of college." After this discussion, each person rated one another on such characteristics as friendliness, consideration, and desirability as a group member. Also, several personality measures were taken.

As might be expected, Falbo found that evaluations of liking and willingness to join in another discussion were more closely associated with the rationality of influence rather than the directness of influence. People who claimed that they influenced others through reasoning, compromise, expertise, bargaining, or persuasion were most favorably evaluated, while those who emphasized deceit, evasion, threat, and emotion-agent received the most negative evaluations. In fact, the strategies in Table 7-2 are listed in order of preference. People claiming that they influenced others through the tactics at the top of the list were more positively evaluated than those who cited the more nonrational strategies farther down the list. In addition, people who used (or at least, reported using) indirect/rational strategies (hinting, persuasion, bargaining) were rated as more considerate and friendlier than people who use direct/nonrational strategies (threat, fait accompli). Lastly, when Falbo examined the relationship between reported strategy and personality traits she found the following:

1. People who are very concerned with being accepted and liked by their fellow group members (high scorers on the Marlowe-Crowne social-desirability scale) tended to use indirect/rational rather than direct/nonrational strategies.
2. People who espouse a Machiavellian, manipulative philosophy of dealing with others (high Machiavellians on a scale developed by Christie and Geiss, 1970) tended to use indirect/nonrational as opposed to direct/rational strategies.
3. People who tend to conform to others' judgments (as assessed by a standard Asch situation paradigm; see Chapter 9) reported using rational/influence more than nonrational/influence strategies.

These findings suggest that (1) personality factors play a role in determining which power tactic a person chooses to use and (2) different power tactics influence attraction and acceptance into the group in different ways. However, we should accept these conclusions with caution given that no evidence is available to indicate whether the essay writers actually used the tactic they described in their papers. Also, other research shows that the dimensions revealed in this study, while generally accurate as descriptors of most group interactions, may not apply to more intimate interactions (Falbo & Peplau, 1980).

Power Processes

We have seen that power permeates many aspects of group life but that to fully understand effects of power we must consider its sources. Given this background, we are now ready to explore some of the power processes evident during group interaction, but we must necessarily restrict our analysis, since the number of topics relevant to power is enormous. Therefore, this section focuses on two areas that have particularly intrigued researchers: (1) factors that influence the willingness of individuals to obey the orders of a powerholder and (2) changing the balance of power through coalition formation.

Obedience in the Face of Power

Imagine yourself as a participant in one of the first experimental investigations of obedience (Milgram, 1963, 1965, 1974). In response to an advertisement in the newspaper or the mail (see box on page 184), you volunteer to take part in a scientific "study of memory and learning" to be conducted at nearby Yale University. When you arrive at the impressively appointed laboratory, you meet the experimenter—a thirtyish man with a crew-cut and dressed in a grey technician's coat—and a fellow subject. This coparticipant looks to be in his late forties, a trifle overweight, and a little nervous. He strikes you as a mild, friendly fellow.

In a matter-of-fact voice, the experimenter begins to explain the study by calling your attention to the relationship between punishment and learning. He notes that while several theories suggest that punishment facilitates learning, little systematic research on the issue has ever been conducted. In the study at hand, designed to fill this gap, one person will play the role of Teacher by reading a series of paired words (for example, blue box, nice day, wild duck, and so on) to the other person, who will play the role of Learner. The Teacher will check the Learner's ability to recall the pairs by reading the first word in the pair and several possible answers (for example, blue: sky, ink, box, lamp). Failures will be punished by electric shock.

After thus describing the procedure, the experimenter announces a "drawing" to decide who will be the Teacher and who will be the Learner. The other subject draws a slip of paper from a hat and reads "Learner." You feel vaguely relieved. The experimenter leads you both to the next room, where you watch as he straps the Learner into a chair ("to prevent excessive movement during the shock"). The subject sits quietly while an electrode is attached to his wrist, but finally asks if the shocks are dangerous. "Oh, no," says the experimenter, "although the shocks can be extremely painful, they cause no permanent tissue damage" (Milgram, 1974, p. 19).

Leaving the Learner strapped in his chair, you follow the experimenter back into the room with the shock generator. The shining machine features a row of 30 electrical switches, each labeled with voltage information. The label to the

---

ANNOUNCEMENT OF THE EXPERIMENT

We will pay you $4.00 for
one hour of your time

Persons Needed for a Study of Memory

- We will pay five hundred New Haven men to help us complete a scientific study of memory and learning. The study is being done at Yale University.
- Each person who participates will be paid $4.00 (plus 50¢ carfare) for approximately one hour's time. We need you for only one hour: there are no further obligations. You may choose the time you would like to come (evenings, weekdays, or weekends).
- No special training, education, or experience is needed. We want:

Factory workers	Businessmen	Construction
City employees	Clerks	workers
Laborers	Professional	Salespeople
Barbers	people	White-collar
	Telephone	workers
	workers	Others

All persons must be between the ages of 20 and 50. High school and college students cannot be used.

- If you meet these qualifications, fill out the coupon below and mail it now to Professor Stanley Milgram, Department of Psychology, Yale University, New Haven. You will be notified later of the specific time and place of the study. We reserve the right to decline any application.

(Source: Milgram, 1974)

switch at the far left indicates that it is 15 volts; the next switch is 30, the next is 45, and so on all the way up to 450 volts. To add to your consternation, verbal labels appear beneath the voltage levels: from left to right they read "Slight Shock," "Moderate Shock," "Strong Shock," "Very Strong Shock," "Intense Shock," "Extreme Intensity Shock," and "Danger: Severe Shock." The final two switches are merely marked "XXX." The rest of the face of the shock generator is taken up by dials, lights, and meters that flicker whenever a switch is pulled.

The experimenter gives you a sample shock of 45 volts to give you an idea of the punishment magnitude (the shock seems fairly painful to you) and asks you to get started. Using a microphone to communicate with the Learner, you read over the list of pairs, and then begin "testing" his memory. Each time you read a word and the alternatives, the Learner indicates his response by pushing one of four numbered switches that are just within reach of his bound hand. His response lights up on your equipment, and as instructed, you deliver a shock when he is incorrect, increasing the voltage one step with each wrong answer. The session proceeds smoothly for a time, but slowly the shock level reaches an alarming intensity. Although you began with just a 15-volt jolt, each failure moves you closer and closer to XXX, 450 volts. You begin wondering what the mild-looking man in the next room is experiencing, and at the 300-volt level you hear a pounding on the wall as the Learner registers his protest at the shock. Turning to the experimenter you suggest that he check on the Learner, but the experimenter looks up from his desk and simply says "Please continue." "Well, one more shock," you think to yourself, "but if he pounds again. . . ." His next error brings a shock of 315 volts, but the pounding subsides. You read the next word, give the possible pair words, and wait for his answer. There is none. You wait, but still there is no answer. Glad that the experiment is over, you rise from your chair, but the experimenter surprises you by repeating "Please continue." When you point out that the Learner has stopped answering, he tells you to treat a failure to respond as a wrong answer and to continue the delivery of shock. You balk, but he says "The experiment requires that you continue." The Learner never again answers as you switch your way up to the maximum voltage level.

This scenario presents the basic paradigm used by Stanley Milgram to investigate obedience to an authority. Subjects were adults of varying occupations recruited from the surrounding community who were paid $4.50 for their participation. The situation, although extremely realistic from the subjects' perspective, was carefully contrived. The drawing for roles was rigged. The Learner was a confederate of the experimenter who in actuality received no shocks. The shock generator, with its elaborate row of switches, was a sham constructed by Milgram himself. The experimenter's off-hand remarks were actually part of a carefully developed and memorized script that was followed for each subject. The **prods** that the experimenter used when the subject expressed a desire to terminate were always given in the following prearranged order (Milgram, 1974, p. 21):

Prod 1: "Please continue" or "Please go on."
Prod 2: "The experiment requires that you continue."
Prod 3: "It is absolutely essential that you continue."
Prod 4: "You have no other choice; you *must* go on."

Each element of the situation had been carefully engineered to create a laboratory analog to a real-world obedience dilemma. The experimenter, while making no claim to special expertise, acted with self-assurance and poise. He gave orders crisply, as if he never questioned the correctness of his own actions, and he seemed surprised that the Teacher would try to terminate the shock sequence. He possessed a good deal of legitimate power, for he was the experimenter in a scientific research project conducted at a prestigious university, and no doubt impressed the subjects as an expert researcher. Yet from the participants' point of view, this legitimate authority was requiring them to act in a way that might be harmful to another person. Although by accepting the $4.50 payment they had implicitly agreed to carry out the experimenter's instructions, they were torn between this duty and their desire to protect the Learner from possible harm. Milgram designed his experiment to determine which side would win this conflict.

THE FINDINGS

Although Milgram realized that his subjects would find the obedience conflict a challenge to their loyalties, he believed that very few would deliver shocks past the 300-volt level. While the experimenter was an authority, the failure of the Learner to respond could only mean that he wished to quit or was seriously hurt, so Milgram felt confident that most people would break off the shocks when the pounding on the wall began. (In fact, Milgram polled a number of psychological researchers and psychiatrists on the subject, and their predictions are summarized by the line in Figure 7-1 marked "Psychologists' predictions." None of these 39 "experts" felt that subjects would shock to the 450-volt level; they predicted most would quit at the 150-volt level). His expectations, however, proved incorrect. Of the 40 individuals who served as Teachers in the experiment, 26 administered the full 450 volts to the helpless Learner. None broke off before the 300-volt level, and several of the eventually disobedient subjects gave one or two additional shocks before finally refusing to yield to the experimenter's prods. The comments made by the subjects during the shock procedure and their obvious psychological distress revealed that they were unwilling to go on but felt unable to resist the experimenter's demands for obedience.

Over a period of several years Milgram studied the responses of nearly 1000 people in a series of replications and extensions of his original study. In these later researches, some of which are discussed below, different aspects of the setting were systematically manipulated, allowing Milgram to assess their influence on obedience rates. Although he continued to search for the limits of obedience, again and again his subjects buckled under the pressure of the experimenter's power.

Proximity of the "victim."   Reasoning that the high rate of obedience observed in the original study could have occurred because the Teacher heard only an ambiguous pounding coming from the other room, Milgram ran three additional conditions that varied the number of cues concerning the Learner's suffering:

1. *Voice-feedback:* Complaints from the Learner could be heard through the walls. He grunted when shocked at levels below 120 volts, and at that point

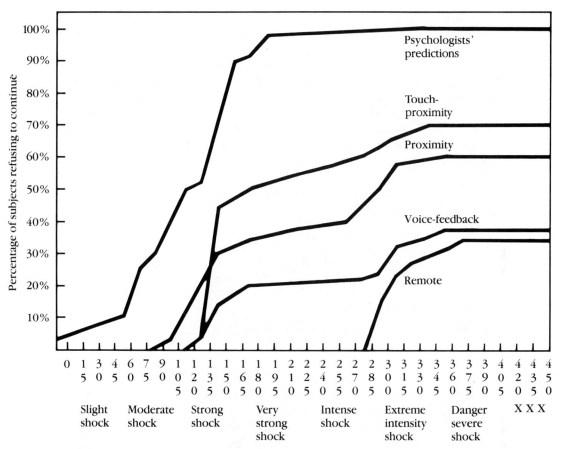

FIGURE 7-1. Obedience rates in several conditions of the Milgram studies. (Source: Milgram, 1974)

began to complain about the pain. At 150 volts he cried out "Experimenter, get me out of here! I won't be in the experiment any more! I refuse to go on!" (Milgram, 1974, p. 23). He continued screaming and demanding release until the 300-volt level, when he refused to answer any more questions.

2. *Proximity:* The Learner sat in the same room as the Teacher, voicing the same complaints used in the voice-feedback condition.

3. *Touch-proximity:* The Learner could only be shocked if he put his hand on a shock plate, and he refused to do so once the shocks reached the 150-volt level. At this point, the experimenter ordered the subject to hold the Learner's hand down on the plate while giving the shocks (the Teacher was protected from the shock).

The results of these three conditions are presented in Figure 7-1, along with the obedience rates from the original condition (the *"remote"* condition). Obedience declined as the proximity of the "victim" increased, dropping down from 65% obedience in the remote condition, to 62.5% in the voice-feedback condition, to 40% in the proximity condition, and to 30% in the touch-proximity condition.

Limiting the experimenter's power.   To examine the sources of the experimenter's surprisingly forceful power, Milgram manipulated the experimenter's surveillance capabilities, prestige, expertise, and legitimacy. In one variation, the situation (as in most of the later studies) was nearly identical to the voice-feedback condition, except that the experimenter left the room after going over the instructions. He continued giving orders by telephone, but when the experimenter could not maintain visual surveillance, only 20% of the participants were obedient (that is, they shocked to the 450-volt level). In fact, many subjects assured the experimenter that they were administering increasingly large shocks with each mistake when they were actually only delivering 15 volts.

To remove another source of power that derived from the link between the study and prestigious Yale University, Milgram moved the research to an office building located in downtown Bridgeport:

> The experiments were conducted in a three-room office suite in a somewhat rundown commercial building located in the downtown shopping area. The laboratory was sparsely furnished, though clean, and marginally respectable in appearance. When subjects inquired about professional affiliations, they were informed only that we were a private firm conducting research for industry [Milgram, 1974, pp. 68–69].

With the prestige component of the experimenter's authority eliminated, obedience dropped to 48%—still a surprisingly large figure given the questionable research setting.

Focusing on the experimenter's legitimate power, Milgram added a second confederate, who was to record information at what had formerly been the experimenter's desk. The experimenter explained the study as in other conditions, but gave no instructions about shock levels before being called away. The confederate, however, filled the role of the authority; he suggested that shocks be given in increasingly strong doses and ordered the subject to continue giving shocks when the Learner started to complain. In this instance obedience dropped to 20%, but when the accomplice began giving shocks at the point the subject had refused to continue, very few subjects were willing to intervene. The majority (68.75%) simply stood by and watched as their fellow subject enthusiastically "electrocuted" the screaming Learner.

Lastly, in a particularly creative episode the experimenter agreed to take the role of the Learner to supposedly convince a reluctant subject that the shocks weren't harmful. However, after the experimenter made a mistake and received a 150-volt shock he shouted "That's enough gentlemen." However the confederate—who had been watching the procedure—gleefully insisted "Oh, no, let's go on. Oh, no, come on, I'm going to have to go through the whole thing. Let's go. Come on, let's keep going" (Milgram, 1974, p. 102). Although the confederate demanded continuation, in all cases the subject released the experimenter; obedience to the ordinary person's command to harm the authority was nil.

Group effects.   Milgram also demonstrated some interesting effects of other group members' behaviors on subjects' obedience. In one variation the subject merely recorded information and performed other ancillary tasks while an accomplice actually pulled the shock switches. In this variation 92.5% obediently fulfilled their tasks without intervening. If, however, the accomplice refused to administer shocks and the experimenter required the subject to take over, only 10% of the subjects were maximally obedient. Also, if two experimenters ran the research but one demanded continued shocking while another argued for stopping the shocks, all subjects obeyed the commands of the benevolent authority.

Similar findings were obtained in an obedience study conducted with Australian college students (Kilham & Mann, 1974). Because the researchers assumed that in many cases orders are passed down from superiors to subordinates through the "chain of command," the basic Milgram-type experiment was modified to include the roles of "transmitter," who relayed orders, and "executant," who actually delivered the shocks. As predicted, transmitters were more obedient than executants (54% vs. 28%). In addition, males were more obedient than females, but other studies have found either no differences between men and women (Milgram, 1974) or heightened obedience among women (Sheridan & King, 1972).

EXPLAINING OBEDIENCE

The obedience observed in Milgram's studies has been interpreted in a variety of ways. According to one explanation, the subjects were irritated by the Learner's slow progress and therefore punished him for his failure. This possibility, which is consistent with frustration/aggression theory (Berkowitz, 1962; see Chapter 4), points to the frustration of the Teacher caught between a demanding experimenter, a dim-witted Learner, and an aggression-eliciting shock machine. Yet the extreme reluctance evidenced by nearly all the subjects during the procedure suggests that their actions were not motivated by a desire to inflict pain. As Milgram reports,

> many subjects showed signs of nervousness in the experimental situation, and especially upon administering the more powerful shocks. In a large number of cases the degree of tension reached extremes that are rarely seen in sociopsychological laboratory studies. Subjects were observed to sweat, tremble, stutter, bite their lips, groan, and dig their fingernails into their flesh [1963, p. 375].

Indeed, the distress of the subjects was so great that the publication of the study sparked a controversy over the ethics of social-psychological research (Baumrind, 1964; Forsyth, 1981; Milgram, 1964, 1977; Schlenker & Forsyth, 1977).

An alternative explanation focuses on the characteristics of the subjects themselves. Just as many people, when first hearing of the Guyana tragedy, wondered "What strange people they must have been to be willing to kill themselves," when people are told about Milgram's findings they react with the question "What kind of evil, sadistic men did he recruit for his study?" Indeed, research has shown that people tend to blame the subjects for their obedience, attributing their actions to their personal characteristics rather than acknowledging the powerful situational forces at work in the experimental situation (Ross, 1977; Safer, 1980). Furthermore, when asked if they would have obeyed in the same circumstances, most people claim they would have stopped at around the 150-volt level. None of the individuals polled answered that they would actually deliver 450-volt shocks (Milgram, 1974), although research suggests otherwise (see box on page 191).

Milgram, as might be anticipated, rejects both these explanations. He believes that his results stem from the unique power of the researcher in a scientific investigation. The control of the experimenter has been demonstrated in other studies, in which, in response to the researcher's demands, subjects have obediently chopped off the heads of live rats with a butcher knife (Landis, 1924), chewed up fried grasshoppers (Zimbardo et al., 1965), swallowed foul-tasking liquids (Riess et al., 1977), eaten vast quantities of soda crackers (Frank, 1944), immersed their hands in what they believed to be acid (Orne & Evans, 1965), and listened to sounds that were supposedly so high in frequency that their hearing would be destroyed (Martin et al., 1976). Although a researcher's position is weak in terms of both reward and coercive power, the legitimate, referent and expert bases are all well established. When subjects agree to take part in a study, they become part of a social hierarchy. They no longer act in an autonomous state where they fulfill their own purposes and goals, but rather are in what Milgram calls the **agentic state**—that is, they become agents of a higher authority (Milgram, 1974). In the obedience research their role as Teacher requires them to pay attention to instructions, carefully monitor their own actions, and try to carry out the orders of the authority. Although they may question the punishment of the Learner, they tend to accept the authority's definition of the situation as a nonharmful one. Also, they feel little responsibility for what is happening to the Learner, since they are only following orders. Disobedience, if it comes, arises only when the effects of obedience become so negative that inner beliefs about the value of human life overwhelm the external pressures of the situation. In the agentic state obedience is easy; disobedience, in contrast, is achieved only with great difficulty and at a considerable psychological cost (Milgram, 1974; see Silver & Geller, 1978).

CONCLUSIONS ABOUT OBEDIENCE

A number of sources, reacting to the seemingly pessimistic implications of Milgram's findings, have argued that the laboratory groups he investigated were unique and that obedience to an experimenter's demands bears little similarity to "real" obedience as it occurs in naturally occurring groups (Orne & Holland, 1968; Patten, 1977). Milgram, however, believes that in any instance of obedience to a malevolent authority—such as the Nazi campaign to exterminate the Jews, the My Lai episode in the Vietnam War, or the kamikaze suicides of World War II—the same processes he observed in his laboratory are at work. In the case of Jonestown, the members were used to following the orders of an absolute authority; they had reached an agentic state. They had no responsibility for their own destiny, and looked to Jones for definitions and order. He emphasized loyalty and self-discipline and extolled the virtues of death for a noble cause. Eventually, when he called for the "ultimate sacrifice" his followers could only obey.

Coalition Formation

When a family joined Jones's congregation, Jones went to great lengths to break down the unity of this small group. First, he discouraged conversation among family members. Second, he prohibited sex between the husband and wife. Third, he encouraged all the family members to inform on one another if any untoward behaviors were observed. Apparently he was worried that, if left intact, the family

WATERGATE AND OBEDIENCE: THE PEOPLE OR THE SITUATION?

Researchers have recently suggested that the tendency for people to react to news of major political/criminal activities—for example, the Watergate crimes, the blind obedience of the Nazis, or the taking of hostages in Iran—by blaming the morality of those involved may reveal actor/observer differences at work (West, Gunn, & Chernicky, 1975). Although dispositional factors are no doubt involved in these types of events, observers often overestimate their causal role whereas actors, in turn, argue that factors in the environment were the major determinants of their fate.

To test this idea Stephen West and his colleagues set up their own "Watergate" break-in by contacting students in criminology classes and asking them to burglarize a local office building. The experimenter was known by all those contacted to be a private detective, and he presented an elaborate plan backed up by aerial photographs, maps of police routes, blueprints, and so on. However, before people were asked to join the team, four different experimental conditions were established:

1. *Immunity*: the burglary was sponsored by a government agency (the IRS) to acquire tax records; if caught, the "agents" would receive immunity from prosecution.

2. *No immunity*: the project was sponsored by the IRS, but immunity could not be guaranteed.

3. *Reward*: participants were told that a rival company would pay to get information from the target company's safe; the subject's share would be $2000.

4. *Control*: subjects were told the burglary would just be a test to see if the plan would work.

As the graph shows, far more subjects agreed to participate in the immunity condition than in the other three, but the subjects' explanations for their agreement to participate are of particular interest. In a second phase of the project the researchers asked those who had complied to give a reason for their decision, and compared these responses to the reasons given by observers who had read a full description of the procedures. As the actor/observer difference would suggest, actors emphasized environmental causes (for example, "The private investigator put pressure on me") more than observers, whereas observers favored dispositional causes (for example, "He seemed to be the kind of person who doesn't care about honesty") more than actors.

(Source: West, Gunn, and Chernicky, 1975)

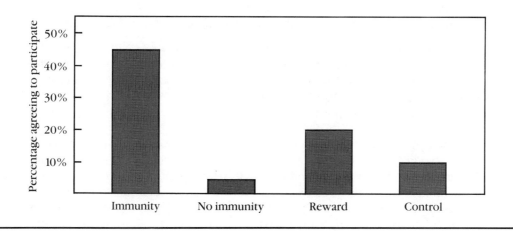

groups would increase their members' resistance to his persuasive efforts; he may have intuitively recognized that several people acting in concert possess more power than people acting as individuals.

A subgroup of individuals within a larger group, such as a family in the People's Temple, is a **coalition.** In most common, everyday groups many coalitions exist, but from a power perspective they become more important during a crisis situation such as a breakdown in group norms, the loss of a group member, a shift in authority, or a disagreement over a key decision. Although an absolute authority could intervene and resolve the crisis, in most groups none of the participants have the dictatorial powers necessary to mandate a solution. Therefore, two or more group members attempt to determine the group's outcome by forming an alliance, which—taken as a whole—has enough power to determine the group's course of action. Although they form for various reasons and may therefore embrace many varied characteristics, most coalitions exhibit the following qualities:

1. They involve participants who disagree on many fundamental issues but decide to ignore these differences until the problem at hand can be settled. As in politics where certain coalitions involve "strange bedfellows," coalitions in small groups sometimes involve the unlikeliest of allies (Murnighan, 1978).

2. They form to facilitate the attainment of certain goals or the achievement of specific outcomes. For a time the members of the subgroup all share a common goal and stand to profit more by forming a coalition rather than remaining independent (Caplow, 1956).

3. They tend to be only temporary liaisons, since members may abandon one alliance to form more profitable ones. Furthermore, once the goals of the coalition are accomplished, the participants' differences again become evident, making cooperation more difficult (Gamson, 1964).

4. They occur in mixed-motive situations. Although allies may wish to compete with one another, no single individual has enough power to succeed alone. Hence, while the coalition exists the competitive motive must be stifled (Gamson, 1964).

5. They involve an adversarial element. Individuals in the coalition work not only to ensure their own outcomes, but also to worsen the outcomes of noncoalition members. Coalitions form between people and against other people, as Thibaut and Kelley (1959, p. 205) point out: "By coalition we mean two or more persons who act jointly to affect the outcomes of one or more other persons."

Because coalitions can cause long-lasting alterations in the group's power structure, we will examine the nature of coalition formation by (1) reviewing the general conclusions of empirical studies of alliances within groups and (2) comparing three of the more prominent theoretical explanations of coalition formation.

EXPERIMENTAL EVIDENCE

Many social-psychological studies of coalition formation have used a "convention" or "legislative" role-play paradigm. Groups of three or more subjects are assembled in the laboratory and told they will be forming coalitions in order to win some points. After the concept of a coalition is defined, *resources* are allocated to each member. As defined by coalition researcher William Gamson, resources are "weights controlled by the participants such that some critical quantity of these weights is necessary and sufficient to determine the decision" [1964, p. 82]. For example, in one study of four-person groups (Murnighan, Komorita, & Szwajkowski, 1977) 17 votes were distributed unevenly among group members; one person was given 8 votes, another 7, and the remaining two people received 1 vote each. Although this distribution seemed to give the person with 8 a considerable edge, a majority of the votes—at least 9—was required to earn the *payoff* (100 points that could be converted to money at the end of the experiment). This procedure might be termed a 9(8–7–1–1) game, where 9 is the number of votes needed to win and 8–7–1–1 is the allocation of resources to the four people in the group. In this situation four winning coalitions are possible: 8–7, 7–1–1, 8–1, and 8–1.

Since none of the members of the group have enough power (votes) to win by themselves, the researcher invites them to contact one another to try to form a coalition. Although the mode of communication varies from study to study, subjects typically either pass written messages, make suggestions to the researcher, or bargain in face-to-face interactions. In most cases, the experiment involves a series of trials in which subjects offer to join with others in a coalition while simultaneously suggesting that the payoff be divided in a particular way. These coalition and payoff negotiations are repeated on each trial, and this paradigm therefore contains two basic dependent variables: the type of coalition formed (for example, 8–7 or 7–1–1) and the manner in which the payoff is distributed. (As an example of the latter variable, when an 8–1 coalition forms, does the person with 8 votes get 85% of the prize while the person with 1 vote gets only 15%?) The following subsections describe the conclusions drawn from detailed reviews of these types of studies (Baker, 1981; Gamson, 1964; Miller & Crandall, 1980; Murnighan, 1978).

Minimum-size effect.   The basic concept of coalition formation—that subgroups will form in a group when no single individual has sufficient resources to break the group's deadlock—has been supported in most studies (Komorita & Meek, 1978; Murnighan, 1978). However, in most instances these coalitions only contain members who are absolutely necessary for victory; in other words, winning coalitions involve only the minimum number of individuals necessary to win with all superfluous parties being excluded from the subgroup. For example, in the 9(8–7–1–1) situation, a friendly coalition of 8–1–1 is very unlikely, since the 8–1 coalition alone is sufficient for success. Although a fair conclusion based on laboratory findings, the minimum-size effect may not apply to political coalitions (see the box on political coalitions).

Three (or more) is a crowd.   Georg Simmel (1950) long ago pointed out that a coalition of two tends to be more stable and more cohesive than a coalition of three or more. The dyad always involves a one-to-one confrontation, and emotions, information, and decisions can be exchanged more rapidly and accurately when only two people are involved. Larger coalitions, in contrast, must develop more complex structures to exchange information adequately, and the multiparty structure means that coalitions can be formed within the coalition! Therefore, confidence and trust among participants in large coalitions are almost always more

---

POLITICAL COALITIONS: MINIMUM WINNING COALITIONS OR OVERWHELMING MAJORITIES?

Although the minimum-size effect has received ample support in the laboratory, studies of coalitions in multiparty parliamentary governments suggest that political coalitions tend to be larger than necessary—ranging all the way up to "overwhelming majorities" that include nearly all the parties in the country (Riker, 1962). Some researchers believe that large coalitions tend to appear after wartime, as if an attempt is being made to overlook differences of opinion and present a unified front. However, given that peacetime coalitions tend to involve more than the minimum number of factions needed to win elections, others argue that large political coalitions ensure that the controlling group can get its legislative programs passed easily (Nachmias, 1974).

---

uncertain. Supporting Simmel's prediction, research indicates that in many instances two-person coalitions are preferred over larger alliances (Shears, 1967; Komorita & Meek, 1978), but that this preference may stem from the laboratory technique of guaranteeing the winning coalition a standard payoff irrespective of the margin of "victory" (Kravitz, 1981).

Weakness is strength.   Available evidence also suggests that individuals with *fewer* resources are often preferred partners in winning coalitions. Although people whose resources are so minimal that they are no help in achieving success are rarely chosen for coalition membership, the person who has just enough to tip the coalition's total resources over the top is typically the most popular partner (Caplow, 1968). This finding is consistent with most of the major theories of coalitions, and probably stems from several factors. First, the weaker individual may be more likely to realize that success can be attained only through a coalition with others who are more powerful. Second, stronger individuals tend to find weaker individuals more attractive partners since they hope weaker persons—realizing that they add only a small fraction to the coalition's total resources—will be satisfied with only a fraction of the payoff. Third, a coalition with a weak partner is likely to be more stable than one with a stronger person, who may be tempted to form a coalition with an alternative partner.

Strength is weakness.   Given the hypothesis that "weakness is strength," it also stands to reason that strength will be a weakness. Study after study has demonstrated that the individual with the greatest resources and power tends to be more frequently excluded from coalitions than weaker, less well off members (Gamson, 1964; Murnighan, 1978). This seemingly paradoxical effect makes sense for several reasons. First, those with few resources tend to avoid powerful partners because (1) their relatively large contributions to the coalition's resources entitles them to a bigger piece of the payoff pie and (2) they may attempt to manipulate or exploit members of the coalition who possess fewer resources. Second, those with large resources frequently fail to realize that they need to join a coalition. Although their power exists only so long as the others don't unite against them, powerful persons often mistakenly believe their power base to be safe and incontrovertible. The strong group member who loses out to a coalition of two weaker members often complains of the "unfairness" of the others.

Sex differences.   Although most studies of coalition formation have examined the behaviors of groups of males, investigations of groups containing females typically find evidence of sex differences in coalition behaviors. As previous summaries of these differences have noted (Miller & Crandall, 1980; Vinacke, 1971), relative to males, females tend to violate the minimum-size rule more frequently, prefer to divide up payoffs equally rather than in proportion to inputs, are less likely to exclude the powerful person from the coalition, and more often refrain from taking full advantage of the weakness of others. In explaining these differences, Gamson (1964) proposed that women tend to adopt an *anticompetitive norm* in coalition situations. While males readily accept the situation as a mixed-motive problem that calls for competition with and exploitation of those who are excluded from the coalition, females tend to coordinate their behavior with the needs of the rest of the group. Therefore, females strive to maintain smooth intermember relations, while males try to maximize their payoffs. Although any group could adopt an anticompetitive norm, female groups seem to accept this norm more readily than all male groups.

THEORIES OF COALITION FORMATION

Consider for a moment the choice you might make if placed in a coalition-formation study. Assuming that the researcher has adopted a three-person game 9(8–7–2) and that you are the 2, would you seek an alliance with 8 or 9? If both indicated that they would accept you in a coalition, who would you side with? How would you react if, after forming a liaison with 7, you discovered that he or she is only willing to give you 20% of the payoff? Would you abandon the alliance and join 8? How would you feel if 7 and 8 formed a coalition, leaving you with no payoff at all? How would you go about breaking up their alliance and forming one of your own?

To understand more fully how most people answer such questions researchers have developed theoretical models to explain when and why certain types of coalitions are likely to form. We must limit our coverage owing to the wealth of such theories (Murnighan's 1978 review mentions 14!) and therefore refrain from discussing several excellent models drawn from game theory, social psychology, and political science. Still, the following brief overview of three perspectives—minimum-resource theory, minimum-power theory, and bargaining theory—will help convey the general direction of theory and research in this important area.

Minimum-resource theory.   Gamson's minimum-resource theory (1961a, 1961b, 1964) is based on two fundamental assumptions. The first is simply that people in group situations will behave hedonistically and will thus be motivated to maximize their power, outcomes, and payoffs by forming coalitions. The second assumption predicts that individuals' expectations concerning the division of the coalition's payoff will conform to a **parity norm:** confreres expect their outcomes to be proportional to their inputs. For example, the parity norm (also called the equity norm) suggests that a person with 20% of the votes in a coalition will anticipate receiving only 20% of the payoff that the coalition earns by succeeding, whereas the individual with 80% of the resources will expect 80% of the payoff.

With these two assumptions in mind, consider the possible coalitions in our 9(8–7–2) triad. As Table 7-3 shows, a coalition between any two group members will be sufficient to win the payoff. However, if the payoff is divided according to a parity norm, only *one* of the three possible coalitions yields comparatively higher payoffs for two of the group members—the 2–7 combination. Therefore, the theory predicts that this coalition is the most likely one to form, because both 7 and 2 should prefer this alliance to one with person 8. Indeed, this coalition is what Gamson calls the *cheapest winning solution*—it reaches the decision point (9 votes), but does so by the smallest margin possible. This approach is called **minimum-resource theory,** since it predicts the most likely coalition to be the grouping that is sufficient to win but involves partners with the fewest resources. (A similar theoretical position, first suggested by Theodore Caplow [1956, 1968] proposed that individuals in a group will form coalitions that maximize their control over the remaining group members. However, because Caplow felt that power typically derives from control over resources, his approach makes predictions that are for the most part identical with those of minimum-resource theory.)

Minimum-power theory.   This theory synthesizes Gamson's resource theory and a mathematical model derived from game theory (Shapley, 1953). The theory begins by suggesting that prior resources are an inadequate indication of a person's power in a coalition situation. In the example triad—9 (8–7–2)—any one of the three members possesses the power to turn a losing coalition into a winning one when a two-person liaison is formed. Even the lowly 2, who controls just 12% of the total resources, can still significantly determine the outcome by joining with one of the other group members in a coalition. In a sense, all three individuals have equal power, even though their resources differ.

Because the minimal-power theory is based on the concept of individuals' power rather than resources, to make it a viable approach we need a systematic way of calculating the power of each group member. To solve this problem, theorists typically focus on **pivotal power:** the power of an individual to turn a winning coalition into a losing one or a losing coalition into a winning one. Individuals have a great deal of pivotal power if (1) by joining a coalition they can increase the total payoff of the clique or (2) by leaving a coalition they can significantly decrease the total payoff of the clique (Miller, 1980a). One can easily estimate the pivotal power of each person by calculating the number of times a person can change a

TABLE 7-3. Parity norm payoffs predicted by minimum-resource theory in a 9(8–7–2) coalition situation

Coalition	Total votes	Payoff to 2	Payoff to 7	Payoff to 8
7–8	15	0	7/15	8/15
2–8	10	2/10	0	8/10
2–7	9	2/9	7/9	0

winning coalition into a losing one by withdrawing, and then dividing this number by the total number of possible coalitions. In the simple example of three persons (2, 7, and 8 votes), we find that all three are equal in terms of pivotal power; there are only three possible coalitions and in each one both partners are pivotal—completely necessary for the success of the coalition (Murnighan et al., 1977). Hence, all three have a pivotal power of 2/3, or .66.

Minimum-power theory also assumes that the parity norm determines payoff allocations, but predicts that the payoff will be in proportion to pivotal power. Thus, the theory predicts the most likely coalition to form is one that wins but contains individuals with the smallest amounts of pivotal power. Forming a liaison with a person who commands a great deal of pivotal power makes little sense, since the parity norm suggests a powerful person will expect, and deserve, a greater payoff than coalition members with little pivotal power.

Bargaining theory. By assuming that group members negotiate with one another while deciding which coalition to join, S. S. Komorita and his colleagues (Komorita & Chertkoff, 1973; Komorita & Meek, 1978) developed an explanation of coalition formation that emphasizes the importance of bargaining, concessions, objections, and threats. As applied to our example triad, the approach assumes that 2, 7, and 8, before beginning negotiations, calculate the payoffs of each possible liaison. For example, person 8, in considering a coalition with 7, could expect to receive 53% of the payoff, but by joining with 2 this payoff could be increased to 80% (see Table 7-4). This expectation, however, is based solely on the parity norm, and bargaining theory suggests that 8 will also estimate payoffs by using an equality norm—equal payoffs to all coalition members irrespective of input or power. Hence, 8 also thinks that a link with either 2 or 7 will yield 50% of the payoffs, if rewards are apportioned based on an equality norm. Although 8 would prefer that rewards be allocated based on the parity norm—since in each case this norm yields a higher payoff—he or she realizes that the actual distribution will fall somewhere in between these two expectations. As shown in Table 7-4, 8's expectation for the 7–8 coalition falls between 50% and 53%, with the 2–8 coalition expectations ranging from 50% to 80%.

On the basis of these mental calculations, 8 will probably prefer a coalition with 2, since such a subgrouping will yield a payoff that most closely approximates that desired (based on averaging the payoffs suggested by the parity and equality norms). Person 8 may, however, be able to negotiate with 7 and 2 to increase his

TABLE 7-4. **Payoff expectations predicted by bargaining theory in a 9(8–7–2) coalition situation**

Individual	Coalition	Parity	Equality	Average expectation
8	7–8	8/15 (53%)	1/2 (50%)	31/60 (51.5%)
	2–8	8/10 (80%)	1/2 (50%)	13/20 (65%)
7	7–8	7/15 (47%)	1/2 (50%)	29/60 (48.5%)
	2–7	7/9 (78%)	1/2 (50%)	23/36 (64%)
2	2–8	2/10 (20%)	1/2 (50%)	7/20 (35%)
	2–7	2/9 (22%)	1/2 (50%)	13/35 (36%)

or her payoff. Although 2, as the individual with the weakest position in terms of resources, will probably "demand" that the payoff be distributed on the basis of equality, 8 may note that unless 2 agrees to a parity distribution he or she will be left out of the coalition and therefore receive no payoff whatsoever. Using this threat, 8 may successfully extract a promise of high rewards if a coalition is formed with 2 rather than with 7.

Komorita's theory is also unique in its consideration of the importance of forming a liaison with a person who won't be tempted to break off the coalition and defect to the "other side." For example, if 2 decides to form a coalition with 7, since 7 promises to divide the payoff on a 65–35% basis, 8 will probably try to talk 2 into leaving the 7–2 coalition. As time goes on, 8 may be willing to make certain concessions to 2 so that 2's payoffs begin to more closely approximate their original expectations as based on the equality norm (50%). According to Komorita, the possibility of later bargaining and concession making suggests that (1) people will prefer to join with others who, because of the resource distribution, will not be tempted to defect, and (2) over a long period of time (or trials), payoff distributions may change as members of the coalition must increase the rewards given to those members who are being tempted away from the subgroup. Thus, bargaining theory, unlike the other two approaches, explains changes that might take place in payoff allocations.

EMPIRICAL TESTS OF THE THEORIES

A *crucial experiment* is one of the most exciting and informative types of studies in any scientific field. In such an experiment, the researcher carefully sets up the conditions in which the hypotheses of two or more rival theories can be compared in the hope of determining which model is more adequate. Although for a number of empirical, logical, and philosophical reasons no experiment can be truly "crucial" (Forsyth, 1976), studies that test the predictions of several theories at once can nevertheless be dramatic in the amount of information they yield.

In the area of coalition behaviors, several recent studies have compared predictions derived from the more prominent coalition theories to determine which can best stand the test (Komorita & Meek, 1978; Komorita & Moore, 1976; Miller, 1980a, 1980b, 1980c; Murnighan et al., 1977). For example, in one project (Komorita & Moore, 1976) four-person groups were instructed to choose others as partners in order to achieve a winning coalition. The resources were allocated on a 10–9–8–3 basis, and a two-thirds majority (20 votes) was needed to win. Hence, only three-party coalitions could successfully win the prize of 100 points, which was to be converted into money at the end of the experiment.

TABLE 7-5. A test of three theories of coalition formation in a 20(10–9–8–3) resource situation

Theory	Predicted coalition	Predicted division of payoff
Minimum resource	9–8–3	45–40–15
Minimum power	Any	33–33–33
Bargaining (first trial)	9–8–3	39–37–24
Bargaining (final trial)	9–8–3	36–34–30

The predictions of the three theories—minimum resource, minimum power, and bargaining—are presented in Table 7-5. First, minimum-resource theory assumes that (1) the person with 10 votes will be left out of the coalition, since the subgroup can succeed with just the 9-vote individual; and (2) payoffs based on the parity norm will be 9/20 (45 points), 8/20 (40 points), and 3/20 (15 points). Second, minimum-power theory considers all four possible coalitions to be equally likely, since all the individuals have the same amount of pivotal power. Since power is equal, payoffs should also be equal—33 points for everyone. Third, bargaining theory predicts a 9–8–3 coalition, but that payoff allocations will change over time. On the first trial the payoff distribution should represent the average of a parity norm and an equality norm (for example, for the person with 9 votes the parity norm suggests a 45-point payoff, but the equality norm recommends 33 points. The average of these two payoffs is 39 points). By the end of the study, however, payoffs to the weaker members should gradually increase, as the high-resource members must bargain with the low-resource members to keep them in the coalition.

The results of the study are quite complex, but in general they seem to lend the most support to bargaining theory. On the first trial, the 9–8–3 coalition occurred most frequently (9 out of 20 times), but this tendency was not statistically significant. Although this "no difference" is consistent with minimum-power-theory hypotheses, the reward allocations in these 9–8–3 coalitions averaged 40–37–23—an almost perfect match of the bargaining-theory predictions. Furthermore, by the end of all the trials the tendency to form the 9–8–3 coalition was highly significant, and the distribution of payoff points had gradually changed to again match the overall prediction of bargaining theory: although the final distribution of 34–35–31 could have been predicted by either bargaining or minimum-power theory, the minimum-resources theory prediction of 45–40–15 seems to be fairly inaccurate.

Despite these findings favorable to bargaining theory, other studies conducted using different payoff strategies and different resource allocations have lent support to other theories. Indeed, as Gamson (1964, p. 92) pointed out in his review, the varying results of the many empirical investigations seem to support just one theory: the utter-confusion theory. However, as research efforts continue, the various strengths and weaknesses of the theories are becoming better known. Undoubtedly at some point in the future our theoretical explanations of coalition formation will become more unified.

The Metamorphic Effects of Power

In 1976 Jim Jones fought for the improvement of housing and progressive political change in the San Francisco area, and his followers worked diligently toward the goals outlined by their leader. In 1978 Jones was accused of human-rights violations, physical assault, and illicit sexual practices while many of his followers labored in the fields in Guyana. In this short period of time, Jones's power had reached dramatic levels, but with this power came strange changes in his behavior and perceptions. Were these changes in Jones unique, or were they evidence of the metamorphic effects of power?

Changes in the Powerholder

As David Kipnis has pointed out, the influence of power on the powerholder has been described and discussed in philosophical, historical, and dramatic works through the ages (Kipnis, 1974). In their tragedies the Greeks often dramatized the fall of heroes who, swollen by past accomplishments, conceitedly compared themselves to the gods. Greek myth is replete with tales of temptations to seek too much power—as in the case of Icarus, whose elation at the power of flight caused his death. In our own century we find examples of political thinkers who, like Jim Jones, began their careers envisioning utopian societies, but became cruel and inhuman dictators when they achieved positions of power. The impact of gaining power seems to be aptly summarized by Lord Acton's maxim "Power tends to corrupt, and absolute power corrupts absolutely."

But what are some of the consequences of power acquisition that have been corroborated through scientific research? To begin at the most fundamental level, researchers have found that people who are delegated power in experimental situations tend to use their power to control others. For example, Kipnis (1972) arranged for advanced business students to participate as managers in a simulated manufacturing company after telling them that their performances would be good indicators of their leadership potential in other executive situations. In one condition the subjects were given a good deal of reward and coercive power over their subordinates; they could award bonuses, cut pay, threaten and actually carry out transfers to other jobs, give additional instructions, or even fire a worker. The subjects in the second condition could only use persuasion or extra instructions to influence their subordinates.

The procedure was designed such that the managers could not actually see their workers, but were kept informed of their production levels by an assistant who brought in the finished products from the four workers. This arrangement was chosen so that Kipnis could carefully control the level of productivity of the fictitious workers (all performed adequately) and also provide a reason for the use of an intercom system in giving orders to subordinates. These communications were surreptitiously recorded, and subsequent analyses revealed that the powerful managers initiated roughly twice as many attempts at influence as the nonpowerful managers and that the difference between the two types of managers became more apparent as the sessions progressed. In addition, the powerful and nonpowerful employed different power tactics: the powerless managers relied on persuasion whereas the powerful managers coerced or rewarded their workers. Other studies have yielded similar support for the idea that people with power tend to make use of it (for example, Deutsch, 1973; Kipnis & Consentino, 1969), but also suggest that the magnitude of this effect depends on many other factors (Bedell & Sistrunk, 1973; Black & Higbee, 1973; Goodstadt & Hjelle, 1973).

Once power has been used to influence others, changes in powerholders' perceptions of themselves and the target of influence may also take place. For example, several sources suggest that the successful use of power as a means of controlling others invariably leads to self-satisfaction, unrealistically positive self-evaluations, and overestimations of interpersonal power (Kipnis, 1974; Raven & Kruglanski, 1970; Sorokin & Lundin, 1959). For example, in the Kipnis simulation described above subjects were asked if their subordinates performed well because of the workers' high self-motivation levels, their manager's comments and suggestions, or their desire for money. Analyses showed that the high-power managers felt their workers were only in it for the money (which the manager could control), while the low-power managers felt that the workers were "highly motivated." In fact, in the powerful-manager condition the correlation between number of messages sent to the workers and agreement with the statement "my orders and influence caused the workers to perform effectively" was quite strong ($r = .65$, Kipnis, 1974). Other studies have also revealed this tendency for powerful individuals to assume that they themselves are the prime cause of other people's behavior (Kipnis, Castell, Gergen, & Mauch, 1976).

Devaluation of the target of the influence attempt also tends to covary with increased feelings of control over people. In a classic study of power dynamics in a mental hospital, Alvin Zander and his colleagues (Zander, Cohen, & Stotland, 1959) found that psychiatrists tended to underestimate the abilities of the psychologists they supervised. Although the psychologists believed themselves to be capable of developing diagnoses and conducting therapy, the psychiatrists considered them qualified only to conduct psychological testing. This study and others (Kipnis, 1972; Sampson, 1965; Strickland, 1958; Strickland, Barefoot, & Hockenstein, 1976) also suggest that powerholders tend to (1) increase the social distance between themselves and the nonpowerful, (2) believe that the nonpowerful are untrustworthy and in need of close supervision, and (3) devalue the work and ability of the less powerful. This tendency to derogate the target person while simultaneously evaluating oneself more positively works to widen the gap between group members who have varying degrees of power (see box on page 202).

In some cases powerholders' inflated views of their power and control over the group can tempt them into overstepping the bounds of their authority. For example, in 1937 Roosevelt was elected president of the United States by an overwhelming majority and subsequently went about increasing the powers of the presidency beyond those specified in the U. S. Constitution. This reaction to increased power brought on by overwhelming support from the group has been labeled the **mandate phenomenon** (Clark & Sechrest, 1976), and has been experimentally verified in small groups. Male college students were told that they would be working on a learning task while being exposed to a nauseating smell. The researchers explained that various odors were used in the research, ranging from ones that cause nausea in 10% of the population to ones that cause nausea in 90% of the population. Groups were instructed to elect a leader who was to pick the smell the group would be exposed to, but they were promised that the fouler the odor, the more money they would receive. Elections were then held, and three conditions were established: in the *mandate condition* the leader was told he had been unanimously selected to be the leader. In the *majority condition* the leader believed he had just won enough votes to get the position. In the *control condition* leaders were told they had been randomly selected to be their group's leader. In the final stage of the research the leaders were asked to select the odor that the group would have to tolerate. Consistent with mandate-phenomenon predictions, individuals who felt that they had the overwhelming support of their group selected more noxious odors than either the leader elected by simple majority or the subjects in the control condition.

Lastly, several sources suggest that acquiring power only serves to stimulate the powerholder into acquiring more power. Because the possession of power may provide the means to achieve many goals, power eventually becomes so closely associated with valued outcomes that people seek it for its own sake (Cartwright & Zander, 1968). Hence, we find that, once in power, individuals take steps to protect their sources of influence (Lawler & Thompson, 1979). Eventually powerholders may become preoccupied with seeking power, driven by a strong motivation to acquire greater and greater levels of interpersonal influence (McClelland, 1975; Winter, 1973). This protective aspect of power translates into a small group version of Michel's "iron law of oligarchy": *individuals in power tend to remain in power.*

Changes in the Powerless

Far fewer studies have been conducted specifically to assess the effects of powerlessness, in part because the range of reactions is very great. When people find themselves the targets of influence in a group they may react passively and accept the situation; rebel against the inequity and attempt to institute a more egalitarian structure; attempt to increase their power covertly through ingratiation or coalition formation; or withdraw from the group entirely (Blau, 1977; Clark, K. B., 1971; Fanon, 1963; Gamson, 1968).

If, however, we limit our examination to changes that occur in the target person who is successfully influenced by the powerholder, several possible consequences can be outlined. First, research suggests that the target person may react to coercive influence with anger, dislike, and hostility (Johnson & Ewens, 1971; Mulder

---

PROFESSORIAL PRESUMPTUOUSNESS

According to William B. Stiles (1978), when high- and low-status individuals meet in interaction, the powerholder often presumes to fully understand the position of the less powerful interactant. Although in some instances the powerholder's assumption of greater knowledge is justified, in many other cases it is completely unwarranted.

Stiles has developed a structured coding system for measuring verbal behavior, and he suggests that presumptuousness exists whenever the powerholder's statements contain relatively large amounts of advisement about what the other person should do (for example, orders, suggestions, prescriptions, permissions), interpretations of the other person's statements (such as explanations, labeling, elucidation), confirmations of the other's viewpoint (agreement or disagree-

ment), and reflections about the other's statements (summarizing, repetitions). In one study he investigated "professorial presumptuousness" by recording and subsequently coding classroom and conversational interactions of university teachers and students (Stiles, Waszak, & Barton, 1979). As expected, the professors were far more presumptuous than their students in the classroom ("Try looking at the bottom of page 24," "I don't understand the point you are making," "Rephrase your question," and "In summarizing our discussion . . ."), but this presumptuousness also carried over into nonclassroom interactions. In a sample collected during a comfortable ten-minute conversation, the greater power of the professors was still in evidence as they continued to make presumptions about the other person's views.

et al., 1964). Hence, while coercive powerholders may be successful in initial encounters, influence becomes more difficult in successive meetings as the target's anger and resistance to pressure grow.

Second, carrying out the demands, orders, or requests of an authority that are inconsistent with one's own attitudes can sometimes cause these attitudes to change. For example, when the subjects in Milgram's obedience studies complied with the experimenter's orders to deliver increasingly powerful shocks to their innocent victim, they ended up performing an action that led to extremely negative consequences. In wondering about their behavior later, these subjects may have asked themselves "Why did I deliver shocks to that person?" and their answer could have been "I am a sadistic person who likes to hurt others." Naturally, Milgram went to great efforts, by discussing the true reasons for the actions at the conclusion of the session, to make certain that the participants in his research did not change their attitudes about themselves.

Third, the use of coercive and reward power can in some instances alter the target person's level of intrinsic motivation. For example, suppose subordinates maintain a high level of productivity because their work is intrinsically satisfying to them—they enjoy it for personal, internal reasons. If, however, a supervisor begins making rewards and punishments contingent upon level of production, the workers may in time come to work to earn rewards and avoid punishments rather than to experience the enjoyment they once felt spontaneously. By introducing external motivators—rewards, promises, threats, or punishments—the supervisor has destroyed the potency of intrinsic motivators. Hence, when the extrinsic motivators are withdrawn or the powerholder fails to maintain surveillance, the productivity levels drop off (Condry, 1977; Lepper & Green, 1975).

Lastly, in extreme instances when a powerholder (such as Jim Jones) inflicts tremendous suffering and misfortune on people, the latter may respond by blaming themselves for their misery. Since most people intuitively "believe that their environment is a just and orderly place where people usually get what they deserve" (Lerner & Miller, 1978, p. 1030), they tend to think that those who suffer must have done something to deserve their misfortunes. However, when we ourselves are the victims, this same "belief in a just world" produces self-blame and self-derogation. For example, the residents of the Jonestown colony totally accepted Jones as their spiritual leader, and yet he punished and abused them. To make sense of their suffering at the hands of their supposed savior they may have assumed that they themselves were responsible for their misfortunes. In blaming themselves instead of Jones, they may eventually have felt so deserving of their punishment that they chose to suffer rather than escape suffering. In part, these feelings of self-condemnation may account for their willingness to take their own lives (Comer & Laird, 1975).

Summary

Although power can be defined in many ways, most definitions emphasize behavioral or psychological change through social influence. At a basic level, power can be traced to the five sources specified by John French and Bertram Raven: reward, coercive, legitimate, referent, and expert power bases. More specifically, these bases of power can be supplemented by considering a variety of power tactics available to group members—such as reasoning, bargaining, fait accompli, or deceit—which vary in terms of rationality and directness.

Many power dynamics are in evidence in group settings, but two processes—obedience and coalition formation—have received much attention from group dynamicists. As Stanley Milgram and other researchers have found, when individuals feel powerless to refuse the orders of an authority, they are capable of actions that they would normally consider immoral. In such an agentic state, disobedience to authority is achieved only with great difficulty, while obedience is easy. However, the balance of power can be changed by group members if they pool their resources by forming a coalition. Evidence indicates that the composition of coalitions can be predicted by considering the strengths, weaknesses, and gender of the group members, and that a bargaining theory seems to account for coalition formation more accurately than either a minimum-resource theory or a minimum-power theory.

These power processes aside, gaining and losing power appears to have metamorphic effects for both the powerful and the powerless. If given the power to influence others, people tend to be quite willing to use it, and the successful influencing of others often leads to increasingly positive self-evaluations, derogations of the "target," and further attempts to increase power. The targets of power, in contrast, generally display a wide variety of reactions to influence, but some of the metamorphic effects of power for the influenced include anger, submission, loss of intrinsic motivation, attitude change, and self-derogation.

8

Leaders and Leadership

L

eadership has long intrigued observers of human behavior. Presumably, ever since the first cave-dweller told the rest of the group "We're doing this all wrong, let's get organized" people have pondered such mysteries as "What actions make up the leadership role?" "What factors determine who becomes the leader?" and "How can a leader change to become more effective?" Like death and taxes, leadership seems to be an inevitable element of life in groups, a necessary prerequisite for coordinating the behavior of group members in pursuit of common goals. Indeed, leadership may be one of the few universals of human behavior, for anthropological evidence indicates that "there are no known societies without leadership in at least some aspects of their social life" (Lewis, 1974, p. 4). Given the significance of leadership, researchers in a variety of areas—anthropology, ethology, political science, management, sociology, and psychology—have focused their empirical and conceptual tools on the phenomenon. Although the topic involves an immensely complicated and intricate aspect of interpersonal relations, these researchers have been resolutely chipping away at questions concerning leadership for nearly four decades. The result: over this period our knowledge of leaders and leadership has expanded dramatically.

This chapter focuses on the processes of leadership that have received the most attention and are best understood at present. Thus, the less-well-understood aspects of the topic will receive only perfunctory attention here. Fortunately, however, several excellent reviews of these areas are available for those who require additional information (see, for example, Bass, 1981; Barrow, 1977; Gibb, 1969; Hollander, 1978; Stogdill, 1974). For the most part our discussions will be aimed at the development of a coherent and defensible theory of leadership processes that is consistent with the findings of research conducted in various scientific fields. However, before we can begin reviewing the empirical research and building our theoretical system, we must explore and, we hope, answer a number of fundamental questions. As a prelude to our review of the research, we will explore the meaning of the term *leadership*. As with many of the topics previously discussed, it will be easier to start by considering what leadership is *not* than what it *is*.

Some Misconceptions about Leadership

Political scientist James McGregor Burns (1978, p. 2) believes that leadership is "one of the most observed and least understood phenomena on earth." Other experts have also expressed dismay at the prevalence of misunderstanding about leadership, complaining that most people "don't have the faintest concept of what leadership is all about" (Bennis, 1975, p. 1), that "the nature of leadership in our society is very imperfectly understood," and that the "many public statements

Leadership is the ability to decide what is to be done, and then to get others to want to do it.
Dwight D. Eisenhower

I must follow the people. Am I not their leader?
Benjamin Disraeli

To be a leader means to be able to move masses.
Hitler

A leader is a man who has the ability to get other people to do what they don't want to do, and like it.
Harry S. Truman

I want to be a President who is a Chief Executive in every sense of the word—who responds to a problem, not by hoping his subordinates will act, but by directing them to act.
John F. Kennedy

The last person in the world to know what the people really want and think.
James A. Garfield

One who implants noble ideals and principles with practical accomplishments.
Richard M. Nixon

The loneliest person in the group.
Anonymous

about it are utter nonsense" (Gardner, 1965, p. 3 and p. 12). Overall, these notables conclude that common-sense conclusions about leadership are based more on myth than reality. In the following subsections, we identify some frequently espoused but erroneous ideas about leadership (Cribbin, 1972).

"Leadership Is Power over Others"

Many people, including some prominent political leaders, assume that good leaders are capable of manipulating, controlling, and forcing their followers into obedience. Hitler, for example, defined leadership as the ability to move the masses, whether through persuasion or violence, and Ho Chi Minh once stated that a good leader must learn to mold, shape, and change the people just as a woodworker must learn to use wood (see the box for these and other views of leadership held by prominent political thinkers). However, to refer to individuals as leaders—be they kings, presidents, bosses, or chairpersons—who influence others through domination and coercion seems incorrect. Instead, the term leader should be reserved for those who act in the best interests of a group with the consent of that group. Leadership is a form of power, but power with people rather than over people; it represents a reciprocal relationship between the leader and the led. Writes Burns (1978, p. 19): "Leadership, unlike naked power-wielding, is thus inseparable from followers' needs and goals."

"Some People Are Born Leaders"

Henry Ford, the amazingly successful founder of a major automotive empire, once remarked that "the question 'Who ought to be Boss?' is like asking 'Who ought to be the tenor in the quartet?' Obviously, the man who can sing tenor." Ford was suggesting that the ability to lead stems from a collection of naturally developing qualities within the person. In other words, ability to lead is a "talent"—

like singing or dancing—that exists in some people but not in others. Because this talent derives from inborn characteristics, the ability to lead cannot be easily developed in a "born follower"; nor can situational factors serve to determine leadership. Research, however, has invalidated Ford's notion of born leaders, indicating rather that the ability to lead is acquired through practice. The search for personality variables associated with effective leadership has, for the most part, proven fruitless (Stogdill, 1974); the more accurate view suggests that leadership "is an *achievement*, not a birthright or happy accident of heredity" (Cribbin, 1972, p. 14).

"A Leader Is a Leader Is a Leader"

The popular corollary of the born-leader notion is that a good leader in one situation will prove to be a good leader in another situation. This notion too undervalues the power of environmental circumstances in determining leader effectiveness. Although a person leading a problem-solving group may do a marvelous job in enhancing group effectiveness and member satisfaction, when placed in charge of a football team this individual could prove completely ineffectual. Similarly, a good discussion-group leader may turn out to be notably poor at leading a 100-person meeting or in passing down executive orders to subordinates. Although "great leaders" no doubt exist, they seem to be a relatively rare commodity (Bales, 1958).

"Good Leaders Are Well Liked"

Niccolo Machiavelli, in his famous treatise *The Prince,* advised the careful ruler to gain the friendship and support of the populace. While few would argue with Machiavelli's enjoinment to secure a leadership position through friendship, leadership is more than a mere popularity contest. As Robert Bales noted many years ago (1958), the recognized leader of a group need not be the best liked member of the group, for in many instances the activities of the leader clash with the satisfactions and happiness of some of the group members. Although some leaders may in fact be well liked by the others in their group (Redl, 1942), the ability to inspire affection is not a key characteristic of a leader.

"Groups Prefer to Be Leaderless"

Although current folk wisdom implies that followers begrudge the authority resting in the leader of a group, the commonness of group leaders suggests that the magnitude of this attitude may be somewhat exaggerated. As a later section will show, in some circumstances groups function well without leaders. However, when group tasks become complicated and the need for coordination grows, group satisfaction and productivity are greater with leadership than without it (Berkowitz, 1953). Indeed, even some frequently recommended forms of "non-leadership," such as participatory democracy (where all group members participate equally in the decision-making process) and distributed leadership (where each group member fulfills one part of the leadership role) can be less effective in some circumstances than a more authoritarian, centralized form of leadership.

A Working Definition of Leadership

Pointing out what leadership is not is far easier than pointing out what it is. Although leadership is a favorite topic of study in many social sciences, researchers typically disagree over its precise definition. The term is used in a variety of contexts and has been accused of a multitude of scientifically reprehensible crimes—excessive ambiguity (Pfeffer, 1977); an overbroad scope (Katz & Kahn, 1978); significant overlap with other descriptive terms (Grimes, 1978); and doubtful theoretical utility (Miner, 1975). Given this disagreement, it is unlikely that any definition of leadership can be suggested that all theorists and researchers would accept. However, some sort of "working" definition of the concept will prove useful in guiding our analysis of leaders and leadership.

Toward this end, let us assume that **leadership** is a reciprocal process in which an individual is permitted to influence and motivate others to facilitate the attainment of mutually satisfying group and individual goals. Although lengthy and somewhat cumbersome as definitions go, this conceptualization succeeds in emphasizing several key features noted by many previous definers. These features will be clearer if we break the definition down into its component parts:

1. Leadership is a reciprocal relationship involving the leader—who directs, guides, and facilitates the group's behavior—and followers—who accept the suggestions of the leader (Hollander, 1978).
2. Leadership is a process of legitimate influence rather than a quality of a person (Grimes, 1978).
3. The right to lead is, in most instances, voluntarily conferred upon the leader by some or all members of the group (Kochan, Schmidt, & DeCotiis, 1975).
4. Leadership involves motivating group members to expend more energy in attaining the goals of the group (Katz & Kahn, 1978).
5. The leader/member relationship is a cooperative interaction, since both parties help one another achieve common goals (Pigors, 1935).

Our working definition is far from the final word on the concept of leadership, but it serves to clear the air and prepare the way for a closer study of the topic. Although in the second half of this chapter we consider what may well be the number one research topic in group dynamics—leader effectiveness—we have three fundamental questions to answer regarding leadership per se: "Who is most likely to become a leader?" "When do groups need a leader?" and "What do leaders do?"

Questions about Leadership

Who Will Lead?

If you have ever wondered how in the world a particular person ever became a group leader, then you have asked a question that has intrigued researchers for many years. Granted, leaders gain their central positions through a variety of means—election by a majority of group members, appointment by an external authority, or implicit recognition by several group members—but group dynamicists assume that the selection process is not an arbitrary one. Rather, a number of specifiable factors determine which individual in a group will eventually become the leader of that group, and this leadership-emergence process is both predictable and understandable.

PERSONALITY TRAITS AND LEADERSHIP EMERGENCE

For many years researchers have puzzled over the viability of a strictly **trait approach to leadership,** which would assume that leaders possess certain personality characteristics that distinguish them from their followers. As noted earlier, no absolute conclusions can be drawn from the hundreds of studies that have tested this assumption by correlating leadership behavior with measures of personality (Bass, 1981; Gibb, 1969); nevertheless, several personality factors tend to be more closely linked with leadership than others. For example, Ralph M. Stogdill, after painstakingly reviewing 124 trait studies in 1948 and 163 studies in 1970 (Stogdill, 1974), points to several personality factors that are often stronger in leaders than followers. Some of these correlates of leadership emergence are presented in Table 8-1, which indicates that leaders tend to be more achievement oriented, adaptable, alert, ascendant, energetic, responsible, self-confident, and sociable than others in the group. This table also indicates, however, that the relationship between leadership and several other personality variables—such as attractiveness, emotional balance, extroversion, and nurturance—is unclear since the findings across the various studies are inconsistent.

In sum, though these findings lend some support to the trait approach to leadership, the strength of the relationship and, in some cases, the inconsistencies across studies indicate that other factors are relevant to leadership emergence. In fact, some theorists favoring a more **situational approach to leadership emergence** argue that the personality data are unclear because emergence depends on factors operating in the group situation rather than on personality factors (Gibb, 1969). While Stogdill cautions against a strict trait approach to leadership, however, he does not accept a strict situational explanation either. He suggests that if a *personality-profile approach* were used to study leadership—whereby leaders were classified on a range of personality traits—then the link between personality and leadership would be clearer. Thus, according to this approach while the indi-

TABLE 8-1. Some personality correlates of leadership behavior

Personality characteristic	Type of relationship
Achievement drive	Positive
Adaptability	Positive
Alertness	Positive
Ascendance	Positive
Attractiveness	Unclear
Dominance (bossy)	Negative
Emotional balance	Unclear
Energetic	Positive
Extroversion	Unclear
Nurturance	Unclear
Responsible	Positive
Self-confidence	Positive
Sociability	Positive

(Source: Stogdill, 1974)

vidual who is alert, dominant, or self-confident probably won't become the leader of the group, the individual who is alert, dominant, *and* self-confident probably will. Further, according to Stogdill, leadership emergence may be influenced by the *interaction* of personality traits and situation factors, a possibility that will be considered in more depth later in the chapter.

OTHER PERSONAL CHARACTERISTICS

Height and weight. As folk wisdom suggests, leaders do in fact tend to be slightly taller than their subordinates. As Stogdill noted in his two reviews, the correlation between height and leadership varies from $-.13$ to $+.71$, but the average is about .30. This relationship may stem, in part, from the desire by group members to be represented by a taller-than-average individual, but evidence indicates that height is certainly not a prerequisite for leadership. For example, many people, such as Napoleon, have managed to reach positions of leadership despite their diminutive stature, so height alone can't be that important a factor. Stogdill reached similar conclusions in discussing the relationship between leadership and weight.

Age. The link between age and leadership emergence is a bit more complicated. Although studies suggest that leaders in informal discussion groups can be older, younger, or the same age as their fellow group members, studies of political and business leadership suggest that those in leadership positions are likely to be older. Many factors could account for this relationship, but no doubt the amount of time it takes to reach a position of leadership and the assumptions group members make about age and ability are relevant. Unless corporate authority is conferred on the basis of family ties, the climb up the organizational hierarchy can take years. While less than a tenth of a percent of the corporate executives listed in the *Register of Corporations, Directors, and Executives* are under 30 years of age (Stanton & Poors, 1967), 74 percent are 50 years of age or older. As Stogdill noted "organizations tend to rely upon administrative knowledge and demonstration of success that comes with experience and age" (1974, p. 76). Further, if group members assume that age is an indicator of wisdom, experience, and sagacity, then they are likely to prefer a leader who is older rather than younger.

Intelligence. Stogdill (1948, 1974) cited 48 studies that report evidence of a link between intellectual ability and leadership. Although the average correlation is small—on the order of .25 to .30—most studies have found that small-group and managerial leaders score higher than average on standard intelligence tests, make superior judgments with greater decisiveness, are more knowledgeable, and speak more fluently. Typically leaders do not, however, exceed their followers in intellectual prowess by a wide margin. Groups appear to prefer leaders who are more intelligent than the average group member, but too great a discrepancy introduces problems in communication, trust, and social sensitivity. Although highly intelligent individuals may be extremely capable and efficient leaders, their groups may feel that large differences in intellectual abilities translate into large differences in interests, attitudes, and values. Hence, while high intelligence may mean skilled leadership, a group prefers to be "ill-governed by people it can understand" (Gibb, 1969, p. 218).

Task abilities.   Possessing skills and abilities that (1) are valued by the other group members or (2) increase the group's chances for achieving success also gives an individual an edge during leadership emergence. In a review of 52 studies of characteristics typically ascribed to the leader, Stogdill (1974) found that the most frequently suggested factor (appearing in 35% of the studies cited) emphasized technical, task-relevant skills. Groups are more accepting of leaders who have previously demonstrated task ability (Goldman & Fraas, 1965) and are more willing to follow the directions of a task-competent person rather than an incompetent person (Hollander, 1965). Furthermore, while high task ability facilitates leadership, low task ability seems to be an even more powerful factor in disqualifying individuals from consideration as leaders (Palmer, 1962). Even marginal group members who frequently violate group norms can become leaders if their task abilities significantly facilitate goal attainment (Hollander, 1964).

PARTICIPATION RATES

One variable that is consistently related to leadership status and that therefore deserves special emphasis is participation rate in group discussion. The surprisingly simple finding is that the person who talks the most in the group is the most likely to emerge as leader (Burke, 1974; Stein & Heller, 1979). While the correlation between leadership emergence and other personal and behavioral characteristics usually averages in the low .20s, the average correlation between participation rate and leadership is .65 (Stein & Heller, 1979). Furthermore, leadership appears to be related more to the sheer quantity of the participation—number of remarks—rather than to the quality of the contributions. That is, the *quality* of what is said doesn't seem to matter as long as quantity is apparent. One study demonstrating this effect manipulated both the quantity and quality of the verbal inputs of a trained confederate in a problem-solving group (Sorrentino & Boutillier, 1975). While the four-person all-male groups worked to solve the experimental tasks, the confederate systematically offered many comments or few comments that were either high in quality (they facilitated success on the tasks) or low in quality (they facilitated failure on the tasks). When subjects later rated, on five-point scales, the confederate's confidence, interest in the problem, competence, influence over others, and contributions to the task solution, only quantity of inputs significantly influenced ratings of confidence and interest. Furthermore, while subjects viewed the confederate as more competent and more influential when he interjected high- rather than low-quality comments, the effects due to quantity were still stronger. That is, differences in quantity explained the variations in the ratings more than differences in the quality of inputs. The only dependent variable that was strongly influenced by the quality of inputs was rating of contribution to problem solution.

Although these findings concerning the quantity and quality of participation may at first seem paradoxical, they make sense when examined from an attributional perspective. Although the individual who offers very high quality suggestions may be perceived to be competent, quantity per se seems to be taken by group members to be an indicator of motivation, involvement, and willingness to work for the group. Thus, high participation rates suggest that the individual is interested in the group and therefore has the "right" to influence others, whereas low participation rates imply that the individual has little interest in the group or its problems. Thus, from the vantage point of the group member, "quality is not positively related to leadership *unless* the competent person demonstrates his willingness to share his resources with the group members and is perceived as seriously trying to contribute to the group's goals" (Sorrentino & Boutillier, 1975, p. 411). These perceptions can apparently be best fostered by participating at high rates.

AN OVERALL LOOK AT LEADERSHIP EMERGENCE

Many of the findings we discussed in this section suggest that we can understand leadership emergence in groups by considering group members' *attributions* about the causes of behaviors and events (Calder, 1976; Green & Mitchell, 1979). According to this analysis, members of a group believe that leadership ability is a dispositional characteristic that must be inferred on the basis of certain environmental and behavioral cues. They therefore monitor the group situation for information they can take as evidence of leadership ability and then implicitly rely on this information to make conclusions about leadership.

An attributional approach to leadership emergence thus suggests that researchers must take group members' assumptions about leadership into consideration before making predictions with any confidence. If members of the group believe that active participation is a good indicator of leadership ability, then the individual who talks the most is the most likely candidate for the leadership slot. If, on the other hand, the group associates leadership with aggressiveness and shrewdness, then an individual who subtly dominates others in the group may be more likely to emerge as leader. An attributional approach to leadership emergence is also consistent with the notion that emergence occurs over time as certain members are eliminated as suitable leadership candidates (Fisher, 1980). Attributionally, time is needed to collect information about others, formulate judgments, and test out the accuracy of these perceptions. In the initial moments of interaction, certain individuals can be eliminated from consideration because they perform behaviors the attributor feels are sure indicants of low leadership ability: refusal to discuss ideas, rigidity in beliefs, inarticulateness, or general obnoxiousness (Geier, 1967), but later decisions are more complicated. Even with the elimination of clearly inappropriate individuals, several more candidates may remain, and the group members must then fix their attention on these potential leaders to determine which one shows the greatest evidence of leadership ability. In many cases, these persons will compete for the role until one succeeds in convincing a majority that he or she would be best.

In sum, while leadership emergence can be related back to certain characteristics of individuals in the group, perceptual and attributional processes seem to be critical as well. If group members believe that dominance, talkativeness, or sensitivity are good indicators of leadership ability, then these characteristics will more than likely be possessed by the emergent leader. For those who are interested in becoming the leaders in their groups, the best advice that researchers can offer is to fulfill the expectations of the group members as closely as possible; if they expect the leader to have Characteristics X, Y, and Z, then the successful candidate for leadership must be able to convince the others that he or she has these characteristics. If, however, you wish to avoid leadership (as many people do), then you should perform actions that can only be interpreted as evidence against the possession of Characteristics X, Y, and Z. Several other "principles" for avoiding leadership are offered in the box.

What Will the Leader Do?

Opportunities for attaining a leadership role abound in everyday life. For example, you may attend the organizational meeting of a club and find yourself elected chair of one of the committees. You may be promoted at your job from a production position to one that involves some supervisory responsibilities. Your fraternity or sorority may hold its annual election of officers and you are elected president. You go to a PTA meeting, complain of the marked disorganization of the group, and for "punishment" the members elect you to the position of president. Although an informal discussion group in one of your classes has no explicitly recognized role designations, you gradually emerge as the group leader.

But what would you *do* if you became the leader in one of these groups? How would you behave? Would you isolate yourself from the rest of the group or try to remain friendly and open? Would you encourage full discussion of problems by the group at large or make most of the decisions yourself? Would you intervene in intragroup conflicts or just let those involved thrash out the problem themselves? Would you boost the morale of the group by emphasizing the importance of group goals or by trying to make everyone feel satisfied with membership? Would you carefully oversee all the group's activities or supervise only minimally? What behaviors would be part of your role as leader?

TWO DIMENSIONS OF LEADERSHIP BEHAVIOR

Naturally, your answer to these questions would depend in part on the kind of group you were leading—work group, discussion group, recreational group, and

---

PRINCIPLES FOR AVOIDING LEADERSHIP DUTIES

B. Aubrey Fisher (1980, pp. 223–224) has recently offered some tongue-in-cheek principles that, if followed carefully, guarantee a position of low status in a group.

Rule 1: Be absent from as many group meetings as possible.

Rule 2: Contribute to the interaction as little as possible.

Rule 3: Volunteer to be the secretary or the recordkeeper of your group's discussions.

Rule 4: Indicate that you are willing to do what you are told.

Rule 5: Come on strong early in the group discussion.

Rule 6: Try to assume the role of joker.

Rule 7: Demonstrate your knowledge of everything, including your extensive vocabulary of big words and technical jargon.

Rule 8: Demonstrate a contempt for leadership.

(Source: Fisher, 1980)

so on. However, researchers who have studied many different types of groups have found that leaders' behaviors usually fall into a finite set of clusters or dimensions. Indeed, the earliest systematic studies of leadership focused on the actions actually taken by leaders with the specific goal of describing how leaders behave in groups. These descriptive analyses began by listing all the possible behaviors associated with leadership—planning, policy making, punishing, rewarding, taking responsibility (Krech & Crutchfield, 1948)—but soon the list grew so long that researchers endeavored to reduce the various types of actions down to the key dimensions of leader behavior. Although some of these attempts, such as the U. S. army's 11 "principles of leadership," were based on intuitive analyses of leadership (Carter, 1952), empirical efforts to identify leadership's basic components tended to rely on either self-report questionnaire methods or observational techniques.

The questionnaire approach is perhaps best represented by the Ohio State University Leadership Studies, which were begun just after the end of World War II. Researchers first developed a list of nine key types of behavior that seemed to characterize military and organizational leaders (initiating new practices, interacting informally with subordinates, representing the group, integrating group action, and so on; see Hemphill, 1950). Second, the investigators designed a questionnaire to measure these behaviors and asked a large number of group members to rate their leader using the instrument. Third, a statistical technique known as factor analysis was used to eliminate overlapping and irrelevant behaviors, and the original nine were narrowed down to four "factors" or dimensions: Consideration, Initiating Structure, Production Emphasis, and Sensitivity (Halpin & Winer, 1952). Of these four factors, the first two seemed to be the most important dimensions; together they accounted for approximately 83.2% of the variation in followers' evaluations of their leaders (see Table 8-2). Indeed, the Ohio State researchers

TABLE 8-2. The two basic dimensions of leadership behavior

Leadership dimensions	Alternative labels	Conceptual meaning	Sample behaviors
Consideration	Relationship orientation Socioemotional Supportive Employee centered Relations skilled Group maintenance	Degree to which the leader responds to group members in a warm and friendly fashion; involves mutual trust, openness, and willingness to explain decisions.	Listens to group members Easy to understand Is friendly and approachable Treats group members as equals Is willing to make changes
Initiating structure	Task orientation Goal oriented Work facilitative Production centered Administratively skilled Goal achiever	Extent to which leader organizes, directs, and defines the group's structure and goals; regulates group behavior, monitors communication, and reduces goal ambiguity.	Assigns tasks to members Makes attitudes clear to the group Is critical of poor work Sees to it that the group is working to capacity Coordinates activity

(Source: Halpin & Winer, 1952; Lord, 1977)

included these two dimensions in their **Leader Behavior Description Questionnaire (LBDQ),** which remains one of the key tools used to assess leadership action (Kerr, Schriesheim, Murphy, & Stogdill, 1974; Stogdill, 1974). To complete this measure, group members rate their leader on a series of items such as those presented in the right-hand column of Table 8-2. The totals from the two separate subscales are assumed to measure the two dimensions of leadership.

By finding evidence of two clusters of leadership activity related to **relationship orientation** (consideration) and **task orientation** (initiating structure), the Ohio State University Studies mesh with other research that emphasizes the dualistic nature of leadership. Although the labels used to designate these two dimensions vary—supportive versus work facilitative (Bowers & Seashore, 1966), employee centered versus production centered (Likert, 1967), relations skilled versus administratively skilled (Mann, 1965), or group maintenance versus goal achievement (Cartwright & Zander, 1968)—these two basic dimensions are discussed with such convincing frequency that most conclude both are essential parts of the leadership role.

Interpersonal relationship activities focus on the feelings, attitudes, and satisfactions of the members of the group and therefore correspond closely to the functions fulfilled by the socioemotional specialist (Bales, 1958; see Chapter 5). Although a group may have formed to complete a particular task or solve a problem, leaders must often act to unify the group at an emotional level before the task goals can be completed. The leader may take steps to ensure that the group atmosphere is positive—boost morale, increase cohesiveness, reduce any interpersonal conflict if necessary—by making certain the nontask needs of the group members are met (Lord, 1977). Rapport between the leader and the rest of the group must be established, and it is hoped that a feeling of concern and consideration will grow as the group members come to realize that the leader is concerned with their welfare and satisfaction.

Task activities, in contrast, focus more heavily on the problem than the personal satisfactions of the group members. Although leadership often involves providing group members with emotional support, leaders must also lead—that is, guide the group in the direction of successful goal attainment. A wide range of behaviors is comprised by this second cluster of actions, including defining problems for the group, establishing communication networks, providing evaluative feedback, planning, activating task-relevant activity, coordinating members' actions, and facilitating goal attainment by proposing solutions and removing barriers (Lord, 1977).

POSSIBLE LIMITATIONS

Studies using questionnaire instruments such as the LBDQ seem to give a clearcut answer to the question "What will the leader do?" Apparently, the leader will improve interpersonal relations in the group and oversee task completion. However, rather than uncritically accept this conclusion, we need to consider the results of research projects that have actually observed leadership behavior. For example, one early study compared the behavior of leaders with that of followers and found relatively few differences in relationship-oriented behaviors (Carter, Haythorn, Shriver, & Lanzetta, 1950). Although 53 different behavior categories were recorded by objective observers, the only clear differences found leaders giving more directions and interpretations of the problem than subordinates. Similarly, a more recent study of leadership behaviors (Lord, 1977) found little evidence of a relationship-oriented dimension, and no relationship between consideration and ratings of leadership and power. A third study, again using observational methods rather than questionnaire responses, found evidence of the two basic leadership dimensions (termed "group goal facilitation" and "sociability" in this investigation), but concluded that the relationship factor was not closely related to ratings of leadership (Couch & Carter, 1952). In fact, in this last investigation a third dimension—termed "individual prominence"—seemed to be more important than those specified in the two-dimensional approach. According to these findings, leaders not only facilitate goal completion and maintain relationships but also act in ways that make them "stand out in the group" (Carter, 1953, p. 269).

One explanation for the conflict between findings based on questionnaire measures and those based on observation methods acknowledges the possibility of biases in group members' perceptions of their leader (Ilgen & Fujii, 1976; Lord, Binning, Rush, & Thomas, 1978; Rush, Thomas, & Lord, 1977). As we noted in our discussion of attributions in groups, the concept of leadership is a familiar topic of discussion in groups. However, if members formulate intuitive but inaccurate conceptions of what actions should make up the leadership role, then these "implicit leadership theories" may bias responses to such measurement instruments as the LBDQ. In other words, the two-dimensional theory of leadership behavior may actually be a theory of followers' perceptions of their leaders. On the other hand, the difficulty may stem from problems in the observational research rather than in the theory itself, but additional research is needed to determine whether (1) certain behaviors—such as personal prominence—constitute an important part of the leadership role, and (2) the importance of consideration has been overstated.

When a Leader?

In many formally organized groups—juries, committees, conferences, workshops, or business meetings—the leadership role is explicitly built into the structure of the group. Yet in groups with no formally defined structures, the role still seems to emerge with remarkable regularity. Informal gatherings such as parties, study groups, discussion groups, or spectators at a sporting event may initially start off as "leaderless groups," because no leader exists, but in time someone steps up to fill the role. The question to consider is when does a group require the services of a leader.

One particularly active researcher in the area, John K. Hemphill, related the group's need for a leader to a number of situational factors, including group size and the type of task confronting the group. According to Hemphill, as a group becomes larger it begins to encounter problems of coordination, administration, and communication that can be easily ameliorated by a leader. Therefore, members are more open to attempts to gain leadership by possible leadership candidates in large than in small groups. To support this prediction, Hemphill compared the behaviors performed by large-group leaders with those of small-group leaders, and found evidence of a greater reliance on the leader to make rules clear, keep members informed, and make group decisions in the larger groups (1951). In a later review of other variables, Hemphill (1961) also suggested that leaders appear in groups when (1) group members feel that success on the group task is within their reach, (2) the rewards for the task success are valued, (3) the task requires group rather than individual effort, and (4) an individual with previous experience in the leadership role is present in the group.

Other researchers have noted that a leader is more likely to emerge in a group when the group faces a stressful situation or experiences a crisis (Hamblin, 1958; Mulder & Stemerding, 1963; Helmreich & Collins, 1967) than at other times. In one illuminating study, college students worked in three-person groups on an easy task. During a second phase, however, the task was changed and the group uniformly performed poorly. The situation posed a crisis for the group, since the experimenter told the failing groups that their performance was being compared to that of high school students who had earlier worked on the task and performed it easily. Faced with the possibility of an embarrassing failure on a task that the younger groups had mastered, the subjects tended to centralize the structure of their groups. During this crisis, substantive, directive comments became localized around one group member, who was soon replaced by another high influencer if the group's performance did not improve. Apparently, during a crisis individual group members tend to prefer the structure and support provided by a leader, but expect the leader to help them deal successfully with the stressful situation (Hamblin, 1958).

A final factor that has recently been related to the development of a leadership role is the absence of **leadership substitutes** in the group situation (Kerr & Jermier, 1978). Although leadership does occur widely in many groups, in some cases substitutes for leadership exist that tend to "negate the leader's ability to either improve or impair subordinate satisfaction and performance" (Kerr & Jermier, 1978, p. 377). When a number of these substitutes are in evidence in a situation, then leadership is both unnecessary and unlikely.

These substitutes are summarized in Table 8-3 which lists characteristics of the group members, the group task, and the group situation that tend to neutralize relationship leadership, task leadership, or both. As the table shows, when a group is composed of competent individuals with a great need for independence, a sense of professional identity, and a disdain for the rewards their work supervisors can offer, then both relationship and task leadership are neutralized. In contrast, only task leadership becomes unnecessary when the group members can work on problems that are unambiguous, routine, and clearly evaluable. Lastly, formal, inflexible, and unambiguous group structures tend to neutralize task-oriented leadership, whereas group cohesiveness, low reward power, and spatial distances make both types of leadership unnecessary.

In an imaginative exploration of these substitutes, researchers asked respondents to complete a questionnaire that measured each of the substitutes for leadership listed in Table 8-3 (for example, to measure Item 1 subjects reported their degree of agreement with the item "Because of my ability, experience, training, or job knowledge, I have the competence to act independently of my immediate superior in performing day-to-day duties;" see Kerr & Jermier, 1978). However, rather than answer as they themselves felt, the subjects were to respond from the viewpoint of a character in one of three well-known nationally televised programs:

Mary Richards in the *Mary Tyler Moore Show,* Hawkeye Pierce in *M.A.S.H.,* and Archie Bunker in *All in the Family* (this study was conducted when the character of Archie worked at the loading dock of the plant). Although the researchers pointed out that the limitations of this role-play procedure require that the findings be interpreted with caution, their results did suggest that the presence of certain leadership substitutes corresponded to the absence of task and relationship leader roles. For example, Mary Richards, as depicted on the program, appears to derive a good deal of intrinsic satisfaction from working on the various tasks that make up her job. Furthermore, her work group seems to be fairly cohesive, and the members express a strong degree of professionalism and intermember respect. According to Table 8-3, these features of the situation should serve as substitutes for relationship-oriented leadership; as the researchers conclude, "on the show she does seem happy in her work despite the erratic attempts at warmth and collegiality displayed by her superior (Lou Grant)" (1978, p. 387). For Hawkeye Pierce, in contrast, his high personal skill and knowledge obviate the need for task leadership, while the combat situation depicted on the program undermines his professionalism and intrinsic satisfaction with the role of surgeon. Hence, these findings suggest that Pierce would benefit from relationship-oriented leadership. These speculations, of course, are most usefully interpreted as examples of the concept of leadership substitutes, but they suggest that future researchers should give greater emphasis to situations in which leadership does not appear in the group.

TABLE 8-3. Substitutes for leadership

	Will tend to neutralize	
Characteristic	*Relationship-oriented leadership*	*Task-oriented leadership*
Of the group member		
1. Ability, experience, training, knowledge		X
2. Need for independence	X	X
3. "Professional" orientation	X	X
4. Indifference toward group rewards	X	X
Of the task		
5. Unambiguous and routine		X
6. Methodologically invariant		X
7. Provides its own feedback concerning accomplishment		X
8. Intrinsically satisfying	X	
Of the organization		
9. Formalization (explicit plans, goals, and areas of responsibility)		X
10. Inflexibility (rigid, unbending rules and procedures)		X
11. Highly specified and active advisory and staff functions		X
12. Closely knit, cohesive work groups	X	X
13. Organizational rewards not within leader's control	X	X
14. Spatial distance between superior and subordinate	X	X

(Source: Kerr and Jermier, 1978)

Leader Effectiveness

The remainder of this chapter examines a question that has been of utmost interest to leadership experts for many years: leader effectiveness. Although theorists are interested in the basis of leadership processes, their fascination springs from pragmatic concerns—a desire to make recommendations concerning how leaders can best lead.

Man is the weak toy of fortune.

Simon Bolivar

If we do not win, we will blame neither heaven nor earth but only ourselves.

Mao Tse-tung

Fiedler's Contingency Model

Alexander the Great governed from a centralized position where he could monitor every important aspect—military, social, and cultural—of his huge empire. Hitler controlled Nazi Germany by developing a complex organization that touched many facets of German life and by inspiring the citizens through his patriotic rhetoric. Gandhi altered the lives of millions of people by giving them examples of vast changes being achieved through nonviolent resistance. Napoleon organized an effective military machine that was victorious in battle after battle. Stalin achieved nearly absolute control over all sectors of the Russian political and social system through careful political maneuvering, party purges, and violence. General George Patton inspired those under his command by displaying high levels of personal confidence, sureness, and an immense strength of character.

Regardless of whether we agree with his values, goals, or methods, we might describe each of these individuals as a great leader who significantly changed the course of history. Yet what precisely was the source of each leader's greatness? Did each of these individuals possess certain skills and abilities that set him apart from others, making him an outstanding leader and military commander? Or did each individual simply respond to his particular historical time and place, the pawn of social forces that were the real determinants of his apparent greatness (Simonton, 1980)?

Many years ago, the historian Thomas Carlyle asserted that prominent political figures were often great geniuses who significantly shaped the times in which they lived. Some individuals, Carlyle proposed in his "Great-Leader Theory" of history, rather than serving as foils for the unfolding of chance events, possess certain characteristics that destine them to greatness. Thus, Carlyle concluded that history can be best studied by considering the contributions of the few great men and women. Russian novelist Leo Tolstoy took a contrasting viewpoint by emphasizing the role situational factors played in determining history. To Tolstoy, such leaders as Alexander and Napoleon came to prominence because the "spirit of the times"— the Zeitgeist—was propitious for the dominance of a single individual, and the qualities of the person were largely irrelevant to this rise to power. Tolstoy would have explained Hitler's rise to power by this theory. Tolstoy thus concluded that the conquests and losses of military leaders such as Napoleon were caused, not by their decisions and skills, but by factors that were beyond their control (Carlyle, 1841; Tolstoy, 1869/1952).

When researchers began examining leadership in small groups, they realized that these two viewpoints explained leadership in completely different terms. If, as Carlyle's Great-Leader Theory suggested, leaders are unique individuals with special characteristics, then we should be able to predict effectiveness by considering the traits of the person. If, however, Tolstoy's Zeitgeist theory is in fact the more accurate explanation, then leadership depends on the situation: the nature of the task, the composition of the group, the group structure, and so on. Of course, as is so often the case when two seemingly incompatible explanations for the same phenomenon are carefully analyzed, group dynamicists soon discovered that both theories contained elements of truth. While early research found few traits that were consistently related to leadership, some individuals did seem to possess a style of interaction that made them more effective in that role (Borgatta, Couch, & Bales, 1954). However, as a scaled-down version of Tolstoy's Zeitgeist notion would predict, a superior leader in one situation sometimes turned out to be an inferior leader when observed in a different context. It was against this background that Fred Fiedler developed his **Contingency Model of Leadership,** a framework that assumed that leadership effectiveness depends on—or is contingent upon—both the personal characteristics of the leader and the nature of the group situation (Fiedler, 1978, 1981).

Fiedler began his program of research in 1951 by examining the relationship between leaders' perceptions of their co-workers and the work group's effectiveness. Although initially he believed that certain leader attitudes—such as openness or regard for others—would be correlated with the success of the group across situations, he soon found that these correlations varied in magnitude and direction depending on the specific group studied. To make sense of these conflicting findings, he studied a large number of groups that fit his definition of interacting groups; they had to produce an evaluable outcome, had to work together as a team, and had to have an appointed, elected, or emergent leader. To summarize his investigations, he developed a theory that explained effectiveness in terms of two basic variables: the *leader's motivational style* and the *leader's control* in the problem-solving situation. Below we will consider each of these variables in detail, but before moving on to the next section take a moment to complete the exercise in the box headed "The LPC Scale."

THE LEADER'S MOTIVATIONAL STYLE

I feel uncomfortable when I have to work too closely with my subordinates—and I think they feel uncomfortable too. My job is to get the work done quickly and efficiently, not to win friends.

The best way to lead a group is to make friends with everyone first, and then get them to work hard on the tasks to be accomplished.

I'm the group leader—and that means I'm supposed to direct the group and give the orders. I wouldn't be fulfilling my duties if I didn't get the job done.

It's not enough to get the job done—the group members have to enjoy their work.

All of these statements reveal some basic, and somewhat incompatible, assumptions about what a leader's job actually involves. While no doubt a person who

THE LPC SCALE

Think of a person with whom you can work least well. She or he may be someone you work with now or someone you knew in the past. He or she does not have to be the person you like least well, but should be the person with whom you have had the most difficulty in getting a job done. Describe this person by circling one of the numbers between each pair of adjectives.

To calculate your score, add up the numbers you have circled for each of the adjective pairs. According to Fiedler, if your score is 56 or less, then you are a low-LPC leader. If, however, your score is 63 or above, then you are a high-LPC leader. If, unfortunately, your score falls between 56 and 63, then you don't fit easily into either category (a motivational style tentatively labeled *socioindependent*).

(Source: Fiedler, 1978)

Pleasant	:	8	7	6	5	4	3	2	1	:	Unpleasant
Friendly	:	8	7	6	5	4	3	2	1	:	Unfriendly
Rejecting	:	1	2	3	4	5	6	7	8	:	Accepting
Tense	:	1	2	3	4	5	6	7	8	:	Relaxed
Distant	:	1	2	3	4	5	6	7	8	:	Close
Cold	:	1	2	3	4	5	6	7	8	:	Warm
Supportive	:	8	7	6	5	4	3	2	1	:	Hostile
Boring	:	1	2	3	4	5	6	7	8	:	Interesting
Quarrelsome	:	1	2	3	4	5	6	7	8	:	Harmonious
Gloomy	:	1	2	3	4	5	6	7	8	:	Cheerful
Open	:	8	7	6	5	4	3	2	1	:	Guarded
Backbiting	:	1	2	3	4	5	6	7	8	:	Loyal
Untrustworthy	:	1	2	3	4	5	6	7	8	:	Trustworthy
Considerate	:	8	7	6	5	4	3	2	1	:	Inconsiderate
Nasty	:	1	2	3	4	5	6	7	8	:	Nice
Agreeable	:	8	7	6	5	4	3	2	1	:	Disagreeable
Insincere	:	1	2	3	4	5	6	7	8	:	Sincere
Kind	:	8	7	6	5	4	3	2	1	:	Unkind

made any one of these statements could become a group leader, his or her behavior once in the role would be heavily influenced by personal assumptions concerning "good" leadership, as well as personal values, and beliefs about leadership goals. Early on in his research Fiedler concluded that he would have to take these kinds of differences into consideration when making predictions about effectiveness. To do so, he posited the existence of two different **motivational styles** of leadership. Essentially, Fiedler felt that some leaders are relationship motivated—that is, strongly motivated to find acceptance within their groups. Such leaders seek to establish strong interpersonal links with the other members of their groups, and are concerned more with these relationships than with task completion. In contrast, the second type of leader is task motivated, concentrating on task completion as the primary goal of the group.

Although these hypotheses are consistent with other research into leader behavior reviewed earlier in the chapter, Fiedler's method of assessing motivational style is unique. Rather than basing his estimates on group members' ratings of the leader, Fiedler asks leaders to complete an indirect measure of motivational style known as the **Least Preferred Co-worker Scale (the LPC Scale).** To complete the instrument respondents are asked to think of the one individual with whom they experienced the most difficulty in working at some time. This person, dubbed the least preferred co-worker, is then evaluated on the scales in the LPC box. According to Fiedler (1978, p. 61),

> An individual who describes the LPC in very negative, rejecting terms (low LPC score, i.e., less than 57) is considered task-motivated. In other words, the completion of the task is of such overriding importance that it completely colors the perception of all other personality traits attributed to the LPC. In effect, the individual says, "If I cannot work with you, if you frustrate my need to get the job done, then you can't be any good in other respects. You are . . . unfriendly, unpleasant, tense, distant, etc."
>
> The relationship-motivated individual who sees his or her LPC in relatively more positive terms (high LPC score, i.e., about 63 and above) says, "Getting a job done is not everything. Therefore, even though I can't work with you, you may still be friendly, relaxed, interesting, etc., in other words, someone with whom I could get along with on a personal basis."

Thus, high LPCs are relationship motivated, while low LPCs are task motivated.

SITUATIONAL CONTROL

By considering LPC scores, Fiedler is able to generate limited predictions about leadership, but more accurate hypotheses can only be formulated by taking situational factors into consideration. In the contingency model Fiedler assumes that the most important feature of any leadership situation is the leader's control and influence therein (in early work Fiedler labeled this variable "situation favorableness" but has since discarded this term as too simplistic). If the leader controls the situation, then the leader can be fairly certain that decisions, actions, and sugges-

TABLE 8-4. The situational-control dimension

Leader/member relations	Good				Bad			
Task structure	High		Low		High			
Position power	Strong	Weak	Strong	Weak	Strong	Weak	Strong	Weak
Octant	I	II	III	IV	V	VI	VII	VIII

(Source: Fiedler and Chemers, 1974)

tions will be carried out by the group members. If, on the other hand, the leader has trouble gaining control, then the outcome of the group's work will be unclear—the group could fall short of its projected performance thus leaving the leader's needs ungratified. Although many factors could be related to control, Fiedler emphasizes three: leader/member relations, the task structure, and the leader's position power.

Leader/member relations.   The leader's acceptance by the group is the most important of all three situational variables. If the group is highly cohesive, relatively conflict free, and cooperative, then the leader will be less concerned with peace keeping and monitoring interpersonal behavior. Further, when group members are loyal to their leaders and acknowledge their ability, leaders can be confident that their suggestions and requests will be heeded. Although leader/member relations can be assessed in a variety of ways, Fiedler and his associates often ask the leader to provide this information by indicating their degree of agreement with such statements as "My subordinates are reliable and trustworthy"; "My subordinates always cooperate with me in getting the job done"; and "I have good relations with the people I supervise" (Fiedler, 1978, p. 63).

Task structure.   The second most important situational factor centers on the group's task. Although the problems some groups work on are relatively straightforward and have only one right solution whose correctness is easily checked, the tasks of other groups are ambiguous, admit to many correct solutions, and offer no "right" way of reaching the goal. Fiedler typically measures task structure by asking the leader's supervisors to indicate degree of agreement with such questions as "Is there a step-by-step procedure or a standard operating procedure that indicates in detail the process to be followed?" and "Is it obvious when the task is finished and the correct solution has been found?" and finally, "Is the evaluation of this task generally made on some quantitative basis?" (Fiedler, 1978, p. 64).

Position power.   The final situational control variable, position power, refers to the leader's power over the other group members. While in some groups—such as informal discussion sessions, classroom groups, social gatherings—the leader's power is low, in others—for example, military units, work departments, and committees—the leader has far more power relative to the subordinates. Fiedler (1978) cites as indicators of position power such factors as leader's control over rewards, punishments, salaries, hiring, evaluation, and task assignment.

Combining the three situational factors.   Fiedler simplifies the control variables by dichotomizing each one: leader/member relations are either good or bad; the task structure is either high or low; and the leader's position power is either strong or weak. Next, Fiedler combines these three factors in a 2 × 2 × 2 framework of situation control such as that presented in Table 8-4. Groups that fall into Octant I are highly favorable for the leader because relations are good, the task is highly structured, and the leader's position power is strong. However, as we

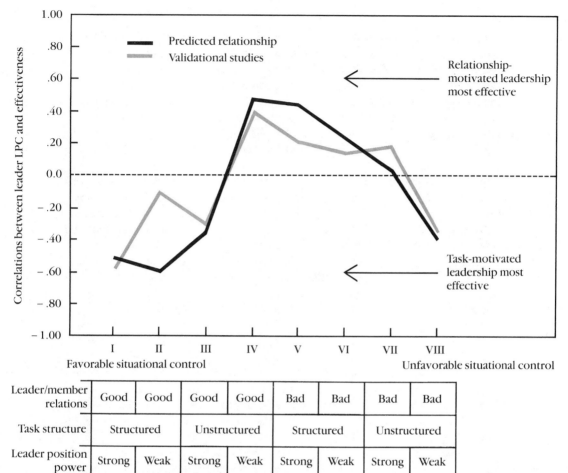

Leader/member relations	Good	Good	Good	Good	Bad	Bad	Bad	Bad
Task structure	Structured		Unstructured		Structured		Unstructured	
Leader position power	Strong	Weak	Strong	Weak	Strong	Weak	Strong	Weak

FIGURE 8-1. The predicted and obtained relationship between LPC score and leadership effectiveness in eight group situations. The correlations, from Octant I to Octant VIII, for the original studies, are $-.52$, $-.58$, $-.33$, .47, .42, xx (Octant VI is missing), .05, $-.43$. The correlations, from Octant I to Octant VIII, for the validational studies, are $-.59$, $-.10$, $-.29$, .40, .19, .13, .17, $-.35$. (Source: Fiedler, 1978)

move from Octant I through to Octant VIII, the situation grows less favorable for the leader. In this last, and worst, type of group the relations are poor, the task is unstructured, and the leader has little power.

THE CONTINGENCY-MODEL PREDICTIONS

According to Fiedler, motivational style and situational control interact to determine leadership effectiveness. Overall, the model predicts that *the low-LPC leader (task motivated) will be most effective in situations that are either highly favorable or unfavorable, while the high-LPC leader (relationship motivated) will be most effective in the middle-range situations.* This prediction is perhaps best elaborated by the graph in Figure 8-1. The horizontal axis represents the eight octants that define situational control. Octant I corresponds to the most controllable and favorable situation, and Octant VIII corresponds to the least controllable and least favorable setting. The vertical axis indicates the predicted relationship between LPC scores and task performance. If the correlation is greater than 0.0 (positive), then effectiveness is positively related to LPC; that is, relationship-motivated leaders are more effective. If, however, the correlation is smaller than 0.0 (negative), then effectiveness is negatively related to LPC; task-motivated leaders are more effective. The predictions of the model for each octant are summarized by the heavy black line.

To see how the model makes predictions about leadership effectiveness, consider two hypothetical antiaircraft artillery crews labeled A and B (Fiedler, 1964). In both crews, the leaders enjoy a strong position power since their authority is determined by rank. In addition, task structure is high in both crews since the same sequence of decisions must be made for each target. However, in Crew A the commander is extremely well liked, while in Crew B the commander is disliked. According to the contingency model, Crew A would be located in Octant I because leader/member relations are good, the task is structured, and position power is strong. Crew B, however, falls into Octant V because while it is identical to Crew A in power and structure, Crew B's leader/member relations are poor. Thus, two different types of leadership would be appropriate for the two crews: for A the low-LPC leader would be most effective, but for B the high-LPC leader would be superior. Supporting this prediction, Fiedler (1955) found that LPC scores were negatively correlated with effectiveness for artillery squads such as Crew A ($r = -.34$), but positively correlated with effectiveness for such crews as B ($r = .49$). Similar predictions for the other six octants of the contingency model can also be derived from Figure 8-1.

To some, the predicted relationship between leader's motivational style, situational control, and effectiveness seems paradoxical and counterintuitive. Why should liking for a co-worker influence a leader's ability? Why would a task-motivated leader do well in unfavorable settings? Why would a relationship-motivated leader do poorly when conditions are favorable for leadership? Fortunately, Fiedler has recently answered some of these questions in his *motivational-hierarchy hypothesis* (Fiedler, 1972, 1978; Fiedler & Chemers, 1974). He assumes that an individual is typically motivated to reach more than one goal. For example, a college student may wish to become an expert in group dynamics, attend many parties, drink beer whenever possible, date attractive persons of the opposite sex, obtain a high grade-point average, and study efficiently. However, given time limitations, the student can attain only some of these goals and must make a decision about which goals come first and which should be left until later. Naturally, if the student is able to attain the top goal (becoming an expert in group dynamics, of course), than he or she will be able to work on other, lower priority activities (attending parties).

This concept of motivational hierarchies, when applied to leadership, suggests that leaders seek a series of goals that can be ordered along a continuum that ranges from "extremely important—top priority" to "not very important—low priority." However, high and low LPCs possess different hierarchies: the high LPC

gives highest priority to establishing and maintaining satisfying interpersonal relations within the group, but the low LPC gives top ranking to successful task completion. Therefore, in an unfavorable situation the low LPC is concerned with
driving the group toward task completion and wastes no time trying to improve
group relations. The high LPC, on the other hand, concentrates on trying to
reestablish satisfying interpersonal relations in a hopelessly irretrievable situation.
Hence, the high LPC is ineffective.

On the opposite side of the ledger—the most favorable situation—leaders become
reasonably certain that their number one priority can be reached, and so they can
shift their focus toward a lower-order priority. From Fiedler (1978, p. 95):

> In other words, assured that they will attain their primary goal, individuals will
> then seek to achieve goals which are next in priority. In groups which provide
> high situational control the leaders have this assurance: High LPC leaders have
> the support of their subordinates; low LPC leaders know that the task will be
> completed (Beach, et al., 1975). Under these high-control conditions, the rela-
> tionship-motivated leader can then turn his attention to other aspects of his sit-
> uation, for example, seeking the approbation of such important others as the boss
> or faculty member who serves as experimenter, as well as gaining more complete
> control of the group. . . . The low-LPC leader who knows the task will get done
> can sit back, relax, and behave in a generally considerate and pleasant manner.

Thus, in favorable situations the low LPCs tend to become more interpersonally
supportive whereas the high LPCs become more task oriented (Green & Nebeker,
1977; Meuwese & Fiedler, 1965). In a favorable situation the strong task emphasis
undermines the high LPCs' effectiveness, but the increase in supportiveness shown
by the low LPCs increases their leadership efficiency.

EVALUATING THE CONTINGENCY MODEL

Fiedler's theory of leadership effectiveness is a data-based model, since its predictions are derived from research findings rather than deductions from theoretical
generalizations. Therefore, Fiedler felt that before the model could be deemed
acceptable, additional studies were needed to validate the original conclusions.
Since he first formulated the model in 1963, more than 300 studies have examined
one or more aspects of the overall theory, suggesting both strengths and weaknesses in the original formulation.

Correlational evidence. The traditional paradigm for testing the contingency
model involves locating various groups (Fiedler has studied navy teams, research
groups, shop departments, supermarkets, engineering groups, hospitals, government panels, athletic teams, and many others), assessing the leader's esteem for
the least preferred co-worker, measuring the situational variables that determine
leader control, and calculating the group's overall effectiveness on an interactive
task. The results of many of these investigations are summarized by the grey line
in Figure 8-1 (Fiedler, 1971a, 1971b). As the contour of this line indicates, the
validation studies tend to track quite closely the earlier findings. Overall, the task-
motivated, low-LPC leader was more effective than the relationship-motivated,
high-LPC leader in the favorable or unfavorable octants—I, II, III, and VIII. This
effect was reversed in the intermediately favorable octants—IV, V, VI, and VII

(Fiedler, 1967, 1971a, 1978). The only exception to this overall confirmation of the model seemed to be specific to Octant II. In this particular cell many validational studies—particularly those conducted in laboratory settings—yielded positive correlations between LPC and effectiveness (Graen, Orris, & Alvares, 1971). Fiedler believes that the inconsistency in the findings related to this octant may stem from the difficulty in simultaneously establishing good leader/member relations, a structured task, and low leader power in a laboratory group. Furthermore, a recent investigation that focused specifically on Octant II groups reports a significant negative correlation, as the original formulation predicted ($r = -.55$; Schneier, 1978).

Experimental evidence.   Experimental studies of the contingency model predictions have yielded results that both contradict (Vecchio, 1977) and support (Chemers & Skrzypek, 1972; Hardy, 1971, 1975) the correlational findings. For example, one study of leadership among male cadets at the United States Military Academy at West Point manipulated all three of the situational-control variables (Chemers & Skrzypek, 1972). Leaders were assigned followers who had previously reported dislike for the designated leader, or were assigned followers who had stated that they liked the leader. Crossing this manipulation, half of the leaders were given a fair amount of power, since they could rate each group member, while the remaining leaders had little evaluative power. Lastly, the groups worked on both structured and unstructured tasks.

The results of this investigation yielded mixed, but generally favorable, support for the contingency model. When LPC score was correlated with group effectiveness across the eight cells of the experimental design that matched the eight octants of the model, the correlations paralleled the model's predictions.

Leadership training studies.   Although many different programs and techniques have been developed to "train" effective leaders, the results of these procedures are typically disappointing (Stogdill, 1974). Fiedler, however, suggests that these programs fail because they place too much emphasis on changing the leaders: making them more supportive, more decisive, more democratic, and so on. In contrast, Fiedler suggests that the situation, and not the leader, should be engineered to fit the leader's particular motivational style. He calls his training program LEADER MATCH because he teaches enrollees to modify their group situation until it matches their personal motivational style (Fiedler, Chemers, & Mahar, 1976). Investigators have tested the effectiveness of this innovative training program, and in general conclude that the procedure is remarkably successful (Csoka & Bons, 1978; Fiedler, 1978). Trained leaders are typically rated as more effective in the group than untrained leaders, apparently because they can change their group's situational favorability.

CRITICISM OF THE MODEL

The contingency model possesses many strengths: it takes into account both personal factors (LPC score) and situational factors (situation control) in predicting effectiveness; a wealth of empirical data generated in a wide variety of groups supports the model's predictions; and a training program based on the theory seems to work well. Yet the model possesses certain limitations, and to provide a balanced picture some of these criticisms should be noted.

First, while the bulk of the research seems to support the contingency-model predictions, several studies report findings that run contrary to the theoretical predictions (Graen et al., 1971; Vecchio, 1977). Second, Fiedler's interpretations of his correlational findings are rejected by some researchers, since they do not always reach conventional levels of statistical significance (Ashour, 1973a, 1973b; McMahon, 1972). Third, because the early research relied heavily on correlational findings, cause/effect conclusions may be inappropriate. Although LPC and situational control may combine to determine effectiveness, it is possible that effectiveness may actually cause changes in LPC and situational control. Fourth, the LPC scale is often the butt of criticisms. Like any psychological instrument, the LPC should be both reliable—that is, internally and temporally consistent—and valid—an accurate index of the corresponding construct it is supposed to assess. Unfortunately, the LPC has been modified many times, and some critics have suggested that the different versions are incompatible and, in general, unreliable (Schriesheim, Bannister, & Money, 1979). In addition, while a precise conceptual understanding of an LPC score has been sought for 25 years, the theoretical meaning of the instrument remains uncertain (Schriesheim & Kerr, 1977).

Given these conflicting appraisals of the model's adequacy, no immutable conclusions can be offered. The contingency model continues to be modified as new research findings come to light, and recent evidence suggests that much progress is being made. For example, one set of reviewers—after statistically combining the results of more than 40 studies—concluded that "the model as a whole was overwhelmingly supported by the available evidence" (Strube & Garcia, 1981, p. 316). Similarly, another reviewer (Rice, 1978a, 1978b, 1979) reports evidence of the reliability of the LPC scale, while also affirming Fiedler's contention that high LPCs are relationship motivated and low LPCs are task motivated. Furthermore, Fiedler (1972, 1978) has elaborated on the dynamics of the LPC/situational control/effectiveness interaction, and argues that the motivational-hierarchy hypothesis provides a parsimonious explanation for the available data. However, as made clear by the box headed "Everybody Can't Be Right," leadership experts are still substantially divided on the question of the model's validity, and more research will be needed before a final answer to the validity question can be given.

Participation Theories of Leadership

The army squad in boot camp begins picking up trash as soon as the sergeant gives the order. The chair of a committee trying to make a decision on a companywide issue asks for input from several members before making a final judgment. A small-business owner studies company productivity levels before deciding to make some organizational changes. Factor workers elect representatives who negotiate with the owners over a wage hike. The manager of a baseball team waits until the team is on the field warming up before revealing the starting lineup. A group of college students gets together with their professor and votes on the topic they wish to research in the coming semester.

In each of these situations individuals are making decisions about issues that will influence the activities, satisfactions, and outcomes of an entire group, but the

EVERYBODY CAN'T BE RIGHT

Although many people think that science should provide answers to questions in absolute right-or-wrong terms, in many cases scientific questions must be debated and argued for some time until a general consensus is reached. As Robert W. Rice has recently pointed out, the controversy over the adequacy of the contingency model is one of those areas where researchers tend to take sides against one another, with partisan identity determining one's appraisal of the value of the model. Some of the polarized comments about the contingency model are quoted below.

In favor of the contingency model

The predictive validity of the contingency model appears to be well supported. Likewise, the recent extension of the model into the effects of leader training and experience promises to be a potentially major advance in our understanding of leadership [Chemers & Rice, 1974, p. 123].

I believe that the model does have some ability to predict group performance on the basis of the leader's LPC score and an appropriate analysis of situational factors [Rice, 1978, p. 1202].

[The] claim that the model lacks empirical validity, contains fatal methodological flaws, and is theoretically inadequate is refuted by the available data [Fiedler, 1973, p. 366].

The model is capable of directing meaningful research, but only as long as traditional research procedures designed to safeguard internal and external validity are carefully exercised [Shiflett, 1973, p. 429].

Against the contingency model

[Available research] casts grave doubts on the plausibility of the contingency model . . . The model has lost the capability of directing meaningful research [Graen et al., 1970, p. 295].

The evidence concerning the LPC instrument does not support its continued use. LPC lacks sufficient evidence of construct, content, predictive, and concurrent validity, and test-retest reliability [Schriesheim & Kerr, 1977, p. 31].

Clearly the contingency model is based on a simplistic scheme that omits essential linkages intervening between leader's traits and group outcomes [Ashour, 1973a, p. 352]. Fiedler's Contingency Model and its related research have serious empirical, methodological and theoretical problems [Ashour, 1973b, p. 375].

Analysis of the model in terms of logic and methodology has revealed serious questions which must be answered if the model's potential is to be realized [McMahon, 1972, p. 708].

Perhaps both sides in the dispute should heed the suggestion of Abraham K. Korman:

Theory, contingency or otherwise, is to help and guide research, not to control it. We should not become so invested in any theory, particularly our own, that it "strangles" us and we ignore the major goal of our work, the understanding of behavior [1974, p. 195].

amount of group member involvement in the decisional process ranges from full to very little. At one end of the participation continuum the group members— with or without the help of the leader—decide (often by vote) the issues in question. At the other end no poll is taken; the leader alone weighs the available information and makes the decision the group is to follow. Between these two extremes are instances in which the leaders make the decision after receiving various amounts of information from the other group members. The question the leader must ask in each situation is clear: Which point along this continuum is the most effective in terms of productivity and satisfaction?

THE LEWIN/LIPPITT/WHITE STUDIES

The issue of group-member participation in decision making was first made salient to group dynamicists by Kurt Lewin, Ronald Lippitt, and Ralph White (1939; White & Lippitt, 1968) in their classic studies of authoritarian, democratic, and laissez-faire leadership. As noted briefly in Chapter 2, these researchers arranged for 10- and 11-year-old boys to meet together after school to work on various hobbies. In addition to the young boys each group included an adult male who adopted one of three particular styles of interaction when dealing with the boys. Some groups were run by an *authoritarian (or autocratic) leader*. This type of leader took no input from the members in making decisions about group activities, did not discuss the long-range goals of the group, frequently emphasized his authority, inevitably dictated who would work on specific projects, and arbitrarily paired the boys with their work partners. In contrast, the *democratic leader* made certain that all group activities were first discussed by the entire group. He assisted during these discussions and sometimes made the final and ultimate decision but was always open to input from the boys. He allowed the group members to make their own decisions about work projects or partners and encouraged the development of an egalitarian atmosphere. The third and final type of leader adopted a *laissez-faire* attitude, rarely intervening in the group activities. Groups with this type of atmosphere made all decisions on their own without any supervision, and their so-called leader functioned primarily as a source of technical information. In some cases the boys were rotated to a different experimental condition so they could experience all three types of participation.

When the behaviors of the boys in the three conditions were compared, a number of differences in efficiency, satisfaction, and aggressiveness seemed to be apparent. As Figure 8-2 reveals, authoritarian groups spent as much time working on their hobbies as the democratic groups, but the laissez-faire groups worked considerably less. However, when the leader left the room, the observers noted that work dropped off dramatically in the authoritarian-led groups, remained unchanged in the democratic groups, and actually increased in the laissez-faire groups. Furthermore, members of groups with an authoritarian leader displayed greater reliance on the leader, expressed more critical discontent, and made more aggressive demands for attention. Democratic groups tended to be friendlier and more group oriented. Overall, the boys preferred democratic leaders over the other two varieties.

Although these findings seem to recommend the democratic-leadership approach over the two alternatives, the findings of the Lewin/Lippitt/White studies were not as clearcut as Figure 8-2 implies. While several of the groups reacted to the authoritarian leader with hostility, negativity, and scapegoating, several others responded very passively to their leaders. In these latter groups productivity was quite high (74%), although it did drop down to 29% if the leader left the room. Aggression, very apparent in some of the authoritarian-led groups, was replaced in these others by apathy and acceptance of the situation. Although the group would become

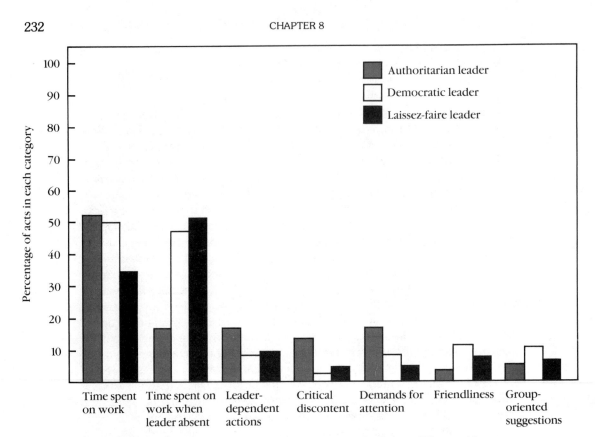

FIGURE 8-2. Findings in the Lewin/Lippitt/White study. (Source: White and Lippitt, 1960)

aggressive if the authoritarian leader was replaced with a more permissive one, when the autocratic supervisor was present the group members worked hard, demanded little attention, only rarely engaged in horseplay, and followed very closely the recommendations of the leader. Apparently, the relationship between participation and effectiveness is not a simple one.

Following the lead of the Lewin/Lippitt/White studies, a plethora of investigations has studied the participation issue, but to an extent the original results—complete with the contradictory conclusions—still hold. In some studies participative leadership seems to be far more effective than nonparticipative leadership. For example, in a classic study of pajama-plant workers' reactions to a change in operating procedures, the researchers established three experimental conditions (Koch & French, 1948). In the *no-participation group* employees were simply told of the changes. In the *participation-through-representation condition* employees selected delegates to work with management in formulating changes. In the *total-participation groups* the members met in groups and decided how the changes would be instituted. Analysis revealed that the workers in the no-participation group displayed more aggression, hostility, turnover, and dissatisfaction, and learned new procedures more slowly than workers in the two participation conditions.

In contrast, other studies found greater productivity and satisfaction when the final decisions were made by a recognized group leader. In a study of 72 groups in industry, business, and government, satisfaction with the group and group cohesiveness were negatively correlated with the leader's permissiveness (Berkowitz, 1953). Similarly, a study of turnover in a factory found that quitting was associated with democratic, rather than autocratic, supervision (Ley, 1966), and a survey of leadership in educational settings suggested that member satisfaction is greatest in authoritarian-led groups (Anderson, 1959). Lastly, studies report both increases and decreases in productivity and satisfaction in permissive, laissez-faire leadership settings (Morse & Reimer, 1956; Weschler, Kahane, & Tannenbaum, 1952).

Ralph Stogdill, after reviewing more than 40 studies of various leadership methods that ranged along the participation/no-participation continuum, concluded that no one participatory technique is more frequently associated with increases in productivity than another (1974). While several studies indicated that productivity decreases when group members participate in decisions, the majority of the research found no differences due to decision centralization. Stogdill goes on to note, however, that satisfaction with the group seems to be highest in democratic groups as opposed to authoritarian and laissez-faire groups. Even this conclusion, however, fails to hold when groups expect an authoritarian leader (Foa, 1957) or when the group is very large (Vroom & Mann, 1960).

A POSSIBLE RESOLUTION

Victor Vroom has recently offered a sophisticated solution to this problem of contradictory findings regarding group-member participation in leadership (1973, 1974, 1976; Vroom & Yetton, 1973). According to Vroom, participation in decision-making processes enhances the satisfaction and effectiveness of the group only in certain situations. He calls his theory a **normative model of leadership** because it makes clear suggestions for the prospective leader; Vroom recommends that individuals who face leadership situations use the theory to determine how much involvement in decisions members should be allowed. Although this complex model cannot be fully described here, the three key features of the approach—the taxonomy of leadership methods, the problem attributes, and the decision tree—are briefly discussed below.

A taxonomy of leadership methods.   Vroom identifies five key types of leadership methods, which fall at varying intervals along the autocratic/participative continuum depicted in Figure 8-3. Beginning at the leader-centered, authoritarian end of the continuum and ranging to the group-centered, democratic end of the continuum, we find the following "methods" of leadership (paraphrased from Vroom & Yetton, 1973, p. 13):

Autocratic I: (AI)	The leader solves the problem or makes the decision using information available to him or her at that time.
Autocratic II: (AII)	The leader obtains necessary information from members, and then decides on the solution to the problem. The leader

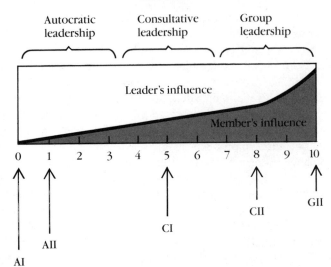

FIGURE 8-3. Vroom's taxonomy of leadership methods. (Source: Vroom & Yetton, 1973)

	may or may not tell the group members what the problem is in getting the information from them. The role played by the group members is one of providing information rather than generating or evaluating alternative solutions.
Consultative I: (CI)	The leader shares the problem with relevant group members individually, getting their ideas and suggestions without bringing them together as a group. Then the leader makes the decision, which may or may not reflect the group members' influence.
Consultative II: (CII)	The leader shares the problem with the members as a group, collectively obtaining their ideas and suggestions. Then the leader makes the decision, which may or may not reflect the group members' influences.
Group II: (GII)	The leader shares the problem with the group members as a group. Together the leader and members generate and evaluate alternatives and attempt to reach agreement (consensus) on a solution. The leader role is much like that of chairperson of a committee. The leader does not try to influence the group to adopt a particular solution, and the leader is willing to accept and implement any solution that is supported by the entire group.

Other leadership methods are, of course, possible (for example, delegative leadership or Group I leadership), but Vroom emphasizes these five.

The problem attributes. In a sense, Vroom's normative model is a "contingency" theory, because it argues that no single leadership method—autocratic (AI or AII), consultative (CI or CII), or group (GII)—will be best in all situations. While the leader may often be well advised to meet with the group whenever a major decision is to be made, in some situations this democratic approach may prove ineffective, time consuming, and dissatisfying to members. In these instances a more autocratic type of leadership may be the most successful approach. The key issue thus focuses on the leadership method/situation contingency: Which leadership approach in which situation?

In answer, Vroom and his colleagues (Vroom, 1976; Vroom & Jago; 1978; Vroom & Yetton, 1973) listed between six and eight attributes of the group situation to consider in judging which type of leadership to use. The seven-attribute list is composed of the following items (paraphrased from Vroom & Yetton, 1973):

A. The importance of the quality of the decision.
B. The extent to which leaders possess sufficient information and expertise to make a high-quality decision by themselves.
C. The extent to which the problem is structured.
D. The extent to which acceptance or commitment on the part of subordinates is critical to effective implementation of the decision.
E. The prior probability that the leader's autocratic decision will be accepted by subordinates.
F. The extent to which subordinates are motivated to attain organizational goals as represented in the objectives made explicit in the statement of the problem.
G. The extent to which subordinates are likely to disagree over the solution.

The decision tree.   Each of the problem attributes listed can be expressed in a yes-or-no question. These seven questions are presented in Figure 8-4, which also contains the normative model's leadership-decision tree. To use this model, the leader starts at the left-hand side of the tree with Question A: Is there a quality requirement such that one solution is likely to be more rational than another? If the answer is no then the leader follows the flow chart to the next query, Question D: Is acceptance of decision by subordinates critical to effective implementation? If, however, the leader's answer to question A is yes, then a different direction is taken in the flow chart and question B must be answered. When the leader reaches a terminal node, he or she is directed to a set of leadership methods that should be most effective—in terms of decision quality, group-member satisfaction, and time efficiency—in the given situation. Figure 8-4 describes 13 different terminal nodes, or *problem types,* and lists a number of leadership options under the column labeled "acceptable methods."

The normative model is still in its formative stages (Hill & Schmitt, 1977), but available evidence seems to support the adequacy of the approach. For example, Vroom and his colleagues have conducted numerous studies in which participants are asked to read a case study of a leadership decision and then make a recommendation about appropriate leader method. Although certain participants tend to opt for a certain style of leadership no matter what the situation, others are able to alter their methods depending upon the characteristics of the problem described (Hill & Schmitt, 1977; Jago, 1978; Vroom & Yetton, 1973). While these studies suggest that the Vroom normative model functions as an adequate descriptive tool, more research is needed to check the specific recommendations of the model. These prescriptions about the "best" method of leadership for each node, while

A. Is there a quality requirement such that one solution is likely to be more rational
than another?
B. Do I have sufficient info to make a high quality decision?
C. Is the problem structured?
D. Is acceptance of decision by subordinates critical to effective implementation?
E. If I were to make the decision by myself, is it reasonably certain that it would be accepted
by my subordinates?
F. Do subordinates share the organizational goals to be attained in solving this problem?
G. Is conflict among subordinates likely in preferred solutions?

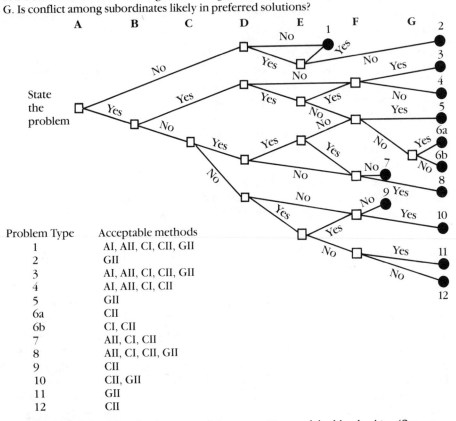

Problem Type	Acceptable methods
1	AI, AII, CI, CII, GII
2	GII
3	AI, AII, CI, CII, GII
4	AI, AII, CI, CII
5	GII
6a	CII
6b	CI, CII
7	AII, CI, CII
8	AII, CI, CII, GII
9	CII
10	CII, GII
11	GII
12	CII

FIGURE 8-4.   The decision tree of the normative model of leadership. (Source:
Vroom & Yetton, 1973)

consistent with prior research, need to be tested by examining the impact of each
of the five key methods in each situation specified by the decision tree (Field,
1979).

Other Perspectives on Leader Effectiveness

The contingency model and normative model are two of the most frequently
cited leadership theories, but some researchers rely on still other theoretical frameworks in their explanations of leadership processes. The number of alternative
approaches has grown so large over the years that we cannot consider all of them,
but at the very least we should look at a subset of these other ideas about leadership.

A TWO-DIMENSIONAL LEADERSHIP-STYLE THEORY

Fiedler, by using the LPC scale as a measure of leader motivations, implicitly assumes that leaders are either relationship motivated *or* task motivated. In contrast, other theorists believe that leaders can be both relationship *and* task oriented or *neither* relationship nor task oriented (Kerr et al., 1974). If it is assumed that leaders can be classified as high or low on the two dimensions specified in the Ohio State Leadership Studies, then crossing the two dimensions in a 2 × 2 yields the typology of leadership styles shown in Table 8-5. Although the labels for the four quadrants vary from theorist to theorist, the basic types remain the same: (1) *relationship-style leaders* focus more on the needs of the group members than on the task; (2) *task leaders* are goal oriented and group structuring; (3) *laissez-faire leaders* satisfy neither leadership function; and (4) *fusion leaders* (Zaleznik, 1966) are able to move the group toward important goals while simultaneously remaining sensitive to the needs of the individual members.

Although research indicates that the leader who is high on both dimensions may be a relatively rare individual (Bales, 1958; Hammer & Dachler, 1973; Kerr et al., 1974), fusion leadership may be most effective across various types of situations. For example, in several early studies of the crews of B-29 bombers flying missions during the Korean War, aircraft commanders were classified into one of the four cells of Table 8-5 on the basis of their crew's responses to the LBDQ (Halpin, 1953, 1954). Two measures of effectiveness were also taken, including ratings provided by the aircraft commanders' superior officers and the crew members' ratings of group morale and commander proficiency. While superiors tended to evaluate more positively leaders who showed a concern for task completion, during training crew members were more satisfied with a relationship-emphasizing leader. However, after the crews had gone into combat, task emphasis also became important; thus, both relationship and task scores on the LBDQ were positively correlated to group-member satisfaction.

Even clearer conclusions are yielded when the laissez-faire and fusion leaders of Table 8-5 are compared. When superiors' evaluations of aircraft commanders were used to classify leaders into two categories—effective or ineffective—analyses revealed that nearly all the effective commanders (8 out of 9) were fusion leaders. In contrast, more of the ineffective leaders (6 out of 10) were laissez-faires (Halpin, 1953). In a similar project, academic leadership was studied by identifying departments known throughout a university for the effectiveness or ineffectiveness of their chairpeople. As in the military studies, chairs with outstanding reputations as administrators received high scores on both scales of the LBDQ, while inept administrators received low scores (Hemphill, 1955).

TABLE 8-5. A two-dimensional theory of leadership style

		Relationship Orientation	
		High	Low
Task Orientation	Low	Relationship leader	Laissez-faire leader
	High	Fusion leader	Task leader

In sum, the two-dimensional approach suggests that leadership effectiveness is related to both task and relationship emphasis. Although this approach received little attention in the 1960s and early 70s, the concept is being revitalized by researchers who are trying to identify the situational variables that alter the magnitude of the relationship between leadership style and effectiveness (Katz, 1977; Kerr et al., 1974). The two-dimensional-style theory also helps to explain sex differences in leadership (see box).

THE THREE-DIMENSIONAL MODEL

Researchers at the Center for Leadership Studies at Ohio State University (Hersey & Blanchard, 1976, 1977) also describe leadership in terms of the relationship and task dimensions, but they feel that a third dimension—effectiveness—must also be considered in applying this approach. Rejecting the notion that the high-relationship/high-task (fusion) leader will be effective across all groups and all situations, the three-dimensional approach suggests that groups benefit from leadership that meshes with the needs of the group members. To a large extent, this "fit" between leadership style and group members' needs is determined by the maturity of the group, where maturity is defined as "the capacity to set high but

---

DO MEN MAKE BETTER LEADERS THAN WOMEN?

Although the sex-role consistency of men's and women's behavior influences many aspects of group dynamics, the relationship between sex roles and leadership behaviors seems particularly marked. As early as 1956, researchers suggested that men in groups tend to provide orientation, opinions, and directions designed to lead the group toward goal attainment, while women emphasize group solidarity, reduction of group tension, and avoidance of intragroup antagonism. Despite the many changes in perceptions of women and men during the years since that study, these findings were recently replicated in both same- and mixed-sex groups: women tend to be relationship oriented while men are task oriented (Piliavin & Martin, 1978; Strodtbeck & Mann, 1956).

Unfortunately, the two-dimensional-style theory suggests that a successful leader should try to satisfy both the relationship and task needs of the groups, raising the possibility that males and females who conform closely to "appropriate" sex roles will be ineffective leaders. Furthermore, research suggests that group members feel that task skills are important qualities for a leader to possess, but devalue interpersonal skills (Leary, Forsyth, & McCown, 1978). This overemphasis on task skills may explain why some group members erroneously assume that men make better leaders than women (Jacobson & Effertz, 1974). Indeed, while research indicates that women and men are *not* differentially effective as leaders (Brown, 1977), group members' assumptions concerning sex differences create biases in their perceptions of the leader's competence. For example, a survey of a number of university employees found that the overwhelming majority preferred male rather than female bosses (Ferber, Huber, & Spitze, 1979). Similarly, an attitude poll of male managers concluded that most rated females more negatively than males when judging aptitudes, leadership skills, motivation, and general temperament (Rosen & Jerdee, 1978). These results suggest that group members' misunderstandings concerning leadership skills and the tendency for women and men to behave in accordance with sex-role stereotypes combine to create biases against female leaders.

attainable goals, willingness and ability to take responsibility, education and/or experience of an individual or a group" (1976, p. 96). In this sense, then, maturity has little to do with age, but rather means experience in working on a particular problem in a particular group.

According to the three-dimensional model, immature group members will work most effectively with a high-task/low-relationship leader. However, as a group matures and begins working adequately on the task, the leader can increase relationship behavior and adopt a high/high fusion style. Still later in the group's development, the leader can ease off on both types of leadership, starting first with task emphasis. In moderately mature groups the high-relationship/low-task style is most effective, and in fully mature work groups a low/low, laissez-faire style is appropriate. Thus, leadership effectiveness depends primarily upon (1) the flexibility of the leader and (2) the maturity of the group. Three-dimensional theorists have developed a measure of leader adaptability in groups of varying maturity (LEAD), and early research returns are encouraging (Hersey & Blanchard, 1976, 1977).

PATH/GOAL THEORY

According to path/goal theory (House, 1971) the leader of a group has two primary functions: facilitation of goal attainment and clarification of the paths to take in reaching these goals. If the leader can fulfill these two functions, then the group members will be satisfied and motivated to work toward the goal. If, however, the leader is perceived to be of little help in making the group's tasks easier, then the motivation of group members will be low. Thus, the path/goal model predicts that leader effectiveness depends in large part on the perceptions, satisfactions, and needs of the members of the group. As with the other approaches, path/goal-theory hypotheses are currently being investigated (see House, 1971; Mawhinney & Ford, 1977).

Some Conclusions

In looking back over the theories and studies discussed in this section, we see a continual growth towards theories that explicitly consider the interaction between the leader's characteristics and the nature of the leadership situation. Virtually all major theories of leadership currently being investigated are based on the "contingency" assumption, although they often emphasize different leader characteristics (for example, the leader's "motivation," "style," or "method") and different features of the situation (such as "situational control," "attributes of the problem," or "maturity"). These theories have, in general, fared well in terms of both research and application to problems of leadership in small groups in business, military, and industrial settings, and we can only hope that these theoretical, empirical, and pragmatic successes will continue in the future.

Summary

In some respects, specifying what leadership is not is easier than specifying what it is. Not necessarily power over others, an inborn ability, a vote of popularity, or an authority grudgingly accepted by others, leadership generally involves a reciprocal process by which an individual is permitted to influence and motivate others to facilitate the attainment of mutually satisfying goals. Many factors—such as height, weight, intelligence, participation rate, and so on—influence who will become the leader in a group—but most leaders tend to perform two types of actions: those designed to improve *interpersonal relations* within the group and those designed to help the group successfully complete its *tasks*. Naturally, whenever other features of the situation fulfill these functions, it is likely that these *leadership substitutes* will make the leadership role unnecessary.

The major issue addressed by much of the theory and research dealing with leadership concerns effectiveness. Although earlier approaches emphasized either a *trait* or *situation approach,* most modern theories are based on the *interaction* between the leader's characteristics and the nature of the group situation. Fred Fiedler's *contingency theory,* for example, clearly shows when leaders with particular motivation styles (either task motivated or relationship motivated as measured by the Least Preferred Co-worker Scale) will function effectively. By taking into consideration the leader/member relations, task structure, and the leader's power, Fiedler's theory predicts that task-motivated leaders (low LPCs) are most effective in situations that are either extremely unfavorable or extremely favorable, while relationship-motivated leaders are most effective in intermediate situations. Taking a different approach, other theorists have extended the early Lewin/Lippitt/White findings regarding the effects of *authoritarian, democratic,* and *laissez-faire* leaders by asking when participatory leadership is effective. Victor Vroom's *normative model* is one of the most sophisticated answers to this question, for it compares the effectiveness of *autocratic, consultative,* and *group-centered* leaders in many different situations. This theory, like Fiedler's model and other theories examined in the chapter (for example, *three-dimensional theory* and the *path/goal model*), is a contingency theory because it is based on the assumption that leadership effectiveness is contingent on the leader's characteristics *and* the nature of the situation.

9

Conformity and Deviancy

They had decided to go out for a pizza once class was over, so ten o'clock found them at a booth in the corner busily perusing a menu. After about 30 seconds of silence, Bob looked up: "Let's get a large, with extra cheese and anchovies."

Although Sean visibly flinched at the word *anchovies,* Jean spoke up quickly in favor of the idea with "Right. Cheese, anchovies, but it's gotta have pepperoni on it, too."

By now Sean was looking both confused and disgusted, but before he could say anything Estelle asked "Is one large pizza going to be enough for us?"

"Sure, plenty," answered Bob, "I've gotten them here before. Is the extra cheese, anchovies, and pepperoni alright with you?"

"Yeah, that's what I usually get anyway," answered Estelle.

By this time Sean had found his voice, and asked "What's this about anchovies? I'm all for the extra cheese and pepperoni, but anchovies too?"

Bob answered reassuringly, "I always get them on pizza—they're really great. Besides, Jean and Estelle, you both want anchovies, don't you? See, we all like 'em."

"Well, I really don't think I like anchovies" mumbled Sean. "Why don't we just get them on half of the pizza; half with, half without?"

Jean entered the fray at this point, and complained "Look, Sean, then we wouldn't get enough ourselves—besides it costs extra that way. If you don't like them, you can just pick them off before you eat your slices." Estelle added "Let's hurry and decide. I'm starved."

As the waiter stood expectantly at the side of the table, Jean, Estelle, and Bob looked at Sean. Sean, feeling as if he had done something wrong, looked desperately at the menu one last time before thinking to himself, "You know, come to think of it, I've never really even tried anchovies before." Facing the waiter, Sean said "I think we're ready to order now."

The above is a mundane example of group dynamics, but this scenario occurs many times a day—with some variations—in pizza parlors all over the world. The group must make a decision on a question that has consequences both for the group as a whole and for each individual member. A majority of the group members is agreed on a particular course of action. Another member, however, holds an opposing opinion and calls into question the accuracy and rationality of the majority's planned decision. The majority, however, reacts to this dissent with group pressure—social influence designed to persuade, cajole, and convince the minority member to adopt its perspective. The incident concludes when the minority member capitulates and conforms to the majority's judgment. Although initially a deviant in the group, the anchovy-hating Sean eventually conformed to the dictates of the others.

As this example makes clear, the groups we belong to do more than supply us with people to talk to or help us in reaching important goals. Groups subtly influence their members; sway their judgments; favor one interpretation of reality over another, equally valid but less preferred; and encourage certain behaviors while discouraging others. To create these effects groups exert pressure on individuals that makes agreement with the norms of the group preferable to deviation from these rules. The person who strays too far from the group's idea of appropriate action, thought, or belief must be convinced of the value in the group's perspective, and encouraged to return again to the fold. The force of social pressure in groups is undeniable.

This chapter considers the processes involved in yielding and refusing to yield to these group pressures—conformity and deviancy. As an introduction to the vast literature relevant to these topics, we begin by considering how one psychologist, Solomon E. Asch, studied the causes and consequences of conformity and deviancy in small groups.

Studies of Conformity

In the early part of this century, researchers sporadically published findings that were either directly or tangentially related to conformity and deviancy in groups (Jenness, 1932a, 1932b; Newcomb, 1943; Sherif, 1936; Thorndike, 1938). For example, Muzafer Sherif, using the autokinetic effect, was able to show that individuals' judgments of the movement of a pinpoint of light in a dark room were influenced by group norms and other members' judgments. Similarly, Theodore Newcomb's classic Bennington study revealed how attitudes, once assumed to be the private territory of individualistically oriented psychologists, were heavily influenced by group forces. Yet while these and other studies were all building up to the same conclusion—that pressures created by group membership exert a pervasive influence on individuals—the topic of conformity did not capture the unified interest of the field until Solomon E. Asch reported the results of his carefully conducted studies of conformity in groups (Asch, 1952, 1955, 1957).

In his research Asch assembled groups of male college students in a group-dynamics laboratory for what was purported to be a psychological experiment in visual perception. The subjects were seated in a semicircle facing the experimenter, who explained that on each of 18 trials he would show the group two cards. One card bore a single line that was to serve as the standard. The second card contained three numbered test lines, as shown in Figure 9–1. The subjects' task was to compare the standard line to the three test lines and pick that line that matched the length of the standard line. Asch found that when making such judgments alone few people made mistakes, since one test line was always the same length as the standard line. Unlike the tasks involved in previous studies (for example, Sherif's perceptual problem), the task was unambiguous and there was always a correct answer.

As the experiment got under way the researcher would display two cards and ask the group members to give their answers out loud, starting at the left-hand side of the semicircle. The task was so clearcut that the subjects began to settle

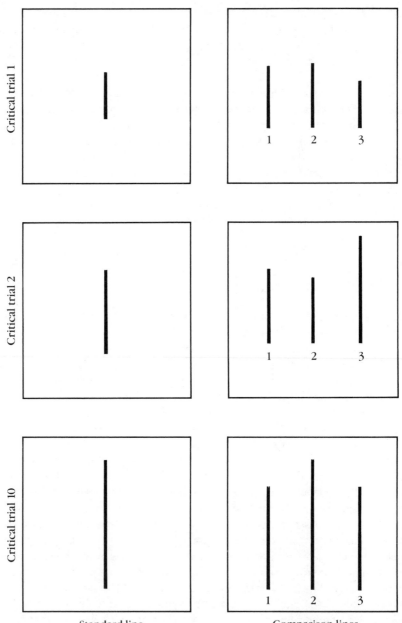

FIGURE 9-1. The Asch experiments. On 12 of the 18 trials, the majority of the group members purposely picked the incorrect comparison line. On the first of these critical trials, the standard line was 3 inches long, and Comparison Line 3 was the correct answer. However, the group chose Line 1, which was actually 3 3/4 inches long. On Critical Trial 2 the correct answer was 1, but the group unanimously answered with 2. Finally, the stimuli used in the tenth critical trial are also shown; the correct answer in this case was 2, but the group suggested 1. (Source: Asch, 1957)

back for what would apparently be a rather boring and unchallenging exercise. However, on the third trial the first person responded with an incorrect answer. The stimulus line was 3 inches long, and the comparison lines were, in order, 3 3/4, 4 1/4, and 3 inches long. Clearly the correct answer was Line 3. However, the first person reported Line 1 as the matching line. Furthermore, as the other group members reported, they all seemed to make the same mistake: each selected Line 1 as the correct answer. Indeed, on 12 of the 18 trials the group members seemed to make a mistaken judgment, sometimes overestimating, sometimes underestimating the length of the standard line.

What caused the inaccuracy of the group members' judgments? As you have probably guessed, only one of the persons in the semicircle was actually a subject. All the others were trained confederates of Asch who deliberately made errors to see if the subject would conform to a unanimous majority's judgments. When the subject entered the room, he was seated so that he responded last or next to last; thus, he would hear the reports of most of the other "subjects" before giving his own response. He would study the lines, identify the correct answer, but hear everyone else make a different selection. Clearly he faced a dilemma.

The results of Asch's initial study of 123 males were fairly surprising. Even though the task was so simple that subjects had to have known they were making errors, 76.4% of the respondents made at least one conforming response. In fact, the average level of conformity was moderately high: more than one-third of the subjects' responses on the critical trials conformed to the incorrect majority solution (4.4 out of 12, or 36.8%). However, as Figure 9-2 shows, a substantial percentage of subjects never conformed to the majority opinion (23.6%), while a smaller percentage of subjects conformed on all 12 trials (5%). Clearly, the situation influenced different individuals in different ways. These variations in reactions among

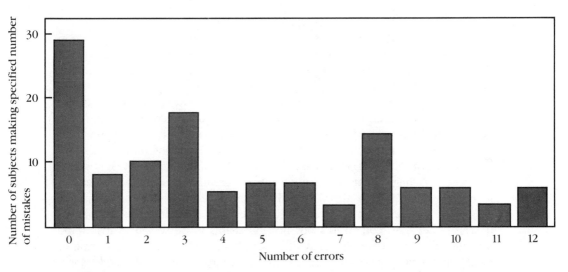

FIGURE 9-2. The number of subjects who made between 0 and 12 errors in the Asch experiment. (Source: Asch, 1957)

subjects became especially evident when Asch later discussed the experiment with participants:

> Among the independent individuals were many who held fast because of staunch confidence in their own judgment. . . . Others who acted independently came to believe that the majority was correct in its answers, but they continued their dissent on the simple ground that it was their obligation to call the play as they saw it. Among the extremely yielding persons we found a group who quickly reached the conclusion: "I am wrong, they are right." Others yielded in order "not to spoil your results." Many of the individuals who went along suspected that the majority were "sheep" following the first responder, or that the majority were victims of an optical illusion; nevertheless, these suspicions failed to free them at the moment of decision [Asch, 1955, p. 33].

Selected Issues in Conformity Research

Asch's demonstration of the remarkable effects of the group on individuals' judgments inaugurated an era of conformity research that persists today. In the years since Asch first startled social scientists with his findings, group dynamicists have conducted hundreds of conformity studies. Although some research parallels the Asch procedures quite closely, other methods, such as that developed by Richard S. Crutchfield (see the box), have also served as the basis of many conclusions. Though laboratory experiments have dominated, some field studies have also shed light on these processes (for example, Lefkowitz, Blake, & Mouton, 1955; Steffensmeier & Terry, 1973). Although space limitations prevent a full consideration of all the conclusions drawn from these many projects (see Allen, 1975; Hare, 1976; Kiesler & Kiesler, 1976 for reviews), several key themes running through these investigations deserve our close scrutiny.

DISPUTES OVER TERMINOLOGY

The number and diversity of terms that describe conformity and deviation in groups, while a testimony to our preoccupation with these topics, can impede the clear, unambiguous analysis of the theoretical concepts. A change in an individual's behavior or cognitions resulting from the influence of other group members has been variously termed *conformity, compliance, identification, uniformity, acquiescence, conventionality, acceptance, internalization,* and *obedience.* Refusing to align one's behaviors and cognitions with the standards of the group has been called *deviancy, dissent, innovation, anticonformity, nonconformity,* and *independence.* Unfortunately, while these terms are often used interchangeably, subtle differences in their meanings create definitional confusions. Despite the need to reach agreement on the meaning of these terms, the field of group dynamics appears to be populated by deviants (or, to use a less pejorative term, *individualists*) rather than conformists, for no one seems to be willing to follow the recommendations of the various theorists who have made reasonable attempts to clarify the terminology (Kelman, 1961; Kiesler & Kiesler, 1976; Stricker, Messick, & Jackson, 1970; Willis, 1963). For purposes of our own discussion, these suggestions are summarized and synthesized below.

THE "CRUTCHFIELD APPARATUS"

Although the Asch paradigm captured the essentials of a conformity situation—face-to-face interaction, unambiguous judgments, and public dissent—the procedure was inefficient. Large numbers of confederates and the services of an experimenter were required to examine the responses of just a single subject. To solve this problem of inefficiency, Richard S. Crutchfield designed a simple apparatus that could be used to assess conformity in behavior. When a group of subjects—say, five in number—reported for the experiment, they were asked to make various group judgments (some were line judgments like those used by Asch, but others, such as that shown here, required them to estimate the area of var-ious figures) while seated in individual cubicles. To report their judgments to the researcher, subjects simply flipped a switch on a response panel, and their answers would supposedly light up on the experimenter's panel as well as the other group members' panels. However, Crutchfield told each person in the group that he or she was to answer last, and he himself simulated the majority's judgments from a master control box. Hence, although the Crutchfield situation sacrifices the face-to-face aspects of the interaction, it allows the experimenter to examine the responses of five or more subjects in a single session without using a single confederate.

(Source: Wrightsman, 1977)

Conformity.   Most investigators agree that at least two very different things can be happening when people respond to group influence by changing their originally stated position (Festinger, 1953; Kiesler & Kiesler, 1976). First, people can be publicly agreeing, when privately they disagree. As Asch reported (1952), many of his subjects knew which answer was correct yet went along with the group because they did not want to seem out of step with the others, anger the experimenter, or appear stupid. This type of conformity is usually labeled **compliance,** a concept that contrasts sharply with **private acceptance,** the personal adoption of the group's position.

Deviancy.   As with conformity, deviancy often involves one of two very different processes (Stricker et al., 1970; Willis & Hollander, 1964). First, the person who refuses to bend to the will of the majority may be displaying **independence—** the public expression of ideas, beliefs, judgments, and so on that are consistent with his or her personal standards. Second, deviancy could stem from **anticonformity,** a tendency to do the opposite of whatever the group recommends. In this latter instance, the individual's behavior is still norm dependent, but it is calculated to violate norms rather than conform to them. Although anticonformity is rarely observed in the Asch situation, other research indicates that this mode of response may depend upon cultural factors (Frager, 1970) and the importance of maintaining behavioral freedom in the group situation (Brehm & Mann, 1975).

These distinctions between conformity and deviancy are summarized in Table 9-1. When individuals' responses are due more to external group pressures than to internal personal standards, then conformity can be labeled compliance while deviancy can be thought of as anticonformity. In the opposite situation, when internal personal standards are more closely linked to the response, conformity becomes private acceptance and deviancy independence. These distinctions, however, are somewhat arbitrary and are purely intended to suggest some plausible distinctions between types of conformity and deviancy. Indeed, much of the research fails to permit us to make these distinctions, thus forcing the use of the more general terms.

THE TYRANNY OF NUMBERS

One of the first issues addressed by Asch concerned the rate of conformity in groups of varying sizes (1952, 1955). On one hand Asch felt that the more people were in the unanimous majority, the greater would be the pressure on the individual to conform. However, Asch also reasoned that eventually a point might be reached where additional pressure would make no difference—that is, a "ceiling

TABLE 9-1. Some terminological distinctions

Source of response	*Type of response*	
	Conformity	Deviancy
Response is most closely linked to external group pressures.	Compliance	Anticonformity
Response is most closely linked to internal, personal standards.	Private acceptance	Independence

effect" would be obtained. To gather empirical data relevant to these hypotheses Asch replicated his procedures with groups ranging in size from 2 to 15 members. His findings, which are shown in Figure 9-3, indicate that increasing the size of a disagreeing majority causes greater conformity, but that conformity rate seems to level off at Group Size 4.

Later studies, however, contradicted these findings. For example, while several investigations reported a ceiling effect similar to Asch's (Buby & Penner, 1974; Gerard, Wilhelmy, & Conolley, 1968; Stang, 1976), other studies using different techniques sometimes found that additional increases in group size went hand in hand with greater conformity (Milgram, Bickman, & Berkowitz, 1969; Nordholm, 1975). Indeed, some studies even found that the number of people in the disagreeing majority had no effect whatsoever on conformity rates (Goldberg, 1954; Kidd, 1958; Reis, Earing, Kent, & Nezlek, 1976).

In part, these differences can be explained by the discrepant procedures used in the studies. Although Asch's initial investigation utilized face-to-face interactions, later studies employed the Crutchfield apparatus (Gerard et al., 1968; Norholm, 1975). Others were field studies in which people were asked to sign a petition that had apparently already been signed by others (Reis et al., 1976; Stang, 1976) or that recorded the number of people who joined groups of varying sizes (Milgram et al., 1969; see Figure 9-3). Furthermore, some of these investigations may not have included groups of sufficient size to reach the ceiling point or a point of downward deflection.

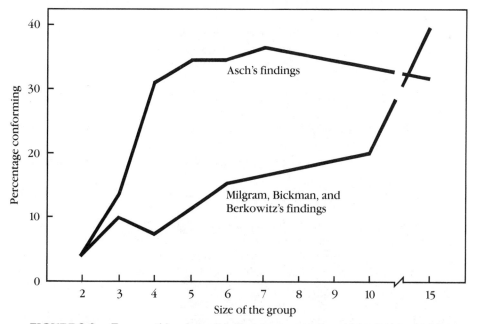

FIGURE 9-3. Two possible relationships between group size and conformity. Asch's results are suggestive of a "ceiling effect," since conformity rates stabilized once the group size reached 4. Milgram, Bickman, and Berkowitz's findings, however, follow a roughly "linear" pattern, since additional members create greater levels of conformity. (Source: Asch, 1955; Milgram, Bickman and Berkowitz, 1969)

In addition to these empirical confusions, several researchers (Gerard et al., 1968; Wilder, 1977) have suggested that subjects' perceptions of the opposing majority must be considered before firm predictions can be advanced. If individuals feel that the first person to respond was the group "leader" and the rest of the respondents were merely following the first person's incorrect statement, then the responses of these others should have less of an influence on the subject's judgments. If, however, the target believes each person in the majority is presenting his or her own individual viewpoint, then conformity pressures should continue to mount as additional members are added. To examine this idea a study was conducted in which subjects were given information about others' judgments concerning a fictitious court case and then asked to formulate their own opinion (Wilder, 1977, Experiment 2). Some subjects were led to believe that these opinions represented the judgments of people working independently, but others believed they reflected the judgments of people working as a group. As predicted, when the information was apparently coming from one single social "entity"—for example, a group of individuals working together—the magnitude of conformity was the same whether the group contained two members or six members. However, when the number of discrete social entities was increased (for example, from two independent individuals to six independent individuals or from one four-person group to two two-person groups), a ceiling effect became evident when the number of entities reached three. These findings clearly suggest that conformity rates differ in accordance with whether the disagreeing majority is perceived to be a "group" or an "aggregate."

CONFORMITY AMONG WOMEN AND MEN

For a number of years, reviewers looking back over the findings reported in studies that assessed the responses of both males and females have agreed that one effect seemed clear: women conform more often than men. For example, one reviewer wrote, "It has also been well established, at least in our culture, that females supply greater amounts of conformity under almost all conditions than males" (Nord, 1969, p. 198). Other commentators have reached similar conclusions, such as, "Women have been found to yield more to a bogus group norm than men" (Hare, 1976, p. 27) and "Females conform to majority opinion more than males" (Shaw, 1981, p. 205).

At least three factors can account for this sex difference in conformity. First, the difference may be traced back to *sex-role stereotypes*. In many Western cultures women tend to adopt a feminine sex role that traditionally includes such characteristics as passivity, reliance on others, submissiveness, and a tendency to yield to the decisions of others. Men, in contrast, often adopt a masculine sex role that emphasizes independence, free thinking, and self-determination. Hence, when women find themselves in a conformity situation they tend to yield to the majority; males, on the other hand, aggressively defend their viewpoints (Crutchfield, 1955, Study 1; Gerard et al., 1968; Tuddenham, 1958, Study 1). In support of this sex-role hypothesis, the number of studies reporting sex differences in conformity dropped during the 1970s, a result, one reviewer suggests, of the recent changes in these sex-role stereotypes (Eagly, 1978). In addition, evidence (Bem, 1975) indicates that people who adopt a feminine sex role—whether they are biologically females or males—tend to conform more frequently than people who adopt a masculine role or a role that combines elements of both masculinity and femininity (an androgynous sex-role orientation).

A second explanation of sex differences in conformity notes that many of the investigations reporting greater conformity among women are methodologically biased, since they used tasks generally considered to be masculine oriented (making economic and political judgments, taking perception tests suggestive of mechanical or mathematical ability). Evidence has consistently indicated that people who feel unskilled on a particular task are much more likely to conform to an incorrect majority opinion (Coleman, Blake, & Mouton, 1958; Endler & Hartley, 1973; Wiesental, Endler, Coward, & Edwards, 1976); thus, the use of "masculine" tasks would cause women to be more willing to conform than men. This proposal has been supported in several studies (Goldberg, 1974; 1975; Javornisky, 1979; Sistrunk & McDavid, 1971), including one in which male and female respondents were asked to indicate agreement or disagreement with a series of feminine-oriented or masculine-oriented items (Sistrunk & McDavid, 1971). The results shown in Figure 9-4 indicate that the bias inherent in the use of sex-role-specific tasks may indeed account for the greater conformity of females; on masculine items males were less conforming than females, but on feminine tasks males were more conforming. On neutral items, the sexes conformed at nearly equivalent rates.

Alice Eagly recently proposed a third explanation for sex differences in conformity (1978). According to Eagly, a careful, unbiased review of the past literature shows that women conform more than men only if the group situation involves direct, face-to-face social pressure. In more anonymous, low-surveillance situa-

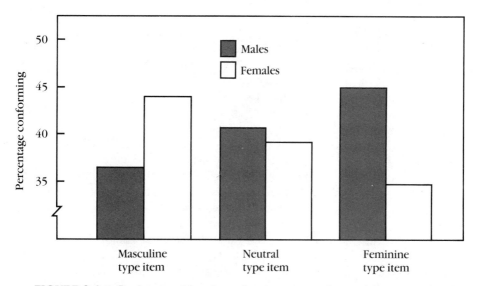

FIGURE 9-4. Conformity of females and males on masculine and feminine tasks. (Source: Sistrunk and McDavid, 1971)

tions such as that developed by Crutchfield, differences between males and females are almost nonexistent. This conclusion, which has been confirmed in two separate reviews that combined the results of dozens of independent studies statistically (Cooper, 1979; Eagly & Carli, 1981), suggests that sex differences in conformity arise from two distinct sources. First, women are more conforming not because they are "yielding" or "compliant" but because they are more concerned with "ensuring group harmony and enhancing cohesiveness" (Eagly, Wood, & Fishbaugh, 1981, p. 385). Second, men conform less because they are especially concerned with seeming independent of others' influence attempts. In support of this interpretation, studies have found that females, in contrast to males, (1) were more likely to express attitudes that were discrepant with their privately held beliefs (Bass & Dunteman, 1964), (2) systematically varied their expressed opinions in order to match the views of attractive male partners (Zanna & Pack, 1975), and (3) were more likely to use opinion conformity as a self-presentational tactic (Braginsky, 1970; Tuthill & Forsyth, 1982). Males, in contrast, have been found to be particularly nonconforming when their responses would be known to other group members (Eagly et al., 1981).

THE INFLUENCE OF A MINORITY

The movie *Twelve Angry Men* particularizes the frustrations and uncertainties of a jury trying to reach a verdict in a murder trial. Although nearly all the group members unhesitatingly agree in the first straw poll that a guilty verdict should be rendered, one member votes "not guilty." The group members react to this dissenting opinion by marshaling their arguments against this perspective, but the disagreeing juror refuses to yield to social pressure. One by one the rest of the group members change their minds until the entire jury has shifted to a verdict of not guilty.

The impact of a dissenting minority on the majority's opinion has been documented by several researchers, most notably Serge Moscovici and his colleagues (Moscovici & Faucheux, 1972; Moscovici & Lage, 1976; Moscovici & Personnaz, 1980). In his research Moscovici reverses the usual Asch situation by studying the reaction of the majority to the disagreeing judgments of a single confederate on a highly subjective task. Care is taken to make certain the subjects don't attribute any special expertise or skill to the minority confederate, and elements in the situation suggest that the minority's responses are not caused by some personal idiosyncrasy. Moscovici (for example, Moscovici & Faucheux, 1972) reports that a minority of one or two members can sometimes considerably influence the majority's judgments, provided (1) the minority's responses are highly consistent over time, (2) the majority is aware of this consistency, and (3) majority members believe the consistency is an indication of the minority's confidence (Moscovici, 1976).

These findings are interesting not only empirically but also theoretically, because they reveal a bias that runs through much of the conformity literature. Researchers in this field have tended to focus on how a majority influences a minority while ignoring the reciprocal process of minority influence. This emphasis stems from the implicit assumption that group change comes about primarily through a one-way process of influence, with the majority members deciding the best course of action and persuading the disagreeing minority to "get in line." Moscovici's findings, in contrast, cite a different source of social change; a consistent, determined minority leading the way during decision making. Naturally, an even-handed perspective on the question of influence suggests that change in a group is a *mutual* process— the majority influences the minority, and the minority influences the majority (Spitzer & Davis, 1978).

A Basic Question: Why Conform?

Many people think of conformity in a negative way, assuming that it reflects a nonassertive concession to others or a "spineless" refusal to stand up for one's personal beliefs. From this common perspective, conformity is a sign of weakness, an indication that the person fears that he or she will be punished by the majority members if they discover this dissent. These pejorative connotations of conformity are, however, inaccurate, for they are based on a misunderstanding of the complexity of the conformity process. Individuals in even a simple situation such as that studied by Asch conform for a variety of reasons; while a fear of punishment for deviancy may be a concern, other equally important causes should also be considered. Four factors that may be operating, either alone or in combination in the conformity setting, are (1) normative influence, (2) informational influence, (3) self-presentational motives, and (4) the conformer's inattention to the situation. Each of these influences is discussed in turn in the following subsections.

NORMATIVE INFLUENCE

You attend a formal dinner and spend much of your time worrying about when to use each fork. At a party everyone is praising the virtues of a rock group you don't particularly care for, but you do your part by claiming to like their latest song. You attend your first class in college wearing your high school ring, but remove it between classes when you realize nobody else is wearing one. At a fast-food restaurant you stand in line to order your food even though there are no directions or signs posted. When the traffic light turns red you bring your car to a halt. You enter a public restroom only to hastily rush out when you discover you have blundered into one reserved for the opposite sex.

According to several theorists, the conformity in these examples stems from **normative social influence** (Aronson, 1980; Deutsch & Gerard, 1955; Kelley, 1952). At one level, the individual feels compelled to act in accordance with the group's norms, since a variety of negative consequences could result from deviance. Violating group norms can create conflict within the group and can lead to losses in status, to rejection, or even to ostracism. This aspect of normative influence seems to be well summarized in the aphorism "To get along you go along." At another level, however, the individual conforms to the norms of the group in order to fulfill personal expectations about "proper" behavior. Because norms are not simply external constraints but also internalized standards, conformity produced by normative influence involves more than just trying to keep in the good graces of the other group members. Individuals feel duty bound to adhere to the norms of the group since, as loyal members, they accept the legitimacy of the established norms and recognize the importance of supporting these norms through behavioral compliance. As applied to a situation such as that studied by Asch, these dualistic bases of normative social influence suggest that people conform because (1) they fear the negative interpersonal consequences—ostracism, ridicule, punishment—that their deviancy may produce and (2) they feel personally compelled to live up to others' expectations.

The role of normative group pressures in producing conformity accounts for a wide variety of empirical relations evident in research. For example, if normative pressures are weakened, perhaps because the majority cannot reach unanimous agreement on the correct responses (Allen, 1975; Morris & Miller, 1975a), or the stimulus is very ambiguous (Crutchfield, 1955), then nonconformity becomes much more likely. Furthermore, if these normative pressures are increased—perhaps by increasing the cohesiveness of the group (Festinger, Schachter, & Back, 1950), creating an expectation of future interaction (Lewis, Langan, & Hollander, 1972), or emphasizing the importance of maintaining a congenial group atmosphere (Rockman & Goethals, 1973)—then conformity tends to increase. Lastly, the concept of normative social influence also explains why certain people, such as those with a high need for social approval (Tuddenham, 1959), conform more than others.

INFORMATIONAL INFLUENCE

Many people who participated in the Asch research were certain that the group was making an error. They would look at the standard line and the three comparison lines and shake their heads in wonder over the baldly incorrect statements of their fellow group members. Yet when the time came to report their judgments, they responded to normative social influence pressures and went along with the group's answer. Some of the subjects, however, later reported that they *believed* the majority's responses to be correct, and that for some reason—poor eyesight, mental strain, an optical illusion, or personal incompetence—they judged the length of the line inaccurately. Hence, they treated the responses of the majority as valuable *information*.

That conformity can sometimes result from informational influence is consistent with the thesis that one primary reason for joining a group is to gain information about the accuracy of one's own perceptions and beliefs (Festinger, 1954; Goethals & Darley, 1977; see Chapter 3). Without social comparisons people are unable to construct meaningful and coherent definitions of social situations or subsequently to validate their conclusions (Fazio, 1979). If we apply this notion to our initial example of a group ordering a pizza with anchovies, the response of the majority conveys a good deal of information to the minority anchovy hater. The three majority-opinion holders, who are apparently friendly enough with each other to share a meal, are unanimous in their liking for anchovies. This information shakes the dissenter's confidence in the accuracy of his own beliefs on the subject, as he begins to think "If all these people like anchovies, then maybe they aren't so bad after all."

Several studies also suggest that the responses of others even more directly influence group members by producing cognitive reinterpretations of the meaning of the situation or actually changing visual perceptions. To demonstrate the possibility of "cognitive restructuring" during conformity, researchers asked subjects to respond to a number of opinion items while seated in standard Crutchfield testing booths (Allen & Wilder, 1980). Although each statement was accompanied by information about the opinions of a previous group of participants, the subjects weren't asked to give their opinions on the items. Rather, they were asked to define certain phrases in the statements. For example, subjects would be shown an item such as "I would never go out of my way to help another person if it meant giving up some personal pleasure," simultaneously learning that a four-person group had unanimously agreed with the statement—clearly an unexpected and unpopular response (Allen & Wilder, 1980, p. 1118). However, the subjects were then asked what the phrase "go out of my way" meant in the sentence and were instructed to choose a number on the following scale:

Be inconvenienced   1 2 3 4 5 6 7 8 9 10   Risk my life

The results of the study indicated that subjects who learned that a group unanimously chose an unpopular response changed the meaning of the opinion statement, which to some extent explained the puzzling response. In the example, they would reinterpret the phrase "go out of my way" as meaning "risk my life" by circling a 9 or a 10 rather than favoring "be inconvenienced."

Although these results show evidence of *cognitive* changes resulting from informational influence, Moscovici's research group (Moscovici & Personnaz, 1980) has recently reported a study that demonstrated *perceptual* changes resulting from social influence. In a clever attempt to make as direct a measure as possible of subjects' actual perceptual responses, these researchers exposed female subjects to a series of blue slides that were consistently labeled green by a confederate. On each trial the subject reported her judgment of the color, but was also asked to look at a blank white screen and report the color of the slide's afterimage. Unknown to the subjects, the afterimage of blue should be yellow-orange, while the afterimage of green should be red-purple. Amazingly, Moscovici and Personnaz report a significant increase in reports of red-purple (the color that subjects would see if the slides were green instead of blue). Although these findings are provocative, other research suggests that they should be interpreted with caution, since several replications have failed to yield similar findings (Doms & Van Avermaet, 1980; Sorrentino, King, & Leo, 1980).

SELF-PRESENTATIONAL MOTIVES

A third reason for conforming to others' opinions and judgments emanates from the general desire to be viewed as a rational, attractive, and likable person. Although in rare instances people try to create the impression of deviancy or peculiarity (Schlenker, 1980), in most cases—particularly those examined in experimental studies of conformity—people use self-presentational tactics to foster an impression of competency and normality. Unfortunately, a situation such as that created by Asch places subjects in a severe *self-presentational dilemma*. From their perspectives the answer is obvious, yet for no discernible reason the rest of the group consistently answers incorrectly, apparently behaving in a bizarre and inexplicable manner. Yet most subjects realize that the rest of the group will no doubt react to disagreement in the same way. They will think the deviant answer (and the answerer) strange and irrational. As Lee Ross and his colleagues comment,

To the subject, the correct judgment appeared so obvious that only perceptual incompetents, fools, or madmen could err. He furthermore had every reason to assume that the right answer appeared equally obvious to his peers. Accordingly by dissenting, he ran the risk of appearing incompetent, foolish, or even mad; at best his dissent promised to be as incomprehensible to his peers as their current judgments were to him. His dissent, in fact, represented a challenge to *their* competence, wisdom, and sanity—a challenge one is loath to offer, particularly when one's own ability to make sense of one's world seems suddenly in question [Ross, Bierbrauer, & Hoffman, 1976, p. 149].

In support of this explanation of conformity, Ross found that subjects who discover a reasonable explanation for the majority's inaccuracy are far less likely to conform.

Studies of ingratiation also reveal that people sometimes create favorable impressions with others by conforming to their opinions (Jones, 1964; Jones & Wortman, 1973; Wortman & Linsenmeier, 1977). For example, in one study high- and low-status college students (seniors and first-year students in an NROTC Naval training program) were given the opportunity to show they either agreed or disagreed with a fellow group member on issues that were relevant or irrelevant to the group situation (Jones, Gergen, & Jones, 1963). Some opinion conformity was evidenced by all the subjects, but this tactic was much more pronounced when a low-status subject was discussing a relevant issue with a high-status subject.

As an aside to those who may be tempted to rush out and use opinion conformity as an ingratiation ploy, a substantial number of studies suggest that in many cases conformity is not the most efficacious self-presentational strategy (Wortman & Linsenmeier, 1977). If the target of the ingratiation attempt believes that the conformity is an insincere attempt to foster a good impression, then opinion agreement may backfire (Jones, Jones, & Gergen, 1963). In other instances dissent, and not conformity, may leave a more positive impression by suggesting an image of power, independence, and sureness (Alexander & Lauderdale, 1977; Morris & Miller, 1975b).

MINDLESSNESS

A final explanation for conformity suggests that people sometimes just don't stop to think about what they are doing. Although psychological theories typically portray people as careful information processors who weigh various factors before selecting a course of action, Ellen Langer and her associates (Langer, Blank, & Chanowitz, 1978; Langer & Newman, 1979) have recently proposed that people in social situations too often respond automatically and hence perform "mindless" actions.

In a study designed to demonstrate mindlessness (Langer et al., 1978, Experiment 1, p. 637), a male or female experimenter approached adults who were using a photocopying machine in a university library and asked, "Excuse me. I have five pages. May I use the Xerox machine?" In the *control condition* no explanation for this surprising request was offered, but in the *real-information condition* the experimenter explained "I'm in a rush." In a third condition a justification was given, but the explanation was essentially absurd: "May I use the Xerox machine, because I have to make copies?" Langer labeled this variation the *placebic-information condition,* because the statement took the form of a justification, which if subjects thought about it would clearly appear to be senseless.

Langer found that 60% of the subjects complied with the request in the control condition, while compliance rates of 94% and 93% were obtained in the real- and placebic-information conditions, respectively. In addition, in a second variation of the study the request was increased from just 5 pages to 20 pages. In this instance the researchers found that compliance rates dropped dramatically, and that people no longer mindlessly reacted to the placebic information. In this case compliance in the control and placebic-information conditions was equal (24%). This study and others reported by Langer and her associates suggest that people sometimes fail to consider the implications of conformity; perhaps future research will explore the generalizability and the limits of mindlessness.

Some Consequences of Conformity and Deviancy

Up to this point we have examined the methods typically employed by researchers unraveling the mysteries of conformity and (in fewer cases) deviancy in groups, a select group of empirical findings pertaining to the magnitude of conformity, and several plausible theoretical explanations of these findings. However, another side of the coin waits to be considered, for we must now turn our attention to the *consequences* of agreement and disagreement in small groups of interacting members. To return to our original example regarding Sean and his dilemma over the anchovies, we must imagine what would have happened had he refused to agree with the rest of the group. Would the other members have insulted him? overtly derogated him? physically attacked him? Would he have lost status within the group and potentially been omitted the next time it got together for pizza? Furthermore, how might the group have reacted to Sean's willingness to conform, and what impact would Sean's agreement have on his own attitudes towards anchovies?

Deviancy, Rejection, and Communication

If Solomon Asch's procedure can be identified as a hallmark experimental analysis of conformity, then Stanley Schachter's 1951 dissertation research should be considered the corresponding classic on deviancy and rejection. The theoretical framework for the study derived in part from an earlier field study of social pressures in informal groups conducted by Schachter in collaboration with Leon Festinger and Kurt Back (Festinger, Schachter, & Back, 1950). This project, which was sponsored by the Research Center for Group Dynamics at MIT, examined the relationship between attraction relations and opinion conformity in two housing developments reserved for married students at MIT. One of the developments, Westgate, was a garden-type complex whose units were arranged in U-shaped courts. The second development, Westgate-West, featured 17 two-story buildings containing 10 apartments each. At the time of the study, the tenants of both complexes were embroiled in a debate over the relative advantages and disadvantages of joining a tenant association, and this topic provided the researchers with a focus for their research.

After sampling the residents' opinions, the experimenters discovered that nearly all the residents of Westgate-West favored the association. In contrast, while the opinions of the Westgate residents were more diverse, agreement within each court was fairly high. Apparently, group pressures tended to create uniformity of opinion in the courts because their physical design promoted interaction among the residents who lived in each courtyard. Furthermore, in Westgate individuals who expressed an opinion that deviated from their court's overall judgment (1) lived in the more physically isolated units and (2) were less well liked than those who agreed with the majority opinion.

Although Festinger and his colleagues followed up on these provocative findings in a number of ways (Back, 1951; Festinger, Gerard, Hymovitch, Kelley, & Raven, 1952; Festinger & Thibaut, 1971; Gerard, 1953), Schachter chose to examine three independent variables—group cohesiveness, topic relevance, and degree of opinion conformity—and several dependent variables related to attraction and rejection. He invited male economics students to join one of four clubs that would be (1) discussing case studies at the behest of a group of local lawyers, (2) advising a new national magazine on editorial policies, (3) screening movies for local theatres, or (4) evaluating material to be used by a local radio station. The potential subjects were asked to indicate their interest in two of these four possible clubs, and cohesiveness was manipulated by putting some of the subjects in clubs that interested them and others in clubs that did not interest them. Schachter assumed that a group of people with common interests would be more cohesive than a group devoted to a topic that did not interest its members.

The relevance of the topic to the group was manipulated in a more straightforward fashion. During what the participants were led to believe was the organizational meeting of their clubs, the experimenter asked them to discuss a legal case. This case, which rather sympathetically described the problems of a young juvenile delinquent named Johnny Rocco, was relevant to the stated purposes of the case-study and the editorial clubs (it was purportedly the basis for a feature article on delinquency) but was irrelevant to those of the radio and movie clubs. Thus Schachter created four different kinds of groups corresponding to his 2×2 factorial design:

1. High cohesiveness/relevant issue groups (Hi Co Rel),
2. Low cohesiveness/relevant issue groups (Lo Co Rel),
3. High cohesiveness/irrelevant issue groups (Hi Co Irrel), and
4. Low cohesiveness/irrelevant issue groups (Lo Co Irrel).

To vary the degree of agreement within the group, Schachter added three confederates to each of the five- to seven-member clubs. These paid participants played one of three carefully controlled roles: *mode, deviant,* and *slider.* As the group discussed the Johnny Rocco case, the members were to decide on a course of treatment for Johnny that could range from "love" (Position 1) to "punishment" (Position 7). Most of the subjects tended to offer fairly lenient recommendations, and the mode confederate would support the group consensus. If during any meeting the group's opinion shifted in any direction, the mode would also shift his position. The deviant, in contrast, adopted a position of extreme discipline (Position 7) and refused to change his opinion during the discussion. The final confederate, the slider, began by championing the extreme-punishment position, but shifted his position during the course of the group meeting to agree with the majority of the members.

Based on Festinger's theory of informal communication (1950), Schachter believed that the deviant would ultimately be rejected by the other group members. He suggested that once the group members realized that two of their members disagreed with the majority opinion, they would put pressure on these two deviants to bring their opinions in line with the overall judgment. If this pressure was successful in creating conformity, as in the case of the slider, then the dissenter would not be rejected interpersonally. If, however, the group failed to persuade the dissenter, as in the case of the deviant, then he would be rejected. The magnitude of this rejection, however, would depend upon the relevance of the deviating belief to the group's purposes and upon the cohesiveness of the group. Schachter hypothesized that both these variables would lead to increases in group pressure in the direction of uniformity, so he predicted rejection would be greater in (1) the Hi Co as opposed to the Lo Co groups, and (2) the Rel groups in contrast to the Irrel groups.

Schachter measured the group members' reactions to the deviant, slider, and mode by collecting sociometric rankings and asking for nominations to various committees. The sociometric data indicated that, across all four experimental conditions, the deviant was given a more negative ranking than either the mode or the slider. In addition, this rejection was more pronounced in the Hi Co groups in comparison to the Lo Co groups (see Table 9-2). Although no differences due to relevancy were obtained on these ratings, effects of this variable were discovered when the nominations to various internal committees were analyzed. Reasoning that the executive and steering committees would be the most desirable assignments while the correspondence committee would be the least desirable assignment, since most members viewed the duties of letter writing and recording with distaste, Schachter asked the members to select members for each committee. He discovered that deviants were saddled with this unpleasant chore more frequently than chance would dictate in all groups save the Lo Co Irrel condition. Overall, this general tendency was more pronounced in the Rel conditions as compared with the Irrel conditions.

Although these findings were somewhat inconsistent, since in each case an effect that occurred for one dependent variable did not occur for the second, subsequent

TABLE 9-2. Some sociometric rankings of the paid participants in the Schachter study of deviancy (higher scores indicate less liking)

Group	Description	Deviant	Mode	Slider
Hi Co, Rel	Highly cohesive group, task is relevant	6.44	4.65	5.02
Lo Co, Rel	Low cohesive group, task is relevant	5.83	4.70	4.56
Hi Co, Irrel	Highly cohesive group, task is irrelevant	6.41	4.68	4.44
Lo Co, Irrel	Low cohesive group, task is irrelevant	5.67	3.83	5.03

(Source: Schachter, 1951)

studies replicated Schachter's basic findings (see Levine, 1980, for a comprehensive review). These later studies typically supported Schachter's conclusions and they frequently pointed out that certain situational factors—task relevance (Lauderdale, 1976; Wiggins, Dill, & Schwartz, 1965), cohesiveness (Emerson, 1954), interdependency (Berkowitz & Howard, 1959), or behavior extremity (Hensley & Duval, 1976; Levine & Ranelli, 1978; Mudd, 1968)—increase the magnitude of this rejection. Conversely, investigations have also uncovered a host of variables that minimize the rejection of deviants—the facilitation of task performance through deviation (Kelley & Shapiro, 1954), apologies for deviation (Dedrick, 1978), and background group norms that encourage innovation (Moscovici, 1976). Overall, however, the general relationship between deviancy and rejection appears to be a fairly robust one.

THE PROCESS OF COMMUNICATION

Although the rejection data were quite consistent with Festinger's (1950) theory, Schachter had also predicted that the pressure put on the deviant would be evident in the frequency of communications directed at the deviant by other group members. At first, communications would be fairly evenly distributed among the mode, deviant, and slider as the group members made public their various positions. However, as soon as it became obvious that the deviant and slider were in disagreement with the others, the bulk of the group's communications would involve these two participants. This focus on the dissenters would increase, it was hypothesized, until (1) the dissenter capitulated to the majority opinion (as in the case of the slider) or (2) the majority concluded that the deviant would not budge from his position (as in the case of the nonchanging deviant). Schachter felt that this latter reaction would probably occur only in the most personally involving groups, Hi Co Rel, and even then for only those group members who strongly rejected the deviant. In these unique circumstances communication would be related to time spent deliberating in a curvilinear fashion; low initially, peaking at the halfway point, and then falling off as the session ends.

To test these rather complicated predictions, Schachter recorded the number of communications addressed to the deviant, mode, and slider during the course of the meeting. When examined, the measurements indicated that communication with the deviant tended to increase throughout the course of the session, apparently as the group tried to identify the appropriate position to take on the issue. However, when subjects who eventually rejected the deviant on the questionnaire measures were studied separately from the others, Schachter found evidence of the hypothesized curvilinear relationship between time and communication in the Hi Co Rel cell of the design; in this specific instance the rate of communication peaked approximately 30 minutes into the discussion but dwindled in the final minutes.

Nevertheless, several problems cloud the interpretation of this finding (Mills, 1962; Berkowitz, 1971). First, an almost exact replication of the study conducted under Schachter's guidance failed to obtain this curvilinear relationship (Emerson, 1954). Second, while Schachter had assumed that pressures toward uniformity were greatest in the Hi Co Rel condition, total amount of communication with the deviant was greatest in the Lo Co Irrel condition, the very group that should have evidenced few attempts at persuading the confederate to agree with the majority.

One possible explanation for this ambiguity in the communications data can be termed the **inclusion/exclusion hypothesis** (Orcutt, 1973). This solution argues that groups' reactions to intractable deviancy may take one of two forms. First, an inclusive reaction may occur that is typified by intensive, hostile communication but little long-term, interpersonal rejection of the deviant. Second, when an exclusive reaction occurs the deviant receives few communications and is subjected to little hostility, but at a covert attitudinal level the deviant is firmly rejected by the majority members. According to this hypothesis, the curvilinear relationship predicted by Schachter will only occur when certain behavioral and situational factors create an exclusive reaction among the group members (Orcutt, 1973).

Available evidence lends partial support to this inclusive/exclusive hypothesis. For example, several studies of deviancy and communication report that majority members send tremendous amounts of information to the most deviant members of their group unless the experimenter increases tendencies towards exclusion by telling the members that their group is extremely heterogeneous (Festinger et al., 1952; Festinger & Thibaut, 1951). In addition, while homogeneous groups are characterized by high rates of communication between modal members and deviants during the initial phases of interaction, when the modal members realize the deviant will not be influenced this communication level decreases. According to the investigator, it seemed as if the group members were "redefining their group boundary" by psychologically rejecting the dissenters (Gerard, 1953). Lastly, even more conclusive findings come from a study of white, all-female groups discussing the case of a black juvenile delinquent (Sampson & Brandon, 1964). Following procedures much like Schachter's, the experimenters manipulated *opinion deviancy* by including a confederate who espoused either a conforming or deviating opinion in each group. Additionally, they manipulated *role deviancy* by letting the group members introduce themselves prior to the group discussion. For half the groups the confederate described herself as a typical liberal college student, much like the other members. However, in the remaining groups the confederate announced that she was a racial bigot—a socially condemned role position. Content analysis of the subsequent group discussion revealed that, overall, hostile statements and requests for information were more frequently directed at the opinion deviant, while statements of solidarity were directed at the conformer. However, far greater differences were produced by the role-deviancy variable. As predicted, the announcement of a prejudiced attitude created an exclusive reaction within the role-deviant groups; rather than argue with this "strange" person the members excluded her from conversations, rated her very negatively on postexperiment evaluations, and in some cases even moved their chairs to avoid facing her (Sampson, 1971).

CHANGING OPINIONS AND GROUP ACCEPTANCE

For a moment, take the role of a "naive" subject in one of Schachter's groups trying to reach consensus on the question of Johnny Rocco. Although you discover that nearly everyone—being reasonable—agrees with your recommendation that Johnny be given a break, the group discussion becomes livelier as two of the members insist on recommending a harsh punishment. You aren't impressed with their reasons for these suggestions, so you and the rest of the majority members try to convince them to change their opinions. Hostility mounts as the disagreement becomes more intense, but finally one of the dissenters begins to show some sense. He nods his head in response to your rationale for the lenient treatment of Johnny, and finally shifts his position around until he agrees with you.

When later asked to evaluate this "slider" (a member who alters his or her expressed opinions during the course of the interaction), what kinds of conclusions would you reach? Would you assume that you had successfully "changed his mind" or that he had just decided to "go along" with the group? Would you admire the slider for his openness to the ideas of others or picture him as a spineless weakling who buckled to group pressure? Would you distrust him because he betrayed the informal alliance he had formed with the other deviant or seek out his opinions on other issues since he seems to be a discerning evaluator? Would you pity him for his lack of self-confidence or be grateful to him for helping to reduce the level of tension in the group?

In Schachter's research the general reaction to the slider was fairly positive, for he was liked just as much as the modal confederate and more than the opinion deviant (1951; Emerson, 1954). However, other studies, while not specifically designed to examine group members' reactions to sliders, suggest other possibilities. For example, investigations of interpersonal attraction suggest that disagreement followed by agreement may often create even greater liking than uniformly consistent agreement (Dutton, 1973; Sigall, 1970), since people are gratified to discover that their persuasive powers are effective. Yet if the slider is blamed for destroying the comraderie of the group by initially dissenting, or if the conformity is taken as evidence of sycophancy, then the slider may be as strongly disliked as the unyielding deviant (Kiesler & Pallak, 1975).

Fortunately, the recent work of John Levine and his associates (Levine, 1980; Levine & Ranelli, 1978; Levine & Ruback, 1980; Levine, Saxe, & Harris, 1976; Levine, Sroka, & Snyder, 1977) has yielded some fairly conclusive evidence concerning reactions to sliders. For example, in one study subjects were seated in individual booths and shown a film portraying the case of a juvenile delinquent named Gary (Levine et al., 1976). Next, the group members were asked to indicate degree of agreement with the item "Gary would benefit more from psychological help than from imprisonment" by flipping one of nine answer switches arranged in order from "very strongly disagree" (1) to "very strongly agree" (9). Although the subjects were led to believe that one set of lights on their own panels showed the other three members' responses, the experimenter actually controlled these lights. During the course of the session subjects voted on the issue five separate times, and between each vote they were asked to send a message to one other person in the group. Their communication partner was supposedly randomly assigned to them, and they were told to limit their notes to criticisms of their partner's vote or to giving the reasons for their own vote.

By manipulating the responses of the three other group members, the experimenters simulated a majority of three (including the subject) facing a minority of one. Subjects were led to believe that two of the three other group members agreed fairly closely with their personal opinion on all five votes (responses 8 and

9, since most people tended to agree very strongly with the item). However, the responses of the third person in the group, who also turned out to be the assigned partner for all subjects, were systematically varied to create the six conditions of the experiment: (1) *no-change/agree* (partner agrees with the subject on all five votes); (2) *neutral/agree* (partner is neutral at Vote 1 but shifts to agree by Vote 5); (3) *neutral/disagree* (partner is neutral at Vote 1 but shifts to disagree by Vote 5); (4) *disagree/agree* (partner disagrees at Vote 1 but shifts to agree by Vote 5); (5) *agree/disagree* (partner agrees at Vote 1 but shifts to disagree by Vote 5); and (6) *no-change/disagree* (partner disagrees with the subject on all five votes).

Ratings of the attractiveness of the four types of sliders and two controls are compared in Figure 9-5. First, the conformer (Condition 1) and the slider who moved from neutrality to agreement (Condition 2) were the best liked. Second, the slider who shifted all the way from nearly complete disagreement to nearly complete agreement (Condition 4) and the slider who actually moved away from the majority opinion (Condition 5) were rated as somewhat attractive (but Condition 4 < Condition 5). Lastly, the slider who moved from neutrality to disagreement and the constant dissenter were the most negatively evaluated of all partners. Overall, these findings suggest that a slider who eventually agrees with the major-

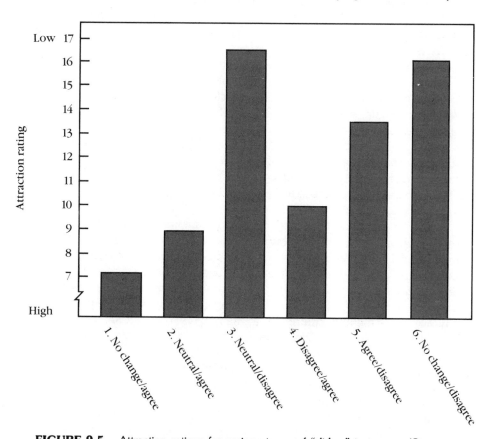

FIGURE 9-5. Attraction ratings for various types of "sliders" in groups. (Source: Levine, Saxe, and Harris, 1976)

ity's opinion will be liked as much but no more than the consistently conforming members. However, if the slider initially expresses an extremely deviant attitude, then subsequent conformity may not be sufficient to create such high levels of attraction (Condition 4). Finally, demonstrating initial conformity and subsequently disagreeing does not shield one from interpersonal rejection (Condition 5); nor does steadfastly refusing to yield to the group's persuasive communications. Apparently most subjects interpreted such a refusal to yield as a sign of close-mindedness rather than independence.

Status and Deviancy

A low-status member suggests the group take an altogether different approach to a problem. This proposal is initially met with angry criticism, but the reaction mellows when the leader endorses the plan. The group decides to revoke two of the new members' voting privileges when they break a group rule, forgetting that one of the group's leaders had broken the same rule the week before with no ill effects. A mail-room employee's suggestion about a profit-sharing plan for the company is dismissed as "an absurdity." When elucidated by one of the company's top executives, the same plan is hailed as "a forward-looking innovation."

A number of years ago, Edwin P. Hollander (1958, 1960) pointed out that groups tend to react more favorably to the nonconformity of a high-status member than that of a low-status member. For example, in one study (Gerson, 1967) 25 males who had recently pledged a fraternity were told that one of their fellow members had violated a group norm: he had sold copies of the fraternity's test files (copies of university examinations collected by members) to an outside party. When the violater was identified as one of the highest status members of the group, the subjects proposed that a formal apology would be sufficient as atonement for the offense. If, however, the accused was a low-ranking member, the subjects recommended either suspension from the fraternity for one semester or revocation of fraternity-house eating and sleeping privileges. Although the gravity of the offense was the same in all instances, the sanctions clearly differed depending upon the status of the offender.

Hollander explained this reaction to high-status nonconformity in terms of a social-exchange model built on the concept of **idiosyncrasy credits.** According to Hollander (1971, p. 573), idiosyncrasy credits can "be considered to be the positive impressions of a person held by others, whether defined in the narrower terms of a small face-to-face group or a larger social entity such as an organization or even a total society." These credits accumulate during the course of interaction, typically as the member contributes to the progress of the group toward desired goals. Because high-status members usually have a greater credit balance—they have contributed more in the past and possess more valued personal characteristics—their nonconformity is more tolerable to the other members. The low-status members' balance of credits is in comparison very low; hence, they are permitted a smaller latitude for nonconformity.

One implication of the idiosyncrasy model suggests that influence levels in a group are increased by careful conformity to group norms during the early phases of group formation followed by dissent when a sufficient balance of credit has been established. To examine this notion, Hollander arranged for male engineering students to work in groups of five on a complex decisional task. One of the members was a confederate who systematically violated certain rules of procedure during the early phases of problem solving or later in the session. Hollander found that the confederate's influence over the others tended to increase over time, but that the confederate who prefaced his deviancy with conformity exerted somewhat more influence than the early deviant. Similar findings were reported when children with well-developed leadership skills were placed in new groups (Merei, 1958). Those who tried to take over and change the group immediately were rejected, whereas those who worked within the group for a time before attempting innovations became successful influencers. Lastly, other researchers report that the greater the perceived competency and group-centered motivation of the individual, the greater the group's toleration of early deviancy (Ridgeway, 1978; Wahrman & Pugh, 1972, 1974).

One major exception to the general tendency to react less negatively to the nonconformity of high-status members occurs when the deviancy is so extreme and damaging in its consequences that it completely "bankrupts" the store of idiosyncrasy credits. This phenomenon has been labeled **status liability,** because it occurs when deviating high-status members are held especially responsible for their actions (Wiggins, Dill, & Schwartz, 1965). Fairly clear evidence of status liability was obtained in a study in which four-person groups worked on a task to try to earn a $50 prize (Wiggins et al., 1965). However, during the task a high-status group member or a medium-status group member was supposedly seen cheating, and in consequence the experimenter deducted a small, medium, or large number of points from the group's overall performance score. While the small penalty did not significantly interfere with the group's performance, the large penalty was harder to overcome. When subjects later evaluated the cheater, evidence of the protective effects of idiosyncrasy credit surfaced in low- and medium-penalty conditions: the low-status member was more disliked than the high-status member. However, status became a liability in the high penalty condition. In this case the high-status cheaters were more disliked than the low-status members. Because status liability seems to occur whenever deviance results in extremely negative consequences, let innovative group leaders be warned: while deviancy that helps the group will be merely tolerated, deviancy that lowers the quality of the group's outcome may lead to rejection, negative sanctioning, and a loss of status.

Deviancy and Identity

By emphasizing the findings of research conducted in the small-groups tradition, our discussion up to this point has virtually ignored the contributions of sociological theories of deviancy. Following a tradition established by Emile Durkheim, a good deal of sociological theory and research has been devoted to the understanding of those in society who are "strange," "odd," or "just different," and the conclusions of this field are relevant to deviancy in small groups. While the earliest sociologists tended to adopt a kind of "medical-model" conception of deviancy—deviancy is a "social disease" and those who suffer from it should be identified and their

behavior corrected—recent theorizing has been dominated by the **labeling perspective** or *societal-reaction theory* (Cullen & Cullen, 1978; Gibbs & Erickson,
1975; Gove, 1980). According to this perspective, the key questions to ask are
not "What causes deviancy?" or "What are the consequences of deviancy?" but
"Why do people label certain actions deviancy?" and "What are the consequences
of this labeling process?" People fail to conform to group and societal norms in a
wide variety of situations, yet these deviations do not become deviancy until
someone reacts to the behavior by labeling it as such. Thus, deviancy is not a
quality of a person or a person's actions, but a *process* that involves one person,
the nonconformer, who is labeled a deviant by others. These general assumptions
are well summarized in the classic statement of one of the perspective's leading
proponents:

> Social groups create deviance by making the rules whose infraction constitutes
> deviance, and by applying these rules to particular people and labeling them as
> outsiders. From this point of view, deviance is not a quality of the act the person
> commits, but rather a consequence of the application by others of rules and
> sanctions to an "offender." The deviant is one to whom that label has been suc-
> cessfully applied; deviant behavior is behavior that people so label [Becker, 1963,
> p. 9].

Although the labeling perspective has been criticized on a number of grounds
(Hagen, 1974; Hirschi, 1973; Schervish, 1973), its definition of deviancy as a
sequence of interactions involving the labeled and the labeler provides a model
for understanding the long-range consequences of deviancy for the self and social
identity. For example, take an instance in which a group of women is discussing
a controversial topic—say, women's rights—and most of the members are expressing a fairly conservative viewpoint with such comments as "I like having doors
opened for me," "I don't think women should be drafted into the army," and "Men
are better at making important decisions than women." However, in the midst of
this discussion one woman loudly states, "I don't agree. I believe that, aside from
a few minor biological characteristics, there are no significant differences between
men and women." At first, the other group members don't react to the comment,
but then they try to discover if the dissenter is serious. When they become convinced she is, they publicly point out that the position is a very "strange" one, and
give the dissenter a number of reasons for changing her attitude. At this point the
dissenter has two choices: conform or once more express a dissenting viewpoint.
According to labeling theory, if she continues to disagree then she will be labeled
by the group members ("You must be one of those women's libber types"), derogated ("You aren't very feminine, you know"), and possibly ostracized. Furthermore, the deviant may also experience significant changes in self-concept and
social identity as a result of this labeling, and thus may come to consider herself
more firmly than ever to be a women's rights advocate.

THE INITIAL GROUP REACTION

In the labeling approach the initial group reaction is the critical first step in the
deviancy process; thus, without a reaction, nothing can be called true deviancy.
In some instances this reaction may not occur, simply because the majority fails

to notice the deviation or because the disagreement is over a minor group rule or issue too insignificant to warrant debate. On the other hand, the members may notice the event but be reluctant to cast aspersions publicly owing to the perpetrator's high status. This greater tolerance afforded the high-status member is, of course, consistent with the concept of idiosyncrasy credit discussed earlier, and has received a number of empirical confirmations. For example, in one study (Steffensmeir & Terry, 1973) reactions to a deviant action were assessed by staging a theft in a public setting. In plain sight of a shopper in a supermarket a high-status (well-dressed and carefully groomed) or low-status (slovenly attired) accomplice would stuff merchandise into his or her coat and then wander off to another part of the store. Immediately after the staged shoplifing an experimenter posing as a store employee would move into the vicinity and pretend to arrange stock. Results confirmed the link between status and rejection, for the unkempt, lower status deviant was far more likely to be reported. Indeed, when turning in the lower status thief the subjects would often add derogatory comments such as "That hippie thing took a package of lunch meat," or "That son of a bitch hippie over there just stuffed a banana down his coat" (Steffensmeir & Terry, 1975, p. 247).

Deviators may also avoid public censure by keeping information about their deviancy private. In a perceptive analysis of the social consequences of deviancy and stigma, Erving Goffman (1963) describes a number of techniques individuals may use to conceal their differences: selective self-disclosure, manipulation of nonverbal cues, avoidance of interactions with those who might object to the deviancy, and the moderation of public statements to reduce disagreement with the majority opinion. In one investigation that examined experimentally this concealment of deviancy (Freedman & Doob, 1968), subjects who had previously been given a number of psychological tests were told that they differed significantly from others (were deviants) or strongly resembled others (were nondeviants) in their group. Furthermore, the subjects were led to believe that the others were aware of their deviancy (public deviancy) or that their scores were known only to themselves (secret deviancy). When asked, the secret deviants expressed a preference for working on the experimental tasks individually rather than in groups, where their "abnormality" may have become evident to the others during the group activity. The public deviants, in contrast, preferred to work in groups; apparently they hoped to disconfirm the negative information by demonstrating their normality to the others.

THE DEVIANT'S RESPONSE

In another of his works dealing with deviancy and everyday interpersonal relations, Erving Goffman suggests that groups typically react to deviancy by challenging the violator and demanding conformity (1967). As our previous review of conformity has shown, in most instances violators respond to this challenge by altering their behavior to match that required by the group. Goffman describes this "interaction ritual" as follows:

> There is, first, the *challenge,* by which participants take on the responsibility of calling attention to the misconduct; by implication they suggest that the threatened claims are to stand firm and that the threatening event itself will have to be brought back into line. . . .

The second move consists of the *offering*, whereby a participant, typically the offender, is given a chance to correct for the offence and re-establish the expressive order. . . .

After the challenge and the offering have been made, the third move can occur: the persons to whom the offering is made can accept it as a satisfactory means of *re-establishing the expressive order* and the faces supported by this order. Only then can the offender cease the major part of his ritual offering [pp. 20–22, 1967].

In one investigation of this process (Moriarty, 1974) male subjects were asked to participate in an "opinion exchange" by reading their positions on ten issues to five other group members via an intercom system. During this exchange the subjects discovered that nearly all the other group members (four of the five) disagreed with their opinions on eight of the ten issues (the group reaction was simulated on a tape recording). To create a public reaction to the deviancy, halfway through the opinion exchange one of the simulated group members interrupted the proceedings by stating,

> May I ask a question . . . without spoiling anything? I've been thinking about what's been going on and . . . it's hard to believe anybody would have answers different from ours—I mean they're *obvious*, a guy would have to be *weird* [Moriarty, 1974, p. 851]!

Other voices murmured agreement and the experimenter could be heard cautioning them to follow the directions.

This public reaction was included in the procedures for half the subjects, but no public reaction occurred in the remaining sessions. In addition, the researchers also manipulated secret versus public deviancy by informing some of the subjects that their microphones were broken and that others would be unable to hear their opinions. In the remaining conditions all were supposedly aware of the aberrancy in the subject's responses. While 20% of the participants reported a desire to alter their opinions when they discovered that they disagreed with the others, 48% expressed this same desire when they had been labeled "weird." Furthermore, although the instructions specifically stated that subjects were simply to read their responses verbatim into the microphone, many of the subjects in the publicly labeled group-reaction condition "cheated" and reported an opinion they felt the group would tolerate. Other research has yielded similar findings: deviants tend to respond to public labeling by complying with the demands of the majority (Filter & Gross, 1975; Freedman & Doob, 1968).

Deviants may also try to avoid the negative consequences of the group's condemnation by accounting for their behavior—providing such a reasonable explanation for the objectionable action that the group can neither blame nor sanction them. While a large number of accounting tactics have been cataloged by researchers (Schlenker, 1980; Schönbach, 1980; Scott & Lyman, 1968), most agree that excuses, justifications, and apologies are the most common types of accounts in groups. For example, if a person who has been accused of some deviant action— say, lying to another group member—wishes to lessen his or her responsibility for the deviancy, he or she would provide an *excuse:* "I didn't know that what I was telling you was untrue" or "I was so tired that I didn't realize what I was saying."

Alternatively, a *justification* would be an attempt to redefine the action as one that was, in the particular situation, allowable or even praiseworthy. For example, the lying group member may claim "I did it to protect your feelings" or "I was only trying to help you out." Failing with these two types of accounts, the deviant may be left with only one course of action: *apologize*—"I'm sorry. I regret it ever happened, and I promise not to do it again."

Several studies have examined the impact of various types of accounts on group reactions to deviancy, and all conclude that they soften the group's negative reaction. To see if group members would be more tolerant of an opinion deviant with a "good excuse," researchers (Levine & Ruback, 1980) exposed subjects to a simulated group member who took a neutral but deviant position on the issue under discussion. However, before the subjects evaluated the deviant they were provided with an explanation of this neutrality that emphasized either indifference (no interest in the task), ambivalence (uncertain, since some issues weighed for, some against), or ignorance (insufficient information to make a valid decision). Attraction ratings indicated that the ambivalent deviant (mean liking score = 11.09) was better liked than the deviant who pleaded ignorance (mean score = 8.06). The indifferent deviant, however, was strongly disliked (mean score = 1.96).

In another study, the effect of the group's reaction to an account was studied by manipulating both accounting tactics and the group's reaction (Dedrick, 1978). Seventh- and eighth-grade boys worked in three-person groups to solve some mathematical problems with slide rules in the hopes of winning $12 through superior performance. Two of the three members, however, were confederates. One acted the role of the deviant by behaving obnoxiously, refusing to work with the group, not bothering to use his slide rule, and ruining the group's performance score. When the experimenter pointed out that, because of the deviant, the group could have only $2, the deviant either apologized for his behavior and claimed that he had tried to help the group or appeared unconcerned and unremorseful. The second confederate took the role of the third party. In some groups he accepted the deviant's account, in others he did not react in any way to the account, and in others he was openly hostile and critical of the deviant.

Some of the results of this study are presented in Figure 9-6. The subjects were asked to indicate how they thought the $2 reward should be divided among the three group members. When the deviant offered no account for his action (the lower line in the figure), most of the subjects suggested that he receive less than 20¢. If, on the other hand, the deviant offered an account for the action and the third party seemed to accept it, then the subjects were more forgiving; their mean suggested allocations to the deviant reached 60.8¢. Lastly, if the third party didn't accept the account, the subjects again recommended unequal payment for the deviator.

SECONDARY DEVIANCY

After the group reaction the deviant may decide to conform and suitably account for the objectionable action. However, if the deviant instead continues to perform behaviors that the group deems unacceptable, then the final phase of the deviancy process begins. Unlike the initial deviant act, secondary deviancy cannot be ignored

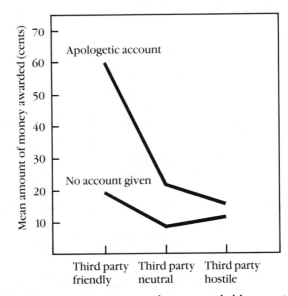

FIGURE 9-6. The mean monetary award recommended for repentant and unrepentant deviants. (Source: Dedrick, 1978)

by the group or explained away by the deviator. Rather, secondary deviancy occurs because the dissenter in the group accepts the group's label of "deviant," and acts in accordance with that role. **Secondary deviancy** "is deviant behavior or social roles based upon it, which becomes a means of defense, attack, or adaptation to the overt and covert problems created by the societal reaction to primary deviation" (Lemert, 1968, p. 17). The individual is no longer one who has committed a deviant act, but one who is a deviant. The societal reaction produces a counterreaction that transforms the group member's self-identity.

The idea that one's self-concept can be influenced by the reactions of others is fully consistent with a theory known as **symbolic interactionism** (Meltzer, Petras, & Reynolds, 1975). According to this perspective, the self is essentially social in nature, since it is built up continually in the course of daily encounters with other human beings. Unlike some theories that portray the self as a static, fixed entity, symbolic interactionism assumes the self to be a dynamic process, the product of the changing transactions between the individual and others. The essence of the approach is summarized in the "looking-glass analogy" of the self:

> . . . as we see our face, figure, and dress in the glass, and are interested in them because they are ours, and pleased or otherwise with them to be; so in imagination we perceive in another's mind some thought of our appearance, manners, aims, deeds, character, friends, and so on, and are variously affected by it [Cooley, 1902, p. 231].

Because the self is, in part, a reflection of the perceived opinions and values of the people with whom one interacts, others' reactions to us will eventually influence our self-identity. If a group reacts to certain behaviors performed in certain situations by labeling them and the individual who commits them deviant, then the logical consequence of the process is the production of a deviant, stigmatized self in the labeled person (see Wells, 1978, for a review of theories dealing with deviancy and changes in self-concept).

Evidence attesting to the internalization of a group's reaction has been reported in studies involving both positive (Meichenbaum, Bowers, & Ross, 1969; Rosenthal & Jacobson, 1968) and negative (Aronson & Mettee, 1968; Kraut, 1973; Snyder & Swann, 1978) labels. Most of the positive labels have been used in educational studies that involved telling teachers that certain students in their classes were "late bloomers" who would soon shine intellectually (Rosenthal & Jacobson, 1968). Although these late bloomers were selected at random by the researchers, the positive expectations created by the label were soon translated into behavioral changes and intelligence gains. The teachers became more positive in their interactions involving the labeled pupils, and the children themselves became better behaved (Meichenbaum et al., 1969). In another study conducted in classrooms, researchers were able to decrease littering and increase math scores simply by repeatedly informing students they were "ecology minded" or mathematically skilled (Miller, Brickman, & Bolen, 1975).

Demonstrating the effects of negative labels, one study gave subjects some rather gloomy information about their personalities ("you are immature, uninteresting, shallow . . ."), positive information ("you are mature, interesting, deep . . ."), or no information. When subjects were subsequently given the opportunity to cheat on an experimental task to win extra money, those who had been negatively labeled were far more likely to do so. In a much different context, individuals who were labeled "uncharitable" when they refused to make a donation to a charity were less likely to give when later contacted by a second charity (Kraut, 1973).

Mark Snyder and William B. Swann (1978) demonstrated the effects of labels and expectations by asking two males to compete in a simple reaction-time game. The subjects were seated in separate rooms and told to press a switch as soon as the signal light came on; the first to press his switch would be declared the winner on that particular trial. However, while total number of wins on the 24 trials was an important determinant of success, the subjects were also told their use of a "noise weapon" would also be considered. On one-half of the trials they could deliver a blast of noise to their opponent that ranged in intensity from very mild to very distracting and irritating. Before play began, however, the subject who had been designated the "labeling perceiver" was given false information suggesting that his opponent was either a hostile or nonhostile individual. Meanwhile, the subject who had been designated the "target" had been subtly encouraged to attribute his behavior during the experiment to his personal dispositional characteristics or to the situation. As predicted, labeling perceivers who expected hostility from their opponents tended to use louder noise levels than those who expected to interact with a nonhostile partner. More interestingly, these expectations received *behavioral confirmation,* since the targets—although unaware that they had been labeled hostile—tended to use higher noise levels than those who had been labeled nonhostile. Snyder and Swann also found that targets who had been labeled hostile and encouraged to make internal attributions continued to use louder noises even when they played a new opponent who had not been given any expectations. In other words, the expectations of the labeling perceiver were confirmed as the target became more aggressive, and the aggressiveness transferred to a new situation and a new interaction partner.

Snyder and Swann (1978, pp. 158, 161) concluded that their "investigation has demonstrated that a perceiver's initially erroneous beliefs about a target individual may initiate a chain of events that channel subsequent social interaction in ways that cause the behavior of the target to confirm the perceiver's beliefs. . . . beliefs can and do create social reality."

Summary

Ever since Solomon Asch's studies demonstrated the powerful pressures to conform that exist in groups, investigators have sought to understand better both conformity (that is, compliance and private acceptance) and deviancy (that is, independence and anticonformity). Looking first at conformity, studies indicate that pressures to agree with others may reach high levels—and then stabilize—in groups with as few as four members, but this relationship between group size and conformity depends upon a number of other factors. Sex of group members and the presence of a consistent minority also influence conformity, which appears to be produced by one or more of the following factors: normative influence, informational influence, self-presentational motives, and mindlessness.

Regarding deviancy, group dynamicists have concentrated on three broad areas: (1) deviancy, communication, and rejection, (2) status and deviancy, and (3) deviancy and identity. Just as Asch's work stimulated many studies of conformity, Stanley Schachter's analysis of group rejection of a deviant initiated a line of research that testifies to the many consequences of nonconformity. These studies have shown that a deviant is generally less well liked by others in the group, and that communication with an unyielding deviant eventually diminishes—at least when cohesive groups are working on relevant tasks. Even members who "change their minds" to conform to the group are no better liked than the consistent conformer, although this rejection is lessened when the high-status deviants' idiosyncrasy credits protect them from rejection.

These rejection mechanisms, when approached from the labeling perspective, hold many long-term implications for the deviant's social identity. After an initial group reaction, deviants may change their actions so they conform or try to account for the deviancy, but in other instances they may refuse to conform. According to the labeling perspective, this secondary deviancy can result in continued rejection of the individual, and through such processes of behavioral confirmation and stigmatization changes in the nonconformist's identity may take place. Hence, by reacting to atypical actions, group members in a sense create deviants.

10

The Environment and Group Behavior

The following is an excerpt from the diary of a young corporate executive:

6:25   Awoke from another lousy night's sleep. Margaret kept rolling over onto my half of the bed. If this keeps up we'll have to get separate beds.

7:30   Herbert drove that little car of his today in the carpool. The six of us sat jammed together like a bunch of sardines. I felt like screaming by the time we got downtown.

9:00   Unlocked my office to discover that the cleaning crew had rearranged my things again. They moved Margaret's picture to the other side of my desk and put the garbage can back in the wrong place.

10:00   I got to the meeting late and the only seat left at the table was right by the boss. I was uncomfortable through the whole thing.

12:30   Frank and I went to lunch at that deli around the corner. The food was good, but it was so noisy and hot in there that I could hardly enjoy it.

2:30   I visited Janice in her new office. She had the entire room decorated in dark brown tones, and the light is so subdued I thought I was in a cave. She sat behind a big dark mahogany desk and complained about her subordinates. I wonder if she keeps it so cold on purpose?

6:30   On the way home I noticed the Wilsons have put up a "Beware of Dog" sign on their gate. That's strange—I don't think they even have a dog.

Although our executive may not notice that his descriptions seem to return again and again to the theme of the environment as a context for interaction, social scientists in many different subfields—environmental psychology, ethology, human ecology, demography, and ecological psychology—have repeatedly found evidence of the importance of environmental variables for human behavior. Individuals and groups exist not in empty, meaningless voids but in dynamic, fluctuating environments that can be too hot, too cold, too impersonal, too intimate, too big, too little, too noisy, too quiet, inadequately furnished, completely unfurnished, or just right. Even more important, people tend to ignore the influences of the environment and are then puzzled when the party thrown in a too-large room goes badly, the meeting held in a busy restaurant accomplishes little, and the seats with the best view in a lecture auditorium are the last to be filled. They feel "uncomfortable" when sitting too close to a colleague, and never obey regulations prohibiting decorations on office walls. Even when an outside observer takes pains to point out environmental influences to the group members, they often react as if such factors as seating arrangements, wall color, temperature, noise, territoriality, and interpersonal distancing were trivial in their effects. Yet, such a judgment would be erroneous.

The scientific literature in this area is enormous, and therefore our intention here is to present only a sampling of the relevant work. The chapter begins with the concept of gaining control over specific parts of a group environment by considering both territoriality within groups and territoriality between groups. In the second section, the relationships linking interpersonal distance and group-member satisfaction and performance are examined in terms of two primary mechanisms: personal space and crowding. The chapter closes with a brief look at several features of the physical environment—temperature, noise, and seating arrangements—that can affect group behavior.

TYPES OF TERRITORIES

Irwin Altman, a leading researcher and theorist in the area of environment and behavior, has recently described three different types of human territories (Altman, 1975). First, *primary territories* are "owned and used exclusively by individuals or groups"; they are "clearly identified as theirs by others, are controlled on a relatively permanent basis, and are central to the day-to-day lives of the occupants" (Altman, 1975, p. 112). Next are *secondary territories*—"places over which an individual or a group has some control,

ownership, and regulatory power, but not the same degree as over a primary territory" (p. 117). Lastly, *public territories* are characterized by "a temporary quality, and almost anyone has free access and occupancy rights" (p. 118). Examples of these territories and a description of the critical ways in which they differ are summarized in the following table. (For some evidence bearing on the validity of the typology, see Taylor and Stough, 1978.)

(Source: Altman, 1975)

Type of territory	Examples	Degree of control and use by occupants	Duration of user's claim to space
Primary	A family's home, a clubhouse, a bedroom, a dorm room, a study	*High.* Occupants control access and are very likely to actively defend this space.	*Long term.* Individuals maintain control over the space on a relatively permanent basis; ownership is often involved.
Secondary	A table in a bar, a seat in a classroom, a regularly used parking space, the sidewalk in front of your home.	*Moderate.* Individuals who habitually use a space come to consider it "theirs." Milder reaction to intrusions.	*Temporary but recurrently occupied.* Others may use the space, but must vacate area if occupant requests.
Public	Elevator, beach, telephone booth, playground, park, bathroom stall, restaurant counter.	*Low.* While occupant may prevent intrusion while present, no expectation of future use exists.	*None.* The individual or group uses the space on only the most temporary basis, and leaves behind no markers.

Territoriality

Although a business executive by profession, Henry Eliot Howard was fascinated by animal behavior and he devoted many years of his life to the careful observation of various species of birds. Every morning before dawn he would awaken, dress, and trudge about the fields and forests of southern England watching the activities of the local bird population, and in time his observations led him to one undeniable conclusion: behavior is strongly influenced by the specific location in which it occurs. According to Howard, birds tend to compete with one another for "choice" areas, and these **territories** are then defended against encroachment by other birds. Bird calls serve as territorial warnings, notifying would-be violators that they will be attacked if they enter the area. Howard also discovered that certain migratory bird species returned to the same location year after year, as if drawn "homeward" by some unerring primordial instinct (Howard, 1920).

H. E. Howard was not the first, nor the last, scholar to comment on the relationship between territory and behavior. Indeed, in the ensuing years researchers collecting data on such diverse types of animals as wolves, lions, seals, geese, seahorses, and human beings described the geographical fixedness of certain patterns of behavior. As the evidence mounted, the concept of territory was frequently used by theorists to describe any area exclusively used and defended by an individual or group. Although precise definitions of the term vary in many minor ways, most conceptions emphasize certain basic aspects of territories. First, the term *territory* necessarily refers to some spatial location, whether on land, in the air, or in the sea, and hence should not be used unless a reference to place is clear. Second, territoriality implies some sort of "possession" over an area, and in humans this possession may or may not also include legal ownership. Third, territories are typically marked by the occupant—whether through the strategic placement of body wastes, glandular secretions, the posting of notices such as "No Trespassing," or threatening graffiti. Finally, intrusion of others into a marked territory can lead to hostility and defensiveness on the occupant's part.

Many fascinating issues concerning territory have been raised in recent years as researchers have questioned its instinctual basis (Ardry, 1970), its role in mating and reproduction (McBride, 1964), the differences between territories established by nonhuman species and those of *homo sapiens* (Altman, 1975), and the basic types of territories established by people (see the box headed "Types of Territories"). However, as group dynamicists our interest in territoriality is more circumscribed. First, both research and everyday experience tell us that groups, as social entities, often establish territories. Second, once in a group, the individual members tend to establish areas they come to consider as theirs, and the study of these areas provides clues concerning status hierarchies and privacy needs in groups. Hence, in the two major divisions of this section we will examine both group territories and individual territories within groups.

Group Territories

Although early ethological studies of birds suggested that territorial defense was carried out by one individual against another, later studies discovered that in some species territories are defended by groups of individuals. For example, South American howler monkeys live together in bands of up to 20 individuals, and these groups forage within a fairly well-defined region. While the bands themselves are cohesive and free of internal strife, when another group of howlers is encountered during the day's wandering a fight begins. Among howlers this territorial defense takes the form of a "shouting match" in which the members of the two bands simply howl at the opposing group until one band, usually the invader, retreats. Indeed, boundaries are rarely violated, because each morning and night the monkeys raise their voices in a communal, and far-carrying, howling session (Carpenter, 1958).

Human groups have also been known to form territories, with the prototypical example being the adolescent gang. Early sociological studies of the social structure of urban communities vividly described the tendency for young males to join forces in defense of a few city blocks that they consider to be their "turf" (Thrasher, 1927; Whyte, 1943; Yablonsky, 1962). For example, many gangs take their names from a street or park located at the very core of their claimed spheres of influence. Like the Nortons, the corner-gang so intensively studied by William F. Whyte (1943), the group members use this central location as a meeting place, coordinate their activities around this "home base," and often defend this ground against invasions by neighboring gangs or those considered to be outsiders. In one study of gangs in Philadelphia, researchers found that part of this defense involves the strategic placement of graffiti on the buildings, signs, and sidewalks of the claimed area. Interestingly, the number of graffiti mentioning the local gang's name increased as one moved closer and closer to the home base, suggesting that the graffiti served as territorial markers warning intruders of the dangers of encroachment. This marking, however, was not entirely successful, for neighboring gangs would occasionally invade a rival's territory to spray-paint their own names over the territorial marker of the home gang, or at least to append a choice obscenity to alter the meaning of the message. In fact, the frequency of graffiti attributable to outside groups provided an index of group power and prestige, for the more graffiti written by opposing gangs in one's territory, the weaker was the home gang (Ley & Cybriwski, 1974a).

Other observers have noted that serious conflicts can arise over territories. For example, Irwin Altman (1975) describes a neighborhood in New York City that contained both Jewish and Irish Catholic residents. These two groups were fairly well isolated from another, and in most instances stayed to their own areas. However, the location of the parochial and public schools necessitated travel across the other group's territory twice a day, so during these times the usual territorial rules were suspended. Altman notes, however, that even though passage through the rival territory was permissible during the specified times, the neighborhood children typically seemed ill at ease and circumspect as they traveled through "enemy territory." Another example of intergroup conflict over territories is described by Doc, the leader of the Norton Street corner boys:

> Once a couple of fellows in our gang tried to make a couple of girls on Main Street. The boy friends of these girls chased our fellows back to Norton Street. Then we got together and chased the boy friends back to where they came from. They turned around and got all Garden Street, Swift Street, and Main Street to go after us. . . . It usually started this way. Some kid would get beaten up by one of our boys. Then he would go back to his street and get his gang. They would come over to our street, and we would rally them. . . .
>
> I don't remember that we ever really lost a rally. Don't get the idea that we never ran away. We ran sometimes. We ran like hell. They would come over to

our street and charge us. We might scatter, up roofs, down cellars, anywhere. We'd get ammunition there . . . Then we would charge them—we had a good charge. They might break up, and then we would go back to our end of the street and wait for them to get together again . . . It always ended up by us chasing them back to their street. We didn't rally them there. We never went looking for trouble. We only rallied on our own street, but we always won there [Whyte, 1943, p. 5].

Doc's allusion to his gang's remarkable success rate when fighting on the home ground is consistent with studies that have examined the superiority of the home team over the visiting team in sporting events (Edwards, 1979). Apparently the home team's greater familiarity with the playing surface and the support of local fans combine to give the home team a considerable edge over an opponent (Altman, 1975).

Studies of territoriality in prisons (Glaser, 1964), naval ships (Heffron, 1973; Roos, 1968), and dormitories (Baum & Valins, 1977) suggest that people feel far more comfortable when their groups can territorialize their living areas. In a clear demonstration of this effect, Andrew Baum, Stuart Valins, and their associates (Baum & Valins, 1977; Baum, Harpin, & Valins, 1975; Baum, Davis, & Valins, 1979) examined the consequences of living in a corridor-style dormitory versus a suite-style dormitory. Much of the project was conducted at a university where incoming students are randomly assigned to one of two types of dormitories. Many lived in the more traditionally designed corridor-style dorm, which featured 17 double-occupancy rooms per floor. A long corridor ran the entire length of the floor and provided the sole means of access to each room. Further, certain facilities—bathrooms and lounges—were shared by all 34 residents of the floor and could only be reached by walking through public corridors. In contrast, the suite-style dorms featured two or three bedrooms clustered around a common lounge and bathroom. Access to these facilities was controlled by the residents of the adjoining bedrooms, and the outside corridor was used only when leaving the building or visiting another suite. Hence, the group living in a suite of rooms maintained a fairly well defined territory, including a private space shared by two roommates as well as the bathroom and lounge controlled by the suitemates. The only territory available to the two-person groups living in the corridor-style dormitories was a small bedroom.

Baum and Valins found that these two types of living conditions produced a range of consequences for the students. Although nearly equal numbers of individuals lived on any floor in the two types of designs, students in the corridor-style dormitories reported feeling more crowded, complained of their inability to control their social interactions with others, and emphasized their unfulfilled needs for privacy. Suite-style residents, on the other hand, developed deeper friendships with their suitemates, worked with one another more effectively, and even seemed more sociable when interacting with people outside the dormitory setting. Baum and Valins concluded that these differences stemmed from the corridor-style residents' inability to territorialize areas that they had to use repeatedly—the bathrooms, the lounges, and hallways. Given the overall design of the dorm and the large number of residents per floor, the only defensible spaces available to corridor-style residents were the bedrooms. Although this limited territory enhanced the cohesiveness of the dyads sharing each room, the design did little to enhance interpersonal relationships among neighbors. The suite-style residents, however, could territorialize and control frequently used spaces with much greater success. These findings have been confirmed by laboratory research (Edney & Uhlig, 1977). Groups given the opportunity to territorialize the rooms in which they worked (by decorating them with posters, ornaments, magazines, flowers, and so on) felt that the rooms "belonged" to the group, considered the rooms more pleasant, reported less arousal, and assumed the rooms could hold fewer people compared with unclaimed rooms.

While these studies attest to the importance of maintaining what Altman would call **primary territories** (see the box), groups have also been found to maintain **secondary** and **public territories** of varying sizes and degrees of exclusiveness. In a rather creative study of space usage at a beach, researchers asked groups of varying sizes to give estimates of their territory by defining an outer boundary (Edney & Jordan-Edney, 1974). Overall, these territories tended to be circular, and increased in size as the number of people in the group increased. However, the size of the territories maintained by groups with five or more members was not appreciably larger than the size of the territories of four-person groups, suggesting that territories do not increase in proportion to the number of group members. Furthermore, territories became smaller as the beach became more crowded; all-female groups maintained smaller group spaces than all-male groups; triads established smaller territories than single individuals, dyads, and larger groups; and the longer the groups remained at the beach the larger their territories became.

Temporary group territories have also been studied by observing outsiders' reluctance to break through group boundaries. Although the area around a group of people may not be marked in any distinctive way, most people feel that it is "rude" or inappropriate to walk through a group of conversing people even if the group has little legitimate right to the space it occupies. In one study of the relative impermeability of groups, two or four confederates talked to one another while standing in a hallway (Knowles, 1973). Individuals who wished to move through this space were forced either to walk between the interactants or to squeeze through the approximately 2.5-foot space between the group and the hallway wall. Seventy-five percent of the passersby observed chose to avoid walking through the group, but this figure dropped to about 25% in a control condition where the interacting individuals were replaced by waste-barrels. Other research indicates that people begin invading group space if the distance between interactants becomes large (Cheyne & Efran, 1972) or the group is perceived to be a crowd rather than a single entity (Knowles & Basset, 1976). Furthermore, mixed-sex groups whose members are conversing with one another seem to have stronger boundaries (Cheyne & Efran, 1972), as do groups whose members are either (1) laughing and joking or (2) angrily arguing (Lindskold, Albert, Baer, & Moore, 1976). Lastly, the perceived size of this invisible territory seems to increase—at least in the eyes of the outsider—as the number of group members grows (see the box headed "Group Spaces" on the next page).

GROUP SPACES

A number of observers have suggested that people in groups seem to be surrounded by a sort of "shell" or "membrane" that forms an invisible boundary for group interaction. Although the space marked by this boundary has been variously labeled *interactional territory* (Lyman & Scott, 1967), *group space* (Edney & Grundmann, 1979), *temporary group territory* (Edney & Jordan-Edney, 1974), *jurisdiction* (Roos, 1968), and *group personal space* (Altman, 1975), evidence indicates that this boundary often effectively serves to repel intruders. For example, in a study (Knowles et al., 1976) conducted in the experimental space pictured below, solitary sub-

jects walking along the right wall of a tunnel that connects two buildings on the University of Wisconsin campus were observed as they passed an alcove. As they approached they could see that the alcove was empty or occupied by one, two, three, or four confederates. An observer positioned in the opposite alcove recorded the deflection of the subject away from the experimental alcove. Analyses revealed that subjects actively avoided the alcove when it was occupied by a group, but that the magnitude of the deflection was limited in part by the unwillingness of subjects to cross to the opposite side of the hallway.

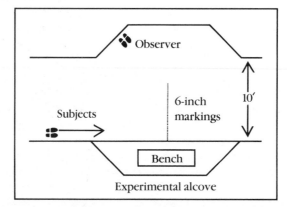

(Source: Knowles, Kreuser, Haas, Hyde and Schuchart, 1976)

Territoriality within Groups

To find evidence of individual territories one need only perform a simple "experiment." First, select several classmates, family members, or work partners as your unknowing "victims." Second, intrude upon their established territory in some way: sit at their usual chairs, put your feet up on their furniture, eat (and spill) your lunch at their desks, arrange to receive telephone calls at their numbers, or put signs up on the walls in their offices. Third, watch for evidence of confusion, discomposure, and mild upset as your victims reveal their reaction to your audacity, and examine your own feelings to see if you are in any way affected. (A note of warning: do not underestimate the importance of even the most temporary of territories. I have witnessed otherwise mild-mannered college students go to great lengths to get back a chair that they feel "belongs" to them.)

If the zealousness of your victims' territorial defenses surprises you, consider some of the important functions territories fulfill for people in groups (Altman, 1975; Edney, 1976). First, in some cases people feel a need to get away from the interaction that typifies group experiences, and retreating back to one's own territory may be an excellent means of effecting this separation. As Irwin Altman (1975) notes, depending upon the situation, people prefer a certain amount of contact with others, and interaction in excess of this level produces feelings of crowding and invasion of privacy. The student in the classroom who is distracted by a jabbering neighbor, employees who are unable to concentrate on their jobs because of their noisy officemates' antics, and the wife who can't enjoy reading a novel because her husband is playing the stereo too loudly are all receiving excessive inputs from a fellow group member. If they moderated their accessibility by successfully establishing and regulating a territorial boundary, then they could achieve a more satisfying balance between contact with others and solitude.

Territories also work as organizers of group members' relationships (Edney, 1976). Once we know the location of others' territories, we can locate—or avoid—them with greater success. Furthermore, because we often grow to like people we interact with on a regular basis (Moreland & Zajonc, 1979), people with contiguous territories tend to like each other. Territories also work to regularize certain group activities—such as the preparation and consumption of food, sleeping, or studying—by providing a place for the performance of these activities. Lastly, territories define what belongs to whom; without a sense of territory the concept of stealing would be difficult to define, since one could not be certain that the objects carried off actually belonged to someone else.

In addition to these privacy and organizing functions, territories also help individual group members to define and express a sense of personal identity. If you enter someone's territory—an office, a dorm room, a bedroom, or a desk in a classroom—you are likely to find evidence of self-definition through marking. Office walls often display posters, diplomas, crude drawings produced by small children, pictures of loved ones, or little signs with trite slogans, even when company regulations specifically forbid such personalizing markings. Although such decorations may seem insignificant to the chance visitor, to the occupant of the space they have personal meaning, and help turn a drab, barren environment into "home."

In an investigation of this function of personal territories, researchers at the University of Utah (Hansen & Altman, 1976; Vinsel, Brown, Altman, & Foss, 1980) photographed the walls over the beds of students living in campus dormitories. As an incidental finding, they discovered that most of these decorations fit into one of the categories listed in Table 10-1. More importantly, however, they also found that students who eventually dropped out of school seemed to mark their walls more extensively—particularly in the personal relationship and music/theater categories—than students who stayed in school. Yet while "stay-ins" used fewer markers, their decorations revealed greater diversity, cutting across several categories. Whereas a drop-out's wall would feature dozens of skiing posters or high school memorabilia, the stay-in's decorations included syllabi, posters, wall hangings, plants, and family photos. The researchers (Vinsel et al., 1980, p. 1114) concluded the wall decorations of dropouts "reflected less imagination or diversity of interests and an absence of commitment to the new university environment."

TABLE 10-1. Categories for wall decorations in dormitory rooms

Category	Decorations
Entertainment/equipment	Bicycles, skis, radios, stereos or components, climbing gear, tennis racquets
Personal relations	Pictures of friends and family, prom flowers, snapshots of vacations, letters, drawings by siblings
Values	Religious or political posters, bumper stickers, ecology signs, flags, sorority signs
Abstract	Prints or posters of flowers, kittens, landscapes, art reproductions
Reference items	Schedules, syllabi, calendars, maps
Music/theater	Posters of ballet, rock or musical groups, theater posters
Sports	Ski posters, pictures of athletes, motorcycle races, magazine covers, mountain climbing-hiking posters
Idiosyncratic	Handmade items (macrame, wall hangings, paintings) plants, unique items (stolen road signs, bearskins)

(Source: Vinsel, Brown, Altman, and Foss, 1980)

TERRITORY AND DOMINANCE

Imagine the surprise of John W. Scott when he discovered the first known mating grounds of the North American sage cock (Scott, 1942). Assembling in groups of 400 to 500 members, the males would arrive well in advance of the hens to secure their individual territories within the selected clearing. Although all the cocks were able to secure small areas, only a few of these territories were "valuable" ones. Indeed, as the hens arrived they would crowd into the territory of the number one male (often labeled the alpha male)—and patiently wait their turn. Cocks who failed to secure and defend one of these coveted locations were completely ignored by the females and hence were unable to mate.

Observers of human groups have likewise noted that the sizes of territories and their locations in the more choice areas occupied by the group seem to match the dominance hierarchy of the group. As one informal observer has noted, in many large corporations the entire top floor of a company's headquarters is reserved for the offices of the upper echelon executives, and can only be reached by a private elevator (Korda, 1975). While the lower floors of the building may be furnished in a mixture of old and new chairs and desks, worn carpeting, and peeling paint, the top floors are elegantly appointed in fine antiques, expensive oil paintings, and heavy wood paneling. Furthermore, within this executive area, offices swell in size and become more lavishly decorated as the occupant's position in the company increases. Substantiating these informal observations, a study of a large chemical company headquarters, a university, and a government agency found a clear link between office size and status (Durand, 1977). The correlation between territory—as reflected by the size of one's office—and status—as reflected by position in the table of organization—was .81 for the company, .79 for the agency, and .29 for the university.

While these anecdotal observations and empirical findings attest to the link between territory and dominance in organizations, evidence from studies of small interacting groups is more equivocal. On one hand, some studies have found that territory size seems to *decrease* as status in the group increases (Esser, 1968; Esser, Chamberlain, Chapple, & Kline, 1965). In contrast, other studies report that territory size *increases* as status increases (Esser, 1973; Sundstrom & Altman, 1974). In an attempt to explain these contradictory results, Eric Sundstrom and Irwin Altman (1974) undertook a longitudinal study of territoriality in a cottage at a boys' rehabilitation center. To assess dominance, each subject ranked the other boys in terms of ability to influence others. In addition, territory was recorded daily by an observer passing through the residence bedrooms, lounge, TV area, and bathrooms. Territoriality was inferred whenever (1) a subject limited his space usage to a few specific areas or (2) an area was used exclusively by a single individual. Lastly, the residents gave their evaluations of these areas in order to determine which territories were more desirable than others.

Although Sundstrom and Altman found evidence of the territory/dominance relation, the strength of this relation varied over time. During the first phase of the project the high-status boys maintained clear control over certain areas, whereas the lower status residents used many areas with equal frequency. In addition, the areas claimed by the high-status boys tended to be more desirable (the best seats in front of the television set), whereas the territory available to the low-status boys was unsatisfying (too close to the supervisor's desk). This period of the study lasted for five weeks, and ended when the administration removed two of the most dominant boys from the group, replacing them with two who would eventually rise to prominent positions. During this second phase of the study, territorial behavior was disrupted as the boys competed with one another for both status and space, and the group was wracked by fighting, teasing, and other forms of misbehavior. However, by the end of the tenth week the group quieted back down, although certain highly dominant members continued to be disruptive. When formal observations were finally terminated, available evidence suggested the group's territorial structures were once more beginning to stabilize.

These findings suggest that dominance/territory relations, like most group processes, are dynamic and multifaceted. While the weight of the evidence supports the notion that higher status members possess larger and more aesthetically pleasing territories, chaotic intermember relations or abrupt changes in membership can create discontinuities in territorial behavior. In addition, the hostility that surfaced in the group when spatial claims were disputed suggests that territories can work as tension reducers by clarifying the nature of the social situation and increasing opportunities for privacy maintenance.

TERRITORIALITY IN ISOLATED GROUPS

During the International Geophysical Year (1957–1958) several countries sent small groups of military and civilian personnel to outposts in Antarctica. Facing some of the harshest weather conditions to be found anywhere on earth, these groups were responsible for collecting various data concerning that unknown portion of the world, but the violent weather forced the staff to remain mostly indoors. Equipment malfunctions occurred regularly, radio contact with the "outside world" was limited, and water rationing restricted bathing and clothes washing. As months went by and these conditions remained unchanged, interpersonal friction often surfaced and the group members found themselves arguing over trivial issues. The members summarized their group malaise with the term *antarcticitis:* lethargy, low morale, grouchiness, and boredom brought on by their unique living conditions (Gunderson, 1973).

These Antarctic groups are by no means unique, for accounts of sailors long confined in submarines (Weybrew, 1963), aquanauts living in Sealab and Tektite (Helmreich, 1974), astronauts in multiperson spacecraft (Fraser, 1966), and work teams on large naval ships (Weiler & Castle, 1972) report evidence of intragroup stress produced by these isolated environmental circumstances. While technological innovations make survival in even the most hostile environments possible, groups living in these space-age settings must learn to cope with problems of interpersonal adjustment—and often territoriality plays a significant role in determining the results of this person/environment interplay.

Some of the best evidence bearing on the effects of isolation on small-group dynamics comes from a series of laboratory studies conducted by Irwin Altman, William Haythorn, and their colleagues at the Naval Medical Research Institute in Bethesda, Maryland (see Altman, 1973, 1977 and Haythorn, 1973 for summaries). In one project, pairs of men worked in a 12 by 12 foot room equipped with beds, toilet cabinet, table and chairs. They worked for several hours each day at various tasks, but were left to amuse themselves with card games and reading the rest of the time. The men in the isolation condition never left their room during the ten days of the experiment, while matched pairs in a control condition were permitted to eat their meals at the base mess and sleep in their regular barracks.

Although a variety of conclusions were drawn from this investigation, one of the most striking findings concerned territoriality. While the control groups seemed to establish few mutually exclusive areas of use, the members of isolated groups quickly claimed particular bunks as theirs. Furthermore, this territorial behavior increased as the experiment progressed, with the isolated pairs extending their territories to include specific chairs and certain positions around the table. While some of the groups used these territories effectively to structure their group dynamics, in other dyads these territories worked as barricades to social interaction and exacerbated the strain of isolation. The cumulative effects of territoriality are evident in Figure 10-1, which shows that withdrawal increased during the three 3-day blocks of the research. The figure also suggests a slight increase in the amount of time spent sleeping during the final stages of the experiment, and a clear decrease in social interaction. Other measures revealed worsened task performance and heightened interpersonal conflicts, anxiety, and emotionality for isolates who drew a "psychological and spatial 'cocoon' around themselves, gradually doing more things alone and in their own part of the room" (Altman & Haythorn, 1967, p. 174).

To follow up these provocative findings, a second experiment manipulated three aspects of the group environment (Altman, Taylor, & Wheeler, 1971); availability of privacy (half of the groups lived and worked in a single room while the remaining groups had small adjoining rooms for sleeping, napping, reading, and so on), expected duration of the isolation (pairs expected the study to last either 4 days or 20 days), and amount of communication with the "outside world" (short music broadcasts, news programs, and taped questions and answers taken from the adviser column of *Playboy* magazine were played to some of the pairs). Although the study was to last for eight days for all the pairs, more than half terminated their participation before the full term was reached. Altman (1973, p. 249) explains this high attrition rate by suggesting that the aborting groups tended to "misread the demands of the situation and did not undertake effective group formation processes necessary to cope with the situation." On the first day of the study these men tended to keep to themselves, never bothering to work out any plans for coping with what would become a stressful situation. Then, as the study wore on, they reacted to increased stress by significantly strengthening their territorial behavior, laying increased claim to particular areas of the room. They also began spending more time in their beds, but seemed simultaneously to be increasingly restless. Access to a private room and an expectation of prolonged isolation only added to the stress of the situation, and created additional withdrawal, maladaptation, and eventual termination.

Groups that lasted the entire eight days seemed to use territoriality to their advantage in structuring their isolation. On the first day they defined their territories, set up schedules of activities, and agreed on their plan of action for getting through the study. Furthermore, the successful groups tended to relax territorial restraints in the later stages of the project, and thereby displayed a greater degree of positive interaction. As described by Altman (1977, p. 310),

> The epitome of a successful group was one in which the members, on the first or second day, laid out an eating, exercise, and recreation schedule; constructed a deck of playing cards, a chess set, and a Monopoly game out of paper; decided how they would structure their lives over the expected lengthy period of isolation.

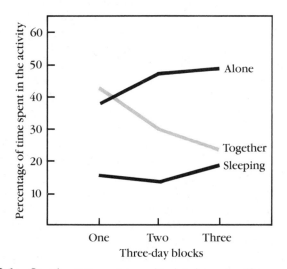

FIGURE 10-1. Social activity patterns of isolated groups. (Source: Altman and Haythorne, 1967)

Thus, although territorial behavior worked to the benefit of some of the groups, the last-minute attempts of some of the abort groups to organize their spatial relations failed to improve their inadequate adaptation to the isolation.

Interpersonal Distance

Birds strung out along a telephone wire at unvaryingly equal distances from one another; solitary moviegoers filing into an empty theater, cautiously selecting chairs several seats removed from their closest neighbors; geese flying south in a precise V formation; friends at a party moving closer together to better hear one another over the din of the conversation and music; Arctic lemmings committing mass suicide to avoid overtaxing available resources; thousands of rock music fans bumping, pushing, and rubbing against one another as they push closer and closer toward the stage.

All these examples revolve around a feature of social interaction that too often goes completely unnoticed: interpersonal distance. Indeed, anthropologist Edward T. Hall (1966) once referred to spatial relations as the "hidden dimension" of social life, and called for the systematic study of this variable. Fortunately, in the years since Hall's suggestion researchers have intensified their studies of the relationship between distance and behavior, with the result that what was once a hidden dimension is now a fairly well understood phenomenon. Many volumes would be needed to describe satisfactorily and catalog all the worthwhile results of these efforts, but our overview will focus only on personal space research and theories of crowding.

Personal Space

Imagine yourself standing in the center of a fairly large room, facing the doorway. As you watch, a stranger appears in the threshold and begins walking toward you with a slow, deliberate step. As the distance between you and the stranger diminishes and the stranger shows no sign of stopping, you begin to experience a vague sense of discomfort. Yet you feel you have no right to complain, at least until the stranger reaches a point that you feel is "too close." But what is "too close?" ten feet? five feet? two feet? so close you can tell the color of the stranger's eyes? so close you can smell the stranger's breath, or hear his or her stomach rumbling? so close the two of you can touch one another?

Most researchers refer to the distance that people like to keep between themselves and others as **personal space.** Often likened to an invisible bubble that surrounds the individual, personal space provides a boundary that limits the amount of physical contact among people. Although this boundary may be irregularly shaped—generally extending farther in the front of the person than behind the back—the individual is always near the center of the bubble. Personal space, in clear contrast to territoriality, is portable, a psychological shell that people carry with them from situation to situation. However, just as territorial encroachments create stress, arousal, and defensive reactions, personal space is actively maintained and defended. When someone violates our personal space we tend to take steps to correct this problem.

A full review of the literature dealing with personal space is well beyond the scope of this chapter, but many excellent summaries are available to aid the interested reader who requires additional information (see, for example, Altman, 1975; Altman & Chemers, 1980; Evans & Howard, 1973; Hayduk, 1978; Knowles, 1980). However, it is possible to consider how a sampling of these research findings can be used to tell us something more about our fellow group members and the many groups that we observe in our day-to-day activities.

For example, several studies suggest that highly cohesive groups occupy smaller spaces than noncohesive gatherings (Evans & Howard, 1973). The concept of personal space logically implies that the spatial distribution of people in groups will be in part determined by the shape of members' "bubbles," so it stands to reason that very compressed groups must enjoy fairly positive internal relations. In a study verifying this hypothesis, members of two- and four-person groups were asked to fill out questionnaires without sitting down or leaning against the walls. When distances were compared, the researchers discovered that groups composed of all friends took up less space than groups composed of strangers (Edney & Grundmann, 1979). Large distances among group members may also tell us that the group faces some sort of threatening situation, for evidence indicates personal space expands when people are stressed (Dosey & Meisels, 1969). E. T. Hall even suggests that the nationality of group members may be reflected in their interpersonal spacings (Hall, 1966); individuals who are socialized in "contact cultures" (Latin America, France, the Middle East) are perfectly comfortable interacting at very close distances, while those reared in "noncontact cultures" (America, England, Scandinavia) prefer large distances.

Spacing may also tell us something about the people who are members of our group. For example, several studies suggest that extroverted people maintain smaller distances from others than do introverts (for example, Patterson & Sechrest, 1970), while higher status members are afforded more space than lower status members (Giesen & McClaren, 1976). Further, people who wish to create a friendly, positive impression usually choose smaller distances than less friendly people (Evans & Howard, 1973), and may combine this intimacy-enhancing positioning with other forms of positive nonverbal behavior, such as increased eye contact. In fact, researchers have continually emphasized the relationship between distance and communication among group members, noting that in different situations the various aspects of spatial behavior must be balanced to maintain the proper degree of intimacy. According to one of the better known explanations of nonverbal behavior in groups, *equilibrium theory* (Argyle & Dean, 1965), four aspects of interaction are critical in defining intimacy: amount of eye contact, personal space, the intimacy of topics discussed, and the amount of smiling among members. According to equilibrium theory, group members will try to maintain each of these factors at an appropriate level for the amount of intimacy acceptable in the group. Hence, if the members of your group make a good deal of eye contact, sit close together, and smilingly discuss the most personal topics, then you can be assured that the group has reached a high level of intimacy (Patterson, 1973).

Lastly, in some group settings it may be more meaningful to apply Hall's extended typology of spatial zones (1966). Rather than considering interpersonal space in dichotomous terms—someone is either in your personal space zone or outside it—Hall suggests the four zones of interpersonal distance shown in Table 10-2. The *intimate zone* is appropriate for only the most involving and personal behaviors, such as love making, wrestling, comforting, and whispering. The *personal zone,* in contrast, is reserved for a wide range of small-group experiences, such as discussions with friends, interaction with acquaintances, and conversation. In the third zone—*social distance*—more routine transactions are expected. Meetings held over large desks, formal dining, and professional presentations to small groups generally take place in this zone. *Public distances* are reserved for even more formal meetings, such as stage presentations, lectures, or addresses.

Personal space has been studied a good deal by researchers for a number of reasons: the manifestations of interpersonal positioning in everyday interactions are readily apparent, the concept is intuitively appealing, and in some respects personal space is fairly easily measured (Hayduk, 1978). The concept, however, is not without its problematic aspects. First, while some of the previously noted findings have been replicated across studies, in some cases subsequent tests lead to contradictory conclusions (Hayduk, 1978). Second, while the concept implies stability across time, evidence indicates personal space size varies widely depending upon the situation and the nature of the group (Patterson, 1975). Third, many methods have been developed to assess the size of personal space (simulation techniques, paper-and-pencil tests, and behavioral measures), but these various measures may not be assessing the same construct (Severy, Forsyth, & Wagner, 1979). Fourth, although personal space implies a discrete, dichotomous spatial process, some researchers believe that theoretical precision can only be gained by viewing distance as a continuous variable (Knowles, 1980). Fifth, some consider the term *personal space* a misnomer, since the process actually refers to interpersonal space (Patterson, 1975). Sixth, while the concept implies that intrusion creates only negative affective reactions, in many instances (for example, in the back seat of an automobile or a secluded spot on a beach) the "violation" of

TABLE 10-2. Hall's zones of interpersonal distance

Zone	Distance	Activities	Zone characteristics
Intimate	Touching to 18 inches	Procreation, massage, comforting, accidental jostling, handshake, slow dancing	Sensory information concerning other is detailed and diverse; stimulus person dominates perceptual field
Personal	18 inches to 4 feet	Friendly discussions, conversations, car travel, watching television	Other person can be touched if desired, but also avoided; gaze can be directed away from the other person with ease
Social	4 feet to 12 feet	Dining, meetings with business colleagues, interacting with a receptionist	Visual inputs begin to dominate other senses; voice levels are normal; appropriate distance for many informal social gatherings
Public	12 feet or more	Lectures, addresses, plays, dance recitals	All sensory inputs beginning to become less effective; voice may require amplification; facial expressions unclear

(Source: Hall, 1966)

personal space can be enjoyable (Shaw, 1981). Perhaps in partial response to these problems, researchers interested in interpersonal distancing have begun to interpret their findings in terms of crowding rather than personal space.

Crowding

Reviews of empirical evidence related to groups working under crowded conditions often begin with John B. Calhoun's classic studies of population density and social pathology in rats (Calhoun, 1962). In his early work, Calhoun established a rat colony in a quarter-acre pen and allowed the animals to breed freely. Although he supplied them with plenty of food and water and protected them from predation, he discovered that the population stabilized at around 150 rats. In addition, the rats tended to organize into subgroups of 10 to 12 members, with larger groupings evidencing aggression and disruptive behavior.

In his other studies, Calhoun systematically increased the size of the population by building a pen that was divided into four sections. If one colony lived in each section, the optimal population level would be 48 rats, but Calhoun arranged the pens so that during feeding times 60 to 80 rats would congregate in one of the sections. Calhoun observed that these high-density conditions created what he called a "behavioral sink": a significant distortion of many aspects of rat behavior, including disruption of courting rituals, mating, nest building, territoriality, aggression, and rearing practices. These results, taken in combination with the findings of other animal studies (for example, Christian, Flyger, & Davis, 1960) and early correlational studies of population density and urban crimes (Galle, Gove, & McPherson, 1972; Galle & Gove, 1979) suggested that crowded groups may undergo a much different set of dynamics than uncrowded groups.

THEORIES OF THE EFFECTS OF CROWDING

To study the consequences of crowding in human groups, researchers began conducting more and more elaborate field and laboratory studies of small groups working in restrictive settings while refining their theoretical assumptions and terminology (Altman, 1978). For example, one important distinction, first noted by Daniel Stokols (1972, 1978) distinguishes between two terms that are often used interchangeably: **density** and **crowding.** According to Stokols, density refers to a characteristic of the environment—literally the number of people per unit of space. Crowding, in contrast, refers to a psychological, experiential state that sometimes but not always corresponds to physical density. Although the density of a given situation, such as a party or a rock concert, may be very high, interactants may not "feel" crowded at all. In contrast, two people sitting in a large room may still report that they feel crowded if they had expected to be alone, were engaged in some private activity, or disliked one another intensely. (It must be pointed out that some researchers [for example, Freedman, 1975] reject this distinction.)

Other theoretical reformulations further elaborated the conditions under which high density translates into the feeling of crowding, until at present the interested researcher can pick and choose from among a vast assortment of theories and models. In selectively sampling some of these ideas, we will consider four different perspectives: overload theory, control models, attributional approaches, and the density-intensity hypothesis.

Overload theory.   The story of country-bred ruralites living in the "big city" is a favorite theme in literature, television, and movies. Typically our privacy-loving protagonists move to the city with enthusiasm and optimism but are startled by the frenzied pace of their new environment—the diversity, confusion, and activity. Psychological suffering invariably follows, lasting until they learn to cope with these new surroundings. Although exaggerated, by emphasizing privacy, stimulation, and coping, this story line parallels some of the essential elements of an overload theory of crowding. Beginning with the assumption that most individuals prefer a certain level of environmental stimulation, overload theories argue that stimulation in excess of this threshold creates psychological stress (Altman, 1975; Milgram, 1970; Saegert, 1978). To reduce this stress, the overloaded individual compensates—by withdrawing, limiting behavior, ignoring certain kinds of information, and so on—and thus avoids overstimulation. In a small-group context, cognitive overload could occur whenever an individual is forced into unwanted social contacts to the point where his or her threshold for privacy and stimulation is surpassed.

In a recent study of compensatory responses to environmental overload, researchers (Greenberg & Firestone, 1977) arranged conversations between male subjects and a male interviewer. Three factors were manipulated in the interview situation. First, subjects were seated in a corner or in the center of the room. Second, the interviews were conducted in the presence of two other people *(surveillance)* or in a private room *(no surveillance)*. Third, during the session the interviewer either physically touched the subject, maintained high eye contact, and leaned toward the subject *(intrusion)* or sat farther from the subject, maintained less eye contact, and leaned backward *(no intrusion)*. Although the corner

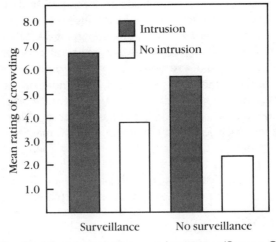

FIGURE 10-2.   Reactions to surveillance and intrusion. (Source: Greenberg and Firestone, 1977)

versus room-center manipulation had little impact on responses, both surveillance and intrusion levels added to feelings of crowding. When subjects later rated the degree of crowding in the setting on a 9-point scale from "not crowded" to "crowded," the results presented in Figure 10-2 were obtained. Both variables added to the degree of overload, with subjects in the intrusion/surveillance condition reporting somewhat larger amounts of crowding.

Control theory.   The idea that people are motivated to achieve a degree of control over their physical and social worlds has been a recurrent theme in social-psychological theorizing. A host of concepts emphasize the importance of behavioral, cognitive, and decisional control (Schmidt & Keating, 1979), and research attests to the impact of control and loss of control on behavior (for example, Abramson, Seligman, & Teasdale, 1978; Glass & Singer, 1972). The concept of control as applied to crowding suggests that high-density situations are unsettling because they undermine our sense of control over our own personal behavior, our ability to understand and process information, and our group's success in reaching sensible decisions (Baron & Rodin, 1978; Sherod & Cohen, 1979; Rodin, 1976; Rodin & Baum, 1978). Although the many approaches that could be subsumed under the rubric *control theory* vary to some extent, most suggest that high density leads to feelings of crowding only when a sense of loss of control occurs concomitantly. This basic assumption can be expressed as

$$\text{high density} + \text{loss of control} = \text{crowding}$$

Although many exciting studies could be cited to show support for control theory, one performed by Judith Rodin and her colleagues is particularly relevant (Rodin, Soloman, & Metcalf, 1978, Experiment 2). Groups of six members (all male) were established in either a small or large laboratory room (14.04 m^2 versus 5.94 m^2) and asked to perform tasks. One problem was a 15-minute open-ended discussion of censorship, and the second involved blindfolding members one at a time and letting them wander about within a circle formed by the rest of the group. To manipulate control, one of the subjects was designated the *coordinator;* he had responsibility for organizing the group, dealing with questions concerning procedures, and blindfolding members for the second task. A second subject, the *terminator,* was given control over ending the discussion and over each member's turn in the center of the circle.

After completing the two tasks, the group members answered a series of questions concerning their perceptions of the room. Significantly, group members who could control the group tasks through coordination or termination were not as bothered by the high-density situation as the four group members who were given no control over the situation. Feeling "in control" partially ameliorated the effects of high density, for even when interacting in the small room the coordinators and terminators tended to downplay the magnitude of the crowding. (The box headed "The Ups and Downs of Crowding" discusses another study conducted by Rodin and her colleagues to further test the effects of controllability on crowding).

Attributional explanations.   A third explanation of crowding suggests that attributional processes mediate reactions to high density (Patterson, 1976; Worchel, 1978). The attributional approach, which is best elaborated in Stephen Worchel's research (Worchel, 1978; Worchel & Teddlie, 1976; Worchel & Yohai, 1979), assumes that the crowding process begins when someone approaches you too closely. This invasion sets off an implicit arousal reaction on your part, and you therefore begin to search the environment for a plausible explanation of your arousal. If you attribute the arousal to others standing too close, then you will conclude "I feel crowded." If, in contrast, you explain the arousal in some other way—"I am fearful," "I drank too much coffee," "I am in love," and so on—then you will not feel crowded.

Several hypotheses derived from the attributional model have been supported empirically. First, the model suggests that interpersonal distance, and not room size, should be closely related to crowding. To test this idea, investigators (Worchel & Teddlie, 1976) varied both of these variables by placing groups in large or small rooms and seating the members either close together or far apart. Significantly, only interpersonal distance was related to crowding. Second, the link between personal space violations and arousal was confirmed in a study of males mictu-

---

THE UPS AND DOWNS OF CROWDING

Imagine yourself standing with eight other people in a small enclosure that measures only about 6 by 4 feet. The enclosure has no windows and no pictures on the walls, but the lighting is so bright that you can see every pore on the nose of the person standing next to you. The air in the booth is both stale and noncirculating, so you can easily tell what cologne the man on your left is wearing, the brand of soap used by the woman on your right, and the type of pizza the person behind you had for lunch. Not one of the occupants says a word to one another, but instead all stand in silence staring at a point in the wall just above the door.

Although you might think that it is highly unlikely that people would willingly enter such a noxious environmental situation, you would of course be incorrect. Our imaginary enclosure is nothing more than a well-loaded elevator, and millions of people force themselves to crowd into these devices each day. Although some people simply cannot adjust to the experience and hence resign themselves to long climbs up and down stairs, most learn to cope with the momentary crowding by concentrating on the background music, carefully avoiding others' eyes, scrutinizing the floor-

indicator lights, or reading any available sign with feigned interest. In addition—as Rodin and her colleagues suggest (Rodin, Solomon, & Metcalf, 1978, Experiment 1)—some individuals cope by situating themselves near the control panel that contains the push buttons for the various floors. According to these researchers, such a position "elevates" one's feeling of control in the situation, and hence makes the elevator ride less distressing. Providing evidence for this hypothesis, these investigators arranged for four confederates to enter an elevator in the Yale University Library whenever a lone individual arrived to use the elevator. These confederates then carefully jockeyed the subject into either the corner opposite the control panel or the corner in front of the control panel. Another member of the research team then trailed the subject when he or she left the elevator, and under the ruse of collecting information for an architecture class, administered a questionnaire that contained several items concerning the elevator. Consistent with control theory, passengers who had been able to manipulate the floor-selection buttons felt that the elevator was less crowded than those who could not reach the buttons.

rating in a public restroom (Middlemist, Knowles, & Matter, 1976). Reasoning that arousal would lead to a general muscular contraction that would delay micturation and reduce its duration, males using wall-mounted urinals were joined by a confederate who used either the next receptacle (*near condition*) or one located farther down the wall (*far condition*). When onset times and duration for males in the near and far condition were compared to those same times for males in a no-confederate control condition, the researchers found that personal space invasion significantly increased general arousal.

The clearest support for the attributional model, however, comes from a study of five-person groups seated in a circle of chairs placed either 20 inches apart or touching at the legs (Worchel & Yohai, 1979). The groups were told to work on a variety of tasks but that during their work subliminal noise would be played in the room. For one-third of the groups the experimenter stated that while the noise was below conscious hearing level it was detectable subconsciously and would lead to stressful, discomforting effects. To another third of the groups the experimenter explained that the noise would be undetectable consciously but in this case would have relaxing and calming effects. The final third of the subjects were given no explanations concerning the effects of the subliminal noise. After this manipulation, the groups worked on tasks, but were not actually exposed to any noise.

Before we consider the results of the study, let us first review the predictions of the attributional framework. First, individuals in the close-interpersonal-distance condition should become aroused by the intrusion of others into their personal space and begin searching for a plausible cause. For subjects in the arousing-noise condition the explanation for their discomfort should be obvious to them—after all, the experimenter had told them that the noise would cause some discomfort. Therefore, they should feel not crowded but rather distressed by the noise. Those in the no-explanation condition would have no reason to interpret noise as a possible source of their stress and therefore should report greater crowding than the arousing-noise groups. Lastly, subjects who had been told the noise would be relaxing should be the most surprised and confused concerning their arousal, since their subjective feelings contradicted what they had been led to expect. Hence, Worchel believed that groups in the relaxing-noise condition would be the most likely to report feeling crowded.

As Table 10-3 shows, subjects' later reports of their feelings of being crowded paralleled these predictions quite closely.

The density-intensity hypothesis. Jonathan Freedman summarizes his theory of crowding in the first few pages of this book *Crowding and Behavior* when he writes,

> Based on research over a period of five or six years by myself and a number of other investigators, we have concluded that crowding does not generally have negative effects on people and that, indeed, it can have either good or bad effects depending upon the situation [1975, p. vii].

Essentially, if something in the situation makes the group interaction unpleasant, then high density will make the situation seem even more unpleasant. If, however,

TABLE 10-3. Results of the experimental test of an attributional model of crowding (low scores imply a low feeling of crowding; higher scores imply more feelings of crowding)

Interpersonal distance	Arousing noise	Relaxing noise	No explanation
Close	4.3	7.1	6.7
Far	3.4	2.7	3.1

(Source: Worchel and Yohai, 1979)

the situation is a very pleasant one, then high density will make the good situation even better. Freedman labels this basic idea the density-intensity hypothesis, for it suggests that crowding (what he calls high density) merely intensifies whatever is already occuring in the group situation (Freedman, 1975, 1979).

Freedman has tested this notion by placing groups of people in large or small rooms and then manipulating some aspect of the group interaction to create unpleasantness or pleasantness. For example, in one investigation groups of six to ten high school students sat on the floor of either a large or small room. Each delivered a speech and then received feedback from the other group members. By prearrangement, Freedman made certain that in some groups the feedback was always positive, whereas in other groups the feedback was always negative. When the subjects later rated the room and their group, people in the little room reported feeling more crowded than those in the big room, but density interacted with pleasantness of the situation such that liking for the group was (1) highest in the high-density/positive-feedback condition but (2) lowest in the high-density/ negative-feedback condition. Furthermore, Freedman found that these effects were clearest for all-female groups as opposed to all-male or mixed-sex groups.

Conclusions.   All four of the theoretical frameworks just described seek to explain crowding in small groups, albeit in somewhat different ways. Although at one level one could compare the four approaches and attempt to select that which best accounts for crowding, more likely each adds something to our understanding that is overlooked or underemphasized in the others. It is to be hoped that future efforts will be directed toward (1) defining the conditions that determine when each alternative theory best applies and (2) integrating these disparate but potentially compatible explanations of crowding.

CROWDING AND GROUP PERFORMANCE

Although theoretical explanations of crowding do much to help us understand reactions to reduced interpersonal distances, one should not lose sight of the practical implications of crowding research. Groups must sometimes live and work in environments that can't be enlarged or rearranged to afford greater space, so it becomes important to know when such high-density conditions will influence group productivity. Naturally, group dynamicists have studied this question in depth, but their complex findings suggest that clear answers can only be offered by oversimplifying the issues involved. Out of the multitude of factors discussed in recent reviews of research (for example, Cohen, 1980; Paulus, 1980) dealing with the relationship between density and performance, we select three for more detailed analysis: (1) the interactive nature of the task, (2) the fit between the group and the situation, and (3) the gender of the group members.

Interactive tasks.   One clear difference distinguishing studies that find no ill effects of crowding (for example, Freedman et al., 1971) and those that do (say, Paulus, Annis, Seta, Schkade, & Matthews, 1976) centers around the interactive quality of the group task. In Freedman's research, subjects sat in crowded and uncrowded rooms and worked on many different memory, reasoning, concentration, and creativity tasks, but all of these problems were individualistic. Subjects never had to interact with the others in their group, and the crowding didn't *directly* interfere with performance. In contrast, other studies have required participants to complete interactive tasks that are more difficult to solve under crowded circumstances (such as Heller, Groff, & Solomon, 1977; Paulus et al., 1976). To demonstrate the importance of considering the degree of interference created by crowding, the designers of one study (Heller et al., 1977) deliberately manipulated both density and interaction. Six-to-eight-member all-male groups were given a task to perform in either a small or large laboratory room. The task itself involved correctly collating eight-page booklets, and to add an incentive the experimenter promised participants a bonus for each booklet correctly assembled. The order of the pages was not constant, however, but was determined by first selecting a card that had the order of pages listed in a random sequence (for instance, 3 5 8 7 6 1 2 4). In the low-interaction condition, the task was simple, since each person was given all eight stacks of pages and a set of sequence cards. In the high-interaction condition, all group members shared the same eight stacks, which were located all around the room. Furthermore, because each sequence differed from the last, subjects constantly had to walk around the room in unpredictable patterns. In fact, the subjects often bumped into one another while trying to move from one stack to another.

The interference created in the high-interaction condition did indeed lead to pronounced decrements in task performance—provided density was high. When the researchers checked the booklets for collating errors, they discovered that crowded/high-interaction groups incorrectly collated their booklets more than 12% of the time. This error rate dropped down to less than 6% in the uncrowded/high-interaction condition and to about 4% in the two low-interaction conditions. These results suggest that performance suffers when high density interferes with a group's ability to successfully solve a task (McCallum et al., 1979; Sundstrom, 1975).

Staffing theory.   Elaborating on the work of ecological psychologists (for example, Barker et al., 1978), Allan Wicker suggests that a given number of people is "right" for each situation (Wicker, 1979; Wicker, Kirmeyer, Hanson, & Alexander, 1976). To choose a common example, consider an office in a small business, university, or government agency that is responsible for typing papers and reports, answering the telephone, duplicating materials, and preparing paperwork on budget, schedules, appointments, and so on. If the number of people working in the office is sufficient to handle all these activities, then the setting is *optimally staffed*

(Wicker uses the phrase *optimally manned* but in the interests of clarity and fairness a more neutral term is used here). If, however, the office is *understaffed*—telephones are ringing unanswered, reports are days late, the photocopy machine is broken and no one knows how to fix it—then the group lacks "enough people to carry out smoothly the essential program and maintenance tasks" in the setting (Wicker, 1979, p. 71). Lastly, if the number of group members exceeds that needed in the situation—if the flow of work is so slight that the staff has little to do, the number of typewriters available is insufficient, only one duplicating machine is available so users must wait their turn, the desk of the new staff member hasn't yet arrived—*overstaffing* exists.

Wicker's staffing theory predicts that the adequacy of staffing in a work setting will have effects on a number of individual and group variables, some of which are listed in Table 10-4. Significantly, the theory hypothesizes that overstaffed groups may not perform inadequately—after all, so many extra people are available to carry out the basic functions—but overstaffing can lead to dissatisfaction with task-related activities and heightened rejection of other group members (Arnold & Greenberg, 1980). Supporting this prediction, Wicker and his associates (Wicker et al., 1976) found that the members of four-person all-male groups, when placed in an overstaffed situation (too few tasks to keep all members active), reported feeling less important, less involved in their work, less concerned with performance, and less needed. These effects were reversed in the understaffed groups.

Sex of group members. While many additional factors could be noted as possible mediators of the density/performance-quality relationship—importance of the task, involvement with the problem, group cohesiveness, and the duration of the crowding experience—we close this section on crowding with a discussion of sex differences. First, while an occasional study suggests that males and females react similarly to high-density situations (for example, MaCallum et al., 1979),

TABLE 10-4. Group members' responses to inadequately staffed worksettings

Members of understaffed groups will tend to:	Members of overstaffed groups will tend to:
Show strong, frequent, and varied actions in carrying out goal-related behavior	Perform tasks in a perfunctory lackadaisical manner
Act to correct inadequate behavior of others	Show a high degree of task specialization
Be reluctant to reject group members whose behavior is inadequate	Demonstrate little concern for the quality of the group product
Feel important, responsible, and versatile as a result of their participation	Exert little effort in helping others in the group
Be concerned about the continued maintenance of the group	Feel cynical about the group and its functions
Be less sensitive to and evaluative of individual differences among group members	Evidence low self-esteem, with little sense of competence and versatility
Think of themselves and other group members in terms of the jobs they do rather than in terms of personality characteristics	Focus on personalities and idiosyncrasies of people in the group rather than on task-related matters

(Source: Wicker, 1979)

most studies with subjects of both sexes report differences. Second, while a minority of these studies find that males react more positively to crowding than females (for example, Marshall & Heslin, 1975), the vast majority suggests that males react negatively to crowding while females sometimes enjoy and work better in high-density situations (Epstein & Karlin, 1975; Paulus et al., 1976; Ross, Layton, Erickson, & Schopler, 1973). For example, in one study in which four-person same-sex groups solved mazes in either large or small rooms, males made more mistakes in the high-density conditions, whereas females made more errors in the low-density conditions (Paulus et al., 1976). Furthermore, other studies suggest that males, relative to females, become more competitive, more vindictive, more hostile, more withdrawn, and more rejecting when crowded (Freedman, 1975; Ross et al., 1973).

Many explanations could be offered for these sex differences—innate needs for larger territories among males, the larger size of males' bodies relative to females' bodies, or the greater socioemotionality of women—but sex-linked normative pressures no doubt play an important role. As one team of researchers concludes, reactions to crowding may be "governed by different sex norms about sharing distress; women perceive that distress should be shared, whereas men perceive that distresses be concealed" (Epstein & Karlin, 1975, p. 39). They go on to suggest that "were men to adopt norms of sharing distress and women to adopt norms of hiding distress, men would display more positive and women more negative behavior" when placed in crowded situations (Epstein & Karlin, 1975, p. 50).

Features of the Physical Environment

When you are part of an interacting group, how sensitive are you to the flood of environmental information conveyed to you by your five senses? Do you notice the color of the surrounding walls, the intensity of the lighting, or the fleeting smile on another's face? Do you pay close attention to peripheral sounds—the noise of traffic on the street below, the scraping of a chair across the floor, the rumbling of someone's stomach—and do you notice the smell of the room, the way it feels to you as you touch it, its temperature, and ambiance? Do you think about the comfort of the chair in which you are seated, how its position in the group facilitates or impedes smooth interaction, or where you would prefer to be seated?

In many instances we don't notice these aspects of the group setting. Our senses may seem overtaxed just in keeping up with the arguments, interjections, and ramblings of other people, and we thus censor out "irrelevant" information in an effort to better comprehend the group discussion. Yet the features of the physical world that we so often overlook can significantly transform the group situation, making incomplete any analysis of a group that lacks a description of the situation. Furthermore, because with practice people can learn more fully to understand the influence of the environment on group behavior, an increased awareness of and sensitivity to the group setting can help us to improve our comprehension and control of our group's dynamics. Therefore, in this final section we consider how certain aspects of the physical setting, such as noise, temperature, and seating patterns, can influence group behavior.

The Ambient Environment

When people gather in groups at specific locations, they are surrounded by an environment that has particular properties and characteristics. For example, the group may meet in a soundproof room or in a hallway outside a children's nursery. The lighting in the room may be bright and glaring or subdued and diffuse. The air in the place may feel uncomfortably hot, too still, odorous, dusty, or smoky. All these features of the room, and many others that we did not mention, make up the group's **ambient environment**—the external, situational stimuli that seem to surround and envelop the group. Although researchers are just now beginning to more fully explore the relationship between the ambient environment and group dynamics (see Beil, Fisher, & Loomis, 1978 and Heimstra & McFarling, 1978 for more detailed reviews), initial findings suggest that group members would do well to remain aware of the ways such factors as lighting, temperature, noise, and even room color influence their behavior (see the box).

To elaborate briefly, studies of temperature suggest that one of the minor miseries of social life occurs when people must work in a room that is too hot or too cold. While a wide range of temperatures—from the mid 60s to the mid 80s is rated as "comfortable" by most people—temperatures that fall outside this range are cause for discomfort, irritability, and reduced productivity (Bell et al., 1978; Baron, 1978; Parsons, 1976). For example, in a study that specifically focused on group members' reactions to temperature (Griffitt & Veitch, 1971) 3 to 16 people were assembled to work on tasks in a normal temperature room (72.4° Fahrenheit) or a hot room (93.5° Fahrenheit). When later questioned about the experience, the overheated group members reported feelings of aggression, fatigue, sadness, and discomfort, while subjects in the normal-temperature room reported feeling more elated, vigorous, and comfortable. Studies also suggest that extremes in temperatures can reduce interpersonal attraction (Griffitt, 1970), interfere with successful task performance (Parsons, 1976), cause severe physical dysfunctions (Folk, 1974), and contribute to increases in aggressive behavior (Baron, 1978). Also, one of the concomitants of high temperatures in groups is exposure to others'

ROOM COLOR AND BEHAVIOR

Although empirical studies of the effect of room color on behavior generally find little evidence of any pervasive influence, the sheer plausibility of the idea that mood, creativity, interpersonal warmth, and so on are linked to room color is so great that lay people continue to insist that color is critical. In fact, officials in one jail have begun painting the cells pink in the belief that this color reduces violence. As one police captain explains, "pink has a 'calming influence' on the prisoners. He said since the holding pen was painted pink, the number of fights among prisoners has declined by 30 percent to 40 percent." He also began "replacing the cells' traditional green with subdued yellow, which he says is even better than pink, because its tranquilizing effect lasts longer."

These informal observations suggest that the effects of color are quite powerful, but research in the area is so limited that we must wait until clearer evidence becomes available before drawing conclusions.

(Source: *Richmond News Leader,* Nov. 12, 1979, p. 14)

body odors—an experience that most people find to be objectionable (McBurney, Levine, & Cavanaugh, 1977).

Lighting also influences perceptions and performance, but these effects depend in large part upon specific characteristics of the illumination such as glare, brightness, color, focus, uniformity, artificiality, and so on (Cuttle, 1973; Martyniuk, Flynn, Spencer, & Hendrick, 1973). For example, in one study of conference-room lighting (Martyniuk et al., 1973) subjects were exposed to various combinations of high- and low-intensity, overhead and peripheral, diffuse and focused lighting. In contrast to certain combinations, the high-intensity overhead lighting was judged to be most acceptable and most helpful in improving perceptual clarity. On the other hand, diffuse overhead lighting and spotlights were less favorably evaluated by the conference-room occupants. This investigation, like those conducted in industrial settings (Sucov, 1973), suggests that increases in illumination may facilitate group performance, but naturally lighting requirements will vary depending upon the group's purposes and goals; vastly different types of illumination would be optimally effective in a task-oriented group discussion as opposed to an informal buzz session.

Noise can also be an important ambient characteristic, since unwanted sounds, if sufficiently loud, significantly inhibit, distort, or even prevent intermember communication. At one level, some noise is to be expected in a group, since people sometimes violate rules of etiquette and politeness when they become immersed in a group discussion. However, excessive interruptions, loud talking, laughter, side conversations, and shouting can make the less voluble members uncomfortable.

Noise that originates outside the group can also cause distraction, irritation, and psychological stress (Cohen & Weinstein, 1981). In a close-up study of noise, researchers (Glass & Singer, 1972; Glass, Singer, & Pennebaker, 1977) arranged for people to work on simple and complex tasks while listening to tape-recorded noise. The noise tape, which was specially prepared by superimposing several sounds upon one another, included two people conversing in Spanish, one person speaking Armenian, and the operating sounds of a mimeograph machine, a desk calculator, and a typewriter. Although the investigators began their research by assuming that people would be unable to work effectively while bombarded with this montage of sounds, they obtained little evidence of the debilitating consequences of noise. Apparently the subjects were able to adjust psychologically to the noise through a process known as *adaptation:* although they had at first been distracted, in time they became so inured to the stimulus that they no longer even noticed it. These findings suggest that a group working in a noisy setting may eventually be able to surmount the problems posed by their excessive environmental stimulation, like a family Robert Sommer (1972, p. 28) once described:

> When friends of mine first moved into a house about 10 miles from Sacramento airport, they were bothered by the noise and billowing black smoke spewing from the jets during takeoff. But when I visit their house now, I am the only one who is disturbed by the noise and black clouds. My friends have adapted to them; conversation continues as the jets roar by, and drinks are poured without a shudder.

Delving deeper into the problem, these same researchers later found that people cannot always adapt successfully to noise. Extremely loud sound, for example, is difficult to ignore, and if exposure is prolonged significant hearing loss can occur. A periodic noise also tends to lead to greater discomfort, particularly if it is unpredictable, and the group is working on a complex task. Thus, if people are working diligently on a hard problem while a pneumatic drill is in use in the street outside the building, fewer negative effects of the noise will be felt if the drill is in continuous use rather than switched off and on with no warning. Additionally, an inability to control the noise aggravates reactions, and at present seems to be the most important factor in predicting the effects of noise. When group members believe they can control the noise, satisfactions, arousal levels, and stress tend to be relatively unaffected. If, however, the group members feel that nothing can be done to reduce the volume of noxious ambient noise, then negative consequences—including headaches, nausea, argumentativeness, irritability, and poor task performance—are more likely (Glass et al., 1977).

Seating Arrangements

Although group members can be found in all sorts of spatial configurations—seated casually on the floor, standing in small clusters scattered about a room, or even waiting in long lines to gain admission to some event—more frequently they occupy various pieces of furniture placed in particular patterns or relationships. While the executive at a conference table, the student seated in the back row of a class, or the lecturer about to speak to a circle of colleagues may take little notice of who is seated where, Robert Sommer (1967) argues that seating arrangements make up an important part of what he calls "small group ecology."

SEATING PREFERENCES

A distinction is often made between **sociopetal** and **sociofugal seating patterns.** The former promotes interaction among group members by heightening eye contact, encouraging verbal communication, and facilitating the development of intimacy. Sociofugal arrangements, in contrast, work to discourage interaction among group members, and can even drive participants out of the situation altogether. Sociopetal environments might include a secluded booth in a quiet restaurant, a park bench, five chairs placed in a tight circle, or a comfortable sofa, while sociofugal environments might include classrooms organized in rows, movie theaters, waiting rooms, and—as Sommer (1969, pp. 121–122) laments—airports:

> In most terminals it is virtually impossible for two people sitting down to converse comfortably for any length of time. The chairs are either bolted together and arranged in rows theater-style facing the ticket counters, or arranged back-to-back, and even if they face one another they are at such distances that comfortable conversation is impossible. The motive for the sociofugal arrangement appears the same as that in hotels and other commercial places—to drive people out of the waiting areas into cafes, bars, and shops where they will spend money.

Investigations of group members' seat selections are fairly consistent in showing a general preference for sociopetal arrangements (Batchelor & Goethals, 1972; Giesen & McClaren, 1976; Sommer, 1969) but this preference depends in part upon the type of task undertaken in the situation (Ryen & Kahn, 1975; Sommer, 1969). For example, Sommer asked college students to indicate which of the various seating arrangements pictured in Figure 10-3 they would prefer when engaged in casual conversation, cooperating on some task, competing, and coacting on individual tasks. As the figure shows, corner-to-corner and face-to-face arrangements were preferred for conversation, while side-to-side seating was selected for cooperation. Competing pairs either took a direct, face-to-face orientation (apparently to stimulate competition) or tried to increase interpersonal distance, while arrangements that effect a visual separation were preferred by coacting pairs (as one student stated, such an arrangement "allows staring into space and not

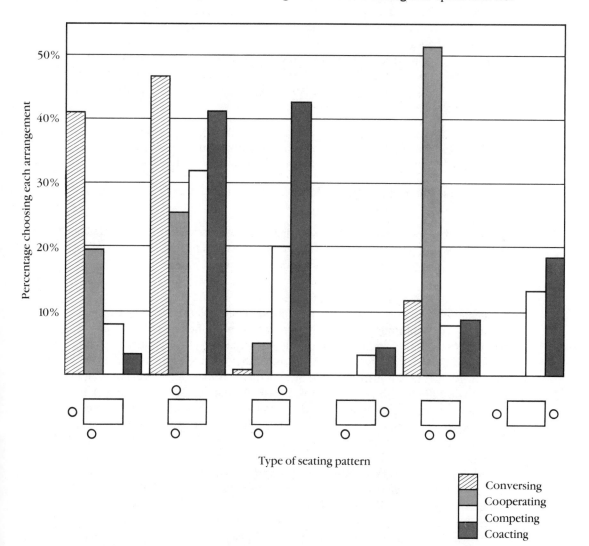

FIGURE 10-3. Seating preferences at rectangular tables. (Source: From the book, PERSONAL SPACE, by Robert Sommer, © 1969 by Prentice-Hall, Inc. Published by Prentice-Hall, Inc., Englewood Cliffs, NJ 07632)

into my neighbor's face"; Sommer, 1969, p. 63). Similar choices were found with round tables.

Gender also seems to be systematically related to seating choices, with males preferring to position themselves across from those they like, while females prefer adjacent seating positions (Sommer, 1959). Furthermore, because individuals tend to reserve favored positions for those they like, when strangers occupy the more intimate locations they are more likely to be rejected. The problem, however, is that males and females don't realize that what one sex considers to be an intimate position is the very position considered to be nonintimate by the other sex. In a study of this source of misunderstanding (Fisher & Byrne, 1975) solitary female and male students working at a library table were approached by a same- or opposite-sex confederate who sat next to the subject or across from the subject. A measure of attraction, affect, crowding, and perceptions administered after the confederate left indicated that males were the least favorably disposed towards the stranger who sat across from them, while females reacted more negatively to the stranger who sat next to them. Elaborating on some possible implications of these findings, the researchers note,

> A female who wants to befriend an unknown male may be surprised to find that a nonthreatening (to her) eyeball-to-eyeball approach causes consternation and alarm. In the same way, a male who attempts to ingratiate himself with an unknown female by sitting down beside her in a nonthreatening (to him) position may be surprised to find that he elicits a "Miss Muffet" reaction [Fisher & Byrne, 1975, pp. 20–21].

Clearly, group members should be sensitive to the possibility that their spatial behaviors will be misinterpreted by others and be willing to take steps to make certain any possible misunderstandings are short lived.

THE IMPACT OF SEATING ARRANGEMENTS ON SOCIAL INTERACTION

Seating arrangements have been found to significantly influence patterns of attraction, communication, and leadership in groups. At the perceptual level, certain types of seating patterns—particularly those featuring large distances among chairs and little chance for eye contact—imply that the interactants are not good friends (Russo, 1967), just as certain arrangements convey an impression of formality (Russell, Firestone, & Baron, 1980). At the behavioral level, certain arrangements tend to promote specific types of actions. For example, in one study conducted with dyads, subjects were seated in chairs that directly faced one another (face to face), were adjacent to one another (simulating sitting together on a couch), or were placed at a 90-degree angle to one another (Mehrabian & Diamond, 1971). By coding verbal and nonverbal behaviors through a one-way mirror, researchers were able to conclude that the 90-degree orientation increased affiliative tendencies, whereas the face-to-face arrangement led to a greater degree of relaxation. In related research comparing circle seating with L-shaped seating (Patterson, Kelly, Kondracki, & Wulf, 1979; Patterson, Roth, & Schenk, 1979) the circle was associated with feelings of confinement but fostered greater interpersonal attraction. People seated in the L-shaped groups, on the other hand, engaged in more self-manipulative behaviors and fidgeting, and paused more during group discussions. Overall, effects of the circle arrangement over the L arrangement were stronger in female groups than in male groups.

In a study of verbal behavior in face-to-face groups, Bernard Steinzor (1949) tried to determine if people seated in certain positions in the group tended to speak at any particular time. Although at first he could find few significant relationships, one day while watching a group he noticed a participant change his seat to sit opposite someone he had argued with during the previous meeting. Inspired by this chance observation, Steinzor reanalyzed his findings (1950) and discovered that individuals tended to speak *after* the person seated opposite them spoke. In explanation, he reasoned that we have an easier time observing and listening to the statements of people who are seated in a position that is central to our visual field, and hence their remarks serve as stronger stimuli for our own ideas and statements. The tendency for members of a group to comment immediately after the person sitting opposite them is now termed the **Steinzor effect.** The phenomenon appears to occur primarily in leaderless discussion groups, for later research suggested that when a strong leader is present group members direct more comments to their closest neighbor (Hearn, 1957).

Researchers have also been able to provide confirmation for the intuitively appealing notion that the leadership role is closely associated with the chair at the head of the table (Sommer, 1967). For example, Sommer (1969) found that people appointed to lead small discussion groups tended to select seats at the head of the table, just as other available evidence indicates that the occupants of this "exalted" position, relative to those in the more "ordinary" seats, tend to possess more dominant personalities (Hare & Bales, 1963), talk more frequently, and often exercise greater amounts of interpersonal influence (Strodtbeck & Hook, 1961). Although many factors could account for this intriguingly consistent spatial relation, Sommer emphasizes two explanations: perceptual prominence and the culture meaning associated with sitting at the head of the table. Looking first at prominence, Sommer suggests that in many groups the chair at the end of the table is the most salient position in the group and that the occupant of this space can therefore easily maintain greater amounts of eye contact with more of the group members, can move to the center of the communication network, and (as the Steinzor effect suggests) can comment more frequently. From the cultural-expectations angle, in the Western cultures where most studies of leadership have been conducted, the head chair at a table has been virtually defined as *the* most appropriate place for the leader to sit. Although Sommer is careful to note that this norm may not hold in other societies, in the Western world people tend to assume that leaders are "supposed" to sit at the head of the table.

Each of these factors seems to play a role in the leadership/head-of-the-table relationship. Examining the role of perceptual prominence, investigators arranged for five-person groups to hold a group discussion while seated at a rectangular table (Howells & Becker, 1962). In a clever manipulation of salience, the researchers arranged for two people to sit at one side of the table, and three people to sit at the other side. Although no one sat at the end seat, the investigators made specific predictions about who should emerge as the leader if eye contact and control of communication were important causal factors. While those seated at the two-person side of the table could maintain easy eye contact with three of the group members, those on the three-person side could best focus their attention on only two members. Therefore, those on the two-person side should be able to influence others more, and hence be the more likely leaders. As predicted, 70% of the leaders came from the two-person side, while only 30% came from the three-person side of the table.

In another study, the tendency for people to automatically associate the head of the table location with leadership was examined by arranging for a confederate to voluntarily choose or be assigned to the end position or some other position around a table (Nemeth & Wachtler, 1974). These confederates then went about systematically disagreeing with the majority of the group members on the topic under discussion, and the extent to which the subjects altered their opinions to agree with the deviant was assessed. Interestingly, deviants succeeded in influencing the others only when they had freely chosen to sit in the head chair. Apparently, disagreeing group members sitting at the "normal" locations around the table were viewed as "deviants," while those who had the confidence to select the end chair were viewed more as "leaders."

Summary

Because groups exist in a physical setting, members' interactions are often influenced by such environmental factors as territoriality, interpersonal distance, and seating arrangements. *Territories*—areas of exclusive use that are generally marked and defended—can be maintained by groups or by individuals in groups. Group territories can be as well established as the "turfs" of urban gangs or as informal and fluctuating as the temporary territories that surround individuals engaged in interaction, but the consequences of territorial processes are often far reaching. Individuals' territories within a group also influence group dynamics, for the size and location of these spatial areas has been shown to be related to group structure, membership termination, dominance, and members' ability to cope with periods of prolonged isolation.

Turning to *interpersonal distance,* we find that group dynamicists have focused on two interrelated concepts: personal space and crowding. Although a good deal can be learned about a group and its members by observing the size of the "invisible bubble" maintained by members, crowding researchers prefer to examine group members' reactions where they feel they have insufficient space to work comfortably. Overload, control, attribution, and density-intensity theories all seek to explain when crowding is experienced, and studies of task-oriented groups find that performance is worsened in *overstaffed* settings, when tasks require interaction, and when the group members are male.

Features of the *ambient environment*—the external, situational stimuli that surround the group—also influence interaction. Many of the consequences of extremes in lighting, temperature, and noise have been documented by researchers, who find that irritating environments can in some cases lead to psychological stress and distraction. The effects of *seating arrangements,* however, have been more closely scrutinized by investigators, who often draw a distinction between sociofugal patterns and sociopetal patterns. Although people generally prefer interaction-promoting sociopetal patterns, these preferences vary with the type of task being attempted and the gender of the interactants. Across a wide variety of groups, however, seating arrangements significantly influence patterns of attraction, communication, and leadership.

PART
FOUR

Problems
in Groups

For the most part groups play a benign role in our social lives. Yet in some instances group behaviors and group processes take a course that can lead to negative consequences. In exploring this darker side of groups, Chapter 11 begins with an analysis of groups whose deindividuated members engage in such destructive behaviors as rioting, panicking, and aggression. Chapter 12 focuses on groupthink—the tendency for highly cohesive groups to formulate poor decisions—and discusses recommendations for its prevention. This part closes with the examination in Chapter 13 of intergroup conflict: conflict between groups rather than solitary individuals.

11

Deindividuation

1096 Literally thousands upon thousands of people answer the call of Pope Urban II to "free the Holy Land from the pagans." All over Europe huge groups of men, women, and children gather to begin the trek to Jerusalem, all captivated by the excitement of the undertaking, the promise of salvation, and the lure of riches. Caught up in their religious fervor, few stop to contemplate the chances for survival.

1789 Groups of French citizens, acting with strikingly singleminded determination, storm through Paris killing government officials and destroying public property. The crowds that form seem to undertake wildly destructive actions, and eventually the government crumbles under the pressure of the rioting population.

1938 On Halloween night Orson Welles broadcasts the radio program *The War of the Worlds*. General panic prevails as listeners, taking the dramatization at face value, react by warning relatives, taking defensive precautions, contemplating suicide, and fleeing from the "invaded areas" (Cantril, 1940).

1943 United States Naval personnel stationed in Los Angeles, California, gather in small groups to roam through the city streets in search of Mexican-Americans wearing zoot suits (a style of clothes, featuring long suit coats and pleated trousers with tight cuffs, popular among men of the Mexican community). Once located, the "zooters" are surrounded, insulted, and brutally beaten. In some cases the sailors force their victims to disrobe (Turner & Surace, 1956).

1954 Rumors that windshields are being damaged by nuclear fallout begin circulating in the Seattle, Washington, area. The rumors escalate into a mild form of mass hysteria as the media devote much attention to the issue, residents jam police telephone lines reporting damage, and civic groups demand government intervention. Subsequent investigation reveals that no damage at all has occurred (Medalia & Larsen, 1958).

1962 Sixty-two persons working in a manufacturing plant experience nausea, pain, disorientation, and muscular weakness; some actually collapse at their jobs or lose consciousness. Although the workers claim that an insect is responsible for transmitting a bizarre type of disease, physicians can find no evidence of any physical illness. They conclude the episode to be completely due to psychological factors (Kerckhoff, Back, & Miller, 1965).

1969 The police force of Montreal, Canada, strikes for 17 hours in a contract dispute. As expected, professional crimes skyrocket, but as night falls the noncriminal population of the city begins to riot. A heterogeneous crowd of people from all walks of life—the impoverished, the rich, and the middle class—rampages along the central business corridor looting and vandalizing. Fires are set, 156 stores are looted, $300,000 worth of glass is shattered, 2 people are killed, and 49 are wounded. Despite the violence, observers comment that the entire incident seems "carnival-like" (Clark, 1969).

1970 The Brazilian soccer team defeats the Italian team in the World Cup Tournament, setting off a series of wild celebrations. Tragically, more than 100 people die and many more are injured by fireworks, brawls, automobile accidents, and shootings.

1979 A crowd in Cincinnati waiting for a concert to be given by the rock group The Who stampedes the entrance to the coliseum. Eleven persons are literally trampled to death and many others are injured. An emergency-room supervisor comments "the bodies were marked with multiple contusions, bruises and the victims had suffered hemorrhages" (Richmond *News Leader,* December 5, 1979, p. 14).

$\overline{\mathbf{A}}$s these historical examples vividly reveal, when people gather together in groups they sometimes perform actions that, as individuals, they would consider unthinkable. To observers through the ages, people in groups seem to possess two different faces—one, a practical, noble visage that draws upon the best qualities of human beings; the second, a dangerous, violent image that surfaces spontaneously as the group members commit violent actions and inflict unspeakable suffering. Indeed, myths and folk tales often emphasize and exaggerate the dualistic nature of people in groups—the humanlike and bestial—suggesting that a group member who seems to be Dr. Jekyll can turn into a Mr. Hyde. In the imagery of such myths, the group member is like the Minotaur, a legendary beast with the head of a bull but the body of a man. Although the Minotaur could walk upright and in many ways seemed to be a rational, humane being, he also displayed the "primordial, destructive instincts" of an animal (Prentice-Dunn & Rogers, 1980, p. 104). Up to now in this book we have focused on the rational, adaptive functions of groups—decision-making strategies, leadership, effective communication. In this chapter we turn our attention to the darker side of human groups.

Theoretical Perspectives

Although scientific accounts of people immersed in crowds appeared as early as 1837 (Milgram & Toch, 1969), a more concerted effort to investigate such phenomena did not begin until after Gustave Le Bon published his classic study *The Crowd* in 1895. Based on his field studies of many kinds of groups, Le Bon became convinced that a crowd of people can, in certain instances, be transformed into a kind of united entity that seems to possess a *collective mind:* a pervasive loss of individuality that results in the domination of bestial, savage emotions over personal moral controls. In the years that followed, theorists in psychology and sociology elaborated on the irrationality of groups that fall prey to wild crazes, fads, rumors, mass hysteria, rioting, and panics, and in time a loosely defined field known as **collective behavior** developed. In a related but conceptually distinct endeavor, other studies were being conducted to investigate the causes and consequences of **deindividuation:** the process of losing one's sense of individuality by becoming submerged in a group. In the following subsections we consider unusual group actions from these two perspectives.

Theories of Collective Behavior

The term *collective behavior* is somewhat misleading, for if taken literally (two or more people acting together) it would encompass most group processes, and therefore could be used interchangeably with the term *group dynamics* (Blumer,

1951). In practice, however, the term is generally reserved for collections of individuals that are more than mere aggregates (random clusterings of people who are not interacting with one another), but are not yet "true" groups (clusterings of people who influence one another through interaction). In consequence, collectives, unlike small groups, tend to (1) be relatively unorganized, (2) lack a specific set of procedures for selecting members and identifying leaders, (3) endorse few specific goals or means to ends, (4) convey a strong sense of unity that transcends individual members, and (5) move in the direction of becoming groups rather than aggregates (Blumer, 1951; Turner & Killian, 1972). Indeed, by convention the term *collective* is typically reserved for two types of social aggregates: *collective outbursts,* including riots, mobs, panics, crazes, and so on, and *collective movements,* including social reforms, political organizations, nationalistic campaigns, and so on (Smelser, 1972). This restriction in topics, however, is by no means formalized or universally recognized (Genevie, 1978).

Over the years investigators in this sociologically oriented field have succeeded in building a number of defensible theories of collective behavior. Like theories in any scientific discipline, these conceptualizations play a major role in organizing our understanding of collectives while simultaneously suggesting avenues for future research. Because theories of collective behavior help us to put our empirical questions and observations into a conceptual perspective, below we will review the basic assumptions of three major approaches to collectives. Although we could have considered many other viewpoints (Turner & Killian, 1972) here, we have chosen to focus on *convergence, contagion,* and *emergent-norm* theories.

CONVERGENCE THEORIES

All movements, however different in doctrine and aspiration, draw their early adherents from the same types of humanity; they all appeal to the same types of mind.

Hoffer (1951, p. 9)

What could the members of such widely disparate and internally heterogeneous collectives as the following possibly have in common: Blacks rioting in Watts, zealots eagerly confessing their sins during a religious crusade, gangs of shoppers rampaging through a department store searching for bargains, and students throwing rocks and bottles at police officers during a "peace rally"? According to **convergence theory,** a great deal, because in all these instances individuals join the group because they possess particular personal characteristics. Although these predisposing features may be latent or virtually unrecognizable, they are the true causes of the formation of both large and small collectives. Such aggregates are not merely haphazard gatherings of dissimilar strangers, but rather represent the convergence of people with compatible needs, desires, motivations, and emotions. By joining in the group the individual makes possible the satisfaction of these needs, and the crowd situation serves as a trigger for the spontaneous release of previously controlled behaviors. Consider some examples. Ghetto dwellers, for instance, may feel angry and bitter over their inability to improve their level of existence, and when they gather together in the streets on a hot summer night they may vent these hostilities through vandalism, looting, and firebombing. Similarly, a group of reticent religious devotees may suddenly become vociferous when they gather together in a group, or an assembly of political radicals may storm off to picket the capitol once inspired by the rhetoric of a soapbox speaker. Although the list of predisposing characteristics differs from one perspective to the next, all convergence theories are similar in that they seek to "identify the latent tendencies in people that will cause them to act alike, the circumstances that will bring people with such tendencies together, and the kinds of events that will cause these tendencies to be released" (Turner & Killian, 1972, p. 19).

Sigmund Freud's theory of group formation, discussed in Chapter 3, is in many respects a convergence theory, for Freud felt that people join collectives to satisfy repressed unconscious desires that otherwise would never be fulfilled (Freud, 1922). He was very much impressed with Gustave Le Bon's description of the changes that overtake the individual immersed in a crowd, but he believed that Le Bon had failed to recognize the role of unconscious needs. Accordingly, Freud extended his psychoanalytic theory to group situations by suggesting that even though individuals may experience sexual impulses, aggressive tendencies, and a strong desire to escape from danger, psychological mechanisms hold those "primitive" libidinal tendencies in check. In the group situation, however, control over behavior is transferred to the leader or other group members, and each person is thus freed from the bonds of restraint and guilt. As a result, formerly repressed needs come to motivate behavior and atypical actions become more likely. Indeed, later writers (Martin, 1920; Meerloo, 1950) extended the psychoanalytic perspective by suggesting that different kinds of groups are formed to satisfy different needs. In this view, violent collective behavior—looting, rioting, lynchings—occurs to satisfy latent aggressive tendencies, flights of panic satisfy a primitive need to flee from danger, and orgies fulfill deep-seated sexual passions.

CONTAGION THEORIES

> Should a horse in a stable take to biting his manger the other horses in the stable will imitate him. A panic that has seized on a few sheep will soon extend to the whole flock. In the case of men collected in a crowd all emotions are very rapidly contagious, which explains the suddenness of panics.
>
> Le Bon (1895, p. 126)

Le Bon did not believe that the unity of the crowds he observed came from any underlying similarities among the people who composed the group. Turning away from a convergence explanation, he proposed that certain processes occur as the crowd action develops and that these situational mechanisms produce what he called the "mental unity of crowds." When describing these mechanisms, Le Bon—who had been trained as a physician—was struck by the tendency for behaviors and emotions to begin at one point in the group and then spread throughout the rest of the crowd. To him this pattern of dispersion seemed to parallel the transmission of contagious diseases, which are involuntarily passed from one person to another until everyone in the vicinity is infected. Based on his observations of many different kinds of crowds, Le Bon concluded that emotions and behaviors can be transmitted from one person to another just as germs and viruses can be passed along, and he felt that this process of **contagion** accounted for the tendency for group members to behave in very similar ways.

The occurrence of contagion in groups is quite common. For example, how often have you caught yourself struggling to stifle a yawn after the person sitting next to you has just yawned broadly? Or have you ever noticed that as one person in a conversation casually crosses his or her arms, the others in the group tend to mirror this position? Recall how in public lectures the question-and-answer sessions following the talks always begin very slowly but soon snowball as more and more questioners begin raising their hands? Although such occurrences are variously explained in terms of the heightened suggestibility of group members (Le Bon, 1895), social facilitation (Wheeler, 1966), and imitation (Tarde, 1903), one particularly noteworthy approach begins by comparing the *circular reactions* of groups experiencing contagion to the *interpretative reactions* of noncontagion groups (Blumer, 1946, 1951, 1957). During interpretative interactions, group members carefully reflect upon the meaning of others' behavior and try to formulate valid interpretations before making any kind of comment or embarking on a line of action. During circular reactions, however, the group's members fail to examine the meaning of others' actions cautiously and carefully, and therefore tend to misunderstand the situation. When they act on the basis of such misunderstandings, the others in the group also begin to interpret the situation incorrectly and a circular process is thus initiated that eventually culminates in full-blown behavioral contagion. If we apply this view to a panic situation as an example, one person in the group may set off the contagion by acting excited, hostile, or fearful. As this source person seems to panic, others nearby assume that "something" is occurring, and they themselves begin to grow nervous. The source of the panic then reacts to the others' nervousness by becoming even more panicky, and the others, in turn, react to the source's behavior by becoming more excited. This spiral of intensifying reactions then multiplies throughout the group until all members are gripped in panic. Indeed, even uninvolved bystanders can become entrapped, for contagion sometimes "attracts and infects individuals, many of whom originally are detached and indifferent spectators and bystanders. At first, people may be merely curious about the given behavior, or mildly interested in it. As they catch the spirit of excitement and become more attentive to the behavior, they become more inclined to engage in it" (Blumer, 1945, p. 176). This kind of circular reaction, which will be discussed in more detail later in the chapter, is humorously depicted in the box on page 314.

EMERGENT-NORM THEORIES

> . . . an individual may know perfectly well what his parents, teachers, and preacher say is right and wrong, *and yet violate this without feelings of guilt if his fellows do not condemn him.*
>
> Sherif and Sherif (1964, p. 182)

The final approach to collective behavior to be considered here was developed by Ralph Turner and Lewis Killian (1972; Turner, 1964) in response to certain shortcomings they attributed to both convergence and contagion theories. In their appraisal, most crowds are not as homogeneous as convergence theories suggest,

A HUMOROUS LOOK AT CONTAGION

The tendency for people to allow their misinterpretations of others' actions to spiral out of control is well described by author James Thurber in this excerpt from his amusing story "The Day the Dam Broke" (Thurber, 1933, p. 41):

Suddenly somebody began to run. It may be that he had simply remembered, all of a moment, an engagement to meet his wife, for which he was now frightfully late. Whatever it was, he ran east on Broad Street (probably toward the Maramor Restaurant, a favorite place for a man to meet his wife). Somebody else began to run, perhaps a newsboy in high spirits. Another man, a portly gentleman of affairs, broke into a trot. Inside of ten minutes, everybody on High Street, from the Union Depot to the Courthouse, was running. A loud mumble gradually crystalized into the dread word "dam." "The dam has broke!" The fear was put into words by a little old lady in an electric, or by a traffic cop, or by a small boy: nobody knows who, nor does it now really matter. Two thousand people were abruptly in full flight.

(Source: Thurber, 1933, 1961)

for group members typically differ from one another in terms of attitudes, motivations, emotions, and so on. Furthermore, while emotions and actions can spread throughout the group, as contagion theories suggest, in many instances bystanders merely stand around without every becoming actively involved. In fact, Turner and Killian reject one of the fundamental assumptions of most collective-behavior theories—that crowds are extremely homogeneous—to conclude that the "mental unity of crowds" is primarily an illusion. Crowds, mobs, and other collectives only *seem* to be unanimous in emotions and actions, since the members all adhere to norms that are relevant in the given situation. Granted, these norms may be unique and sharply contrary to more general societal standards, but as they emerge in the group situation they exert a powerful influence on behavior.

Turner and Killian apply their **emergent-norm theory** to many types of collective actions, but their case-study analysis of a weekend religious retreat is especially informative. This particular retreat, which took place in California, proceeded along fairly typical lines for several days as the members met in small Bible discussion groups, listened to short sermons, and sang hymns. The attendees also gathered together at night to talk over their feelings about God and their church, and again these meetings followed a routine pattern as the members made matter-of-fact statements about their goals and satisfactions. However, toward the end of the retreat one well-known member of the group gave a long, emotional commentary on her relationship to God, and eventually broke down as she sobbed about her selfishness and unworthiness. During the statement the atmosphere of the group was marked by tension for, unlike some denominations, such confessions were not encouraged and hence rarely occurred. Yet when the woman finished, a second person stood and gave a similarly emotion-laden oration, and others soon followed suit: "One after another individuals would arise, confessing everything from cheating on exams to fornication, each apparently outdoing the preceding in describing the intensity of his sinfulness" (Hamilton, 1972, p. 17).

In their analysis, Turner and Killian suggest that a norm of confession emerged during the retreat, and that many of the group members conformed to this norm by publicly admitting their shortcomings. While many of the participants realized that public confessions were clearly contrary to the doctrines of the church, they remained silent during the proceedings and thereby lent implicit support to the emergent norm. As in the norm-formation studies of Muzafer Sherif (1934) and the conformity experiments of Solomon Asch (1952), a powerful but incongruous norm developed in the group and became the standard for behavior. Thus, while the actions—when viewed from a wider, more objective perspective—may have seemed out of control and very strange, for the retreat participants they were consistent with the emergent norms.

CONCLUSIONS

The three perspectives on collective behavior—convergence, contagion, and emergent-norm theory—are in no sense incompatible with one another. Although each approach emphasizes different mechanisms, to achieve a fuller understanding of collective behaviors we need to draw from each theoretical viewpoint. For example, consider the behavior of *baiting crowds*—groups of people who urge on a person threatening to jump from a building, bridge, or tower (Mann, 1981). Applying the three theories, the convergence approach suggests that only a certain "type" of person would be likely to bait the victim to leap to his or her death. These shouts could then spread to other bystanders through a process of contagion until the onlookers were infected by a norm of callousness and cynicism that made their actions seem consistent with the structure of the setting. Hence all three processes—as well as others—may contribute to baiting, as an archival study conducted by Leon Mann suggests. Although Mann was unable to determine if the baiters in a crowd possessed any identifying personality or demographic characteristics (as convergence theory would suggest), he did note that baiting became more likely as crowd size increased. This effect, which is generally consistent with contagion theory, may be due to the "greater probability that in a large crowd at least one stupid or sadistic person will be found who is prepared to cry 'Jump!' and thereby provide a model for suggestible others to follow" (Mann, 1981, p. 707). In addition, Mann reports evidence of an antilife norm in several of the crowds where members not only encouraged the victim to "end it all," but also jeered and booed as rescuers attempted to intervene.

Mann's study also indicated that other variables—such as the anonymity of the crowd, dehumanization of the victim, and frustration due to waiting—influenced baiting. While these factors are not inconsistent with the processes emphasized by collective-behavior theorists, they lie at the core of another perspective on atypical group behavior known as **deindividuation theory**. This theory is reviewed in the next sections.

Deindividuation Theory

Although many early collective-behavior theorists alluded to a process like **deindividuation** in their work (Blumer, 1946; Freud, 1922; Le Bon, 1895; Tarde, 1903), the term itself was first introduced in 1952 in a research report published by Leon Festinger, Albert Pepitone, and Theodore Newcomb. They hypothesized that there

> occurs sometimes in groups a state of affairs in which the individuals act as if they were "submerged in the group." Such a state of affairs may be described as deindividuation; that is, individuals are not seen or paid attention to as individuals. The members do not feel that they stand out as individuals. Others are not singling a person out for attention nor is the person singling out others [p. 382].

Elaborating, they suggested that deindividuation results in the "reduction of inner restraints" and thereby allows group members to engage in aberrant actions.

In a preliminary investigation of these general hypotheses, these researchers performed a correlational study utilizing all-male groups ranging in size from four to seven members. For the atypical behavior that would be increased by feelings of deindividuation, the investigators selected expression of hatred for parents. They felt that in most group settings strong restraints exist that prevent individuals from harshly criticizing their own parents. If, however, the group members were made to feel deindividuated, and the discussion was focused on attitudes toward parents, then critical comments would become more likely. To create this focus, the researchers told the groups that a recent study had discovered that the vast majority of college students (87%) harbors a deep-seated hatred for one or both parents. These statistics were, of course, fictitious, but the experimenter apparently succeeded in convincing participants that the survey was accurate and, further, that those who deny having such feelings of animosity were likely to be those who most hated their parents. The groups then discussed the topic for 40 minutes, during which the expression of a negative attitude toward one's parents was taken to be an index of atypical behavior. (The researchers calculated this quantity by subtracting the number of positive comments from the number of negative ones.)

Deindividuation was not manipulated in the investigation, but Festinger, Pepitone, and Newcomb felt that the ability to identify who said what during the group discussion would be a suitable indicator. After the discussion, subjects were exposed to a series of statements that had been made during the 40 minutes and were asked to recall which group member had made each particular claim. If the respondent could correctly associate each statement with the member who had made it, then the group must have been individuated. If, on the other hand, the subject made many errors in linking statements to members, then deindividuation must have been high. When this index of deindividuation was computed (and corrected for overall memory differences) and correlated with the measure of negative attitudes toward parents, evidence of a significant relationship between the two variables was obtained; $r = .57$.

Although this study provided suggestive evidence concerning the effects of deindividuation, it left a number of questions unanswered. For example, while Festinger, Pepitone, and Newcomb felt that unidentifiability had caused the greater incidence of negative commentary, the correlational findings could also be explained by reasoning that subjects, embarrassed by the high levels of negativity towards parents, simply refused to identify other group members' comments. In addition, the researchers assumed that low identifiability was an indicator of deindividuation, but they presented no firm data to support this contention. While the investigators recognized these limitations and proposed that other researchers follow up their efforts, with only a few exceptions (Singer, Brush, & Lublin, 1965; Ziller, 1964), the area attracted little systematic study until 1969, when Philip Zimbardo developed a more elaborate theory of deindividuation.

In an attempt to organize our knowledge of atypical group actions, Zimbardo's theory drew on anecdotal observations, systematic small-group research, and prior theorizing in collective behavior. To begin, he proposed that deindividuation is best visualized as a *process* that involves a series of input variables present in the group situation leading to changes in the individual group member that in turn culminate in "a lowered threshold of normally restrained behavior" (1969, p. 251). Essentially, Zimbardo breaks this complex process down into the three components shown in Table 11-1. First, he specifies the conditions of deindividuation—features of the group situation such as anonymity and responsibility that stimulate or retard the onset of the process. Second, he describes the deindividuated state—a subjective experience in which the individual group members experience losses in self-awareness and self-regulation. (In Table 11-1, this component of the model is modified on the basis of theorizing that followed Zimbardo's work. This adaptation of the original deindividuation model is discussed later in this section.)Third, the model ends by listing a series of deindividuated behaviors that represent the outputs of the process. Although Zimbardo notes that deindividuation could result in a range of "positive" outcomes, for the most part he emphasizes "antisocial behaviors" such as violence, destruction, and hostility.

Before we consider each of these components of Zimbardo's theory, let us apply the overall model to a specific case of deindividuated action. Consider the case in which concert goers forced their way into an arena, and in the process crushed 11 people to death. To begin the analysis, we must examine those features of the specific situation that could have contributed to the creation of a state of deindividuation. Rather than seek out one single cause of the occurrence, we must develop an array of contributory-input variables: the size of the group; the reliance on unreserved, first-come-first-served seating; the limited number of entrance doors; on-going alcohol consumption and marijuana use; and prevalent rumors that the concert had already begun. Next, the effects of these input variables can be traced to changes in the rock fans themselves: a loss of inner restraints; an

TABLE 11-1. The process of deindividuation

Conditions of deindividuation		The state of deindividuation		Deindividuated behaviors
1. Anonymity 2. Responsibility 3. Group membership 4. Arousal 5. Others (sensory overload, novel situations, drug usage, altered states of consciousness, and so on)	→	Loss of self-awareness ↓ Loss of self-regulation 1. Low self-monitoring 2. Failure to consider relevant norms 3. Little use of self-generated reinforcements 4. Failure to formulate long-range plans	→	Behavior is emotional impulsive, irrational, regressive, with high intensity 1. Not under stimulus control 2. Counternormative 3. Pleasurable

(Source: Zimbardo, 1969)

uncaring, hostile attitude toward those in the front of the mob; and a single-minded drive to enter the concert hall no matter what the cost. Lastly, as a result of these intrapsychic changes, behavior is affected: group members push, shove, and step on people, ignoring those who are in the group. The intensity of these output behaviors is reflected in the comments of those who survived the stampede:

- People were hitting other people, and a girl fell down in front of me. I helped her up finally.
- All of a sudden, I went down. . . . I couldn't see anything. My face was being pressed to the floor. I felt I was smothering.
- I saw people's heads being stepped on. I fell and couldn't get up. People kept pushing me down.
- People just didn't seem to care. I couldn't believe it. They could see all the people piled up and they still tried to climb over them just to get in [Richmond *News Leader*, December 5, 1979, p. 14].

Keeping this overall process in mind, let us now consider each part of the model in more detail. Although the three components—input conditions, the deindividuated state, and output behaviors—are so closely intertwined that each is reflected in the other two, for clarity of exposition we will consider each segment separately.

CONDITIONS OF DEINDIVIDUATION

While many theorists have pointed to factors that might play a causal role in the production of aberrant group actions—the historical context (Le Bon, 1895), psychodynamic needs (Freud, 1922), social structures (Smelser, 1963), and the unique norms that form in collectives (Turner & Killian, 1972)—Zimbardo emphasizes social-psychological causes in his explanation of deindividuation. As the left-hand column of Table 11-1 suggests, deindividuation occurs more frequently when the group members feel anonymous; "others can't identify or single you out, they can't evaluate, criticize, judge, or punish you" (Zimbardo, 1969, p. 255). When group members are disguised, masked, or dressed in uniforms they may come to feel that they have no individual identity apart from the group, and hence they become submerged in the crowd. Darkness can also play a role in the production of feelings of anonymity, as can feelings of social alienation. Zimbardo and others suggest that the anonymity that comes with living in a large city may promote violent, destructive behavior such as rioting and vandalism (Ley & Cybriwsky, 1974b).

Group members' feelings of responsibility for the consequences of the group's action is another important input variable, with the occurrence of deindividuation increasing in likelihood as factors in the situation limit feelings of personal accountability. For example, if an authority who demands compliance is present, then group members may feel that they are not personally responsible for the consequences of their actions (Milgram, 1974). In addition, if the consequences are somehow separated from the act itself—as when a bombardier presses a bomb-release switch, a technician in an underground bunker launches a missile aimed at a site a thousand miles away, or the "learner" you are shocking remains unseen and unheard—then a sense of responsibility for the negative consequences is lessened.

Personal responsibility is also minimized whenever **diffusion of responsibility** occurs in the group. As researchers investigating both helping behavior (Darley & Latané, 1968) and decision making (Clark, 1971) have noted, people in groups sometimes feel that they have less personal responsibility when full responsibility is shared equally with the other group members. To provide an example of this process occurring in an emergency situation, consider the well-publicized case of Kitty Genovese who in 1964 was stabbed to death on the street outside her New York City apartment. Although she called for help and police later estimated that 38 people were aware of the attack, not a single person either directly intervened or summoned the police. As a consequence, the murderer, who had initially fled the scene, felt it was safe to return to finish off his victim. Apparently, the "knowledge that others are present and available to respond, even if the individual cannot see or be seen by them, allows the shifting of some of the responsibility for helping to them" (Latané & Nida, 1981, p. 309). Zimbardo supplies examples of groups in a much different context that actually take steps to ensure the diffusion of responsibility, as when murderers pass around their weapons from hand to hand so that responsibility for the crime is distributed through the entire group rather than concentrated in the one person who pulls the trigger or wields the knife. Similarly, Zimbardo notes that at one time some executions using the electric chair were carried out by three executioners. Each one flipped a switch to electrify the chair, but only one of the mechanisms actually turned on the current. The executioners, however, never knew which one was the "live" switch, and each one could therefore believe himself free of responsibility for the death of the condemned prisoner. A similar practice was supposedly utilized in firing squads: typically, one gun would be loaded with blanks so that the squad members, if bothered by guilt, could later tell themselves that they had not shot another human being.

For a number of reasons, group membership is another key input variable in the deindividuation process. First, being part of a group increases both feelings of anonymity and makes diffusion of responsibility possible. Second, contagion becomes more likely in groups, since more people are present to facilitate communication and provide behavioral examples. Third, compresence—the presence of other people—can, in some instances, trigger general arousal and even excitement (Zajonc, 1965; see Chapter 6). Fourth, acting in concert with a large group of people can give participants a feeling of invincibility and power, particularly if they occupy a central position in the group. Indeed, Le Bon had earlier emphasized the impact of large numbers of people on individual behaviors when he wrote,

> . . . The individual forming part of a crowd acquires, solely from numerical considerations, a sentiment of invincible power which allows him to yield to instinct which, had he been alone, he would have perforce kept under restraint. He will be less disposed to check himself from the consideration that, a crowd being anonymous, and in consequence irresponsible, the sentiment of responsibility which always controls individuals disappears entirely [1895, p. 30].

Although Zimbardo lists a number of *other* input variables—altered temporal perspective, sensory overload, heightened involvement, lack of situational structure, and the use of drugs—that function as facilitators of deindividuation, we will consider only one other factor: personal arousal. As any high school football coach knows, a group must sometimes be "psyched up" to perform its violent best, and the inspirational talk given before the game, the pep rally, and the stands teeming with throngs of cheering fans can do much to excite and motivate the most listless team. Zimbardo even suggests that certain war rituals—such as war dances and group singing—enacted prior to the onset of battle are actually designed to arouse participants and to thus enable them to be deindividuated when the fighting starts. "Among cannibals, like the Cenis or certain Maori and Nigerian tribes, the activity of ritual bonfire dance which precedes eating the flesh of another human being is always more prolonged and intense when the victim is to be eaten alive or uncooked" (Zimbardo, 1969, p. 257). Personal arousal no doubt also plays a large part in panic reactions, which occur when groups of individuals react unthinkingly in potentially dangerous situations. Although many incidents of panic have been documented by social scientists, historians, and other observers of human behavior, one gruesome but typical example of the total transformation of people into a mindless mass of movement is presented in the box.

PANICS OF ESCAPE

Studies of one of the most intensely frightening experiences some human beings must face—entrapment in a burning building—suggest that people don't always react by panicking (Keating & Loftus, 1981). However, in those instances in which a large group of people tried to escape from the threat of a fire by bolting for exits, tragedy invariably resulted. For example, in 1903 a fire broke out in Chicago's Iroquois Theater. Although the management tried to calm the audience, when the lights went out and fire was visible behind the stage, the crowd stampeded for the exits. Some were burned or died by jumping from the fire escapes to the pavement, but many more were killed as fleeing patrons trampled them. As one observer described the panic,

In places on the stairways, particularly where a turn caused a jam, bodies were piled seven or eight feet deep. Firemen and police confronted a sickening task in disentangling them. An occasional living person was found in the heaps, but most of these were terribly injured. The heel prints on the dead faces mutely testified to the cruel fact that human animals stricken in terror are as mad and ruthless as stampeding cattle. Many bodies had the clothes torn from them, and some had the flesh trodden from their bones [Foy & Harlow, 1928].

Although the fire department arrived promptly and extinguished the blaze in only ten minutes, more than 600 people were either burned, trampled, or smothered to death.

THE DEINDIVIDUATED STATE

In Zimbardo's theory of deindividuation, the input variables create certain changes in the group members, and these changes are the most immediate causes of the abnormal social behaviors that are eventually observed. Although Zimbardo described these intervening psychological changes briefly, a more refined analysis emphasizing the loss of self-awareness and self-regulation has been provided by Edward Diener (1977, 1980). Drawing from research dealing with *self-awareness* (Carver & Scheier, 1981; Wicklund, 1980), Diener assumes that people generally focus their attention outward, onto other group members or environmental objects, or inward, onto the self. When this focus is on the self, people become more self-aware and are more likely to attend to their emotional and cognitive states, care-fully consider their behavioral options, and monitor their actions closely. When this focus is on features of the situation that are external to the person, people fail to monitor their actions and may therefore overlook any discrepancies between moral and social standards and their behavior:

> People who are deindividuated have lost self-awareness and their personal iden-tity in the group situation. Because they are prevented by the situation from awareness of themselves as individuals and from attention to their own behavior, deindividuated persons do not have the capacity for self-regulation and the ability to plan for the future. Thus, prevented from self-attention and self-monitoring by the group situation, they become more reactive to immediate stimuli and emotions and are unresponsive to norms and the long-term consequences of behavior [Diener, 1980, p. 210].

Tracing the formula of deindividuation shown in Table 11-1 further, we find that this loss of self-awareness culminates in an overall reduction in self-regulation. Once more drawing from relevant work in psychology—in this instance, social-learning theory (Bandura, 1977, 1978)—Diener proposes that self-aware people take responsibility for regulating their own behavior across situations. In the exam-ple of a family that wants to purchase a color television set, social-learning theory suggests that the group would consider various means of achieving this goal. Although the family may be tempted to buy the television on credit, it may decide that dangers of missing payments are too great and therefore opt for simply saving the necessary funds over time. It may then monitor family spending closely, making certain no money is wasted, and periodically see how far along the family is in the fund raising. In fact, as the family successfully saves more and more of the needed funds, members will probably reinforce themselves by reviewing their determination, pointing out the proximity of their goal, praising their own will-power, and encouraging one another. When self-awareness is minimized, how-ever, such self-regulatory mechanisms break down. The family may not consider the long-range consequences of its actions and thus may rush out and buy the television it cannot afford. Next, members may fail to monitor their spending, and when the time for paying for the television set comes around, they will therefore be unable to make the payment. Self-reinforcement will also be low, and members will thus fail to feel gratified whenever they manage to economize. Indeed, at extremely low levels of awareness the family may even fail to consider the rela-tionship between its actions and relevant social norms. As a result, it may elect to steal a television set from a store or a next-door neighbor.

Diener summarizes this loss of self-regulation by listing the various consequences of low self-awareness: (1) poor likelihood of behavior monitoring, (2) the failure to examine the relationship between behavior and relevant norms, (3) the minimal use of self-generated reinforcements, and (4) a failure to make long-range plans and to formulate goals. When these consequences combine, a group may not even consider the moral implications of its actions and thus will lose the ability to understand fully the violent actions it performs. For example, Zimbardo tells of a teenage boy who was beaten mercilessly during a hazing ritual for a junior high school club. The club members, caught up in the heat of the moment, did not realize the damage they were inflicting on their hapless victim and became more and more determined to make the inductee cry. When the new member refused to shed a single tear, the violence escalated until the boy was beaten into unconsciousness. A similar example, mentioned earlier, of unthinking behavior comes from observations of crowds that gather whenever someone threatens to commit suicide by jumping from a building. To the amazement of many observers, these crowds often cheer the potential suicide on with calls of "Jump, jump," "Chicken," and "Get it over with." In their unaware state they somehow manage to overlook the morality of their actions as they fail to consider that they are actively contributing to the death of another person.

DEINDIVIDUATED BEHAVIORS

What kinds of actions are likely to be performed by deindividuated group members? Altruistic contributions to charity? Attempts to establish meaningful relationships with others? Goal-oriented achievement strivings? Clearly not, for in Zimbardo's words, deindividuated behaviors are "emotional, impulsive, irrational, regressive, or atypical for the person in the given situation" (1969, p. 259). To consider again only a subset of those features outlined by Zimbardo, let us turn our attention to three questions: Is the behavior under stimulus control? Is the behavior counternormative? Is the behavior pleasurable?

Stimulus control.   In the language of behaviorism, certain stimuli in the environment are assumed to serve as signals to the organism that a particular behavior, if performed, will be reinforced or punished. For example, for the individual taking care of some errands in the downtown district of a city, traffic signals indicate when to stop and when to cross the street, signs convey information about where to wait or which line to use, and symbols of authority—police officers or bank guards—make lawful actions more likely. In behavioristic terminology, these features of the environment exert a degree of stimulus control over behavior, since when presented to the organism they increase the likelihood of some behaviors while decreasing the likelihood of others.

Viewed from this perspective, most "normal," nondeindividuated social behaviors are under some degree of stimulus control. Indeed, without environmental cues, we would be at a loss to know which behaviors to perform when, and what the consequences of our actions might be. Deindividuated behaviors, however, are not "stimulus bound"; they occur with seemingly unpredictable spontaneity and tend to contradict previously observed patterns of behavior. While the group would normally listen to the advice of a leader, when deindividuation occurs the leader's orders no longer have any significant effect on the group members. Although the appearance of legal authorities—police cars, officers, attack dogs—is sufficient to warn a group of bystanders that riotous actions will be punished, when a mob becomes deindividuated these symbols of authority lose their power to control action. As a result of deindividuation, completely blameless victims may be attacked, perceptions of the environment may be massively distorted while little information about the specific situation is either noticed or remembered, and violent actions intensify as feedback-control mechanisms break down. In consequence, deindividuated actions are often difficult to terminate, since environmental cues are no longer interpreted as signals to stop.

Counternormativeness.   The answer to the query "Is deindividuated behavior counternormative?" depends largely upon who is asking the question. From the viewpoint of the objective observer, deindividuated actions clearly violate societal norms concerning restraint, obedience to authority, respect for public property, and the valuing of human life. Yet to the group member, the actions may be completely consistent with emergent norms that are idiosyncratic to the particular group situation (Turner & Killian, 1972; Zimbardo, 1969). In discussing this distinction, Zimbardo elaborately analyzes the degree of conflict between societal and group norms regarding car stripping. Although most residents of large cities would readily admit that it is "wrong" to remove parts from parked cars, smash car windows, or use damaged autos as garbage receptacles, these actions are carried out hundreds of times a day in cities all over the world. In explanation, Zimbardo suggests that automobile vandalism is considered counternormative from a societal perspective, but is norm consistent from the community perspective (see the box).

Pleasure.   To close this section on the nature of deindividuated behavior, let us briefly examine one final question: Is the behavior pleasurable? Zimbardo answers in the affirmative, and proposes that this aspect of deindividuation explains why

---

A FIELD EXPERIMENT ON AUTO STRIPPING

In order to collect observational data on acts of vandalism, Philip Zimbardo purchased two cars, parked them on city streets in New York City and Palo Alto, California, removed the license plates, opened the hoods, and waited. In his words,

> What happened in New York was unbelievable! Within ten minutes the 1959 Oldsmobile received its first auto strippers—a father, mother, and eight-year-old son. The mother appeared to be a lookout, while the son aided the father's search of the trunk, glove compartment, and motor. He handed his father the tools necessary to remove the battery and radiator. Total time of destructive contact: seven minutes. . . .
>
> In less than three days what remained was a battered, useless hulk of metal, the result of 23

incidents of destructive contact. The vandalism was almost always observed by one or more other passersby, who occasionally stopped to chat with the looters. Most of the destruction was done in the daylight hours and not at night (as we had anticipated), and the adults' stealing clearly preceded the window-breaking, tire-slashing fun of the youngsters. The adults were all well-dressed, clean-cut whites who would under other circumstances be mistaken for mature, responsible citizens demanding more law and order. . . .

In startling contrast, the Palo Alto car not only emerged untouched, but when it began to rain, one passerby lowered the hood so that the motor would not get wet [1969, p. 287].

(Source: Zimbardo, 1969)

members of mobs, even when engaged in intensely violent and aggressive actions such as lynchings and rioting, can appear joyous, boisterous, and happy. While in part the pleasure of deindividuation stems from the feeling of security that can be gained by immersion in a group, Zimbardo suggests that action is evaluated as pleasurable at a more basic emotional level. To return to the example of auto-mobile vandalism, he recounts some of his own affective reactions as a member of a group damaging a car with a sledge hammer:

> . . . it feels so good after the first smack that the next one comes more easily, with more force, and feels even better. . . . Once one person has begun to wield the sledge hammer, it was difficult to get him to stop and pass it to the next pair of eager hands. . . . Group members later reported that feeling the metal or glass give way under the force of their blows was stimulating and pleasurable [Zim-bardo, 1969, p. 290].

Deindividuation: Empirical Evidence

Although Zimbardo was able to muster a good deal of suggestive evidence for his concept of deindividuation, his attempts to construct an adequate theory were in some respects hampered by the lack of empirical evidence concerning the process. While related phenomena had been of considerable interest to social scientists for many years, much of this interest had been focused on the develop-ment of elaborate theories and the collection of evidence through informal obser-vations of crowds and mobs. Although Zimbardo masterfully wove together bits and pieces of information gleaned from a variety of sources, many of his hypotheses were based largely on conjecture and intuition. As a consequence, the many issues he raised begged for empirical investigation.

Although only a little more than a decade has transpired since Zimbardo's theory fanned group dynamicists' scientific curiosities, a significant dent has already been made in the task of evaluating the strengths and weaknesses of the model. Admit-tedly, certain portions of the theory—particularly those segments dealing with the form, diversity, and frequency of deindividuated actions—remain relatively unstud-ied, but other aspects have been examined in sufficient detail to enable us to draw certain limited conclusions. In this section we will focus on the two broad areas that have received the most attention up to this point—the causes of dein-dividuation and the nature of the deindividuated state—but in so doing we must overlook other relevant work. Readers who require more detailed information should consult more in-depth reviews (see, for example, Diener, 1977, 1980; Dipboye, 1977).

Causes of Deindividuation

IDENTIFIABILITY

One of the first factors noted by Zimbardo as a potential source of aberrant group action was low identifiability. While identifiability is avoided through a variety of means—wearing disguises, using an alias, avoiding acquaintances, or perform-ing actions in a group whose members are very similar to one another—these methods are similar in that they enhance feelings of anonymity. If group members are conforming to societal laws and norms simply because they fear legal reprisals and social sanctions, then anonymity eases the likelihood that those in authority will locate and punish them for engaging in "strange" or illegal activities. Zimbardo felt that anonymity was a variable of paramount importance in the deindividuation process.

In one of the few pre-Zimbardo studies of deindividuation identifiability was directly manipulated in a laboratory setting (Singer, Brush, & Lublin, 1965). College women who signed up as participants in a study of concept formation were asked in advance to wear old clothes or to come in more formal attire (dresses). Once they arrived for the study, those in old clothes were asked to put on oversized white lab coats, which they wore throughout the experimental session. The researchers felt that wearing lab coats would create a feeling of anonymity, and that anonymous subjects would be more likely to display atypical behaviors. Consistent with this hypothesis, when subjects in the low-identifiability condition discussed the topic of pornography in four-woman groups, they (1) used more obscenities, (2) interrupted each other more frequently, (3) reported liking the group more, and (4) allowed fewer seconds of silence to pass during the discussion than subjects in the high-identifiability condition. When a more neutral topic was discussed (attitude toward the value of a liberal education), no differences between the two conditions were obtained.

Zimbardo, in his own research, also manipulated identifiability experimentally to determine its effects on deindividuated actions (1969). Once more, female college students were made to feel identifiable (Id) or nonidentifiable (non-Id). Non-Id subjects wore large lab coats (size 44) and hoods over their heads. The experimenter pointed out that they were not to mention their names, and maintained that they could in no way be identified. In the Id condition subjects were greeted by name and wore large name tags, and the experimenter emphasized their uniqueness and individuality.

To disguise the true purposes of the study the participants were told that the research involved a test of an empathy-theory hypothesis: that the more active your involvement with other persons the more accurate is your perception of them. Ostensibly as a test of this notion the subjects were to rate two "stimulus persons" (both female) after becoming actively involved with them; active involvement, however, would entail giving them a series of 20 electric shocks! The justification for this unique method of getting acquainted was that the stimulus persons were subjects in another study and were to receive the shocks anyway, so to make things easier the two investigations had been combined. Unknown to the subjects, two different "targets" were included in order that a second independent variable could be manipulated. Prior to each shock session the subjects listened to what were supposedly taped interviews with the up-coming target person. These tapes were carefully constructed to make one of the women seem attractive ("nice, accepting, altruistic, sweet"; p. 266) while the other seemed obnoxious ("obnoxious, self-centered, conceited, and critical"; p. 266). Naturally, the order of the interview tapes was counterbalanced across groups.

Subjects were seated in a darkened room, and through a one-way mirror watched the first target person. Each was required to depress a switch on signal, and the experimenter emphasized the group's responsibility for the action. When the switch was depressed, the target would jump from the pain of the electric shock. Indeed, halfway through the 20 trials the target—who was actually a confederate and received no shocks—pretended to react so severely that her hand ripped out of the restraints. At that point the experimenter strapped her hand down again and 10 more shock trials were carried out. This entire procedure was then repeated with a second stimulus person, who was also a confederate.

The results of this intriguing study provided some support for Zimbardo's belief that aggressive behavior would be greatest among non-Id subjects. Although both groups gave an equal number of shocks (an average of 17 of 20), the non-Id subjects gave significantly longer shocks than the Id subjects. Apparently the instructions were so strong that most of the subjects felt compelled to administer the shocks whenever the signal light was on, but non-Id subjects held their switches down nearly twice as long as the Id subjects (.90 seconds versus .47 seconds). In addition, while the differences in shock duration for obnoxious and attractive targets did not reach statistical significance, Id subjects tended to be more influenced by the targets' characteristics than were the non-Id subjects. The nonanonymous subjects seemed to administer shorter and shorter shocks to the nice victim over trials, while the anonymous subjects continually increased the length of the shocks they gave. Also, the correlation between shock duration and ratings of the target was significant for Id subjects ($r = .67$), but nonsignificant for non-Id subjects ($r = .10$), suggesting that the anonymous subjects were simply unaffected by the characteristics of the victim. Hence, this study not only attests to the importance of low identifiability, but also lends some support to Zimbardo's assumption that the aggressive actions of deindividuated group members are not under stimulus control.

While the generalizability of the Zimbardo shock study may be limited given the uniqueness of the laboratory situation and the possibility that the participants saw through his elaborate deceptions, no such criticism can be leveled at a cross-cultural study of real-world violence and anonymity-enhancing rituals (Watson, 1973). Through the use of the Human Relations Files maintained by anthropologists, ethnographers, and sociologists, a number of cultures were classified as either high or low in violence. Violent cultures were those that engaged in such practices as headhunting, the torturing of captives, fighting to the death in battles, and mutilation, while low-violence cultures were those that spared prisoners or engaged in only minor raids on neighboring groups. Cultures that instituted a "specific change in appearance of the individual before battle" (p. 343) were also noted, as were those that featured no changes. Results indicated that 92.3% of the highly aggressive cultures (12 of 13) featured rituals that disguised the appearance of warriors, while only 30.0% of the low aggression cultures (3 of 10) featured similar rituals.

GROUP MEMBERSHIP

Although the three studies reviewed in the preceding section suggest that anonymity produces deindividuation, not all studies support this overall conclusion (for example, Diener & Kasprzyk, 1978; Zimbardo, 1969). For example, when Zimbardo later replicated his shock study using different subjects and altered instructions, he found that the hooded participants tended to be *less* aggressive than the identified subjects. Although this inconsistency stems in part from the tremendous psychological complexity of the various manipulations used in various experiments to create anonymity (Diener, 1980), failures to find a clear relationship between identifiability and deindividuation occur more frequently in studies that examine the responses of solitary individuals rather than the responses of individuals in groups. This tendency raises a critical issue: Should the concept of deindividuation be applied only to people in groups and not to lone individuals?

The clearest answer to this question comes from a study conducted by Ed Diener and his colleagues that took advantage of a unique tradition: Halloween trick-or-treating (Diener, Fraser, Beaman, & Kelem, 1976). The subjects in the research were 1352 children from the Seattle, Washington, area who went trick-or-treating at one of the 27 experimental homes scattered throughout the city. The entrance to each home was set up so that as the children entered, they would necessarily notice a low table with two bowls on it—one containing small candy bars and a second filled with pennies and nickels. Although a female (who did not live at the house) greeted the children, she simply told them to take one candy before explaining "I have to go back to my work in another room." At that point she left the room, leaving behind the children standing before the two bowls. As you may have guessed, an observer hidden behind a decorative panel recorded transgressions—that is, number of extra candy bars taken and amount of money stolen.

While several independent variables were examined in the study, the two of critical interest in the current discussion were group membership and anonymity. Since the children came to the house alone or in small groups, group membership varied naturally and was simply recorded by the observer (exceedingly large groups were not included in the study; nor were groups that included an adult). Furthermore, since the children were already disguised, the problem was to make some of them identifiable while leaving others unidentified. Therefore, nothing was done to children assigned to the anonymous condition, whereas those in the nonanonymous condition were asked to give their names and addresses. The experimenter repeated this information aloud and seemed to be memorizing their identities.

The percentages of children transgressing in the four conditions of the experiment are shown in Figure 11-1. As the chart indicates, each variable contributed somewhat to transgression, with more money and candy being taken by children in groups rather than alone and by anonymous rather than nonanonymous children. However, the effects of anonymity on solitary children were not very pronounced, whereas in the group conditions the impact of anonymity was enhanced. These findings, which have been supported in other investigations (Cannavale, Scarr, & Pepitone, 1970; Mathes & Guest, 1976; Mathes & Kahn, 1975) suggest that the term deindividuation is used most appropriately in reference to people who perform atypical behavior while members of a group.

SIZE OF THE GROUP

It is impossible to make clearcut predictions based on deindividuation theory regarding the effects of group size on atypical group behavior. While on the one hand many factors associated with deindividuation—anonymity, diffusion of responsibility, and social arousal—should become stronger as crowds grow in size, in large groups communication among members requires more time than in small

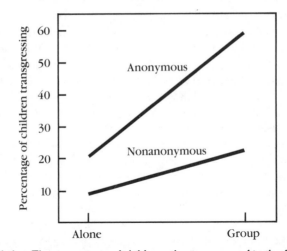

FIGURE 11-1. The percentage of children who transgressed in the four conditions of the Diener et al. trick-or-treat study. (Source: Diener, Fraser, Beamon, and Kelem, 1976)

groups, problems of coordination arise, and the likelihood of heterogeneity increases. Thus, from a theoretical perspective the link between group size and aberrant actions is unclear.

In one of the few laboratory studies of this question, Diener and his colleagues (Diener, Lusk, DeFour, & Flax, 1980, Experiment 1) asked people in groups of varying sizes to perform "silly and probably embarrassing tasks" such as "acting like a chimp, making 'gross' sounds, 'fingerpainting' with one's nose, and sucking on a baby bottle" (p. 451). While they performed these actions, their behaviors were recorded by eight observers, and after each task the participants completed a measure of self-consciousness. Concern about being watched and overall self-consciousness were also measured.

Some of the findings of this study are presented in Table 11-2. As this table shows, behavior did not intensify in larger groups and the mild increase in two-person groups was not statistically significant. However, the other measures did reveal effects of group size, with the general effect suggesting a drop in self-

TABLE 11-2. Group size and self-consciousness

Dependent variable	Number of persons in groups				
	1	2	4	8	16
Behavior intensity	19.3	20.4	18.0	19.9	19.4
Overall self-consciousness	5.2	4.9	4.4	4.1	3.7
Summed self-consciousness	243.3	221.4	206.4	185.1	161.7
Concern for onlookers	4.7	4.5	4.1	3.8	3.5

Note. Behavior intensity was the sum of the four behaviors, each scored on a 10-point scale, and therefore varied from 0 to 40. For overall self-consciousness and concern for onlookers, subjects responded on 7-point scales after performing all four behaviors. Summed self-consciousness was the sum of four behaviors on 0 to 100 scales, and thus this score could vary from 0 to 400.

(Source: Diener, Lusk, DeFour, and Flax, 1980)

consciousness and concern about onlookers as group size increased. This finding, when paired with the general tendency for individuals who are less self-conscious to exhibit more intense behaviors ($r = -.47$), suggests that atypical actions are more likely in larger groups.

Additional evidence comes from a recent study of persuasion during religious crusade meetings (Newton & Mann, 1980). In most such meetings, when the speaker ends the lecture and sermon he or she enjoins the listeners to make a public "decision" to accept the espoused teachings. For example, at the end of religious meetings conducted by the Billy Graham Evangelistic Association the audience members are invited to become *inquirers* by coming forward and declaring their dedication to Christ. Although the crusaders consider this dedication to be a spiritual experience caused by divine prompting, from a group-dynamics perspective the actions can be viewed as crowd responses to a persuasive communication. Accordingly, if deindividuation is associated with larger groups, then the proportion of listeners who become inquirers will be greater in large groups than in small groups. Supporting this contention, across 57 religious meetings a significant relationship between crowd size and the proportion of people who moved down to the stage to become inquirers was obtained ($r = .43$). Indeed, on Sunday the correlation rose to .78 and on weekdays the correlation was .84. Thus, these findings are consistent with Mann's conclusions concerning group size and crowd baiting (1981).

AROUSAL

The final factor to be considered here—personal arousal—was heavily emphasized by Zimbardo as a cause of deindividuation. He felt that arousal "increases the likelihood that gross, agitated behavior will be released, and that cues in the situation that might inhibit responding will not be noticed." Continuing, he proposed that "extreme arousal appears to be a necessary condition for achieving a true state of 'ecstasy'—literally, a stepping out of one's self" (1969, p. 257).

While Zimbardo may have been overstating his case in labeling arousal a necessary condition, certainly research has shown that reactions are intensified when group members are physiologically aroused. To cite just a few of the relevant findings, (1) many investigators have found that individuals who have unknowingly received doses of stimulants such as epinephrine experience stronger affective reactions and display more intensely emotional behaviors than individuals who are not aroused (for example, Schachter & Singer, 1962, 1979; Erdman & Janke, 1978); (2) flight reactions in animals have been found to increase dramatically when physiologically aroused animals are placed in fearful situations (for example, Singer, 1963; Haroutunian & Riccio, 1977); (3) arousal produced by anger has been repeatedly linked to increases in aggressive responses in humans (Rule & Nesdale, 1976); and (4) studies indicate that emotionally neutral activities such as exercise and physical exertion can create a state of general physiological arousal that in certain situations is misinterpreted as excitement, anger, and hostility (Zillman & Cantor, 1976). Furthermore, evidence indicates that Zimbardo was correct in suggesting that aroused individuals are more likely to ignore inhibitory situational cues (Zillmann, Bryant, Cantor, & Day, 1975).

Experiencing Deindividuation

... I had the knife in my right hand and I was just swinging with the knife, and
I remember hitting something four, five times repeatedly behind me. I didn't see
what it was I was stabbing.

Testimony of S. Atkins during the grand jury investigation of the Manson crimes,
reported in Bugliosi, 1974, p. 239

.. Everyone was pushing and I pulled out my knife. I saw this face—I never seen
it before, so I stabbed it. He was laying on the ground lookin' up at us. Everyone
was kicking, punching, stabbing. I kicked him on the jaw or someplace; then I
kicked him in the stomach. That was the least I could do was kick 'im.

Gang member's account of the stabbing of a polio victim in New York City,
reported in Yablonsky, 1959, p. 113

... I began to have intervals of liberty—for waves of glory swept over me and
when they came I praised God with a loud voice and in the spirit I clapped my
hands and rejoiced.

A. T. Boisen describing his conversion to a religious sect known as the Holy
Rollers, 1939, pp. 188–189

Each of these accounts of a deindividuating experience suggests the operation of
one or more of the processes noted by Zimbardo (1969) and Diener (1980): a
lack of self-monitoring and self-restraint, interruptions in memory, feelings of power
and excitement, and a general failure to consider the normativeness of action. Yet
from these accounts the essential nature of the deindividuation experience remains
unclear. In other words, what precisely transpires when an individual becomes
deindividuated? What feelings and emotions lie at the very core of this unique
experience?

In a series of studies, Edward Diener sought to answer this very question by
examining the retrospective accounts of group members who had been placed in
deindividuating situations (Diener, 1979, 1976; Diener, Dineen, Endresen, Beaman, & Fraser, 1975). In two of these projects (Diener, 1976; Diener et al., 1975),
he approached the problem by creating a simulated deindividuation situation in
the laboratory. College students were placed in a dimly lit room and told they
could perform any sorts of actions that interested them. In the room was a "passive
role player," who simply sat on the floor in the middle of the room. On the table
in the room were various instruments of simulated aggression, including several
foam rubber swords, three buckets of newspaper balls, a large bowl of rubber
bands, three pellet pistols, and foam "bricks." Observers hidden behind concealed
observation windows carefully recorded the incidence of aggressive actions, such
as throwing things at the target person or striking him with a sword.

After this session subjects completed a questionnaire measure of many of the
variables that are assumed to covary with feelings of deindividuation—self-consciousness, memory for behavior, concern about others' perceptions, memory for
peripheral information, and thoughts about the past and future. When these
responses were analyzed, Diener was surprised to find that the correlations among
these variables were quite small and formed no coherent pattern. While deindividuation theory would predict that decreases in self-awareness, memory loss,

anonymity, and distorted time perceptions would be linked to increases in disinhibited aggressive actions, these hypothesized relationships were not found.

Diener felt that one of two possible explanations could account for his results. First, it is possible that deindividuation is not a useful construct and does not refer to a "unitary experiential and behavioral phenomenon" (Diener, 1979, p. 1161). Second, and more likely, his attempt to simulate deindividuation had been unsuccessful; he had included many of the necessary ingredients for producing deindividuation (group membership, anonymity, arousal, and so on), but the strange laboratory situation made subjects feel ill at ease and self-conscious. To choose between these two alternative explanations, Diener conducted another study that included three experimental conditions: self-aware, non-self-aware, and deindividuated. Although this experiment was also conducted in a laboratory situation, he carefully controlled the group interaction by including a large number of confederates in each interacting group. While subjects felt that they were members of eight-person groups, in actuality six of the group members were Diener's accomplices trained to facilitate or inhibit the development of deindividuation.

In the *self-aware condition* various steps were taken to emphasize the individuality of the subjects. While waiting for the study to begin, the confederates seemed restless and fidgety. The actual subjects were then separated from the confederates—supposedly to work on different experimental tasks—and once apart they were asked to wear name tags and long-sleeved coveralls to "protect their clothes." While alone, the two subjects also worked on tasks designed to heighten self-awareness, such as providing personal responses to questions, sharing their opinions on topics, and disclosing personal information about themselves. Following these procedures, they rejoined the confederates, who were still wearing their street clothes; hence, the subjects were dressed quite differently from the others.

In the *non-self-aware condition* an attempt was made to shift subjects' focus of attention outward by having them perform a series of mildly distracting tasks. In no case was their individuality emphasized, and while the problems were not difficult, they required a good deal of concentration and creativity.

In the *deindividuation condition* the experimenter and confederates went to great lengths to try to foster a feeling of group cohesiveness, unanimity, and anonymity. Confederates always addressed their questions and comments to the group as a whole, and they even adopted a group name when the experimenter suggested this would be appropriate. During the study all eight group members wore coveralls, and the experimenter referred to them only by the group name. Lastly, the groups undertook a series of tasks and games designed to increase arousal, cohesiveness, and external focus:

> Group members sang together and then did "elevation"—getting "psyched up" and together lifting an assistant high in the air. The group next formed a circle by interlocking arms and were told to prevent one of the assistants from breaking into the circle. The next activity, African dancing, was designed to continue the group-cohesive activities, but was also intended to produce the arousal, group coordination, and kinesthetic sensory experience that seems to be a part of many groups in which disinhibition occurs (Sargant, 1975). During the loud Burundi drum music, the group clapped in unison, swayed in unison, and danced around the circle together. The lights in the room were dimmed [Diener, 1979, p. 1163].

Immediately after their group experience subjects were given the opportunity to perform uninhibited tasks (for example, playing in the mud, writing down the faults of their friends, sucking liquids from baby bottles, writing down all the obscenities they could think of) or more inhibited tasks (such as working on crossword puzzles, reading an essay on disarmament, answering moral dilemmas). While the subjects worked, their statements and actions were unobtrusively recorded by several of the confederates. Additionally, participants later completed a memory test and a questionnaire like that used in the simulation studies.

Because Diener was fundamentally interested in obtaining a valid description of the deindividuated state, he used a statistical procedure called factor analysis to search for clusters of highly intercorrelated variables in his observational and self-report data. Based on this analysis, he concluded that the two clusters or factors shown in the box headed "The Two Factors of Deindividuation" summarize subjects' experiences in the situation. The first factor, which is labeled *self-aware-ness* in the box, seems to be most closely related to the core of the hypothesized process. It encompasses a lack of self-consciousness, little planning out of action, high group unity, and disinhibited action. The second dimension, *altered experiencing,* is also consistent with theory in that it ties together a number of related processes such as "unusual" experiences, altered perceptions, and a loss of individual identity. When Diener compared the responses of subjects in the three conditions of his experiment, he discovered that (1) deindividuated subjects displayed greater losses of self-awareness than both the non-self-aware and the self-aware subjects and (2) deindividuated subjects reported more extreme altered experiencing than the self-aware subjects. On the basis of this research Diener was able to reject the null findings of his simulation studies to conclude that a unique experiential state does occur in deindividuated group members.

These findings, which have been replicated (Prentice-Dunn & Rogers, 1980) and extended (Rogers & Prentice-Dunn, 1981) weigh in favor of a *multicomponent theory* of deindividuation involving (at minimum) a loss of self-awareness

---

THE TWO FACTORS OF DEINDIVIDUATION

Through factor analysis Diener concluded that the two factors described below summarize individuals' experiences when deindividuated. While Diener called the self-awareness factor deindividuation, other investigators (Prentice-Dunn & Rogers, 1980) reserve that label for the entire experiential state. Deindividuated group members don't experience a loss of self-awareness alone; they also report a range of altered experiences involving perceptual distortions and loss of identity.

(Source: Diener, 1979)

Factor One: Loss of Self-awareness
Minimal self-consciousness
Lack of conscious planning as behavior becomes spontaneous
Lack of concern for what others think of you
Subjective feeling that time is passing quickly
Liking for the group and feelings of group unity
Disinhibited speech
Performing disinhibited tasks

Factor Two: Altered Experiencing
Reports of "unusual experiences" such as hallucinations
Reports of altered states of consciousness
Subjective loss of individual identity
Feelings of anonymity
Liking for the group and feelings of group unity

and altered experiencing. Yet, while these findings are compatible with extant models of deindividuation, they raise a second question: Does this multifactor deindividuated state actually mediate the effects of the situational variables on aberrant behavior? While the basic model suggests that

situational variables → deindividuated state → atypical behavior,

Diener was unable to verify conclusively the existence of a causal relationship between the deindividuated state and atypical behavior. However, investigators who have systematically manipulated levels of self-awareness report that in certain situations an external focus of attention produces disinhibited actions, including heightened susceptibility to incorrect interpretations of social situations (Scheier, Carver, & Gibbons, 1979), reductions in willingness to help others (Wegner & Schaefer, 1978), and increases in aggression (Carver, 1975) and stealing (Beaman, Klentz, Diener, & Svanum, 1979). Furthermore, in a study in which deindividuated and nondeindividuated subjects delivered electric shocks to a confederate, aggression was negatively correlated with self-awareness but positively correlated with altered experiencing (Prentice-Dunn & Rogers, 1980). These studies are similar in their suggestion that deindividuation causes aberrant actions.

In sum, research indicates that the three-step conception of deindividuation presented in Table 11-1 remains a viable approach to understanding disinhibited group behavior. While large gaps in the empirical domain remain, the influence of certain situational variables (for example, anonymity, group members, and personal arousal), the nature of the deindividuated state and the causal links among the three components of the process model have been tentatively confirmed. As investigators continue to expand their efforts in this area, we can hope that the puzzling behavioral and emotional misfirings of people in groups—riots, vandalism, gang violence, and panics—will become more predictable and thus more preventable.

Alternative Perspectives on Deindividuation

In his writings Philip Zimbardo implicitly conveys the impression that deindividuation results in a "perversion of human potential," a regrettable replacement of reason and order with impulse and chaos (1969, 1975, 1977). According to Zimbardo (1975, p. 53), "conditions that reduce a person's sense of uniqueness, that minimize individuality are the wellsprings of antisocial behaviors, such as aggression, vandalism, stealing, cheating, rudeness, as well as a general loss of concern for others." Yet he hints at an alternative way of considering deindividuation, suggesting that in some instances it may give rise to positive behaviors, "intense feelings of happiness or sorrow, and open love for others" (1969, p. 251). To end this chapter, let us reexamine some of our assumptions about individuality, deindividuation, and group behavior.

Deindividuation and Prosocial Behavior

Consider the following experiment (Gergen, Gergen, & Barton, 1973). The subject arrives for a study of "environmental psychology" and is told to fill out some questionnaires. After about 20 minutes, the subject is led by an experimenter to another room, where just before entering he or she is told,

You will be left in the chamber for no more than an hour with some other people. There are no rules . . . as to what you should do together. At the end of the time period you will each be escorted from the room alone, and will subsequently depart from the experimental site alone. There will be no opportunity to meet the other participants [Gergen et al., 1973, p. 129].

The subject finds a fairly small room (10 by 12 feet) that features padded walls and floors. Occupying this comfortable space are approximately eight other people, some male and some female, all of whom are utter strangers to one another.

Would you be surprised if told that some of the subjects in this experiment intimately embraced and kissed one another? That of the nearly 50 persons who participated, 100 percent accidentally touched one another. That 89 percent purposefully touched one another? That 51 percent hugged one another? That 78 percent reported that they felt sexually aroused? That over 50 percent changed their positions in the room every five minutes?

No doubt you find these statistics a bit difficult to believe, but only because one crucial bit of information about the study was omitted: the room was completely dark. When a well-lit room was used, none of these intimate actions occurred (see Figure 11-2). Only in the darkened chamber were individuals completely anonymous, and thus able to engage in many behaviors that, under more usual circumstances, would have been considered counternormative and bizarre. However, in no case did the anonymous (and possibly deindividuated) group members exhibit hostility, aggressiveness, or violence. Rather, nearly all became more intimately involved with one another in a positive fashion. In the words of one participant, a "group of us sat closely together, touching, feeling a sense of friendship

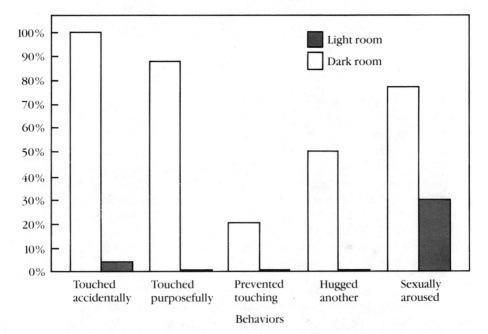

FIGURE 11-2. Frequency of assorted behaviors under light and dark conditions. (Source: Gergen, Gergen, and Barton, 1973)

and loss as a group member left. I left with a feeling that it had been fun and nice." Apparently the situation helped people express feelings that they would have otherwise kept hidden, but these feelings were those of affection rather than aggression.

In explanation, several investigators have proposed that deindividuation does not necessarily lead to violent actions (Johnson & Downing, 1979; Diener, 1980). Rather, deindividuation sets the stage for the performance of either prosocial or antisocial behaviors, depending upon the needs that are prominent for group members or the nature of the situation. In a study that investigated this possibility, female college students were told that they were to be members in four-person groups that would be administering shocks to a male taking part in a learning study (Johnson & Downing, 1979). Each time the male made an error, the subject could elect to administer either high, moderate, or slight increases in shock voltage ($+3$, $+2$, $+1$) or high, moderate, or slight decreases in shock voltage (-3, -2, -1). To manipulate anonymity, some subjects were told that their names and decisions regarding the voltage level would be known to other group members, while others were told that names and decisions could not be linked to any particular group member. To manipulate situational cues, subjects were given costumes to wear under the guise of masking individual difference characteristics. In the *prosocial-cues condition* nurses' gowns were used; the experimenter explained "I was fortunate the recovery room let me borrow these nurses' gowns." In the *antisocial-cues conditions* the costumes resembled Ku Klux Klan outfits: "I'm not much of a seamstress; this thing came out looking kind of Ku Klux Klannish" (p. 1534).

The researchers hypothesized that the effects of anonymity would largely depend upon the valence of the situational cues. They predicted that when prosocial cues were present, then anonymity would lead to a reduction in the intensity of the punishment. If, however, the situation contained antisocial cues, then anonymity should promote increases in punishment. As Figure 11-3 shows, these hypotheses were supported. When taken in combination with other studies that have found significant effects of situational cues on deindividuated group members (Diener et al., 1975; Prentice-Dunn & Rogers, 1980; Singer et al., 1965), this orientation suggests that deindividuation is neither "good" nor "bad." As Diener summarizes,

> The deindividuated person in a certain situation might be more likely to donate a large amount of money to charity, might be more likely to risk his or her life to help another, and might be more likely to kiss friends—all behaviors that many consider laudatory. However, a deindividuated person might also be more likely to throw rocks at others, participate in a lynching, or set a building ablaze. Thus, less concerned with norms, personal punishment, or long-term consequences, the deindividuated person is quite reactive to emotions and situational cues that may lead to uninhibited behaviors that are judged to be prosocial, antisocial, or neutral by the individual's society [1980, p. 232].

Balancing Individuation and Deindividuation

Robert L. Dipboye (1977), in his recent review of deindividuation, calls attention to a paradox that permeates analyses of group membership and individuality. On the one hand, many theorists assume that deindividuation—and the freedom to

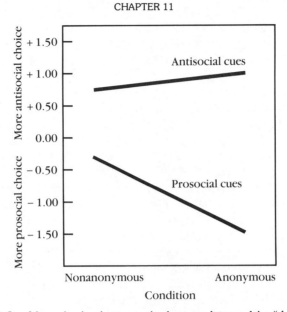

FIGURE 11-3. Mean shock selection in the four conditions of the "deindividuation and cues" experiment. (Source: Johnson and Downing)

act that it spawns—is a pleasurable, gratifying, and often-sought experience (Hoffer, 1951; Le Bon, 1895; Zimbardo, 1969). Submersion in a group results in the attainment of power and an escape from societal inhibitions; hence group members seek and try to maintain the experience of deindividuation. In contrast, humanistic theorists (for example, Fromm, 1965; Laing, 1960; Maslow, 1968) maintain that human beings can enjoy psychological well-being only when they are able to establish and maintain their own unique identities. In the words of R. D. Laing (1960, p. 44), "A firm sense of one's own autonomous identity is required in order that one may be related as one human being to another. Otherwise, any and every relationship threatens the individual with loss of identity." Thus, from this perspective deindividuation is unpleasant and identity-threatening; group members who feel "lost" in a group will try to reestablish their individual identities.

When deindividuation is considered an experience to be avoided rather than sought after, some of the output behaviors that had previously been interpreted as disinhibited, impulsive actions can be recast as identity-seeking behaviors. For example, while riots may stem from the loss of responsibility, anonymity, arousal, and group presence of deindividuation, rioters may also be attempting to reaffirm their individual identities. As one resident of the riot-torn community of Watts in California explained, "I don't believe in burning, stealing, or killing, but I can see why the boys did what they did. They just wanted to be noticed, to let the world know the seriousness of their state of life" (Milgram & Toch, 1969, p. 576). Similarly, members of large groups, such as industrial workers, students in large lecture-type classrooms, people working in bureaucratic organizations, and employees in companies with high turnover rates may perform atypical actions just to stand apart from the "crowd."

In one of the few studies that report evidence of the need to seek individuation (Maslach, 1972), members of four-person groups were led to expect that one of their members was to be chosen to work on a particular task. During this screening interview, two of the subjects were made to feel individuated; the experimenter referred to them by name, made more personal comments to them, and maintained a significant amount of eye contact. The other two subjects were made to feel deindividuated, since the experimenter avoided close contact with them and addressed them impersonally. When these individuals were later given the opportunity to engage in a free-response group discussion and complete some questionnaires, the deindividuated subjects evidenced two different types of identity-seeking reactions. Some attempted to make themselves seem as different from the other group members as possible by giving more unique answers to the questions, making longer comments, joining in the discussion more frequently, and attempting to capture the attention of the experimenter. In contrast, other subjects seemed to redefine their identities by revealing more intimate details of their personalities and beliefs through longer and more unusual self-descriptions.

In fairness to both of these perspectives, in some situations group members may prefer to become deindividuated while at other times the need to be individuated may predominate (Diener, 1980; Ziller, 1964). Spectators at a college football game, celebrants at the Mardi Gras, shy listeners in a large audience, and soldiers standing for inspection may all feel quite comfortable when submerged in the group. Yet when these same persons seek rewards for their personal skills and contributions, wish to make lasting impressions with others, or hope to establish one-to-one relationships with other group members, then they would no doubt prefer to stand out as individuals. Indeed, it is a reflection on the value of groups in human affairs that joining with others makes both of these goals possible; only by becoming members of groups can we both lose ourselves in the crowd while also securing an audience for our identity-defining self-presentations.

Summary

Instances of atypical group behavior, such as riots, mobs, panics, and mass violence, have been studied by both collective-behavior theorists and deindividuation theorists. As collective behavior, bizarre group actions can be traced back to the convergence of individuals with similar needs and desires, the transmission of feelings and actions through contagion processes, or the emergence of unique group norms. As deindividuated action, the reduction of inner constraints that is sometimes seen in groups is viewed as a process involving three components: 1) inputs (anonymity, diffusion of responsibility, group membership, arousal), 2) internal changes (loss of self-awareness and self-regulation), and 3) outputs (counternormative but pleasant actions that are not under stimulus control).

Empirically, researchers have succeeded in demonstrating the validity of both perspectives in field and laboratory settings. For example, Philip Zimbardo's study of group members administering shocks to others indicated that aggression is more likely if members can't be identified, and Edward Diener's study of Halloween trick-or-treaters showed that group membership combined with anonymity leads to the highest rate of transgression. Group size and arousal have also been linked to deindividuation, which seems to involve at least two interrelated mechanisms: losses in self-awareness and altered experiencing.

Although group dynamicists tend to emphasize the negative consequences of deindividuation, atypical, violent actions do not always follow losses of identity and self-awareness. In fact, evidence indicates that, given certain prosocial cues, deindividuated group members may behave altruistically and that some of the atypical behaviors that had previously been interpreted as disinhibited, impulsive actions were actually attempts to reestablish a sense of individuality. Thus, deindividuation has both a positive and a negative side.

12

Groupthink

Irving Janis is an expert group dynamicist. For more than 20 years he has systematically studied group structure, leadership, stress, and conflict, and his research has often attested to the powerful effects of the social forces that shape group behavior. Yet as he read historical accounts of the invasion of Cuba at the Bay of Pigs, he found himself puzzling over many questions: How could such a disastrous decision be reached? Why didn't anyone object to the patently obvious shortcomings of the plan? What could account for the flawed judgments made by such shrewd decision makers as John F. Kennedy and his advisors?

As he became more intrigued by this defective decision, Janis began to collect other examples of people in groups reaching wrong conclusions. In the realm of politics and military planning he found that many of history's most profound fiascoes—the failure to defend Pearl Harbor from Japanese air attack, the escalation of the Vietnam War, the Watergate burglary—resulted from the decisions of groups. In the newspapers he read of ordinary citizens seriously misjudging issues— for example, a complacent community that ignored warnings of a mining disaster until it was too late or a committee that approved placing a coal-storage facility so close to a school that its accidental collapse killed all the town's school-aged children. Turning to the business world, he found that certain infamous industrial projects, such as the marketing of Thalidomide and the decision to build a car that nobody wanted (the Edsel), were the result of group deliberations. Lastly, in reviewing his own experiences and observations in many kinds of groups—infantry platoons, air crews, therapy and encounter groups, seminars, and experiments—he recalled a number of instances in which group members sacrificed effective decisional processes during the course of group discussions. One particularly revealing incident occurred in a group of heavy cigarette smokers who, unable to quit on their own, had joined together in a sort of Alcoholics Anonymous for smokers. As members, they agreed to attend all the group's meetings and make a conscientious effort to stop smoking cigarettes.

However, during the second meeting of the group a curious thing happened. Two of the more vocal members brought up the issue of how best to stop smoking, and offered what they thought was the only possible answer. Smoking is a difficult habit to break, they said, amounting to a nearly incurable addiction. Therefore, the best way to stop is by gradually cutting back step by step over a prolonged period of time. After some discussion they had convinced virtually the entire group of their position, but one particularly heavy smoker broke the consensus; he claimed that through willpower alone he had stopped smoking just a few weeks before and had not smoked a cigarette since. He recommended his cure to all the others, sparking an animated debate. Rather than considering the possibility of quitting "cold turkey," the group members attacked his idea in a lengthy argument that continued out into the hallway once the meeting was adjourned. But even more surprisingly, at the next meeting the group "deviant" stood up and announced that he had reconsidered his position. He concluded that the group was right, and so had gone back to smoking two packs of cigarettes a day. In response, the group members applauded his decision, welcoming him back into their midst with open arms. Janis, as the psychological consultant for the group, pointed out that the group members were violating the primary reason for the group by encouraging smoking, but the group members refused to listen to his criticisms.

Janis decided that this group, like the others he had noted, had fallen victim to **groupthink;** a strong concurrence-seeking tendency that interferes with effective group decision making (Janis, 1972, 1979; Janis & Mann, 1977). At the core of the process is the tendency for group members to strive for solidarity and cohesiveness to such an extent that they carefully avoid any questions or topics that could lead to disputes. If members anticipate arguments over an issue, they never raise it. If they will be unable to answer a question, they never ask it. If they can find shortcuts and reach simplistic solutions, they take them. Thus, as a result of an irrational emphasis on maintaining unanimity and cohesiveness, the group's decisions are ill-considered, impractical, and unrealistic (see box).

In his book *Victims of Groupthink,* Janis (1972) relies on case-study methods both to develop and to provide suggestive evidence for the validity of his hypotheses concerning groupthink. Focusing only on groups whose gross errors of judgment virtually doomed their plans to failure, he succeeded in finding many well-documented instances of suspiciously similar group-planned fiascoes. Many of these cases highlighted prominent policy-making groups dealing with sensitive political issues, and by scouring historical documents Janis was therefore able to uncover clues to the resulting debacles. Although Janis describes many fiascoes, we will concentrate on one case that he examined in detail and which we described briefly in Chapter 1: the decision formulated by John F. Kennedy's ad hoc advisory committee on the Bay of Pigs invasion. After reviewing the incident from a historical perspective, we will note some of the symptomatic group processes that suggest the group was experiencing groupthink and outline some possible causes

---

WHY THE WORD "GROUPTHINK?"

I use the term "groupthink" as a quick and easy way to refer to a mode of thinking that people engage in when they are deeply involved in a cohesive in-group, when the members' strivings for unanimity override their motivation to realistically appraise alternative courses of action. "Groupthink" is a term of the same order as the words in the newspeak vocabulary George Orwell presented in his dismaying *1984*—a vocabulary with terms such as "doublethink" and "crimethink." By putting groupthink with those Orwellian words, I realize that groupthink takes on an invidious connotation. The invidiousness is intentional: Groupthink refers to a deterioration of mental efficiency, reality testing, and moral judgment that results from in-group pressures [p. 9].

(Source: Janis, 1972)

of groupthink to determine what kinds of groups are most susceptible to defective decision making. However, we will end the chapter on an optimistic note, concentrating on how groupthink might be prevented.

The Bay of Pigs Invasion: A Case Study

In the early-morning darkness of April 17, 1961, eight landing craft made their way toward Giron Beach in the Bahía De Cochinos (Bay of Pigs) on the southern coast of Cuba. The 1400 men in the craft had been recruited, armed, trained, and transported to the battle site by the CIA; they were anti-Castro Cuban exiles who hoped to establish a new government in their homeland by armed insurgency. Though small, the group believed it could retake Cuba if a beachhead at the Bay of Pigs could be established and defended, Castro's air force was disabled by covert U. S. air force strikes, the invasion sparked a general uprising of the population, and Castro's own troups defected to the exiles' forces.

Unfortunately, little went according to plan. In its approach to the beach the craft were grounded on a coral reef that hadn't been spotted. Then, as the men moved into Giron, they realized that despite CIA assurances that the residents of the small town didn't even have telephones, sophisticated communications equipment had been used to inform Castro of the invasion. Furthermore, U. S. air strikes had been curtailed and, as the sun rose over the beach, Castro's air forces began riddling the landing party and attacking its supply ships. When the invasion force's air cover finally arrived, the old B-26s were no match for the Cuban jets and many were soon shot down. In the fatal blow, Castro sent his well-trained troops to Giron, along with tanks, howitzers, rocket launchers, and more air support. The invaders, unable to retreat since their ships had been sunk or damaged, fled into the surrounding swamps. Eventually, nearly 1200—some near starvation—were rounded up by the Cuban forces and after a mock trial were ransomed back to the U. S. government for more than $50 million in food and medical supplies (Houseman, 1981).

The Decision Makers

Janis (1972, p. 14) describes the Kennedy administration's decision to invade Cuba as one of the "worst fiascoes ever perpetrated by a responsible government," but he does not attribute the mistake to the inabilities of the decision makers. After all, the plan to achieve the overthrow of Fidel Castro's communist regime was the brainchild of some of the United States' most intelligent government advisors: John F. Kennedy, a dazzlingly successful politician with a string of accomplishments; Secretary of State Dean Rusk, who had weighed complex issues in the political arena for years; Secretary of Defense Robert McNamara, a one-time faculty member of Harvard Business School, statistician, and researcher into rational approaches to decision making; Secretary of the Treasury Douglas Dillon, a Republican whose reputation as an "objective and analytic thinker" earned him a place in the otherwise partisan group; Special Assistant for National Security Affairs McGeorge Bundy, a former dean of Harvard University; and the well-respected historian Arthur Schlesinger, Jr. In addition, as Figure 12-1 indicates, the formal meetings included experts on Latin American affairs, the director and deputy director of the CIA, and, as representatives of the military, the Joint Chiefs of Staff. The input of other White House staff members, most notably Robert Kennedy and Richard Goodwin, was also solicited during the decisional process.

No, the plan's failure could not be explained by pointing to the shortcomings of the men who approved it; all were quite competent individuals. Furthermore, at a surface level of analysis they seemed to work well together in a group. Although the Joint Chiefs of Staff kept to themselves, the other discussants worked hard and long at improving the plan. Soon a strong feeling of unity and cohesiveness pervaded the group, and mutual respect for others' opinions was quite high since the qualifications of each member seemed unquestionable. While a newly formed group attempting to decide a complex issue that it had not even raised (the CIA had developed the scheme at the request of the previous administration), Kennedy's leadership style ensured that the group approached the problem in an orderly businesslike fashion. Although the group uncovered several minor wrinkles in the CIA's strategy during the three months of planning, it ironed out these problems with dispatch. Discussion was carefully controlled by Kennedy, and norms concerning who could ask questions, the order of questioning, and even the proper phrasing for comments and inquiries were rarely broken. The group seemed to deal with problems like a smoothly functioning machine.

Symptoms of Groupthink

Hidden beneath these amiable, conflict-free interactions were the signs of groupthink. Although Janis initially isolated eight major indicators of groupthink, he later elaborated on these symptoms, as did other theorists (Janis, 1972, 1979; Janis & Mann, 1977; Longley & Pruitt, 1980; Wheeler & Janis, 1980). To summarize these ideas, we consider two general categories of symptoms below: (1) premature concurrence seeking and (2) illusions and misperceptions.

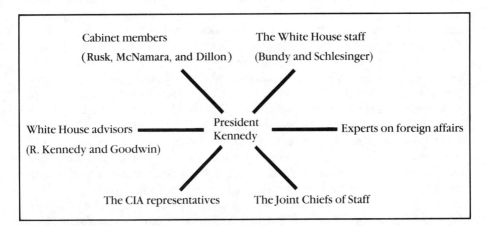

FIGURE 12-1. The decision makers.

PREMATURE CONCURRENCE SEEKING

Imagine yourself a member of a group trying to agree on the answer to the following "duck problem":

> A number of ducks swim downstream in formation. Two are in front, two in the middle, and two bring up the rear. What is the smallest number of ducks that could swim by in such a formation [Raven & Rubin, 1976, p. 206]?

The members of your group would probably approach the problem by expressing their opinions about the correct solution with some arguing "six," others "eight," and still others simply confessing confusion. However, as the discussion continues and no objections are raised against the majority opinion, pleas for a quick decision will probably be voiced. Dissenters may express doubts with suggestions that it may be a "trick question," but soon they will show some agreement as the discussion of new points is curtailed.

While this kind of *concurrence seeking* is necessary when reaching closure on issues, unwarranted conformity can sometimes undermine the quality of the group's decision. If without thinking the problem through completely several members, including the leader, boldly state, "This is simple. It's obviously six ducks," and call for a voice vote, then the group might never realize that the correct answer is four (if the ducks were in single file, the first two would be in front, the second and third would be in the middle, and third and fourth would be bringing up the rear.) When we consider the advisory committee's interactions for evidence of premature concurrence seeking, we find that four separate symptoms reveal a tendency towards early agreement due to excessive in-group pressures: (1) high conformity pressures; (2) self-censorship of dissenting ideas; (3) mindguards; and (4) apparent unanimity.

High-conformity pressures. As noted in Chapter 9, pressures to conform are present to some degree in nearly all groups. However, when groupthink occurs, these pressures become pronounced and overpowering. Tolerance for any sort of disagreement over even the most minor issue seems virtually nil, and in some cases exceedingly harsh measures are taken to bring those who dissent into line. In the ad hoc advisory committee, a group taboo against criticizing the plan soon developed, apparently because members felt that the two CIA representatives who were responsible for the project would be offended if anything negative was said. These two men were fully accepted members of the team, and every attempt was made to keep them within the inner circle. Thus, if anyone raised minor criticisms, President Kennedy would ask the CIA to reply *prior* to any full discussion by the group. As a result, norms soon developed that ruled out criticism, and group pressure ensured the compliance of the members with this norm.

Other aspects of Kennedy's leadership style also contributed to conformity pressure in the group, for he would make his opinion clear at the outset of each meeting, as if daring the members to disagree. For example, in one particularly important meeting Senator William Fulbright joined the group to discuss the plan. However, rather than simply turning the floor over to this newcomer who may have had a fresh viewpoint, Kennedy ran the meeting by asking those individuals seated around the conference table to vote for or against the plan in a straw poll.

Although Fulbright broke the majority consensus by disagreeing with the plan, he was seen as an outsider by the group, and the rest of the advisory committee banded together to oppose him. Ironically, President Kennedy's procedures for requiring a voice vote by individual without prior group discussion parallel quite closely the methods used by Solomon Asch (1952) to heighten conformity pressures in discussion groups.

Self-censorship of dissenting ideas.   Although the maxim claims "silence is golden," in decision-making groups reluctance in expressing disagreement can often undermine critical thinking. In this case, although many of the members of the group privately felt uncertain about the plan, their discomfort over expressing their doubts openly prompted them to remain silent. In some instances they would raise questions by sending private memoranda to the president before or after a meeting, but when the group convened the doubting Thomases sat in silence. As historian Arthur Schlesinger later wrote,

> In the months after the Bay of Pigs I bitterly reproached myself for having kept so silent during those crucial discussions in the Cabinet Room, though my feelings of guilt were tempered by the knowledge that a course of objection would have accomplished little save to gain me a name as a nuisance. I can only explain my failure to do more than raise a few timid questions by reporting that one's impulse to blow the whistle on this nonsense was simply undone by the circumstances of the discussion [1965, p. 225].

Mindguards.   Just as a bodyguard protects a person from injurious physical assault, a mindguard takes steps to protect group members from information that they think will destroy their confidence in the group and its ability to formulate a good solution. These self-appointed mindguards can protect the group through a number of channels, including *gate keeping* and *dissent containment*. As a gate-keeper, the mindguard diverts controversial information away from the group by "losing" it, "forgetting" to mention it, or deeming it irrelevant and thus unworthy of the group's attentions. Alternatively, the mindguard may practice containment of dissent by taking dissenting members aside and pressuring them to keep silent. The mindguard may use a variety of strategies to achieve this pressure—requesting the change as a personal favor, pointing out the damage that might be done to the group, or informing the dissenter that in the long run disagreement would damage his or her position in the group (Uris, 1978). But whatever the method the overall goal is the same: quash dissent before it reaches the level of group awareness.

In the ad hoc advisory group both President Kennedy and Secretary of State Rusk acted, at times, as mindguards by keeping information relevant to the decision to themselves. Kennedy had received memoranda from both Schlesinger and Fulbright condemning the plan, yet he never discussed the memos with the group. Indeed, in one instance when a straw poll was being taken he ended the vote and the meeting before group members who opposed the plan had a chance to either vote or express their doubts. Similarly, Rusk suppressed information that his own staff had given him. One extreme example of this mindguarding occurred when Rusk, unable to attend the meeting, sent Undersecretary of State Chester Bowles.

Although Bowles was "horrified" by the plan under discussion, President Kennedy—perhaps acting as a mindguard—never gave Bowles the opportunity to speak during the meeting. Therefore, Bowles later followed bureaucratic channels by voicing his critical misgivings in a memorandum to his superior, Rusk. Rusk, however, kept silent during the next advisory committee and informed Bowles that the plan had been revised. (Ironically, Bowles was fired several weeks after the Bay of Pigs fiasco.)

Robert Kennedy, although not a formal member of the group, also acted as a mindguard on occasion by trying to contain dissent. In a private discussion with Schlesinger he made it clear that dissent should be avoided at all costs. After listening to Schlesinger criticize the invasion plan, he told him "You may be right, or you may be wrong, but the President has made his mind up. Don't push it any further. Now is the time for everyone to help him all they can" (quoted in Janis, 1972, p. 42).

Apparent unanimity. The high conformity pressures, self-censorship, and mindguarding in the group added up to an illusory concurrence of opinions. Almost from the outset the entire group seemed to agree to the man that the basic plan presented by the CIA was the only solution to the problem and in later discussions appeared to just be "going through the motions" of debate. Although retrospective accounts revealed that many of the group's members objected to the plan, these objections never surfaced during the meetings. Instead, a "curious atmosphere of assumed consensus" (Schlesinger, 1965, p. 250) characterized discussion, as each person wrongly concluded that everyone liked the plan. As Janis (1972, p. 39) explains, the group members played up "areas of convergence in their thinking, at the expense of fully exploring divergences that might disrupt the apparent unity of the group." Apparently, the members felt that it would be "better to share a pleasant, balmy group atmosphere than be battered in a storm."

ILLUSIONS AND MISPERCEPTIONS

In objective terms, the plan for the Bay of Pigs invasion entailed the following components: attacking a small neighboring country; smuggling arms into another nation in the hopes of creating a civil war; hiring mercenaries to do most of the actual fighting; attacking without declaring war; misinforming other nations—both allies and enemies—about the U.S. role in the invasion; misinforming U.S. citizens, including elected members of Congress, concerning the details of the invasion; and launching a major military offensive without carefully examining key assumptions about the morale of the Cuban exile invaders, the expertise of the defenders, the suitability of the landing site, the adequacy of planned air support, and the likelihood of a general uprising in Cuba.

However, in spite of all these aspects of the plan spelling failure and hinting at the possible occurrence of severely negative consequences, the members of the advisory committee plunged ahead without pause. Although each member, as an individual, may have experienced misgivings over the plan, when the men joined together at a conference table they forgot their qualms. Critical reasoning faculties seemed to be impeded as the group continually formulated, and failed to further revise, a range of invalid appraisals of the power of their own forces and the strengths of their plan. After studying the advisory committee closely, Janis concluded that these errors in judgment stemmed from four basic illusions and misperceptions symptomatic of groupthink: (1) illusions of invulnerability, (2) illusions of morality, (3) biased perceptions of the out-group, and (4) collective rationalizing.

Illusions of invulnerability. In each of the meetings, a feeling of assurance and confidence engulfed the group. The members felt that their error-riddled plan was virtually infallible, the product of a committee that could not make major errors in judgment. Kennedy had just been elected president despite all odds against him, and he had assembled a seemingly peerless cadre of consultants. The atmosphere in the new group could almost be described as euphoric, for members felt that such a powerful group of men would be invulnerable to dangers that could arise from bad decisions or ill-considered actions. As Janis notes, such feelings of confidence and power may help athletic teams or combat units reach their objectives, but the feeling that all obstacles can be easily overcome through power and good luck tends to cut short clear, analytic thinking in decision-making groups.

Illusions of morality. Although the plan to invade Cuba could unsympathetically be described as an unprovoked sneak attack by a major world power on a small, virtually defenseless country, the decision makers never questioned the morality of their plan. No doubt as individuals each of the members endorsed basic principles of human rights and justice, but when the members joined together in the group they seemed to lose their principles in the group's desire to bravely end Castro's regime. While the means used to defeat the spread of communism may have been considered questionable, the group felt the ends certainly justified them; the cause of democracy was offered as justification enough for the planned attack. In this regard the advisory committee was similar to many other United States administrative groups that suffered from groupthink. As revealed by one recent archival study of committees that made groupthinklike decisions (for example, the decision to invade North Korea or to escalate the Vietnam War) or well-reasoned decisions (such as the formulation of the Marshall Plan or the handling of the Cuban missile crisis), decision makers in groupthink crises tend to make more positive statements about their own country and causes than do decision makers in nongroupthink crises (Tetlock, 1979).

Biased perceptions of the out-group. As we will find in Chapter 13, conflict among groups often leads to, and in some cases is fed by, biased perceptions of out-group members. For example, the members of the ad hoc advisory committee all shared a negative opinion of Castro and his political ideology, and this opinion often found expression during the group discussions. Castro was depicted as a weak leader, an evil communist, and a man too stupid to realize that his country was about to be attacked. His ability to maintain an air force was discredited, as was his control over his troops and the citizenry. The group participants' underestimation of their enemy was so pronounced that they sent a force of 1400 men to fight a force of 200,000 and expected an easy success. The group wanted to believe that Castro would prove to be an ineffectual leader and military officer, but this oversimplified picture of the dictator turned out to be merely wishful thinking.

Although little evidence of this devaluation of the out-group was found in the previously mentioned archival study of several decision-making groups (Tetlock, 1979), a study of one groupthink crisis—the decision to escalate the Vietnam War—found a consistent theme in American justifications for U.S. intervention. In many of President Lyndon B. Johnson's speeches on the subject, he depicted the North Vietnamese as "savages" who were driven by an irrational desire to subjugate others by military force (Ivie, 1980).

Collective rationalizing.   Once people commit themselves to a particular course of action, they often begin to reduce their conflict over the choice by avoiding information that weighs against that choice while emphasizing data that confirm its correctness. When the decision maker is part of a committee, these defensive decisional tactics can be communicated to others during the discussion. In the Kennedy advisory committee, the injustice being done to the Cubans and the exiles was explained away with rhetoric of democratic ideals and the importance of freedom. Warnings that the world would condemn U.S. involvement in Cuban affairs were dismissed as ludicrous, as were arguments that Castro might prevent a general uprising when the invasion took place. Similarly, while the attack depended heavily on the element of surprise, when the U.S. newspapers leaked the story the group members continued on with the plan as if nothing had changed. Even though President Kennedy himself complained, "Castro doesn't need agents over here. All he has to do is read our papers. It's all laid out for him" (quoted in Salinger, 1966, p. 194), the group members dealt with the secrecy problem by minimizing the importance of surprise and reiterating the weakness of the Cuban forces.

CONCLUSIONS

The talented advisors worked long and hard over the planned invasion of Cuba, and yet they approved an "operation so ill conceived that among literate people all over the world the name of the invasion site has become the very symbol of perfect failure" (Janis, 1972, p. 49). Although we cannot be certain that the group actually suffered from groupthink, close study of historical documents and retrospective accounts of the meetings suggest that the committee evidenced the major symptoms. The president tried to force the members to reach a consensus on the difficult issue too soon, and in response pressures to conform became so strong that dissenting opinions were rare. Most members believed that the group was unanimously in favor of the plan, and hence censored any private misgivings they may have had, while mindguarding members of the group prevented the less reticent dissenters from expressing disagreement. Other symptoms of groupthink—illusions of power, morality, images of the enemy as a savage, and blatant disregard of warnings that the plan would fail—also surfaced in the group, justifying Janis' decision to stamp the label *groupthink* on the committee's proceedings.

Causes of Groupthink

Although the conformity pressures, illusions, and misperceptions that characterized the advisory committee may have been causally related to the development of groupthink, Janis prefers to label them *symptoms* of the problem rather than actual *causes*. Critics of the theory have pointed out that such a distinction is arbitrary and difficult to test empirically (Longley & Pruitt, 1980), but Janis prefers to concentrate on a more limited set of factors when considering the causal antecedents of faulty decision making in groups (Janis, 1972, 1979; Janis & Mann, 1977). In this section we review four of these causal factors cataloged by Janis— cohesiveness, the isolation of the group, the style of the leader, and the stress on the group to reach a good decision. Additionally, a related process that also occurs in decision-making groups—group polarization—is described and related to the development of groupthink.

Cohesiveness

Of the many factors that contribute to the rise of groupthink, Janis emphasizes cohesiveness above all others. Although cohesion plays an important, and generally positive, role in groups by linking members together through bonds of attraction, Janis notes that where cohesiveness is extreme the effects can be detrimental.

COHESIVENESS DEFINED

Although the origin of the term *cohesiveness* in group dynamics is murky, most scholars trace the concept back to the early theoretical efforts of Kurt Lewin and his colleagues at the Research Center for Group Dynamics (originally located at MIT but later moved to the Institute for Social Research at the University of Michigan) (Zander, 1979b). Although not rigorously defined, the term has been traditionally used to summarize the strength of the forces that bind members to a group, including both liking for the group as a whole and the attraction of each member to every other member. Thus, at the group level *cohesiveness* refers to the "spirit of the group," that "we-feeling" that joins people together to form a single unit. At a more individualistic level, cohesiveness refers to the member's attraction to other group members, whether this attraction is based on liking, respect, or trust. Furthermore, because those who are members of cohesive groups tend to remain in the group for a longer period of time, the more formal definitions of cohesiveness often focus on membership maintenance. For example, Dorwin Cartwright defined cohesiveness as "the degree to which the members of the group desire to remain in their group" (1968, p. 91) and Leon Festinger called it "the resultant of all the forces acting on the member to remain in the group" (1950, p. 274).

Because cohesiveness is a high-order theoretical construct, the concept is not directly tied to any observable, measurable aspect of the group in a one-to-one fashion. In other words, the question of how best to measure cohesiveness remains open, and in consequence different researchers have operationalized cohesiveness in different ways (see Cartwright, 1968, for a more detailed review). For example, one often-used measurement technique focuses on patterns of attraction among individual group members (Lott & Lott, 1965). Such a method of assessing cohesiveness was used by Leon Festinger and his colleagues in their well-known study of groups of people living in the same court of a housing project (Festinger, Schachter, & Back, 1951). After residents supplied the names of all their good friends, the investigators calculated the ratio of in-court choices and outside-court choices. The greater the ratio, the greater was the cohesiveness of the court. Of course, attraction could also be assessed simply by asking each group member to rate the attractiveness of every other group member using a standard questionnaire format.

A second measurement approach assumes that group members are accurate observers of their group's cohesiveness and, if asked, are willing to communicate their perceptions to the researcher. For example, in a recent study of surveying parties formed from students in an engineering class, cohesiveness was measured by assessing subjects' responses to such questions as "How would you describe the way you and the other members of your survey party 'got along' together on this task?" using 7-point rating scales (Terborg, Castore, & DeNinno, 1976, p. 785). Similarly, the cohesiveness measures presented in the box headed "Paper-and-Pencil Measures of Group Cohesiveness" emphasize subjective estimates of "we-feeling."

In a third tack the strength of members' identification with the group is considered. Although identification can be assessed by merely asking people to rate their sense of belonging or commitment to the group (Steers, 1977), more unobtrusive measures can also be used. For example, in one project, identification with one's group—in this case, a college—was measured by recording the proportion of observed students wearing apparel that connected them with their university; examples of group identifiers included pins, jackets, shirts, books, and notebooks displaying the school name, nickname, mascot, or university insignia (Cialdini et al., 1976, Experiment 1). In a second study, identification with one's college football team was measured by engaging students in a telephone conversation about a recent game. During the conversation the number of references to the football team that expressed a link between the subject and the team (for example "We won that game" or "We are a good team") were noted, along with the number of nonidentification responses (such as "They won that game" or "They are a good team"). Incidentally, both studies showed that individuals tended to emphasize the link between themselves and their school more heavily when their school's football team was successful rather than unsuccessful. Although the researchers interpret this increase as an attempt to "bask in the reflected glory" of the team, these findings are also consistent with the many studies showing an increase in group cohesiveness immediately after group success (Cartwright, 1968).

Cohesiveness can also be assessed by calculating the group's ability to retain its members for prolonged periods of time. Self-report measures include asking people to indicate their desire to remain in the group (for instance, Marshall & Heslin, 1975), more behaviorally oriented approaches that give subjects the opportunity to leave the group before its tasks have been completed (for example, Anderson, 1975), and field approaches that examine actual membership turnover and resignation rates (such as Mobley et al., 1979).

PAPER-AND-PENCIL MEASURES OF GROUP COHESIVENESS

Group cohesiveness can be measured in many different ways, but investigators often rely on questionnaires since they are relatively easy to administer and interpret. In many cases, a researcher might measure the group members' perceptions of their group's unity with a single item, such as:

- Do you want to remain a member of this group (Schachter, 1951)?
- How did you like your team (Schachter et al., 1951)?
- How strong a sense of belonging do you feel you have to the people you work with (Indik, 1965)?

In contrast, other methods call for the use of multi-item *scales* that include many questions concerning cohesiveness; once a group member answers the items, his or her responses can then be combined to yield a single index of cohesiveness. For example, Rudolph H. Moos' *Group Environment Scale* (GES; Moos & Humphrey, 1974; Moos, Insel, & Humphrey, 1974) measures co-hesiveness by asking for yes/no answers to items such as:

- There is a feeling of unity and cohesion in this group.
- Members put a lot of energy into this group.

(An extremely useful instrument, the GES also contains subscales assessing degree of leader support, expressiveness, independence, task-orientation, self-discovery, anger/oppression, order/organization, leader control, and innovation in the group.) Similarly, sports researchers (for example, Martens, Landers, & Loy, 1972) often use the *Sports Cohesiveness Questionnaire* to assess group unity. This particular instrument includes items that focus on three aspects of group cohesiveness, including the strength of member-to-member bonds, the strength of member-to-group bonds, and perceptions of group unity (Carron, 1980; Carron & Chelladurai, 1981). In general, multi-item scales are superior to single-item measures.

While clearcut measures of cohesiveness were, of course, never collected for the advisory committee on the Bay of Pigs invasion, archival evidence suggests that cohesiveness was high in the group. Indeed, irrespective of the particular type of measure chosen, retrospective analysis points again and again to the unity of the group. First, the majority of the men on the committee were close personal friends, and at minimum confessed to a profound respect for one another. Undoubtedly, interpersonal attraction was strong among members. Second, later comments and memoirs are repleat with laudatory evaluations of the group, suggesting that attitudes toward the group were exceptionally positive. Third, identification with and commitment to the group and its goals were quite high, for all the members were proud to proclaim their membership in such an elite body. The magnitude of this identification is suggested by the frequent use of *we* and *us* in the following remark made by Robert Kennedy as he described the group (quoted in Guthman, 1971, p. 88; italics added):

> It seemed that with John Kennedy leading *us* and with all the talent he had assembled, nothing could stop *us*. *We* believed that if *we* faced up to the nation's problems and applied bold, new ideas with common sense and hard work, *we* would overcome whatever challenged *us*.

Lastly, the group retained all its members for the duration of the decision-making process, testimony to the strength of the forces working to keep members from leaving the group.

THE CONSEQUENCES OF COHESIVENESS

In his review of research dealing with cohesiveness, Dorwin Cartwright (1968) outlines a number of positive and negative consequences of in-group unity. On the positive side, enjoyment and satisfaction are usually much more pronounced in highly cohesive groups than in less cohesive groups. In closely knit groups members tend to participate more fully and communicate more frequently while absences are much less likely. Furthermore, Cartwright reviews studies indicating that people in cohesive groups experience heightened self-esteem and lowered anxiety, apparently because the group provides a source of security and protection. Such groups have also been found to be more effective than less cohesive groups in achieving goals that the members themselves consider to be important (although this finding may not necessarily entail heightened productivity or output), and increases in cohesiveness generally go hand in hand with increases in the group's capacity to retain its members. Thus, cohesiveness "contributes to a group's potency and vitality; it increases the significance of membership for those who belong to the group" (Cartwright, 1968, p. 91).

On the negative side of the ledger, cohesive groups exert a more powerful influence over their members than do noncohesive groups. In accord with Festinger's conceptualization of cohesiveness, if the individual is not attracted to the group but is being pressured to perform certain behaviors, then that person will probably simply terminate his or her membership. In highly cohesive groups, however, the resultant force acting upon the individual to remain in the group is very great. Therefore, the group can set up a correspondingly large degree of influence against the group member, who will remain in the group so long as these internal pressures don't exceed the resultant force produced by the group's cohesiveness (Festinger, 1950). Social-exchange theory leads to a similar prediction when it is assumed that cohesive groups offer members a satisfyingly high reward/cost ratio that far exceeds their comparison level for alternatives (Thibaut & Kelley, 1959).

At an empirical level, this theoretically predicted relationship between cohesiveness and group power has, for the most part, been confirmed. For example, studies reviewed by Cartwright indicated that people in cohesive groups tend to more readily accept the group's goals, decisions, and norms. Furthermore, and more closely related to the process of groupthink, people in cohesive groups are also more likely to evidence greater conformity during decision-making sessions. For example, in an early test of Festinger's theory of informal group communication (Festinger, 1950), cohesiveness was directly manipulated by telling subjects that they would either enjoy being in the group, since care had been taken in assembling highly compatible teams (*high-cohesiveness condition*) or that membership in the two-person groups would not be particularly pleasurable, since the members were clearly incompatible (*low-cohesiveness condition;* Back, 1951). Subsequent analyses revealed that when subjects discovered that they disagreed with their partners' interpretations of three ambiguous stimuli, they attempted to influence their partners more if they had been led to expect their groups to be cohesive. Additionally, conformity to the opinion of their partners also increased in the cohesive groups, apparently because of this added social pressure. Other evidence indicates that conformity to a contrived group opinion correlates significantly with sociometric indices of cohesiveness (Lott & Lott, 1961), members of cohesive groups tend to bring greater pressures to bear on dissenters (Festinger et al., 1952), and the more cohesive the group, the greater was the rejection of an unyielding deviant (Schachter, 1951). Furthermore, investigators have also found that the power of cohesive groups over their members can be further increased if members are trying hard to cooperate with one another (Thibaut & Stickland, 1956), if members are uncertain of their acceptance by the other members of the group (Dittes & Kelley, 1956; Harvey & Consalvi, 1960), and if attraction to particular members in the group is high (Sakurai, 1975).

A second, less-well-researched negative consequence of cohesiveness concerns the strength of hostile reactions to threats from outside sources. In one of the few studies in this area, two-person all-male groups were recruited to participate in a survey of college students' attitudes (Pepitone & Reichling, 1955). In half the sessions, the dyads were given cohesiveness instructions—supposedly they had been selected to work together because they possessed extremely compatible personality profiles. The other dyads were told that the researcher had been unable to schedule compatible pairs, and therefore the dyad members would probably not get along well together. The next step in the procedure called for insulting and degrading the subjects; thus, the investigators arranged for a third party to enter the experimental setting and verbally attack the groups. This third party, labeled the instigator, acted out as naturally and as realistically as possible the script presented in the box headed "How to Create Hostility in Groups." The researchers took the precaution of pretesting this step of the procedure to make certain that the instigator was sufficiently insulting, and, as one might expect after reading through the passage, most people who were subjected to this scathing attack felt that they had been unjustly criticized.

Following the attack, the groups were left on their own for six minutes, during which time an observer watched members' actions through a one-way mirror while listening via a hidden microphone. As anticipated, the cohesive groups, relative to the noncohesive groups, spent more of their time in the free-interaction period venting their hostilities (95.7 seconds versus 43.6 seconds). The members of cohesive groups also performed more unrestrained behaviors, criticized the instigator more harshly, and tended to complain more about the way they had been treated. Of course, at the end of the study the researchers discussed their hypotheses and procedures with the subjects, who had an opportunity to ask questions and express their feelings about the experience. Furthermore, before "the subjects were dismissed, apologies were tendered and, happily, in all cases accepted" (Pepitone & Reichling, 1955, p. 331).

COHESIVENESS AND GROUPTHINK

The members of the Bay of Pigs advisory committee probably felt they were fortunate to belong to a group that boasted such high morale and esprit de corps.

HOW TO CREATE HOSTILITY IN GROUPS

Instigator: (Enters after a deliberate, three-minute delay. To Assistant.) "Hello." (Looks annoyed.) "I see these groups finally got here. Do you have their application forms?"

Assistant: "Yes, here they are."

Instigator: (Looks through forms.) "This is terrible. How did these people get here?"

Assistant: "The campus doesn't have much to offer."

Instigator: "I can see that." (To one of the subjects.) "What's your name?" (To the other subject.) "And yours is?" (To one subject.) "How old are you?" (Sarcastically, before he answers.) "We don't want kids for this survey—we need mature adults." (To second subject.) "What's your age?" (Disgustedly, after person responds.) "That's just fine. Do either of you take part in any activities?" (Aside to Assistant.) "These people won't have any idea what's going on around campus." (To one participant.) "Do you ever go out with girls? How often?" (After response, cynically.) "Great!" (To other subject.) "And you?" (Moans as answer is given.) (To apparently poorer-dressed subject.) "Do you always come to appointments dressed like that?" (To Assistant.) "Well, let's see if we can use these groups anyway. I'll give them a sample question." (To one person.) "How do you feel about student-faculty relations on campus?" (Subject is cut off before completing the answer. To other subject.) "How about you?" (After response.) "Well, that's a profound observation!" (To Assistant.) "I can't waste the Association's time and money on drivel like this. I can't give them lab credit." (Volunteers had been promised an excuse from one lab paper.) "You might check with Professor Jason (fictitious) to find out if he can use them. He'll use almost anyone." (Exit.)

(Source: Pepitone & Reichling, 1955)

Problems could be handled without too much internal bickering, personality clashes were rare, the atmosphere of each meeting was congenial, and replacements were never needed since no one ever left the group. However, these benefits of cohesiveness did not offset one fatal consequence of a closely knit group: in-group pressures so strong that critical thinking degenerated into groupthink. Although Janis carefully explains that cohesive groups are not necessarily doomed to be victims of groupthink, he hypothesizes that a "high degree of *group cohesiveness* is conducive to a high frequency of *symptoms of groupthink,* which, in turn, are conducive to a high frequency of defects in decision-making" (Janis, 1972, p. 199).

A recent doctoral dissertation by John A. Courtright tested this hypothesis by examining the decision-making strategies of groups of male and female students discussing the question "What is the best method for recruiting new students to the university?" (Courtright, 1978). To manipulate the degree of cohesiveness in these zero-history, virtually leaderless groups, participants assigned to the high-cohesiveness condition were (1) allowed to interact with one another for ten extra minutes before considering the issue; (2) told that the members would be extremely compatible given participants' scores on a personality test; and (3) shown a bogus but realistic-looking graph illustrating the similarity of group members' opinions on a previously completed questionnaire. Subjects assigned to the low-cohesiveness condition were (1) not allowed a warm-up session as a group; (2) told that the attempt to bring together compatible people had failed and that there was no reason therefore to expect group members to like one another very much; and (3) shown a graph that illustrated the dissimilarity of members' opinions.

A second variable—constraints imposed on the group's discussion—was manipulated along with cohesiveness. This second variable had three levels:

1. A *freeing condition,* in which group members were told that sufficient time was available to fully discuss the issue, and that "the best solutions usually come from vigorous competition among a large number of incompatible ideas" (p. 233).
2. A *limiting condition,* in which the instructions suggested that little time was left for discussion and that "the best solutions usually come when one good idea cooperatively evolves from a small number of initial ideas" (p. 233).
3. A *no-instructions condition* that served as a control group.

Based on Janis' theory of groupthink, Courtright predicted that the two independent variables—cohesiveness and constraints on the group discussion—would interact to determine when poor decision making would occur. He predicted that groups in the freeing condition would formulate better decisions when they were cohesive rather than noncohesive but that this relationship would reverse when discussion was limited by time and cooperation restraints. In this condition cohesive group members would tend to agree more with one another, disagree less with one another, and formulate poorer decisions.

The results of the project provided partial support for these hypotheses. Although no differences occurred among the six experimental conditions in terms of number of solutions offered or degree of agreement within the group, the frequency of disagreement among members followed the predicted pattern. As Figure 12-2 reveals, among cohesive group members disagreement tended to be greatest in the freeing condition, less in the no-instruction condition, and least in the limiting condition—the very group that, theoretically, should have suffered from groupthink. Furthermore, these relationships tended to reverse in the low-cohesiveness condition, although the overall differences were not as pronounced.

Turning to the quality of the solution, Courtright arranged for independent judges to read and rate the quality of the groups' solutions to the issue on such dimensions as effectiveness, feasibility, creativity, and significance. Once more, the predicted interaction was statistically significant; the best solutions tended to come from the cohesive/freeing-instructions groups, while the worst solutions generally came from the cohesive/limiting-instructions groups.

Although Courtright's study provides fairly strong support for the adequacy of Janis' prediction concerning the relationship between cohesiveness and groupthink, several qualifications apply. First, the usual limitations of generalizing from a laboratory study involving college students to real-world policy-making groups are particularly relevant in this instance. Second, given that another study (to be discussed shortly) found little evidence of the effect of cohesiveness on the development of groupthink (Flowers, 1977), more research is needed before any firm conclusions can be drawn. Third, Courtright's study drives home Janis' caveat that highly cohesive groups need not always suffer from groupthink—rather, cohe-

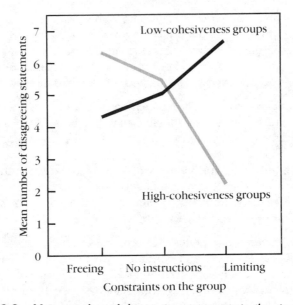

FIGURE 12-2. Mean number of disagreeing statements in the six experimental conditions of the Courtright experiment. (Source: Courtright, 1978. Reprinted by permission.)

siveness only sets the stage for the rise in in-group pressures that, when paired with other factors (in this case, limitations on the group discussion), can result in defective decision making.

Isolation, Leadership, and Decisional Conflict

One of the more obvious characteristics of the Bay of Pigs advisory committee was its *isolation* from outside experts. The members all felt that secrecy was a critical factor in planning the invasion, and that the fewer people knowing of the plan the better. The committee did not need to report its conclusions to anyone, including Congress, so there was no final review of the decision before putting the plan into action. This isolation also meant that very few outsiders ever came into the group to participate in the discussion, and thus the committee was virtually insulated from any possible criticisms. Therefore, while many experts on military questions and Cuban affairs were available and, if contacted, could have warned the group about the limitations of the plan, the committee closed itself off from these valuable resources.

President Kennedy's *style of leadership* in conducting the problem-solving sessions is another parameter of the group situation that contributed to groupthink. By tradition, the advisory committee meetings, like cabinet meetings, were very formal affairs that followed a rigid protocol. The president, as chairperson of the meeting, could completely control the group discussion by raising only certain questions and asking for input from particular conferees. Open, free-wheeling discussion was possible only at the suggestion of the president, but since Kennedy tended to follow traditions while also sanctioning any dissenting opinions, the group really never got down to the essential issues.

The leader's impact on the course of a group discussion was recently examined by Matie L. Flowers (1977) through the use of a role-playing procedure. She asked members of four-person mixed-sex groups to pretend they were part of an administrative team that had been given a perplexing problem by the local school board. The issue concerned what to do with a 62-year-old high school algebra teacher, a Miss Simpson, who was apparently so senile that she could no longer handle the duties of classroom teaching. Parents had begun complaining about the education her students were receiving, and the president of the local school board had requested that the committee formulate an immediate solution to the problem that would not involve the expenditure of additional funds. Flowers chose this particular problem in order to incorporate some of the many aspects noted by Janis in his archival studies of group decisions: a controversial problem with no clear solution, a situation with moral overtones, a time crisis, implied competition with an outside group (parents), and a lack of complete knowledge and background on which to base a solution.

Each member of the group was assigned a role to play. One individual, the leader, was designated the superintendent of schools and was thus responsible for running the meeting. Other roles included a principal of Miss Simpson's school, a school counselor, and a member of the school board. Each individual was also given a list of six or seven problem-relevant facts that they could raise during the discussion. For example, the superintendent knew that all the other schools in the district had supposedly refused to accept Miss Simpson as a transfer; the principal's fact sheet stated that Miss Simpson had suffered a mild stroke several years earlier; one of the counselor's facts described the large number of As and Bs given out by Miss Simpson to her students; and the school board member's sheet included the fact that, ten years earlier, the board member had enjoyed an English class under Miss Simpson.

The "superintendent of schools" had been previously trained to adopt either an *open* or *closed* style of leadership. Open leaders didn't describe their solution to the problem until the other members had made their recommendations, they encouraged open discussion, and at two times during the meeting stated "The most important thing, I think, is that we air all possible viewpoints in order to reach a wise decision. Now, what does each of you think should be done?" (Flowers, 1977, p. 891). In contrast, the closed leaders described their solution before yielding the floor to the other participants, limited discussion whenever possible, and at two times during the meeting stated "The most important thing, I think, is that we all agree on our decision. Now, what I think should be done is. . . ." (The cohesiveness of the groups was also manipulated by examining two types of teams—those composed of strangers and those composed of friends—but in contrast to Courtright's study this manipulation yielded few effects.)

Flowers' content analysis of tape recordings of the problem-solving sessions focused on two primary dependent variables: the number of different solutions proposed during the 30- to 45-minute period and the number of facts (taken from the role assignment sheets) that emerged during the group discussion. As expected, the leader's behavior produced obvious effects during the discussion. The number of solutions proposed was higher in the open-leader condition than in the closed-leader condition (the respective means were 6.5 and 5.1), and prior to the reaching of a solution more facts were mentioned in the open leadership group than in the closed leadership group (the means were 15.5 and 8.2). Thus, while little support was found for Janis' cohesiveness prediction, the effects of leadership were both pervasive and hypothesis confirming.

A final variable listed by Janis as an important cause of groupthink concerns the degree of *pressure on the group* to arrive at a "good" decision. Although intuitively one might think that the more important the issue at hand, the more carefully the group members would consider their solution, Janis suggests that the opposite case is more likely. In general, as the importance of the problem to be solved increases, group members become more concerned with reducing their misgivings about their answer and less concerned with processing information rationally and adequately. According to Janis, people make decisions only with great reluctance and are "beset by conflict, doubts, and worry, struggling with incongruous longings, antipathies, and loyalties, and seeking relief by procrastinating, rationalizing, or denying responsibility for choices" (Janis & Mann, 1977, p. 15). These tendencies become especially pronounced when consequential, ego-involving decisions must be formulated, and can thereby further undermine efficient problem solving.

As an example, try to recall the thoughts and feelings you experienced when you found yourself in a situation that required a choice between several alternatives. Such a decision might concern which college to attend, which of three job offers to accept, whether to quit a job, or whether to terminate an intimate relationship. All these decisions will culminate in personally important long-range consequences. Yet it is in precisely these kinds of situations that we often fall prey to a number of coping strategies that, while adaptive in helping us deal with our **decisional conflict,** are maladaptive in terms of making the decision (Janis, 1959; Janis & Mann, 1977). For example, we may simply avoid making the decision altogether, and hence *procrastinate* our way out of the dilemma. Alternatively, we may quickly but arbitrarily formulate a decision without thinking things through completely, but then *bolster* our preferred solution by exaggerating the favorable consequences and minimizing the importance and likelihood of unfavorable consequences. A group can *deny responsibility* by delegating the decision to a subcommittee or by diffusing accountability throughout the entire assemblage. Decision makers can also utilize the fine art of *muddling through* (Lindblom, 1965) by considering "only a very narrow range of policy alternatives that differ to only a small degree from the existing policy" (Janis & Mann, 1977, p. 33). Members can also reduce decisional conflict by using *satisficing* strategies: accepting as satisfactory any solution that meets only a minimal set of criteria instead of working to find the best solution. While superior solutions to the problem may exist, the "satisficer" is content with any alternative that surpasses the minimal cutoff point. Lastly, as is consistent with *The Law of Triviality* (see the box), the group may avoid dealing with larger issues simply by focusing on minor issues. All in all, these strategies may help the group members deal with decisional conflicts, but in the long run they will lead to groupthink.

THE LAW OF TRIVIALITY

British humorist C. Northcote Parkinson, perhaps best known for the "law" that bears his name—work expands so as to fill the time available for its completion—also argues for the validity of the "law of triviality"—the time spent on any item of the agenda will be in inverse proportion to the consequentiality of the item (Parkinson, 1957, paraphrased from page 24). Providing a fictitious example, he describes a finance committee dealing with Item 9 on a long agenda—a $10 million allocation to build a nuclear reactor. Discussion is terse, lasts about two and a half

minutes, and the committee unanimously approves the item. However, when the group turns to Item 10—the allocation of $2350 to build a bicycle shed to be used by the office staff—everyone on the committee has something to say. As Parkinson explains, "A sum of $2350 is well within everybody's comprehension. Everybody can visualize a bicycle shed. Discussion goes on, therefore, for forty-five minutes, with the possible result of saving some $300. Members at length sit back with a feeling of achievement" (p. 30).

Polarization Processes

In 1961 newly elected President John F. Kennedy was asked to finalize and approve the plan for the invasion of Cuba. As we saw earlier, the plan itself had been carefully designed by U.S. intelligence officers, but the scheme was still a risky one; success depended upon the falling into place of certain key factors, but a victory would earn the United States many rewards. Kennedy faced a host of complicated questions in trying to decide to implement the plan: Are the risks too great? Do the positive consequences of a successful attack justify the risks involved? Should steps be taken to reduce the risks and thereby ensure victory? Naturally, he could have answered these questions without consulting anyone, but he decided instead to form a group to explore these issues. While historians cannot say why he relied on a group, he may have acted on the intuitively appealing notion that group solutions tend to be more conservative and cautious than individuals' solutions. Unfortunately for Kennedy, his advisors, and the members of the attack force, in this instance the assumption that groups are conservative turned out to be a myth.

THE DISCOVERY OF THE RISKY SHIFT

At about the time that Kennedy's advisory committee was grappling with the problems inherent in the invasion plan, group dynamicists were initiating studies of the effects of group discussion on decision making. While several of these investigations suggested that groups do indeed offer more conservative solutions than individuals (for example, Atthowe, 1961; Hunt & Rowe, 1960), in others a surprising shift in the direction of greater riskiness was found after group interaction (Stoner, 1961; Wallach, Kogan, & Bem, 1962). For example, in one of the most frequently cited projects male and female college students responded to twelve story problems individually and in small groups (Wallach et al., 1962). All the problems used in the investigation followed the same basic form, each one describing a hypothetical situation in which an individual had to choose between one of two possible courses of action. Unfortunately for the decision maker, the alternative that offered the more desirable rewards was also the course of action least likely to be carried out successfully. The question put to the subject after reading each situation was "What would the probability of success have to be before you would advise the character in the story to choose the riskier course of action?" The box headed "Item Number One . . ." presents the first story item from this "Choice-Dilemmas Questionnaire" along with the format used to measure subjects' responses.

To test for changes following group discussion, the investigators followed a fairly simple procedure. First, subjects filled out and turned in their answers to the choice dilemmas. Second, they discussed the items in five- or six-person groups in an attempt to reach a unanimous decision concerning the degree of tolerable risk. Third, the group members were instructed to separate and once more answer the questions to determine if the change induced by the group setting had any carry-over effects. In addition, (1) a control condition was included in which subjects merely filled out the questionnaire twice without an intervening discussion; (2) some subjects were contacted several weeks after the session and asked to complete the questionnaire again.

Table 12-1 contains the results of the investigation. In adding together choices from all 12 items, the investigators found that the mean of prediscussion individual decisions was 66.9 for males and 65.6 for females. The mean of the group's consensual decision, however, was 57.5 for males and 56.2 for females—a shift of 9.4 points in the direction of greater risk. As Table 12-1 reveals, this shift also occurred when individual judgments were collected after the group discussion and when the individual postdiscussion measures were delayed two to six weeks (the

---

ITEM NUMBER ONE FROM THE CHOICE-DILEMMAS QUESTIONNAIRE

Mr. A, an electrical engineer who is married and has one child, has been working for a large electronics corporation since graduating from college five years ago. He is assured of a lifetime job with a modest, though adequate, salary and liberal pension benefits upon retirement. On the other hand, it is very unlikely that his salary will increase much before he retires. While attending a convention, Mr. A is offered a job with a small, newly founded company which has a highly uncertain future. The new job would pay more to start and would offer the possibility of a share in the ownership if the company survived the competition of the larger firms.

Imagine that you are advising Mr. A. Listed below are several probabilities or odds of the new company proving financially sound. Please check the *lowest* probability that you would consider acceptable to make it worthwhile for Mr. A to take the new job.

____ The chances are 1 in 10 that the company will prove financially sound.
____ The chances are 3 in 10 that the company will prove financially sound.
____ The chances are 5 in 10 that the company will prove financially sound.
____ The chances are 7 in 10 that the company will prove financially sound.
____ The chances are 9 in 10 that the company will prove financially sound.
____ Place a check here if you think Mr. A should *not* take the new job no matter what the probabilities.

(Source: Wallach, Kogan, and Bem, 1962)

TABLE 12-1. Shifts toward risk following group discussion

Comparison	Males	Females
Individual pretest versus group decision	−9.4	−9.4
Individual pretest versus individual posttest	−10.4	−8.2
Individual pretest versus individual delayed posttest	−12.3	——

Note. Negative scores indicate a shift in the direction of greater risk.
(Source: Wallach, Kogan, and Bem, 1962)

delayed posttests were collected from male subjects only). Lastly, participants in the no-group-discussion control condition shifted very little.

The finding that groups seem to make riskier decisions than individuals was promptly dubbed the **risky-shift phenomenon** and in the decade from 1960 to 1970 hundreds and hundreds of studies were conducted in an attempt to better understand this rara avis. During that period studies demonstrated that the risky shift was not limited to the types of decisions required on the choice-dilemmas questionnaire, but that group discussion seemed to intensify all sorts of attitudes, beliefs, values, judgments, and perceptions (Myers, 1982). The shift was reliably demonstrated in many countries around the world (for example, Canada, the United States, England, France, Germany, New Zealand) and with many different kinds of group participants (Pruitt, 1971a). Although commentators sometimes wondered about the generality and significance of the phenomenon (Smith, 1972), laboratory findings were eventually bolstered by field studies (Lamm & Myers, 1978).

During this research period, however, some investigators hinted at the possibility of the directly opposite process: *a cautious shift.* For example, when the early risky-shift researchers examined the amount of postdiscussion change revealed on each item of the choice-dilemma questionnaire, they frequently found that group members consistently advocated a less risky course of action than did individuals on one particular item (Wallach et al., 1962). Intrigued by this anomalous finding, subsequent researchers wrote additional choice dilemmas and they too occasionally found evidence of a cautious shift. Then in 1969 researchers reported evidence of individuals moving in *both* directions after a group discussion, suggesting that both cautious and risky shifts were possible (Doise, 1969; Moscovici & Zavalloni, 1969).

Somewhat belatedly, group dynamicists realized that risky shifts after group discussions were a part of a larger, more general process. When people discuss issues in groups, there is a tendency for them to decide upon a more extreme course of action than would be suggested by the average of their individual judgments, but the direction of this shift depends upon what was initially the dominant point of view. After examining dozens of risky-shift studies in this light, David G. Myers and Helmut Lamm (1976, p. 603; Lamm & Myers, 1978) summarized the many findings in terms of the **group-polarization hypothesis:** "The average postgroup response will tend to be more extreme in the same direction as the average of the pregroup responses." As graphically depicted in the box headed "Group Polarization," when the average choice of the group members—before discussion—was closer to the risky pole of the continuum than to the cautious pole (as would be the case in a group composed of persons A, B, C, and D), then

GROUP POLARIZATION

If the group members were working on an item from the choice-dilemmas questionnaire such as that one presented in the box headed "Item Number One . . ." they could vary in their choices from 1 (risky) to 10 (cautious). If Group 1 included Person A (who chose 1), B (who chose 3), C and D (who both chose 5), then the average of pregroup choices would be (1 + 3 + 5 + 5)/4 or 3.5. Because this mean is less than 5, a risky shift would most likely occur in Group 1. If, in contrast, Group 2 contained persons C, D, E, and F, their pregroup average would be (5 + 5 + 7 + 9)/4 or 6.5. Because this mean is closer to the caution pole, a conservative shift would most likely occur in the group.

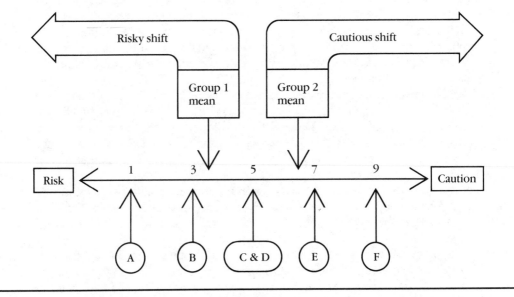

a risky shift will occur. If, in contrast, the group was composed of persons C, D, E, and F, then a cautious shift would take place, since the pregroup mean of 6.5 falls closer to the cautious pole. This example is, of course, something of an oversimplification, since the shift depends upon distance from the psychological rather than the mathematical midpoint of the scale. As Myers and Lamm (1976) note, on choice dilemmas an initial pregroup mean of 6 or smaller is usually sufficient to produce a risky shift, while a mean of 7 or greater is necessary to produce a cautious shift. If the pregroup mean falls between 6 and 7, shifting is unlikely.

POLARIZATION PROCESSES AND GROUPTHINK

Although Janis does not emphasize polarization as a major antecedent of faulty group decision making, he clearly hints at this possibility when he states that "members show interest in facts and opinions that support their initially preferred policy and take up time in their meetings to discuss them, but they tend to ignore facts and opinions that do not support their initially preferred policy" (1972, p.

10). In concordance with Janis' viewpoint, Lamm and Myers (1978) cite a number of studies in which, after engaging in group discussions, subjects became more aggressive, made more extreme and unreasonable demands, became more competitive, and formulated more negative appraisals of out-group members. For example, in one particularly relevant study, college students, army officers, and ROTC cadets made decisions about how the U.S. armed forces should best deal with an international conflict involving the United States and another world power. Each of the hypothetical problems centered around a potential military crisis, and the decision makers were asked to select one course of action from a list of alternatives ranging from bilateral negotiation to the use of nuclear weapons. Consistent with the polarization hypothesis, the "dovish" college students shifted in the direction of less militaristic responses after group discussion, while the "hawkish" army officers advocated even more forceful tactics after the group meeting. The ROTC cadets, who began at an intermediate position on the six problems, shifted very little (Semmell, 1976).

Such studies suggest that polarization may have contributed to the faulty decision making that went into the Bay of Pigs invasion plan, but significant empirical questions still remain unanswered. First, while polarization has been established as a stable group phenomenon, too much of the published research relies on artificial, uninvolving decisions; before these results are accepted as applicable to groupthink crises, they need to be replicated in more naturalistic settings. Second, while continued empirical probing has resulted in the virtual elimination of the early theories dealing with choice shifts, experts remain divided in their discussions of the persuasion and value approaches (see Burnstein & Vinokur, 1977; Lamm & Myers, 1978; Miller, 1978; Sanders & Baron, 1977; Stasser, Kerr, & Davis, 1980). As explained in the box headed "The Path of Progress and Theories . . .", some favor a **persuasive-arguments approach,** emphasizing the distribution of arguments among members. Others strongly endorse a **social-comparison** approach derived from the general value theories in which a decision must await the accumulation of additional data. Lastly, while studies have succeeded in illuminating the kinds of situations in which polarization is most likely to occur, researchers have yet to explore ways of reducing or preventing decision extremization during group discussion. The question of prevention, however, is the topic of the final section of this chapter.

Preventing Groupthink

For thirteen days in October of 1962 the world swayed on the brink of nuclear holocaust. The Soviet Union, perhaps at the request of a Cuban government frightened by the misguided Bay of Pigs invasion, was rapidly constructing a missile base on Cuban soil that, once completed, would be capable of launching nuclear weapons that could wipe out more than 80 million Americans. To seek a solution to this crisis, the president of the United States—again, John F. Kennedy—called together his top advisors to form the Executive Committee of the National Security Council. Though somewhat larger than the Bay of Pigs advisory group, many of the same individuals attended Executive Committee meetings. For five days these men considered the issues, debated possible solutions, and disagreed

THE PATH OF PROGRESS AND THEORIES OF GROUP POLARIZATION

Group dynamicists have been prolific in their attempts to explain the causes of risky shifts, cautious shifts, and polarization in groups. Briefly tracing the theoretical roots of current perspectives on the issue, we find that the earliest period of research (which focused almost exclusively on risky shifts) generated a number of explanations:

1. *Diffusion-of-responsibility theory.* Group members, feeling that they have less personal responsibility for the negative consequences of excessively risky decisions when the decision is a group effort, experience less anxiety over recommending a risky course of action.
2. *Leadership theories.* Shifts occur because high-risk takers tend to exercise more influence over the group members due to their greater persuasiveness, confidence, assertiveness, and involvement in the discussion.
3. *Familiarization theory.* As individuals discuss the problems with others they become more familiar with the items; as familiarity increases, uncertainty decreases, creating a willingness to advocate more risky alternatives.
4. *Value theories.* Since taking risks and dares is a positively valued attribute in many cultures, participants prefer to think of themselves (and

prefer to be seen by others) as willing to take a chance; when members discover that others in the group favor riskier alternatives, they change their original positions to agree with the riskiest group member.

Although most theorists came to endorse the "value" perspective (for example, Clark, 1971; Dion, Baron, & Miller, 1970; Myers & Lamm, 1975, 1976; Pruitt, 1971a, 1971b; Vinokur, 1971), two schools of thought later developed *within* this general approach. On the one hand, *persuasive-arguments theorists* proposed that group members shift in the direction of the "valued" pole (either risk or caution) because the members can generate more arguments favoring the more valued pole (Burnstein & Vinokur, 1973, 1977; Vinokur & Burnstein, 1974, 1978). In contrast, *social-comparison theorists* suggest that polarization stems from the general tendency to compare one's viewpoints with those of other group members (Goethals & Zanna, 1979; Myers & Lamm, 1976; Myers, 1978; Myers et al., 1980; Sanders & Baron, 1977). Although both perspectives have some merit, at this point the theoretical issues remain unresolved.

---

over strategies until they hammered out a plan that involved a naval blockade of all Cuban ports. Although the Soviet Union denounced the naval quarantine as "piracy," ships believed to be carrying nuclear armaments were successfully directed away from Cuba. Eventually, the Cuban missile crisis was resolved, as the Russians agreed to dismantle the launch sites while the Americans promised never to invade Cuba.

The parallels between the two decisions—the Bay of Pigs invasion and the resolution of the Cuban missile crisis—and the two groups that worked on each plan are obvious. To a large extent both decisions were formulated by the same people, meeting in the same room, guided by the same leader, and working equally hard under the same time pressures. Both crises occurred in reference to the same area of the world, involved the same foreign powers, and could have led to equally serious consequences. Yet despite these similarities, the Executive Committee worked with admirable precision and effectiveness. Members thoroughly analyzed a wide range of alternative courses of action, deliberately considered and then reconsidered the potential effects of their actions, consulted experts, and made detailed contingency plans in case the blockade failed to stop the Russians. Clearly, this group, in contrast to its unfortunate predecessor, avoided the pitfall of groupthink. Janis (1972) feels that three sets of factors led to this beneficial about-face: limiting premature concurrence seeking, correcting group members' misperceptions, and utilizing effective decision techniques.

Limiting Premature Concurrence Seeking

When it became obvious that the Cuban invaders had failed in their quest, the members of the advisory committee reacted with self-condemnation and outrage over their shortsightedness. The members did not, however, blame one another or become demoralized or bitter. Rather, they realized they had failed and willingly shouldered the blame, but at the same time they managed to maintain their cohesiveness. Thus, at the time of the Cuban missile crisis the core of the newly formed Executive Committee was still highly cohesive and had the potential to become a victim of groupthink once more.

However, President Kennedy had not taken his failure lightly. In the months following the Bay of Pigs fiasco, he set up a commission of inquiry to locate the source of the debacle. Then, acting on this information and on his own hunches, he insititued a number of procedural changes that improved communication, promoted independent thinking, and altered the atmosphere of the meetings. In many respects these changes worked to limit premature concurrence seeking without sacrificing group cohesion.

PROMOTING OPEN INQUIRY

While debating their proposed solutions to the missile crisis, the group members rarely succumbed to conformity pressures. In Robert Kennedy's words, tensions and conflicts ran high: "And so we argued, and so we disagreed—all dedicated, intelligent men, disagreeing and fighting about the future of their country, and of mankind" (1969, p. 35). This dissension, however, was beneficial: no norm of conformity was given the slightest opportunity to develop, and each person in the group was able to express doubts and worries openly. Rules of discussion were suspended, agendas avoided, and new ideas were welcomed. Although pressures to conform surfaced from time to time during the discussion, the members felt so comfortable in their roles of skeptical critical thinkers that they were able to resist the temptation to go along with the consensus. In fact, the group never did reach 100% agreement on the decision to turn back Soviet ships.

EFFECTIVE LEADERSHIP

The atmosphere of open inquiry can be credited to changes designed and implemented by Kennedy. He not only diagnosed the sources of his earlier errors, but also successfully moderated his directiveness in order to avoid the creation of pressures towards uniformity. Essentially, he dropped his closed style of leadership to become an open leader as he (1) carefully refused to state his personal beliefs at the beginning of the session, instead waiting until others had let their views be known; (2) required a full unbiased discussion of the pros and cons of each possible course of action; (3) convinced his subordinates that he would welcome healthy criticism but condemn "yea-saying;" and (4) arranged for the group to meet without him on several occasions. Although some observers interpreted his refusal to rule the meetings with an authoritarian hand as a sign of weakness, the results more than justified Kennedy's open leadership approach.

MULTIPLE GROUPS

To further break down pressures to conform unthinkingly to the majority opinion, Kennedy arranged for the members to meet separately in two subgroups. The committee members had practiced this approach on other policy-issue decisions, and the members were satisfied that it yielded many benefits: arbitrary agreement with the views of the other subgroup was impossible, the lower level staff members felt more at ease expressing their viewpoints in the smaller meetings, and the presence of two coalitions in the subsequent combined meetings virtually guaranteed a spirited debate. Generalizing this approach to other situations, Janis and his colleague Daniel D. Wheeler suggest that organizations that rely on groups as vehicles for decision making should use this duplicating process:

> If groupthink takes over in one of the groups, the contrasting recommendation from the other group might serve as a caution. A new or combined group can explore the reasons for the difference and make a single recommendation. If the two groups agree in their findings, it is less likely that either group has overlooked or ignored any of the important considerations. The decision can be implemented with more confidence than if only a single group had worked on it [Wheeler & Janis, 1980, p. 207].

THE DEVIL'S ADVOCATE

During the group discussions and in private meetings, President Kennedy encouraged his brother Robert to play the role of the devil's advocate by trying to find fault with any argument that might be offered as valid (see the box headed "Formalizing Dissent"). Accordingly, the younger Kennedy would continually raise questions about undiscussed consequences and potentially ruinous oversights, a practice that failed to earn him a place of popularity in the group. However, the undeniable benefits of Kennedy's argumentativeness—forcing discussion of both sides of any proposal while motivating members to present their ideas more carefully—outweighed the harmful effects of increased interpersonal conflict. Furthermore, Janis suggests that the stresses created by having to disagree continually with one's coparticipants can be reduced if (1) the devil's advocate is careful to

---

FORMALIZING DISSENT

The term "devil's advocate" originated centuries ago during investigations of proposals for sainthood in the Roman Catholic Church. Because such decisions were critically important to the church and its members, the deciding panel felt that explicit, formalized procedures should be used to guarantee examination of both supporting and disconfirming evidence. Hence, the position of devil's advocate was developed to ensure that someone would explore and present any information that might lead to the disqualification of the candidate for sainthood. The technique is now utilized by many legal, corporate, academic, and parliamentary decision-making bodies with positive results (Herbert & Estes, 1977).

present his or her arguments in a low-key, nonthreatening manner; (2) the leader publicly and unambiguously assigns the role; and (3) the role is shifted from one group member to another.

Correcting Misperceptions and Errors

Janis' image of people as reluctant decision makers does not quite match the Executive Committee members. The participants fully realized that *some* course of action had to be taken, and they resigned themselves to their difficult task. Their decisional conflict was fanned by doubts and worries over questions they could not answer, and at times they must have been tempted to ease their discomfort by overestimating American superiority, belittling the Russians, and denying the magnitude of the dangers. Yet, through vigilant appraisal of the crisis situation they succeeded in avoiding these misperceptions, illusions, and errors.

ACKNOWLEDGING LIMITATIONS

No trace of the air of confidence and superiority that permeated the planning sessions of the Bay of Pigs invasion was in evidence during the Executive Committee meetings. The men knew that they, and their decision, were imperfect and that wishful thinking would not improve the situation. President Kennedy repeatedly told the group that there was no room for error, miscalculation, or oversight in their plans, and at every meeting the members openly admitted the tremendous risks and dangers involved in taking coercive steps against the Russians. Each solution was assumed to be flawed, and even when the blockade was painstakingly arranged the members developed contingency plans should the naval intervention fail.

Members also admitted their personal inadequacies and ignorance, and therefore willingly consulted experts who were not members of the group. No group member's statements were taken as fact until independently verified, and the ideas of younger, lower level staff members were solicited at each discussion. Participants also discussed the group's activities with their own staffs, and entered each meeting armed with the misgivings and criticisms of these unbiased outsiders.

Lastly, instead of assuming that the Russians' "immoral," "warlike" actions justified any response (including full-scale invasion of Cuba), the committee discussed the ethics of the situation and the proposed solutions. For example, while some members felt that the Russians left themselves open to any violent response the Americans deemed appropriate, the majority argued that a final course of action had to be consistent with "America's humanitarian heritage and ideals" (Janis, 1972, p. 157). Illusions of morality and invulnerability were successfully minimized.

EMPATHIZING

Tempers flared in the first meeting of the Executive Committee as members expressed their anger over Russia's action, but the men soon realized that their emotions were clouding their thinking. Reacting at a more empathic level, they tried to understand why the Russians had started constructing the missiles and how they would respond to the blockade. Soviet leaders, especially Premier Khrushchev, were credited with intelligence, insight, and caution, and the typical assumption that the enemy was bent on total destruction of the United States was rejected. Nonhumiliation also became a theme during the group's deliberations, as President Kennedy continually insisted that the American response should not humiliate, threaten, or embarrass Khrushchev. Press releases initiated in the meetings went so far as to compliment the Soviet premier on his statesmanship and diplomacy. Kennedy hoped that by leaving the premier a "way out" of the crisis an all-out war could be avoided, and he was ever careful in making certain his messages to the Kremlin sounded more like requests and suggestions than threats and ultimatums. As Robert Kennedy later stated, "A final lesson of the Cuban missile crisis is the importance of placing ourselves in the other country's shoes" (1969, p. 124).

SECOND-CHANCE MEETINGS

In listing possible ways to correct errors in perceptions, Janis (1972, p. 218) suggests that groups should "hold a 'second-chance' meeting at which every member is expected to express as vividly as he can all his residual doubts and to rethink the entire issue before making a definite choice." The Executive Committee frequently held such meetings, and the conferees needed little urging to criticize their plans, construct imaginative but black scenarios of the possible consequences, and openly express their doubts. Janis suggests that the second-chance meeting is most appropriate when the group moves to a consensus on an important issue too quickly and he endorses the strategy used by Alfred P. Sloan, the outstanding executive who designed and implemented the organizational structure of the monolithic corporation, General Motors. Supposedly Sloan, while running a meeting of his executives, once announced,

> Gentlemen, I take it we are all in complete agreement on the decision here. . . . Then I propose we postpone further discussion of this matter until our next meeting to give ourselves time to develop disagreement and perhaps gain some understanding of what the decision is all about [quoted in Drucker, 1966, p. 148].

Janis also recommends that the second-chance meeting be held in a different, more relaxing setting, citing as precedent the decisional methods of the ancient Persians. As Herodotus reported in about 45 B.C., the Persians always made their decisions twice, once sober and once while enjoying the liberating influence of wine.

Effective Decision Techniques

Janis did not cite the Executive Committee as an example of a "good" decision-making body simply because its solution to the missile crisis worked. Rather, Janis felt that—just as the Bay of Pigs advisors "deserved" to fail given the approach they took to the problem—the Executive Committee "deserved" to succeed, since it used effective, time-proven decision-making techniques. For example, an early push to agree on a military intervention as the best solution was quick to be rejected by the majority of the members, who instead insisted that other alternatives be explored. This demand led to an expanded search for alternatives, and soon a list that ran from a "hands-off" policy to full military involvement was developed. The ten most seriously discussed alternatives were these:

1. Doing nothing
2. Exerting pressure on the Soviet Union through the United Nations
3. Arranging a summit meeting between the two nations' leaders
4. Secretly negotiating with Castro
5. Initiating a low-level naval action involving a blockade of Cuban ports
6. Bombarding the sites with small pellets, rendering the missiles inoperable
7. Launching a surgical air strike with advance warning to reduce loss of life
8. Launching a surgical air strike without advance warning
9. Carrying out a series of air attacks against all Cuban military installations
10. Invading Cuba

Once this listing of alternatives was complete, the men focused on each course of action before moving on to the next. They considered the pros and cons, fleshed out unanticipated drawbacks, and estimated the likelihood of successful implementation. During this process outside experts were consulted to give the members a better handle on the problem and contingency plans to follow in case of failure were briefly explored. Even those alternatives that had initially been rejected (for example, doing nothing) were resurrected and discussed, and the group invested considerable effort in trying to find any overlooked detail. When consensus on the blockade plan finally developed, the group went back over this alternative, reconsidered its problematic aspects, and meticulously reviewed the steps required in its implementation. Messages were sent to the Russians, military strategies were worked out to prevent any conflict-escalating slip-ups, and a graded series of actions to undertake should the blockade fail was developed. Allies were contacted and told of the U.S. intentions, the legal basis of the intervention was established by arranging for a hemispherewide blockade sanctioned by the Organization of American States, and African countries with airports that could have been used by Russia to circumvent the naval blockade were warned not to cooperate. To quote Robert Kennedy once more, "nothing, whether a weighty matter or a small detail, was overlooked" (1969, p. 60).

The techniques utilized by Kennedy and his team conform well to a model of decision making recommended by Janis and his colleagues (Janis & Mann, 1977; Wheeler & Janis, 1980). During Stage 1 the group must *accept the challenge* by electing to seek the best possible solution. While tendencies toward defensive avoidance may create complacency on the part of the members, the group needs to confront the crisis while deciding what procedures to utilize in seeking a solution. This initial stage of the process represents an important starting point, and research has shown that groups that skip this first step by failing to consider procedural matters will, in the long run, end up with poorer solutions (Hirokawa, 1980). Stage 2, however, is also critical, for at this juncture the group must *search for alternatives*. Alternatives are not evaluated at this point, but only listed, and group members must mainly concentrate on conducting a thorough search. Good ideas may be missed by prematurely terminating this stage, and Janis suggests that brainstorming rules or the synectics spectrum policy, discussed briefly in Chapter 6, may help to ensure a more adequate range of solutions.

Stage 3 probably takes the most time, for it requires the systematic *evaluation of alternatives* developed during Stage 2. Effective group decision makers must research each course of action, and try to rely only on facts that can be objectively verified. Through forecasting the consequences of the alternatives should be predicted, and a careful balance sheet should be kept for both the pros and cons. To be fair, all alternatives are given full consideration, even those that were initially viewed with disfavor.

Stages 4 and 5 represent the culmination of the procedure. It is hoped that by the end of Stage 3 the members have shifted toward a consensus, so the goal of the fourth stage is to turn this consensus into *commitment to the decision*. A full-scale second-chance meeting should be held, the final choice restudied, and contingency plans ironed out. When the decision is at last made, Stage 5—*adherence to the decision*—officially begins as the group puts the plan in motion. In some cases strategies must be changed, unforeseen setbacks overcome, and contingency plans redesigned, but the members should be willing to follow through on their decision.

Thus, Janis' five-stage model calls for accepting the challenge, searching for alternatives, evaluating alternatives, becoming committed, and adhering to the decision. Although he does admit that this sequence may be inappropriate in some instances and that even rigorous adherence to the five steps does not guarantee success, Janis recommends the method as an effective preventative of groupthink.

Summary

Groupthink is a strong concurrence-seeking tendency that interferes with effective group decision making. This process, which is believed to be responsible for many fiascoes and blunders perpetrated by groups—such as the decision to invade Cuba at the Bay of Pigs—can potentially occur whenever members strive for solidarity and cohesiveness to such an extent that any questions or topics that could lead to disputes are avoided.

In describing the *symptoms* of groupthink, Irving Janis emphasizes premature concurrence seeking (high conformity pressures, self-censorship of dissenting ideas, mindguards, and apparent unanimity) and various illusions and misperceptions (illusions of invulnerability and morality, biases in perceptions of the out-group, and collective rationalizing), but when considering the *causes* of groupthink he focuses on a more limited set of conditions. First and foremost, Janis predicts that groupthink occurs only in highly cohesive groups where pressures to conform are strong, and this hypothesis has been partially supported experimentally. Second, groupthink is more likely to occur in isolated groups, if the leader adopts a closed rather than open style, and if the group is working on a crucially important but extremely complicated issue. Third, polarization mechanisms can work to undermine the group's decision by shifting opinions toward the extremes.

Turning to ways to prevent poor decision making, Janis notes that groups need not sacrifice cohesiveness in order to avoid the pitfall of groupthink. To limit premature concurrence seeking, Janis recommends promoting an atmosphere of *open inquiry* in the group through effective leadership, establishing multiple decisional groups, and including a devil's advocate in all group discussions. *Misperceptions and errors* can also be corrected if the group members are careful to acknowledge their limitations, empathize with out-groups, and hold second-chance meetings to reconsider decisions. Lastly, the group members can be more certain that their final solution is adequate if they employ effective *decisional strategies* during their deliberations. Although decision making involves many steps, Janis and his colleagues emphasize five key stages, including accepting the challenge, searching for alternatives, evaluating alternatives, becoming committed, and adhering to the decision.

13

Conflict Between Groups

$\mathbf{T}$he experiment finally got under way on June 19, 1954. The preceding months had been taken up with careful preparations and planning as the research team headed by Muzafer and Carolyn Sherif (Sherif, Harvey, White, Hood, & Sherif, 1961) formulated hypotheses, selected subjects, and designed an experimental procedure. Already more than 300 hours had been spent solely in finding and recruiting the 22 subjects for the study—a homogeneous group of 11-year-old boys attending the fifth grade in Oklahoma City schools. Their teachers had been interviewed, their academic records scrutinized, their family backgrounds noted, and their behavior in school and on the playground unobtrusively observed. The researchers sought "average" adolescent males; "normal, well-adjusted boys of the same age, educational level, from similar sociocultural backgrounds and with no unusual features in their personal backgrounds" (Sherif et al., 1961, p. 59).

The parents of these 22 boys paid a nominal $25 fee, signed some consent forms, and packed their sons off to a three-week summer camp. For ethical reasons the parents had been told that the camp was actually part of a research project in intergroup relations, but the boys themselves knew nothing of the camp's true purpose. They were transported by buses to the 200-acre campsite, which had been carefully selected because it could offer many activities that would appeal to the young campers while remaining isolated from outsiders. The site was situated in the Sans Bois Mountains in southeastern Oklahoma in the midst of Robbers Cave State Park, which took its name from a cave that was located very near the boys' campsite. Later the study would be known as the **Robbers Cave Experiment.**

During Stage 1 of the research the experimenters created two separate groups of 11 members each. Basing their strategy on earlier studies (Sherif & Sherif, 1953; Sherif, White, & Harvey, 1955), the staff brought the children to camp in two separate trips and strictly segregated the two factions for one week. During that week the boys camped, hiked, swam, and played sports while group norms, roles, and intragroup structures developed naturally. Leaders and captains for the baseball teams emerged as status hierarchies formed, and territories within the camp were quickly established (see Figure 13-1). The two groups invented names and slogans for their "gangs"—the Rattlers and the Eagles—and stenciled these names on their shirts and painted them onto flags. Clear group norms developed as both groups standardized certain rules about their games, meals, and camping activities. By the end of this first stage of the research the staff members—who were actually the unobtrusive data collectors—noted clear increases in group-oriented behaviors, cohesiveness, and positive in-group attitudes. The following excerpt describes a good example:

General layout of the campsite and
respective areas of the two groups

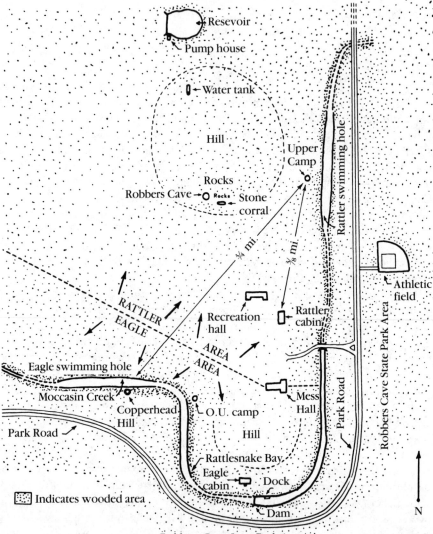

FIGURE 13-1.   The Robbers Cave campsite. (Source: Sherif, Harvey, White, Hood, and Sherif, 1961)

At the hideout, Everett (a non-swimmer when camp started) began to swim a little. He was praised by all and for the first time the others called him by his preferred nickname. Simpson yelled, "Come on, dive off the board!" All members in the water formed a large protective circle into which Everett dived after a full 2 minutes of hesitation and reassurance from the others. While he repeated the performance, little Barton, a frightened non-swimmer, plunged forward and started swimming a little too. He was called to the board and he too jumped in. Allen, a swimmer who was afraid to go off the board, now followed. Harrison, on the bank with an injured hand, was assured by the others that when his hand was healed they would all help him "so that we will *all* be able to swim" [p. 79].

Although the researchers had initially thought they would have to take steps to create tension between the Rattlers and the Eagles, the groups themselves set the stage for intergroup conflict. Toward the end of the first phase each group realized that it was sharing the camp facilities with another group, and references to "those guys," "they," and "outsiders" became increasingly frequent. Both teams wanted to compete with the other group, and asked the staff to set up a tournament. Of course, a series of competitions between the two groups was exactly what the staff had in mind, so on Day 1 of the second stage of the research both groups were told that a tournament would be held. The winning team would receive a trophy and members would all receive prizes (four-bladed pocket knives) and medals; therefore, both groups took the competition seriously.

The series of events lasted four days and included baseball games, tug-of-war contests, tent-pitching competitions, cabin inspections, and a (rigged) treasure hunt. At first, the tension between the two groups was limited to verbal insults, name calling, and teasing. Soon, however, the intergroup conflict escalated into full-fledged hostilities. After losing a bitterly contested tug-of-war battle, the Eagles sought revenge by taking down a Rattler flag and burning it. The next day, when the Rattlers discovered the charred remains of their flag they

> went to the Eagles and asked if they burned the flag, which they admitted. The Rattlers followed up Simpson, calling invectives; Martin worked his way close to the Eagle flag, grabbed it and ran down the road with some other Rattlers and with Mason (Eagle) in hot pursuit.
>
> In the meantime, on the field, the Eagles ran for the Rattlers' second flag which they had left on the field. The remaining Rattlers tried to get it, but the Eagles tore it up. Swift (Rattler) grabbed Craig and held him in a wrestling hold, asking which Eagle had burned the flag. Craig said they all had. Simpson (R) had gotten Cuttler (E) down in a fist fight, and the physical encounters had to be stopped [pp. 105–106].

Next, raiding began, as the Rattlers sought revenge by attacking the Eagles' cabin during the night. The raiders—in dark clothes and with blackened faces—swept through the Eagles' cabin tearing out mosquito netting, overturning beds, and carrying off personal belongings. (The Rattlers even got away with a pair of blue jeans belonging to the Eagle leader; they turned them into a flag and on each leg painted "The Last of the Eagles.") The angered Eagles, who wanted to reciprocate that evening with a raid, were deterred by the staff because they planned to use rocks. However, when the Rattlers went to breakfast the following morning, the Eagles struck:

> After making sure that the Rattlers were in the mess hall, they started off, armed with sticks and bats, and led by Cutler who had balked at participating in a raid the previous night. The Eagles messed up the Rattlers' cabin, turning over beds, scattering dirt and possessions, and then returned to their cabin where they entrenched and prepared weapons (socks filled with rocks) for a possible return raid by the Rattlers [p. 108].

During this period the attitudes of each group toward the other became more and more negative but the cohesiveness of each became increasingly stronger. Although every defeat was associated with initial dejection and internal bickering, the groups were quickly able to channel this animosity in the direction of the opponent. As time passed, the groups became better organized and the group structure solidified. As the observers noted,

> The afternoon of the first day was spent by both groups in intensive preparation for other events. The Rattlers had cabin clean-up, practiced for tug-of-war, and washed their Rattler shirts which they decided to wear at every game. Mason delivered a *lecture* to the Eagles on how to win, and the group practiced at tug-of-war for 45 minutes. Mason had organized a cabin-cleaning detail before lunch, insisting on full participation, although prior to the tournament he himself had shown no interest at all in such chores. Later in the tournament, Mason was to urge his group to practice other activities in which he personally had little interest, such as the skits. When he felt they were not trying hard enough, his usual procedure was to declare he was going home, even starting for the door [p. 103].

The Eagles won the overall contest by a slim margin and were awarded the trophy, knives, and medals. During the Eagles' celebration swim, however, the Rattlers raided the Eagle cabin:

> The Rattlers raided while the Eagles were gone, messing up beds, piling personal gear in the middle of the cabin, setting loose boats at the dock, and absconding with the prize knives and medals. When the Eagles found what had happened, they rushed to the Rattler cabin shouting invectives. Mason (E) was in the lead, furious and ready to fight. . . . The Rattlers told the Eagles that if they would get down on their bellies and crawl, they would return the prize knives and medals they had taken. Mason (E) begged the Rattlers to take out their two big boys and fight, which the Rattlers refused to do. Martin (R) got into a fist fight with Lane (low status E). Mills (R) was scuffling with Clark (E). At this point, it was decided to stop the interaction altogether to avoid possible injury [pp. 110–111].

The two groups were then taken do different parts of the camp amid expostulations concerning those "poor losers," "bums," "sissies," "cowards," and "little babies."

In just two weeks the researchers at the Robbers Cave camp had managed to change a group of "normal" boys into two gangs of scheming, physically assaultive hellions. How had this change taken place? What factors in the situation were contributing to the animosity between the two groups? Perhaps even more important, how could the conflict between the two groups be reduced? This chapter focuses on the Robbers Cave Experiment in an attempt to answer these questions about intergroup conflict. In seeking a better understanding of this phenomenon, we will examine three general areas: (1) the factors that lead to tension between groups, (2) the consequences of intergroup conflict, and (3) ways to reduce group conflict.

Sources of Intergroup Conflict

Two gangs from the West Side of New York City battle one another with knives, zip guns, and chains in an effort to drive the opposing group from a local park. Machine operators in a factory view the management with distrust and resentment, and decide to call a general strike after the factory owner fires one of the workers. The students at a large university complain that the faculty members teach poorly, assign grades unfairly, and impose arbitrary restrictions, while the faculty believes the students to be unmotivated and intellectually lacking. The Black residents of Liberty City in Miami attack White residents and their businesses when several police officers accused of killing a Black robbery suspect are not sent to jail. Since Israel was established, to be an Israeli has always meant that you hate Arabs, while to be an Arab has meant that you hate Israelis.

Conflicts between groups occur at all levels of social organization—from fighting between street gangs to the organized disputes in industrial settings to inner-city riots stemming from breakdowns in racial relations to conflicts between nations. Although intergroup conflict is one of the most complicated phenomena studied by social scientists, the goal of greater understanding—and the promise of better interpersonal relations—remains enticing. The natural starting point for such an investigation is the deceptively simple query "What causes intergroup conflict?" To provide a partial answer, we will consider first the factors that contributed to the development of conflict between the Rattlers and the Eagles.

Competition

On the ninth day of the Robbers Cave Experiment the Rattlers and the Eagles were told what they would receive if they won the tournament. When the two groups breakfasted, the boys saw the tournament-prize exhibit for the first time: a large shining trophy, medals for each of the boys, and—best of all—four-bladed camping knives. The boys *wanted* these prizes, and made it clear that nothing, especially the other group, would stand in the way of their success. From that point on, all the group activities revolved around the ultimate goal of winning the tournament. Unfortunately, while both groups aspired to win the prizes, success for one group meant failure for the other. The groups were now adversaries, enemies who had to be overcome if the prize was to be won.

The idea that intergroup conflict stems from competition over limited resources is the central hypothesis of what has been called **realistic-group-conflict theory** (Campbell, 1965; LeVine & Campbell, 1972). According to this theory, the things that people value—money, prestige, natural resources, energy—are too limited for everyone to share them. If the members of one group manage to acquire a scarce commodity, the members of another group will go without it. Naturally, groups would prefer to be "haves" rather than "have-nots," and they therefore take steps designed to achieve two interrelated outcomes: attaining the desired resources and preventing the other group from reaching its goals. The simple hypothesis that conflict is caused by competition over valued but scarce resources has been used to explain the origin of class struggles (Marx & Engels, 1947), rebellions (Gurr, 1970), international warfare (Streufert & Streufert, 1979), and the development of culture and social structure (Simmel, 1955; Sumner, 1906).

In the more limited arena of conflict between small groups, the realistic-group-conflict theory has been well supported (for example, Bass & Dunteman, 1963; Campbell, 1965; Blake & Mouton, 1979). The Robbers Cave Experiment, for example, demonstrated the power of competition in the production of conflict. In addition, Robert Blake and Jane Mouton (1970, 1979) have conducted a series of experiments that replicated the Sherifs' findings, but their subjects were corporate executives rather than small boys. In their studies Blake and Mouton assigned executives attending a two-week management-training program to small groups that worked on a series of problem-solving tasks. Although the researchers never explicitly mentioned competition, the teams knew that their performances would be evaluated by a group of experts who would decide which group had produced the most adequate solution.

After studying more than 150 such groups, Blake and Mouton concluded that the implicit competitivenes of the business-oriented situation inevitably led to intergroup conflict. The group members became very involved in what they thought was a contest to see who was "best," and wholeheartedly accepted the importance of "winning." Leaders who helped the group "beat" the opponent became strong in their influence, while leaders of defeated groups were replaced. The opposing groups bonded together tightly during work and coffee breaks, and only rarely did any participant show liking for a member of another group. In one interesting variation, Blake and Mouton had representatives of each team meet and decide which team had done the best work. Although most of these meetings resulted in complete and utter deadlocks, occasionally one representative would agree that the other group's product was best. Representatives who gained success in these meetings were greeted as "heroes" and showered with praise and appreciation, but those who capitulated were branded "traitors" and were either ignored by the group or ridiculed and criticized.

Laboratory studies of competition and conflict have also supported realistic-conflict theory. In one illustrative study (Worchel, Andreoli, & Folger, 1977), subjects worked in one of two small groups on "industrial" tasks to earn money. Before actually starting the problems, however, the experimenter explained how their performances would be evaluated. Subjects in *competitive groups* were told that only the team whose performance was best would earn the prize money. In the *cooperation condition* instructions stated that, as in industry, the output of the two groups would be combined, and this combined product would then be evaluated. If the two groups managed to perform well, then both would receive the reward. If not, then both would fail. Lastly, some groups were told that each session involved two groups rather than one simply for the sake of convenience. The groups would be evaluated separately and the outcomes of one would in no way influence the other. In addition to this manipulation of interdependence—competitive, cooperative, or individualistic—half the groups were told that they had succeeded but the other half were told they failed.

After receiving feedback about their group's performance, subjects were asked to indicate liking for members of the other group on a 31-point scale. The results of these ratings, which are partially reported in Figure 13-2, indicated that a group's failure when competing with another group leads to considerably greater rejection of the competitor than failure when cooperating or independent. Furthermore, irrespective of type of interdependence, success was associated with positive rankings of the members of the other groups. These findings support the competition/conflict hypothesis, but they also suggest a qualification. The losing group may

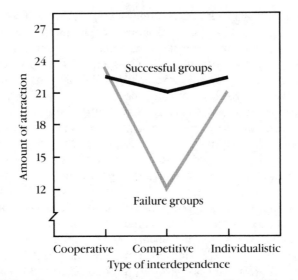

FIGURE 13-2. Competition and intergroup attraction. (Source: Worchel, Andreoli, and Folger, 1977)

respond with hostility and rejection, but the group that succeeds may still be willing to accept interpersonally members of the other group. After all, the victors can afford to be charitable: they owe their success to the failure of the other team.

Social Categorization

The Sherifs (Sherif et al., 1961, p. 94) note that intergroup conflict began to develop between the two groups even before the idea of a competitive tournament was mentioned. Indeed, the Rattlers and Eagles had not even seen each other when the boys began to refer to members of the "other" group in a derogatory way.

> When the in-group began to be clearly delineated, there was a tendency to consider all others as out-group. . . . The Rattlers didn't know another group existed in the camp until they heard the Eagles on the ball diamond; but from that time on the out-group figured prominently in their lives. Hill (Rattler) said "They better not be in our swimming hole." The next day Simpson heard tourists on the trail just outside of camp and was conviced that "those guys" were down at "our diamond" again.

Although the Sherifs argued that the conflict between the two groups resulted from their competitions, this explanation cannot fully account for the almost automatic rejection of members of the other group. Is it possible that group membership per se—even in the absence of any competition—is sufficient to produce intergroup conflict?

Henri Tajfel (1978a, 1978b, 1978c; Tajfel & Turner, 1979) answers this question in the affirmative. Tracing conflict back to processes underlying social cognition, Tajfel suggests that people learn to understand their social environments by classifying objects—both animate and inanimate—into categories. This categorization process, when applied to social perception, suggests that while many different kinds of people exist in the world, all can ultimately be fit into various perceptual categories. Although the perceiver may make use of a wide range of possible categories for classifying people (for example, female, neighbor, stranger, Catholic, jock, friend), two very basic social categorizations are (1) member of my group and (2) member of another group (Hamilton, 1979).

Although this **social categorization** helps people understand their social environment, Tajfel (Tajfel & Turner, 1979, p. 38) proposes that the "mere perception of belonging to two distinct groups—that is, social categorization per se—is sufficient to trigger intergroup discrimination favoring the in-group." To test this hypothesis, Tajfel and his colleagues have studied what they call *minimal groups*. In the basic paradigm subjects are randomly divided up into two groups but are told that the division is based on some irrelevant characteristic such as art preference. Next, the subjects read over a series of booklets asking them to decide how a certain amount of money is to be allocated to other participants in the experiment. The names of the individuals are not given in the booklets, but the subject can tell which group a person belongs to by looking at his or her code number. Tajfel calls the result a minimal group because (1) members of the same group never interact in a face-to-face situation, (2) the identities of in-group and out-group members remain unknown, and (3) no personal economic gain can be secured by granting more or less money to any particular person. In essence, the groups are "purely cognitive"; they exist only in the minds of the subjects themselves.

Tajfel's research revealed a systematic in-group bias even in this minimal-group situation. Participants did not know one another, would not be working together in the future, and their membership in the so-called "group" had absolutely no personal or interpersonal implications. Yet subjects not only tended to award more money to members of their own group, but they also seemed to try actively to keep money from members of the other group. Indeed, the in-group favoritism seemed to persist even when the researcher went to great lengths to make it clear that assignment to group was done on a random basis and giving money to the out-group would not cause any monetary loss for any in-group member. Tajfel's startling conclusion was this: "the mere awareness of the presence of an out-group is sufficient to provoke intergroup competition or discriminatory responses on the part of the in-group" (Tajfel & Turner, 1979, p. 38; for an in-depth look at this topic see Brewer, 1979a).

Intergroup Aggression

The final source of conflict between the Eagles and the Rattlers is perhaps the most obvious one. While the existence of two groups in the camp and the competitive tournament may have set the stage for conflict, the negative intergroup exchanges—insults, humiliations, destruction of personal property, and threats—were the elements that sparked the explosion of hostilities. On the first day of the tournament the disconsolate Eagles were harassed and insulted by the Rattlers. In retaliation, the Eagles burned the Rattlers' team flag. When the Rattlers discovered their loss, they confronted the unrepenting Eagles. The Rattlers then burned the Eagles' flag, and the Eagles then tore up the second Rattler flag.

Physical attacks began at that point and from then on intergroup conflict remained at high levels.

Like most episodes of intergroup conflict, (and intragroup conflict; see Chapter 4), the conflict at the Robbers Cave started with mildly negative exchanges between group members, but soon escalated as intergroup aggression intensified. In similar fashion the infamous Hatfield/McCoy feud, which began with the theft of some hogs by Floyd Hatfield, escalated from a verbal argument over ownership to a court case and eventually a series of bloody interfamily battles (see box). Likewise, studies of gang "rumbles" indicate that many street fights stem from some initial negative action that in reality may pose little threat to the offended group. The target of the negative action, however, responds to the threat with a counterthreat and the intensity of the conflict spirals upward. Battles resulting in the death of gang members have begun over an ethnic insult, the intrusion of one group into an area controlled by another group, or the theft of one gang's property by another gang (Gannon, 1966; Yablonsky, 1959).

Larger scale intergroup conflict also has its seeds in relatively minor negative events. Studies of American race riots in the late 1960s reveal that the larger conflicts were preceded by series of reciprocating hostile actions between police forces and Black activists (Goldberg, 1967). Rioting in Detroit, for example, was precipitated by a police raid on a "blind pig" (a private drinking and gambling establishment). A crowd gathered during the arrests, and looting began after a window was broken by one spectator. Police withdrew for several hours in the hope that the area would quiet down, but the looting continued unabated. To quell the disorder, elite riot troops, complete with bayonets, swept through the streets. Blacks responded with a series of fire-bombings, and officials asked that the state police and national guard be brought in to control the mob. Rumors of sniping activity, the removal of restraints concerning the use of firearms, the lack of clear organization, and a desire for revenge prompted police violence, which in turn led to more widespread rioting.

Robert North and his associates (Holsti & North, 1965; North & Holsti, 1964) cite Germany as the ultimate example of a country embroiled in a conflict spiral.

THE HATFIELDS AND THE McCOYS

One of the best-known stories of frontier America is that of the feud between two families living in the valleys of Appalachia: the Hatfields and the McCoys. Although historians are uncertain of all the details (Rice, 1978), it seems that the feud began in 1863 when a Hatfield stole some hogs from a McCoy. The McCoys countered by stealing hogs from another member of the Hatfield clan, but soon members of the two families began taking pot-shots at one another. Then, in 1865 Harmon McCoy was killed by an unknown assailant; most of the residents assumed that Devil Anse, a Hatfield, was to blame. After this incident, things quieted down until 1878, when Randolph McCoy accused Floyd Hatfield of stealing more hogs, and filed a civil suit for damages. A jury, composed of six Hatfields and six McCoys, decided in favor of Hatfield, and from this point on full-scale violence gripped the families. In the years between 1878 and 1890, more then ten men and women lost their lives as a direct result of interfamily violence.

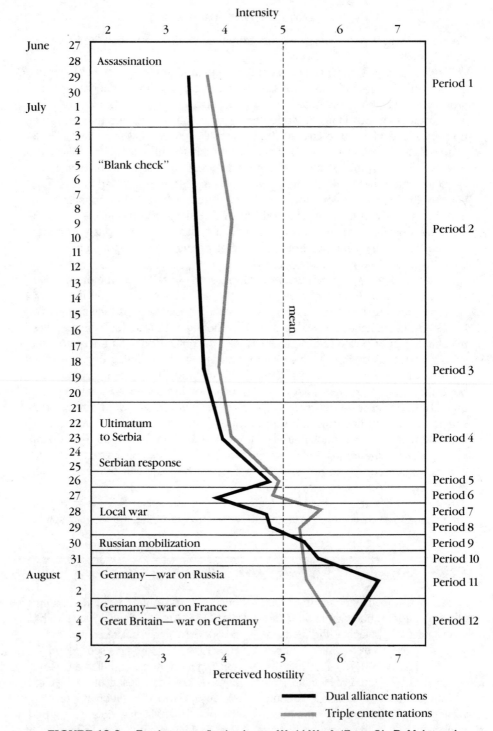

FIGURE 13-3. Escalating conflict leading to World War I. (From Ole R. Holsti and Robert C. North, "The History of Human Conflict," in THE NATURE OF HUMAN CONFLICT, ed., by Elton B. McNeil, © 1965, p. 162. Reprinted by permission of Prentice-Hall, Inc., Englewood Cliffs, N.J.)

They suggest that Germany did not initiate World War I in order to amass more territories and greater wealth for the Dual Alliance nations (Austria/Hungary and Germany), and indeed analysis of the personal documents of the key German decision makers indicates that these leaders did not think their nation could possibly win a full-scale European conflict. Instead, North concludes, the war was the product of escalating threats and minor aggressions that ballooned into international conflict. The data presented in Figure 13-3 support North's conclusions. Graphing the leaders' of the two groups perceptions of hostility and threat from the time of the assassination of Archduke Francis Ferdinand to the outbreak of full-scale war, we see a gradual increase on both sides up to August 4, 1914. Each side felt it was only reacting to the aggressions and hostilities of its future enemies.

A spiral model of conflict intensification accurately describes the unfolding of violence at the Robbers Cave. The conflict began with minor irritations and annoyances but quickly built in intensity. The mildest form of rejection—verbal abuse—began as soon as the groups met for the tournament. Verbal insults were exchanged, members of the opposing team were given demeaning names, and verbal abuses ran high. Next, groups began to actively avoid contact with one another, and intergroup discrimination also developed. The groups isolated themselves from each other at meals and the boys expressed the belief that it was wrong for the other team to use the camp facilities or be given an equal amount of food. Last came the acts of physical violence—the raids, thefts, and fist-fights. Thus the conflict at the Robbers Cave built in a series of progressively more dangerous stages from verbal abuse to avoidance to discrimination and finally to physical assault (Allport, 1954).

Consequences of Intergroup Conflict

In his classic treatise *The Nature of Prejudice,* Gordon W. Allport (1954, p. 226) stated "realistic conflict is like a note on an organ. It sets all prejudices that are attuned to it into simultaneous vibration. The listener can scarcely distinguish the pure note from the surrounding jangle." He was suggesting that conflict, even if rooted in objective characteristics of the situation, will eventually create subjective biases that will further divide the opposing factions. Although the Eagles could reasonably blame the Rattlers for their losses, their reactions went far beyond the simple rejection of a competitor. Each defeat at the hands of the "enemy" brought greater dislike for out-group members and increases in affection for in-group members. Once conflict began, the two groups tried to draw clear distinctions between one another, and finally the team members began attributing negative characteristics and malevolent intentions to the opposing group on the basis of inadequate information.

Studies of intergroup conflict suggest that these consequences are not unique to the Robbers Cave groups, for such conflicts typically produce a rather predictable set of changes in the involved groups. In general, two basic reactions seem to take place. First, changes within the groups create increases in cohesiveness, out-group rejection, and greater group differentiation. Second, intergroup conflict seems to produce misperceptions of the motives and qualities of the out-group members. Both kinds of reactions are discussed below.

Changes in Intragroup Processes

Intrigued by the development and ramifications of intergroup conflict, Lewis Coser (1956) developed a series of propositions that were consistent with previous sociological theorizing (Park & Burgess, 1921; Simmel, 1955; Sumner, 1906). Rejecting the idea that social conflict is "bad"—a disease that society should cure whenever possible—Coser pointed out that conflict between groups has positive as well as negative consequences. Although space limitations prevent a complete analysis of all 16 of Coser's propositions concerning the functions of social conflict, discussion of some of his most important hypotheses follows.

CONFLICT AND COHESION

Hypothesis: Conflict with out-groups increases internal cohesion (Coser, 1956, p. 87). The idea that a conflict with another group will solidify in-group structure was well supported in the Sherif research. During the competitions both the Eagles and the Rattlers became more tightly organized units. Although each failure of the group was followed by a brief period of internal strife, the groups would soon counter with increased organization, strengthened leadership, and demands for stricter conformity to group norms.

Even clearer evidence of increased cohesion in the face of intergroup conflict was obtained by the Sherifs in an earlier study (Sherif & Sherif, 1953; see the box headed "Other Studies by the Sherifs"). In that research the boys were not separated into groups until a full week of campwide activities had been held. Naturally, many of the boys formed close friendships during this period, and the researchers took pains to try to break up these natural alliances when the two separate groups—the Red Devils and the Bull Dogs—were later created. Thus, when groups were first formed many of the Red Devils had friends on the Bull Dog team and many Bull Dogs accepted Red Devils as friends.

After intergroup conflict these out-group friendship choices were virtually obliterated. Boys who continued to interact with members of the out-group were branded "traitors" and threatened with bodily harm unless they broke off their friendships. One member of the Bull Dogs who did not completely identify with the group was partially ostracized, and eventually his parents had to remove him

---

OTHER STUDIES BY THE SHERIFS

Although the Robbers Cave Experiment is perhaps the best known of the Sherifs' field studies of intergroup conflict, this project was actually the third in a series. The first experiment was conducted in the summer of 1949 in a camp in northern Connecticut and followed, for the most part, the procedures of the Robbers Cave study (Sherif & Sherif, 1953). The teams in that study called themselves the Red Devils and the Bull Dogs, and conflict was eventually dispelled by (1) breaking up the two groups during meals and other camp activities and (2) staging a softball game between the entire camp and a team from another camp. A 1953 study (Sherif, White, & Harvey, 1955) was designed to test hypotheses concerning status and estimates of task performance but had to be aborted when the two groups—the Panthers and the Pythons—realized that the camp administration was creating the intergroup friction.

from the camp. A Red Devil who suggested that the two groups get together for a party was punished by the Red Devil leader. This observational evidence was buttressed by the sociometric-choice data collected before and after the groups were formed. As Figure 13-4 shows, prior to intergroup conflict most of the boys reported that their best friends were members of what would eventually become the out-group. Later, however, friendship choices were generally limited to members of one's own group.

The increases in cohesiveness suggested by Coser and the Sherifs have also been found in laboratory studies of the effects of conflict. In one early investigation (Wilson & Miller, 1961) subjects rated teammates and opponents both before and after a competition. Provided the subject's team had won the competition, shifts in the direction of greater favorability were much more pronounced on teammate ratings as compared to opponent ratings. Other studies have confirmed this effect (Dion, 1973, 1979; Ryen & Kahan, 1970, 1975), suggesting increases in cohesiveness during conflict may be greater when the in-group maintains the advantage.

CONFLICT AND OUT-GROUP REJECTION

Hypothesis: Conflict with out-groups sometimes, but not always, increases out-group rejection (Coser, 1956, p. 55). Although Coser points out that groups in conflict often come to arbitrarily reject out-group members, he also states that hostility is not a necessary consequence of conflict. Rejection helps the group carry out aggressive actions against the opposing group, but out-group hatred, rejection, and contempt do not always covary with in-group cohesion, acceptance, and attraction. Marilynn Brewer's more recent reviews of empirical evidence agree

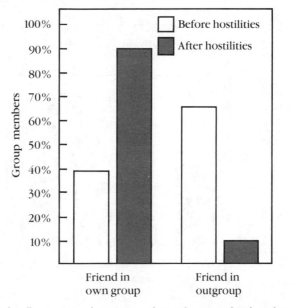

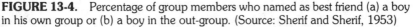

FIGURE 13-4. Percentage of group members who named as best friend (a) a boy in his own group or (b) a boy in the out-group. (Source: Sherif and Sherif, 1953)

with Coser's conclusions, for they indicate that conflict creates "the perception that one's own group is better, although the out-group is not necessarily depreciated" (Brewer, 1979a, p. 322; 1979b). She suggests that the expression of out-group hostility depends upon a number of situational factors, including (1) the similarity of in-group and out-group members, (2) anticipated future interactions, (3) reward structures, and (4) the type of evaluation being made.

At the Robbers Cave, however, in-group favoritism did seem to go hand in hand with out-group rejection. With increases in cohesiveness came the tendency to insult, criticize, and deride out-group members. To record this rejection the Sherifs had the boys rate their own group and the other group on a series of adjective scales (brave, tough, friendly, sneaky, smart aleck, and stinkers). As Figure 13-5 shows, the boys tended to use the more negative characteristics to describe the out-group, but rated their own group more favorably.

GROUP DIFFERENTIATION

Hypothesis: Conflict serves to establish and maintain the identity and boundary lines of groups (Coser, 1956, p. 38). As the conflict between the Eagles and the Rattlers escalated, each group tended to emphasize the major distinctions between the two combatants. The groups began to isolate themselves from one another and asked that they be allowed to eat separately. Unique group norms also began to develop, and if one group adopted a style of action this behavior was soundly rejected by the other. For example, the Rattlers cursed frequently, and, to distinguish themselves from those "bad cussers," the Eagles adopted the norm of no profanity. Later their leader decided that the Rattlers were such poor sports that "the Eagles should not even talk to them anymore" (p. 106). Proprietary orientations toward certain portions of the camp also developed, along with mottoes, uniforms, and secret passwords.

According to Coser these tendencies toward group differentiation typify groups in conflict. Rather than noting the similarities that link the groups together, the

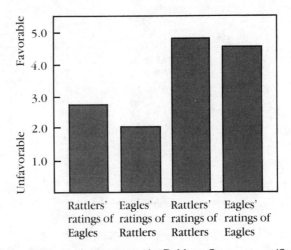

FIGURE 13-5. Patterns of attraction in the Robbers Cave groups. (Source: Sherif, Harvey, White, Hood, and Sherif, 1961)

groups tend to emphasize their differences. While all the boys at the Robbers Cave were extremely similar in their appearances, backgrounds, and attitudes, the Rattlers were nevertheless viewed as completely different from the Eagles. Furthermore, once groups expected to find these differences, their expectations were confirmed as they perceptually accentuated and exaggerated minor between-group differences (Cooper & Fazio, 1979).

Changes in Intergroup Perceptions

Being a member of a group is more than simply interacting with certain individuals on a regular basis, keeping personal behavior within the bounds prescribed by group norms, or sitting with certain people during lunch. Rather, groups can influence us as individuals in many ways, ranging from forcing attitude and value changes to altering our basic beliefs and behaviors (Triandis, 1979). Group membership also exerts a subtle but pervasive influence on our perceptions, and as a result people who are members of different groups often have divergent perceptions of the world. Naturally, these divergent social perceptions add an additional complicating factor to the already complex problem of intergroup conflict, because they tend to create mistrust, misunderstanding, and impediments to communication. Some of these outcomes (which closely parallel the symptoms of groupthink documented by Janis, 1972; see Chapter 12) are described in the next section.

MISPERCEPTIONS AND MIRROR-IMAGE THINKING

Ralph White has long been interested in better understanding the psychology of war. More than any other researcher, his studies have continually emphasized the causal importance of certain misperceptions that increase the strain between adversary groups (White, 1965, 1966, 1969, 1970, 1977). As noted in Chapter 4, individuals come to understand the social world by attributing behaviors and events to specific causes. Although formulating attributions is an individualistic process, these causal inferences are influenced by social comparison between, and information exchange with, members of one's group (Forsyth, 1980). Hence, group members come to develop similar perceptions of their social environments and, in particular, their antagonists. These perceptions, however, when viewed by an outside observer often fail to follow logically from the events that actually took place. It follows that where a conflict is involved group members' views of the situation can often be more accurately described as misperceptions rather than perceptions.

The diabolical-enemy image.   According to White, one of the more frequently occurring misperceptions develops when group members transform members of the other group into the "enemy." For example, during the Robbers Cave Experiment members of the two groups tended to belittle, humiliate, and derogate out-group members. Although the only difference between the two sets of boys was their group identification—Rattler or Eagle—the boys acted as if the out-group members came from a different world. They were the "enemies," "bums," "bad guys," and "those damn campers" rather than opponents in a simple contest. They considered the out-group members capable of doing practically anything to win the prize, and were certain that the others would cheat if they got the chance. No out-group boy could be trusted to tell the truth, and the group as a whole was believed to be continually planning to raid the other team's cabin, invade its sacrosanct swimming and camping areas, destroy its foodstuffs, and steal its property. Friendship with those "bums" would be out of the question.

White contends that such diabolical-enemy images are prevalent in more widespread conflicts. In general, the other side is dehumanized and branded with various uncomplimentary labels—"commies," "capitalist swine," "hippies," "rednecks," "wops," and "spics." Furthermore, because in-group members assume that the other group is composed of evil, immoral, nearly inhuman barbarians, they tend to associate malevolent intentions with even the most benevolent actions on the out-group's part. Even Hitler, who should have realized that other countries were only reacting to his aggressive international policies, felt that his aggressions were motivated by atrocities committed by Poland, the encirclement of Germany by communists, a conspiracy led by the Jews to destroy the German republic, and France's willingness to launch air attacks against German industry. Hitler was certain that all things evil were personified in the Jewish people and that Germany had a duty to protect the world from this menace.

The moral-group image. The Sherifs report no evidence that suggests the boys at the Robbers Cave ever considered their aggressions against the other team to be "wrong." Poor sportism, verbal derision, destruction of others' property, theft, vandalism, and physical violence were all condoned as actions taken against the enemy. The boys felt that their own group had the right to seek victory at all costs, and that the home group's actions were somehow more moral than those of the other team. The Eagles even held prayer meetings before each contest to ask for God's help in vanquishing their foe; several boys were certain that their success was the result of divine intervention.

The combination of a moral-group image and a diabolical-enemy image results in the tendency to view the actions of our own group as good and the actions of the other group as bad. When the other group "aggresses" against us, we respond with "defensive retaliation." When we refuse to yield to threats (which the other side called requests), we are courageous, though they consider us stubborn. Pride in our own group is nationalism, while the other group takes it as evidence of ethnocentrism. We offer them concessions, but they interpret them as ploys. Examining such perceptual differences in Arabs' and Israelis' attributions concerning the cause of the major Middle East wars of 1948, 1956, 1967, and 1973, White (1977, p. 205) found that both sides believed the other side to be the aggressor in all four wars. In two of these wars (1956, 1967) the Arabs believed that Israel simply attacked without provocation. In the remaining two (1948, 1973) the Arabs admitted that they initiated hostilities but believed they were forced to do so by the expansionistic policies of Israel. Conversely, the Israelis felt that the 1948 and 1973 wars were "instances of naked, obvious Arab aggression" while the 1956 and 1967 battles were indirectly caused by the threats and malevolent intentions of the Arabs.

Thus a *double standard* seems to exist when groups evaluate their own actions and those of another group. People will consider an action performed by their own group in the most positive light possible while ascribing numerous negative attributions to the identical action when performed by the out-group. Double standards in perceptions of international relations were demonstrated by researchers who asked American college students to read a list of 50 governmental actions and rate them on a scale from -3 to $+3$ (Oskamp & Hartry, 1968). Unknown to the students, however, the experimenters had prepared two different versions of the questionnaire. On half of the questionnaires the actions were supposedly taken by the United States in opposition to Russian influence, but on the other half the actions were supposedly taken by Russia in opposition to the United States. Consistent with the concept of a double standard, the subjects evaluated the actions positively if they were ascribed to the United States but negatively if ascribed to Russia.

Double standards are also frequently used when groups make judgments about the performance and products of in-group and out-group members. After the tournament was completed at the Robbers Cave, the boys were asked to compete in a bean-collecting game to win $5. The simple task involved picking up beans scattered on the ground within a one-minute time limit. The beans were then collected from the boys and exhibited on a screen via an overhead projector, and the boys from both groups were told to estimate the number of beans shown. However, the projector showed not the beans the boys had actually collected, but the same 35 beans over and over again in slightly different configurations. The boys' biases are evident in the data presented in Table 13-1. Rattlers overestimated the number of beans collected by Rattlers and slightly underestimated the number of beans supposedly collected by Eagles. The estimates provided by the Eagles were inflated for both in-group and out-group members, but the error was much greater for in-group evaluations. Subsequent laboratory studies have found similar biases in groups evaluating their own and others' products, but they suggest that the bias is minimized (1) in losing rather than winning teams and (2) when the judgments are made privately rather than publicly (Hinkle & Schopler, 1979).

The virile-group image. When the groups at the Robbers Cave were first told about the tournament, their members expressed total confidence in their ability to beat the opposing team. To admit otherwise would, of course, have suggested that the in-group was not as good as the other group and such was unthinkable. The group members had an image of power and toughness to live up to, and they were determined to demonstrate their strength and ability. According to White, such sentiments are typical during conflicts between groups. Indeed, in many instances groups seem to be more concerned with being—and appear-

TABLE 13-1. Errors in judging performance

| Group judging | Group being judged | | Mean differences |
	Rattlers	Eagles	
Rattlers	3.40	−.29	3.69
Eagles	4.56	11.80	7.24

(Source: Sherif, Harvey, White, Hood, and Sherif, 1961)

ing—strong and victorious rather than right and peaceful. These virile group-images, naturally, can get the group into difficulties since they can create over-confidence that might eventually lead to the overextension of the group's resources.

Mirror images. The distorted images that create misperceptions when two groups come into conflict are common to both groups. That is, just as Group A thinks of Group B as evil and deceptive, B thinks of A as wicked and treacherous. Just as A thinks of its actions as benevolent and peaceful, B thinks of its own actions as tranquil and benign. Lastly, both A and B believe they can win any challenge to their might. This tendency for conflicting groups to adopt the same distorted picture of one another has been called **mirror-image thinking** (Bronfenbrenner, 1961). In the Arab/Israeli conflict, for example, both sides assume their opponent to be the aggressor, intent upon war and destruction, unwilling to make any concession for peace, and motivated by selfish desires and deeply ingrained hatred (White, 1977). As a result, both sides continue to misunderstand one another completely and the conflict continues to escalate. As White laments,

> There is supreme irony in this mirror-image type of war. It seems utterly ridiculous that *both* sides should be fighting because of real fear, imagining the enemy to be a brutal, arrogant aggressor, when actually the enemy is nerving himself to fight a war that he too thinks is in self-defense. Each side is fighting, with desperate earnestness, an imagined enemy, a bogey-man, a windmill [1969, p. 29].

STEREOTYPING

To the anti-Semite, Jews are sly, penurious, clannish, and overbearing. To the White racist, Blacks are unintelligent, lazy, musical, and superstitious. To the sexist, women are talkative, illogical, dainty, and emotional. To the ultraconservative, college students are hippies, dope smokers, and communists. To the Rattlers, Eagles are cheats, thieves, and bums.

Each of these generalizations is based on a stereotype: "a set of expectations held by the perceiver regarding members of a social group" (Hamilton, 1979, p. 65). Although in many ways stereotypes function as cognitive "labor-saving devices" by helping the perceiver place other people into meaningful categories, stereotypes lead to misunderstandings when they are inaccurate or biased. Because stereotyping errors are particularly likely when emotions are running high and the tendency to overgeneralize about others is strong, their impact on intergroup conflict is considerable. Some of the dangers of stereotyping are described below.

1. *Individuals tend to overestimate the similarity of out-group members.* Participants in one study watched a videotape of four persons stating their opinions concerning who should be blamed in a civil court case (Wilder, 1978). The experimenter pointed out that the people in the tape had reached their decisions individually and that the group members did not know one another, since the groups had been arbitrarily formed with volunteers for research. The experimenter also described the group in one of three different ways. Some observers were told that the four persons were (1) an aggregate of individuals who would not interact as a group, some that the four were (2) a discussion group meeting for the first time, and some that the four were (3) two two-member discussion groups each meeting

for the first time. After the portion of the tape was played in which Person One stated her attitude, observers were asked to make an estimate of Person Three's attitude on the case. In the aggregate condition only 23% of the subjects felt that Person Three would agree with Person One. In the single-group condition this percentage rose to 50%, and in the two-group condition dropped down to 26%—after all, Person One and Person Three were in different discussion groups. Thus, even though the experimenter had stressed the lack of relationship among the people in the group, observers still felt that they could tell something about other group members based on the response of a single group member.

Extending these findings, other researchers (Quattrone & Jones, 1980) arranged for subjects to watch videotapes of a student making a simple decision (choose to join a group, select some music to listen to, or pick a problem to work on). Half the observers were told that the actor in the tape was from their own college, but the other half were led to believe that the actor was from a rival university. This manipulation was introduced to test the prediction that people tend to assume that all members of an out-group act in the same way. If observers see a person in Group A make a particular choice, they tend to assume that other members of Group A will make similar choices. This interesting hypothesis was confirmed when the observers were later asked to estimate the percentage of the students at the actor's college that would have made the same decision as the actor. Observers tended to think that other group members would have made similar choices, especially if the person being watched attended the rival college. Thus, the tendency to overestimate the similarity of group members is especially pronounced for out-groups in conflict.

2. *Stereotypes create an oversimplified picture of out-group members.* Although most perceivers are quick to point out the many characteristics that distinghish them from their fellow group members ("Why I'm not like them at all!"), when their attentions turn to evaluations of out-groups they tend to overlook the heterogeneity of these groups while emphasizing their homogeneity ("They all look the same to me"). According to recent research, people possess complex and extremely differentiated conceptions of their own groups but relatively simplistic and nonspecific pictures of out-groups (Linville & Jones, 1980; Quattrone & Jones, 1980). Their appraisals are usually structured in black-and-white terms—*all* out-group members are either *all* good or *all* bad—and perceptions of within-group variability are minimized. Indeed, the basic evaluative processes utilized by perceivers seem to be more complex when applied to in-group than to out-group members, making it easy to generalize from the behavior of one person to that of the entire group. Furthermore, the larger the group, the more likely are these oversimplications to occur (Rothbart, Fulero, Jensen, Howard, & Birrell, 1978).

3. *Stereotypes are self-fulfilling.* Allport (1954, p. 252) tells the tale of an Irishman and a Jew who

> encounter each other in casual contact, perhaps in a small business transaction. Neither has, in fact, any initial animosity toward the other. But the Irishman thinks, "Ah, a Jew; perhaps he'll skin me; I'll be careful." The Jew thinks, "Probably a Mick; they hate the Jews; he'd like to insult me." With such an inauspicious start both men are likely to be evasive, distrustful, and cool.

This story suggests that stereotypes, once accepted, subtly influence intergroup interactions in such a way that the stereotype is behaviorally confirmed. By way of example, assume that Julia thinks that members of Group X tend to be over-bearing and manipulative. When she meets Tony and discovers he is an X, she begins to notice evidence of overconfidence and craftiness in his actions. The non-Machiavelian Tony, on the other hand, is a bit put off by Julia's suspiciousness and so becomes less friendly toward her. Quite naturally she interprets this change as further evidence of his manipulativeness. The initial expectation about Group X and Tony has been fulfilled.

The self-fulfilling nature of stereotypes was aptly demonstrated in a study of stereotypes concerning physical appearance (Snyder, Tanke, & Berscheid, 1977). Reasoning that most people assume physically attractive people possess more pleasant personalities than unattractive people, researchers arranged for pairs of males and females to get acquainted with each other via a telephone conversation. To activate the stereotype concerning physical attractiveness males were shown a picture of their female partners. The pictures however, were actually snapshots of women who had been previously identified as extremely attractive (8s on a 10-point scale) or rather unattractive (2.5s on the scale). They were not photographs of their actual partners, who in reality did not vary greatly from one another in terms of physical attractiveness.

As predicted, males who thought their partners were physically attractive rather than unattractive rated them positively (sociable, poised, humorous, and socially adept) even before they had the opportunity to converse. More striking, however, were the differences in the females' actual behaviors as revealed by evaluations provided by objective raters who listened to tape recordings of all the conversa-tions. A woman talking to a man who thought she was attractive *sounded* more attractive—more sociable, poised, sexually warm, outgoing—than a woman talk-ing to a man who thought she was unattractive. The women were never directly told what the men believed, but apparently the initial expectation of the males set up a positive (or negative) atmosphere during the interaction that influenced the females' responses.

Although this research indicates that stereotypes are sometimes confirmed behaviorally, other studies indicate that they are cognitively confirmed as well. For example, when perceivers expect members of a group to act in a certain way, they tend to recall more accurately instances that confirm rather than disconfirm this expectation. Hence, if a person believed a group of people to be stupid, he or she would tend (1) to remember instances in which one of these people was confused in class or failed a test but would tend (2) to forget instances in which one of these people achieved a 4.0 grade point average or became class valedic-torian (Rothbart, Evans, & Fulero, 1979). In addition, given perceivers' initial tendency to make less favorable appraisals of out-group members, these biased memory processes cause perceivers to remember the negative actions of out-group members better than the negative actions of in-group members (Howard & Rothbart, 1980).

In summary, intergroup conflict sets in motion a number of perceptual and behavioral reactions that tend for the most part only to add to the confusion of the original disagreement. In-group solidarity increases along with out-group rejection, and antagonists tend to draw clearer differentiations between the groups. Perceptions of the situation are also influenced by the conflict, as interactants fall prey to diabolical-enemy images, moral-group images, virile-group images, and double standards. Finally, self-fulfilling stereotyped thinking ensures that the disputants will develop oversimplified views of out-groups that will overestimate the similarity of their members. Given these numerous complicating factors contributing to the escalation of intergroup conflict, obviously the next question to ask is "How can conflict between groups be resolved?"

Intergroup-Conflict Reduction

The Robbers Cave researchers were left with a major problem. The manipulations of the first two phases of the experiment had worked very well, for the intense conflict between the Rattlers and the Eagles conveyed a great deal of information about how conflict develops and escalates. Unfortunately, the manipulations were almost too successful, for the members of the two groups now despised one another. Certainly no conscientious social scientist could turn his or her back on these groups without trying to undo some of the negative interpersonal effects of the study. Therefore, the Sherifs and their colleagues felt compelled to seek a method through which harmony and friendship could be created at the Robbers Cave campsite.

Intergroup Contact

In keeping with a notion labeled the **contact hypothesis,** the Sherifs considered bringing the members of the two groups together during some pleasant group activity in the hope that intergroup bonding would result. The Sherifs, however, weren't very optimistic about the effectiveness of intergroup contact as a means of reducing conflict. Indeed, they predicted that a "contact phase in itself will not produce marked decreases in the existing state of tension between groups" (Sherif et al., 1961, p. 51). The researchers set up a series of seven contact situations in which the Rattlers and the Eagles ate, played games, viewed films, and shot off firecrackers as a single group. Despite these activities, the contact between the groups seemed to increase rather than decrease conflict. During all these events the lines between the two groups never broke, and antilocution, discrimination, and physical assault continued unabated. When contact situations occurred during meals, "food fights" were particularly prevalent:

> After eating for a while, someone threw something, and the fight was on. The fight consisted of throwing rolls, napkins rolled in a ball, mashed potatoes, etc. accompanied by yelling the standardized, unflattering words at each other. The throwing continued for about 8–10 minutes, then the cook announced that cake and ice cream were ready for them. Some members of each group went after their dessert, but most of them continued throwing things a while longer. As soon as each gobbled his dessert, he resumed throwing [p. 158].

At one level the failure of the intergroup contact to produce decreases in friction between the groups is surprising. After all, the hypothesized curative effects of contact are the basis of many social and political policies such as school and housing integration, foreign-student exchange programs, and international sporting events such as the Olympics. All such policies are based on the principle that in-group/out-group biases are caused in large part by mistaken assumptions about out-group members that would be cleared up by contact between interactants. Yet the contact hypothesis wasn't confirmed at the Robbers Cave.

At another level the outcome of the contact phase of the Sherif's study should be no shock to proponents of the contact hypothesis, since the *nature* of the contact was uncontrolled. Few would propound the theory that any type of contact produces intergroup harmony. If group members who are meeting together begin to insult, argue with, physically attack, cr discriminate against the out-group, then certainly such contact should not be expected to yield beneficial effects. Hence, the success of contact as a means of reducing intergroup conflict will depend upon what happens during the contact itself. Apparently the researchers at the Robbers Cave did not create the appropriate contact situation to produce intergroup harmony.

Subsequent empirical work has helped to identify the elements in intergroup contact necessary to maximize conflict reduction (Amir, 1969, 1976; Cook, 1972; Foley, 1976). After conducting a ten-year study of the reduction of racial prejudice via contact in small groups, Stuart Cook concluded that five situational factors seem critical. First, the interacting group members in the contact situation should all have the same degree of status. If interactants are of unequal status, then in-group biases will only be reinforced and conflict could escalate. Second, the contact should involve personal or intimate interactions with out-group members as opposed to superficial contacts. Third, the social climate of the contact situation should emphasize friendly, helpful, and egalitarian attitudes. Fourth, the out-group members should attempt to contradict as much as possible the prevailing stereotypes concerning their behavior. After all, if the contact only lends added support to the in-group members' negative evaluations of the out-group, then it will not have improved matters greatly. Fifth, the situation should be structured such that competition with out-group members goes unrewarded or is punished, while cooperation is reinforced.

Bearing these five characteristics in mind, we can discern why intergroup contact in the Robbers Cave Experiment failed to alleviate group tensions. The two groups were brought together immediately after a week of competition. The Eagles were the victors and in all likelihood they viewed themselves as "winners" having higher status than those "losers." Thus, all interactants did not necessarily share equal status. Next, the contact situations, which involved watching a movie, eating, and playing a game together, afforded little opportunity for members of the opposing groups to get to know out-group members on an intimate basis. For the most part, no real intermingling among the two sets of boys ever took place, and the requirement for personal association appears to have been unmet. In addition, the two groups had been competitors for the preceding week and no explicit attempt was made to change the norms from a situation emphasizing competition to one calling for cooperation. Indeed, little payoff was afforded those group members who did try to work with out-group members, for they earned no special rewards and were usually criticized by their fellow group members. In sum, little incentive existed for treating the other group in a friendly, cooperative way, so the failure of the contact to create a reduction in intergroup conflict should not be surprising.

Cooperation Between Groups

When the simple contact between group members failed to ease intergroup animosity, the Sherifs took the contact situation one step further. Rather than simply placing the two groups together and allowing them to interact in whichever way they wished, the researchers tried to instill cooperation by prompting the boys to try to reach **superordinate goals:** goals that could only be attained if the two groups worked together as a team. According to the Sherifs, superordinate goals would force the groups to forget their previous disagreements and combine their efforts to solve the more important problems they now faced. Because failure for all interactants would be a certainty if the groups remained antagonistic, a strong spirit of cooperation should develop that would eventually create increased intergroup harmony. Hence, like the disagreeable neighbors who unite forces when a severe thunderstorm threatens to flood their homes, failing college students who study together to try to get better grades on the next test, or warring nations in the recurring science fiction theme who pool their technological skills in attempting to prevent the collision of the earth with an asteroid, the Rattlers and the Eagles could be reunited if they sought goals that could not be solved by a single group working alone.

To create these superordinate goals the staff staged a series of crises and explained to the two groups that their combined help was needed to reach solutions. For example, the staff secretly sabotaged the water supply and then asked the boys to find the source of the problem by tracing the water pipe from the camp back to the main water tank, located about three-quarters of a mile away. The boys became quite thirsty during their search, and worked together to try to correct the problem. Eventually they discovered that the main water valve had been turned off by "vandals," and cheered when the problem was repaired. Later in this stage the boys pooled their monetary resources to rent a movie that they all wanted to see, worked together to pull a broken-down truck, prepared meals together, exchanged tent materials, and took a rather hot and dusty truck ride together.

After six days of cooperation the original tensions between the groups were fairly well wiped out. When it came time to return to Oklahoma City, several of the group members asked if everyone could go in the same bus:

> When they asked if this might be done and received an affirmative answer from the staff, some of them actually cheered. When the bus pulled out, the seating arrangement did not follow group lines. Many boys looked back at the camp, and Wilson (E) cried because camp was over [p. 182].

Through the power of superordinate goals the Robbers Cave experiment had a happy ending.

Of course, the Sherifs could have induced cooperation between the two groups in other ways. For example, in the 1949 research the Red Devils and the Bull Dogs were partially reconciled by the formation of a softball team made up of members from both the groups and pitted against a team from an outside camp (Sherif & Sherif, 1953). This *common-enemy approach* was partially successful in that during the game the boys cheered one another on, and when the home team won they congratulated themselves without paying heed to group loyalties.

The Sherifs point out, however, that while combining groups in opposition to a common enemy works for a short period of time (during the actual competition or crisis), once the enemy is removed the groups tend to return to the original status quo. In fact, the 1949 groups never were successfully reunited despite the experimenters' extended efforts.

It should be noted that the use of a common enemy to create cooperation actually enlarges a conflict—in the Sherifs' research the tension that once divided a single camp now divided two different camps. At the international level, this method would amount to solving the disagreements between the Soviet Union and the United States by forming a Soviet/American alliance to attack China. Thus, the common-enemy approach can in some instances amount to no more than scapegoating (see the box).

Investigators might also elicit cooperation between groups simply by instructing groups to work together, but the Sherifs found that creating trust and cooperation between groups that had previously disagreed can be extremely difficult. In their 1949 research the camp administrators frequently urged the boys to sit together at dinner, cooperate when playing games, and help each other with camp chores, but despite these encouragements the in-group cliques remained. In explanation, Svenn Lindskold has recently (1978, 1979a) suggested that the barriers to inter-group-conflict reduction can only be overcome very gradually. Given the misunderstandings, misperceptions, reciprocated hostility, and general distrust between groups, interactants often find that attempts at cooperation are misinterpreted by the opponents as attacks. According to Lindskold this mutual distrust can be successfully eroded if the groups follow a series of steps designed to increase gradually trust and cooperation. These steps are all part of a conflict-reduction

SCAPEGOATING

And Aaron shall lay both his hands upon the head of the live goat, and confess over him all the iniquities of the children of Israel, and all their transgressions in all their sins, putting them upon the head of the goat, and shall send him away by the hand of a fit man into the wilderness [Leviticus 16:21].

When the Eagles lost the contests on the first day of the tournament they felt frustrated and angrily blamed the Rattlers for their misfortunes. Later they would vent their anger by burning the Rattler flag. But what would have happened if the Eagles had been unable to aggress against the Rattlers? What if the Eagles were too fearful of retaliation to attack openly? How would the Eagles then have reacted to the frustrating losses?

In most instances, if Group A interfered with Group B, B would respond by retaliating against A. If, however, Group A is extremely powerful, too distant, or difficult to locate, Group B may respond by turning its aggression onto Group C. This other out-group, although in no way responsible for the negative event B experienced, would nonetheless be blamed and thereby become the target of B's aggressive actions. Group C, in this case, would be the *scapegoat*—a label derived from the biblical guilt-transference ritual. Anger originally aroused by one group becomes displaced upon another, more defenseless group. Attacking the guiltless group provides an outlet for pent-up angers and frustrations, and the aggressive group may then feel satisfied that justice has been done.

model developed by Charles Osgood (1979), which he labeled the *Graduated and Reciprocal Initiative in Tension Reduction (GRIT)* proposal.

The ten steps of the GRIT model are listed in Table 13-2 along with some of the principles that go along with each phase and an example drawn from international disarmament negotiations. The first three points call for adequate communication between the groups in the hope of establishing the "rules of the game." The next three stages, on the other hand, are designed to increase trust between the two groups as the consistency in each group's responses demonstrates credibility and honesty. (Lindskold suggests that these phases are crucial to overwhelm the skepticism of the opponents as well as the tendency for other parties to assume that the concessions are merely "smokescreens" or propaganda tactics.) The final

TABLE 13-2. GRIT: Graduated and reciprocal initiative in tension reduction

GRIT point	Relevant principles	Example
1. General statement that sets the stage for reciprocation.	Creates framework for interpreting subsequent actions; forces consistency in actions through commitment; activates third party interest; must be a voluntary action.	Leader of Country X announces an important plan to change relations with Country Y.
2. Public announcement of each unilateral initiative.	Works against misinterpretation due to communication breakdown; explains relationship to entire plan; contains no moralizing.	Leader of X announces that a satellite-destroying laser weapon will not be developed.
3. Reciprocation is invited but not demanded.	Nonmanipulative; demonstrates vulnerability; prevents reactance in other group.	Country X notes it would welcome similar moves from Country Y but will take its action regardless.
4. Each initiative is carried out exactly as described.	Credibility is built as promises are kept.	Country X destroys preliminary model of laser weapon.
5. Initiatives continued even when no reciprocation.	Credibility is further reinforced; reciprocity norms pressure for concessions.	X relinquishes certain air bases; halts nuclear tests even though Y takes no action.
6. Initiatives are unambiguous and can be verified.	Open communication between parties; caution to make certain that publicity is not excessive.	Country X invites representatives of the world press to evaluate its initiatives.
7. Initiatives must be risky and meaningful, but retaliatory capacity is retained.	Conciliation, though not the only available strategy, is chosen; aggression and retaliation remain possible; attack capability maintained but not used.	X offers major concessions but retains nuclear superiority over Y.
8. Precise retaliation to aggression.	Overretaliation avoided to limit possibility of conflict spiral; norm of reciprocity makes precise retaliation admissible.	Y establishes a missile base too close to X; X blockades the base until the missiles are removed.
9. Diversified initiatives	Diversified attempts made at cooperation to establish communication, trust, and increased conciliation.	X not only makes concessions concerning arms, but also human rights issues and X/Y trade.
10. Match any reciprocation in future initiatives	Any conciliation from the other group must be bilateral; each conciliation should be followed by an equal or more important initiative.	Y also destroys its laser weapon, and X follows by halting construction of its latest strategic bomber.

(Source: Lindskold, 1978)

four steps are necessary only in extremely intense conflict situations in which the breakdown of intergroup relations implies a danger for the group members. In the example used in the table—military conflict—the failure to stem the conflict could have disastrous consequences. Hence, each side must make concessions at a fixed rate while at the same time maintaining retaliatory capability.

Although the GRIT proposal may seem to be overly elaborate and therefore inapplicable to all but the most intense conflicts, the model does clarify the difficulties inherent in establishing mutual trust between parties who have been involved in a prolonged conflict. Although some of the stages are not applicable to all conflicts, the importance of clearly announcing intentions, making promised concessions, and matching reciprocation are relevant to all but the most transitory conflicts. Furthermore, case studies (Etzioni, 1967), simulations (Crow, 1963), and experiments (Lindskold, 1979; Lindskold & Aronoff, 1980; Lindskold & Collins, 1979) have lent considerable support to the recommendations of the GRIT model as a means of inducing cooperation. At minimum, the model offers a good deal of promise as a guide for better relationships between groups.

Although creating cooperation among groups may sound like a universal panacea for intergroup conflict, we should note two limiting conditions suggested by research before wholeheartedly accepting this solution. First, in all likelihood several cooperative encounters will be needed before conflict is noticeably reduced. In the Robbers Cave research a whole series of superordinate goals was required prior to the reduction of animosity. In a more direct test of the importance of multiple cooperative encounters (Wilder & Thompson, 1980), students from two different colleges worked together on problems—sometimes with students from their own schools but sometimes with students from a different school. The results indicated that a cooperative encounter led to increased liking for members of the out-group only when it occurred twice. Students who worked with the out-group just once or not at all rated the members of the out-group more negatively (the mean on a 9-point scale was 5.9) than students who worked with the out-group twice (this mean was 7.0).

Second, if the cooperative venture ends in failure for both groups then the magnitude of the resulting intergroup attraction will almost certainly be reduced. As a reinforcement position would suggest, when cooperating groups manage to succeed, then the "warm glow of success" may generalize to the out-group and create greater intergroup attraction. If, however, the group fails, the negative effect associated with a poor performance will spread to the out-group. In addition, if the cooperative encounter ends in failure, then each group may blame the other for the misfortune and intergroup relations may further erode (Worchel, 1979). The problem of failure was aptly demonstrated in one study in which groups that had previously competed with one another were asked to work together to solve a problem (Worchel, Andreoli, & Folger, 1977). However, half the groups failed during the cooperative phase, while the other half succeeded. As predicted, when the intergroup cooperation ended in failure, out-group members were still rejected. Other studies have replicated this effect (for example, Blanchard, Adelman, & Cook, 1975) and indicate that unless some excuse for the failure exists (Worchel & Norvell, 1980) a disastrous performance during cooperation will only serve to further alienate groups.

Alternative Modes of Conflict Resolution

While contact and cooperation may be two of the most frequently noted methods of resolving intergroup tensions, many other techniques offer equally viable alternatives. For example, group conflict could be easily reduced if the groups were broken apart so that interactants responded as individuals rather than as members of a group. In the Sherifs' earlier research this method involved instituting a series of games that the boys played as individuals, thus enabling them to succeed or fail apart from the rest of the group. Although this technique proved to be somewhat successful, it required the sacrifice of the groups themselves.

Individuation of out-group members has also been shown to be an effective method of reducing in-group/out-group biases (Wilder, 1978b). In one experiment the out-group (Group B) acted as a jury making decisions that were clearly detrimental for another group (Group A). Later, the members of Group A were given the opportunity to allocate payment to members of both groups. Results indicated that members of A were strongly biased against members of B unless they had information that someone in Group B had disagreed with their fellow group members. That is, the decisions of Group B had not been unanimous because one out-group member consistently dissented. Other studies that heightened out-group individuation by arranging for each member of the out-group to send a personal message to the in-group lent further support to the idea that individuation reduces intergroup biases.

A more frequently used method of conflict resolution involves intergroup *bargaining and negotiation.* Emphasizing rationality, this approach involves meetings of parties to discuss their grievances and recommend solutions. Typically, both sides draw up a list of problem areas that are sources of dissatisfaction. Next, the two groups together consider each issue and seek a solution that is satisfying to both sides. When one issue is solved, then the negotiations proceed to the next item on the agenda. In industry, conflicts between management and employees are often solved through bargaining. Production-line workers may feel that their salaries are too low, the work setting is unsafe,or health benefits are poor. Because such dissatisfaction could cause low morale and undermine productivity, negotiations are set up in which the grievances of the workers can be discussed in an atmosphere of mutual cooperation and objectivity. Negotiations are often effective means of conflict resolution because they involve many interpersonally advantageous elements: (1) open communication between disputants (Deutsch, 1973); (2) mutual cooperation in seeking a solution (Worchel, 1979); (3) intergroup contact (Cook, 1972); and (4) conflict *fractionation*—the breakdown of the general conflict into smaller, specific issues that can be dealt with one at a time (Fisher, 1964; see the box on page 400).

Although disputes between very small groups can be negotiated directly, in most cases this arrangement is impractical. Usually authority is delegated to a group representative who meets with a representative from the other side in a discussion of the issues. Unfortunately, while the advantages of group representation are numerous, disadvantages are also often involved. On the positive side of the ledger, representatives are often skilled in negotiations and therefore work more effectively toward acceptable solutions. Second, with just a few participants fewer communications problems crop up, and issues can be considered rapidly and

A GLOSSARY OF NEGOTIATORS' TERMS

Over the years a vocabulary has developed for some of the strategies that can be used to gain the "upper hand" through bargaining and negotiation. Some of the more colorful terms include the following:

Bad guys   Members of the negotiation team who take a harsh stance toward members of the other group. They make unreasonable demands and behave obnoxiously, refusing to make even the smallest concessions. Others on their team then put on a show of trying to reason with them.

Dancer   A member of the negotiation team that can speak for long periods of time without saying anything.

Heckling   "Shaking up" members of the other group by insulting them, making excessive noise while they speak, joking around, or threatening them.

Last-chancing   A standard negotiation tactic in which one announces "Alright, this is my last and final offer. Take it or leave it," before the middle ground is even reached.

Log-rolling   When negotiators on each side have a list of grievances, they make concessions back and forth; when A gives in on one issue, B gives in on the next.

Scrambling eggs   When negotiations go poorly, teammates may deliberately try to confuse the issue by misinterpreting others, expressing themselves badly, and dragging in irrelevant issues.

Tiger teams   A squad made up of experts that is brought in to unfreeze deadlocked negotiations or try to reclaim ground lost earlier.

---

efficiently. Third, when negotiators take their roles seriously they often strive to seek the best solution while controlling their emotions, keeping the overall problem in perspective, and refusing to commit themselves to positions the rest of their group may reject. On the negative side representatives may lack the power to make a final decision and therefore must continually consult their group before any concession can be made. Second, the group members may become dissatisfied with their negotiators and refuse to support the solutions they may have spent long hours negotiating. Group members are often shocked when they discover their representative has made agreements with the other side and then take steps to replace the "traitor" with a more "loyal" representative (Blake & Mouton, 1979). Lastly, the negotiators may become so concerned with presenting themselves as tough, dogged bargainers that they become hopelessly deadlocked even when a solution is in fact possible (Brown, 1977).

With as many positive features as negative, the use of representatives to solve conflicts may not always be a successful strategy. Indeed, in the Sherifs' 1949 study an informal attempt by one of the Bull Dog leaders to negotiate with the Red Devils ended in *increased* antagonism:

> Hall . . . was chosen to make a peace mission. He joined into the spirit, shouting to the Bull Dogs, "Keep your big mouths shut. I'm going to see if we can make peace. We want peace."
> Hall went to the Red Devil cabin. The door was shut in his face. He called up that the Bull Dogs had only taken their own . . . and they wanted peace. His explanation was rejected, and his peaceful intentions were derided. He ran from the bunkhouse in a hail of green apples [Sherif & Sherif, 1953, p. 283].

A final conflict-reduction technique that deserves brief mention introduces a third party into the negotiation process. All such interventions, however, are not equivalent, since the power of this third party can vary considerably (LaTour, 1978; LaTour, Houlden, Walker, & Thibaut, 1976). In an *inquisitorial* procedure the third party simply questions the two parties and then hands down a verdict that the two parties must accept. In *arbitration* the disputants present their arguments to the third party, who then bases his or her decision on the information they provide. In a *moot* the disputants and the third party discuss, in as open and informal a meeting as possible, the problems and possible solutions. While these third parties cannot make any binding decisions, they facilitate communication, make suggestions, and enforce standing rules. When the third party has no power to enforce participation or make recommendations, the intervention is known as *mediation.*

Third-party negotiators facilitate conflict reduction by performing a number of important functions. For example, they help in the following ways:

1. Reducing emotionalism by giving both sides an opportunity to vent their feelings.
2. Presenting alternative solutions, by recasting the issues in different or more acceptable terms.
3. Providing opportunities for "graceful retreat" or facesaving in the eyes of one's adversary, one's constituency, the public, or oneself.
4. Facilitating constructive communication between the opposing sides.
5. Planning the meeting for the two adversaries, including such aspects as the neutrality of the meeting site, the formality of the setting, the time constraints, and the number and kinds of other people (if any) who should be there [Raven & Raven, 1976, p. 462].

Naturally, satisfaction with the use of a third party depends on how well the intermediary fulfills these functions, but research suggests that people most prefer arbitration, followed by a moot, then mediation, and lastly inquisitorial procedures (LaTour et al., 1976).

Summary

Many of the causes of, consequences of, and possible solutions to conflict between groups were evident in the *Robbers Cave Experiment,* a field study conducted by Muzafer and Carolyn Sherif and their colleagues. Soon after the investigators separated the young participants into two groups, conflict developed as the boys on the two "teams" (1) competed for scarce resources, (2) drew distinctions between in-group and out-group members on the basis of social categorization, and (3) acted aggressively toward out-group members. In addition to recording the growing antipathy between the groups, the Sherifs also noted the occurrence of a number of consequences of the conflict. Some of these consequences—such as increases in internal cohesion, out-group rejection, and group differentiation—occurred at an intragroup level. Others—misperceptions, illusions (diabolical-enemy images, moral-group images, virile-group images, and mirror images), and stereotyping—influenced intergroup perceptions. Overall, these consequences of conflict only heightened the animosity between the two groups.

The Sherifs explored several options as they worked to reduce the conflict between the two groups. First, they introduced intergroup contact by providing opportunities for the groups to perform interesting activities together. However, because these *contact situations* did not include the components necessary for successful conflict reduction (equal status, intimacy, positive social climate, unfulfilling stereotypic action, and cooperation), the attempts failed. However, when the researchers established cooperation between the groups by prompting the boys to work toward a *superordinate goal*—one that could be achieved only through unified effort—conflict lessened. Other methods that could have been utilized include a "common-enemy approach," direct instruction, *GRIT* (Graduated and Reciprocal Initiative in Tension reduction), individuation of out-group members, bargaining, and negotiation, but introducing the superordinate goal was sufficient to reduce conflict at the Robbers Cave campsite.

PART
FIVE

Applications

Since its inception group dynamics has shown two faces: one turning toward theory development and scientific research designed to clarify group processes, and a second seeking insight into and improvements in "real" groups. Although we have referred to this second side of group dynamics throughout this book wherever applications of theory and research were relevant, in this final section we concentrate solely on groups found in everyday, nonresearch settings. In Chapter 14 we focus on groups that exist in organizations, businesses, and industries. Chapter 15 covers three different, but very interesting kinds of groups: classrooms, juries, and teams. Finally, Chapter 16 analyzes interpersonal-skills training and therapy in groups.

14

Groups in Organizations and Industry

Please read the following statements carefully before marking each one either true (T) or false (F).

T F 1. In most work settings people are more concerned with their personal performances than with their groups' performances.

T F 2. People are invariably more productive when they work in cohesive than in noncohesive groups.

T F 3. People are more satisfied working alone rather than in groups.

T F 4. To maximize the impact of rewards, they should be given to specific individuals rather than to a group of individuals.

T F 5. It is easier to change solitary individuals than individuals in a group.

T F 6. The best conference meetings are characterized by strong leadership, animated discussion, and aggressive debate.

T F 7. The best meeting leaders don't use agendas.

T F 8. *Robert's Rules of Order* are the best standards for conducting any kind of organizational or business meetings.

This quiz is not easy; in fact, the questions it raises have been debated by experienced industrial leaders and studied by applied group dynamicists for many years. As a result of this intensive effort to apply group-dynamics concepts to problems in industry, investigators have succeeded in accumulating a wealth of information that, if taken seriously, offers many insights into group behavior in organizational settings.

As always, this chapter serves only as an introduction to this important area, and therefore items for discussion were chosen selectively. The questions posed above, however, serve as a partial outline of topics we will consider. In the first section we examine two related topics: (1) group goals and performance and (2) satisfaction and group membership. We raise many issues in relation to these two topics, but the general point made is that individuals work not in organizations, businesses, and industries, but in small groups that combine to form larger organizations, businesses, and industries. Hence, all the processes explored in previous chapters are relevant to organizational behavior.

In the second major section of the chapter we turn to questions of how change is achieved in organizational and industrial settings. Much of this analysis can be directly traced to Kurt Lewin's (1951, p. 228) dictum "It is easier to change individuals formed into a group than to change any of them separately" and the contemporary expression of this insight in a set of approaches known as organizational-development. Modern organizational-development interventions are heavily dependent upon groups for achieving improvements in performance, and here we focus on four basic techniques for promoting change: survey feedback, process consultation, team building, and laboratory training.

The chapter closes with an analysis of a much maligned group setting, the meeting, by offering practical suggestions to both rank-and-file members and chairpersons. In this final section we do not review research on meetings—since little good empirical work has, in fact, been done—but rather show how principles and findings from other areas of group dynamics can be applied to improve the effectiveness of meetings. Thus, the overall objectives of the chapter are to explain groups in organizations and industry in terms of group-dynamics theory and research and, in a practical sense, to show how these "action" groups can be improved. And in the course of meeting these objectives we will have demonstrated that all the true/false questions in the above list are false.

Organizational Group Behavior

Interpersonal relations among group members is a topic of little relevance to any manager who assumes that people work solely to make money. Such a viewpoint, which was popularized in the early decades of this century by the so-called scientific-management theories (Taylor, 1923), is based on the premise that human beings, like reluctant donkeys, must be goaded into action by promises of financial carrots. This philosophy of human nature presumes that although people don't enjoy working, because they enjoy starvation even less they will labor simply to avoid the more unpleasant alternative. In consequence, early managerial methods emphasized *situational* determinants of behavior: financial incentives directly tied to production, close supervision of workers to prevent loafing, and clear, simple goals set by management rather than workers.

More modern approaches to organizational behavior, however, fully recognize the impact of interpersonal processes on performance. These *interpersonal* approaches, which can be traced back to industrial research projects conducted in such places as the Hawthorne plant of the Western Electric Company (Mayo, 1933, 1945; see Chapter 2), assume that a strict focus on situational factors overlooks many important determinants of behavior, such as motivations, attitudes, satisfactions, aspirations, and personal goals. Whereas workers were once thought of as the mere "adjuncts of machines" (March & Simon, 1958), contemporary approaches to management seek to incorporate social and psychological variables as well as situational factors in analyses of worker productivity (Katz & Kahn, 1978).

To achieve an understanding of interpersonal relations within industrial settings, many researchers focus on group-level processes; after all, industrial behavior generally takes place in groups. In fact, some approaches—such as Rensis Likert's **linking-pin model** (see box)—suggest that organizations can be conceptualized as systems of interdependent groups. Viewed from this perspective, people work not in organizations, but in small groups or "families" that are nested in organizations. In consequence, organizational behavior is intimately tied to small-group behavior.

To gain a sense of the possible applications of group dynamics to organizational behavior, consider how you might use the processes studied in Chapter 3 (group formation) to explain why individuals seek particular jobs with particular companies and how those individuals become accepted within the organizations. Or

THE LINKING-PIN MODEL OF ORGANIZATIONAL STRUCTURE

Rensis Likert (1961, 1967) believes that most complex organizations can be easily conceptualized as hierarchies of "families" that are tied together by "linking pins"—individuals who are leaders in one group but peer-group members at the next highest organizational level. Unlike many other organizational theories, Likert's model emphasizes group concepts—leadership, group goals, group responsibility—instead of individual concepts—personal motivation and responsibil-

ity. In general, Likert recommends that organizations be adapted to his scheme, since his system (1) limits intergroup conflicts, (2) increases communication effectiveness, (3) ensures that formal structures match informal structures, and (4) capitalizes on group processes for improving motivation.

(Source: Likert, 1961)

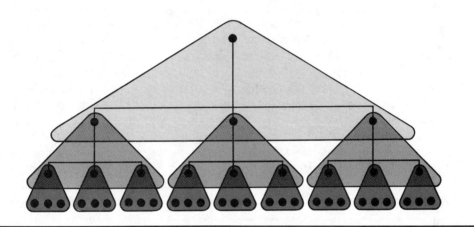

consider the parallel between the sources of disputes among workers and the sources of intragroup conflict examined in Chapter 4. Or, again, think about roles, examined in Chapter 5, as they function in industrial settings, where, along with norms they determine leadership practices, interaction patterns, and levels of productivity. At a general level, all the processes examined in the preceding chapters—conflict, performance, obedience, leadership, conformity, intergroup relations—are relevant, for organizational behavior is in large part group behavior.

Rather than simply reapply material discussed in earlier chapters to industrial groups in the two major sections that follow, we will restrict our analysis to two topics: goals and group satisfaction. First, in an attempt to clarify work motivation, we will examine group goals and compare them with individuals' goals. In the following section, we will turn to our second question: Does working in a group promote employee satisfaction?

Motives and Goals in Groups

Many analyses of work motivation, in emphasizing individualistic psychological factors (for example, need for achievement, drive to self-actualization, desire for success, or fear of failure; see Pinder, 1977, for a review) overlook the significance of group goals as motivators. As Alvin Zander explains in *Motives and Goals in Groups* (1971), in many instances people are as interested in helping their groups reach their goals as in satisfying their own personal needs. For example, when Zander asked women working an assembly line in a slipper factory to rate the importance of personal success and their group's success, the women strongly emphasized their group's goals. When he asked the same question of men working in a Swedish brewery, they also emphasized the importance of their work team's success—even though their concern for the company as a whole was minimal. Executives serving on the boards of 46 United Funds gave similar responses, suggesting that "team spirit" may be as important in determining productivity as the striving for individual achievement (Zander, 1974, 1977).

COHESIVENESS AND GROUP GOALS

The impact of group goals on productivity depends, of course, on members' commitment to the group and its objectives. We have all worked in groups that had little unity or sense of camaraderie, groups where individual goals dominated group goals. As Zander (1977) explains, group members typically have the choice of working for the group, for themselves, for both the group and themselves, or for neither, and thus do not always choose to strive for group success. If, however, group cohesiveness is so strong that all members feel united in a common effort, then group-oriented motives should replace individualistic motives and the desire among members for group success should be strong.

This line of reasoning suggests that cohesive groups will be more productive than noncohesive groups. However, this prediction overlooks one significant problem: the group's goal may not necessarily be to maximize productivity. For example, a major survey of 5871 factory workers in 228 groups found that the more cohesive the group, the less the productivity levels varied among members; members of cohesive groups produced nearly equivalent amounts, but individuals in noncohesive groups varied considerably more in their productivity. Furthermore,

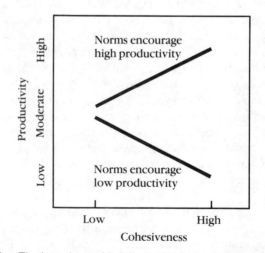

FIGURE 14-1. The hypothesized link between productivity and cohesiveness.

fairly low standards of performance had developed within some of the highly cohesive groups, and thus productivity was uniformly low among these groups. In contrast, in groups with relatively high performance goals, members of cohesive groups were extremely productive (Seashore, 1954). This evidence can be expressed in a hypothesis that predicts a link between cohesiveness and productivity: so long as group norms encourage high productivity, cohesiveness and productivity are positively related—the more cohesive the group, the greater its productivity. If, however, group norms encourage low productivity the relationship is negative. This hypothesized link between cohesiveness and productivity is graphically summarized in Figure 14-1.

This hypothesis appeared to be confirmed in an experimental study of productivity in which female college students worked in three-person teams on an assembly-line project in a laboratory setting (Schachter, Ellertson, McBride, & Gregory, 1951). First, half of the subjects were led to believe that they were members of cohesive groups, while the other subjects were convinced that their groups were noncohesive. Second, during the task, messages were ostensibly sent from one worker to another to establish performance norms. In some instances the messages called for increased production (positive messages), but in other instances the messages requested a slow-down (negative messages). As expected, the impact of the messages was significantly greater in the cohesive groups than in the noncohesive groups. Furthermore, the decreases in productivity brought about by the negative messages were greater than the increases brought about by the positive messages.

GROUP GOALS: CLARIFYING THE MEANS AND ENDS

Members of even the best-run groups sometimes lose sight of their group's original purpose. As multiple meetings are held, ambiguous issues raised, and divergent opinions voiced, members can become sidetracked, pursuing questions that are only tangentially related to their real goals. In an illuminating example of this process, John Z. DeLorean, a former top executive with General Motors Corporation, describes how even highly qualified executives can become disoriented (Wright, 1979). He writes of regularly-held pointless meetings, where trivial issues alone were discussed, attended by sleepy executives earning $100,000-plus salaries. DeLorean felt that General Motors had become overly centralized and that problems that could have been easily rectified at lower corporate levels were brought to the top executives. Thus the group virtually forgot its true task—planning for the corporation's future needs and goals—as the GM executives became the highest paid supervisors in the world.

While DeLorean's examples document the harmful consequences of unclear goals, several fascinating studies can be cited that demonstrate the beneficial effects of clear goals. For example, in one field investigation, truck drivers who hauled logs from the woods to the mill were initially told to "do their best" when loading the logs (Latham & Baldes, 1975). Unfortunately, with these vague instructions the men only carried about 60% of what they could legally haul. When the drivers were later encouraged to reach a goal of 94% of the legal limit, they increased their efficiency and met this specific goal. In financial terms, this clarification of goals saved the company more than a quarter of a million dollars. Other investigations have yielded similar results (see Locke, K. Shaw, Saari, & Latham, 1981, for a review), leading Zander (1971, p. xi) to conclude "A working group is more likely to be effective if it has a clear criterion of success since members can better comprehend where the group is going and whether it is getting there."

A possible exception to Zander's general conclusion concerning goal clarity arises when the *goal* is clear but the *path* to reaching it is unclear. The problem of the top-executives group at General Motors might well have stemmed as much from goal/path ambiguity as from goal ambiguity alone. Although they were supposed to plan for the corporation's future needs, the members had all been promoted from positions within the organization that had not prepared them for this task. In consequence, they simply did not know how to "tackle" the problem, for the path to follow in achieving this broad goal was unknown to them.

Similarly, goal/path ambiguity may be encountered by individuals who want to perform well but who are uncertain as to which factors their supervisors are concerned with in performance-quality evaluations. In one experiment, the subjects were telephone operators whose problem-solving abilities were being tested by their supervisor (Cohen, 1959). The employees' goal in this situation was clearcut—to achieve a high evaluation—but the means of achieving this goal were unclear, since the questions were ambiguous and difficult to answer. Therefore, where the supervisor informally told subjects how the problems could be solved, the operators worked well. In contrast, where the supervisor's informal hints were inconsistent and of little help, the subjects reported feeling less secure, rated themselves more negatively, evidenced less motivation, and worked less efficiently. The investigator therefore concluded that clear goals are not always enough; in some instances the paths to these goals must be clear as well.

SETTING GROUP GOALS

If indeed group effectiveness is dependent on clear goals and unambiguous paths, then it stands to reason that workers in industrial settings who have definite goals and clearcut paths to achieving them will perform better than those who do not. This suggestion, however, raises a question that has long intrigued group dynamicists: should goals be made difficult so that group members must work hard to achieve them, or should they be made fairly easy so that the group can be certain to succeed?

This question is addressed by **level-of-aspiration theory,** a theoretical perspective developed by Kurt Lewin that explains how people set goals for themselves and their groups (Lewin, Dembo, Festinger, & Sears, 1944). According to Lewin, people enter achievement situations with an ideal outcome in mind—for example, earning an A in the course, hitting a home run, turning out a given number of products, or making a specific amount of money. However, as they gain experience in a particular setting, people may revise these ideals to match more realistic expectations. For example, students entering a class may hope for a final grade of A, but if they fail the first two tests they may have to revise their goals. Lewin used the term level of aspiration (LOA) to describe this compromise between ideal goals and more realistic expectations.

Groups, like individuals, also develop levels of aspiration. For example, in one study Zander arranged for high school boys to play a simple skills game that required batting a wooden ball down a runway through team effort; scores could range from 5 to 50 points (Zander & Medow, 1963). The subjects wrote down their performance predictions before each trial and discussed their expectations among themselves until they reached complete agreement. Over a series of 14 trials Zander found that the group aspirations accurately reflected individual aspirations; groups did not opt for either extremely difficult or extremely easy goals, but rather for goals that matched the capabilities of their members. The group LOA was, however, slightly more optimistic than a strict forecast based on past performance would predict; groups averaged 36 points across the trials but the mean LOA was 38. During the group-discussion session members frequently exchanged encouraging suggestions, and this advice may have been partly responsible for the success-oriented LOAs in the groups.

Zander also reports that groups tended to revise their LOAs as feedback about performance levels became available. As with individuals, whenever groups succeeded in reaching their LOAs, they tended to raise their expectations on the next trial. Conversely, groups that failed to reach their preset goals tended to lower their LOAs. The only exception to this general "success-raise/failure-lower" rule involved relative change: groups lowered their LOA less after failure than they raised it after success. In one exemplifying study, Zander recorded the fund-raising goals set by United Funds. While 40% of the funds that failed to reach their previous year's goal lowered their LOAs slightly, 8% kept the same goals and 52% actually raised their goals. In contrast, 80% of the successful funds raised their LOAs, while 20% lowered or kept the same goals (Zander, 1971). For some of these groups, this continual raising of LOA resulted in a vicious cycle of failure. Pressured by outside forces to raise more funds, the members of the fund's executive board refused to admit defeat and continued to set overly optimistic goals. Some of these funds had not reached their goals in more than four years, and this consistent history of failure adversely affected group morale, work enjoyment, and group efficiency. Thus, while the optimistic goal setting of successful groups challenged members to work harder and improve performance, the refusal to revise overly idealistic goals in unsuccessful groups set the stage for future failure.

Satisfaction and Group Membership

Managers can ill afford to ignore the satisfactions of their workers. While satisfaction does not necessarily ensure smooth organizational functioning, dissatisfaction has been consistently linked with poor performance (Wanous, 1974), high turnover (Mobley, Griffeth, Hand, & Meglino, 1979), absenteeism (Porter & Steers, 1973), illness, and even accidents (Hersey, 1955). Given this important relationship between satisfaction and organizational outcomes, the following question arises: Does working in a group promote employees' satisfaction?

SATISFACTION AND SOCIAL INTERACTION

Anecdotal accounts abound of the beneficial effects of laboring in a cohesive, supportive group. For example, one particularly vivid account written by a newcomer to a group of men operating punch presses tells of the monotony and fatigue of the first few days (Roy, 1973). Quite soon, however, the newcomer began taking part in the group's informal social activities, which ranged from conversation to horseplay to out-and-out silliness. Many rituals were followed daily to help break up the monotony, such as the habitual unplugging of the machine of one worker, Sammy. Each day Sammy would leave his post for a few minutes to get a drink from the water fountain, and in his absence someone would disconnect his machine. Like clockwork, Sammy would return, try to start working, and then angrily reproach his comrades when his machine failed. The newcomer initially thought that Sammy must be very stupid to repeatedly "fall" for this simple practical joke, but in time he realized the supportive, healthy function of this social ritual: "It captured attention and held interest to make the long day pass" (Roy, 1973, p. 417).

The effects of group membership on satisfaction were clearly documented in an early study of bricklayers and carpenters working on a housing development (Van Zelst, 1952). For the first five months of the project the men worked at various assignments in groups formed by the supervisor. This period gave the men a chance to get to know virtually everyone working on the development, and natural likes and dislikes soon surfaced. The researcher assessed these relationships sociometrically, and established groups so that in nearly every instance men were able to work with those they liked the best. As anticipated, the new arrangement had many beneficial effects. In the words of one worker, "Seems as though everything flows a lot smoother. . . . The work is a lot more interesting when you've got a buddy working with you. You certainly like it a lot better anyway" (Van Zelst, 1952, p. 183). The work teams finished units more quickly and used fewer materials in the process when they were sociometrically compatible than when their associations were arbitrary. The turnover for the period also dropped substantially (from 3.1 men per production period to 0.3 men per period) and an overall 5% reduction in total project costs was realized.

SATISFACTION AND GROUP INCENTIVES

Given our current understanding of the effects of reinforcement on behavior, it stands to reason that when rewards (for example, bonuses, salaries, advancement) are contingent upon performance, productivity increases (Lawler, 1973). However, individual incentive programs sometimes run into problems: workers, fearful of rejection by their peers, may restrict output; intrinsic motivation may be undermined; or competition among work-group members for the limited reinforcements may escalate.

To prevent these problems from arising, several management specialists recommend the use of group rather than individual incentive plans (Bass & Ryterband, 1979; Farr, 1976; Lawler, 1973). An early study illustrating the benefits of the group-incentive approach involved switching sales clerks from a traditional commission system to a group commission system. While sales were satisfactory under the original plan, the clerks tended to ignore maintenance duties, compete with one another for customers, and suffer low morale. Under the group plan, in contrast, a stronger feeling of teamwork developed and members reported greater feelings of satisfaction (Babchuk & Goode, 1951). Similar successes with group-incentive schedules have been obtained in experimental studies as well (for example, Farr, 1976), but certain limitations should be noted. If group members are not contributing to the group's product in roughly equal proportions, a group-incentive plan can be very frustrating for the hard worker and seriously abused by the lazy worker. Furthermore, other evidence suggests that group payment is less effective in large work groups (say, more than ten members) and when group members are not given a voice in the setting of the standards for incentives (Bass & Ryterband, 1979).

SATISFACTION, SUCCESS, AND FAILURE

When the team loses the game, the production line fails to earn the bonus, the leader lambasts the group members for their inadequacies, or the executives fail to reach their fund-raising goal, a large number of positive and negative processes can be set in motion. On the plus side, failure may be motivating. Frustrated in their attempt to secure the group goal, members may strive even harder in their next group effort and thereby ensure a more satisfying outcome. When the failure is attributed to outside factors—such as interference by another group or another segment of the organization—the group may be welded into a more cohesive unit boasting high morale. Failure may also force the group to reconsider its aspirations and formulate a more realistic set of expectations.

Factors on the minus side of the equation, however, tend to outweigh these positive consequences of failure. While in most instances groups are motivated by a "desire for group success" (Zander, 1974), repeated failures can undermine this source of motivation. Members of failing groups can develop a strong "desire to avoid group failure," and begin utilizing various interpersonal strategies to overcome the embarrassment brought on by failure. For example, the group members may derogate the importance of the group's task by claiming that they are not personally concerned with the outcome or that failure is irrelevent to them personally (Forsyth & Schlenker, 1977). Alternatively, the group members may make success unlikely by setting unreasonably high goals, thus providing a justification for potential failures (Zander, 1971). Or members might reinterpret the feedback they receive in more positive terms (Janssens & Nuttin, 1976).

Table 14-1 is a sampling of embarrassment-avoiding tactics used by members of failing groups. As the table shows, many of these tactics are group serving—that is, they help the group as a unit to cope with the failure. In contrast, other tactics are self-serving, since they are designed to help individuals overcome their personal embarrassment at the expense of other group members. Naturally, group-serving tactics tend to unite the group while self-serving tactics can result in interpersonal conflict and a gradual reduction in cohesiveness (Jacobs, 1974). For example, in one study two teams competed against one another in a game situation (Shaw & Breed, 1970). Certain members of each team were confederates of the researcher, and these confederates systematically blamed one of the actual subjects for the team's losses. Unfairly accused group members, relative to others who had escaped blame, were less satisfied with their teams, belittled their teammates' abilities, and preferred to work with other groups on future tasks. Similar consequences of self-serving reactions in the face of failure were obtained in the study discussed in the box headed "Some Consequences of Grabbing Credit and Avoiding Blame" on page 415.

In sum, group members generally begin working on a task with fairly high expectations for success but through feedback sometimes discover that their initial

TABLE 14-1. A sampling of embarrassment-avoiding tactics used by members of failing groups

Tactic	Example
Group-serving tactics	
1. Minimizing the importance of success	1. "This goal isn't worth the trouble."
2. Seeking impossibly difficult goals	2. "No team could have done any better."
3. Denying embarrassment	3. "You have to expect to lose some."
4. Blaming the procedures	4. "We could do well if we could change the system."
5. Reinterpreting the feedback	5. "All things considered, I think we did pretty well."
Self-serving tactics	
1. Minimizing the importance of personal success	1. "The rest of the group thinks this goal is valuable, but I don't care."
2. Claiming personal success	2. "Personally speaking, I did well."
3. Blaming other group members	3. "My co-workers are incompetent."
4. Withdrawing from the group	4. "I'm not really part of that group anymore."
5. Shirking responsibility	5. "I am not responsible for my group's performance."

level of aspiration was overly optimistic. If the group continues to fail, group-serving rationalizations may keep the team from splitting apart, but the true source of the failure may remain unexcised. Perhaps even more damaging, the need to protect one's sense of personal competence may eventually dominate the desire to protect the group from embarrassment, and these self-serving reactions may turn members against one another. Although studies have not yet been conducted to identify the most effective means of coping with failure or maintaining success, Zander (1971) summarizes his own research with two general suggestions. First, because frustration and dissatisfaction can disrupt performance when the group's goals are either too easy or too difficult, Zander recommends that members set realistic goals. Second, because group members who are motivated by a desire to avoid failure sometimes utilize self-serving coping strategies that are, in the long run, detrimental to the group as a whole, Zander rejects a desire to avoid failure as a motivator. Instead, he consistently recommends the development of a desire for success within the group.

Groups and Change

One of Kurt Lewin's earliest studies of group dynamics grew out of the beef shortages resulting from wartime demands (Lewin, 1943). At the behest of the Food Habits Committee of the National Research Council, Lewin conducted a simple study to see if food preferences could be changed more efficiently through group discussion or through persuasion. He had only 45 minutes to convince the volunteer homemakers to serve undesirable (but readily available) meat products (beef hearts, sweetbreads, kidneys) to their families, so he developed two basic approaches that could be utilized in the experimental setting. The first approach, which was used for three groups, featured an "attractive" lecture that stressed the patriotic importance of serving these meats, ways to prepare the foods, and the

SOME CONSEQUENCES OF GRABBING CREDIT AND AVOIDING BLAME

Have you ever worked with someone who, after discovering the group had failed, exclaimed "You really blew that one"? How did you react? Similarly, when someone in the group moans "I deserve all the blame for what happened," do you appreciate the modesty and self-sacrifice of the blame taker?

To study group members' reactions to such responsibility claims, investigators assigned college students to small groups working on a simulated survival exercise (Forsyth, Berger, & Mitchell, 1981). After they learned whether they had succeeded or failed at their task, the subjects ranked themselves regarding personal responsibility for the outcome and ranked others regarding credit (or blame) due. Finally, the subjects evaluated other group members who had apparently claimed high, moderate, and low responsibility for the outcome.

As shown in the figure, when the group failed, the self-serving low-responsibility claimer was liked significantly less than the more group-serving moderate and high-responsibility claimers. Con-

versely, when the group did well, individuals who claimed all the credit were liked the least and moderate-responsibility claimers were liked the most. Overall, group members who tried to place themselves in the best light at the expense of the rest of the group were not well liked.

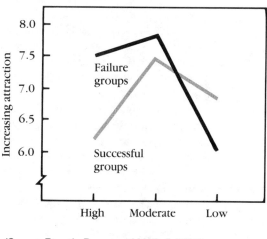

(Source: Forsyth, Berger, and Mitchell, 1981)

food's nutritional value. Although the participants listened to the persuasive lecture in a group, they did not interact with one another. In contrast, a second approach applied to three other groups involved the homemakers in a group discussion of the meat products. In this second approach the participants discussed the same information used in the lecture, but they were also urged to reach a group consensus on the issue. Thus, the focus in the first approach was on changing the individual's opinion, while the focus in the second approach was on changing the group's opinion.

A follow-up yielded striking differences between the two approaches. While only 3% of the members who heard the lecture served the unique meats, 32% of the group discussants served at least one dish containing the less desirable foods. Intrigued by these findings, Lewin and his colleagues conducted a series of similar studies on work production, alcoholism, and prejudices, and in study after study they found strong effects of groups on individual behavior change (see Lewin, 1953, for a review). Summarizing these studies, Lewin (1951, p. 228) stated, "It is easier to change individuals formed into a group than to change any of them separately." In this section we will see how Lewin's "law" of achieving change through group participation explains organizational development and change.

The Group as Change Agent

In the late 1940s the management of the Harwood Manufacturing Corporation was grappling with a thorny production problem. The plant turned out a fairly basic product—pajamas—but due to engineering advances and product alterations, changes in production methods occurred frequently. Unfortunately, these changes called for job changes as well, and each reform was met with protests and grievances from the line workers. To the women working in the factory, it seemed that the management was taking fiendish pleasure in changing their jobs as soon as they had learned them perfectly. In consequence, turnover was high, productivity was down, and the amount of time needed for retraining after each production change was excessive.

To solve these problems, two group dynamicists—Lester Coch and John R. P. French, Jr.—conducted a field study in which they compared three types of training programs (Coch & French, 1948). The first method, *no participation,* served as a control condition. As had always been the case in the company, employees were not involved in the planning and implementation of the changes but were given an explanation for the innovations. The second method involved *participation through representation,* since a group meeting was held with all employees present. The need for change was discussed openly, and an informal decision was reached. A subgroup of the employees was then chosen to become the "special" operators who would serve as the first training group. The third method, *total participation,* followed much the same procedures as those used in the second method, but here all the employees, not a select group, were transferred to the training system.

As briefly noted in Chapter 8, the results of the innovation were impressive. The control group improved very little, and hostility, turnover, and inefficiency within it remained high. In fact, 17% of the control-condition workers quit rather than relearn the new procedure, and those that remained never reached the goals set by time/motion experts. The two participation conditions, in contrast, responded well. These workers learned their new tasks quickly, and their productivity soon surpassed prechange levels and the time/motion goals. Morale was high, only one hostile action was recorded, and none of the employees quit in the 40 days following the change. Furthermore, when the members of the control condition were run through a participation program several months later, they too reached appropriate production levels.

Although among the earliest systematic studies, the Coch/French experiments are not the only examples of groups being used as agents of organizational change. For instance, beginning in the late 1940s the executives at Texas Instruments laid the foundations for what would become a billion-dollar-a-year enterprise. Showing remarkable insight into group processes, the TI management organized employees into small groups whenever possible, took steps to build up team cohesiveness, and went to great lengths to establish clear goals based on realistic levels of aspiration (Bass & Ryterband, 1979). In a related effort, the Esso Standard Oil Company began utilizing group-level processes in the 1950s to develop and implement a series of carefully planned organizational changes (Esso Research Division, 1960). In the 1960s the Banner Company, one of the largest packing manufacturers in the United States, systematically manipulated five organizational variables (emphasis on the work group, supportive supervision, participant leadership, organizational overlap among groups, and intensity of group interaction) highlighted in Likert's linking-pin model (Likert, 1961; see the box earlier). This study went on for several years, revealing consistent improvements in employee satisfaction, waste reduction, and turnover (Seashore & Bowers, 1970). At about the same time as the Banner project, the innovative management at the Harwood pajama plant began an elaborate series of changes designed to rework the organization of the recently purchased Weldon Company (Marrow, Bowers, & Seashore, 1967). Although in some respects these interventions went beyond the bounds of small-group behavior by manipulating individualistic and organizational factors as well as group variables, in many instances group dynamics played a pivotal role in the organizational changes. Furthermore, because these efforts were generally quite effective, in recent years managers have been relying ever more heavily on group approaches to organizational change. Often these systematic programs for achieving change in business and industry are referred to as **organizational-development.**

Organizational-Development

The "organizational-development movement" has been steadily growing in popularity for the last 15 years. Typically referred to as simply OD, organizational-development techniques are management programs specifically designed to improve organizations. For example, if a company is having difficulty retaining employees—say, the annual turnover rate is 65%—the management may wish to interview workers and locate the source of the problem. If the executives of an international conglomerate become ensnared in petty squabbles during board meetings, they may hire a consultant who initiates a series of communication-improvement workshops. If two companies are considering a merger, elaborate planning may be undertaken to link the two organizations in the most profitable manner possible. Of course, the company executives could deal with these kinds of problems without recourse to OD, but in certain instances they may opt for an innovative, carefully planned analysis grounded in social-science theory and research. Outside experts—OD consultants and/or social scientists—are often "imported" to carry out the project, which (to oversimplify greatly) generally involves one or more of the following components:

1. *Description:* determining the organization's current stage of development through systematic observation and survey work;
2. *Goal specification:* elaborating, clarifying, and determining the priority of objectives of the organization;
3. *Planning:* developing a plan for achieving organizational goals; and
4. *Innovation:* implementing the plan and evaluating its effectiveness.

As recent overviews of the organizational-development literature are careful to note, managers and their consultants can use a wide variety of techniques when addressing the four kinds of concerns (see, for example, Beckard, 1969; McGill, 1977; Varney, 1977). However, the techniques that are considered briefly below— survey feedback, process consultation, team building, and laboratory training— are among the most frequently encountered approaches to organizational-development.

SURVEY FEEDBACK

Bill Busman, as director of personnel for the central office, was responsible for recruiting, training, and promoting employees in a wide range of positions. Therefore, he was well aware of the fact that a problem was developing in the office staff unit. Recent months had seen an increase in turnover among the unit's secretaries, stenographers, receptionists, and clerks, and despite several extensive conferences with office managers the source of the difficulty remained elusive. Losses in efficiency were growing more noticeable, and Busman realized that unless steps were taken to reverse the trend, upper-level management would soon be demanding answers.

In this type of situation an OD consultant might very well recommend using a strategy known as **survey feedback.** Developed in the 1950s by members of the Survey Research Center of the Institute for Social Research of the University of Michigan (Mann & Likert, 1952), the survey-feedback approach emphasizes description as a means of locating sources of organizational dysfunction. During the initial stages of OD, the consultant gathers information about the current state of the organization through observation, employee interviews, and surveys. Next, these findings are synthesized to form an overall picture of the organization that pinpoints both adequacies as well as inadequacies. These findings are then channeled back into the organization in the form of feedback, and in some instances the consultant develops a plan for changing the more problematic aspects of the organization.

Applied to our fictitious case of office-worker turnover, a survey-feedback analysis would begin by systematically assessing employees' attitudes toward their duties, their managers, and the organization as a whole. In a small company this poll may be taken by informally interviewing employees, but if the company is large and a wide sampling is required, then the consultant might use a standard survey instrument such as that in Figure 14-2. This questionnaire, which was developed by Rensis Likert (1967), assesses several key dimensions of organizational climate, with higher scores reflecting smoother, more efficient functioning. In the abridged version shown in Figure 14-2, the management diagnosis questionnaire includes 18 questions focusing on leadership (1–3), motivation (4–6), communication (7–10), decision making (11–13), goals (14 and 15), and control (16–18). After collecting an adequate sampling of employees' perceptions, the consultant typically summarizes these responses in the form of an organizational profile. The average of employees' responses to each item is plotted on a diagnostic chart, which can be shared with the participating employees as well as the office managers. For example, if a profile such as that graphed in Figure 14-2 were obtained, the OD consultant may conclude that the high turnover was caused by poor leadership practices of the office managers, a lack of goal-oriented motivation among employees, and the company's centralized decision-making procedures. His or her recommendations for organizational development might therefore emphasize a more elaborate training program for corporate managers, a revitalized

FIGURE 14-2. A hypothetical profile of averaged responses to Rensis Likert's "Management Diagnosis Chart" (shortened version). (Source: Likert, 1967)

	Organizational Variables	System 1	System 2	System 3	System 4	Item No.
Leadership	How much confidence and trust is shown in subordinates?	Virtually none	Some	Substantial amount	A great deal	1
Leadership	How free do they feel to talk to superiors about job?	Not very free	Somewhat free	Quite free	Very free	2
Leadership	How often are subordinates' ideas sought and used constructively?	Seldom	Sometimes	Often	Very frequently	3
Motivation	Is predominant use made of 1 fear, 2 threats, 3 punishment, 4 rewards, 5 involvement?	1, 2, 3, occasionally 4	4, some 3	4, some 3 and 5	5, 4, based on group	4
Motivation	Where is responsibility felt for achieving organization's goals?	Mostly at top	Top and middle	Fairly general	At all levels	5
Motivation	How much cooperative teamwork exists?	Very little	Relatively little	Moderate amount	Great deal	6
Communication	What is the usual direction of information flow?	Downward	Mostly downward	Down and up	Down, up, and sideways	7
Communication	How is downward communication accepted?	With suspicion	Possibly with suspicion	With caution	With a receptive mind	8
Communication	How accurate is upward communication?	Usually inaccurate	Often inaccurate	Often accurate	Almost always accurate	9
Communication	How well do superiors know problems faced by subordinates?	Not very well	Rather well	Quite well	Very well	10
Decisions	At what level are decisions made?	Mostly at top	Policy at top, some delegation	Broad policy at top, more delegation	Throughout but well integrated	11
Decisions	Are subordinates involved in decisions related to their work?	Almost never	Occasionally consulted	Generally consulted	Fully involved	12
Decisions	What does decision-making process contribute to motivation?	Not very much	Relatively little	Some contribution	Substantial contribution	13
Goals	How are organizational goals established?	Orders issued	Orders, some comments invited	After discussion, by orders	By group action (except in crisis)	14
Goals	How much covert resistance to goals is present?	Strong resistance	Moderate resistance	Some resistance at times	Little or none	15
Control	How concentrated are review and control functions?	Very highly at top	Quite highly at top	Moderate delegation to lower levels	Widely shared	16
Control	Is there an informal organization resisting the formal one?	Yes	Usually	Sometimes	No—same goals as formal	17
Control	What are cost, productivity, and other control data used for?	Policing, punishment	Reward and punishment	Reward, some self-guidance	Self-guidance, problem-solving	18

motivational system of group incentives and job enrichment, and a decentralization of goal-setting procedures.

PROCESS CONSULTATION

Darlene Boss was delighted when she was promoted to director of the research and development unit, but as the weeks went by her delight turned into worry. Upper management had asked Darlene's unit to evaluate the potential profit to be gained from manufacturing two new items, but the personnel Darlene had chosen to complete the projection had already missed several deadlines. To spur the group's creativity, Darlene had scheduled weekly meetings to consider new ideas, but these sessions were characterized by so much in-group bickering, irrelevant conversation, and yawning, that little was accomplished. Other problems were also surfacing in the unit, but Darlene was not sure whether the fault lay with the staff, her leadership abilities, or the difficulty of the tasks facing the group.

OD experts called in to assist Ms. Boss in her diagnosis of the problem might decide to explore the unit's difficulties through **process consultation.** This approach, which has been most strongly advocated by Edgar Schein (1971), typically involves informal observation of the group as it goes about its everyday business. The consultant(s), who are well versed in the intricacies of group behavior, focus on the many aspects of groups that we have considered in earlier chapters, including patterns of communication and attraction, decision-making procedures, sources of power, informal social norms, potency of in-group pressures, and varieties of intermember conflict. Once the consultants are confident that they understand how the group is working, they discuss their conclusions with the unit and ask "Did you realize that you were working this way?" and "Would you like to change any of these processes?" If the group answers "yes" to the second question, the consultants offer suggestions designed to improve the group's dynamics.

Applied to the example, process consultation might begin with the observation of the unit's weekly meetings. The consultant would note such factors as where people sit around the conference table, who attends, who speaks to whom, and who offers task versus socioemotional comments, and would try to integrate this information in an overall portrayal of the group. As a result of this unstructured observational period, the consultant might realize that one of the males in the group is the focus of many of the comments made by others, and that this male frequently changes the direction of the discussion. After later interviewing some of the unit members, the consultant could conclude that this male, who has been with the company for many years, is the informal leader of the group. Many of the employees look to him for guidance, and because he partly resents the presence of Ms. Boss he tends to take action on his own. Furthermore, the newer employees accept Ms. Boss as their leader, but this acceptance contributes to the development of a conflict-laden coalition situation. The consultant would then cautiously describe these dynamics to the group during their next meeting, and after much discussion the members might begin to understand the implications of this structural breakdown. The group would then agree to take special precautions, such as meeting in nominal groups, relocating offices to break up coalitions, and regulating information flow through Ms. Boss' office, and soon the efficiency of the unit would be regained.

TEAM BUILDING

As he prepared for the weekly meeting, Arthur recalled how the previous session had been interrupted by a personal argument between two members, a 20-minute discussion of the company's new office furniture, and the loud snoring of one less-than-enthusiastic member. Overcoming an impulse to skip the meeting, Arthur is first to arrive despite being five minutes late. As others trickle in they sit around the table in silence, and the few feeble attempts at conversation are short lived. Not too surprisingly, about a third of the members never show up.

Arthur's group could profit from a **team-building** intervention. This OD technique begins with the assumption that success in work groups results from a collaborative interdependence that develops through practice. The work-group-as-team analogy is fundamental to this approach, so in many ways team building in the work place parallels team building in sports. For example, a game such as football—with its high interdependence among players and emphasis on group goals—requires elaborate teamwork if played with any degree of expertise. Each play must be practiced again and again until the athletes function as a single unit, and desire for personal success must be transformed into a desire for group success. The team's coach may create situations designed to foster a sense of team spirit, and he or she may encourage the players to formulate group goals, identify weaknesses in the team, and strive for cooperation and integration. Similarly, during team building in the work setting the manager/consultant acts as the "coach" by helping the group develop a sense of team unity. Just as athletes must learn how to pool their individual abilities and energies to maximize the team's performance, employees must learn to coordinate their efforts with those of the other group members. Group goals must be set, work patterns structured, and a sense of group identity developed. Individual members must learn how to coordinate their actions, and any strains and stresses in interpersonal relations need to be identified and resolved. Thus, team building emphasizes the analysis of work procedures, the development of positive member-to-member relationships, and the role of the manager as "coach" (Dyer, 1977; Ends & Page, 1977; McGill, 1977).

Applied to Arthur's group, the imaginary team-building instruction begins with a "retreat" or workshop held at a site away from the work setting. This workshop (given the ideal circumstances) lasts for several days to enable members to move past surface problems to more essential issues. A consultant is structuring the workshop, and she chooses to start things off with a discussion of the unit's "problems." To show the group members that they can work together smoothly and efficiently, the consultant utilizes a special decisional procedure—the Nominal Group Technique (see Chapter 6)—to stimulate productivity. As the day continues the results of the discussion are written on newsprint so that they can be posted around the conference room and visibly remind participants that progress is being made.

Once Arthur's group reaches agreement concerning the group's difficulties—say, unclear goals, unstructured work procedures, and poor group decision-making skills—then the consultant introduces specific activities designed to solve these problems. A structured goal-setting session is used to obtain members' agreement on a set of realistic objectives, and work procedures are reviewed and redesigned to make better use of the group's resources. To improve group communication skills the consultant arranges for the unit to work on tasks that are very similar to the types of activities that the group generally performs. A videotape is made of this activity to be critiqued later by the consultant and the group, and once specific limitations are noted the group practices improved problem-solving behaviors. Lastly, on the final day of the workshop the consultant asks the members to relax and "open up" by publicly voicing any gripes or dissatisfactions that they may have been suppressing thus far. While the session begins slowly, things soon heat up as participants discuss their comembers' limitations and irritating work habits. Although some members feel threatened, for the most part the open communication of grievances results in a substantial reduction of interpersonal friction within the group.

LABORATORY TRAINING

When Daphne's boss received another complaint he decided that the problem had to be confronted and resolved. He knew that Daphne was a talented executive, but her subordinates were complaining that she was insensitive to their needs, brusque in manner, hard to talk to, and highly critical of even their best work. When confronted with the "charges," Daphne insisted that the fault lay with her subordinates and not with herself.

In this hypothetical example the boss could deal with the difficulty by asking Daphne to participate in a *laboratory training program* or *T-group* (see the box). Like team-building OD, T-groups meet in isolated settings away from the workplace. Unlike team building, Daphne would be the only executive from her company present; the other 10 to 12 members of her T-group would be executives from other organizations. While from time to time the conferees might meet in

ORIGINS OF T-GROUPS

Group-dynamics folklore suggests that the first human-relations training group, or T-group for short, was serendipitously initiated by Kurt Lewin in 1946. As part of a series of problem-solving workshops, Lewin arranged for his graduate students to observe and later discuss the dynamics of work groups. These discussions were held in private until one evening a few of the work-group members asked if they could listen to the interpretations. Lewin reluctantly agreed to their request, and sure enough the participants confirmed Lewin's expectations by sometimes vehemently disagreeing with the observations and interpretations offered by Lewin's students. However, the animated discussion that followed proved to be highly educational, and Lewin realized that everyone in the group was benefiting enor-

mously from the analysis of their group's processes and dynamics.

Lewin helped organize the National Training Laboratory (NTL) at Bethel, Maine, which later flourished under the leadership of Leland P. Bradford. This center further developed the concept of training groups in special workshops or "laboratories," and during the sixties and seventies thousands of executives participated in programs offered by NTL and other training centers. Although the long-term effectiveness of T-groups is still being debated (compare, for example, Aronson, 1980; Bednar & Kaul, 1979; Kaplan, 1979) and recent years have seen a decline in the technique's popularity (McGill, 1977), laboratory-human-relations training remains an important method of achieving positive change in people.

large groups to hear lectures or presentations, during the program most learning would take place in the small group. Advocates of laboratory training believe that significant increases in self-knowledge and sensitivity toward others can be gained by actually experiencing an intensive, long-term group relationship, and training can therefore last as long as three weeks. Although each group includes a professional leader—often called *facilitator* or *trainer*—this individual acts primarily as a catalyst for discussion rather than as director of the group. Indeed, in the first few days of a T-group's existence, the members often complain of the lack of structure and the situational ambiguity, blaming the trainer for their discomfort. From the very start, the facilitator works to shift responsibility for structuring, understanding, and controlling the group's activities to the participants themselves.

Daphne's group members begin their training by introducing themselves to one another. This process takes only a few minutes, however, so soon the ten executives are raising questions of agenda, goals, and structure. When the leader refuses to "lead," the members begin to institute a structure for their group. Daphne takes a major role at this point, and makes a variety of suggestions ranging from planned activities to nominating a group member to act as the recorder. She dominates the group for nearly an hour until one of the more quiet members complains "Who put you in charge here? You sure are pushy." Daphne reacts defensively by denying any attempt to boss others around, but soon the interactants are all drawn into a discussion of the group's dynamics and the personal behaviors of individual members. In time, Daphne realizes that she has hardly understood herself, much less the meaning of her interactions with others. Through feedback from the other group members, she improves her ability to communicate and gains awareness of herself and her fellow members. She learns to disclose her feelings honestly, gains conflict-reduction skills, and finds enjoyment from working in collaborative relationships. When Daphne returns to her post in her company, her subordinates are struck by the dramatic change in her interpersonal skills.

In summary, the T-group approach is an experiential learning procedure. Although Daphne could learn more facts about effective interpersonal relations by attending lectures or by reading a book about group dynamics, the proponents of T-group methods argue that good group skills are most easily acquired by actually experiencing human relations. Hence, during laboratory training members are encouraged to actively confront and resolve interpersonal issues with the goal of better understanding of self and others. As one advocate of group training explains,

> The training laboratory is a special environment in which they learn new things about themselves. . . . It is a kind of emotional re-education. It teaches that the modern executive to be truly efficient must understand as much about feelings as he does about facts [Marrow, 1964, p. 25].

Meetings

No discussion of groups in industry and organizations would be complete without examining that hallowed institution, the meeting. Surveys indicate that the average corporate executive spends well over three hours a week in regularly scheduled formal conferences and another nine and one-half hours in more informal group sessions (Tilman, 1960). The number of required committee member-ships proliferates as one moves up the corporate ladder, making the committee meeting a critically important structure within the organization. Yet, while most executives agree that committees are "the best way to ensure informed decisions," a substantial number of the respondents sampled in one study (more than 50%) felt that committees, while useful, waste too much time (Tilman, 1960). A small number even suggested abolishing all committees in their organizations, express-ing a sentiment that many of us have probably felt at one time or another.

Citing the negative features of meetings is relatively easy. They can be boring affairs, dominated by a few powerful individuals who quash dissent. They are expensive, for by definition they often involve several highly paid individuals (one two-hour meeting attended by 20 executives matches in time and money spent the cost of one individual's entire work week). They can waste time in making minor decisions, and their participants can become mired in conflict and fall prey to groupthink. Rather than concentrating on the weaknesses and pitfalls often characteristic of everyday committee meetings, however, let us consider some actions that participants—both rank-and-file members and group leaders—can take to enhance their committees' effectiveness (for more detailed discussions of "meeting tips" see Auger, 1972; Donaldson & Scannell, 1978; Doyle & Straus, 1977; Kirkpatrick, 1980; Lord, 1981; Nadler & Nadler, 1980; Potter & Andersen, 1976; Snell, 1979).

Becoming a Good Group Member

Books on "how to improve your group" tend to focus primarily on the leader of the meeting, as if he or she alone determined the committee's destiny. Clearly, such an assumption overlooks the fact that the general members can make or break even the most elaborately planned, carefully orchestrated meetings. Thus, participants should not simply sit back and listen to the group discussion, secure in the belief that the possible failure of the meeting could be blamed on the discussion leader or other participants. Rather, group members should do all they can to make the meeting a positive, productive experience. Undoubtedly partic-ipants sometimes find this task difficult, but they may increase the meeting's use-fulness if they keep in mind some of the following suggestions.

PREPARATION

Like Boy Scouts, group members should be prepared. Premeeting preparations need not be time consuming or elaborate, but merely sufficient to enable the participant to contribute maximally. The kind of preparation required before a staff meeting, workshop, discussion, or planning session depends in large part upon the *function* of the particular meeting. In most organizations meetings are held for specific reasons, and adequate preparation means tailoring premeeting activities to these functions. First, if the primary function of the meeting is *information distribution*—the reporting of activities of various subcommittees, the summarizing of the year's successes, or the reviewing of new work procedures—then partici-pants should be ready to present information as it is called for. The chair of one of the reporting subcommittees has the added responsibility of reviewing the subgroup's conclusions just prior to the full meeting, perhaps developing handouts or visual aids required for a smooth presentation. Second, if the meeting is an initial *fact-finding discussion* focused on a problem or issue, participants would profit from reviewing their own ideas and understandings of relevant facts before the meeting. They might even wish to bring along materials to share with the rest of the group. Third, before *decision-making sessions* participants might wish to go over notes and the minutes from previous meetings held concerning the issue, informally discussing the matter with comembers and trying to anticipate criticisms of the solution they favor. Fourth, if the meeting serves an *organizational* function—for example, goal setting, revision of work procedures, sharing of feedback, or developing better interunit coordination—then participants' preparations may be as simple as collecting their thoughts and energies as they focus on the task at hand. Lastly, if the meeting serves more than a single purpose, as if often the case, then members would be well advised to prepare for each aspect of the meeting.

COMMUNICATION

The success of any meeting is heavily dependent upon the participants' ability to communicate effectively with one another. If the discussion shoots off on tangents, members ignore one another's comments, and ideas are poorly presented, the conferees will no doubt leave feeling "Another wasted meeting; we accomplished nothing." In contrast, if the recommendations are followed for effective group process offered by communication theorists (see Chapter 6), then members will walk away from the meeting with a sense of progress and self-satisfaction. Researchers are only beginning to accumulate enough empirical information to generate pragmatic suggestions, but experience in groups recommends a number of "rules" for the active communicator:

1. Make your statements brief and clear.
2. Try to add your own comments, suggestions, statements, and questions at the "right" point in the discussion; timing can be critical.
3. Make long verbal presentations to the group interesting by using imaginative phrasings, colorful analogies and similes, and eye-catching visual aids.
4. Actively listen to what others are saying.
5. Ask for clarification of statements that you do not understand.
6. Draw silent participants into the discussion through questioning.
7. Explore rather than avoid sources of disagreement and tension.
8. Follow the course of the discussion carefully, keeping in mind the points that have been made while anticipating profitable directions to follow.

SUPPORTIVENESS

In general, meetings should be cooperative endeavors built on openness and trust rather than competitive debates emphasizing power tactics and the verbal manipulation of others. To achieve this state of healthy interdependency, participants must be supportive in their interactions. As Rensis Likert explains,

All the interaction, problem-solving, decision-making activities of the group occur in a supportive atmosphere. Suggestions, comments, ideas, information, criticisms are all offered with helpful orientation. Similarly, these contributions are received in the same spirit. Respect is shown for the point of view of others both in the way contributions are made and in the way they are received [1961, p. 167].

Conducting the Meeting

Inevitably among the participants at any meeting is that one person with the special duty of conducting the meeting. Although the chairperson's responsibilities vary depending upon the nature and function of the meeting, the successful chair acts to achieve the two basic leadership goals noted in Chapter 8: improving task performance and maintaining good intermember relations. Unfortunately, most chairs have learned their leadership techniques in boring, time-wasting groups conducted by chairpersons who are similarly "on-the-job trained." Thus, ineffective tactics and techniques are passed down from one generation of chairpersons to the next. No wonder meetings and those who conduct them are generally described as "plodding," "petty," "nonproductive," and "rigid." This reputation could be changed if chairs would adopt some of the policies recommended below.

PREPARATION

The premeeting activities of the chairperson are usually much more varied and detailed than those of the rank-and-file member. Even before walking through the door of the conference room a chair deals with questions of time, place, function, participants, priorities, and agenda. To begin, the chair must clearly understand the purpose of the meeting, since other preparations depend heavily on this basic question. In addition, the chair must grapple with agenda development and circulation, for the members who are to be "invited" themselves must be given adequate time to prepare.

Unfortunately, harried chairpersons sometimes fail to send out agendas or circulate sketchy ones hastily tossed together, and in consequence their meetings go badly. Some frequently seen agenda-based errors are (1) topic lists so long that the group dispenses with only the most insignificant items in the time allotted; (2) poor sequencing of topics, in which low-priority items are discussed at length while high-priority items are slighted; and (3) the inclusion of items that should be addressed and resolved elsewhere. Naturally, to develop a "good" agenda, the chair must keep his or her finger on the pulse of the group, including only topics the members truly wish to discuss, identifying controversial issues in advance, and allotting sufficient time for item resolution. Once the chairperson has prepared by determining the function of the meeting and the agenda, then he or she can turn to some of the more mundane aspects of conference preparation, such as selecting an appropriate room, arranging for refreshments, checking equipment needs, preparing figures, charts, and other visual aids, and so on.

STRUCTURING THE GROUP

The first few meetings of any new group are often ambiguous events characterized by uncertainty. By the third or fourth meeting the group will have developed a fairly clear structure of norms, roles, and intermember relations, but in the early sessions members aren't sure how they should relate to one another. While this temporary confusion may create some problems for the rank-and-file members, it presents the group's leader with a golden opportunity to shape the group's structure. For example, if members initially feel that the chairperson should "run" the meeting, the chair can dispel this preconception from the outset by defining his or her role as a *process facilitator* rather than a *process controller*. The farsighted chairperson can also work to instill norms that promote effective group functioning during this formative phase of group development. To prevent difficulties from arising farther down the road, the chairperson can make certain that the group's unspoken rules of conduct include such standards as "Prepare in advance for each meeting," "Take an active role in all discussions," "Do not engage in side conversations during the meeting," and "Arrive on time."

STRUCTURING THE MEETING

The chairperson not only guides the development of a promotive group structure but also works to structure each individual meeting. Although most members enter meetings expecting to follow the usual rituals—open with statement of goal, discuss various perspectives, push for consensus, vote if necessary—a chairperson who can modify these procedures can help the group to function more efficiently while avoiding the monotony of the routine. For example, if the group needs to

ROBERT'S RULES OF ORDER

For a number of years army engineer Henry M. Robert had been irritated by the chaos and confusion that characterized many of the meetings he attended. Realizing that a solution to this problem lay in the development of a set of rules for standardizing meetings, he published the guidelines that now bear his name: *Robert's Rules of Order* (first published in 1876). Patterned after the operating principles of the U. S. House of Representatives, *Robert's Rules* explicate not only "methods of organizing and conducting meetings, the duties of officers, and the names of ordinary motions," but also such technicalities as how motions should be stated, amended, debated, postponed, voted upon, and passed (Robert, 1915/1971). For example, no less than seven pages are used to describe how the group member "obtains the floor," including suggestions for proper phrasings of the request, appropriate posture, and timing. More complex issues, such as the intricacies of voting, require as many as 20 pages of discussion.

Robert's Rules are the traditionally adopted regulations for many groups. Thus, to increase their effectiveness group members should study them carefully and use them to advantage during meetings. However, while the rules are extremely useful in organizing meetings, they are not without certain drawbacks. Robert purposely designed them to "restrain the individual somewhat," for he assumed that "the right of any individual, in any community, to do what he pleases, is incompatible with the interests of the whole" (1915/1971, p. 13). In consequence, the rules promote a formal, technically precise form of interaction, sometimes at the expense of openness, vivacity, and directness. Additionally, the rules can create a "win/lose" atmosphere in the group, for members expect to debate differences and to solve these disagreements through voting rather than a discussion to consensus. Lastly, groups using the rules can become so highly structured that little room is left for group development, interpersonal adjustment, and role negotiation. Because in a sense the rules take the "dynamics" out of group dynamics, leaders should remain ever mindful of their weaknesses as well as their strengths.

agree on a creative solution to a problem, then the chairperson might ask that the group's usual discussion guidelines (probably *Robert's Rules of Order;* see the box) be suspended so that ideas can be discussed more openly. The chairperson could also explain brainstorming, nominal groups, or synectics procedures to the group (see Chapter 6), and use these special performance techniques whenever meetings bog down or conflicts become so strong that face-to-face discussion is ineffectual.

FACILITATING EFFECTIVE GROUP PROCESS

Chairpersons, and rank-and-file members to a lesser extent, are also responsible for facilitating effective group process, where *process* refers to all the various actions undertaken by members during the meeting. At the start of each session the chair should remind conferees about the function and objectives of the meeting (information distribution, fact finding, and so on) before running down the list of topics to be considered. Keeping one eye on the *content* of the discussion—points raised, ideas offered, questions resolved—and one eye on *process*—who is talking most, what conflicts are developing, where the discussion is headed—the chairperson works to make the meeting move along smoothly. To achieve this goal chairs should monitor the amount of time spent on each topic and encourage resolution when appropriate. Group discussions can bog down if members are not reminded of time constraints, and chairpersons can win many friends and admirers by keeping meetings interesting, lively, and fast-paced. The chairperson can also work to improve communication among members by providing clear transitions from topic to topic (especially when a change in topic also involves a change in function), summarizing and synthesizing the points made in discussion, providing feedback to discussants, and drawing out reticent members through questioning.

Summary

Although nearly all the topics considered in previous chapters are relevant to human behavior in industrial and organizational settings, in this introduction to the area we focused on three major topics: organizational group behavior, achieving change through groups, and improving the efficiency of meetings. Like Rensis Likert's *linking-pin theory* of organizations, our approach assumed that much organizational behavior is actually group behavior, and that performance can therefore be improved through a consideration of group goals and group satisfactions. For example, while cohesive groups often outperform noncohesive groups, evidence indicates that tightly knit groups will actually perform poorly if their norms emphasize low levels of productivity. Performance is also influenced by the clarity of goals, paths to these goals, level of aspiration, and group members' overall satisfaction with group membership.

Because research tends to support Kurt Lewin's "law" concerning *achieving change through groups,* most organizational-development techniques focus on groups rather than individuals. Exploring several OD techniques we found that (1) survey-feedback strategies are useful for objectively assessing the organizational climate, (2) process consultation—when carried out by a consultant skilled in group-process analysis—can detect formerly unrecognized dysfunctions under-lying organizational interactions, (3) team building can succeed in promoting unity and "team spirit" in disjointed work groups, and (4) laboratory training (or T-groups) can increase individuals' understanding of themselves and their rela-tions with others.

In the final section of the chapter we turned our attention to *meetings*. Although very little empirical evidence exists that directly addresses the source of dysfunction in meetings and ways to alleviate these problems, by extending basic group prin-ciples elaborated in previous chapters we were able to offer some definite rec-ommendations to group members. For the rank-and-file member, premeeting preparation should be consistent with the function of the meeting, whether it be informational, fact finding, decision making, or organizational. During the meeting participants should also try to maintain effective communication patterns while remaining supportive of others. The individual who conducts the meeting should also be prepared for the conference, and must work to structure both the group and the meeting itself. The effective group leader is able to facilitate effective group process while contributing to the substantive content of the discussion.

15

Groups in Educational, Judiciary, and Athletic Contexts

i

n one respect group dynamicists are more fortunate than scientists in other disciplines. For example, subatomic physicists, simply to record phenomena of interest, require elaborate equipment costing millions of dollars. Anthropologists studying preliterate societies may be forced to travel long distances to do their field work. Astronomers must sometimes be content to observe important solar processes just once in their lifetimes. In contrast, the group dynamicist has no trouble finding appropriate entities suitable for study, for in everyday life, everywhere we turn, we encounter groups: gangs, clubs, committees, communes, juries, families, teams, choirs, fraternities, sororities, airplane crews, audiences, orchestras, dance troupes, and so on. As researchers, our objective in studying these naturally occurring "action" groups is twofold: first, to gauge the explanatory power of existing group-dynamics theories and second, on the more pragmatic side, to improve group members' means of achieving group goals. Also, of course, as human beings we are drawn to the study of groups simply because they are so interesting.

Even when we restrict our range to groups not discussed in the other chapters of this section (see Chapter 14 for a discussion of work groups in business and industry and Chapter 16 for a review of therapeutic groups), we are still faced with a myriad of possible groups demanding detailed analysis. To reduce the range of groups we study in order to cover a few in detail, this chapter focuses on three uniquely different kinds of action groups: classes, juries, and teams. As we examine each of these types we will ask again and again the two basic questions implied above: "Do theory and research in group dynamics help to explain this group's processes?" and "How can the group be improved?"

Classes

When children reach age five they gain membership into uniquely influential and long-lasting groups known as classes. While some of the little newcomers join their groups rather reluctantly, sobbing and sighing as they leave their fathers and mothers at the doorway, membership in this group will result in a wide range of cognitive, social, and intellectual changes through the years. Admittedly, educational processes can be viewed from many different perspectives, such as child development, the psychology of learning, and identity growth, but as group dynamicists we are interested in the class as a group: an aggregate of individuals who influence one another through social interaction (Trow, Zander, Morse, & Jenkins, 1950).

The Class as a Group

Classes have all the characteristics of groups first noted in Chapter 1. First, *interaction* among classmates is typically quite intense, ranging from nonverbal winks, nods, smiles, and shoves to more audible whispers, giggles, conversations, and shouts. Second, roles (teacher, student, principal, class clown), norms (no talking during tests, no cheating, no sticking gum under your desk), and patterns of intermember relations provide classes with *structures* that promote group stability. Third, classes possess *goals,* although the objectives of the teacher may not, in all instances, match the desires of the students. Fourth, while classes vary in the extent to which they are perceived to be unified, organized *Gestalts,* most classrooms are high in *groupness* (or entitativity). The members not only refer to themselves as "Mr. Rose's sixth graders" or "the Algebra III class" but nonmembers refer to them with similarly general labels. Lastly, classes are *dynamic,* almost always in flux. As a single year passes a class develops its own atmosphere, but this developmental process rarely culminates in a static, unchanging group; from year to year classes are continually reformed as new students enter, pupils are promoted, new teachers are hired, and former teachers leave to take jobs elsewhere.

Given these parallels between classes and groups in general, it is no wonder that many of the processes discussed in previous chapters influence classroom dynamics. For example, dating from the time of the classic Lewin/Lippitt/White studies (1939) of the relative impact of autocratic, democratic, and laissez faire leaders (see Chapter 8), educational researchers have scrutinized the relationships linking classroom climate, teacher control, and learning. In one early study this issue was explored by observing 275 female third- and fourth-grade teachers as they worked with their pupils (Ryans, 1952). When these teachers were rated on a number of bipolar adjectives—such as democratic/autocratic, kindly/harsh, and disorganized/orderly—the researchers found that students seemed more interested, cooperative, constructive, and participative in democratically organized classes as compared with more autocratic ones. Laissez faire classes, however, evidenced the most negative outcomes, for when teachers were aloof and unresponsive students became bored, unruly, and inattentive. Apparently the most effective teachers work to maintain a midpoint between a climate of complete control by students and complete control by the teacher; effective teachers take much of the responsibility for structuring class activities, but partly share this responsibility with their students (Schmuck & Schmuck, 1979).

In related research, investigators of the bases of power (see Chapter 7) in the classroom find significant differences between teachers who maintain authority through the use of coercive power and those who maintain authority through referent power. While many teachers rely more heavily on coercion than on other bases of power when trying to regulate students' actions (French & Raven, 1959), evidence indicates that coercive power is one of the least effective means of influencing others (Kounin, 1970). For example, in one study coercive-control techniques, such as physical punishment, displays of anger, and shouting, not only failed to change the target student's behavior but also led to negative changes in the classroom's atmosphere (Kounin & Gump, 1958). When the misbehaving student was severely reprimanded, the observing students would often become more disruptive and uninterested in their schoolwork and negative, inappropriate social activity seemed to spread from the troublespot throughout the classroom. This disruptive contagion, which the investigators labeled the *ripple effect,* was found to be especially strong when the reprimanded students were powerful members of the classroom authority structure or when commands by teachers were vague and ambiguous. On the basis of these findings the researchers suggested that teachers avoid the ripple effect by building up their referent and expert power bases while downplaying the use of coercive power.

Moving from the realm of teacher/student relations to student/student relations, we find that students may learn as much from association with their classmates as from their instructors. Interactions in the peer group provide the setting for a host of critically important developmental changes—from the socialization of attitudes, beliefs, and values, to the perfection of social skills, to the emergence of empathy and personal identity—and integration into the classroom group therefore promotes psychological adjustment and emotional well being. Good peer relations have been found to correlate positively with achievement strivings, feelings of self-worth, and willingness to cooperate with others (Johnson, 1980; Ide, Parkerson, Haertel, & Walberg, 1981; Lewis & St. John, 1974; Schmuck & Schmuck, 1979) while isolation within the classroom group has been linked to "high anxiety, low self-esteem, poor interpersonal skills, emotional handicaps, . . . psychological pathology, . . . disruptive classroom behavior, hostile behavior and negative affect, and negative attitudes toward other students and school" (Johnson, 1980, p. 132). These clearcut consequences of group rejection suggest that teachers should remain sensitive to the patterns of attraction in their classes in order to encourage potential isolates during their peer-group interactions.

Peer-group norms also play a dramatic role in educational settings, since these implicit rules, like productivity norms in industry, can either encourage academic goal striving or discourage high achievement. For example, one especially noteworthy study of secondary school boys in England found that the students tended to work up to, or down to, the standards established by their peer group (Hargreaves, 1967). In that particular school system students were divided into various subgroups that, in time, developed their own unique set of norms. For example, one group adopted a normative system that directly conflicted with school rules. Poor academic performance was encouraged; tardiness, vandalism, and truancy were considered commendable and students who obeyed teachers were subject to physical punishment. In contrast, another subgroup in the same school developed norms that were completely consistent with institutional guidelines. "Mucking around" in class, fighting, laziness, and disobedience were all condemned, while striving for achievement, hard work, and honesty were positively sanctioned. Obviously, the performance of the first group was consistently worse than that of the second (for additional information, see Strain, 1981).

Issues

At this point we have achieved the first of our primary goals: by noting how classroom dynamics can be interpreted in terms of group structure, leadership, and power we have demonstrated the potential applicability of some general group-dynamics principles to the class. However, we have so far ignored the question of whether a group approach to educational settings has pragmatic utility. Thus, we turn now to some current issues in education to determine whether an understanding of group process yields any suggestions for improving classes.

CLASS COMPOSITION AND ACHIEVEMENT

Until quite recently **tracking** (or *streaming*)—establishing homogeneous classes by grouping together students of approximately equal levels of ability—was a common practice in our schools. Going on the assumption that tracking solved some of the problems encountered by teachers trying to satisfy the intellectual needs of a classroom containing students with all sorts of backgrounds and abilities, proponents of homogeneous-ability grouping argued that tracking (1) made teaching easier, (2) exposed students to material more suited to their level of achievement, and (3) protected less able students from identity-damaging comparisons with students of high ability. In time, however, these assumptions were called into question. Taking each of the assumed benefits of tracking in turn, adversaries of the practice argued that grouping made life easier for the teachers fortunate enough to be assigned classes composed of the brightest students, but those who worked with classes composed of only less able students faced an overwhelming task. Second, students who were assigned to one of the "slow" tracks throughout their public school careers were disadvantaged at graduation, since they had never been taught certain topics; in a sense, they never caught up to their schoolmates in the "faster" tracks. Lastly, students were quick to realize that their assignments were not based on chance and suffered losses in self-esteem in being "condemned" to classes "full of dummies."

Although the relative benefits of homogeneous- versus heterogeneous-ability grouping are still being debated, empirical studies of the issue tend to weigh against streaming (homogeneous classes) and in favor of **mainstreaming** (heterogeneous classes). For example, one study of achievement-score changes in thousands of students in more than 300 classes found that streamed students performed no better than mainstreamed students (Millman & Johnson, 1964). Similarly, while a two-year study of 2200 children attending 45 different schools found only small effects of classroom composition, in nearly every instance these differences showed students in the heterogeneous classes to be outperforming students in the homogeneous classes (Goldberg, Passow, & Justman, 1966). The self-esteem data from studies of students in heterogeneous classes is less clearcut (some researchers report positive gains in self-image—Budoff & Gottlieb, 1976—but others document losses, particularly among less able students—Goldberg et al., 1966). However, the coupling of these data with evidence that grouping discriminates against minorities and the handicapped prompted the U. S. government in 1975 to pass Public Law 94-142. This statute virtually outlaws streaming across classrooms, although individual teachers may continue to separate students into homogeneous learning groups (such as the "Red Bird" reading group or the "Blue Jay" math group) within the classroom.

CLASS CREATIVITY

An interesting exception to the general rule that heterogeneous grouping is superior to homogeneous grouping occurs when creativity, rather than achievement, is considered. E. Paul Torrance, a long-time researcher in the field of creativity measurement and development, many years ago noted that the tendency for creative children to work alone increases from grades two through six (1963). To explore the cause of this reluctance to join with others in groups, Torrance arranged for students to work in small groups on various creativity and learning exercises (1963, 1965). Upon observing the groups at work, Torrance watched as the children he had previously identified as highly creative (willing to work on difficult tasks, imaginative, unconventional in ideas and actions) suffered rejection at the hands of the group. Although in 17 of the 25 groups the creative members accounted for most of the group's ideas, in many instances the group members refused to recognize the value of the creative students' contributions. Furthermore, by the time the students had reached the sixth grade they had developed methods for dealing with the unusual behavior of the creative student that included hostility, physical aggression, criticism, rejection, and pressuring to reduce creativity. Torrance found that these normative pressures ease off in homogeneous creative-ability groups, and thus suggests that creative students may fare better if they are able to work with other highly creative individuals.

STRUCTURING CLASS GOALS

When Janice started her first year in college she expected difficult courses, but the many different grading techniques used by her professors took her by surprise. In one class in mathematics she worked through a series of tape-recorded modules taking tests on each unit whenever she felt she was ready. In her psychology class the instructor graded "on the curve," so Janice worked hard to outdo her fellow students. Lastly, in her art class she developed projects in a group with four other students, and the teacher assigned each member of the team the same grade.

Janice's classes exemplify three types of goal structures to be found in classes. First, when goals are *individualistic* students' outcomes are totally independent of one another; success or failure by one student has no impact on any other student's grade. Second, if the classroom is *competitively* structured, students can earn good grades only if other students earn poor grades; grading "on the curve" involves a mild form of competition, since students' performances are judged relative to the average student performance (see the box on page 436). Third, in *cooperation-based* classes students can succeed only if the other members of the class (or subgroup) succeed. In this regard, classrooms are like groups discussed in earlier chapters, especially those dealing with conflict (Chapter 4), performance (Chapter 6), and productivity (Chapter 14).

If the teacher asked a group dynamicist to recommend one of these classroom structures—individualist, competitive, or cooperative—for use in most educational settings, the group dynamicist would have to balance the advantages and disadvantages of each structure in drawing a conclusion. For example, an individualistic class, while promoting independence and instilling a sense of personal responsibility for one's work, may fail in other ways: students may not have the personal motivation to do well, opportunities for student-to-student learning experiences may go untapped, and the students may not have the chance to acquire important interpersonal skills. In contrast, a competitive classroom—where students must strive to outdo others—may be highly motivating and good preparation for careers in competitively oriented occupations. However, as our analyses of the sources of conflict in groups showed (Chapter 4), competition is a major factor in precipitating interpersonal conflict, loss of trust, and aggression. For this reason, the group dynamicist may recommend that the cooperative class—with its potential prob-

HOW TEACHERS CREATE COMPETITION BY ASSIGNING GRADES

Although there are probably as many methods of assigning grades as there are people who teach, a distinction is often drawn between norm-referenced grading and criterion-referenced grading. *Norm-referenced grading,* or grading "on the curve," begins by calculating the mean of all students' scores on the test. Next, letter grades of A, B, C, D, and F are assigned by giving students who score at or near the mean Cs, higher and lower scoring students Bs and Ds, and still higher or still lower scoring students As and Fs. In contrast, with *criterion-referenced grading* the standards for performance are established before students take the test, making the average performance of the classroom irrelevant in the grade-assignment process.

Both of these methods possess weaknesses and strengths (see Ebel, 1978 and Popham, 1978 for two opposing viewpoints), but the normative system entails one particularly significant drawback:

students realize that they can only earn high grades if others perform poorly, and an element of competition is thus introduced into the class. High-scoring students (sometimes labeled curve setters by their lower scoring classmates) are sometimes warned by other students about the negative consequences of "pushing up" the class's average performance, and the competition for grades can become so extreme that students refuse to help one another learn material—since it is to their advantage to outperform others—or destroy learning materials before others in the class have had the chance to study them. Because of these negative consequences of norm-referenced grading, some educators prefer to assign grades using a criterion-referenced system or some other approach that does not create competitive norms in the classroom (for example, pass/fail grading, grading by growth, and so on).

---

lems of low personal motivation and loss of individuality—be utilized to promote harmony, trust, and teamwork. From a group-dynamics perspective, the advantages of a cooperative classroom outweigh the disadvantages.

The relative benefits of each of these classroom practices are still being debated, but empirical evidence increasingly ranks cooperative classrooms over individualistic or competitive classrooms. Although the findings are not uniformly positive, a recent review of more than 120 studies conducted in educational and performance settings concluded that "cooperation is considerably more effective than interpersonal competition and individualistic effort" (Johnson, Maruyama, Johnson, Nelson, & Skon, 1981, p. 47) and that competition only helps when students cooperate in small groups competing against other groups. David W. Johnson (1980, p. 140), a leading researcher in this area, goes so far as to predict that an "emphasis on positive goal interdependence among students not only will create the supportive, accepting, and caring relationships vital for socialization but will also promote achievement, perspective-taking ability, self-esteem, psychological health, liking for peers, and positive attitudes toward school personnel." He feels that, given the divergent effects of cooperation, competition, and individualistic goal structures shown in Table 15-1, teachers should make learning a cooperative enterprise.

TEAM LEARNING

Taking into consideration the positive impact of cooperative goals in classes, several educators have suggested transforming classes into teams. Although coop-

TABLE 15-1. Goal structures and group processes that affect learning

Cooperative	Competitive	Individualistic
High interaction	Low interaction	No interaction
Effective communication	No misleading, or threatening communication	No interaction
Facilitation of other's achievement: helping, sharing, tutoring	Obstruction of other's achievement	No interaction
Peer influence toward achievement	Peer influence against achievement	No interaction
Problem-solving conflict management	Win-lose conflict management	No interaction
High divergent and risk-taking thinking	Low divergent and risk-taking thinking	No interaction
High trust	Low trust	No interaction
High acceptance and support by peers	Low acceptance and support by peers	No interaction
High emotional involvement in and commitment to learning by almost all students	High emotional involvement in and commitment to learning by the few students who have a chance to win	No interaction
High utilization of resources of other students	No utilization of resources of other students	No interaction
Division of labor possible	Division of labor impossible	No interaction
Decreased fear of failure	Increased fear of failure	No interaction

(Source: Johnson, 1980)

eration, taken in isolation, promotes achievement, teams further motivate students by establishing a supportive, achievement-oriented atmosphere; ensuring a high degree of interaction by linking together students' outcomes; and heightening group cohesiveness. Some team programs that have been found to be effective are described in the following subsections.

The Jigsaw class. In the Jigsaw method (Aronson, Stephan, Sikes, Blaney, & Snapp, 1978) the teacher gives a group an assignment that can only be completed if each individual member contributes his or her share—that is, provides a piece of the overall puzzle. In general, a unit of study is broken down in various subareas, and each member of a group is assigned one of these subareas; students must then become experts on their subjects and teach what they learn to other members of the group. For example, in a class studying government, the teacher might separate the pupils into three-person groups, with each member of the group being assigned one of the following topics: the judiciary system (the Supreme Court of the United States), the duties and powers of the executive branch (the president's office), and the functions of the legislative branch (Congress). In developing an understanding of their assigned topic, the students would leave their three-person groups and meet with their counterparts from other groups. Thus, everyone assigned to study one particular topic—such as the Supreme Court— would meet to discuss it, answer questions, and decide how to teach the material to others. Once they had learned their material, these students would then rejoin their original groups and teach their fellow group members what they had learned. Thus, the Jigsaw class utilizes both group-learning and student-to-student teaching techniques.

Teams/Games/Tournaments.   The TGT technique (DeVries, Edwards, & Fennessey, 1973) evolved from the old idea of spelling bees, but includes a healthy emphasis on group interaction and student instruction. First, students are assigned to four- to five-person *teams*. Next, the groups work on material the teacher has recently presented to the class, playing various *games* designed to test and extend their understanding of the information. At the end of the week the class plays the *tournament:* students compete with representatives from other teams for points. In TGT the teams are carefully designed to include members of varying levels of ability, and in tournaments the students only compete with students of equal ability. Hence, even the less able students can earn points for their team.

Student Teams Achievement Divisions.   The final teaching method, STAD, involves group learning followed by a quiz (Slavin, 1977). Students in small teams review a unit as a group, testing one another until they feel confident that they know their material. While the method is similar to the TGT, since students teach one another, in STAD the students' knowledge is measured on individual quizzes. Evaluations, however, are based on comparisons with students of equivalent past performance, so again all the team members can potentially contribute to the team effort.

All these team techniques capitalize on the self-correction processes operating in interacting learning groups, where members have the opportunity to teach one another by detecting, correcting, and explaining the sources of co-members' errors (Webb, 1980). The team procedures also seem to strike a responsive motivational chord in most students, who often become dedicated learners as they strive for both personal and group achievement. The effects of a desire for group success sometimes become so strong that it is not unusual for formerly bored students to seek out teachers after class to ask for extra materials in the hopes of improving their inputs to the group. These team techniques have also been used effectively in reducing out-group rejection in recently integrated classrooms by promoting cross-racial interactions. While rejection of another student on the basis of race is possible in the traditional classroom, such discrimination becomes self-defeating when the other student, as a teammate, possesses valued information and skills. During team learning racially different children are no longer competitors seeking a limited number of good grades, but teammates participating in an equal-status setting.

TEAM TEACHING

Given that students seem to learn well in groups, the next logical question to ask is "Do teachers teach well in groups?" Team teaching takes many forms, as Table 15-2 indicates, and the basic strengths underlying a team approach to education are both many and varied. For example, in a team situation the best abilities of each teacher can be identified and fully utilized, thereby improving the quality

TABLE 15-2. Types of team-teaching strategies

Type	Description
1. Team with leader	One individual within the group is designated the team leader or director, and given special responsibility for organizing the team.
2. Associates	All members of the team are equal in status, although an informal leader may emerge over time.
3. Apprenticeships	One person in the team is the "veteran" teacher who helps in the training and acculturation of new teachers.
4. Coordinated teams	Although in this method the teachers do not instruct the same group of students, they teach the same material to their own students using jointly developed lesson plans, activities, exams, and so on.
5. Rotational teams	Each member of the team takes responsibility for teaching one particular part of the course during the semester or school year.

(Source: Cunningham, 1960)

of instruction and reducing the workloads of individual teachers. In addition, teachers working in close conjunction with other educators are certain to be exposed to new ideas and suggestions for improving their teaching, and become more strongly motivated to improve their methods, since they are working before an audience of their colleagues. Closer student/teacher relationships may also evolve when the team approach makes individualized contacts more likely, and the possibility that pupils will find at least one teacher with whom they can work well increases when more teachers are present. Lastly, team teaching ensures that potentially critical decisions about students will be made by a group of educators rather than a single individual, thereby guarding against biases and unverified personal assumptions (Armstrong, 1977).

Recognizing these strengths, many educators favor the use of teams in teaching, though their advocacy is often based on conjecture rather than systematic empirical investigation. While teaching teams, in theory, should be effective pedagogical devices, studies comparing the achievements of students taught by teams and by solitary teachers generally find few major differences. For example, one major review of nearly 20 studies conducted between 1959 and 1973 showed that team teaching often results in some gains in specific areas but that overall the teams are no more effective than solitary teachers. In fact, in some instances students performed more poorly in classes taught by teams (Armstrong, 1977). These findings suggest that the potential of team teaching frequently goes unrealized in classrooms, perhaps because problems of organization, planning, leadership, and coordination stand in the way of team effectiveness. Teachers who have participated in team teaching often complain of planning and administrative problems as well as breakdowns in coordination that result in chaotic classrooms, interpersonal conflicts, and team members doing less than their fair share (Rutherford, 1975). Evidence indicates that teaching teams require at least three years of experience before members report feeling comfortable with the innovation (Hall & Rutherford, 1975), and the ineffectiveness of team teaching may therefore stem more from inexperience than from a basic flaw in the concept. In any case, more evidence is needed before a decision can be made for or against team teaching.

Juries

Imagine yourself ensnared in the following predicament. After stopping you for a routine traffic violation a police officer notices that your appearance matches the description of an at-large suspect believed to be responsible for a series of armed robberies. He takes you down to the station where, to your horror, no fewer than seven eyewitnesses identify you as the robber. You can't provide a good alibi for the nights when the robberies occurred, so the police, ignoring your protestations of innocence, charge you with the crimes. The ordeal drags on until the day comes when you must face your accusers. As you enter the courtroom you realize that the only barrier between you and an undeserved prison sentence is a small group of your peers—strangers to one another, chosen at random from your community, unschooled in legal principles, and unpracticed in group decision making. Your fate lies in the hands of a **jury.**

The practice of asking a group of people to serve as the final arbiter of guilt and innocence has formed the foundations of judicial systems for centuries (see Hyman & Tarrant, 1975, and Moore, 1973, for a discussion of the history of juries). As far back as the 11th century the neighbors of those accused of wrongdoing were asked both to provide information about the actions of the accused and to weigh the evidence. In time, the duty of providing evidence was shifted to witnesses and experts, but the jury remained the "finder of fact," responsible for weighing the testimony of each person before deciding if a law had, in fact, been broken. In theory, the jury serves as the "voice" of the community by ensuring "citizen participation in government" and applications of laws in ways that are "consistent with present-day community values" (Kadish & Paulsen, 1975, p. 1317).

The Jury as a Group

In recent years research focus on juries has burgeoned. Social scientists have become increasingly interested in all aspects of the judicial process and the participants in this process—judges, lawyers, and prosecutors—have begun looking to these scientists for answers to such practical questions as "Are jurors influenced by pretrial publicity?" "How many people should make up a jury?" and "When are judges and juries likely to disagree?" At base, some of these questions call for a focus on the characteristics of individual jurors—their personalities, memories, abilities, and biases. In contrast, other issues call for an analysis of the jury as a functioning unit—its structures, decisional procedures, and outcomes. Naturally, in this brief review we will rely more heavily on the latter approach as we examine the group dynamics of juries (for more extensive reviews see Davis, Bray, & Holt, 1977; Dillehay & Nietzel, 1980; Elwork, Sales, & Suggs, 1981; Gerbasi, Zuckerman, & Reis, 1977; Saks, 1977; Saks & Hastie, 1978; Simon, 1980; Wrightsman, 1978).

STATUS AND INFLUENCE IN JURIES

In the mid-1950s Fred L. Strodtbeck and his colleagues, in conjunction with the University of Chicago's Law and Behavioral Science Project, conducted a series of studies of status and influence in deliberating juries (Strodtbeck & Hook, 1961; Strodtbeck & Mann, 1956; Strodtbeck, James, & Hawkins, 1957). Enlisting the cooperation of the court, Strodtbeck repeatedly selected 12 individuals from the pool of eligible jurors, simulated voir dire (the pretrial-interview process designed to eliminate biased jurors), and assembled the group in the courtroom. A bailiff would then play a tape recording of a trial and ask the group to retire to a jury room to decide upon a verdict. In virtually all respects—other than the use of a tape-recorded trial—the groups were treated exactly like actual juries.

In studying the deliberations of these "juries," Strodtbeck and his associates found that certain irrelevant status characteristics (occupation, gender of jurors) significantly influenced the authority, attraction, and communication relations in the groups. Juries tended to favor people of high socioeconomic status (proprietors and clerical workers) over those of low socioeconomic status (skilled and unskilled workers) when choosing a foreperson, even though no mention of occupation was made. Higher status members also participated more heavily in the jury's discussion, generally by offering more suggestions and providing more orientation to the task (categories 4 and 6 in the Bales Interaction Process Analysis; see Table 5-1). Members of low status, in contrast, tended to show more agreement with others. Given these communication patterns, Strodtbeck and his co-workers found that the members with high socioeconomic status were the most successful in convincing the others that their judgments on the case were the most accurate. The correlation between private predeliberation opinion and the jury's final decision was .50 for proprietors, but dropped all the way down to .02 for the laborers (Strodtbeck et al., 1957).

Sex differences were also apparent, for women joined in the discussion less frequently than men (James, 1959; Strodtbeck et al., 1957). Furthermore, females' comments were more often socioemotional in nature—showing solidarity and agreement—while males' comments were more task focused (Strodtbeck & Mann, 1956). Whether or not these differences continue to persist is unclear, since research conducted in the mid-1970s using a mock jury has both confirmed and disconfirmed the original Strodtbeck findings (Nemeth, Endicott, & Wachtler, 1976).

THE DELIBERATION PROCESS

Although juries conduct their deliberations in secret, by relying on alternative sources of information—such as recordings of mock-jury discussions and post-decision interviews with jurors—researchers have succeeded in piecing together a fairly coherent picture of the *deliberation process*. Broken down into its simplest components, the process starts at the close of the trial when the jurors formulate their preliminary personal decisions; this process is represented by Step 1 of Figure 15-1 (Penrod & Hastie, 1979, 1980). Next, the jurors join together and, after settling basic "housekeeping" matters (selecting a foreperson, clarifying the judge's instructions), review the facts in the case until they take the first vote (Step 2). This initial check to determine if consensus has been reached is often a critical turning point in the deliberations, for the vote brings the divergent viewpoints of the individual group members into the open. In a sense, the group "gets down to serious business" with the taking of the first vote (Saks & Hastie, 1978, p. 93).

Naturally, few juries will (1) achieve quorum (Step 3) or (2) be so pessimistic that they feel deadlocked (Step 5) after one vote, so in most instances the jury deliberates for a time before taking a new ballot (Step 7). In general, a small

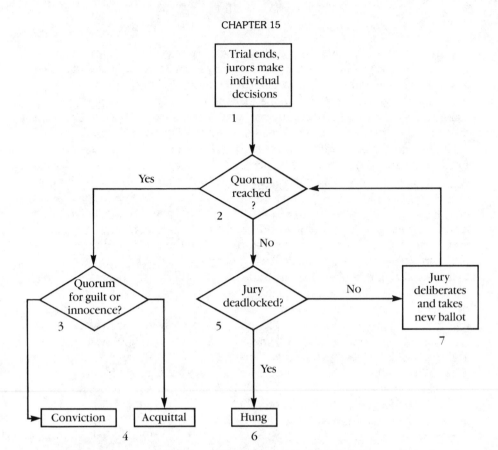

FIGURE 15-1. A flowchart diagraming the sequence of decisions made during deliberation. (Source: Penrod and Hastie, 1980)

subgroup of four to five individuals takes a very active role during this phase, essentially carrying out the bulk of the discussion while more reticent members add occasional comments. This working core accounts for as many as 70% of the verbal statements exchanged during deliberation (Levine, Fattell, & Perrotta, 1981), with the foreperson alone contributing about 20 to 25% of the group communication (R. James Simon, 1980). This discussion phase continues in a cycle from Step 2 to Step 5 to Step 7 until eventually the jury either admits it is "hung" (Step 6) or renders a verdict (Step 4). While some juries may require many days to work through the entire process diagramed in Figure 15-1, most juries (55%) reach a verdict in one hour or less (Kalven & Zeisel, 1966).

Irrespective of the jury's eventual conclusion the deliberation process itself sets in motion many of the mechanisms highlighted in previous chapters. Topics such as persuasion, conformity, obedience, and attitude change are all relevant to an understanding of juries, but here we focus on a subset of these mechanisms: pressures for consensus, minority influence, and verdict polarization.

Pressures for consensus. Surveys of jury verdicts indicate that despite clear differences in jurors' personal opinions prior to deliberation, the "hung" jury is a statistical rarity, occurring in fewer than 6% of the criminal and civil cases heard by juries (Kalven & Zeisel, 1966). In explanation, investigators suggest that pressures for conformity to the majority opinion are so powerful that those in the minority can rarely withstand them. In essence, once the first vote is taken and the majority's position is identified, the jurors not only reexamine the evidence but also begin pressuring the dissenting minority to adopt the majority decision (Saks & Hastie, 1978). The pervasive tendency for the minority to conform to the opinion of the majority was documented in one study that compared the first-ballot voting pattern with the jury's final verdict (Kalven & Zeisel, 1966). If from one to five jurors (a minority) favored acquittal, in 90% of the cases the jury returned a verdict of guilt. If, in contrast, only from one to five voted guilty on the first ballot, then a not-guilty verdict occurred in 86% of the cases. Other studies of the social-decision rules implicitly adopted by juries indicate that if a significant majority of the members (say, two-thirds) favor a verdict, then in all likelihood the jury will return to the courtroom with that verdict (for reviews, see Davis, Bray, & Holt, 1977; Penrod & Hastie, 1979).

Minority influence. Although the majority opinion tends to "win" in most deliberations, the statistics in Table 15-3 show that staunch minorities can sometimes hang a jury, or even persuade the majority to adopt its viewpoint. For example, in the Mitchell/Stans Watergate-conspiracy trial the first vote was 4 to 8 in favor of a guilty verdict (Wrightsman, 1978; Zeisel & Diamond, 1976). However, one of the members of the minority coalition, a vice president of a bank, had achieved a position of high status by doing favors for the other jurors such as paying for their small expenses and arranging for entertainment while the jury was sequestered. In time he managed to enlarge the size of the minority coalition until the jury's stance shifted to acquittal. Thus, a minority can potentially influence the majority, but likelihood of successful influence is closely tied to the size of the minority (Penrod & Hastie, 1980). As suggested by the conformity research discussed in Chapter 9, a lone dissenter will generally change his or her vote, but as the minority swells in size its power increases exponentially. In fact, a computer model that simulates jury deliberations (DICE) assumes that a 3-person coalition in a standard 12-person jury will be relatively weak but a 4- or 5-person coalition will be fairly stable and influential (Penrod & Hastie, 1980).

Verdict polarization. The tendency for juries to shift toward guilty or not-guilty verdicts depending upon the distribution of predeliberation opinions in the

TABLE 15-3. Outcomes of deliberations in juries with and without minority coalitions on the first vote

Outcome	Number of juries	Percentage
Total agreement on first ballot	69	31.0
Jury adopts majority's decision	127	56.5
Jury adopts minority's decision	6	2.5
Minority "hangs" jury	13	5.6
Split 6–6 on first ballot	10	4.4

(Source: Penrod and Hastie, 1980)

group parallels the process of group polarization (see Chapter 12). In one study that aptly demonstrates this polarization process, researchers carefully constructed fictitious court cases that made the defendant seem either innocent or guilty (Myers & Kaplan, 1976). College-student subjects were then asked to read the cases and provide judgments of guilt and punishment. When the predeliberation judgments were compared to the postdeliberation judgments, the researchers found that "for both guilt and punishment ratings, cases designed to elicit harsh initial judgments obtained even harsher judgments after deliberation, while cases eliciting lenient initial judgments were rated more lenient after deliberation" (Kaplan & Schershing, 1981).

THE FINAL PRODUCT

Determining the effectiveness of juries as deciders of guilt or innocence is a complicated task, for we can never know when the jury has been "correct" or "incorrect" in condemning or freeing a defendant. After all, if a clear criterion for determining guilt existed, then juries would not be necessary in the first place. However, we can cite several bits of evidence that provide partial support for the effectiveness of juries as decision makers, although the evidence is by no means indisputable.

First, most studies of jury behavior suggest that the participants take their role very seriously and therefore strive to reach the fairest decision possible. As jury expert Rita James Simon noted after studying the responses of more than 2000 jurists participating in the Chicago Law project,

> . . . the jurors spent most of their time reviewing the court record. By the time they finished deliberating they had usually considered every bit of testimony, expert as well as lay, and every point offered in evidence. The most consistent theme that emerged from listening to the deliberations was the seriousness with which the jurors approached their job and the extent to which they were con-cerned that the verdict they reached was consistent with the spirit of the law and with the facts of the case [1980, p. 52].

Second, a major survey of verdicts conducted a number of years ago (Kalven & Zeisel, 1966) evaluated juries by comparing the judge's preferred decision with the jury's decision in nearly 8000 actual criminal and civil trials. Overall, the judge and jury disagreed on only 20% of the cases; for criminal trials the jury was somewhat more lenient than the judge, but for civil trials the disagreements were evenly split for and against the defendant. Furthermore, subsequent analysis indi-cated that 80% of these disagreements occurred when the weight of the evidence was so close that the judge admitted the verdict could have gone either way. This concordance between verdicts may explain why a later survey of judges indicated that 77% felt the jury system was satisfactory, 20% felt it had disadvantages that should be corrected, but only 3% felt that the system was so unsatisfactory that its use should be curtailed (Kalven, 1968).

Lastly, while individual jurors seem to be influenced by a range of irrelevant factors—such as the attractiveness of the defendant or the eloquence of the pros-ecutor—the reliance on a group-judgment process works to limit the influence of these biases. Given that the jury faces an optimizing, unitary, disjunctive task (see Chapter 6), on theoretical grounds alone we would expect its solution to be "better" than the solution offered by individuals.

Issues

For decades the jury system operated in its traditional, unchanging manner, seemingly as constant as the motion of the earth around the sun. However, recent years have brought several breaks from tradition as innovations in the jury system have been suggested and, in some instances, implemented. In this section we will consider the contributions that group-dynamics theory and research make to the understanding of the long-term consequences of three significant modifications: reductions in the number of required jurors, easing of the unanimity-decision rule, and increasingly sophisticated jury-selection procedures.

JURY SIZE

In 1970 the United States Supreme Court returned a landmark ruling in the case of Williams v. Florida. Williams sought to have his conviction overturned on the grounds that the deciding jury included only six persons. The Supreme Court, however, found in favor of the State, ruling that the jury's performance of its role

> . . . is not a function of the particular number of the body that makes up the jury. To be sure, the number should probably be large enough to promote group deliberation, free from outside attempts at intimidation, and to provide a fair possibility for obtaining a representative cross-section of the community. But we find little reason to think that these goals are in any meaningful sense less likely to be achieved when the jury numbers six, than when it numbers twelve—particularly if the requirement of unanimity is retained. And certainly the reliability of the jury as a factfinder hardly seems likely to be a function of its size [Williams v. Florida, 1970, pp. 100–101].

Thus the court answered affirmatively the question "Are six-person juries equivalent in all important respects to the twelve-person juries?" sparking a widespread revision in jury systems throughout the country (NCSC, 1976).

Unfortunately, when this question is approached from a perspective grounded in group-dynamics theory and research, the answer becomes less clear. According to Michael J. Saks, one of the leading researchers in this area (Saks, 1977; Saks & Hastie, 1978), modifying the size of the jury leads to numerous other changes, including the following.

1. *Changes in communication patterns.* In two experiments Saks (1977) systematically manipulated the sizes of mock juries while coding the pattern and content of communications. Overall, he found that participation was more equally distributed among the members of small groups, but that the larger groups communicated more since they took longer to deliberate. As an incidental finding, he also reported that the members of the smaller juries rated each other more positively.

2. *Changes in representativeness.* Saks (1977) also found that 6-person juries were not as representative of the community as 12-person juries. Although this loss was anticipated by the Supreme Court members in their ruling, Saks showed that the magnitude of the effect could be quite large. For example, in one com-

munity that was 10% Black and 90% White, 80% of the 12-person juries included at least one Black but only 41% of the 6-person juries contained a Black.

3. *Changes in minority/majority pressures.* In the review of conformity pressures in Chapter 9 we found that once the group reaches a certain size—typically, four members—conformity rates remain essentially constant as the group increases in size. However, conformity pressures may be greater in 6-person juries since the likelihood of finding a dissenting "ally" is smaller. Thus, while the Court assumed that a 5–1 vote in a 6-person jury was essentially the same as a 10–2 split in a 12-person group, psychologically the situation is dramatically different. With the 10–2 vote one's opinion is buttressed by the presence of a dissenting partner, while in the 5–1 vote one must face the majority alone.

4. *Changes in conviction and acquittal rates.* From a practical standpoint differences in communication, representativeness, and majority/minority pressures are of secondary importance. Of primary interest is the impact of the change on conviction and acquittal rates, and evidence bearing on this consequence is encouraging. On the negative side, many studies conducted to investigate this issue are methodologically flawed, and therefore difficult to interpret (Saks, 1977; Vollrath & Davis, 1980). On the positive side, studies that yield interpretable data suggest that verdict differences between 6- and 12-member juries are slight (Padawer-Singer, Singer, & Singer, 1977; Saks, 1977). As the Supreme Court's ruling suggested, the impact of jury size may be negligible on the overall product of the deliberation.

In conclusion, 6- and 12-person juries each possess strengths and weaknesses, and the use of either size will necessarily call for some trade-offs: smaller juries ensure full member participation and increase efficiency, but members of larger juries communicate with each other more and represent the community more adequately, and the larger size of the group may ease conformity pressures. Furthermore, while many of the assumptions that formed the basis for the Court's favorable decision for smaller juries are inaccurate, its overall belief in the similarity of 6- and 12-person jury's verdicts has been empirically confirmed.

THE UNANIMITY RULE

In 1972 three men were convicted in separate trials of assault, grand larceny, and burglary by the court system of the State of Oregon. In a united appeal to the U. S. Supreme Court, these three men contested the verdicts by claiming that their right to a fair trial had been violated since the votes of the juries were not unanimous; in the first two trials the vote was 11–1 for conviction, while in the burglary trial the decision was 10–2. To the defendants' dismay, the Supreme Court ruled in favor of the State of Oregon (Apodoca v. Oregon, 1972), concluding that the Sixth Amendment only guarantees that a "substantial majority of the jury" must be convinced of the defendants' guilt. Later in the ruling, the Court suggested that 75% agreement constitutes an acceptable minimum quorum for most juries.

From an empirical perspective, the Court's conclusion was in part reasonable, but in part unreasonable. First, as our review of the effect of the minority opinion on the majority demonstrated, the verdict preferred by the majority of the jurors on the first vote becomes the final verdict in a large percentage of the cases. Referring back to Table 15-3, we see that in juries with minority and majority coalitions the minority converted to the majority position in 56.5% of the cases. Second, the minority's opinion prevailed in only 2.5% of the juries summarized in Table 15-3, and in most of these cases the minority was so substantial that a 10 out of 12 quorum would not have been reached anyway. Third, studies of informal decision rules in juries suggest that despite the judge's instructions to deliberate to unanimity, most juries nonetheless seem to implicitly operate according to a basic two-thirds or 10 out of 12 quorum rule (Davis, Kerr, Atkin, Holt, & Meek, 1975; Davis, Kerr, Stasser, Meek, & Holt, 1977). While all three of these points lend support to the Court's decision, a final point does not: when groups use a quorum rule, such as two-thirds majority, then deadlocks become very unlikely (Kerr, Atkin, Stasser, Meek, Holt, & Davis, 1976). As Michael Saks and Reid Hastie note (1978, pp. 84–85), this last consequence of relaxing unanimity requirements implies that juries will reach "decisions on the basis of weaker evidence; and this means that more errors of both types will occur: convictions when the correct decision is acquittal; acquittals when the correct decision is conviction." Saks and Hastie feel that "increased efficiency is purchased at some cost in accuracy," but that the magnitude of this inaccuracy is not yet clearly known.

CHANGES IN VOIR DIRE PROCEDURES

For a number of years the courts have selected jury members from a pool of potential participants through a process known as *voir dire*. Voir dire, which literally means "to speak true," calls for verbal or written questioning of prospective jurors to uncover any biases or prejudices that may stand in the way of fairness and impartiality.

Until the 1970s voir dire was primarily left up to judges' discretion; defense lawyers could submit questions to be used in voir dire, but judges were free to omit them if they desired. However, in the face of certain Supreme Court rulings in which convictions were overturned because trial judges disallowed defense participation in voir dire (for example, Ham v. S. Carolina, 1973), courts began opening up the procedure to defense attorneys. In consequence, defense lawyers began to use *systematic jury selection* methods that involved (1) development of a "psychological profile" for pinpointing the characteristics of sympathetic and antagonistic jurors, and (2) utilizing the voir dire process as a means of identifying prospective jurors who fit these two types. For example, defense attorneys used systematic jury-selection techniques when picking the panel for political activist Angela Davis, who was brought to trial in 1972 to face charges of murder and kidnaping. The defense attorneys spent a total of 13 days selecting the 12 jurors and 4 alternates for the trial, and they based their choices on detailed analyses of each juror prepared by a team of five psychologists. The trial, once begun, lasted for more than two months, but in the end the elaborate voir dire process apparently paid off: the jury found Davis "not guilty."

Systematic jury selection based on elaborate pretrial research and intensified voir dire has sparked a controversy over the purposes of voir dire. On the one hand, proponents of the technique argue that in many political and criminal trials biases produced by unfair publicity, regional prejudices, and unrepresentative jury rosters must be controlled if the defendant is to receive just treatment. Critics, in contrast, feel that systematic selection is tantamount to jury rigging, since it produces lenient rather than fair juries (see Wrightsman, 1978). Unfortunately, neither of these positions can be either confirmed or rejected on the basis of empirical evidence, for many questions remain unanswered: How valid are the "psychological profiles" developed to identify sympathetic jurors? Can biased jurors be detected through voir dire? and What impact does systematic selection have on the group dynamics of the jury? (Saks & Hastie, 1978; Wrightsman, 1978).

Teams

Games and sports, both informal and organized, can influence our lives in many ways. Sporting events capture our interest as fans as we find entertainment in cheering on our favorite players and teams. As participants, we can exercise, relax, and have fun playing our favorite games and sports. As gamblers, owners, or professional players, we can achieve financial gains (or losses) by playing with or betting on teams.

As group dynamicists, however, we are drawn to the study of sports because many of these athletic contests pit group against group. While sports such as tennis, golf, and boxing involve individual competition, other sports—football, basketball, baseball, and rugby—are played by teams. From our perspective, teams taking part in athletic or sporting events are simply one more variety of groups that warrants closer examination.

The Team as a Group

The word *team* is used to describe a wide assortment of human aggregations. For example, in business settings work units are sometimes referred to as *production teams* or *decision-making teams*. In a university, professors and graduate students may form a *research team* to conduct experiments cooperatively. In organizational development a *team of experts* may make recommendations to the corporation. In schools, a *teaching team* may be responsible for the education of 500 students. These divergent types of groups, though considerably different from one another, are all labeled *teams* because they resemble the sorts of groups we commonly find competing in athletic and sporting events. Like all groups, teams are influenced by the characteristics (norms, roles, structures, size, goals) and processes (conformity pressures, power, leadership, deindividuation) examined in earlier chapters, but teams playing sports also boast some unique properties. As Alvin Zander (1975) explains, the team "conducts its major business (engaging in athletic contests) before the eyes of observers" who can be as concerned about team performance as the members themselves (p. 26). Activities of the group also tend to be rigidly structured, for the sport must be played according to certain rules and regulations; on the field, norm violations end in sanctions administered by unforgiving officials. The quality of performance is also critically important in sports, and perhaps in consequence players sometimes display "wide extremes of emotional reaction" ranging from "boredom to pride to shame" (p. 26). Lastly, the motivational bases of team performance are often extremely complex, since players' desires for personal and group success may not be completely compatible.

Despite these unique qualities, the team remains essentially a small group, a social unit whose internal processes conform to the theories and models developed by group dynamicists. However, rather than simply accepting this claim on faith, let us examine the explanatory power of two group-level variables—cohesiveness and group continuity—with regard to team performance.

COHESIVENESS AND SUCCESS

When the American hockey-team members skated onto the ice before the semifinals of the 1980 Winter Olympic Games, most observers felt that their chances for victory were slim. Although most of the players were on college teams, they faced a seasoned Russian team that outclassed them in terms of skill, strength, and experience. The Americans were talented, but few felt that they could survive the onslaught of a Russian team that had trained long and hard for the tournament.

Unexpectedly, the Americans won, and by way of explanation many analysts underscored the *spirit* of the team—its unity, cohesiveness, comraderie, esprit de corps. They suggested that the Russian team may have been more skilled but that the American team played as a cohesive, integrated unit and this greater cohesiveness proved to be the winning edge. As Zander explains (1974, p. 65), most coaches, players, and spectators assume that high team cohesiveness is a prerequisite for team victory, that "in spite of the individual athletes who make headlines when they strike off for themselves, team spirit is the rule rather than the exception in sports. In fact, both amateurs and professionals generally feel that a team can't become a winner without it."

Systematic analyses of the link between cohesiveness and performance, however, indicate that the relationship between these two factors is not so simple as some would assume. One the one hand, a host of studies has reported significant correlations between measures of team cohesiveness and the team's win/loss record. For example, in one study of female volleyball teams the winning teams tended to be more cohesive than the losing teams (Bird, 1977). Similarly, when predicting the successfulness of baseball teams, one researcher found that cohesiveness was a better predictor than indices based on skill levels (Long, 1972). For all kinds of sports—basketball, baseball, football, soccer, and volleyball— studies uncovered evidence favoring a positive correlation between performance and cohesion.

In contrast, other studies suggest that performance is negatively correlated with cohesion. For example, in one oft-cited study of German rowing teams, the researcher was surprised to find that the greater the internal conflict, the greater the group's effectiveness (Lenk, 1969). In one team the conflicts were so intense that the members contemplated dissolution of the team, but managed to keep the group in existence by forming various coalitions. In spite of this animosity and disunity, the team won the Olympic Games that year (for reviews, see Carron, 1980; Cratty, 1982; Nixon, 1976).

Should the researchers have been surprised when they discovered that cohesiveness and team performance were not correlated in a simple one-to-one fashion? Probably not, for in retrospect these disparate findings can be explained when we take into account the nature of group cohesiveness and the methods used in the various research projects. At the conceptual level, the cohesiveness studies performed in industrial and educational settings should have warned investigators that the impact of cohesiveness cannot be predicted without taking into account other aspects of the group situation. For example, in Chapter 14 we found that cohesive work groups, while satisfying environments for members, are highly productive only if their norms emphasize productivity. If the norms call for low production, then the relationship between cohesiveness and productivity reverses as highly cohesive groups become particularly unproductive. Applied to teams, cohesiveness will be positively correlated with performance only if the norms of the team emphasize the importance of success. In some extremely cohesive teams the members may become so wrapped up in the social aspects of the group that interaction becomes the primary goal, while winning takes on secondary importance.

Additionally, at the methodological level, the contradictory findings may have stemmed from inadequacies in the measures, differences in the types of teams studied, and the heavy reliance on correlational data. As we noted in Chapter 12, cohesiveness is a higher order theoretical construct, and in consequence it typically proves difficult to operationalize in research; so many different measures of cohesiveness have been used that the divergent results may be due to assessment discrepancies alone (Carron & Chelladurai, 1981). Furthermore, cohesiveness may have different effects depending upon whether or not the sport calls for *interaction* between teammates—as in football, rugby, or soccer—or simply *coaction*—as in bowling, team swimming, or archery (Landers & Luschen, 1974). Lastly, as Zander's (1971) work on motives and goals in groups indicates, correlations between performance and cohesiveness may indicate that performance causes changes in cohesiveness, rather than cohesiveness causing changes in performance (see box).

WHICH CAME FIRST: THE COHESIVENESS OR THE PERFORMANCE?

As noted in Chapter 2, one major problem with correlational research concerns causal interpretation. While investigators may find that two variables, such as team performance and team cohesiveness, are highly correlated, they cannot be certain which causal sequence best accounts for the results. While Condition 1 below coincides with common-sense notions of team dynamics, it may well be that as the team becomes successful, interpersonal relations among the players grow more positive; as Condition 2 suggests, the performance actually causes changes

in cohesiveness. In addition, some mediating (or intervening) variable, such as the mysterious X in Condition 3, may be the actual causal culprit. For example, increases in cohesiveness may cause the players to come to practice more, with the result that the increase in practice changes performance. Lastly, as a systems approach to team performance would suggest, the relationship between the two variables may be a reciprocal one (Condition 4): cohesiveness influences performance, and performance changes further influence cohesiveness.

$$\text{Cohesiveness} \rightarrow \text{Performance}$$
$$(1)$$

$$\text{Performance} \rightarrow \text{Cohesiveness}$$
$$(2)$$

$$\text{Cohesiveness} \rightarrow X \rightarrow \text{Performance}$$
$$(3)$$

$$\text{Cohesiveness} \circlearrowright X \circlearrowright \text{Performance}$$
$$(4)$$

CONTINUITY AND TEAM SUCCESS

Teams are *open* rather than *closed* groups (Ziller, 1965). As each new season begins the coaches make adjustments in the starting line-ups, recruit new players, and release veterans who are no longer needed. However, some teams tend to retain more of their players from year to year than others, so the question arises: Do groups with more stable memberships perform better than more unstable groups?

A number of studies have tried to answer this query by relating the records of various teams to the amount of turnover among the teams' players. For example, John Loy and his colleagues (Loy, McPherson, & Kenyon, 1978), in summarizing the results of studies conducted with teams playing such sports as baseball, basketball, football, and gymnastics, report that turnover rates and performance are negatively related; groups with a high rate of personnel loss perform less well than more stable groups. This tendency for teams with members who have played together for a longer period of time to be more successful was also found in a study of line-up changes and success rates in German soccer teams (Essing, 1970). Apparently, substituting a reserve team player for a starting player disrupts the coordination between teammates, for (1) stable team line-ups generally covaried with team success, and (2) high turnover rates covaried with team failure. Relationships between the replacement rate for coaching personnel and performance have also been demonstrated empirically (Eitzen & Yetman, 1972; Grusky, 1963).

These consistent effects of group stability on success stem from at least two basic group processes. First, virtually all developmental approaches to groups note that groups need time to reach a point at which members work well with one another. In open groups, where new members join the group and old members leave, performance may be of uneven quality as the members learn to adjust to their new teammates. In essence, turnover heightens "process loss." Second, a high rate of turnover may be a symptom of organizational dysfunction. While in some cases a high succession rate may be caused by neutral events, such as graduation of the senior-class team members or retirement, in other instances turnover may be produced by such factors as intermember conflict, leader/member disputes, or low cohesion. In this instance the high succession rate is significantly correlated with performance because it reflects other difficulties disrupting the group.

Issues

The team-as-a-group approach provides a unique perspective for examining a host of issues of interest to sports educators, coaches, athletes, and sports researchers. Here, however, we consider only two such issues: coaching for group successes and aggression in sports.

COACHING FOR GROUP SUCCESS

In many respects, coaches are leaders, for their role in the group requires them to influence and motivate others in order to improve the team's chances for success. Indeed, evidence indicates that coaches can have a tremendous impact on their players, both on the field and off (Snyder, 1972), and that a good coach is very much appreciated by the team (Percival, 1971). Players apparently prefer their coach to be supportive, providing a conducive atmosphere for performance, but also a task master who can "psych up" the team, provide technical information, and explain sources of errors (Percival, 1971). Unfortunately, one poll of 382 athletes found that the majority of the players (55%) rated their coach in fairly negative terms, which implies that the coaching role, like the leadership role, is a complex and difficult one to fill.

Although researchers are only beginning to apply some of the leadership theories discussed in Chapter 8 to coaching (for an application of Vroom's 1976 normative model see Chelladurai & Haggerty, 1978; for an application of Fiedler's 1978 contingency model see Bird, 1977), Alvin Zander believes that the essence of good team coaching lies in building up a **desire for group success.** While some coaches appeal to player-centered motivations by supporting each player individually, emphasizing personal performance, and reinforcing individual expertise, Zander feels that the advantages of a team-centered approach are too great to justify an individualistic coaching style. He argues that athletes who take pride in their team's performance will be more supportive of one another, work harder to coordinate their individual efforts, and derive more satisfaction from victory, and he therefore recommends that coaches instill a strong desire for group rather than individual success. To achieve this objective, he offers the coaching guidelines shown in the box headed "Coaching for Group Success." These guidelines, which Zander derives from his research on groups performing in many kinds of settings, describe ways to develop team unity, set appropriate group goals, and cope with fears of group failure.

AGGRESSION IN SPORTS

The positive consequences of team sports for both participants and spectators are numerous and undeniable. For participants, team sports provide exercise, enhance fitness, give pleasure, and teach teammates to work with others. For the spectator, watching sports can be a stimulating and entertaining form of recreation that is as involving as it is satisfying (for reviews, see Sloan, 1979; Zillmann, Bryant, & Sapolsky, 1979).

When we turn to the issue of aggression, however, the consequences of participation in team sports change from positive to negative. Although early speculations suggested that playing or watching physically violent sports "drained off" aggressions and hostilities, evidence indicates that violence in sports tends to promote two types of aggressive conflicts: conflict between players of opposing teams and the violent action of a crowd. While both forms of aggression are worrisome to those involved in sports—athletes, spectators, coaches, announcers, and owners—both reflect the "natural" operation of group dynamics. For example, violence between players fits the model of intergroup conflict developed by Muzafer and Carolyn Sherif in their Robbers Cave Experiment (Sherif et al., 1961). Because the encounter occurs in a sporting context, all the elements identified by the Sherifs as determinants of conflict—competition, categorization, and physical contact—are present. Furthermore, factors specified by other aggression theories, such as physiological arousal (Zillmann & Cantor, 1970) and frustration (Berkowitz, 1978), further compound the situation, enhancing the probability that the competitive situation will escalate into an aggressive situation.

COACHING FOR GROUP SUCCESS: SOME GUIDELINES

1. Emphasize the importance of pride in the group, its sources, and its consequences for the team. . . .

2. Make sure that each member understands that his or her contribution to the team is valued.

3. Use various means to underscore how each teammate depends upon the work of each other for the success of their unit.

4. Emphasize the unity of the group, the score as a product of team effort, and the perception that all members are within the group's boundary.

5. Indicate to members separately how membership helps each individual, so that each will see the group as an attractive entity.

6. Take care in the selection of group goals so that these are realistic challenges, not unreasonably hard or easy ends. Set standards of excellence for all skills and activities.

7. Don't be afraid to change goals that are found to be unreasonably difficult.

8. Once goals have been set, consider what obstacles might prevent fulfillment of these goals and how the obstacles might be overcome.

9. Encourage talk in the group about how performance can be improved and how the boring parts of athletics can be made more involving.

10. Avoid fear of failure and the tendency to evade challenges that are engendered thereby.

(Source: Zander, 1975)

Unfortunately, the brawls of baseball, the bodychecks in ice hockey, and the late hits of football also serve as starting points for another form of violence: spectator aggression. When violence occurs during the course of a game or when a referee makes a debatable call, spectators often erupt with counteraggression and mass violence. As several reviewers have noted (Boire, 1980; Leonard, 1980), spectators attending games involving physical contact between players on opposing teams tend to be particularly prone to violence, apparently because the crowd situation contains the predisposing ingredients specified in theories of collective behavior. First, through *contagion* processes the fans become aroused by observations of fouls committed on the field and violence in the stands. Second, *convergence* factors may be operating, since many of the spectators are true "fans"— dedicated followers and supporters of their team. Third, *norms* promoting "hooliganism" or "rowdyism" may develop during the course of the game, so that disruptive actions—the throwing of objects on the field, the assaulting of officials, the destruction of property—become a regular part of the sports situation (Mann, 1979).

Obviously, when all these factors combine we find increased fan violence and rises in deindividuation. In fact, sports spectators are infamous for their moblike reactions, for in recent years many instances of out-of-control crowd actions have occurred. For example, in Peru 293 people were murdered or trampled to death during a soccer game in 1964. In 1971, 66 fans were crushed when they tried to jam through a stadium exit in Scotland. In 1974, the Cleveland Indians had to forfeit a game to the Texas Rangers because the hometown fans attacked the Rangers' players (Leonard, 1980). Unfortunately, because of the nature of the sports situation, these instances of collective behavior may be difficult to prevent through direct physical means. While some changes in the structure of the sporting stadium or arena and increases in "crowd-control personnel" may help to limit fan attacks on players, mobs continue to become unruly. From a group-dynamics perspective, a more effective approach would entail altering the norms of the sporting situation to emphasize respect among players and fan restraint. If implicit norms in the sports settings did not condone aggression, then violence would be a less frequently observed phenomenon.

Summary

In studying three uniquely different "action" groups—classrooms, juries, and teams—we showed how the behaviors of individuals in these groups could be readily interpreted in terms of group processes; we also explored ways for improving the functioning of these groups. Beginning first with groups in educational settings, we found that class behaviors can be better understood once such group-dynamics concepts as group structure, leadership, and power are considered, and that many suggestions can be offered for improving classrooms. For example, evidence indicates that mainstreaming (the practice of placing students of varying levels of ability in the same classroom) is more effective than streaming, except when tasks call for creativity. Furthermore, individualistic or competitive learning does not appear to be as effective as cooperative learning, which can be achieved through many team-learning techniques. The effectiveness of team teaching, however, is less clear.

Like classrooms, juries are influenced by many group processes. Jurors are, in a sense, group decision makers, so we find that mechanisms that were discussed earlier operate during jury deliberations, including pressures for consensus, minority influence, and opinion polarization. Looking beyond these processes, however, we find evidence to indicate that juries are satisfactory vehicles for making legal decisions, and that the recent changes that have taken place in the legal system have not substantially undermined this effectiveness. These modifications, which include reducing the number of jurors from 12 to 6, relaxing the unanimity rule, and selecting jurors through more sophisticated voir dire procedures, do not seem to have resulted in dramatic changes in the general functioning of these groups.

Groups in athletic settings can also be better understood when approached from the group-dynamics perspective. For example, team performance appears to be related to cohesiveness, but many factors determine whether this relationship is positive, negative, or causal. Similarly, team performance is also dependent upon the stability of the group's membership, although the underlying basis of this relationship is not yet known. However, just as we generated pragmatic recommendations for classrooms and juries, group dynamicists can also offer suggestions for improving team performance, such as coaching for a "desire for team success" and reducing the amount of violence that sometimes occurs among both players and spectators by changing the group norms.

16

Interpersonal-Skills Training in Groups

Thomas V. McGovern

U sing groups to accomplish therapeutic goals is not new. Long before professionals in mental-health or medical fields began to pay attention to the curative power of the group, religious and political leaders were aware of its emotional and persuasive potential. Historically, the processes of healing and change have been social ones, rooted more in a communal context than in private, one-to-one interactions. It was in this century, however, that both practitioners and scientists rediscovered the power of the group.

Early therapeutic groups occurred in medical settings, where physicians brought together patients who suffered the same malady. At first, such grouping was done for economy's sake, to save both time and money, and for convenience of treatment. Soon, however, perceptive doctors became aware of the curative nature of the support, caring, and alternatives provided by fellow sufferers. Other groups were developed in community settings. They were based on the concept that in a group one could experience a reenactment of one's family life. In this context, human warmth, the opportunity to express one's sorrows to attentive listeners, and the candor of other members were the basic advantages of the group experience.

Since the inception of the group as a therapeutic tool, group methods have been viewed by the public alternatively as panacea and pandemonium. During the 1960s, when group approaches reached a zenith in popularity, clients and therapists flocked to marathon groups and other innovative formats of emotional and sensory stimulation. Many politically conservative persons looked upon such encounters as communist-inspired political tools or as indications of the society's spiritual bankruptcy and decadence. Despite this stormy period, group method survived and now quietly flourishes.

Throughout this checkered history, and despite the diversity in theoretical approaches, a consistent emphasis in groups has been on the learning of interpersonal skills. This emphasis reflects Kurt Lewin's (1948, 1951) basic assumption that participating in groups is the most effective way to learn new social skills. Participants' attainment of such skills has been viewed by both researchers and practitioners as either a desirable by-product or a specific goal of every group experience.

The purpose of this chapter is to review the methods and research support, past and present, that exist for **interpersonal-skills training** in groups. In the first section, we emphasize traditional group approaches. We use a hypothetical case study of a college student, Joe Flynn, to illustrate the similarities and differences in four of the most commonly used group approaches. The controversy regarding the effectiveness of these traditional approaches and the empirical research documenting their utility are covered in the second section. Finally, the third section describes contemporary group approaches to interpersonal-skills training. Many of these newer methods, such as assertion training and human-resource development programs have as their primary objective participants' acquisition of interpersonal skills. Two additional hypothetical case studies, of Maria Diaz and Judith Miller, show how supervisors in work settings can use these recently developed group methods to help their staffs increase their effectiveness.

Traditional Group Approaches

Once again it was September and Joe Flynn left his family and friends in a rural part of the state to return to college in the city. For the most part, Joe enjoyed college and, as the first college student in his family, was an eager and willing learner. His biggest problem at school was not educational but personal. After two years, Joe could name only about five people whom he could call acquaintances and not a single person he could label friend. While he had never been outgoing back home, at least he had belonged to a group of guys who always "hung around together and mixed it up every weekend." At school, he continually felt isolated and alone and had begun to spend increasingly more time studying in the library or sleeping in his dorm room.

Last year, his roommate had tried to arrange a date for Joe. The rendezvous point was in the library where Joe was working on a paper for a philosophy class. As the time grew near for the meeting, Joe found himself growing more and more anxious. He began to perspire, felt a mild headache develop, and had an awful sensation of churning acid in his stomach. Ten minutes before his date was to arrive, Joe retreated to the men's room to splash some water on his face. He began to rehearse his opening lines to Karen into the mirror when he heard someone behind him laugh. "Next time I'll check if anyone is in here!" Joe responded nervously.

As Joe started back to his work table, he saw that Karen had arrived and seemed to be looking around for him. He mustered up his courage and strode across the study area. "Hello, there . . ." Joe's voice cracked and its pitch could have shattered glass. Startled, Karen turned around in time to watch the crimson splotches rise up Joe's neck and cover his face. After a couple of minutes of awkward small talk, Karen suggested they head for a restaurant to get a cup of coffee. Joe agreed but the same thoughts kept racing through his head. "What do I say to this girl?" "She must think I'm a jerk." "She seems really nice but I'm really blowing it."

Over coffee, the talk was a little freer, but Joe still felt that he just wasn't making contact or saying the right things. A lot of long pauses took place while Karen sipped her coffee and Joe looked around and fidgeted. They talked about the psychology class that they were in that semester and how awful it was to face the instructor at eight o'clock in the morning. They talked about life in the dorms, away from home, and trying to get along with disagreeable roommates. In many ways, Joe felt that he and Karen had a number of things in common, but he never felt confident about the impression he was making. Karen, in contrast, seemed relaxed and able to talk easily about anything.

When they finished their coffee, Joe walked Karen back to her dormitory. Over and over he rehearsed to himself how he would ask her out again. At the building entrance, they both exchanged the ritual remarks: "Thanks, it was great"; "Maybe

I'll see you again sometime"; and "Yeah, if I'm awake in that eight o'clock psych class." And then Karen was gone. All the way back to his room, Joe was furious with himself: "If only I had asked her about Friday night . . . Why can't I carry on a conversation? . . . The best chance I've had and I messed it up!" All the next day Joe felt depressed. He slept late and cut all of his classes.

Personal Growth in Groups

The case of Joe Flynn is a realistic one. Many people have Joe's problems to a greater or lesser degree, particularly in late adolescence and early adulthood. In search of solutions to these social difficulties and to find alternative ways to interact with other people, some students seek professional assistance at their university counseling centers or other agencies in their community. Let's suppose that Joe Flynn chose this course of action. What could he reasonably expect from a counseling agency?

On his first visit Joe would meet and talk with a staff counselor trained in psychology, social work, education, or rehabilitation. This person would listen to Joe's problems and help him to identify their causes and their consequences. Counselors generally approach their clients' problems in accordance with the particular theoretical assumptions about human behavior they were trained in. The procedures they recommend to solve these problems are consistent with these theoretical assumptions and should be scientifically established as effective.

The most conventional procedure for helping a person like Joe would be to set up a one-to-one interaction with a counselor on a weekly basis until the client's problems were satisfactorily resolved. In these individual sessions, Joe and his counselor might focus on his feelings, thoughts, actions, or some combination of these factors. Individual counseling remains the most widely used method for a multitude of client problems. Nevertheless, for the specific purpose of helping a client to develop interpersonal skills, individual counseling is often ineffective and always inefficient. Although clients in one-to-one counseling can establish and develop interpersonal relations with the counselor, a group setting offers a richer context for acquiring and practicing effective social skills. As the next section will show, however, the desirability of a group over an individual approach to problems of adjustment and personal growth depends in part upon the *type* of group approach being considered.

Four Approaches

If Joe were seeking assistance between approximately 1960 to 1970, he probably would have found himself in a group-counseling situation. During that decade, therapeutic groups generally met on a weekly basis for two to three hours and, in the academic context, lasted for one to two semesters. In fact, such groups were often offered as credit courses in the departments of education, psychology, or social work. The actual format of the group sessions depended on the training, experience, and theoretical position of the group leader. The box headed "Types of Groups" gives an overview of the types of groups that emerged during that period.

In the following subsections we describe in detail the four group approaches that were used most widely from 1960 to 1970—T-groups, psychoanalytic groups,

TYPES OF GROUPS

A major source of difficulty for the lay consumer is the wide diversity of group approaches. While textbook descriptions of these groups emphasize their uniqueness, group leaders are more often eclectic in their actual practice. Such an eclecticism has both advantages and disadvantages. Though group practice evolves as new techniques are developed to meet client needs, as techniques and approaches are "mixed and matched" by group leaders, empirically demonstrating a group's effectiveness becomes ever more difficult.

All the groups listed below are currently in use. They may be advertised as therapy, counseling, growth, or training groups by the person who leads them.

Adlerian
Encounter
Existential/experiential
Gestalt
Group dynamic
Marathon
Psychoanalytic
Psychodrama
Rational/emotive
Reality
Sensitivity training
Synanon
Tavistock
T-group
Transactional analysis

Many texts offer full descriptions of these groups (Corey, 1981; Hansen, Warner & Smith, 1980; Shaffer & Galinsky, 1974).

---

encounter groups, and Gestalt groups. We discuss the historical roots and basic goals of each approach, but our emphasis is mainly on Joe Flynn and how he would learn more effective interpersonal skills in these groups.

TRAINING GROUPS (T-GROUPS)

T-groups have been among the most widely used methods of interpersonal-skills training. As you may recall from Chapter 14, the original T-group model was developed in 1946 as part of a project designed by Kurt Lewin. The purpose of the project was to aid a group of state employees in implementing a Fair Employment Practices Act by working together to develop clear communication patterns. Through the years, the original objective of the T-group—to provide a laboratory for learning, based upon group-dynamics principles, in which participants could develop interpersonal skills to apply in their workplaces—has survived. A variation of the T-group, the **sensitivity-training group,** emphasizes the individual member's emotional experiences during the session more than his or her interactions on the job.

The T-group has basic goals: to enable participants (1) to learn how to learn inductively from their own experiences, (2) to learn about themselves, (3) to learn about group dynamics, and (4) to learn some behavioral skills. Typically, on first entering a T-group, Joe's initial reactions would be uncertainty, ambiguity, and perhaps annoyance. He would find a characteristic absence of defined group structure, roles, and agendas. The members would be told that they were responsible for their own learning and together would have to establish a set of norms and goals for themselves. As the group members developed their working relationships, they would become increasingly willing to express their reactions to what was said and who was saying it.

In this laboratory environment, Joe would presumably gain increased cognitive insight into the patterns of his interpersonal behavior with men and women. He would receive *feedback,* or reports by other members on their perceptions of how he "came across." Both the members and the trainer/role model would support Joe's attempts to be more emotionally expressive and communicative about his thoughts. For Joe, the desired outcome of his T-group experience would be increased self-confidence and the desire to try his newly learned behaviors in his daily interactions. It is hoped that he would develop a rational insight about interpersonal behavior in general and his communication style in particular.

PSYCHOANALYTIC GROUPS

Sigmund Freud created his theory of personality development and designed his therapeutic methods for work with individual patients. However, a number of Freud's followers adapted his psychoanalytic techniques for use in group settings. In practice, this adaptation takes the form of individual analysis in the presence of members/observers. However, this format may vary if the therapist is not too controlling but rather allows members to interact with each other freely or helps them to aid one another in resolving individual problems.

In a psychoanalytic group, Joe Flynn would meet a heterogeneous mix of people. The psychoanalytic group would not be designed to focus specifically on interpersonal-communications problems. Rather, interpersonal skills might be only one of a variety of issues raised by group members. Joe would be asked to focus on his feelings for and associations with other members in the group as they discussed their personal problems or related with one another. One central theoretical concept would be presented to Joe at some point during the group sessions: that Joe's responses to group members could be reflections of his feelings toward his original family members. It could well be hypothesized that his inability to speak freely to a Marcia in a group or to a Karen outside the group might stem from early conflicts with a female sibling or perhaps his mother. The group environment would provide him with the opportunity to discover these patterns of his interpersonal communications, which, it would be assumed, were motivated more strongly by past relationships than by present reality.

By reacting spontaneously to others Joe's behavior might initially come across as "irrational" or "inappropriate." In the heat of an argument in the group, Joe might actually act as if another member were his older brother or the therapist were his father or mother. (This would be an instance of the phenomenon known as *transference.*) After such a critical incident took place and Joe had let down his defenses, the therapist would lead him to an understanding of what had taken place. Using a technique called *interpretation,* the therapist would help Joe recognize how such behavior functioned in the context of his earlier family interactions. The psychoanalytic approach strongly emphasizes insight into the origins of one's problems. Most psychoanalysts assume that the failure to attend to these roots of an interpersonal problem fosters its continuance.

As he listened to the therapist's interpretations and to the support and criticisms offered by other members, Joe would presumably feel gradually less defensive and less conflicted about his interpersonal relationships. Understanding the sources of one's problems is the primary objective in the traditional psychoanalytical group. It is assumed that with his new emotional and cognitive insight into the root causes of his fears about relationships, Joe would quite naturally change his behaviors and find himself speaking more directly and assertively to others outside of his group.

ENCOUNTER GROUPS

Unlike T-groups or psychoanalytic-therapy groups, encounter groups rest upon no one theoretical framework. Both critics and disciples aptly characterize the encounter-group method as a smorgasbord of techniques and experiences intended to guide normal individuals toward a deepening of interpersonal intimacy. With defensiveness and socially motivated facades eliminated by means of specific techniques, group members encounter each other "authentically." Perhaps the fundamental principle is that one's interpersonal relationships are of primary importance, a principle that is consistent with the counterculture movement in our technological—and to some extent "dehumanized"—society.

The history of the encounter-group model is diverse. In a 1914 poetic writing, *Invitation to an Encounter,* Moreno described the encounter concept in this way:

A meeting of two: eye to eye, face to face. And when you are near I will tear your eyes out and place them inside of mine, and you will tear my eyes out and place them inside of yours, then I will look at you with your eyes and you will look at me with mine [Moreno, 1953, p. 7].

The T-group was a precursor of the encounter group. However, with the encounter group the focus shifted from the learning of group dynamics for implementation in the workplace to a more clinical emphasis on self-awareness through therapeutic feedback. Thus, the sensitivity-training group and the encounter group became indistinguishable. Carl Rogers' *basic encounter group* (1970) and William Schutz's *open encounter group* (1967) both offered distinct rationales and methods and brought two charismatic spokespersons into association with the encounter-group approach. These two clinicians fashioned a "therapy for normals" designed to increase participants' openness to new experiences, especially those of an interpersonal nature.

Let's return now to Joe Flynn, who remains anxious about his interpersonal relations. He sees himself as neither likable nor desirable. Owing to his poor self-concept, he distorts, denies, and discounts the value of his interpersonal experiences. In an encounter group of Carl Rogers' style, Joe would receive unconditional positive regard and empathic understanding from his leader and the other members. In contrast to the predominantly rational feedback he would receive in a T-group, Joe would experience more emotionally charged confrontations here. He would be encouraged to experience and express intense feelings of anger, caring, loneliness, and helplessness, and a norm of authentic self-disclosing behavior would emerge within the group. In an encounter group of William Schutz's style, sensory-physical awareness would also be heavily emphasized. In such a setting, the leader might introduce structured exercises designed to heighten the members' physical and emotional contact with one another.

Thus, we could describe Joe's encounter-group experience as a return to "basics."
In this approach, Joe would be seen as having lost sight of his basic goodness due
to his unmet needs for approval and love. His lack of self-acceptance would be
viewed as impeding his self-expression and thus his capacity to interact meaning-
fully with other people. The goal of the encounter group would be to restore to
Joe his ability to trust his feelings, his most personal qualities, and thereby to free
him to relate to others naturally, without fear.

GESTALT GROUPS

More than any other type of group experience, Gestalt therapy drew its energy
and popularity from the charismatic qualities of its founder. Before his death in
1970, Fritz Perls had developed a unique approach from a blend of rather divergent methods and theories. Basically, Gestalt therapy was grounded in the perceptual theory of the Gestalt psychologists and was intended as a repudiation of
the rigid prescriptions of psychoanalysis. Perls' richly textured, sometimes sensa-
tional method comprised elements of the existential movement, psychodrama
exercises, and a focus on bodily awareness that came to be the hallmark of the
Esalen Institute in Big Sur, California. An active speaker throughout the late 1960s,
plus an easily grasped writer in such books as *Gestalt Therapy Verbatim* (1969)
and a personable demonstrator in numerous films and videotape materials, Perls
attracted a large following both to himself and his Gestalt-therapy approach. In
the process, he demonstrated the guru/disciple tendencies inherent in the method.

In a Gestalt therapy group, Joe Flynn would be struck first by the central role
played by the leader. A highly skilled Gestalt leader is like a symphony conductor
working with a featured soloist. If Joe were the soloist, all attention in the group
would focus on him as the leader directed him to concentrate intensely on his
feelings at the present moment, on his physical sensations and nonverbal actions,
and on the blockages he was experiencing caused by emotional conflict or impasse.
In the group, Joe would be asked to "play out his piece" on the theme of inter-
personal-relationship difficulties. He would find himself repeating the lines he had
rehearsed to say to Karen or the conversational tools he armed himself with to
break the ice in class. The leader might ask Joe to play the part of Karen, and
thus to demonstrate how he projected onto her a critical attitude about his own
interpersonal style. *Why* he had done so would matter little to the Gestalt leader;
of more concern would be helping Joe to become aware of *how* he was responsible for interacting with others in a stereotypical way. In taking on the role of
Karen, the leader might ask Joe to play himself and to attend to his own fears and
anxieties. The origin of Joe's avoidance of interpersonal relationships might be
revealed to be a fear of intimacy, a devaluation of himself as a male, or even a
piece of "unfinished business" dating from an earlier relationship turned sour.

The Gestalt-group leader works not with a predetermined plan but with a spontaneous orchestrating technique that moves the client to deeper and deeper emotional experiences. In Joe's case the desired outcome would be a heightened
insight into Joe's particular interpersonal style and experience. Joe would experience emotional release, a newly discovered awareness, and a kind of exhilaration
that is often linked to the leader's mystically powerful style. After taking his turn
on the "hot seat," Joe would blend back into the group and watch with empathy

and vicarious enthusiam as a new soloist moved onto center stage. After such a session, Joe would leave the group with the distinct feeling that all things were possible in his interpersonal relationships. To complete the musician metaphor, he would have been elevated from a back-row player to soloist, or even an improviser and composer, in performing interpersonally in a new and satisfying style.

Comparing the Approaches

We can compare these four approaches to group therapy on several dimensions: the function of the leader, the role of group members, the degree to which individuals are focused upon within the group, and the emphasis on growth and skill learning versus deep-seated personality changes.

As a starting point, it is important to evaluate the basic assumptions in each of these approaches regarding how and what members learn. The learning goals may be new insights about oneself or new behaviors such as interpersonal skills. The psychoanalytic and Gestalt group-therapy approaches assume that members learn most from the words and actions of the group leader. To achieve their common goals of guiding participants to self-understanding and new insight, both the psychoanalytic and the Gestalt group leader focus on one member at a time, using techniques that were originally developed for one-to-one interactions. The other group members watch with awe, reverence, and vicarious emotions, and patiently await their turns while the leader works with a single member. Thus, the principal focus in these approaches is on individual members, not on the group, and the expert leader directs whatever learning takes place.

The T-group and encounter group operate on a different assumption: that members can learn from one another as well as from the leader. As noted in Chapter 14, the small-group leader functions as a *facilitator* of member interactions. In these approaches, leaders are catalysts for discussions in which members can learn about themselves by attending to their interactions with one another. The encounter-group leader goes one step further, even fully participating as a member in the emotional experiences of the group. In this view, leaders cannot be distant or expert if they are fully to aid members in learning about themselves (see the box headed "Communication Patterns in Counseling Groups" on page 464).

All four types of groups are similar in their underlying assumption that groups are effective vehicles for promoting healthy personal change. However, the effectiveness of groups for this purpose depends upon many interrelated factors, such as the practitioner's theoretical assumptions and methodology and the members' own experiences. In recent years researchers have sought to assess just how effective group approaches really are. We turn now to a detailed consideration of this central topic.

The Effectiveness Controversy

Although early group therapists and counselors advocated group approaches to interpersonal-skills training on purely theoretical, logical, or clinical grounds, eventually questions arose as to the measurable impact of groups on individuals, and a number of empirical studies were performed to measure effectiveness.

COMMUNICATION PATTERNS IN COUNSELING GROUPS

A recent synthesis of a social-psychological perspective and group approaches was accomplished by Stanley Strong in his book with C. A. Claiborn, *Change Through Interaction* (1982). Strong uses Shaw's analysis of group-communication patterns to compare various group-counseling approaches. He describes the traditional forms—psychoanalytic, Gestalt, transactional analysis, and behavioral groups—as examples of the *wheel pattern,* with the therapist as the hub and the clients as the spokes. In contrast, encounter and T-groups represent the *comcon pattern,* in which each person communicates with every other person including the therapist. Norms, group tasks, group goals, cohesiveness, and member changes all become predictable consequences of the chosen communication pattern. After reviewing the encounter-group findings (Lieberman, Yalom and Miles, 1973), Strong reframes earlier writers' conclusions about changes in comcon group members. He defines caring and self-disclosure as norms that foster the processes of deindividuation and cohesiveness, the necessary conditions for therapeutic intervention and change, and suggests that the potential of comcon groups to accomplish powerful and long-lasting changes is quite high. Wheel groups, he argues, are more successful with clients whose behavior is "deviant"—that is, pathological, aggressive, or generally unresponsive to social influence. Strong's conceptual model of interaction should receive increasing attention as the fields of group dynamics and group-practice approaches continue to influence one another.

Taking an historical approach to this research, this section begins by reviewing the first of these studies, which concentrated on the positive and negative consequences of participation in groups. Next, we cover the shift in research focus that led investigators to search for both the beneficial and limiting factors common to all groups approaches. Lastly, we synthesize the results of this research by reviewing the *interactional* approach to skills training in groups.

Early Research

Early research on group treatments was quite primitive, especially when compared with the group-dynamics research covered in preceding chapters. Whereas the latter generally involved experiments in which member variables, leader variables, task variables, and experimental conditions were defined and controlled, research on group counseling and therapy research began by taking a global approach. At first, researchers began with such questions as "Is Gestalt therapy more effective than no treatment at all?" and set up, say, a three-group design (A, a Gestalt-group condition; B, a placebo/discussion-group condition; and C, a no-treatment/waiting-list control condition). An "expert" leader would be recruited for Group A, and usually he or she would not lead Group B. The typical measure of change would be a self-report instrument administered to subjects before and after the treatment to assess differences in their values, attitudes, personality characteristics, and levels of adjustment. In short, psychotherapy in general, perceived as a package of leadership and group techniques leading to positive changes in subjects, was hypothesized to be better than no treatment at all. Many of the studies of this genre documented just that conclusion.

DO GROUPS PRODUCE CASUALTIES?

Two terms often appear in the descriptive and empirical literature on groups: *premature terminations* and *casualty*. While these terms are sometimes used synonymously, their meanings are not identical. A participant who leaves a group before its planned completion and who is neither harmed nor positively affected is a *premature termination*. Such people leave groups because they may lack motivation or because their expectations about groups are unmet. The latter reason has been the most often reported in the available literature (Bednar & Kaul, 1978).

A *casualty* is quite different, although the term has been defined differently by different authors. The number of casualties reported in studies has ranged from none among 94 participants in a human-relations training lab followed up after five months (Smith, 1975) to a high of 8% of encounter-group participants (Lieberman, Yalom, & Miles, 1973). Definitions variously refer to physical or psychological distress, self-reports of negative effects of participation, and assorted measures taken after termination, from immediately to a follow-up period of six months.

Two conclusions are supported by the available research. Persons with serious psychological difficulties prior to a group experience are more prone to becoming group casualties than those without serious problems. Clearly, much work is necessary in developing screening variables for prospective group members. Second, the personality of the member, the leadership style of the group leader, and the overall expectations of both seem to interact in a somewhat predictable fashion. The laissez faire leader or the highly emotional, highly energizing leader seem to be most frequently associated with member casualties (Lieberman, Yalom, & Miles, 1973). Again, continued work is necessary to define these relationships empirically.

In an important review of the literature on current perspectives in group research, Richard L. Bednar and Theodore J. Kaul (1978) summarized the major methodological problems associated with these early research efforts. First, they pointed out that most researchers failed to employ multiple groups in their designs. Investigators assumed that error variance was based solely on subject differences within groups and gave no consideration to the possibility that the unique ecology of a particular group could contribute to error variance among groups, thus confounding positive treatment effects based upon the group method. A second problem was the sensitization effects of pretesting, especially in group research where pre- and posttesting and an experimental/control group design were used. A third methodological problem was a tendency to ignore possible placebo or expectancy effects. In many studies authors concluded that a particular group-therapy method was effective although they showed no significant differences between the theoretical treatment condition and the placebo/discussion-group condition.

Bednar and Kaul (1978) draw several conclusions from their review. They show that while a growing body of literature indicates that groups "work," evidence also exists to show that groups not only don't work, but may produce casualties (see the box headed "Do Groups Produce Casualties?"). The authors also conclude that the reported effectiveness of group methods should be assessed in light of the methodological problems just described and the types of measurement employed. Most of the effective changes reported were yielded by self-report instruments designed to measure self-concept, attitude, or personality. If Joe Flynn's groups had been the focus of these studies, the subjective measures might have given positive effects though no actual behavior changes had been assessed. In sum, Joe may have become more "self-actualized" according to his measurement results while his ability to talk less anxiously and more effectively with another person remained undocumented. Behavioral measurement did not gain sophistication until the early 70s, when new strides were made in group therapy (described in the section headed "Contemporary Group Approaches"). Still, valuable insights into why groups worked were gained following the early research efforts.

Comparative Research on Traditional Groups

In 1970, Irvin Yalom wrote a seminal work entitled *The Theory and Practice of Group Psychotherapy* (a second edition was published in 1975). Based upon his experiences as an active practitioner, teacher, and group researcher, Yalom identified eleven **curative factors** that cut across the various schools of group work. In describing these factors of change in group members, he created a new perspective for group-therapy research: he specified definable mechanisms that may operate in all groups. (Yalom's factors are listed in the box headed "Yalom's Curative Factors.") In his text, Yalom reviewed a series of studies that assessed directly the importance of these curative factors from both the group members' and the group leaders' perspectives. He concluded that these factors are interdependent in groups, that certain ones may vary based upon a particular method, and that much work is necessary to define the interactions among these factors and such variables as member differences, group development, group goals, leadership differences, and the methods used to evaluate group outcomes.

Subsequent to the appearance of Yalom's important text, he and two other colleagues (Lieberman, Yalom, & Miles, 1973) sought to demonstrate empirically the curative elements within all group treatments. They designed and conducted a large-scale study at Stanford University. As part of a 30-hour academic course, 206 students were assigned to 18 different groups representing 9 widely used

---

YALOM'S CURATIVE FACTORS

1. Instillation of hope (if other members can change, so can I).
2. Universality (we all have problems).
3. Imparting of information (alternative methods to solve problems are taught).
4. Altruism (I can help others in my group).
5. Corrective recapitulation of the primary family group (my group was like reliving and understanding my family relationships).
6. Development of socializing techniques (basic social skills).
7. Imitative behavior (observational learning-modeling effects).
8. Interpersonal learning (group is a social microcosm).
9. Group cohesiveness (members accept one another).
10. Catharsis (I am able to express emotions freely).
11. Existential factors (I am responsible for my own life despite its circumstances).

(Source: Yalom, 1975)

approaches plus one "Tape Group" that had no leader but utilized tape-recorded exercises. The 16 group leaders had been identified by their colleagues as the best in the San Francisco area. The researchers measured participant variables, leader characteristics, leader methods, group characteristics, participants' reports of the experience, discrete types of participant outcomes, and the interactions among variables. They took measures before, during, immediately after, and six months following the group experience. Measurement methods included self-reports by leaders and members, members' ratings of other members and their leaders, external ratings of leaders by expert observers, and ratings of members by non-participating friends.

This complex study on time-limited groups yielded a number of important results. First, the study demonstrated that it is not a "school of psychotherapy" and its packaged set of methods that contributes most to changes in members. The best outcomes obtained by members were the results of interaction effects among group-member characteristics, group-environment conditions (for example, norms and cohesiveness), and group-leadership styles. For example, two separate Gestalt groups with different Gestalt therapists were part of this study. On a composite score of several variables, one Gestalt group was ranked second highest both immediately after the experience and six months later. The other Gestalt group was ranked last—that is, as yielding the least benefit—at both measurement points! This pattern was evident for most of the theoretical orientations.

Second, the overall effects of these traditional groups seemed to be in the areas of value and attitude changes and in the self-perceptions of the participants. The authors concluded that the traditional types of groups they studied produced more "internal" than "external," or behavioral, changes. These internal changes were still evident at the six-month follow-up point.

Third, four leadership functions emerged from an analysis of 27 variables measuring leadership behavior. First, *emotional stimulation* refers to leader behavior that emphasizes confrontation, emotional self-disclosure, demands, exhortations, and the modeling of intense emotional expressions of love or anger. An emotionally stimulating leader is a center of attention, often charismatic, and frequently unpredictable and dramatic in style. Next, a *caring* leader style is characterized by warmth, friendliness, genuineness, and kind attention to the needs of group members. Such a leader gives members support and encouragement consistently and humanistically. *Meaning attribution* refers to leader behavior marked by teaching and the translating of members' feelings and actions into ideas and understandable concepts. This function includes clarification, explanation, and interpretation. The meaning-attributing leader emphasizes the cognitive understanding of group members rather than just an immediate emotional expression. Finally, *executive function* refers to such leader behaviors as setting time limits, management, pacing of activities, defining rules and boundaries, and focusing on group decision making.

When the investigators related these four leadership functions to various member-outcome scores, a clear profile emerged. The most effective leaders were high in caring and moderate in the other three functions. The least effective leader was characterized as low in caring, low in meaning attribution, very low or very high in emotional stimulation, and very low or very high in executive function.

Regarding the traditional forms of groups overall, the researchers also concluded that from the members' perspective such groups could be beneficial, neutral, or downright damaging. At the conclusion of the 30 hours, 60% of the participants reported having benefited. Six months later, 10 to 20% of this group was less positive in its evaluation of benefit. Leaders' evaluations of member benefits were not as critical. Leaders judged 90% of the participants to have benefited. For those members who did not experience benefit, no "late-blooming effect" was detected in the six-month follow-up. Finally, of the 206 subjects, 16 (7.8%) suffered significant psychological injury. They were the casualties of this experience.

To date, this comparative study has neither been replicated nor even approximated in the number of groups, participants, and measures employed. Numerous criticisms of the methodology and the conclusions have been forwarded. However, this effort represented an important transition from group research that focused on comparing global approaches to studies that addressed more specific member, treatment, and leadership variables.

Effectiveness: An Interactional Model

In 1966, Donald Kiesler proposed that an interactional model be used to evaluate effectiveness in one-to-one treatment methods. Recent authors (Bednar & Kaul, 1978; Goldfried, 1980; Parloff, 1979) have echoed this call for research that asks the question: Why does this therapy method work? Laboratory research in group dynamics has reflected an interactional orientation for many years. However, in the group-counseling and -training field, this model is only just gaining support. We can state the interactionist approach succinctly with respect to group effectiveness merely by iterating the salient question researchers and practitioners should ask: (1) What kinds of changes are produced by (2) what kinds of group methods applied to (3) what kinds of group members by (4) what kinds of group leaders under (5) what kinds of group environment conditions? This rather bulky query encompasses the five factors interacting to determine group-treatment effectiveness.

Contemporary Group Approaches

In this section, we cover contemporary group approaches. While these approaches no more lay to rest the effectiveness question than the more traditional methods do, they draw on the contributions made by previous group workers and focus especially on interpersonal-skills training. Most contemporary group approaches are based on the principles and methods of **behavior therapy.** The fundamental assumptions of behavior therapy are listed in the box headed "Basic Assumptions of Behavior Therapy." These assumptions, which differ sharply from those of the traditional approaches, are elaborated in the following subsection.

Behavior Therapy in Groups

Recent authors (Flowers, 1979; Rose, 1977) have described a rationale and method for behavior group therapy. The most common definition of behavior group therapy actually parallels those of psychoanalytic or Gestalt group therapy.

Behavior group therapy can be seen as individual **behavior therapy** conducted in a group setting. That is, within the group setting the therapist defines and treats an individual member's problems according to specific learning principles. Other members watch and await their turns. A second definition of behavior group therapy emphasizes the use of specific behavioral techniques in an already existing group. For example, a group leader may promote the growth of cohesiveness in a group by using specific positive-reinforcement techniques when members interact. The leader sets specific goals for increasing the level of cohesiveness and intervenes accordingly.

A third definition of behavior group therapy involves teaching members to perceive their problems behaviorally and to then use the group as a whole in modifying the problematic behaviors. Groups that focus on interpersonal-skills development best exemplify this third definition. Group members such as Joe Flynn, for example, are selected for a group because their problems involve a lack of interpersonal skills. The leader teaches them to analyze their problems in behavioral terms and then involves all the group members in helping, supporting, and criticizing one another. The leader introduces structured exercises designed to develop new and more effective interpersonal skills. These groups exist only briefly (from 12 to 20 hours) and are highly structured around one set of problems and the best techniques to modify them.

In behavior group therapy, effectiveness is solely defined as behavioral change as measured before and after the group experience and again after an extended follow-up. In contrast to the assessment methods used in the traditional approaches described above, assessment in behavior therapy involves the observation and rating of a client's actual behavior in a real or simulated interaction. For example, before beginning such a group, the leader would ask Joe to interact with several persons on several topics chosen by the leader. These interactions would be videotaped and rated by independent judges on such behaviors as amount of eye contact, speech fluency, appropriate content, and voice loudness or pitch. When the same interactions were filmed and rated after the group experience, Joe would

---

BASIC ASSUMPTIONS OF BEHAVIOR THERAPY

1. Behavior therapy emphasizes the problem behavior itself (e.g., lack of interpersonal skills), rather than any presumed, underlying cause (e.g., early childhood conflict).
2. Just like any other behavior, problematic behavior is acquired through learning.
3. Behavior therapy assumes that psychological principles drawn from learning theory are most effective to modify problematic behavior.
4. The goals of behavior therapy are always specific and clearly defined as behaviors which need to increase (e.g., assertiveness during a job interview) or to decrease (e.g., smoking, eating too much or often).
5. A behavior therapist tailors the treatment method to the specific needs of the client. One method may never exactly match all client differences.
6. A behavior therapist uses only those treatment methods which have been empirically tested and have been found relatively effective for a specific client problem.

(Source: Rimm & Masters, 1974)

---

be expected to show tangible behavior changes reflecting a more relaxed, interpersonal style.

In sum, behavior group therapy is brief, aimed at specific changes in problem behavior, and highly structured in its methods to accomplish those changes. The

---

CURATIVE FACTORS IN GROUP-BEHAVIOR THERAPY

1. *Instillation of hope.* The expectations and goals for behavior change are clearly stated to the client before the group begins. Research evidence from prior groups and clients is presented to inspire confidence.
2. *Universality.* Clients for a group are chosen on the basis of a single target problem behavior. The recognition that all members share a common difficulty and common expectations is demonstrated in the first session.
3. *Imparting of information.* The reasons for problem behaviors and their consequences are continually analyzed and discussed. The rationale behind all structured exercises to accomplish change is presented. Alternative strategies for problem solving outside of group are taught.
4. *Altruism.* After members learn to analyze the antecedents and consequences of their own behavior, they can offer alternative perspectives to others in the group. Techniques of positive reinforcement are taught and members are actively encouraged to help one another in a specific, discriminating fashion.
5. *Corrective recapitulation of the primary family group.* Since problem behaviors are learned behaviors, how one's family may support or discourage more adaptive behavior is explored. The emphasis, however, is on the present and on seeking alternatives for new behavior and a contemporary support system.
6. *Development of socializing techniques.* In groups where interpersonal skills are the goal, this factor is central. In groups organized to address other problems (for example, smoking or eating excesses), members are taught

to give feedback clearly after listening carefully to one another's problems.

7. *Imitative behavior.* Group-behavior therapy continually uses modeling by the leader and role playing among the members. The structured exercises are designed to stress the following sequence: watch/listen to a rationale, practice new behaviors, receive alternative suggestions, try again until satisfied.
8. *Interpersonal learning.* Group members are selected on the basis of a homogeneous set of problems but are often a heterogeneous mix of age, sex, status, and educational characteristics. The group is seen as a social microcosm in which new skills are practiced in vivo before they are used outside the group.
9. *Group cohesiveness.* This concept is defined behaviorally as the quantity and quality of actual intermember interactions. Verbal and nonverbal reinforcement can be rated for its effect on how the members relate to one another.
10. *Catharsis.* Strong emotions such as anger and frustration can be readily expressed in group-behavior therapy. Release, however, is not the curative factor. Members must learn alternate, more effective ways to express a wide range of emotions. They must also learn to discriminate clearly the effects that their emotional expressions have on others.
11. *Existential factors.* Behavior therapy strongly advocates responsibility for one's own life. In contrast to "accepting life's circumstances," behaviorism seeks to discern scientifically the causes and effects of such circumstances. In the group, the individual must ultimately choose that style of behavior that he or she considers most authentic.

group focuses on one problem at a time rather than indirectly seeking to effect changes by global shifts in attitudes or values or by gaining insight into oneself. While behavior group therapy and the traditional approaches differ in many ways, they also exhibit many similarities. The box headed "Curative Factors . . ." is a synthesis of Yalom's factors with the methods of the behavioral approach.

Several forms of behavioral groups and their applications to specific types of interpersonal-skills training and development are described in the following subsections. Included are assertion training, interpersonal-skills training workshops, and counselor-skills training programs.

Assertion Training

Let's return to the case of Joe Flynn and conclude his hypothetical journey through the forms of group treatment likely to be offered by his university counseling center. Recall that during the period from 1960 to 1970 he would probably have been placed in a traditional-type group, such as a T-group, encounter group, Gestalt group, psychoanalytic group, or one of the other groups listed in the box on page 459. Since 1970, however, Joe's interpersonal problems would have led a counselor to place him in a behavior-therapy group, particularly assertion training.

Early definitions of assertive behavior were broad, comprising all socially acceptable expressions of rights and feelings (Wolpe & Lazarus, 1966). As the concept received more research attention, however, formal definitions of assertive behavior became more specific. Some authors (Gambrill & Richey, 1975) labeled an actual set of situations in which a person would need to respond assertively (see box headed "Types of Assertive Response Situations"). In a major review of the existing literature, two other authors (Rich & Schroeder, 1976) gave their definition: "Assertive behavior is the skill to seek, maintain, or enhance reinforcement in an interpersonal situation through an expression of feelings or wants when such expression risks loss of reinforcement or even punishment" (p. 1082). In the same review these authors described how effective training in assertive behavior must include asser-

---

TYPES OF ASSERTIVE RESPONSE SITUATIONS

1. Initiating a conversation or making a request of a person whom you do not know
2. Confronting a person about their opinions or behavior, usually over something about which you disagree
3. Giving negative feedback to an intimate friend or to someone about an intimate topic
4. Responding to other person's criticism of your opinions or behavior
5. Turning down a request to do something, to borrow or lend something to another

6. Handling service situations in a restaurant or similar retail settings
7. Resisting peer pressure to drink or to use drugs
8. Receiving a compliment; making a positive statement about one's accomplishment
9. Complimenting another person
10. Admitting personal error or ignorance
11. Handling a bothersome situation with another person

(Source: Gambrill & Richey, 1975)

A BEHAVIOR-REHEARSAL SCRIPT

Trainer: I'd like to start off this session by asking if anyone has any questions about the home-work assignment I gave at the conclusion of the last session. Joan?

Joan: As I tried to write down the thoughts that went through my mind before I called my mother, I felt artificial and even depressed about having so many.

Trainer: Almost like there were too many to handle and writing it down made it even worse?

Joan: Yes, that's it.

Trainer: [Brief minilecture and coaching period about the importance of recognizing how thoughts do influence our behavior] Yes, I know this seems artificial at first, but it not only gets easier to list those thoughts, the thoughts tend to decrease in importance once you've made them explicit. Anyone else?

Joe: I've got a perfect situation to report and I want to practice today if I can. It happened a couple of days ago but I still feel pretty anxious and stupid about how I handled an interaction with this girl Karen.

Notice the level of self-disclosure and self-aware-ness demonstrated in Joe's comment. Because of the norms of acceptance, caring, problem-solving together, Joe can readily make such a comment after six to ten hours in an assertion-training group.

Trainer: That sounds fine. Let me first check to see who else would like to work today so we can manage our time. Beth? Michael? O.K. That should keep us busy. Joe, let's start with you. I'd like you to describe to the group some of the thoughts that went through your mind while you were with . . . Karen, was it?

Joe: Yes, that's her name. Well, we were set up by my roommate to meet in the library for sort of a blind date. My voice cracked when I met her. I had nothing to talk about when we went to the restaurant and I never said anything, although I really wanted to, before she went back to her dorm.

Trainer: I think that a number of us in the group may have experienced a similar scene at some time in our own lives. Can anyone identify with Joe's spot?

Michael: That's almost the same bit that I was going to look at in my turn.

Trainer: Joe, describe your thoughts about relating to Karen. You gave us a good account before of the events. Now focus on your thoughts.

Joe: That's easy. I knew that I had to be bright, fairly witty, and keep the conversation going or else this girl would never like me at all.

Trainer: Group? What are your comments?

Michael: I had similar thoughts and they always get in my way, like I have to perform.

Joan: From the other side of the interaction, that's not what makes for a good interaction for me. I'm looking for someone who doesn't have to be using the little rituals and looking-good games all the time. Relax. Talk about what you like and know something about. If she isn't interested, you can't make anyone change unless they want to.

Trainer: Those were helpful comments, Michael and Joan. Joe, let's go with Joan's suggestion about talking about something you know or think you might have in common. I want you to recall how we practiced in our second group session those principles of carrying on conver-sations and the technique of asking open-ended questions. Would you be willing to practice that now?

Joe: Yes, let's give it a try. I'd like to have Joan play the role of Karen. She always seems so confident in here and looks just like her.

Trainer: Joan?

Joan: I'm not sure about the self-confidence, but I'll do it with him.

Trainer: Good. Before we start, Joe, what are two nonverbal behaviors that you want to focus on during this interaction? Positive ones.

(continued)

A BEHAVIOR-REHEARSAL SCRIPT

Joe: Well, I want to keep steady eye contact and try to keep my voice from cracking.

Trainer: That sounds good. All right, let's set the scene at the restaurant again. You're sitting across the table from Karen (Joan) and you begin a conversation about the early-morning psych class. Now, I want the group to pay special attention to those two nonverbal behaviors Joe wants to focus on. Let's go, now.

Joe: Boy, that psych class is pretty hard to get into at that hour.

Joan: Yes, I find myself very sleepy, especially with his monotone voice.

Joe: What other courses are you taking?

Trainer: Good, let's stop. Group, I want you to give Joe some positive comments, first about his two nonverbal behaviors and second about what he said.

The behavior-rehearsal sequence continues in this fashion until Joe has acquired a number of concrete responses through models and has practiced for his interaction with Karen. The trainer actively orchestrates the sequences, sometimes coaching, perhaps asking a group member to model a technique, soliciting comments from the members about Joe's performance, and summarizing the learning that takes place.

---

tive-response acquisition, assertive-response reproduction, assertive-response shaping and strengthening, and the generalization of assertive behavior.

The book *Responsible Assertive Behavior: Cognitive/Behavioral Procedures for Trainers* (Lange and Jakubowski, 1976) describes an assertion-training program directly applicable to Joe Flynn's problems. Joe would first read about his assertion-training group in an advertisement in the campus newspaper. However, the ad would refer not to "therapy" but rather to the assertion-training group as an educational program with an emphasis on skills development in a time-limited, structured environment. The stated objectives would include

1. Learning to discriminate between assertion and aggressive behavior;
2. Learning to identify and accept personal needs, opinions, and rights;
3. Learning to explore and refute irrational thinking that limits assertive communication;
4. Learning in a laboratory setting to develop new ways of responding more assertively to previously problematic situations.

A series of systematic exercises is used to accomplish the first three objectives listed above. In this group, Joe would be directed to participate in the structured exercises during every session. By applying two distinct methods, he would learn how to be attentive to the verbal and nonverbal aspects of his own interpersonal behavior. First, he would listen to the comments made by others about his style; then he would define for himself those aspects of his style that he would like to expand or modify. Next, the leader or trainer would teach him how to respond specifically to the other participants regarding their characteristic styles. In the early sessions Joe would actively learn through a structured give-and-take process. In the later meetings (the last 12 to 18 hours of the 30-hour course) the group would devote itself to a complex but systematic procedure called *behavior rehearsal*. This technique has been identified as the most important element in any assertion-training group (Heimberg, Montgomery, Madsen, & Heimberg, 1977; Lange &

Jakubowski, 1976). It is exemplified in detail in the box headed "A Behavior-Rehearsal Script," where the technique has been adapted to Joe Flynn's case.

Since the mid-1970s a rapidly increasing amount of empirical research has focused both on specific components of assertive behavior and on assertion-training technologies. But a broader term, **social-skills training,** has come to be applied to a wide range of interpersonal behaviors—including assertiveness—and the most effective group methods for accomplishing their enhancement or modification. In the course of the evolution of the social-skills-training concept, populations with serious and sometimes severe psychological problems have been assessed for social-skills deficits in an effort to identify those individual behaviors that severely limit people's social interactions. Furthermore, not only has assessment become more discriminating, but training methods have become more comprehensive and more carefully matched to subjects' cognitive, emotional, and behavioral difficulties.

Social-skills training (for comprehensive reviews, see Bellack & Hersen, 1979; Curran, 1977; Galassi & Galassi, 1979) reflects the interactional model described earlier with respect to effectiveness. Thus, social-skills changes are produced by structured group-behavior therapy applied to a homogeneous set of individuals with interpersonal deficits. Though the structured method focuses on behavior at all times, depending on the participant's particular difficulty, attention might also be given to participants' perceptions of interpersonal relationships or modes of expressing specific emotions (for example, love or anger) during interactions. In the empirical research to date, two components of the interactional model—types of group leaders and types of group-environment conditions—have received less attention than the other three components—kinds of changes, methods, and members.

Group leaders of assertion-training or social-skills-training groups often structure their group environments to reflect the *wheel* pattern of communication, where the leader is at the hub and the clients are the spokes. The behavior-therapy tradition has always assumed that a well-researched technique, such as behavior rehearsal, applied directly by the therapist is most effective. This leads to one-on-one social-skills or assertion-training done *in a group.* As several behavior-group therapists (Flowers, 1979; Rose, 1977) have emphasized however, training *by the* group members has the most potential to be effective.

Interpersonal Skills in Work Settings

The emphasis in this chapter so far has been on the use of groups to promote the acquisition of effective interpersonal skills regardless of the type of setting. Thus, such groups could exist in hospitals, universities, prisons, or community centers. Nor have we made distinctions as to types of group members; interpersonal-skills groups might be composed of psychiatric patients, students, prisoners, or community members. Group approaches go beyond the boundaries of what we typically think of as "therapy," for they can be applied not only in clincial settings but also wherever interactants are dissatisfied with their social skills. In this section, we concentrate on ways to increase interpersonal skills in a work setting.

THE CASE OF MARIA DIAZ

Maria Diaz was recently appointed as supervisor of the state office for unemployment benefits. One of her first priorities was to observe the members of her staff as they routinely dealt with the applicants. In her meetings with the personnel who processed claims for benefits, these employees consistently complained about the initial training for this position. The new employee-training program, they told her, covered using the correct forms, writing employer-approval correspondence, making referrals for employment interviews, and eliciting declarations of previous income levels. Furthermore, the training was excellent with respect to acquainting staff members with proper procedures. However, after a very short time on the job new employees realized that their training in communication skills had been inadequate, and it was this weakness that elicited complaints.

With this information at hand, Maria observed the staff at work during a typical week. Among her other observations, she recorded the following. On Monday, a middle-aged woman came into the office with two young children. She quietly filled out all of her eligibility forms and brought them to the counter to be approved. Upon reviewing her application, the staff member informed her that she was ineligible for unemployment benefits. The woman burst into tears and began to describe the dire financial problems that she faced as a single parent. The staff member began by listening politely but grew impatient with her story, and finally snapped that he was "no social worker," and that she should "pull herself together and work something out somewhere else."

On Wednesday, a man came into the office in the early afternoon and talked loud enough to be heard on the next floor. His behavior seemed somewhat erratic and fairly bothersome. After waiting in line, he staggered up to the counter and demanded service. Maria watched a staff member answer the man's questions as best he could while the applicant leaned farther and farther across the counter and bellowed ever louder about the "stupid bureaucracy, red tape, and harassment that a veteran was made to endure just to collect his just benefits."

On Thursday, one of Maria's clerks asked her to help him at the counter. He thought that the applicant he was helping was a "foreigner," "probably Mexican" and that Maria could translate the procedures into Spanish for him. As she spoke with the man, slowly and in English, Maria discovered—and revealed to the clerk—that this elderly person was rather confused about the details on the forms and was completely literate in English though somewhat timid in responding to the clerk's rapid questions.

At the weekly staff meeting on Friday, Maria's employees complained at length about their stress level and their lack of training in coping with demanding clients. It had become evident to Maria that some form of skills-development workshop on interpersonal communications would greatly benefit her workers.

INTERPERSONAL-SKILLS TRAINING WORKSHOPS

Interpersonal-skills training is no less appropriate to meet the needs of Maria's staff than to meet those of Joe Flynn, different though those needs are. Maria's staff had indeed been trained well to use proper forms and to follow appropriate eligibility procedures, but they were ill-prepared to handle claimants' personal idiosyncracies and aggressive actions when they arose in the course of their inter-actions. Inadequate interpersonal-skills training is common among both public-service and private-sector workers, such as retail sales workers, state police officers, receptionists, nurses, and others whose primary task is to interact with the public in accomplishing their agency's goals.

The interpersonal-skills-development workshop designed to meet the needs of Maria Diaz's staff might be offered in a two-day, 16-hour format. Its program would be tightly structured, drawing heavily upon the assertion-training model described in the previous section. The basis of the program would be a conceptualization of the communication process depicted in Figure 16-1. First, participants would listen to and participate in four lectures with demonstrations/modeling/discussion: How to Understand Your Client (focusing on listening and empathy skills), How to Assess Yourself and Communicate in an Assertive Manner, How to Manage Emo-tionally Intense Interactions, and How to Cope with Stress. One of these presen-tations would be given during each morning and afternoon session.

The heart of the program would be a role-play rehearsal sequence. In such a procedure, workshop members are asked to identify two critical situations that actually occur on the job and that they would like particularly to practice in order to explore alternative methods of handling them. Over the course of the two days, all participants have the opportunity to describe the situations they have chosen, recruit antagonists/role players from the group, state their desired goals, and prac-tice the interchanges. Feedback and discussion are generated by the group and the sessions are videotaped to enable members to observe their own strengths and weaknesses in managing situations that admittedly give them trouble on the job.

During the afternoon of the second day of the workshop, the trainer, in sum-marizing, reiterates the different components of interpersonal skills, places this

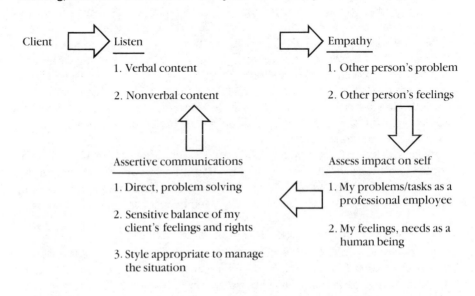

FIGURE 16-1.   Interpersonal-communications model.

behavioral program in the context of broader mental-health concerns, and introduces the concept of stress management both on and off the job.

As with social-skills training in general, there is an important emphasis in such workshops on developing interpersonal skills through interactions with other group members. The group leader imparts information, structures a set of exercises that have proven effective, and facilitates the members' working relationships with each other, but it is the members themselves who know most about the content of their procedures. While the leader establishes a framework in which members can understand their interpersonal communications, group members themselves are best able to suggest alternative behaviors and styles for handling the difficult clients. The social skills related directly to on-the-job interactions are thus demonstrated, practiced, and enhanced by modeling and feedback from group members.

The interpersonal skills emphasized in this paradigm—listening, empathy, and assertiveness—are most relevant to brief interactions on the job. They are intended to help staff members increase the professionalism of their contacts with clients. The goal is not to offer counseling to the client despite the often dire circumstances or predicaments he or she might describe. Rather, the group members' objectives are to improve their abilities to gather information, respond to specific questions, and help customers solve their own problems.

Interpersonal Skills in Counseling

Because the objectives of interpersonal-skills training enumerated above are important for counselors as well as other service workers, they have been incorporated in behavioral programs for teaching interpersonal skills to counselors. We turn now to survey some of the approaches specifically designed to help therapists, social workers, counselors, consultants, and other facilitators to improve their interpersonal skills.

THE CASE OF JUDITH MILLER

At a recent board meeting of the United Way Agency directors in a large metropolitan area, Judith Miller, Program Coordinator, informed her colleagues about a new clientele in need of services. The already established crisis-intervention program had begun to receive an increasing number of calls and drop-in visits from elderly persons. With recent budget cuts and the continued rise in the cost of living, old people on fixed incomes were experiencing increasingly high levels of stress and were using the crisis-intervention service more frequently than ever before. While the agency was pleased to be able to extend its services to this new group, the volunteer staff was becoming increasingly concerned that it was unable to meet the specific needs of the elderly.

Judith had discussed these concerns with the volunteer counselors and was able to identify three problem areas:

1. All the volunteers at Crisis Intervention were 35 or under and had little or no experience with old people.
2. The initial training program and the established referral network were designed to help volunteers serve the needs of post-adolescent to middle-adult-aged clients.

3. The contacts with the elder clients tended to take about five times the average time of interactions with the younger clients. The volunteers perceived the older people as highly dependent, disorganized, overly emotional, and unwilling to accept their problem-solving suggestions.

Judith recruited a task force to review the problem, solicit advice from the agencies in the city that dealt solely with the elderly, and make specific recommendations for more effective ways of serving these new clients. This group contacted a number of agencies and received suggestions from directors of the Departments of Gerontology at several universities. The group's proposal was to establish a peer-counseling program in which older volunteers would be trained to work with older clients and to set up a referral system especially designed for services for this target group. Such a program had received considerable support in other cities and there was even the possibility of federal grant monies to set up a pilot project.

Judith presented this proposal to the United Way directors, who unanimously approved the proposal. Her next task was to develop a peer-counselor training program that would cover those interpersonal skills found effective in working with elderly clients.

COUNSELOR-SKILLS TRAINING PROGRAMS

Judith Miller's volunteer-staff consisted of men and women who wanted to help others; their educational level ranged from that of high school graduate to that of college graduate. Before they began to staff the agency's hotline or to handle walk-in clients, these volunteer counselors received intensive and specialized group training focusing on basic interpersonal skills, technical knowledge about the problems typical in the 20–55 age range (for example, drug or alcohol abuse and suicide), and accurate information about the most appropriate referral resources (Wolber & McGovern, 1977). These three content areas are stressed to a greater or lesser extent in training programs for all crisis-intervention services, depending on the stated goals of the particular program. The training of volunteers to communicate empathetically with others is the characteristic common to all such programs.

Judith Miller's staff's new clientele demanded interpersonal skills and technical information not presented in the initial training. Their recommendation was to establish a peer-counselor program in which elderly volunteers would be trained in groups to work with elderly clients. Such a goal too, is completely consistent with the desired outcomes of interpersonal-skills-training groups. One of two established approaches is generally taken in training groups of volunteers in counseling skills. Both approaches are structured in their format and specific in their goals. These approaches were developed by Robert Carkhuff and Allen Ivey.

Carkhuff's human-resource-development approach.   Volunteer-counselor training programs emerged on the mental-health scene in the late 1960s, about the same time that behavior-therapy groups emerged. These training programs represented a unique synthesis of two traditionally divergent views: Carl Rogers' client-centered approach and the behavioral-training approach. The person most responsible for this important synthesis was Robert Carkhuff. He called his approach **human-resource development.**

Carkhuff's early work was on the identification and measurement of the "core conditions" necessary for the success of counseling and psychotherapy. Using the research of Carl Rogers and others, Carkhuff identified a set of interpersonal skills (for example, empathy, respect, genuineness, concreteness) that helped clients in their self-exploration. Further, he popularized the notion that if such basic "skills-of-helping" interactions could be specified, then they could also be taught in a systematic fashion to both professional and volunteer, or paraprofessional, counselors. To accomplish this goal, Carkhuff adopted the group-training methods of the behavioral approaches. He wrote that such skills as empathy could be taught in groups in the following step-by-step fashion: define the skill, model the skill, practice the skill in role play with another group member, receive concrete feedback from group members about strengths and weaknesses on that skill, practice again, and practice with others outside the group. Notice how similar this sequence is to the steps of assertion training.

Ivey's microcounseling approach. A somewhat different approach to counselor training in groups was developed by Allen Ivey (Ivey & Authier, 1978). This complex counseling process, called *microcounseling,* is broken down into discrete, identifiable, and therefore trainable interpersonal skills. In his taxonomy of helper behavior, Ivey identifies two broad categories of skills: *attending* and *initiating.* Within these categories are very specific skills such as asking open and closed questions, paraphrasing, giving directions, and making interpretations. What is most appealing about the microcounseling approach, however, is not its content but the group process by which these skills are taught.

Borrowing from behavioral-training approaches, the microcounseling method uses the following systematic and progressive sequence:

1. The trainee videotapes a 5 to 15 minute role-play counseling session with another group member to establish a baseline performance.
2. Trainees read a programed text or manual on the target interpersonal skill—for instance, paraphrasing.
3. Trainees watch a live or videotaped model of the target skill that demonstrates both an *effective* and clearly *ineffective* response.
4. Trainees review the tape of the individual member (see Step 1). Both the trainer and group members give feedback on the trainee's skill performance as revealed in the tape and suggest alternatives.
5. Trainee role plays the target skill in the group and receives continued feedback.
6. Trainee videotapes a second role-play counseling session to show outcome performance and further training needs in the skill.
7. Trainee completes a "DO-USE-TEACH" homework assignment that emphasizes a generalization of the learned (*do*) response by *use* of the skill and by *teaching* it to another person or group.

This format offers multiple advantages over the Carkhuff approach. The use of videotape equipment has become a sine qua non for all interpersonal-skills training. The feedback and modeling potential inherent in videotape techniques enable the trainer to attend more fully to group dynamics, since group members' performance will be documented automatically. The generalization of the skill through the specific homework assignments is another strong feature of this format.

JUDITH MILLER'S PROGRAM

Let us return now to the group-training program necessary to aid the elderly volunteers in gaining the interpersonal skills necessary for their work with elderly clients. In developing such a program, Judith Miller could draw upon the elements of either the microcounseling approach or the human-resource-development approach. One important component of this training program would be the group interactions among the new volunteers. Both approaches utilize feedback from group members and the identification by group members of alternative approaches. In this case, a particularly fruitful opportunity exists for individuals to learn from their fellow group members, since the trainees, being elderly themselves, will undoubtedly bring to bear personal understanding to the problems of old age and the inadequacy of prevailing stereotypes of the elderly. Thus, while the trainer can impart correct information by lectures, the exchange of information among group members will be a weighty aspect of the training. In short, the actual group program (see Alpaugh & Haney, 1978) to train new volunteers will best be accomplished *by* the group itself, not merely by a teacher *in* a group setting.

Summary

The behavioral approaches have contributed substantially to the more precise definition of group-member and group-method variables. The recent emphasis on social-skills assessment has yielded increasing specificity to group-member characteristics. This is especially true for those verbal and nonverbal qualities of member behavior that seem to elicit positive support or avoidance from other persons both inside and outside a group. *Behavior therapy* in general has also supplied much in the way of methods that produce concrete outcomes. Interpersonal-skills exercises, behavior rehearsal, modeling, feedback, videotape techniques, and homework assignments have all been identified and evaluated primarily within the behavioral-training paradigms.

While the training technologies of the behavioral approaches are robust in their work on the first three areas (member, method, outcome), group leadership and group conditions have been neglected. The emphasis on specific techniques to use with specific member problems could easily lead to an understanding of leadership as technician competence alone. Work within the group-dynamics field as well as on the nonbehavioral methods suggests that there is more to leadership than a controlled task orientation. When leadership is defined so narrowly, group-environment conditions will also be narrowly defined. A number of authors have recognized that the communications prevalent in behavioral groups reflects the preference to do individual behavior therapy *in* groups rather than behavior therapy *by* all of the group.

This area seems to be rich in possible research topics. How can we combine specific methods to accomplish particular goals with particular clients while relying heavily on the other group members as agents of change? The behavioral group may prove to be ever more of a social microcosm, an environment where members can be validated and critiqued and learn interpersonal skills by being both the helpers and the helped. To achieve such a blending, both scientist and group worker in this field need to learn from one another, across disciplines and theoretical perspectives.

Glossary

Accounts   Verbal statements designed to explain away deviant actions including excuses (attempts to lessen responsibility), justifications (attempts to redefine the action in more positive terms), and apologies.

Action research   Lewin's term for the use of the scientific method in solving research questions having significant social value.

Actor/observer hypothesis   The tendency for the observer to focus on internal causes when explaining an actor's behavior, and the tendency for the actor to focus on external causes when explaining his or her own behavior.

Additive tasks   Tasks that can be solved by adding together cumulatively individual group members' inputs.

Agentic state   The loss of autonomy one experiences as one becomes the agent of a higher authority.

Ambient environment   The external situational stimuli that surround the group; the environmental "envelope."

Androgyny   The possession of characteristics that are typical of both masculine and feminine sex roles.

Anomie   A state of normlessness.

Anticonformity   The public expression of ideas, beliefs, judgments, and so on opposed to the group's standards simply to disagree with the group.

Assertiveness (or assertion) training   A development program, usually conducted in a group setting, aimed at increasing participants' skills in expressing their feelings, defending their beliefs, negotiating with others, and dealing with awkward social settings.

Attraction relations   Patterns of liking and disliking in a group; often represented sociometrically.

Attribution theory   A social-psychological explanation of how individuals make inferences about the causes of behaviors and events.

Audience setting   A context for task performance in which there is a passive spectator.

Authority relations   Patterns of status or power in a group; the "chain of command" or hierarchy of dominance.

Autistic (or false) conflicts   Disputes among group members that stem from mistaken beliefs about the group situation.

Autokinetic effect   The apparent movement of a stationary pinpoint of light in an otherwise completely darkened room.

Balance   A satisfying equilibrium in a group's attraction patterns that exists when all relationships among members are positive or the number of negative relationships is even.

Bargaining theory   An explanation of coalitions that predicts the formation of coalitions through bargaining, negotiation, promises, threats, and concessions.

Behavioral assimilation   The eventual matching of the behaviors displayed by cooperating or competing group members.

Behavior therapy   Treatment of interpersonal and psychological problems through the application of learning principles; applying specific behavioral techniques in already existing groups.

Bonding   An hypothesized genetic predisposition for individuals to join with others in groups; some theorists argue bonding is stronger among males than in females.

Brainstorming   A technique for increasing creativity in groups that calls for heightening expressiveness, inhibiting evaluation, emphasizing quantity, and building on earlier ideas.

Case study   A research technique that involves examining, in as much detail as possible, the dynamics of a single group.

Charismatic leaders   Individuals whose tremendous referent power enables them to influence large masses of people.

Choice/dilemma questionnaire (CDQ)   An instrument developed by Wallach, Kogan, and Bem to measure riskiness in decisions.

Coaction   Performing a task while others in the same physical setting are engaged in a similar activity.

Coalition   A subgroup within a larger group.

Coercive power   Power based on the individual's ability to threaten and punish others.

Cohesiveness   The forces that bind members to a group, including both liking for the group as a whole and the attraction of each member to every other member.

Collective behavior   Interaction among members of social collectives that are more than random aggregations of individuals but not yet structured groups.

Communication networks   Well-defined patterns of communication in a group that describe who speaks to whom (for example, wheel, circle, chain).

Communication relations   Patterns of information exchange in a group.

Comparison level   In Thibaut and Kelley's social-exchange theory, the standard by which the individual evaluates the quality of any social relationship.

Comparison level for alternatives   In Thibaut and Kelley's social-exchange theory, the standard by which the individual evaluates the quality of other groups that he or she may join.

Compensatory tasks　Tasks that can be completed by averaging together individual group members' inputs to form a "statisticized" group solution.

Competition　The working against one another of individuals where the success of any one individual depends on the failure of the others.

Compliance　Conformity to group standards without personal acceptance of these standards.

Compresence　The performance of actions when others are present.

Conflict　A confrontation between two or more group members that occurs when the actions and/or beliefs of one party are incompatible with and hence are resisted by the other party.

Conflict grid　Blake and Mouton's theory of interpersonal styles based on two dimensions: concern for people and concern for results.

Conflict spiral　Escalating patterns of conflict whereby mild levels of group conflict are transformed into intense conflict.

Conformity　Changes in behavior that result from group influence including compliance (change without internal acceptance) and private acceptance (change in behavior and belief).

Conjunctive tasks　Tasks that require input from all group members.

Contact hypothesis　The prediction that contact among group members in conflict will be sufficient to reduce the magnitude of the conflict.

Contagion　The transmission of behaviors and emotions from one member of a collective to another.

Contingency model of leadership　Any model predicting that leadership effectiveness depends upon both personal characteristics of the leader and the nature of the group situation; usually used in reference to the leadership theory of Fiedler that is based on the leader's motivational style and situation control.

Contingent conflicts　Disputes among group members that are caused by some minor, and easily changed, feature of the group interaction.

Control theory　An explanation of crowding suggesting that high-density situations are stressful because they undermine our sense of control.

Convergence theory　An explanation of collective behavior that assumes that individuals with similar needs, values, goals, and so on tend to converge to form a single group.

Cooperation　The working together of individuals because the success of any one individual improves the chances of success by the others.

Coordination losses　Inefficiency that results from group members' inability to combine their resources in a maximally productive fashion.

Criterion-referenced grading　A system of assigning grades based on previously identified standards for acceptable and unacceptable performance.

Crowding　The psychological reaction to high-density settings.

Curative factors in groups　Elements present in group settings that aid and promote personal growth and adjustment.

Decisional conflict　Uncertainty over important decisions that culminates in emotionality, defensiveness, irrational coping, and rationalizing.

Defensive communication An ineffective pattern of information exchange that occurs whenever members of a group feel personally threatened.

Deindividuation An experiential state brought about by group membership, anonymity, loss of responsibility, arousal, and other inputs that leads to losses of self-awareness and atypical behavior.

Delphi technique A group-performance method that involves repeated assessment of members' opinions via questionnaires as opposed to face-to-face meetings.

Density The number of individuals per unit of space.

Density-intensity hypothesis An explanation of crowding predicting that high density makes unpleasant situations more unpleasant but pleasant situations more pleasant.

Dependent variable The variable systematically measured by the researcher in an experiment; the effect factor in a cause/effect relationship.

Desire for group success According to Zander, the underlying motive accounting for individuals' striving for group goals.

Desire to avoid group failure According to Zander, a self-defeating motive that can become very strong in groups that consistently fail.

Deviancy A refusal to change one's behavior to conform to group standards of action; refers to both independence (public expression of dissenting personal opinions) and anticonformity (disagreement with majority opinion).

Devil's advocate The group member who consistently finds fault with the decisions and recommendations of other group members.

Diffuse-status characteristics Skills, abilities, and attributes that members generally consider determinants of status and authority (for example, sex, race, age).

Diffusion of responsibility A reduction of personal responsibility that results from membership in a group.

Discretionary tasks Relatively unstructured problems that can be solved by using a variety of social-combination procedures.

Disjunctive tasks Either/or and yes/no tasks that are completed only when the group members reach agreement on a single answer that will stand as the group's product.

Distraction/conflict theory An explanation of social facilitation that assumes the distraction and attentional conflict produced by the presence of others facilitates productivity on simple tasks but inhibits performance on complex tasks.

Divisible tasks Tasks that can be split up into component subtasks.

Dominant responses Well-learned behaviors that are performed more efficiently in the presence of others.

Double-barrelled items Questionnaire items that ask individuals to respond to two (or more) issues at the same time.

Effect dependence The dependence of people on others for positive consequences and desirable outcomes.

Emergent-norm theory An explanation of collective behavior that suggests that aberrant behaviors in groups stem from unique norms that develop in the group situation.

Encounter groups   A form of sensitivity training that provides individuals with the opportunity to gain deep interpersonal intimacy with other group members.

Entitativity   The quality of being an entity; perceived groupness.

Equality norm   A standard of reward distribution suggesting that group members should all receive equal outcomes.

Equity norm   A standard of reward distribution suggesting that group members should receive outcomes in proportion to their inputs.

Eureka tasks   Tasks with solutions that, once suggested, seem obviously correct.

Evaluation-apprehension   Concern over being appraised by observers; a possible mediator of social-facilitation effects.

Expectation-states theory   An explanation of authority relations in groups that emphasizes the individual's standing on positively and negatively valued status characteristics.

Experiment   A study in which the researcher manipulates one or more independent variables while systematically assessing the dependent variables and controlling other possible contaminating factors.

Expert power   Power that derives from group members' belief that the powerholder possesses superior skills and abilities.

FIRO (Fundamental Interpersonal Relations Orientation)   Schutz's theory of group formation that emphasizes compatibility among three basic needs: inclusion, control, and affection.

Fundamental-attribution error   The tendency for observers to assume that other people's behavior is caused by personal factors rather than situational factors.

Fusion leaders   Leaders who fulfill both the socioemotional and task needs of the group.

Gestalt groups   Training groups that are based on Perls's theory of interpersonal adjustment and that emphasize gaining a deeper understanding of emotions and feelings through leader-guided group exploration.

Goal/path ambiguity   Situations in which the goal may be clearly understood but the steps to this goal are unclear.

GRIT (Graduated and Reciprocal Initiative in Tension Reduction)   A tenstep system for reducing intergroup conflict by increasing trust and cooperation.

Group   Two or more individuals who influence one another through social interaction.

Group differentiation   The processes whereby group members establish and maintain boundary lines between their group and other groups.

Group dynamics   The scientific study of groups; also a general term for group processes.

Group-incentive systems   Delivering bonuses and other organizational rewards to work groups rather than to individuals in the groups.

Groupmind (or collective conscious)   A unifying mental force linking group members together.

Group-polarization hypothesis   An explanation of risky and cautious shifts in judgments following group discussion that assumes judgments made after group discussion will be more extreme in the same direction as the average of individual judgments made prior to discussion.

Group structure A stable pattern of relationships among members of a group.

Groupthink A strong concurrence-seeking tendency that interferes with effective group decision making.

Hawthorne effect A change in behavior that occurs when individuals know they are being observed by researchers.

Heterogeneous-ability grouping Placing together individuals with diverse abilities.

Homogeneous-ability grouping Placing together individuals with approximately equal levels of the same ability (see *tracking*).

Human-resource development Carkhuff's technique for training counselors and therapists through the application of group-learning experiences that relies on a behavioral sequence of skill definition, modeling, practice, and feedback.

Idiosyncrasy credits Hypothetical "credits" granted to high-status members that permit them to deviate from group norms without fear of sanction.

Inclusion/exclusion hypothesis The proposition that reactions to deviancy take two forms: inclusive (deviant is pressured to conform while remaining in group) and exclusive (deviant is ostracized).

Independence The public expression of ideas, beliefs, judgments, and so on that are consistent with one's own personal standards, irrespective of group pressure to conform.

Independent variable The variable manipulated by the researcher in an experiment; the causal factor in a cause/effect relationship.

Individuation Maintaining a sense of unique individual identity.

Informational social influence Social influence that results from discovering new information about a situation by observing others' responses.

Information dependence The dependence of people on others for information about social reality.

Information saturation The point at which the individual can no longer efficiently monitor, collate, or route incoming and outgoing messages.

Interaction The mutual influence of two or more components of a system (see also *social interaction*).

Interaction process analysis A structured coding system developed by Bales that can be used to classify group behavior into socioemotional or task-oriented categories.

Interactionist approach to leadership A framework that assumes leadership emergence is determined by the interaction of personality traits and situational factors.

Interchange compatibility The degree to which the members of a group agree concerning level of inclusion, control, and affection to be exchanged in the group.

Interdependence Situations in which the behaviors of one or more individuals can influence and can be influenced by the behaviors of others.

Interference Incompatibility between group members' behaviors and/or goals.

Intergroup conflict Disputes between members of two or more groups.

Intermember relations   Patterns of interaction and influence that link individual members to one another including authority, attraction, and communication relations.

Interpersonal-skills training   A general label for experiential training techniques designed to teach group members new social skills; also, recently developed training methods that emphasize the acquisition of specific behavioral skills.

Interpersonal style   An individual-differences variable that describes variations in group members' general behavioral orientations; in Blake and Mouton's theory, interpersonal style depends upon concern for people and concern for results.

Interrole conflict   Incompatibility between two simultaneously enacted roles.

Intragroup conflict   Disputes among members of a single group.

Intrarole conflict   Incompatibility among the behaviors that make up a single role, often resulting from inconsistent expectations on the part of the role taker and the role sender.

Jigsaw classrooms   A team-learning technique that involves assigning topics to each group member, allowing students with the same topics to study together, and then requiring these students to teach their topics to the other members of their groups.

Jury   A group of individuals chosen from the community who weigh evidence presented in a court case before deciding guilt or liability.

Labeling perspective (societal-reaction theory)   A theoretical framework that argues deviancy is "created" by group members who react to others' actions.

Leader behavior description questionnaire (LBDQ)   An instrument used for measuring two dimensions of leadership: interpersonal relationships (consideration) and task orientation (initiating structure).

Leadership   A reciprocal process in which an individual is permitted to influence and motivate others to facilitate the attainment of mutually satisfying group and individual goals.

Leadership substitutes   Factors in the group situation that take the place of the leader.

Least Preferred Co-worker scale (LPC)   A questionnaire used to measure a leader's motivational style; those with a high LPC score are relationship motivated, while those with a low LPC score are task motivated.

Legitimate power   Power that stems from the target person's belief that the powerholder has a justifiable right to require and demand the performance of certain behaviors.

Level-of-aspiration theory   A theoretical perspective developed by Kurt Lewin that explains how people set goals for themselves and their groups; the theory generally predicts that goals are revised upward after success but downward after failure.

Lifespace   In Lewin's field theory, the total of all personal and environmental variables present in the situation.

Linking-pin model   Likert's model of organizations that suggests they be organized into a set of hierarchical "families" tied together by linking pins—individuals who are leaders in one group become general members in the next highest level of organization.

Mainstreaming Establishing heterogeneous classrooms by grouping together students with a wide range of abilities and backgrounds.

Mandate phenomenon A tendency to overstep the bounds of authority when one feels he or she has the overwhelming support of the group.

Maximizing tasks Tasks calling for maximal production of some product; the more produced the better.

Mere-exposure effect Increased liking for stimuli that are merely presented repeatedly to individuals.

Microcounseling Ivey's technique for training counselors and therapists in two basic skill areas—attending and initiating; utilizes behavioral training methods in a group setting.

Mindguard A group member who "protects" others from the damaging effects of negative information by gatekeeping and dissent containment.

Mindlessness A tendency for people to perform actions without considering their meaning.

Minimax principle The notion that people seek to minimize negative outcomes (costs) while maximizing positive outcomes (rewards).

Minimum-power theory An explanation of coalitions that predicts the formation of a coalition that is sufficient to win but includes partners with the most minimal pivotal power.

Minimum-resource theory An explanation of coalitions that predicts the formation of a coalition that is sufficient to win but involves partners with the most minimal resources.

Mirror-image thinking The tendency for groups in conflict to adopt the same distorted misperceptions about one another.

Mixed-motive situations Situations in which the interdependence among interactants involves both cooperative and competitive goal structures.

Motivational style of leadership In Fiedler's contingency theory, the degree to which the leader is concerned with interpersonal relations (relationship motivated) or the task (task motivated); assessed via the LPC scale.

MUM effect The reluctance to relay bad news to other group members.

N-affiliation A personality trait that reflects a need to associate with other people.

Negative reciprocity A norm calling for harming those who harm you.

Nominal group technique A group performance method that calls for combining individuals' inputs in a structured group setting.

Nondominant responses Newly learned behaviors that are performed less efficiently in the presence of others.

Normative model of leadership A theory of leadership developed by Vroom that predicts the effectiveness of group-centered, consultative, and autocratic leaders across a number of group settings.

Normative social influence Social influence that results from pressures to conform to group norms.

Norm-referenced grading A system of assigning grades that may promote competition among class members since grades depend on the average performance level.

Norms Group "rules" that describe what actions should and should not be performed by group members; the standards by which group members regulate their actions.

Observational research The systematic description and recording of events that transpire in groups by observers.

Optimizing tasks Tasks that call for matching some predetermined standard of performance; a good performance is one that most closely approximates the optimum performance.

Organizational development (OD) A general label for a wide variety of organizational interventions designed to assess current level of development, clarify and prioritize goals, promote adequate planning, and create innovation.

Originator compatibility The degree to which the members of a group have complementary needs; for example, originator compatibility is high if Person A needs to express affection while Person B needs to receive affection.

Overload theory An explanation of crowding that emphasizes privacy, stimulation, and environmental coping.

Parity norm A norm of resource allocation that suggests individuals' payoffs should be proportional to their inputs; similar to an equity norm.

Participant observation Basing analyses of group process on observations collected as a participating member of the group.

Path/goal theory of leadership A model of leadership that emphasizes two key functions: facilitation of goal attainment and clarification of paths to goals.

Personal space The distance that people like to keep between themselves and others.

Persuasive-arguments approach An explanation of polarization in groups that assumes that group members shift in the direction of the more valued pole because they can generate more arguments favoring the more valued pole.

Pivotal power The power of an individual to turn a winning coalition into a losing one by withdrawing his or her resources.

Polarization The tendency for individuals to become more extreme when formulating decisions in groups than as individuals (see *group-polarization hypothesis*).

Power The ability (or authority) to effect behavioral or psychological change in others through the process of social influence.

Power bases Sources of group members' power; French and Raven specify five bases: reward, coercive, legitimate, referent, and expert.

Power tactics Specific methods of social influence, such as persuasion, threat, and promises.

Primary groups Groups, such as a family or very close friends, that are characterized by high interdependency, identification, and interaction.

Primary tension An atmosphere of discomfort and awkwardness that characterizes interactions in newly formed groups.

Primary territories Well-controlled areas that are possessed on a relatively permanent basis.

Prisoners Dilemma Game (PDG) A laboratory procedure used for studying cooperation, competition, and the development of mutual trust.

Private acceptance   Conformity to group standards resulting from a personal acceptance of the appropriateness of these standards.

Process consultation   An organization-development technique that calls for the analysis of the group or organization by an observing expert.

Process losses   Aspects of the group's dynamics that inhibit successful performance; these losses include coordination losses and social loafing.

Psychoanalytic training groups   A form of group therapy that traces reactions in the group setting back to deep-seated psychodynamic needs.

Psychodynamic theory   A psychological theory of behavior developed by Freud; it emphasizes the impact on behavior of childhood experiences, deep-seated needs, and strong psychological drives.

Public territories   Areas that are controlled only when occupied; no expectation of future use exists.

Reactance   A psychological response to situations that threaten one's freedom of choice; often associated with behavioral attempts to reestablish freedom.

Realistic-group-conflict theory   The assumption that conflict between groups is caused by competition over valued but scarce resources.

Reciprocity principle   That people like those who admire them and dislike those who do not.

Recurring-phase models of group development   Any models hypothesizing that groups pass through various phases over time but that these phases can reoccur later in the life of the group.

Reference group   A group that is so central to its members that it influences their basic attitudes and beliefs.

Referent power   Power based on the group members' identification with, attraction to, or respect for the powerholder.

Relationship-orientation   The relative emphasis placed on interpersonal relations within the group by a leader; synonymous concepts include interpersonal orientation, consideration, supportiveness, and socioemotionality.

Replacement theory   Freud's belief that individuals join groups as adults in order to "replace" the original family group.

Resources   Skills, abilities, tools, materials, equipment, and so on needed to complete a task; members' inputs in a group setting.

Reward power   Power based on the powerholder's control over the positive and negative reinforcements desired by other group members.

Ringlemann effect   The inverse relationship between the number of people in a group and the quality and/or magnitude of individual performance on additive tasks.

Ripple effect   The contagious spread of negative, inappropriate social activity in classrooms.

Risky-shift phenomenon   The tendency for groups to make riskier decisions than individuals.

Robbers Cave Experiment   A study performed by the Sherifs and their colleagues in an attempt to better understand the causes and consequences of intergroup conflict.

Role   A behavior characteristic of persons in a context; the "part" played by a member of a group.

Role conflict   Intragroup and intraindividual conflict that results from incompatibility in role relations.

Role differentiation   The development of distinct roles in a group, such as leader, follower, isolate.

Schismatic group   Any group whose members take widely disparate stances on key issues.

Secondary deviance   Behavior that occurs because the deviant accepts the group's label of "deviant" and acts in accordance with that role.

Secondary tension   A form of conflict that occurs in groups that have passed through an earlier period of primary tension.

Secondary territories   Areas that are controlled on a regular basis, although other individuals may utilize the space as well.

Self-awareness   A focus on the self as an object, often accompanied by emotional and cognitive monitoring and careful consideration of behavioral options.

Self-perception   An attributional theory that assumes that people infer their attitudes, beliefs, and values from observations of their own actions.

Self-report measures   Assessment devices, such as questionnaires, tests, or interviews, that ask respondents to describe their current feelings, attitudes, or beliefs.

Sensitivity-training group   A variety of the T-group that focuses on the individual's emotional experiences during the sessions; generally designed to increase the individual's social sensitivity.

Sequential-stage models of group development   Any models hypothesizing that groups generally pass from one stage of development to the next without repetition.

Situational approach to leadership emergence   A framework that assumes leadership emergence is determined by factors operating in the group situation and not personality characteristics of the group members.

Situation control   In Fiedler's contingency theory, the degree to which the leader can control and influence the situation; generally used to describe situation favorability; control is determined by leader/member relations, the task structure, and the leader's position power.

Slider   A deviant who revises his or her opinion when pressured by the group.

Social categorization   The perceptual classification of people into various social groups.

Social-combination rules   The procedures used by group members for combining individuals' inputs to yield a group product.

Social-comparison processes   The exchange of information about social reality achieved through affiliation.

Social-exchange theory   An economic model of group behavior that predicts that individuals join groups offering many rewards with few costs.

Social facilitation   The enhancement of well-learned responses in the presence of others.

Social interaction   Patterns of mutual influence linking two or more persons.

Social loafing   A reduction of individual effort when working with others on an additive group task; one component of the Ringlemann effect.

Social-skills training   A structured intervention designed to help participants improve their interpersonal skills; social skills training is generally conducted in group settings.

Social traps   Situations that prompt individuals to act in their own immediate self-interest to the detriment of other group members' needs or their own long-term outcomes.

Sociobiology   A theory of social behavior based on the assumption that recurring behaviors in animals ultimately stem from evolutionary pressures that increase the likelihood of adaptive social actions while extinguishing nonadaptive practices.

Socioemotional activity   Behavior that focuses on interpersonal relations in the group.

Socioemotional specialist   In Bales's terminology, the supportive, interpersonally accommodative group leader.

Sociofugal seating patterns   Seating arrangements that discourage or prevent interaction among group members.

Sociograms   "Maps" of attraction among groups' members created through sociometry.

Sociometry   A measurement technique developed by Moreno that can be used to summarize graphically and mathematically patterns of interpersonal attraction in groups.

Sociopetal seating patterns   Seating arrangements that promote interaction among group members.

Specific-status characteristics   Skills, abilities, and attributes that are prerequisites for succcess in the given group situation.

Staffing theory   An ecological explanation of the consequences of overstaffed, understaffed, and optimally staffed behavior settings.

Status incongruency   Inconsistency in the individual's standing on various status-determining characteristics.

Status liability   The condition that prevails when deviancy is so extreme that high-status individuals' idiosyncrasy credits are no protection against sanction and they are held especially responsible for the negative consequences.

Status-organizing processes   Mechanisms by which authority relations are developed in groups.

Steinzor effect   The tendency for members of a group to speak immediately after the person sitting opposite them finishes speaking.

Stereotype   A set of expectations about others based on their membership in a social group.

Streaming   See *tracking*.

Structured coding system   An observational method that involves classifying (coding) observed group behavior under well-defined (structured) categories. The Bales Interaction Process Analysis (IPA) and SYMLOG are examples of such coding systems.

Student teams achievement divisions   A team-learning technique that involves group learning followed by an individual quiz.

Superordinate goals   Goals that can only be attained if the members of two or more groups work together by pooling their efforts and resources.

Survey feedback   An organizational-development technique that focuses on describing the current state of the organization through surveys and then sharing this descriptive information through feedback.

Symbolic interactionism   A broad theoretical perspective that argues that the self results from a dynamic interchange between individuals.

SYMLOG   A system of multiple-level observations of groups developed by Bales for the classification of group behavior.

Synectics   A specialized group-performance technique designed to increase creativity through certain discussion norms, the expression of wishes and goals, and excursions.

Systems   Series of units linked in reciprocal causal relationships.

Task activity   Behavior that addresses the task facing the group.

Task-orientation   The relative emphasis placed on task-related matters by a leader; synonymous concepts include initiating structure, goal-orientation, work facilitation, and task specialization.

Tasks   Activities undertaken by groups, including solving problems, creating products, making decisions, generating ideas, learning facts, and achieving goals.

Task specialist   In Bales's terminology, the goal-oriented, task-focused group leader.

Team building   An organizational-development technique that utilizes workshops, member-to-member training, and changes in work procedures aimed at creating a team atmosphere.

Teams/games/tournaments   A team-learning technique that involves playing vaious team-learning games and holding competitive tournaments.

Territory   Any physical location that is exclusively used and defended by a group or individual.

Three-dimensional theory of leadership   A model of leadership effectiveness that predicts that leaders who emphasize task versus socioemotional concerns will be effective at different times during the development of the group.

Threshold theory of group tension   A theory that assumes that conflict serves a useful function in groups so long as it does not surpass the tolerance threshold for too long.

Tracking (or streaming)   Establishing homogeneous classrooms by grouping together students of approximately equal levels of ability.

Trait approach to leadership   A framework that assumes that leaders possess certain personality characteristics distinguishing them from nonleaders.

Trust   The feeling, belief, or expectation that the statements of others can be relied upon.

Truth-supported wins rule   The assumption that a group working on a disjunctive task will correctly solve the problem only if the correct answer, once suggested, is supported by a significant proportion of the group's members.

Truth-wins rule   The assumption that a group working on a disjunctive task will correctly solve the problem if one of the group members knows the correct answer.

Unanimity rule   A decision rule in groups (such as juries) that requires the decision be recommended by all the group members.

Unitary tasks   Tasks that cannot be broken down into simpler subtasks.

Value theories of risky shift   An explanation of group risk taking that emphasizes the value of risk in this society; since risk is seen as a positively valued trait, when individuals discover that others take more risks, they shift their decisions in a riskier direction.

Voir dire   The verbal or written questioning of prospective jurors by counsel.

References

Abramson, L. Y., Seligman, M. E. P., & Teasdale, J. D. Learned helplessness in humans: Critique and reformulation. *Journal of Abnormal Psychology*, 1978, *87*, 49–74.

Adams, J. S. Inequity in social exchange. In L. Berkowitz (Ed.), *Advances in experimental social psychology* (Vol. 2). New York: Academic Press, 1965.

Alexander, C. N., Jr., & Lauderdale, P. Situated identities and social influence. *Sociometry*, 1977, *40*, 225–233.

Allen, H. Cults: The battle for the mind. In C. A. Krause (Ed.), *Guyana massacre: The eyewitness account.* New York: Berkley, 1978.

Allen, V. L. Social support for nonconformity. In L. Berkowitz (Ed.), *Advances in experimental social psychology* (Vol. 8). New York: Academic Press, 1975.

Allen, V. L., & Wilder, D. A. Impact of group consensus and social support on stimulus meaning: Mediation of conformity by cognitive restructuring. *Journal of Personality and Social Psychology*, 1980, *39*, 1116–1124.

Allport, F. H. The influence of the group upon association and thought. *Journal of Experimental Psychology*, 1920, *3*, 159–182.

Allport, F. H. *Social psychology.* New York: Houghton Mifflin, 1924.

Allport, G. W. *The nature of prejudice.* New York: Addison-Wesley, 1954.

Alpaugh, P., & Haney, M. *Counseling the older adult: A training manual.* Los Angeles: University of Southern California Press, 1978.

Altman, I. An ecological approach to the functioning of socially isolated groups. In J. E. Rasmussen (Ed.), *Man in isolation and confinement.* Chicago: Aldine, 1973.

Altman, I. *The environment and social behavior.* Monterey, Calif.: Brooks/Cole, 1975.

Altman, I. Research on environment and behavior: A personal statement of strategy. In D. Stokols (Ed.), *Perspectives on environment and behavior.* New York: Plenum, 1977.

Altman, I. Crowding: Historical and contemporary trends in crowding research. In A. Baum & Y. M. Epstein (Eds.), *Human response to crowding.* Hillsdale, N. J.: Erlbaum, 1978.

Altman, I., & Chemers, M. M. *Culture and environment.* Monterey, Calif.: Brooks/Cole, 1980.

Altman, I., & Haythorn, W. W. The ecology of isolated groups. *Behavioral Science*, 1967, *12*, 169–182.

Altman, I., & Taylor, D. A. *Social penetration.* New York: Holt, Rinehart, & Winston, 1973.

Altman, I., Taylor, D. A., & Wheeler, L. Ecological aspects of group behavior in social isolation. *Journal of Applied Social Psychology*, 1971, *1*, 76–100.

Amir, Y. Contact hypothesis in ethnic relations. *Psychological Bulletin*, 1969, *71*, 319–342.

Amir, Y. The role of intergroup contact in change of prejudice and ethnic relations. In P. A. Katz (Ed.), *Towards the elimination of racism.* New York: Pergamon, 1976.

Anderson, A. B. Combined effects of interpersonal attraction and goal-path clarity on the cohesiveness of task-oriented groups. *Journal of Personality and Social Psychology*, 1975, *31*, 68–75.

Anderson, L. R. Groups would do better without humans. *Personality and Social Psychology Bulletin*, 1978, *4*, 557–558.

Anderson, R. C. Learning in discussions—a resume of the authoritarian-democratic studies. *Harvard Educational Review*, 1959, *29*, 201–215.

Anthony, W., & Drasgow, J. A human technology for human resource development. *The Counseling Psychologist*, 1978, *7*, 58–65.

Apfelbaum, E. On conflicts and bargaining. In L. Berkowitz (Ed.), *Advances in experimental social psychology* (Vol. 7). New York: Academic Press, 1974.

Apodoca v. Oregon, 406 U.S. 404 (1972).

Archibald, W. P. Psychology, sociology, and social psychology: Bad fences make bad neighbors. *British Journal of Sociology*, 1976, *27*, 115–129.

Argyle, M., & Dean, J. Eye-contact, distance, and affiliation. *Sociometry*, 1965, *28*, 289–304.

Armstrong, D. G. Team teaching and academic achievement. *Review of Educational Research*, 1977, *47*, 65–86.

Arnold, D. W., & Greenberg, C. I. Deviate rejection within differentially manned groups. *Social Psychology Quarterly*, 1980, *43*, 419–424.

Aronson, E. *The social animal* (3rd ed.). San Francisco: Freeman, 1980.

Aronson, E., & Mettee, D. R. Dishonest behavior as a function of differential levels of induced self-esteem. *Journal of Personality and Social Psychology*, 1968, *9*, 121–127.

Aronson, E., & Mills, J. The effect of severity of initiation on liking for a group. *Journal of Abnormal and Social Psychology*, 1959, *59*, 177–181.

Aronson, E., Stephan, C., Sikes, J., Blaney, N., & Snapp, M. *The Jigsaw classroom*. Beverly Hills, Calif.: Sage, 1978.

Aronson, E., Willerman, B., & Floyd, J. The effect of a pratfall on increasing interpersonal attractiveness. *Psychonomic Science*, 1966, *4*, 227–228.

Aronson, E., & Worchel, P. Similarity versus liking as determinants of interpersonal attractiveness. *Psychonomic Science*, 1966, *5*, 157–158.

Asch, S. E. *Social psychology*. Englewood Cliffs, N.J.: Prentice-Hall, 1952.

Asch, S. E. Opinions and social pressures. *Scientific American*, 1955, *193*(5), 31–35.

Asch, S. E. An experimental investigation of group influence. In *Symposium on preventive and social psychiatry*, 15–17 April 1957, Walter Reed Army Institute of Research. Washington, D.C.: U.S. Government Printing Office.

Ashour, A. S. The contingency model of leadership effectiveness: An evaluation. *Organizational Behav-ior and Human Performance*, 1973, *9*, 339–355. (a)

Ashour, A. S. Further discussion of Fiedler's contingency model of leadership effectiveness. *Organizational Behavior and Human Performance*, 1973, *9*, 369–376. (b)

Atkinson, J. W. (Ed.). *Motives in fantasy, action, and society*. Princeton, N.J.: Van Nostrand, 1958.

Atthowe, J. M., Jr. Interpersonal decision making: The resolution of a dyadic conflict. *Journal of Abnormal and Social Psychology*, 1961, *62*, 114–119.

Auger, B. Y. *How to run better business meetings*. New York: AMACOM, 1972.

Babchuk, N., & Goode, W. J. Work incentives in a self-determined group. *American Journal of Sociology*, 1951, *16*, 679–687.

Bachrach, P., & Baratz, M. S. Decisions and non-decisions: An analytical framework. *American Political Science Review*, 1963, *57*, 632–642.

Back, K. W. Influence through social communication. *Journal of Abnormal and Social Psychology*, 1951, *46*, 9–23.

Baker, P. M. Social coalitions. *American Behavioral Scientist*, 1981, *24*, 633–647.

Bales, R. F. *Interaction process analysis: A method for the study of small groups*. Reading, Mass.: Addison-Wesley, 1950.

Bales, R. F. How people interact in conferences. *Scientific American*, 1955, *192*(3), 31–35.

Bales, R. F. Task roles and social roles in problem-solving groups. In E. E. Maccoby, T. M. Newcomb, & E. L. Hartley (Eds.), *Readings in social psychology*. New York: Holt, Rinehart, & Winston, 1958.

Bales, R. F. The equilibrium problem in small groups. In A. P. Hare, E. F. Borgatta, & R. F. Bales (Eds.), *Small groups: Studies in social interaction*. New York: Knopf, 1965.

Bales, R. F. *Personality and interpersonal behavior*. New York: Holt, Rinehart, & Winston, 1970.

Bales, R. F. *SYMLOG case study kit*. New York: Free Press, 1980.

Bales, R. F., Cohen, S. P., & Williamson, S. A. *SYMLOG: A system for the multiple level observation of groups*. New York: Free Press, 1979.

Bales, R. F., & Strodtbeck, F. L. Phases in group problem solving. *Journal of Abnormal and Social Psychology*, 1951, *46*, 485–495.

Bales, R. F., Strodtbeck, F. L., Mills, T. M., & Roseborough, M. E. Channels of communication in small groups. *American Sociological Review*, 1951, *16*, 461–468.

Bandura, A. Self-efficacy: Toward a unifying theory of behavioral change. *Psychological Review*, 1977, *84*, 191–215.

Bandura, A. The self system in reciprocal determinism. *American Psychologist*, 1978, *33*, 344–358.

Barker, R. G. (Ed.). *Habitats, environments, and human behavior: Studies in ecological psychology and eco-behavioral sciences from the Midwest Psychological Field Station, 1947–1972.* San Francisco: Jossey-Bass, 1978.

Barnard, C. I. *The functions of the executive.* Cambridge, Mass.: Harvard University Press, 1938.

Baron, R. A. Aggression and heat: The "long hot summer" revisited. In A. Baum, J. E. Singer, & S. Valins (Eds.), *Advances in environmental psychology* (Vol. 1). Hillsdale, N. J.: Erlbaum, 1978.

Baron, R. M., & Rodin, J. Personal control as a mediator of crowding. In A. Baum, J. E. Singer, & S. Valins (Eds.), *Advances in environmental psychology* (Vol. 1). Hillsdale, N.J.: Erlbaum, 1978.

Baron, R. S., Moore, D. L., & Sanders, G. S. Distraction as a source of drive in social facilitation research. *Journal of Personality and Social Psychology*, 1978, *36*, 816–824.

Barrow, J. C. The variables of leadership: A review and conceptual framework. *Academy of Management Review*, 1977, *2*, 231–251.

Bass, B. M. *Stogdill's handbook of leadership.* New York: Free Press, 1981.

Bass, B. M., & Dunteman, G. Biases in the evaluation of one's own group, its allies, and opponents. *Journal of Conflict Resolution*, 1963, *7*, 16–20.

Bass, B. M., & Dunteman, G. Defensiveness and susceptibility to coercion as a function of self-, interaction-, and task-orientation. *Journal of Social Psychology*, 1964, *62*, 335–341.

Bass, B. M., & Ryterband, E. C. *Organizational psychology* (2nd ed.). Boston: Allyn and Bacon, 1979.

Batchelor, J. P., & Goethals, G. R. Spatial arrangements in freely formed groups. *Sociometry*, 1972, *35*, 270–279.

Batson, C. D. Rational processing or rationalization?: The effect of disconfirming information on a stated religious belief. *Journal of Personality and Social Psychology*, 1975, *32*, 176–184.

Baum, A., Davis, G. E., & Valins, S. Generating behavioral data for the design process. In J. R. Aiello & A. Baum (Eds.), *Residential crowding and design.* New York: Plenum, 1979.

Baum, A., Harpin, R. E., & Valins, S. The role of group phenomena in the experience of crowding. In S. Saegert (Ed.), *Crowding in real environments.* Beverly Hills, Calif.: Sage, 1976.

Baum, A., & Valins, S. *Architecture and social behavior: Psychological studies of social density.* Hillsdale, N.J.: Erlbaum, 1977.

Baumrind, D. Some thoughts on ethics of research: After reading Milgram's "Behavioral study of obedience." *American Psychologist*, 1964, *19*, 421–423.

Bavelas, A. A mathematical model for group structures. *Applied Anthropology*, 1948, *7*, 16–30.

Bavelas, A. Communication patterns in task oriented groups. *Journal of the Acoustical Society of America*, 1950, *22*, 725–730.

Bavelas, A., & Barrett, D. An experimental approach to organization communication. *Personnel*, 1951, *27*, 367–371.

Beach, B. H., Mitchell, T. R., & Beach, L. R. *Components of situational favorableness and probability of success.* Tech. Rep. 75–66. Seattle: University of Washington, Organizational Research Group, 1975.

Beaman, A. L., Klentz, B., Diener, E., & Svanum, S. Objective self-awareness and transgression in children: A field study. *Journal of Personality and Social Psychology*, 1979, *37*, 1835–1846.

Becker, H. S. *The outsiders.* New York: Free Press, 1963.

Beckhard, R. *Organization development: Strategies and models.* Reading, Mass.: Addison-Wesley, 1969.

Bedell, J., & Sistrunk, F. Power, opportunity, costs, and sex in a mixed-motive game. *Journal of Personality and Social Psychology*, 1973, *25*, 219–226.

Bednar, R. L., & Kaul, T. Experiential group research: Current perspectives. In S. Garfield & A. Bergin (Eds.), *Handbook of psychotherapy and behavior change* (2nd ed.). New York: Wiley, 1978.

Bednar, R. L., & Kaul, T. Experiential group research: What never happened. *Journal of Applied Behavioral Science*, 1979, *15*, 311–319.

Bednar, R. L., & Lawlis, F. Empirical research in group psychotherapy. In A. Bergin & S. Garfield (Eds.), *Handbook of psychotherapy and behavior change.* New York: Wiley, 1971.

Bell, P. A., Fisher, J. D., & Loomis, R. J. *Environmental psychology.* Philadelphia: W. B. Saunders, 1978.

Bellack, A., & Hersen, M. (Eds.). *Research and practice in social skills training.* New York: Plenum, 1979.

Bem, D. Self-perception theory. In L. Berkowitz (Ed.), *Advances in experimental social psychology* (Vol. 6). New York: Academic Press, 1972.

Bem, S. L. Sex role adaptability: One consequence of psychological androgyny. *Journal of Personality and Social Psychology*, 1975, *31*, 634–643.

Benne, K. D., & Sheats, P. Functional roles of group members. *Journal of Social Issues*, 1948, *4*(2), 41–49.

Bennis, W. G. Where have all the leaders gone? *Federal Executive Institute*, 1975.

Bennis, W. G., & Shepard, H. A. A theory of group development. *Human relations*, 1956, *9*, 415–437.

Berger, J., Cohen, B. P., & Zelditch, M., Jr. Status characteristics and social interaction. *American Sociological Review*, 1972, *37*, 241–255.

Berger, J., Conner, T. L., & Fisek, M. H. (Eds.). *Expectation states theory: A theoretical research program.* Cambridge, Mass.: Winthrop, 1974.

Berger, J., Fisek, M. H., Norman, R. Z., & Zelditch,

M., Jr. *Status characteristics and social interaction.* New York: Elsevier, 1977.

Berger, S. M., Hampton, K. L., Carli, L. L., Grandmaison, P. S., Sadow, J. S., Donath, C. H., & Herschlag, L. R. Audience-induced inhibition of overt practice during learning. *Journal of Personality and Social Psychology,* 1981, *40,* 479–491.

Berkowitz, L. Sharing leadership in small, decision-making groups. *Journal of Abnormal and Social Psychology,* 1953, *48,* 231–238.

Berkowitz, L. *Aggression: A social psychological analysis.* New York: McGraw-Hill, 1962.

Berkowitz, L. Reporting an experiment: A case study in leveling, sharpening, and assimilation. *Journal of Experimental Social Psychology,* 1971, *7,* 237–243.

Berkowitz, L. Some determinants of impulsive aggression: Role of mediated associations with reinforcements for aggression. *Psychological Review,* 1974, *81,* 165–176.

Berkowitz, L. Whatever happened to the frustration-aggression hypothesis? *American Behavioral Scientist,* 1978, *32,* 691–708.

Berkowitz, L., & Geen, J. A. The stimulus qualities of the scapegoat. *Journal of Abnormal and Social Psychology,* 1962, *64,* 293–301.

Berkowitz, L., & Howard, R. C. Reactions to opinion deviates as affected by affiliation need (n) and group member interdependence. *Sociometry,* 1959, *22,* 81–91.

Berkowitz, L., & Walster, E. (Eds.). *Equity theory: Toward a general theory of social interaction. Advances in experimental social psychology* (Vol. 9). New York: Academic Press, 1976.

Bertram, B. C. R. Living in groups: Predators and prey. In P. P. G. Bateson & R. A. Hinde (Eds.), *Behavioral ecology: An evolutional approach.* London: Blackwell, 1978.

Bickman, L. The social power of a uniform. *Journal of Applied Social Psychology,* 1974, *4,* 47–61.

Biddle, B. J. *Role theory: Expectations, identities, and behavior.* New York: Academic Press, 1979.

Billig, M. *Social psychology and group relations.* New York: Academic Press, 1976.

Bion, W. R. *Experiences in groups.* New York: Basic Books, 1961.

Bird, A. M. Team structure and success as related to cohesiveness and leadership. *Journal of Social Psychology,* 1977, *103,* 217–223.

Bixenstine, V. E., Chambers, N., & Wilson, K. V. Effect of asymmetry in payoff on behavior in a two-person non-zero-sum game. *Journal of Conflict Resolution,* 1964, *8,* 151–159.

Black, T. E., & Higbee, K. L. Effects of power, threat, and sex on exploitation. *Journal of Personality and Social Psychology,* 1973, *27,* 382–388.

Blake, R. R., & Mouton, J. S. *The managerial grid.* Houston, Tex.: Gulf, 1964.

Blake, R. R., & Mouton, J. S. The fifth achievement. *Journal of Applied Behavioral Science,* 1970, *6,* 413–426.

Blake, R. R., & Mouton, J. S. *The new managerial grid.* Houston, Tex.: Gulf, 1978.

Blake, R. R., & Mouton, J. S. Intergroup problem solving in organizations: From theory to practice. In W. G. Austin & S. Worchel (Eds.), *The social psychology of intergroup relations.* Monterey, Calif.: Brooks/Cole, 1979.

Blanchard, F. A., Adelman, L., & Cook, S. W. Effect of group success and failure upon interpersonal attraction in cooperating interracial groups. *Journal of Personality and Social Psychology,* 1975, *31,* 1020–1030.

Blascovich, J., Nash, R. F., & Ginsburg, G. P. Heart rate and competitive decision making. *Personality and Social Psychology Bulletin,* 1978, *4,* 115–118.

Blau, P. M. Cooperation and competition in a bureaucracy. *American Journal of Sociology,* 1954, *59,* 530–535.

Blau, P. M. Patterns of choice in interpersonal relations. *American Sociological Review,* 1962, *27,* 41–55.

Blau, P. M. *Exchange and power in social life.* New York: Wiley, 1964.

Blau, P. M. *Inequality and heterogeneity.* New York: Free Press, 1977.

Bleda, P. R., & Sandman, P. H. In smoke's way: Socioemotional reactions to another's smoking. *Journal of Applied Psychology,* 1977, *62,* 452–458.

Blumer, H. Collective behavior. In A. M. Lee (Ed.), *New outline of the principles of sociology.* New York: Barnes and Noble, 1946.

Blumer, H. Collective behavior. In A. M. Lee (Ed.), *Principles of sociology.* New York: Barnes and Noble, 1951.

Blumer, H. Collective behavior. In J. B. Gittler (Ed.), *Review of sociology: Analysis of a decade.* New York: Wiley, 1957.

Bogardus, E. S. Group behavior and groupality. *Sociology and Social Research,* 1954, *38,* 401–403.

Boire, J. A. Collective behavior in sport. *Review of Sport and Leisure,* 1980, *5*(1), 2–45.

Boisen, A. T. Economic distress and religious experience. A study of the Holy Rollers. *Psychiatry,* 1939. *2,* 185–194.

Bonner, H. *Group dynamics: Principles and applications.* New York: Ronald, 1959.

Bonney, M. E. Popular and unpopular children: A sociometric study. *Sociometry Monographs,* 1947, No. 9.

Booth, A. Sex and social participation. *American Sociological Review,* 1972, *37,* 183–193.

Borah, L. A., Jr. The effects of threat in bargaining: Critical and experimental analysis. *Journal of Abnormal and Social Psychology*, 1963, *66*, 37–44.

Borgatta, E. F. The small groups movement: Historical notes. *American Behavioral Scientist*, 1981, *24*, 607–618.

Borgatta, E. F., Cottrell, L. S., Jr., & Mann, J. H. The spectrum of individual characteristics: An interdimensional analysis. *Psychological Reports*, 1958, *4*, 279–319.

Borgatta, E. F., Cottrell, L. S., Jr., & Meyer, H. J. On the dimensions of group behavior. *Sociometry*, 1956, *19*, 223–240.

Borgatta, E. F., Couch, A. S., & Bales, R. F. Some findings relevant to the great man theory of leadership. *American Sociological Review*, 1954, *19*, 755–759.

Bormann, E. G. *Discussion and group methods: Theory and practices* (2nd ed.). New York: Harper & Row, 1975.

Bouchard, T. J. Training, motivation, and personality as determinants of the effectiveness of brainstorming groups and individuals. *Journal of Applied Psychology*, 1972, *56*, 324–331. (a)

Bouchard, T. J. A comparison of two group brainstorming procedures. *Journal of Applied Psychology*, 1972, *56*, 418–421. (b)

Bouchard, T. J., Barsaloux, J., & Drauden, G. Brainstorming procedure, group size, and sex as determinants of the problem-solving effectiveness of groups and individuals. *Journal of Applied Psychology*, 1974, *59*, 135–138.

Bouchard, T. J., Drauden, G., & Barsaloux, J. A. comparison of individual, subgroup, and total group methods of problem solving. *Journal of Applied Psychology*, 1974, *59*, 226–227.

Bouchard, T. J., & Hare, M. Size, performance, and potential in brainstorming groups. *Journal of Applied Psychology*, 1970, *54*, 51–55.

Bowers, D. G., & Seashore, S. E. Predicting organizational effectiveness with a four-factor theory of leadership. *Administrative Science Quarterly*, 1966, *11*, 238–263.

Bradley, P. H. Power, status, and upward communication in small decision-making groups. *Communication Monographs*, 1978, *45*, 33–43.

Braginsky, D. D. Machiavellianism and manipulative interpersonal behavior in children. *Journal of Experimental Social Psychology*, 1970, *6*, 77–99.

Bramel, D., & Friend, R. Hawthorne, the myth of the docile worker, and class bias in psychology. *American Psychologist*, 1981, *36*, 867–878.

Brandon, A. C. Status congruence and expectations. *Sociometry*, 1965, *28*, 272–288.

Bray, R. M., Kerr, N. L., & Atkin, R. S. Effects of group size, problem difficulty, and sex on group performance and member reactions. *Journal of Personality and Social Psychology*, 1978, *36*, 1224–1240.

Brechner, K. C. An experimental analysis of social traps. *Journal of Experimental Social Psychology*, 1977, *13*, 552–564.

Brehm, J. W. Responses to loss of freedom: A theory of psychological reactance. In J. W. Thibaut, J. T. Spence, & R. C. Carson (Eds.), *Contemporary topics in social psychology*. Morristown, N.J.: General Learning Press, 1976.

Brehm, J. W., & Mann, M. Effect of importance of freedom and attraction to group members on influence produced by group pressure. *Journal of Personality and Social Psychology*, 1975, *31*, 816–824.

Brehm, J. W., & Sensenig, J. Social influence as a function of attempted and implied usurpation of choice. *Journal of Personality and Social Psychology*, 1966, *4*, 703–707.

Brehm, S. S., & Brehm, J. W. *Psychological reactance: A theory of freedom and control.* New York: Academic Press, 1981.

Breiger, R. L., & Ennis, J. G. Personae and social roles: The network structure of personality types in small groups. *Social Psychology Quarterly*, 1979, *42*, 262–270.

Brewer, M. B. In-group bias in the minimal intergroup situation: A cognitive-motivational analysis. *Psychological Bulletin*, 1979, *86*, 307–324. (a)

Brewer, M. B. The role of ethnocentrism in intergroup conflict. In W. G. Austin & S. Worchel (Eds.), *The social psychology of intergroup relations*. Monterey, Calif.: Brooks/Cole, 1979. (b)

Brickman, P., Becker, L. J., & Castle, S. Making trust easier and harder through two forms of sequential interaction. *Journal of Personality and Social Psychology*, 1979, *37*, 515–521.

Brockner, J., Shaw, M. C., & Rubin, J. Z. Factors affecting withdrawal from an escalating conflict: Quitting before it's too late. *Journal of Experimental Social Psychology*, 1979, *15*, 492–503.

Brockner, J., & Swap, W. C. Effects of repeated exposure and attitudinal similarity on self-disclosure and interpersonal attraction. *Journal of Personality and Social Psychology*, 1976, *33*, 531–540.

Bronfenbrenner, U. The mirror image in Soviet-American relations: A social psychologist's report. *Journal of Social Issues*, 1961, *17*(3), 45–56.

Brown, B. R. Face-saving and face-restoration in negotiation. In D. Druckman (Ed.), *Negotiations*. Beverly Hills, Calif.: Sage, 1977.

Browning, L. A grounded organizational communication theory derived from qualitative data. *Communication Monographs*, 1978, *45*, 93–109.

Buby, C. M., & Penner, L. A. Conformity as a function of response position. *Psychological Reports*, 1974, *34*, 938.

Buckley, W. *Sociology and modern systems theory*. Englewood Cliffs, N.J.: Prentice-Hall, 1967.

Budoff, M., & Gottlieb, J. Special class students mainstreamed: A study of an aptitude (learning potential) × treatment interaction. *American Journal of Mental Deficiency*, 1976, *81*, 1–11.

Bugliosi, V. *Helter Skelter*. New York: Bantam, 1974.

Burke, P. J. The development of task and social-emotional role differentiation. *Sociometry*, 1967, *30*, 379–392.

Burke, P. J. Participation and leadership in small groups. *American Sociological Review*, 1974, *39*, 832–842.

Burns, J. M. *Leadership*. New York: Harper, 1978.

Burnstein, E., & Vinokur, A. Testing two classes of theories about group-induced shifts in individual choice. *Journal of Experimental Social Psychology*, 1973, *9*, 123–137.

Burnstein, E., & Vinokur, A. Persuasive arguments and social comparison as determinants of attitude polarization. *Journal of Experimental Social Psychology*, 1977, *13*, 315–332.

Burwitz, L., & Newell, K. M. The effects of the mere presence of coactors on learning a motor skill. *Journal of Motor Behavior*, 1972, *4*, 99–102.

Buss, A. H. *The psychology of aggression*. New York: Wiley, 1961.

Buys, C. J. Humans would do better without groups. *Personality and Social Psychology Bulletin*, 1978, *4*, 123–125. (a)

Buys, C. J. On humans would do better without groups: A final note. *Personality and Social Psychology Bulletin*, 1978, *4*, 568. (b)

Byrne, D. Anxiety and the experimental arousal of affiliation need. *Journal of Abnormal and Social Psychology*, 1961, *63*, 660–662.

Byrne, D. *The attraction paradigm*. New York: Academic Press, 1971.

Byrne, D., Ervin, C. R., & Lamberth, J. Continuity between the experimental study of attraction and real-life computer dating. *Journal of Personality and Social Psychology*, 1970, *16*, 157–165.

Calder, B. J. An attribution theory of leadership. In B. M. Staw & G. R. Salancik (Eds.), *New directions in organizational behavior*. Chicago: St. Clair Press, 1976.

Calhoun, J. B. Population density and social pathology. *Scientific American*, 1962, *206*, 139–148.

Campbell, D. T. Common fate, similarity, and other indices of the status of aggregates of persons as social entities. *Behavioral Science*, 1958, *3*, 14–25. (a)

Campbell, D. T. Systematic error on the part of human links in communication systems. *Information and Control*, 1958, *1*, 334–369. (b)

Campbell, D. T. Ethnocentric and other altruistic motives. In D. Levine (Ed.), *Nebraska symposium on motivation* (Vol. 13). Lincoln: University of Nebraska Press, 1965.

Cannavale, F. J., Scarr, H. A., & Pepitone, A. Deindividuation in the small group: Further evidence. *Journal of Personality and Social Psychology*, 1970, *16*, 141–147.

Cantril, H. *The invasion from Mars*. Princeton: Princeton University Press, 1940.

Caple, R. B. The sequential stages of group development. *Small Group Behavior*, 1978, *9*, 470–476.

Caplow, T. A theory of coalitions in the triad. *American Sociological Review*, 1956, *21*, 489–493.

Caplow, T. *Two against one*. Englewood Cliffs, N.J.: Prentice-Hall, 1968.

Carkhuff, R. R. *Helping and human relations: Selection and training* (Vol. 1). New York: Holt, Rinehart, & Winston, 1969. (a)

Carkhuff, R. R. *Helping and human relations: Research and practice* (Vol. 2). New York: Holt, Rinehart, & Winston, 1969. (b)

Carkhuff, R. R. *The art of helping III*. Amherst, Mass.: Human Resource Development Press, 1972/1977.

Carlyle, T. *On heroes, hero-worship, and the heroic*. London: Fraser, 1841.

Carment, D. W. Rate of simple motor responding as a function of coaction, competition, and sex of the participants. *Psychonomic Science*, 1970, *19*, 340–341.

Carpenter, C. R. Territoriality: A review of concepts and problems. In A. Roe & G. G. Simpson (Eds.), *Behavior and evolution*. New Haven: Yale University Press, 1958.

Carron, A. V. *Social psychology of sport*. Ithaca, N. Y.: Mouvement Publications, 1980.

Carron, A. V., & Chelladurai, P. The dynamics of group cohesion in sport. *Journal of Sport Psychology*, 1981, *3*, 123–139.

Carter, J. H. Military leadership. *Military Review*, 1952, *32*, 14–18.

Carter, L. F. Leadership and small group behavior. In M. Sherif & M. O. Wilson (Eds.), *Group relations at the crossroads*. New York: Harper, 1953.

Carter, L. F. Recording and evaluating the performance of individuals as members of small groups. *Personnel Psychology*, 1954, *7*, 477–484.

Carter, L. F., Haythorn, W., Shriver, B., & Lanzetta, J. The behavior of leaders and other group members. *Journal of Abnormal and Social Psychology*, 1951, *46*, 589–595.

Cartwright, D. A field theoretical conception of power. In D. Cartwright (Ed.), *Studies in social power*. Ann Arbor, Mich.: Institute for Social Research, 1959.

Cartwright, D. The nature of group cohesiveness. In D. Cartwright & A. Zander (Eds.), *Group dynamics:*

Research and theory (3rd ed.). New York: Harper & Row, 1968.

Cartwright, D. Theory and practice. *Journal of Social Issues*, 1978, *34*(4), 168–175.

Cartwright, D. Contemporary social psychology in historical perspective. *Social Psychology Quarterly*, 1979, *42*, 82–93.

Cartwright, D., & Harary, F. Structural balance: A generalization of Heider's theory. *Psychological Review*, 1956, *63*, 277–293.

Cartwright, D., & Harary, F. Ambivalence and indifference in generalizations of structural balance. *Behavioral Science*, 1970, *14*, 497–513.

Cartwright, D., & Zander, A. *Group dynamics: Research and theory* (3rd ed.). New York: Harper & Row, 1968.

Carver, C. S. Physical aggression as a function of objective self-awareness and attitudes toward punishment. *Journal of Experimental Social Psychology*, 1975, *11*, 510–519.

Carver, C. S., & Scheier, M. F. *Attention and self-regulation: A control-theory approach to human behavior.* New York: Springer Verlag, 1981.

Castore, C. H., & Murnighan, J. K. Determinants of support for group decisions. *Organizational Behavior and Human Performance*, 1978, *22*, 75–92.

Chapanis, A., Garner, W. R., & Morgan, C. T. *Applied experimental psychology: Human factors in engineering design.* New York: Wiley, 1949.

Chelladurai, P., & Haggerty, T. R. A normative model for decision styles in coaching. *Athletic Administrator*, 1978, *13*, 6–9.

Chemers, M. M., & Skrzypek, G. J. Experimental test of the contingency model of leadership effectiveness. *Journal of Personality and Social Psychology*, 1972, *24*, 173–177.

Cheyne, J. A., & Efran, M. G. The effect of spatial and interpersonal variables on the invasion of group controlled territories. *Sociometry*, 1972, *35*, 477–487.

Christian, J. J., Flyger, V., & Davis, D. E. Factors in the mass mortality of a herd of silka deer *Cervus nippon. Chesapeake Science*, 1960, *1*, 79–95.

Christie, R., & Geis, F. L. (Eds.). *Studies in Machiavellianism.* New York: Academic Press, 1970.

Cialdini, R. B., Borden, R., Thorne, A., Walker, M., Freeman, S., & Sloane, L. R. Basking in reflected glory: Three (football) field studies. *Journal of Personality and Social Psychology*, 1976, *34*, 366–375.

Clark, G. What happens when the police strike? *New York Times Magazine,* 1969, November, 45.

Clark, K. B. The pathos of power. *American Psychologist*, 1971, *26*, 1047–1057.

Clark, R. D., III. Group-induced shift toward risk: A critical appraisal. *Psychological Bulletin*, 1971, *76*, 251–270.

Clark, R. D., III, & Sechrest, L. B. The mandate phenomenon. *Journal of Personality and Social Psychology*, 1976, *34*, 1057–1061.

Clore, G. L., & Byrne, D. A reinforcement-affect model of attraction. In T. Huston (Ed.), *Foundations of interpersonal attraction.* New York: Academic Press, 1974.

Coch, L., & French, J. R. P. Overcoming resistance to change. *Human Relations*, 1948, *1*, 512–532.

Cohen, A. R. Situational structure, self-esteem, and threat-oriented reactions to power. In D. Cartwright (Ed.), *Studies in social power.* Ann Arbor, Mich.: Institute for Social Research, 1959.

Cohen, D. J., Whitmyre, J. W., & Funk, W. H. Effect of group cohesiveness and training upon group thinking. *Journal of Applied Psychology*, 1960, *44*, 319–322.

Cohen, S. Aftereffects of stress on human performance and social behavior: A review of research and theory. *Psychological Bulletin*, 1980, *88*, 82–108.

Cohen, S., & Weinstein, N. Nonauditory effects of noise on behavior and health. *Journal of Social Issues*, 1981, *37*(1), 36–70.

Coleman, J. F., Blake, R. R., & Mouton, J. S. Task difficulty and conformity pressures. *Journal of Abnormal and Social Psychology*, 1958, *57*, 120–122.

Collins, B. E., & Guetzkow, H. *A social psychology of group process for decision-making.* New York: Wiley, 1964.

Collins, B. E., & Raven, B. H. Group structure: Attraction, coalitions, communication, and power. In G. Lindzey & E. Aronson (Eds.), *Handbook of social psychology* (Vol. 4, 2nd ed.). Reading, Mass.: Addison-Wesley, 1968.

Comer, R., & Laird, J. D. Choosing to suffer as a consequence of expecting to suffer: Why do people do it? *Journal of Personality and Social Psychology*, 1975, *32*, 92–101.

Condry, J. Enemies of exploration: Self initiated versus other initiated learning. *Journal of Personality and Social Psychology*, 1977, *35*, 459–477.

Cook, M. The social skill model and interpersonal attraction. In S. Duck (Ed.), *Theory and practice in interpersonal attraction.* New York: Academic Press, 1977.

Cook, S. W. Motives in a conceptual analysis of attitude-related behavior. In J. Brigham & T. Weissbach (Eds.), *Racial attitudes in America: Analyses and findings of social psychology.* New York: Harper & Row, 1972.

Cook, S. W. Ethical implications. In L. H. Kidder (Ed.), *Research methods in social relations* (4th ed.). New York: Holt, Rinehart, & Winston, 1981.

Cooley, C. H. *Human nature and the social order.* New York: Scribner, 1902.

Coon, A. Brainstorming—a creative problem solving technique. In R. Cathart & L. Somovan (Eds.), *Small group problem solving: A reader.* New York: William C. Brown, 1976.

Cooper, H. M. Statistically combining independent studies: A metaanalysis of sex differences in conformity research. *Journal of Personality and Social Psychology*, 1979, *37*, 131–146.

Cooper, J., & Fazio, R. H. The formation and persistence of attitudes that support intergroup conflict. In W. G. Austin & S. Worchel (Eds.), *The social psychology of intergroup relations.* Monterey, Calif.: Brooks/Cole, 1979.

Coser, L. A. *The functions of social conflict.* Glencoe, Ill.: Free Press, 1956.

Cottrell, N. B. Social facilitation. In C. G. McClintock (Ed.), *Experimental social psychology.* New York: Holt, Rinehart, & Winston, 1972.

Cottrell, N. B., & Epley, S. W. Affiliation, social comparison, and socially mediated stress reduction. In J. M. Suls & R. L. Miller (Eds.), *Social comparison processes.* Washington: Hemisphere, 1977.

Cottrell, N. B., Wack, D. L., Sekerak, G. J., & Rittle, R. H. Social facilitation of dominant responses by the presence of an audience and the mere presence of others. *Journal of Personality and Social Psychology*, 1968, *9*, 245–250.

Couch, A. S., & Carter, L. F. *A factorial study of the rated behavior of group members.* Paper presented at the Annual Meetings of the Eastern Psychological Association, 1952.

Courtright, J. A. A laboratory investigation of groupthink. *Communication Monographs*, 1978, *43*, 229–246.

Cratty, B. J. *Social psychology in athletics.* Englewood Cliffs, N. J.: Prentice-Hall, 1981.

Cribbin, J. J. *Effective managerial leadership.* New York: American Management Association, 1972.

Crook, J. H. The evolutionary ethology of social processes in man. In H. Kellerman (Ed.), *Group cohesion.* New York: Grune & Stratton, 1981.

Crosbie, P. V. Effects of status inconsistency: Negative evidence from small groups. *Social Psychology Quarterly*, 1979, *42*, 110–125.

Crow, W. J. A study of strategic doctrines using the Inter-Nation Simulation. *Journal of Conflict Resolution*, 1963, *7*, 580–589.

Crutchfield, R. S. Conformity and character. *American Psychologist*, 1955, *10*, 191–198.

Csoka, L. S., & Bons, P. M. Manipulating the situation to fit the leader's style—Two validation studies of Leader Match. *Journal of Applied Psychology*, 1978, *63*, 295–300.

Cullen, F., & Cullen, J. *Toward a paradigm of labeling theory.* Lincoln: University of Nebraska Press, 1978.

Cummings, L. L., Harnett, D. L., & Stevens, O. J. Risk, fate, conciliation and trust: An international study of attitudinal differences among executives. *Academy of Management Journal*, 1971, *14*, 285–304.

Cunningham, J. D., Starr, P. A., & Kanouse, D. E. Self as actor, active observer, and passive observer: Implications for causal attributions. *Journal of Personality and Social Psychology*, 1979, *37*, 1146–1152.

Cunningham, L. L. Team teaching: Where do we stand? *Administrator's Notebook*, 1960, *8*, 1–4.

Curran, J. P. Skills training as an approach to the treatment of heterosexual-social anxiety: A review. *Psychological Bulletin*, 1977, *84*, 140–157.

Cuttle, C. The sharpness and the flow of light. In R. Kuller (Ed.), *Architectural psychology: Proceedings of the Lund conference.* Stroudsburg, Penn.: Dowden, Hutchinson, & Ross, 1973.

Dahrendorf, R. Toward a theory of social conflict. *Journal of Conflict Resolution*, 1958, *2*, 170–183.

Dahrendorf, R. *Class and class conflict in industrial society.* Palo Alto, Calif.: Stanford University Press, 1959.

Dalkey, N. C. *Experiment in group prediction.* Santa Monica, Calif.: The Rand Corporation, 1968.

Dalkey, N. C. *The Delphi method: An experimental study of group opinion.* Santa Monica, Calif.: The Rand Corporation, 1969.

Dance, F. E. X. The "concept" of communication. *Journal of Communication*, 1970, *20*, 201–210.

Darley, J. M., & Aronson, E. Self-evaluation vs. direct anxiety reduction as determinants of the fear-affiliation relationship. *Journal of Experimental Social Psychology*, 1966, Supplement 1, 66–79.

Darley, J. M., & Latané, B. Bystander intervention in emergencies: Diffusion of responsibility. *Journal of Personality and Social Psychology*, 1968, *8*, 377–383.

Dashiell, J. F. An experimental analysis of some group effects. *Journal of Abnormal and Social Psychology*, 1930, *25*, 190–199.

Davis, J. H. *Group performance.* Reading, Mass.: Addison-Wesley, 1969.

Davis, J. H. Group decision and social interaction: A theory of social decision schemes. *Psychological Review*, 1973, *80*, 97–125.

Davis, J. H., Bray, R. M., & Holt, R. W. The empirical study of decision processes in juries: A critical review. In J. L. Tapp & F. J. Levine (Eds.), *Law, justice, and the individual in society.* New York: Holt, Rinehart, & Winston, 1977.

Davis, J. H., Kerr, N. L., Atkin, R. S., Holt, R., & Meek, D. The decision processes of 6- and 12-person juries assigned unanimous and 2/3 majority rules. *Journal of Personality and Social Psychology*, 1975, *32*, 1–14.

Davis, J. H., Kerr, N. L., Stasser, G., Meek, D., & Holt, R. Victim consequences, sentence severity, and decision processes in mock juries. *Organizational Behavior and Human Performance*, 1977, *18*, 346–365.

Dedrick, D. K. Deviance and sanctioning within small groups. *Social Psychology*, 1978, *41*, 94–105.

Defoe, D. *The life and strange surprising adventures of Robinson Crusoe, of York, mariner, as related by himself.* Philadelphia: Altemus, 1908.

DeLamater, J. A. A definition of "group." *Small Group Behavior*, 1974, *5*, 30–44.

Delbecq, A. L., & Van de Ven, A. H. A group process model for problem identification and program planning. *Journal of Applied Behavioral Science*, 1971, *7*, 466–492.

Delbecq, A. L., Van de Ven, A. H., & Gustafson, D. H. *Group techniques for program planning.* Glenview, Ill.: Scott, Foresman, 1975.

Dember, W. Birth order and need affiliation. *Journal of Abnormal and Social Psychology*, 1964, *68*, 555–557.

Deutsch, M. A theory of cooperation and competition. *Human Relations*, 1949, *2*, 129–152. (a)

Deutsch, M. An experimental study of the effects of cooperation and competition upon group process. *Human Relations*, 1949, *2*, 199–231. (b)

Deutsch, M. Trust and suspicion. *Journal of Conflict Resolution*, 1958, *2*, 265–279.

Deutsch, M. The effect of motivational orientation upon trust and suspicion. *Human Relations*, 1960, *13*, 123–139.

Deutsch, M. Socially relevant science: Reflections on some studies of interpersonal conflict. *American Psychologist*, 1969, *24*, 1076–1092.

Deutsch, M. *The resolution of conflict.* New Haven, Conn.: Yale University Press, 1973.

Deutsch, M., & Gerard, H. B. A study of normative and informational social influences upon individual judgment. *Journal of Abnormal and Social Psychology*, 1955, *51*, 629–636.

Deutsch, M., & Krauss, R. M. The effect of threat upon interpersonal bargaining. *Journal of Abnormal and Social Psychology*, 1960, *61*, 181–189.

Deutsch, M., & Krauss, R. M. Studies of interpersonal bargaining. *Journal of Conflict Resolution*, 1962, *6*, 52–76.

Deutsch, M., & Lewicki, R. J. "Locking in" effects during a game of Chicken. *Journal of Conflict Resolution*, 1970, *14*, 367–378.

Deutsch, M., & Solomon, L. Reactions to evaluations by others as influenced by self-evaluations. *Sociometry*, 1959, *22*, 93–112.

DeVries, D. L., Edwards, K. J., & Fennessey, G. M.

Using Teams-Games-Tournaments (TGT) in the classroom. Baltimore, Md.: Center for Social Organization in Schools, Johns Hopkins University, 1973.

Diener, E. Effects of prior destructive behavior, anonymity, and group presence on deindividuation and aggression. *Journal of Personality and Social Psychology*, 1976, *33*, 497–507.

Diener, E. Deindividuation: Causes and consequences. *Social Behavior and Personality*, 1977, *5*, 143–155.

Diener, E. Deindividuation, self-awareness, and disinhibition. *Journal of Personality and Social Psychology*, 1979, *37*, 1160–1171.

Diener, E. Deindividuation: The absence of self-awareness and self-regulation in group members. In P. B. Paulus (Ed.), *Psychology of group influence.* Hillsdale, N.J.: Erlbaum, 1980.

Diener, E. Dineen, J., Endresen, K., Beaman, A. L., & Fraser, S. C. Effects of altered responsibility, cognitive set, and modeling on physical aggression and deindividuation. *Journal of Personality and Social Psychology*, 1975, *31*, 328–337.

Diener, E., Fraser, S. C., Beaman, A. L., & Kelem, R. T. Effects of deindividuating variables on stealing by Halloween trick-or-treaters. *Journal of Personality and Social Psychology*, 1976, *33*, 178–183.

Diener, E., & Kasprzyk, D. *Causal factors in disinhibition by deindividuation.* Unpublished research report, University of Illinois, 1978.

Diener, E., Lusk, R., DeFour, D., & Flax, R. Deindividuation: Effects of group size, density, number of observers, and group member similarity on self-consciousness and disinhibited behavior. *Journal of Personality and Social Psychology*, 1980, *39*, 449–459.

Dillehay, R. C., & Nietzel, M. T. Constructing a science of jury behavior. In L. Wheeler (Ed.), *Review of personality and social psychology* (Vol. 1). Beverly Hills, Calif.: Sage, 1980.

Dion, K. K., & Stein, S. Physical attractiveness and interpersonal influence. *Journal of Experimental Social Psychology*, 1978, *14*, 97–108.

Dion, K. L. Cohesiveness as a determinant of ingroup-outgroup bias. *Journal of Personality and Social Psychology*, 1973, *28*, 163–171.

Dion, K. L. Intergroup conflict and intragroup cohesiveness. In W. G. Austin & S. Worchel (Eds.), *The social psychology of intergroup relations.* Monterey, Calif.: Brooks/Cole, 1979.

Dion, K. L., Baron, R. S., & Miller, N. Why do groups make riskier decisions than individuals? In L. Berkowitz (Ed.), *Advances in experimental social psychology* (Vol. 5). New York: Academic Press, 1970.

Dipboye, R. L. Alternative approaches to deindividuation. *Psychological Bulletin*, 1977, *84*, 1057–1075.

Dittes, J. E., & Kelley, H. H. Effects of different conditions of acceptance upon conformity to group norms. *Journal of Abnormal and Social Psychology*, 1956, *53*, 100–107.

Doise, W. Intergroup relations and polarization of individual and collective judgments. *Journal of Personality and Social Psychology*, 1969, *12*, 136–143.

Doms, M., & Van Avermaet, E. Majority influence, minority influence, and conversion behavior: A replication. *Journal of Experimental Social Psychology*, 1980, *16*, 283–292.

Donaldson, L., & Scannell, E. E. *Human resource development.* Reading, Mass.: Addison-Wesley, 1978.

Donohue, W. A. An empirical framework for examining negotiation processes and outcomes. *Communication Monographs*, 1978, *45*, 247–256.

Dosey, M., & Meisels, M. Personal space and self-protection. *Journal of Personality and Social Psychology*, 1969, *11*, 93–97.

Doyle, M., & Straus, M. *How to make meetings work.* Chicago: Playboy Press, 1977.

Drucker, P. F. *The effective executive.* New York: Harper & Row, 1966.

Druckman, D. (Ed.). *Negotiations.* Beverly Hills, Calif.: Sage, 1977.

Dunnette, M. D., Campbell, J., & Jaastad, K. The effect of group participation on brainstorming effectiveness for two industrial samples. *Journal of Applied Psychology*, 1963, *47*, 30–37.

Durand, D. E. Power as a function of office space and physiognomy: Two studies of influence. *Psychological Reports*, 1977, *40*, 755–760.

Durkheim, E. *The division of labor in society.* New York: Free Press, 1964.

Durkheim, E. *Suicide.* New York: Free Press, 1897/1966.

Dutton, D. Attribution of cause for opinion change and liking for audience members. *Journal of Personality and Social Psychology*, 1973, *26*, 208–216.

Dyer, W. G. *Team building: Issues and alternatives.* Reading, Mass.: Addison-Wesley, 1977.

Eagly, A. H. Sex differences in influenceability. *Psychological Bulletin*, 1978, *85*, 86–116.

Eagly, A. H., & Carli, L. L. Sex of researchers and sex-typed communications as determinants of sex differences in influenceability: A meta-analysis of social influence studies. *Psychological Bulletin*, 1981, *90*, 1–20.

Eagly, A. H., Wood, W., & Fishbaugh, L. Sex differences in conformity: Surveillance by the group as a determinant of male nonconformity. *Journal of Personality and Social Psychology*, 1981, *40*, 384–394.

Ebel, R. L. The case for norm-reference measurements. *Review of Educational Research*, 1978, *48*, 3–5.

Edman, I. *Human traits and their social significance.* New York: Houghton Mifflin, 1919.

Edney, J. J. Human territories: Comment on functional properties. *Environment and Behavior*, 1976, *8*, 31–48.

Edney, J. J. The commons problem: Alternative perspectives. *American Psychologist*, 1980, *35*, 131–150.

Edney, J. J., & Grundmann, M. J. Friendship, group size, and boundary size: Small group spaces. *Small Group Behavior*, 1979, *10*, 124–135.

Edney, J. J., & Jordan-Edney, N. L. Territorial spacing on a beach. *Sociometry*, 1974, *37*, 92–104.

Edney, J. J., & Uhlig, S. R. Individual and small group territories. *Small Group Behavior*, 1977, *8*, 457–468.

Edwards, J. D. The home field advantage. In J. H. Goldstein (Ed.), *Sports, games, and play.* Hillsdale, N.J.: Erlbaum, 1979.

Eitzen, D. S., & Yetman, N. R. Managerial changes, longevity, and organizational effectiveness. *Administrative Science Quarterly*, 1972, *17*, 110–116.

Ellis, D. G., & Fisher, B. A. Phases of conflict in small group development. *Human Communication Research*, 1975, *1*, 195–212.

Elwork, A., Sales, B. D., & Suggs, D. The trial: A research review. In B. D. Sales (Ed.), *The trial process.* New York: Plenum, 1981.

Emerson, R. M. Deviation and rejection: An experimental replication. *American Sociological Review*, 1954, *19*, 688–693.

Endler, N. S., & Hartley, S. Relative competence, reinforcement, and conformity. *European Journal of Social Psychology*, 1973, *3*, 63–72.

Ends, E. J., & Page, C. W. *Organizational team building.* Cambridge, Mass.: Winthrop, 1977.

Epstein, Y. M., & Karlin, R. A. Effects of acute experimental crowding. *Journal of Applied Social Psychology*, 1975, *5*, 34–53.

Erdmann, G., & Janke, W. Interaction between physiological and cognitive determinants of emotions: Experimental studies on Schachter's theory of emotions. *Biological Psychology*, 1978, *6*, 61–74.

Esser, A. H. Dominance hierarchy and clinical course of psychiatrically hospitalized boys. *Child Development*, 1968, *39*, 147–157.

Esser, A. H. Cottage Fourteen: Dominance and territoriality in a group of institutionalized boys. *Small Group Behavior*, 1973, *4*, 131–146.

Esser, A. H., Chamberlain, A. S., Chapple, E. D., & Kline, N. S. Territoriality of patients on a research ward. In J. Wortis (Ed.), *Recent advances in biological psychiatry.* New York: Plenum, 1965.

Essing, W. Team line-up and team achievement in European football. In G. S. Kenyon (Ed.), *Contem-*

porary psychology of sport. Chicago: Athletic Institute, 1970.

Esso Research Division. *An action research program for organization development.* Ann Arbor, Mich.: Foundation for Research on Human Behavior, 1960.

Etzioni, A. The Kennedy experiment. *The Western Political Quarterly,* 1967, *20,* 361–380.

Evans, G. W., & Howard, R. B. Personal space. *Psychological Bulletin,* 1973, *80,* 334–344.

Exline, R. Effects of need for affiliation, sex, and the sight of others upon initial communications in problem solving groups. *Journal of Personality,* 1962, *30,* 541–556.

Falbo, T. The multidimensional scaling of power strategies. *Journal of Personality and Social Psychology,* 1977, *35,* 537–548.

Falbo, T., & Peplau, L. A. Power strategies in intimate relationships. *Journal of Personality and Social Psychology,* 1980, *38,* 618–628.

Fanon, F. *The wretched of the earth.* New York: Grove, 1963.

Farr, J. L. Incentive schedules, productivity, and satisfaction in work groups: A laboratory study. *Organizational Behavior and Human Performance,* 1976, *17,* 159–170.

Fazio, R. H. Motives for social comparison: The construction-validation distinction. *Journal of Personality and Social Psychology,* 1979, *37,* 1683–1698.

Festinger, L. Informal social communication. *Psychological Review,* 1950, *57,* 271–282.

Festinger, L. An analysis of compliant behavior. In M. Sherif & M. O. Wilson (Eds.), *Group relations at the crossroads.* New York: Harper, 1953.

Festinger, L. A theory of social comparison processes. *Human Relations,* 1954, *7,* 117–140.

Festinger, L. *A theory of cognitive dissonance.* Evanston, Ill.: Row, Peterson, 1957.

Festinger, L., Gerard, H. B., Hymovitch, B., Kelley, H. H., & Raven, B. The influence process in the presence of extreme deviates. *Human Relations,* 1952, *5,* 327–346.

Festinger, L., Pepitone, A., & Newcomb, T. Some consequences of deindividuation in a group. *Journal of Abnormal and Social Psychology,* 1952, *47,* 382–389.

Festinger, L., Riecken, H. W., & Schachter, S. *When prophecy fails.* Minneapolis: University of Minnesota Press, 1956.

Festinger, L., Schachter, S., & Back, K. *Social Pressures in informal groups.* New York: Harper, 1950.

Festinger, L., & Thibaut, J. Interpersonal communication in small groups. *Journal of Abnormal and Social Psychology,* 1951, *46,* 92–99.

Fiedler, F. E. The influence of leader-keyman relations on combat crew effectiveness. *Journal of Abnormal and Social Psychology,* 1955, *51,* 227–235.

Fiedler, F. E. A contingency model of leadership effectiveness. In L. Berkowitz (Ed.), *Advances in experimental social psychology* (Vol. 1). New York: Academic Press, 1964.

Fiedler, F. E. *A theory of leadership effectiveness.* New York: McGraw-Hill, 1967.

Fiedler, F. E. Note on the methodology of Graen, Orris, and Alvarez studies testing the Contingency Model. *Journal of Applied Psychology,* 1971, *55,* 202–204. (a)

Fiedler, F. E. *Leadership.* Morristown, N.J.: General Learning Press, 1971. (b)

Fiedler, F. E. Personality, motivational systems, and behavior of high and low LPC persons. *Human Relations,* 1972, *25,* 391–412.

Fiedler, F. E. The contingency model—A reply to Ashour. *Organizational Behavior and Human Performance,* 1973, *9,* 356–368.

Fiedler, F. E. The contingency model and the dynamics of the leadership process. In L. Berkowitz (Ed.), *Advances in experimental social psychology* (Vol. 12). New York: Academic Press, 1978.

Fiedler, F. E. Leadership effectiveness. *American Behavioral Scientist,* 1981, *24,* 619–632.

Fiedler, F. E., & Chemers, M. M. *Leadership and effective management.* Glenview, Ill.: Scott, Foresman, 1974.

Fiedler, F. E., Chemers, M. M., & Mahar, L. *Improving leadership effectiveness: The Leader Match Concept.* New York: Wiley, 1976.

Field, R. H. G. A critique of the Vroom-Yetton contingency model of leadership behavior. *Academy of Management Review,* 1979, *4,* 249–257.

Filley, A. C. *Interpersonal conflict resolution.* Oakland, N. J.: Scott, Foresman, 1975.

Filter, T. A., & Gross, A. E. The effects of public and private deviancy on compliance with a request. *Journal of Experimental Social Psychology,* 1975, *11,* 553–559.

Fisher, B. A. *Small group decision making* (2nd ed.). New York: McGraw-Hill, 1980.

Fisher, J. D., & Byrne, D. Too close for comfort: Sex differences in response to invasions of personal space. *Journal of Personality and Social Psychology,* 1975, *32,* 15–21.

Fisher, R. Fractionating conflict. In R. Fisher (Ed.), *International conflict and behavioral science: The Craigville papers.* New York: Basic Books, 1964.

Flowers, J. Behavioral analysis of group therapy and a model for behavioral group therapy. In D. Upper & S. Ross (Eds.), *Behavioral group therapy, 1979: An annual review.* Champaign, Ill.: Research Press, 1979.

Flowers, M. L. A laboratory test of some implications of Janis' groupthink hypothesis. *Journal of Personality and Social Psychology,* 1977, *35,* 888–896.

Foa, U. G. Relation of worker's expectation to satisfaction with supervisor. *Personnel Psychology*, 1957, *10*, 161–168.

Foa, U. G., & Foa, E. B. Resource exchange: Toward a structural theory of interpersonal relations. In A. W. Siegman & B. Pope (Eds.), *Studies in dyadic communication*. New York: Pergamon Press, 1971.

Foley, L. A. Personality and situational influences on changes in prejudice: A replication of Cook's railroad game in a prison setting. *Journal of Personality and Social Psychology*, 1976, *34*, 846–856.

Folk, G. E., Jr. *Textbook of environmental physiology*. Philadelphia: Lea & Febiger, 1974.

Forsyth, D. R. Crucial experiments and social psychological inquiry. *Personality and Social Psychology Bulletin*, 1976, *2*, 454–459.

Forsyth, D. R. The function of attributions. *Social Psychology Quarterly*, 1980, *43*, 184–189.

Forsyth, D. R. A psychological perspective on ethical uncertainties in behavioral research. In A. J. Kimmel (Ed.), *New Directions for Methodology of Social and Behavioral Science: Ethics of Human Subject Research* (No. 10). San Francisco: Jossey-Bass, 1981.

Forsyth, D. R., Berger, R., & Mitchell, T. The effects of self-serving vs. other-serving claims of responsibility on attraction and attribution in groups. *Social Psychology Quarterly*, 1981, *44*, 59–64.

Forsyth, D. R., & Schlenker, B. R. Attributing the causes of group performance: Effects of performance quality, task importance, and future testing. *Journal of Personality*, 1977, *45*, 220–236.

Fox, J., & Moore, J. C., Jr. Status characteristics and expectation states: Fitting and testing a recent model. *Social Psychology Quarterly*, 1979, *42*, 126–134.

Foy, E., & Harlow, A. F. *Clowning through life*. New York: Dutton, 1928, 1956.

Frager, R. Conformity and anticonformity in Japan. *Journal of Personality and Social Psychology*, 1970, *15*, 203–210.

Frank, F., & Anderson, L. R. Effects of task and group size upon group productivity and member satisfaction. *Sociometry*, 1971, *34*, 135–149.

Frank, J. D. Experimental studies of personal pressure and resistance: I. Experimental production of resistance. *Journal of General Psychology*, 1944, *30*, 43–56.

Franke, R. H. The Hawthorne experiments: Re-view. *American Sociological Review*, 1979, *44*, 861–867.

Fraser, T. M. *The effects of confinement as a factor in manned space flight*. NASA Contractor Report, NASA CR-511. Washington, D.C.: NASA, 1966.

Freedman, J. L. *Crowding and behavior*. San Francisco: Freeman, 1975.

Freedman, J. L. Reconciling apparent differences between responses of humans and other animals to crowding. *Psychological Review*, 1979, *86*, 80–85.

Freedman, J. L., & Doob, A. N. *Deviancy: The psychology of being different*. New York: Academic Press, 1968.

Freedman, J. L., Klevansky, S., & Ehrlich, P. R. The effect of crowding on human task performance. *Journal of Applied Social Psychology*, 1971, *1*, 7–25.

Freeman, L. C. A set of measures of centrality based on betweenness. *Sociometry*, 1977, *40*, 35–41.

French, E. G. Motivation as a variable in work-partner selection. *Journal of Abnormal and Social Psychology*, 1956, *53*, 96–99.

French, E. G., & Chadwick, I. Some characteristics of affiliation motivation. *Journal of Abnormal and Social Psychology*, 1956, *52*, 296–300.

French, J. R. P., Jr. The disruption and cohesion of groups. *Journal of Abnormal and Social Psychology*, 1941, *36*, 361–377.

French, J. R. P., Jr., & Raven, B. The bases of social power. In D. Cartwright (Ed.), *Studies in social power*. Ann Arbor, Mich.: Institute for Social Research, 1959.

Freud, S. *Group psychology and the analysis of the ego*. London: Hogarth, 1922.

Froman, L. A., Jr., & Cohen, M. D. Threats and bargaining efficiency. *Behavioral Science*, 1969, *14*, 147–153.

Fromm, E. *Escape from freedom*. New York: Holt, Rinehart, & Winston, 1965.

Galassi, J. P., & Galassi, M. D. Modification of heterosocial skills deficits. In A. S. Bellack & M. Hersen (Eds.), *Research and practice in social skills training*. New York: Plenum, 1979.

Galle, O. R., & Gove, W. R. Crowding and behavior in Chicago, 1940–1970. In J. R. Aiello & A. Baum (Eds.), *Residential crowding and design*. New York: Plenum, 1979.

Galle, O. R., Gove, W. R., & McPherson, J. M. Population density and pathology: What are the relationships for man? *Science*, 1972, *176*, 23–30.

Gallo, P. S., Jr. Effects of increased incentives upon the use of threat in bargaining. *Journal of Personality and Social Psychology*, 1966, *4*, 14–20.

Gambrill, E. D., & Richey, C. A. An assertion inventory for use in assessment and research. *Behavior Therapy*, 1975, *6*, 547–549.

Gamson, W. A. A theory of coalition formation. *American Sociological Review*, 1961, *26*, 373–382. (a)

Gamson, W. A. An experimental test of a theory of coalition formation. *American Sociological Review*, 1961, *26*, 565–573. (b)

Gamson, W. A. Experimental studies of coalition formation. In L. Berkowitz (Ed.), *Advances in experimental social psychology* (Vol. 1). New York: Academic Press, 1964.

Gamson, W. A. *Power and discontent*. Homewood, Ill.: Dorsey Press, 1968.

Gamson, W. A. SIMSOC: Establishing social order in a simulated society. In M. Inbar & C. S. Stoll (Eds.), *Simulation and gaming in social science.* New York: Free Press, 1972.

Gannon, T. M. Emergence of the "defensive" group norm. *Federal Probation*, 1966, *30*(4), 44–47.

Gardner, J. W. *The antileadership vaccine.* Annual Report of the Carnegie Corporation. New York: Carnegie Corporation, 1965.

Garner, K., & Deutsch, M. Cooperative behavior in dyads: Effects of dissimilar goal orientations and differing expectations about the partner. *Journal of Conflict Resolution*, 1974, *18*, 634–645.

Geen, R. G. The effects of being observed on performance. In P. B. Paulus (Ed.), *Psychology of group influence.* Hillsdale, N. J.: Erlbaum, 1980.

Geen, R. G. Evaluation apprehension and social facilitation: A reply to Sanders. *Journal of Experimental Social Psychology*, 1981, *17*, 252–256.

Geen, R. G., & Gange, J. J. Drive theory of social facilitation: Twelve years of theory and research. *Psychological Bulletin*, 1977, *84*, 1267–1288.

Geier, J. G. A trait approach to the study of leadership in small groups. *Journal of Communication*, 1967, *17*, 316–323.

Genevie, L. E. (Ed.). *Collective behavior and social movements.* Itasca, Ill.: Peacock, 1978.

Gerard, H. B. The effect of different dimensions of disagreement on the communication process in small groups. *Human Relations*, 1953, *6*, 249–271.

Gerard, H. B. Emotional uncertainty and social comparison. *Journal of Abnormal and Social Psychology*, 1963, *66*, 568–573.

Gerard, H. B., & Mathewson, G. C. The effect of severity of initiation on liking for a group: A replication. *Journal of Experimental Social Psychology*, 1966, *2*, 278–287.

Gerard, H. B., & Rabbie, J. M. Fear and social comparison. *Journal of Abnormal and Social Psychology*, 1961, *62*, 586–592.

Gerard, H. B., Wilhelmy, R. A., & Conolley, E. S. Conformity and group size. *Journal of Personality and Social Psychology*, 1968, *8*, 79–82.

Gerbasi, K. C., Zuckerman, M., & Reis, H. T. Justice needs a new blindfold: A review of mock jury research. *Psychological Bulletin*, 1977, *84*, 323–345.

Gergen, K. J., Gergen, M. M., & Barton, W. H. Deviance in the dark. *Psychology Today*, 1973, *10*, 129–130.

Gerson, L. W. Punishment and position: The sanctioning of deviants in small groups. *Case Western Reserve Journal of Sociology*, 1967, *1*, 54–62.

Gewirtz, J. L. Mechanisms of social learning: Some rules of stimulation and behavior in early human development. In D. A. Goslin (Ed.), *Handbook of socialization theory and research.* Chicago: Rand McNally, 1969.

Gewirtz, J. L., & Baer, D. M. Deprivation and satiation of social reinforcers as drive conditions. *Journal of Abnormal and Social Psychology*, 1958, *57*, 165–172. (a)

Gewirtz, J. L., & Baer, D. M. The effect of brief social deprivation on behaviors for a social reinforcer. *Journal of Abnormal and Social Psychology*, 1958, *56*, 49–56. (b)

Gibb, C. A. Leadership. In G. Lindzey & E. Aronson (Eds.), *The handbook of social psychology* (Vol. 4, 2nd. ed.). Reading, Mass.: Addison-Wesley, 1969.

Gibb, J. R. Defensive level and influence potential in small groups. In L. Petrullo & B. M. Bass (Eds.), *Leadership and interpersonal behavior.* New York: Holt, Rinehart, & Winston, 1961.

Gibb, J. R. Defensive communication. In W. G. Bennis, D. E. Berlew, E. H. Schein, & F. I. Steele (Eds.), *Interpersonal dynamics* (3rd ed.). Homewood, Ill.: Dorsey, 1973.

Gibbs, J. P., & Erickson, M. Major developments in the sociological study of deviance. *Annual Review of Sociology*, 1975, *1*, 21–42.

Giesen, M., & McClaren, H. A. Discussion, distance, and sex: Changes in impressions and attraction during small group interaction. *Sociometry*, 1976, *39*, 60–70.

Gilchrist, J. C. The formation of social groups under conditions of success and failure. *Journal of Abnormal and Social Psychology*, 1952, *47*, 174–187.

Glaser, B. G., & Strauss, A. L. *The discovery of grounded theory: Strategies for qualitative research.* Chicago: Aldine, 1967.

Glaser, D. *The effectiveness of a prison and parole system.* Indianapolis: Bobbs-Merrill, 1964.

Glass, D. C., & Singer, J. E. *Urban stress.* New York: Academic Press, 1972.

Glass, D. C., Singer, J. E., & Pennebaker, J. W. Behavioral and physiological effects of uncontrollable environmental events. In D. Stokols (Ed.), *Perspectives on environment and behavior.* New York: Plenum, 1977.

Goethals, G. R., & Darley, J. M. Social comparison theory: An attributional approach. In J. M. Suls & R. L. Miller (Eds.), *Social comparison processes: Theoretical and empirical perspectives.* Washington, D.C.: Hemisphere, 1977.

Goethals, G. R., & Zanna, M. P. The role of social comparison in choice shifts. *Journal of Personality and Social Psychology*, 1979, *37*, 1469–1476.

Goetsch, G. G., & McFarland, D. D. Models of the distribution of acts in small discussion groups. *Social Psychology Quarterly*, 1980, *43*, 173–183.

Goffman, E. *Stigma: Notes on the management of*

spoiled identity. Englewood Cliffs, N.J.: Prentice-Hall, 1963.

Goffman, E. *Interaction ritual.* Garden City, N.Y.: Doubleday, 1967.

Goldberg, C. Sex roles, task competence, and conformity. *Journal of Psychology,* 1974, *86,* 157–164.

Goldberg, C. Conformity to majority type as a function of task and acceptance of sex-related stereotypes. *Journal of Psychology,* 1975, *89,* 25–37.

Goldberg, L. Ghetto riots and others: The faces of civil disorder in 1967. *Journal of Peace Research,* 1968, *2,* 116–132.

Goldberg, M. L., Passow, A. H., & Justman, J. *The effects of ability grouping.* New York: Teachers College Press, 1966.

Goldberg, S. C. Three situational determinants of conformity to social norms. *Journal of Abnormal and Social Psychology,* 1954, *49,* 325–329.

Goldfried, M. Toward the delineation of therapeutic change principles. *American Psychologist,* 1980, *35,* 991–999.

Goldman, M., & Fraas, L. A. The effects of leader selection on group performance. *Sociometry,* 1965, *28,* 82–88.

Goodstadt, B. E., & Hjelle, L. A. Power to the powerless: Locus of control and use of power. *Journal of Personality and Social Psychology,* 1973, *27,* 190–196.

Gordon, B. Influence, social comparison, and affiliation. *Dissertation Abstracts,* 1965, *26*(4), 2366.

Gordon, W. *Synectics: The development of creative capacity.* New York: Harper & Row, 1961.

Gormally, J., & Hill, C. Guidelines for research on Carkhuff's training model. *Journal of Counseling Psychology,* 1974, *21,* 539–547.

Gove, W. R. (Ed.). *The labelling of deviance.* Beverly Hills, Calif.: Sage, 1980.

Graen, G. Role-making processes within complex organizations. In M. D. Dunnette (Ed.), *Handbook of industrial organizational psychology.* Chicago: Rand McNally, 1976.

Graen, G. B., Alvares, K. M., Orris, J. B., & Martella, J. A. The contingency model of leadership effectiveness: Antecedent and evidential results. *Psychological Bulletin,* 1970, *74,* 285–296.

Graen, G. B., Orris, J. B., & Alvares, K. M. Contingency model of leadership effectiveness: Some experimental results. *Journal of Applied Psychology,* 1971, *55,* 196–201.

Green, R. B., & Mack, J. Would groups do better without social psychologists? A response to Buys. *Personality and Social Psychology Bulletin,* 1978, *4,* 561–563.

Green, S. G., & Mitchell, T. R. Attributional processes of leaders in leader-member interactions. *Organizational Behavior and Human Performance,* 1979, *23,* 429–458.

Green, S. G., & Nebeker, D. M. The effects of situational factors and leadership style on leader behavior. *Organizational Behavior and Human Performance,* 1977, *19,* 368–377.

Greenberg, C. I., & Firestone, I. J. Compensatory responses to crowding: Effects of personal space intrusion and privacy reduction. *Journal of Personality and Social Psychology,* 1977, *35,* 637–644.

Greenstein, T. N. Scope conditions and crucial tests: Comment on Lee and Ofshe. *Social Psychology Quarterly,* 1981, *44,* 381–383.

Greenstein, T. N., & Knottnerus, J. D. The effects of differential evaluations on status generalization. *Social Psychology Quarterly,* 1980, *43,* 147–154.

Griffitt, W. Environmental effects on interpersonal affective behavior: Ambient effective temperature and attraction. *Journal of Personality and Social Psychology,* 1970, *15,* 240–244.

Griffitt, W., & Veitch, R. Hot and crowded: Influence of population density and temperature on interpersonal affective behavior. *Journal of Personality and Social Psychology,* 1971, *17,* 92–98.

Griffitt, W., & Veitch, R. Preacquaintance attitude similarity and attraction revisited: Ten days in a fall-out shelter. *Sociometry,* 1974, *37,* 163–173.

Grimes, A. J. Authority, power, influence and social control: A theoretical synthesis. *Academy of Management Review,* 1978, *3,* 724–737.

Gross, E., & Stone, G. P. Embarrassment and the analysis of role requirements. *American Journal of Sociology,* 1964, *70,* 1–15.

Grush, J. E. A summary review of mediating explanations of exposure phenomena. *Personality and Social Psychology Bulletin,* 1979, *5,* 154–159.

Grusky, O. Managerial succession and organizational effectiveness. *American Journal of Sociology,* 1963, *69,* 21–31.

Gulley, H. E., & Leathers, D. G. *Communication and group process.* New York: Holt, Rinehart, & Winston, 1977.

Gunderson, E. K. E. Individual behavior in confined or isolated groups. In J. E. Rasmussen (Ed.), *Man in isolation and confinement.* Chicago: Aldine, 1973.

Gurr, T. R. *Why men rebel.* Princeton, N.J.: Princeton University Press, 1970.

Guthman, E. *We band of brothers.* New York: Harper & Row, 1971.

Gustafson, D. H., Shukla, R. M., Delbecq, A. L., & Walster, G. W. A comparative study of differences in subjective likelihood estimates made by individuals, interacting groups, Delphi groups, and nominal groups. *Organizational Behavior and Human Performance,* 1973, *9,* 280–291.

Gustafson, J. P. Schismatic groups. *Human Relations*, 1978, *31*, 139–154.

Haas, D. F., & Deseran, F. A. Trust and symbolic exchange. *Social Psychology Quarterly*, 1981, *44*, 3–13.

Hackman, J. R., Brousseau, K. R., & Weiss, J. A. The interaction of task design and group performance strategies in determining group effectiveness. *Organizational Behavior and Human Performance*, 1976, *16*, 350–365.

Hackman, J. R., & Morris, C. G. Group tasks, group interaction process, and group performance effectiveness: A review and proposed integration. In L. Berkowitz (Ed.), *Advances in experimental social psychology* (Vol. 8). New York: Academic Press, 1975.

Hagan, J. Conceptual deficiencies in an interaction's perspective on "deviance." *Criminology*, 1974, *11*, 383–404.

Hall, G. E., & Rutherford, W. L. *Concerns of teachers about implementing the innovation of team teaching.* Austin, Tex.: Research and Development Center for Teacher Education, University of Texas, 1975.

Hall, E. T. *The hidden dimension.* New York: Doubleday, 1966.

Halpin, A. W. Studies in aircrew composition: III. In *The combat leader behavior of B-29 aircraft commanders.* Washington, D.C.: Human Factors Operations Research Laboratory, Bolling Air Force Base, 1953.

Halpin, A. W. The leadership behavior and combat performances of airplane commanders. *Journal of Abnormal and Social Psychology*, 1954, *49*, 19–22.

Halpin, A. W., & Winer, B. J. *The leadership behavior of the airplane commander.* Columbus: Ohio State University Research Foundation, 1952.

Ham v. South Carolina, 409 U.S. 524 (1973).

Hamblin, R. L. Leadership and crises. *Sociometry*, 1958, *21*, 322–335.

Hamilton, D. L. A cognitive-attributional analysis of stereotyping. In L. Berkowitz (Ed.), *Advances in experimental social psychology* (Vol. 12). New York: Academic Press, 1979.

Hamilton, R. W. Weekend retreat. In R. H. Turner & L. M. Killian (Eds.), *Collective behavior* (2nd ed.). Englewood Cliffs, N.J.: Prentice-Hall, 1972.

Hammer, T. H., & Dachler, H. P. *The process of supervision in the context of motivation theory.* College Park: University of Maryland, 1973.

Hansen, J., Warner, R., & Smith, E. *Group counseling: Theory and process* (2nd ed.). Chicago: Rand McNally, 1980.

Hansen, W. B., & Altman, I. Decorating personal places: A descriptive analysis. *Environment and Behavior*, 1976, *8*, 491–504.

Hardin, G. The tragedy of the commons. *Science*, 1968, *162*, 1243–1248.

Hardy, R. C. Effect of leadership style on the performance of small classroom groups: A test of the Contingency Model. *Journal of Personality and Social Psychology*, 1971, *19*, 367–374.

Hardy, R. C. A test of poor leader-member relations cells of the contingency model on elementary school children. *Child Development*, 1975, *45*, 958–964.

Hare, A. P. *Handbook of small group research* (2nd ed.). New York: Free Press, 1976.

Hare, A. P., & Bales, R. F. Seating position and small group interaction. *Sociometry*, 1963, *26*, 480–486.

Hare, A. P., Borgatta, E. F., & Bales, R. F. *Small groups: Studies in social interaction.* New York: Knopf, 1955.

Hargreaves, D. *Social relations in a secondary school.* New York: Humanities Press, 1967.

Harkins, S. G., Latané, B., & Williams, K. Social loafing: Allocating effort or taking it easy. *Journal of Experimental Social Psychology*, 1980, *16*, 457–465.

Harlow, H. F., & Harlow, M. K. Learning to love. *American Scientist*, 1966, *54*, 244–272.

Harnett, D. L., Cummings, L. L., & Hamner, W. C. Personality, bargaining style, and payoff in bilateral monopoly bargaining among European managers. *Sociometry*, 1973, *36*, 325–245.

Haroutunian, V., & Riccio, D. C. Effect of arousal conditions during reinstatement treatment upon learned fear in young rats. *Developmental Psychobiology*, 1977, *10*, 25–32.

Harper, N. L., & Askling, L. R. Group communication and quality of task solution in a media production organization. *Communication Monographs*, 1980, *47*, 77–100.

Harrison, A. A. Mere exposure. In L. Berkowitz (Ed.), *Advances in experimental social psychology* (Vol. 10). New York: Academic Press, 1977.

Hartman, J. Small group methods of personal change. *Annual Review of Psychology*, 1979, *30*, 453–476.

Harvey, O. J., & Consalvi, C. Status and conformity to pressures in informal groups. *Journal of Abnormal and Social Psychology*, 1960, *60*, 182–187.

Harvey, P. H., & Greene, P. J. Group composition: An evolutionary perspective. In H. Kellerman (Ed.), *Group cohesion.* New York: Grune & Stratton, 1981.

Hastorf, A. H., & Cantril, H. They saw a game. *Journal of Abnormal and Social Psychology*, 1954, *49*, 129–134.

Hayduk, L. A. Personal space: An evaluative and orienting overview. *Psychological Bulletin*, 1978, *85*, 117–134.

Haythorn, W. W. The miniworld of isolation: Laboratory studies. In J. E. Rasmussen (Ed.), *Man in isolation and confinement.* Chicago: Aldine, 1973.

Hearne, G. Leadership and the spatial factor in small

groups. *Journal of Abnormal and Social Psychology*, 1957, *54*, 269–272.

Heckel, R., & Salzberg, H. *Group psychotherapy: A behavioral approach*. Columbia, S.C.: University of South Carolina Press, 1976.

Heffron, M. H. The naval ship as an urban design problem. *Naval Engineers Journal*, 1972, *12*, 49–64.

Heider, F. *The psychology of interpersonal relations*. New York: Wiley, 1958.

Heimberg, R. G., Montgomery, D., Madsen, C. H., Jr., & Heimberg, J. S. Assertion training: A review of the literature. *Behavior Therapy*, 1977, *8*, 953–971.

Heimstra, N. W., & McFarling, L. H. *Environmental psychology* (2nd. ed.). Monterey, Calif.: Brooks/Cole, 1978.

Heller, J. F., Groff, B. D., & Solomon, S. H. Toward an understanding of crowding: The role of physical interaction. *Journal of Personality and Social Psychology*, 1977, *35*, 183–190.

Helmreich, R. L. Evaluation of environments: Behavioral observations in an undersea habitat. In J. Lang, C. Burnette, W. Moleski, & D. Vachon (Eds.), *Designing for human behavior*. Stroudsburg, Penn.: Dowden, Hutchinson, & Ross, 1974.

Helmreich, R. L., Aronson, E., & LeFan, J. To err is humanizing—sometimes: Effects of self-esteem, competence, and a pratfall on interpersonal attraction. *Journal of Personality and Social Psychology*, 1970, *16*, 259–264.

Helmreich, R. L., & Collins, B. E. Situational determinants of affiliative preference under stress. *Journal of Personality and Social Psychology*, 1967, *6*, 79–85.

Hemphill, J. K. *Leader behavior description*. Columbus: Ohio State University Personnel Research Board, 1950.

Hemphill, J. K. Relations between the size of the group and the behavior of superior leaders. *Journal of Social Psychology*, 1952, *32*, 11–22.

Hemphill, J. K. Leadership behavior associated with the administrative reputation of college departments. *Journal of Educational Psychology*, 1955, *46*, 385–401.

Hemphill, J. K. Why people attempt to lead. In L. Petrullo & B. M. Bass (Eds.), *Leadership and interpersonal behavior*. New York: Holt, Rinehart, & Winston, 1961.

Henchy, T., & Glass, D. C. Evaluation apprehension and the social facilitation of dominant and subordinate responses. *Journal of Personality and Social Psychology*, 1968, *10*, 446–454.

Hensley, V., & Duval, S. Some perceptual determinants of perceived similarity, liking, and correctness. *Journal of Personality and Social Psychology*, 1976, *34*, 159–168.

Herbert, T. T., & Estes, R. W. Improving executive decisions by formalizing dissent: The corporate devil's advocate. *Academy of Management Review*, 1977, *2*, 662–667.

Hermann, M. G., & Kogan, N. Effects of negotiators' personalities on negotiating behavior. In D. Druckman (Ed.), *Negotiations*. Beverly Hills, Calif.: Sage, 1977.

Hersey, P., & Blanchard, K. H. Leader effectiveness and adaptability description (LEAD). In J. W. Pfeiffer & J. E. Jones (Eds.), *The 1976 annual handbook for group facilitators* (Vol. 5). La Jolla, Calif.: University Associates, 1976.

Hersey, P., & Blanchard, K. H. *Management of organizational behavior: Utilizing human resources* (3rd ed.). Englewood Cliffs, N.J.: Prentice-Hall, 1977.

Hersey, R. *Zest for work*. New York: Harper, 1955.

Hill, T. E., & Schmitt, N. Individual differences in leadership decision making. *Organizational Behavior and Human Performance*, 1977, *19*, 353–367.

Hill, W. F., & Gruner, L. A study of development in open and closed groups. *Small Group Behavior*, 1973, *4*, 355–381.

Hinkle, S., & Schopler, J. Ethnocentrism in the evaluation of group products. In W. G. Austin & S. Worchel (Eds.), *The social psychology of intergroup relations*. Monterey, Calif.: Brooks/Cole, 1979.

Hirokawa, R. Y. A comparative analysis of communication patterns within effective and ineffective decision-making groups. *Communication Monographs*, 1980, *47*, 312–321.

Hirschi, T. Procedural rules and the study of deviant behavior. *Social Problems*, 1973, *21*, 159–173.

Hoffer, E. *The true believer*. New York: Harper & Row, 1951.

Hollander, E. P. Conformity, status, and idiosyncrasy credit. *Psychological Review*, 1958, *65*, 117–127.

Hollander, E. P. Competence and conformity in the acceptance of influence. *Journal of Abnormal and Social Psychology*, 1960, *61*, 365–369.

Hollander, E. P. *Leaders, groups, and influence*. New York: Oxford University Press, 1964.

Hollander, E. P. Validity of peer nominations in predicting a distant performance criterion. *Journal of Applied Psychology*, 1965, *49*, 434–438.

Hollander, E. P. *Principles and methods of social psychology* (2nd ed.). New York: Oxford University Press, 1971.

Hollander, E. P. *Leadership dynamics: A practical guide to effective relationships*. New York: Free Press, 1978.

Holmes, J. G., & Miller, D. T. Interpersonal conflict. In J. W. Thibaut, J. T. Spence, & R. C. Carson (Eds.), *Contemporary topics in social psychology*. Morristown, N.J.: General Learning Press, 1976.

Holsti, O. R., & North, R. The history of human conflict. In E. B. McNeil (Ed.), *The nature of human conflict.* Englewood Cliffs, N.J.: Prentice-Hall, 1965.

Homans, G. C. *The human group.* New York: Harcourt, Brace, & World, 1950.

Homans, G. C. *The nature of social science.* New York: Harcourt, Brace, & World, 1967.

Homans, G. C. *Social behavior: Its elementary forms.* New York: Harcourt Brace Jovanovich, 1974.

Horai, J. Attributional conflict. *Journal of Social Issues,* 1977, *33*(1), 88–100.

Hottes, J. H., & Kahn, A. Sex differences in a mixed-motive conflict situation. *Journal of Personality,* 1974, *42,* 260–275.

House, R. J. A path goal theory of leader effectiveness. *Administrative Science Quarterly,* 1971, *16,* 321–338.

Houseman, M. P. With intelligence botched, it was downhill from the start. *Richmond Times Dispatch,* April 12, 1981, J-1, J-7.

Hovland, C. I., Janis, I. L., & Kelley, H. H. *Communication and persuasion.* New Haven: Yale University Press, 1953.

Howard, H. E. *Territory and bird life.* London: John Murray, 1920.

Howard, J. W., & Rothbart, M. Social categorization and memory for in-group and out-group behavior. *Journal of Personality and Social Psychology,* 1980, *38,* 301–310.

Howells, L. T., & Becker, S. W. Seating arrangement and leadership emergence. *Journal of Abnormal and Social Psychology,* 1962, *64,* 148–150.

Huesmann, L. R., & Levinger, G. Incremental exchange theory: A formal model for progression in dyadic social interaction. In L. Berkowitz (Ed.), *Advances in experimental social psychology* (Vol. 9). New York: Academic Press, 1976.

Hunt, E. B., & Rowe, R. R. Group and individual economic decision making in risk conditions. In D. W. Taylor (Ed.), *Experiments on decision making and other studies.* Arlington, Va.: Armed Services Technical Information Agency, 1960.

Hyman, H. M., & Tarrant, C. M. Aspects of American trial jury history. In R. J. Simon (Ed.), *The jury system in America.* Beverly Hills, Calif.: Sage, 1975.

Ide, J. K., Parkerson, J., Haertel, G. D., & Walbey, H. J. Peer group influence on educational outcomes: A quantitative synthesis. *Journal of Educational Psychology,* 1981, *73,* 472–484.

Ilgen, D. R., & Fujii, D. S. An investigation of the validity of leader behavior descriptions obtained from subordinates. *Journal of Applied Psychology,* 1976, *61,* 642–651.

Indik, B. P. Organization size and member participation: Some empirical tests of alternate explanations. *Human Relations,* 1965, *15,* 339–350.

Ingham, A. G., Levinger, G., Graves, J., & Peckham,

V. The Ringelmann effect: Studies of group size and group performance. *Journal of Personality and Social Psychology,* 1974, *10,* 371–384.

Insko, C. A., & Schopler, J. *Experimental social psychology.* New York: Academic Press, 1972.

Insko, C. A., & Wilson, M. Interpersonal attraction as a function of social interaction. *Journal of Personality and Social Psychology,* 1977, *35,* 903–911.

Isenberg, D. J., & Ennis, J. G. Perceiving group members: A comparison of derived and imposed dimensions. *Journal of Personality and Social Psychology,* 1981, *41,* 293–305.

Iverson, M. A. Personality impressions of punitive stimulus persons of differential status. *Journal of Abnormal and Social Psychology,* 1964, *68,* 617–626.

Ivey, A. E., & Authier, J. *Microcounseling: Innovations in interviewing, counseling, psychotherapy, and psychoeducation.* Springfield, Ill.: Charles C Thomas, 1978.

Ivie, R. L. Images of savagery in American justifications for war. *Communication Monographs,* 1980, *47,* 279–294.

Jablin, F. M. Superior-subordinate communication: The state of the art. *Psychological Bulletin,* 1979, *86,* 1201–1222.

Jackson, J. M., & Latané, B. All alone in front of all those people: Stage fright as a function of number and type of co-performances and audience. *Journal of Personality and Social Psychology,* 1981, *40,* 73–85.

Jacobs, A. The use of feedback in groups. In A. Jacobs (Ed.), *The group as agent of change.* New York: Behavioral Publications, 1974.

Jacobs, R. C., & Campbell, D. T. The perpetuation of an arbitrary tradition through several generations of a laboratory microculture. *Journal of Abnormal and Social Psychology,* 1961, *62,* 649–658.

Jago, A. G. Configural cue utilization in implicit models of leader behavior. *Organizational Behavior and Human Performance,* 1978, *22,* 474–496.

James, R. Status and competency of jurors. *American Journal of Sociology,* 1959, *64,* 563–570.

Janis, I. L. Group identification under conditions of external danger. *British Journal of Medical Psychology,* 1963, *36,* 227–238.

Janis, I. L. *Victims of groupthink.* Boston: Houghton-Mifflin, 1972.

Janis, I. L. *Preventing groupthink in policy-planning groups: Theory and research perspectives.* Paper presented at the Second Annual Meetings of the International Society of Political Psychology, Washington, D.C., 1979.

Janis, I. L., & Mann, L. *Decision making: A psychological analysis of conflict, choice, and commitment.* New York: Free Press, 1977.

Janssens, L., & Nuttin, J. R. Frequency perception of

individual and group successes as a function of competition, coaction, and isolation. *Journal of Personality and Social Psychology*, 1976, *34*, 830–836.

Javornisky, G. Task context and sex differences in conformity. *Journal of Social Psychology*, 1979, *108*, 213–220.

Jenness, A. Social influence in the change of opinion. *Journal of Abnormal and Social Psychology*, 1932, *27*, 29–34. (a)

Jenness, A. The role of discussion in changing opinion regarding a matter of fact. *Journal of Abnormal and Social Psychology*, 1932, *27*, 279–296. (b)

Jennings, H. H. *Leadership and isolation* (2nd ed.). New York: Longmans & Green, 1950.

Johnson, D. W. Group processes: Influences of student-student interaction on school outcomes. In J. H. McMillan (Ed.), *The social psychology of school learning*. New York: Academic Press, 1980.

Johnson, D. W., & Johnson, F. P. *Joining together*. Englewood Cliffs, N.J.: Prentice-Hall, 1975.

Johnson, D. W., Maruyama, G., Johnson, R., Nelson, D., & Skon, L. Effects of cooperative, competitive, and individualistic goal structures on achievement: A meta-analysis. *Psychological Bulletin*, 1981, *89*, 47–62.

Johnson, M. P., & Ewens, W. Power relations and affective style as determinants of confidence in impression formation in a game situation. *Journal of Experimental Social Psychology*, 1971, *7*, 98–110.

Johnson, R. D., & Downing, L. L. Deindividuation and valence of cues: Effects on prosocial and antisocial behavior. *Journal of Personality and Social Psychology*, 1979, *37*, 1532–1538.

Jones, E. E. *Ingratiation*. New York: Appleton-Century-Crofts, 1964.

Jones, E. E., Gergen, K. J., & Jones, R. G. Tactics of ingratiation among leaders and subordinates in a status hierarchy. *Psychological Monographs*, 1963, *77*(3), Whole No. 566.

Jones, E. E., Jones, R. G., & Gergen, K. J. Some conditions affecting the evaluation of a conformist. *Journal of Personality*, 1963, *31*, 270–288.

Jones, E. E., & Nisbett, R. E. *The actor and observer: Divergent perceptions on the causes of behavior*. Morristown, N.J.: General Learning Press, 1971.

Jones, E. E., & Wortman, C. *Ingratiation: An attributional approach*. Morristown, N.J.: General Learning Press, 1973.

Jourard, S. *Self-disclosure*. New York: Wiley, 1971.

Kadish, S. H., & Paulsen, M. G. *Criminal law and its processes*. Boston: Little, Brown, 1975.

Kahn, R. L., Wolfe, D. M., Quinn, R. P., Snoek, J. D., & Rosenthal, R. A. *Organizational stress: Studies in role conflict and ambiguity*. New York: Wiley, 1964.

Kalven, H., Jr., & Zeisel, H. *The American jury*. Boston: Little, Brown, 1966.

Kandel, D. B. Similarity in real-life adolescent friendship pairs. *Journal of Personality and Social Psychology*, 1978, *36*, 306–312.

Kaplan, M. F., & Schersching, C. Juror deliberation: An information integration analysis. In B. D. Sales (Ed.), *The trial process*. New York: Plenum, 1981.

Kaplan, R. E. The conspicuous absence of evidence that process consultation enhances task performance. *Journal of Applied Behavioral Science*, 1979, *15*, 346–360.

Katz, D., & Kahn, R. L. *The social psychology of organizations* (2nd ed.). New York: Wiley, 1978.

Katz, R. The influence of group conflict on leadership effectiveness. *Organizational Behavior and Human Performance*, 1977, *20*, 265–286.

Katz, R., & Tushman, M. Communication patterns, project performance, and task characteristics: An empirical evaluation and integration in an R & D setting. *Organization Behavior and Group Performance*, 1979, *23*, 139–162.

Kaul, T., & Bednar, R. Conceptualizing group research: A preliminary analysis. *Small Group Behavior*, 1978, *9*, 173–191.

Keating, J. P., & Loftus, E. F. The logic of fire escape. *Psychology Today*, 1981, *15*(6), 14–19.

Kelley, H. H. Communication in experimentally created hierarchies. *Human Relations*, 1951, *4*, 39–56.

Kelley, H. H. Two functions of reference groups. In G. E. Swanson, T. M. Newcomb, & E. L. Hartley (Eds.), *Readings in social psychology* (2nd ed.). New York: Holt, 1952.

Kelley, H. H. Interpersonal accommodation. *American Psychologist*, 1968, *23*, 399–410.

Kelley, H. H. *Personal relationships: Their structures and processes*. Hillsdale, N.J.: Erlbaum, 1979.

Kelley, H. H., & Shapiro, M. M. An experiment on conformity to group norms where conformity is detrimental to group achievement. *American Sociological Review*, 1954, *19*, 557–567.

Kelley, H. H., & Stahelski, A. J. Errors in perceptions of intentions in a mixed-motive game. *Journal of Experimental Social Psychology*, 1970, *6*, 379–400. (a)

Kelley, H. H., & Stahelski, A. J. The inference of intentions from moves in the Prisoner's Dilemma Game. *Journal of Experimental Social Psychology*, 1970, *6*, 401–419. (b)

Kelley, H. H., & Stahelski, A. J. Social interaction basis of cooperators' and competitors' beliefs about others. *Journal of Personality and Social Psychology*, 1970, *16*, 66–91. (c)

Kelley, H. H., & Thibaut, J. W. Group problem solving. In G. Lindzey & E. Aronson (Eds.), *The handbook of social psychology* (Vol. 4, 2nd ed.). Reading, Mass.: Addison-Wesley, 1969.

Kelley, H. H., & Thibaut, J. W. *Interpersonal relations: A theory of interdependence.* New York: Wiley, 1978.

Kelman, H. C. Processes of opinion change. *Public Opinion Quarterly*, 1961, *25*, 57–78.

Kennedy, R. F. *Thirteen days.* New York: Norton, 1969.

Kerckhoff, A. C., Back, K. W., & Miller, N. Sociometric patterns in hysterical contagion. *Sociometry*, 1965, *28*, 2–15.

Kerr, N. L., Atkin, R. S., Stasser, G., Meek, D., Holt, R. W., & Davis, J. H. Guilt beyond a reasonable doubt: Effect of concept definition and assigned decision rule on the judgments of mock jurors. *Journal of Personality and Social Psychology*, 1976, *34*, 282–294.

Kerr, N. L., & Bruun, S. E. Ringelmann revisited: Alternative explanations for the social loafing effect. *Personality and Social Psychology Bulletin*, 1981, *7*, 224–231.

Kerr, S., & Jermier, J. M. Substitutes for leadership: Their meaning and measurement. *Organizational Behavior and Human Performance*, 1978, *22*, 375–403.

Kerr, S., Schriesheim, C. A., Murphy, C. J., & Stogdill, R. M. Toward a contingency theory of leadership based upon the consideration and initiating structure literature. *Organizational Behavior and Human Performance*, 1974, *12*, 62–82.

Kidd, J. S. Social influence phenomena in a task-oriented group situation. *Journal of Abnormal and Social Psychology*, 1958, *56*, 13–17.

Kidder, L. H. *Research methods in social relations* (4th ed.). New York: Holt, Rinehart, & Winston, 1981.

Kiesler, C. A. *The psychology of commitment: Experiments linking behavior to belief.* New York: Academic Press, 1971.

Kiesler, C. A., & Kiesler, S. B. *Conformity* (2nd ed.). Reading, Mass.: Addison-Wesley, 1976.

Kiesler, C. A., & Pallak, M. S. Minority influence: The effect of majority reactionaries and defectors, and minority and majority compromisers, upon majority opinion and attraction. *European Journal of Social Psychology*, 1975, *5*, 237–256.

Kiesler, D. J. Some myths of psychotherapy research and the search for a paradigm. *Psychological Bulletin*, 1966, *65*, 110–136.

Kilham, W., & Mann, L. Level of destructive obedience as a function of transmitter and executant roles in the Milgram obedience paradigm. *Journal of Personality and Social Psychology*, 1974, *29*, 696–702.

Kilmann, P., & Sotile, W. The marathon encounter group: A review of the outcome literature. *Psychological Bulletin*, 1976, *83*, 827–850.

Kipnis, D. Does power corrupt? *Journal of Personality and Social Psychology*, 1972, *24*, 33–41.

Kipnis, D. *The powerholders.* Chicago: University of Chicago Press, 1974.

Kipnis, D., Castell, P. J., Gergen, M., & Mauch, D. Metamorphic effects of power. *Journal of Applied Psychology*, 1976, *61*, 127–135.

Kipnis, D., & Consentino, J. Use of leadership powers in industry. *Journal of Applied Psychology*, 1969, *53*, 460–466.

Kirkpatrick, D. L. *How to plan and conduct productive business meetings.* New York: Dartnell, 1980.

Kissel, S. Stress-reducing properties of social stimuli. *Journal of Personality and Social Psychology*, 1965, *2*, 378–384.

Kleiner, R. J. The effects of threat reduction upon interpersonal attractiveness. *Journal of Personality*, 1960, *28*, 145–155.

Knight, H. C. *A comparison of the reliability of group and individual judgment.* Unpublished master's thesis, Columbia University, 1921.

Knowles, E. S. Boundaries around group interaction: The effect of group size and member status on boundary permeability. *Journal of Personality and Social Psychology*, 1973, *26*, 327–331.

Knowles, E. S. An affiliative conflict theory of personal and group spatial behavior. In P. B. Paulus (Ed.), *Psychology of group influence.* Hillsdale, N.J.: Erlbaum, 1980.

Knowles, E. S., & Bassett, R. L. Groups and crowds as social entities: The effects of activity, size, and member similarity on nonmembers. *Journal of Personality and Social Psychology*, 1976, *34*, 837–845.

Knowles, E. S., Kreuser, B., Haas, S., Hyde, M., & Schuchart, G. E. Group size and the extension of social space boundaries. *Journal of Personality and Social Psychology*, 1976, *33*, 647–654.

Kochan, T. A., Schmidt, S. M., & DeCotiis, T. A. Superior-subordinate relations: Leadership and headship. *Human Relations*, 1975, *28*, 279–294.

Kogan, N., & Wallach, M. A. *Risk taking: A study of cognition and personality.* New York: Holt, Rinehart, & Winston, 1964.

Kohler, W. *Gestalt psychology.* New York: Liveright, 1947.

Komorita, S. S., & Chertkoff, J. M. A bargaining theory of coalition formation. *Psychological Review*, 1973, *80*, 149–162.

Komorita, S. S., & Meek, D. D. Generality and validity of some theories of coalition formation. *Journal of Personality and Social Psychology*, 1978, *36*, 392–404.

Komorita, S. S., & Moore, D. Theories and processes of coalition formation. *Journal of Personality and Social Psychology*, 1976, *33*, 371–381.

Korda, M. *Power! How to get it, how to use it.* New York: Ballantine, 1975.

Korman, A. K. Contingency approaches to leadership:

An overview. In J. G. Hunt & L. L. Larson (Eds.), *Contingency approaches to leadership*. Carbondale, Ill.: Southern Illinois University Press, 1974.

Kounin, J. S. *Discipline and group management in classrooms*. New York: Holt, Rinehart, & Winston, 1970.

Kounin, J. S., & Gump, P. V. The ripple effect in discipline. *Elementary School Journal*, 1958, *59*, 158–162.

Krause, C. A. *Guyana massacre: The eyewitness account*. New York: The Washington Post, 1978.

Krauss, R. M., & Deutsch, M. Communication in interpersonal bargaining. *Journal of Personality and Social Psychology*, 1966, *4*, 572–577.

Kraut, R. Effects of social labeling on giving to charity. *Journal of Experimental Social Psychology*, 1973, *9*, 551–562.

Kravitz, D. A. Effects of resources and alternatives on coalition formation. *Journal of Personality and Social Psychology*, 1981, *41*, 87–98.

Kravitz, D. A., Cohen, J. L., Martin, B., Sweeney, J., McCarty, J., Elliott, E., & Goldstein, P. Humans would do better without other humans. *Personality and Social Psychology Bulletin*, 1978, *4*, 559–560.

Krebs, D., & Adinolfi, A. A. Physical attractiveness, social relations, and personality style. *Journal of Personality and Social Psychology*, 1975, *31*, 245–253.

Krech, D., & Crutchfield, R. S. *Theory and problems of social psychology*. New York: McGraw-Hill, 1948.

Kriesberg, L. *The sociology of social conflicts*. Englewood Cliffs, N.J.: Prentice-Hall, 1973.

Lacoursiere, R. B. *The life cycle of groups*. New York: Human Sciences Press, 1980.

La Gaipa, J. J. Interpersonal attraction and social exchange. In S. Duck (Ed.), *Theory and practice in interpersonal attraction*. New York: Academic Press, 1977.

Laing, R. D. *The divided self*. London: Tavistock, 1960.

Lambert, M., & DeJulio, S. Outcome research in Carkhuff's human resource development training programs. Where is the donut? *The Counseling Psychologist*, 1977, *6*, 79–86.

Lamm, H., & Myers, D. G. Group-induced polarization of attitudes and behavior. In L. Berkowitz (Ed.), *Advances in Experimental Social Psychology* (Vol. 11). New York: Academic Press, 1978.

Lamm, H., & Trommsdorff, G. Group versus individual performance on tasks requiring ideational proficiency (Brainstorming): A review. *European Journal of Social Psychology*, 1973, *3*, 361–388.

Landau, R., & Gewirtz, J. L. Differential satiation for a social reinforcing stimulus as a determinant of its efficacy in conditioning. *Journal of Experimental Child Psychology*, 1967, *5*, 391–405.

Landers, D. M., & Luschen, G. Team performance outcome and the cohesiveness of competitive coacting teams. *International Journal of Sport Sociology*, 1974, *9*, 57–71.

Landis, C. Studies of emotional reactions, II. General behavior and facial expression. *Journal of Comparative Psychology*, 1924, *4*, 447–509.

Landsberger, H. A. *Hawthorne revisited*. Ithaca, N.Y.: Cornell University, 1958.

Lange, A. J., & Jakubowski, P. *Responsible assertive behavior: Cognitive/behavioral procedures for trainers*. Champaign, Ill.: Research Press, 1976.

Langer, E. J., Blank, A., & Chanowitz, B. The mindlessness of ostensibly thoughtful action. *Journal of Personality and Social Psychology*, 1978, *36*, 635–642.

Langer, E. J., & Newman, H. M. The role of mindlessness in a typical social psychology experiment. *Personality and Social Psychology Bulletin*, 1979, *5*, 295–298.

Lanzetta, J. T., & Roby, T. B. The relationship between certain group process variables and group problem-solving efficiency. *Journal of Social Psychology*, 1960, *52*, 135–148.

Latané, B. The psychology of social impact. *American Psychologist*, 1981, *36*, 343–356.

Latané, B., & Bidwell, L. D. Sex and affiliation in college cafeterias. *Personality and Social Psychology Bulletin*, 1977, *3*, 571–574.

Latané, B., & Glass, D. C. Social and nonsocial attraction in rats. *Journal of Personality and Social Psychology*, 1968, *9*, 142–146.

Latané, B., & Nida, S. Ten years of research on group size and helping. *Psychological Bulletin*, 1981, *39*, 308–324.

Latané, B., Williams, K., & Harkins, S. Many hands make light the work: The causes and consequences of social loafing. *Journal of Personality and Social Psychology*, 1979, *37*, 822–832.

Latham, G. P., & Baldes, J. J. The "practical significance" of Locke's theory of goal setting. *Journal of Applied Psychology*, 1975, *60*, 122–124.

LaTour, S. Determinants of participant and observer satisfaction with adversary and inquisitorial modes of adjudication. *Journal of Personality and Social Psychology*, 1978, *36*, 1531–1545.

LaTour, S., Houlden, P., Walker, L., & Thibaut, J. Some determinants of preference for modes of conflict resolution. *Journal of Conflict Resolution*, 1976, *20*, 319–356.

Lauderdale, P. Deviance and moral boundaries. *American Sociological Review*, 1976, *41*, 660–676.

Laughlin, P. R. Social combination processes of cooperative problem solving groups on verbal intellective tasks. In M. Fishbein (Ed.), *Progress in social psychology*. Hillsdale, N.J.: Erlbaum, 1980.

Laughlin, P. R., & Adamopoulos, J. Social combination processes and individual learning for six-person cooperative groups on an intellective task. *Journal of Personality and Social Psychology*, 1980, *38*, 941–947.

Lawler, E. E., III. *Motivation in work organizations*. Monterey, Calif.: Brooks/Cole, 1973.

Lawler, E. J., & Thompson, M. E. Impact of a leader's responsibility for inequity on subordinate revolts. *Social Psychology Quarterly*, 1978, *41*, 264–268.

Lawler, E. J., & Thompson, M. E. Subordinate response to a leader's cooptation strategy as a function of type of coalition power. *Representative Research in Social Psychology*, 1979, *9*, 69–80.

Lazarus, A. A. *Behavior therapy and beyond*. New York: McGraw-Hill, 1971.

Leary, M., Forsyth, D. R., & McCown, N. *Self-presentational determinants of leaders*. Paper presented at the 24th Annual Meetings of the Southeastern Psychological Association, 1978.

Leavitt, H. J. Some effects of certain communication patterns on group performance. *Journal of Abnormal and Social Psychology*, 1951, *46*, 38–50.

Le Bon, G. *The crowd*. London: Ernest Benn, 1895.

Lefkowitz, M., Blake, R. R., & Mouton, J. S. Status factors in pedestrian violation of traffic signals. *Journal of Abnormal and Social Psychology*, 1955, *51*, 704–706.

Lemert, E. M. Human deviance, social problems, and social control. Englewood Cliffs, N.J.: Prentice-Hall, 1967.

Lenk, H. Top performance despite internal conflict. In J. W. Loy & G. S. Kenyon (Eds.), *Sport, culture, and society*. New York: Macmillan, 1969.

Leonard, W. M., II. *A sociological perspective on sport*. Minneapolis: Burgess, 1980.

Lepper, M. R., & Green, D. Turning play into work: Effects of adult surveillance and extrinsic rewards on children's intrinsic motivation. *Journal of Personality and Social Psychology*, 1975, *31*, 479–486.

Lerner, M. J. Social psychology of justice and interpersonal attraction. In T. Huston (Ed.), *Perspectives on interpersonal attraction*. New York: Academic Press, 1974.

Lerner, M. J., & Miller, D. T. Just world research and the attribution process: Looking back and ahead. *Psychological Bulletin*, 1978, *85*, 1030–1051.

Lerner, M. J., Miller, D. T., & Holmes, J. G. Deserving and the emergence of forms of justice. In L. Berkowitz & E. Walster (Eds.), *Equity theory: Toward a general theory of social interaction. Advances in experimental social psychology* (Vol. 9). New York: Academic Press, 1976.

Leventhal, G. S. The distribution of rewards and resources in groups and organizations. In L. Berkowitz & E. Walster (Eds.), *Equity theory: Toward a general theory of social interaction. Advances in experimental social psychology* (Vol. 9). New York: Academic Press, 1976.

Levine, J. M. Reaction to opinion deviance in small groups. In P. B. Paulus (Ed.), *Psychology of group influence*. Hillsdale, N.J.: Erlbaum, 1980.

Levine, J. M., & Ranelli, C. J. Majority reaction to shifting and stable attitudinal deviates. *European Journal of Social Psychology*, 1978, *8*, 55–70.

Levine, J. M., & Ruback, R. B. Reaction to opinion deviance: Impact of a fence-straddler's rationale on majority evaluation. *Social Psychology Quarterly*, 1980, *43*, 73–81.

Levine, J. M., Saxe, L., & Harris, H. J. Reaction to attitudinal deviance: Impact of deviate's direction and distance of movement. *Sociometry*, 1976, *39*, 97–107.

Levine, J. M., Sroka, K. R., & Snyder, H. N. Group support and reaction to stable and shifting agreement/disagreement. *Sociometry*, 1977, *40*, 214–224.

Levine, M., Farrell, M. P., & Perrotta, P. The impact of rules of jury deliberation on group developmental processes. In B. D. Sales (Ed.), *The trial process*. New York: Plenum, 1981.

LeVine, R. A., & Campbell, D. T. *Ethnocentrism: Theories of conflict, ethnic attitudes, and group behavior*. New York: Wiley, 1972.

Lewin, K. Forces behind food habits and methods of change. *Bulletin of the National Research Council*, 1943, *108*, 35–65.

Lewin, K. *Resolving social conflicts: Selected papers on group dynamics*. New York: Harper, 1948.

Lewin, K. *Field theory in social science*. New York: Harper, 1951.

Lewin, K. Studies in group decision. In D. Cartwright & A. Zander (Eds.), *Group dynamics: Research and theory*. Evanston, Ill.: Row, Peterson, 1953.

Lewin, K., Dembo, T., Festinger, L., & Sears, P. S. Level of aspiration. In J. McV. Hunt (Ed.), *Personality and the behavior disorders*. New York: Ronald, 1944.

Lewin, K., Lippitt, R., & White, R. Patterns of aggressive behavior in experimentally created "social climates." *Journal of Social Psychology*, 1939, *10*, 271–299.

Lewis, H. S. *Leaders and followers: Some anthropological perspectives*. Reading, Mass.: Addison-Wesley, 1974.

Lewis, M., & Kreitzberg, V. S. Effects of birth order and spacing on mother-infant interactions. *Developmental Psychology*, 1979, *15*, 617–625.

Lewis, R., & St. John, N. Contribution of cross-racial friendship to minority group achievement in desegregated classrooms. *Sociometry*, 1974, *37*, 79–91.

Lewis, S. A., Lagan, C. J., & Hollander, E. P. Expectation of future interaction and the choice of less desirable alternatives in conformity. *Sociometry*, 1972, *35*, 404–447.

Ley, D., & Cybriwsky, R. Urban graffiti as territorial markers. *Annals of the Association of American Geographers*, 1974, *64*, 491–505. (a)

Ley, D., & Cybriwsky, R. The spatial ecology of stripped cars. *Environment and Behavior*, 1974, *6*, 53–68. (b)

Ley, R. Labor turnover as a function of worker differences, work environment, and authoritarianism of foremen. *Journal of Applied Psychology*, 1966, *50*, 497–500.

Lieberman, M. Change induction in small groups. *Annual Review of Psychology*, 1976, *27*, 217–250.

Lieberman, M. Group methods. In F. Kanfer & A. Goldstein (Eds.), *Helping people change*. New York: Pergamon, 1980.

Lieberman, M., & Borman, L. *Self-help groups for coping with crises*. San Francisco: Jossey-Bass, 1979.

Lieberman, M., Yalom, I., & Miles, M. *Encounter groups: First facts*. New York: Basic Books, 1973.

Likert, R. *New patterns of management*. New York: McGraw-Hill, 1961.

Likert, R. *The human organization*. New York: McGraw-Hill, 1967.

Lindblom, C. E. *The intelligence of democracy*. New York: Free Press, 1965.

Lindskold, S. Trust development, the GRIT proposal, and the effects of conciliatory acts on conflict and cooperation. *Psychological Bulletin*, 1978, *85*, 772–793.

Lindskold, S. Managing conflict through announced conciliatory initiatives backed with retaliatory capability. In W. G. Austin & S. Worchel (Eds.), *The social psychology of intergroup conflict*. Monterey, Calif.: Brooks/Cole, 1979. (a)

Lindskold, S. Conciliation with simultaneous or sequential interaction. *Journal of Conflict Resolution*, 1979, *23*, 704–714. (b)

Lindskold, S., Albert, K. P., Baer, R., & Moore, W. C. Territorial boundaries of interacting groups and passive audiences. *Sociometry*, 1976, *39*, 71–76.

Lindskold, S., & Arnoff, J. R. Conciliatory strategies and relative power. *Journal of Experimental Social Psychology*, 1980, *16*, 187–198.

Lindskold, S., & Collins, M. G. Inducing cooperation by groups and individuals. *Journal of Conflict Resolution*, 1978, *22*, 679–690.

Lindzey, G., & Borgatta, E. F. Sociometric measurement. In G. Lindzey (Ed.), *Handbook of social psychology*. Cambridge, Mass.: Addison-Wesley, 1954.

Linville, P. W., & Jones, E. E. Polarized appraisals of out-group members. *Journal of Personality and Social Psychology*, 1980, *38*, 689–703.

Lippitt, R. Kurt Lewin, 1890–1947: Adventures in the exploration of interdependence. *Sociometry*, 1947, *10*, 87–97.

Locke, E. A., Shaw, K. N., Saari, L. M., & Latham, G. P. Goal setting and task performance: 1969–1980. *Psychological Bulletin*, 1981, *90*, 125–152.

Long, G. *Cohesiveness of high school baseball teams*. Unpublished master's thesis, Southern Illinois University, 1972.

Longley, J., & Pruitt, D. G. Groupthink: A critique of Janis's theory. In L. Wheeler (Ed.), *Review of personality and social psychology* (Vol. 1). Beverly Hills, Calif.: Sage, 1980.

Lord, R. G. Functional leadership behavior: Measurement and relation to social power and leadership perceptions. *Administrative Science Quarterly*, 1977, *22*, 114–133.

Lord, R. G., Binning, J. F., Rush, M. C., & Thomas, J. C. The effect of performance cues and leader behavior on questionnaire ratings of leadership behavior. *Organizational Behavior and Human Performance*, 1978, *21*, 27–39.

Lord, R. W. *Running conventions, conferences, and meetings*. New York: AMACOM, 1981.

Lorenz, K. *On aggression*. New York: Harcourt, Brace, & World, 1966.

Lorge, I., Fox, D., Davitz, J., & Brenner, M. A survey of studies contrasting quality of group performance and individual performance, 1920–1957. *Psychological Bulletin*, 1958, *55*, 337–372.

Lorge, I., & Solomon, H. Two models of group behavior in the solution of Eureka-type problems. *Psychometrika*, 1955, *20*, 139–148.

Lott, A. J., & Lott, B. E. Group cohesiveness communication level, and conformity. *Journal of Abnormal and Social Psychology*, 1961, *62*, 408–412.

Lott, A. J., & Lott, B. E. Group cohesiveness, as interpersonal attraction: A review of relationships with antecedent and consequent variables. *Psychological Bulletin*, 1965, *64*, 259–309.

Lott, A. J., Lott, B. E., Reed, T., & Crow, T. Personality-trait descriptions of differentially liked persons. *Journal of Personality and Social Psychology*, 1970, *16*, 284–290.

Loy, J. W., McPherson, B. D., & Kenyon, G. *Sport and social systems: A guide to the analysis, problems, and literature*. Reading, Mass.: Addison-Wesley, 1978.

Luce, R. D., & Raiffa, H. *Games and decisions*. New York: Wiley, 1957.

Lyman, S. M., & Scott, M. B. Territoriality: A neglected sociological dimension. *Social Problems*, 1967, *15*, 236–249.

Mack, R. W., & Snyder, R. C. The analysis of social conflict—Toward an overview and synthesis. *Journal of Conflict Resolution*, 1957, *1*, 212–248.

MacNeil, M. K., & Sherif, M. Norm change over subject generations as a function of arbitrariness of prescribed norm. *Journal of Personality and Social Psychology*, 1976, *34*, 762–773.

McBurney, D. H., Levine, J. M., & Cavanaugh, P. H. Psychophysical and social ratings of human body odor. *Personality and Social Psychology Bulletin*, 1977, *3*, 135–138.

McCallum, R., Rusbult, C. E., Hong, G. K., Walden, T., & Schopler, J. Effects of resource availability and importance of behavior on the experience of crowding. *Journal of Personality and Social Psychology*, 1979, *37*, 1304–1313.

McClelland, D. C. *Power: The inner experience*. New York: Irvington, 1975.

McCranie, E. W., & Kimberly, J. C. Rank inconsistency, conflicting expectations, and injustice. *Sociometry*, 1973, *36*, 152–176.

McDougall, W. *An introduction to social psychology*. London: Methuen, 1908.

McGill, M. E. *Organization development for operating managers*. New York: AMACOM, 1977.

McGrath, J. E. *Social Psychology: A brief introduction*. New York: Holt, 1964.

McGregor, D. *The human side of enterprise*. New York: McGraw-Hill, 1960.

McMahon, J. T. The contingency model: Logic and method revised. *Personnel Psychology*, 1972, *25*, 697–710.

Maier, N. R. F. The quality of group decisions as influenced by the discussion leader. *Human Relations*, 1950, *3*, 155–174.

Maier, N. R. F., & Solem, A. R. The contribution of a discussion leader to the quality of group thinking: The effective use of minority opinions. *Human Relations*, 1952, *5*, 277–288.

Maki, J. E., Thorngate, W. B., & McClintock, C. G. Prediction and perception of social motives. *Journal of Personality and Social Psychology*, 1979, *37*, 203–220.

Manis, M., Cornell, S. D., & Moore, J. C. Transmission of attitude-relevant information through a communication chain. *Journal of Personality and Social Psychology*, 1974, *30*, 81–94.

Mann, F. C. Toward an understanding of the leadership role in formal organizations. In R. Dubin, G. C. Homans, F. C. Mann, & D. C. Miller (Eds.), *Leadership and productivity*. San Francisco: Chandler, 1965.

Mann, F. C., & Likert, R. The need for research on the communication of research results. *Human Organization*, 1952, 14–19.

Mann, L. Sports crowds viewed from the perspective of collective behavior. In J. H. Goldstein (Ed.), *Sports, games, and play: Social and psychological viewpoints*. Hillsdale, N.J.: Erlbaum, 1979.

Mann, L. The baiting crowd in episodes of threatened

suicide. *Journal of Personality and Social Psychology*, 1981, *41*, 703–709.

March, J. G., & Simon, H. A. *Organizations*. New York: Wiley, 1958.

Markus, H. The effect of mere presence on social facilitation: An unobtrusive test. *Journal of Experimental Social Psychology*, 1978, *14*, 389–397.

Markus, H. The drive for integration: Some comments. *Journal of Experimental Social Psychology*, 1981, *17*, 257–261.

Marquart, D. I. Group problem solving. *Journal of Social Psychology*, 1955, *41*, 103–113.

Marrow, A. J. *Behind the executive mask*. New York: American Management Association, 1964.

Marrow, A. J. *The practical theorist: The life and work of Kurt Lewin*. New York: Basic Books, 1969.

Marrow, A. J., Bowers, D. G., & Seashore, S. E. *Management by participation*. New York: Harper & Row, 1967.

Marshall, J., & Heslin, R. Boys and girls together: Sexual composition and the effect of density and group size on cohesiveness. *Journal of Personality and Social Psychology*, 1975, *31*, 952–961.

Martens, R., & Landers, D. M. Evaluation potential as a determinant of coaction effects. *Journal of Experimental Social Psychology*, 1972, *8*, 347–359.

Martens, R., Landers, D. M., & Loy, J. *Sports cohesiveness questionnaire*. American Association of Health, Physical Education, and Recreation, 1972.

Martin, E. D. *The behavior of crowds*. New York: Harper, 1920.

Martin, J., Lobb, B., Chapman, G. C., & Spillane, R. Obedience under conditions demanding self-immolation. *Human Relations*, 1976, *29*, 345–356.

Martyniuk, O., Flynn, J. E., Spencer, T. J., & Hendrick, C. Effect of environmental lighting on impression and behavior. In R. Kuller (Ed.), *Architectural psychology: Proceedings of the Lund conference*. Stroudsburg, Penn.: Dowden, Hutchinson, & Ross, 1973.

Marx, C., & Engels, F. *The German ideology*. New York: International Publishers, 1947.

Maslach, C. Social and personal bases of individuation. *Proceedings of the 80th Annual Convention of the American Psychological Association*, 1972, *7*, 213–214.

Maslow, A. H. *Toward a psychology of being*. New York: Van Nostrand Reinhold, 1968.

Mathes, E. W., & Kahn, A. Diffusion of responsibility and extreme behavior. *Journal of Personality and Social Psychology*, 1975, *5*, 881–886.

Mathes, E. W., & Guest, T. A. Anonymity and group antisocial behavior. *Journal of Social Psychology*, 1976, *100*, 257–262.

MaWhinney, T. C., & Ford, J. D. The path goal theory of leader effectiveness: An operant interpretation.

Academy of Management Review, 1977, *2*, 398–411.

Mayer, T. *Mathematical models of group structure*. New York: Bobbs-Merrill, 1975.

Mayo, E. *The human problems of an industrial civilization*. Cambridge, Mass.: Harvard University Press, 1933.

Mayo, E. *The social problems of an industrial civilization*. Cambridge, Mass.: Harvard University Press, 1945.

Meadow, A., Parnes, S. J., & Reese, H. Influence of brainstorming instructions and problem sequence on a creative problem solving test. *Journal of Applied Psychology*, 1959, *43*, 413–416.

Medalia, N. Z., & Larsen, O. N. Diffusion and belief in a collective delusion: The Seattle windshield pitting epidemic. *American Sociological Review*, 1958, *23*, 180–186.

Meerloo, J. A. *Patterns of panic*. New York: International Universities Press, 1950.

Mehrabian, A., & Diamond, S. G. Effects of furniture arrangement, props, and personality on social interaction. *Journal of Personality and Social Psychology*, 1971, *20*, 18–30.

Meichenbaum, D. H., Bowers, K. S., & Ross, R. R. A behavioral analysis of teacher expectancy effect. *Journal of Personality and Social Psychology*, 1969, *13*, 306–316.

Meltzer, B. N., Petras, J. W., & Reynolds, L. T. *Symbolic interactionism: Genesis, varieties, and criticism*. Boston: Routledge & Kegan Paul, 1975.

Merei, F. Group leadership and institutionalization. In E. E. Maccoby, T. M. Newcomb, & E. L. Hartley (Eds.), *Readings in social psychology* (3rd ed.). New York: Holt, Rinehart, & Winston, 1958.

Messé, L. A., Stollak, G. E., Larson, R. W., & Michaels, G. Y. Interpersonal consequences of person perception in two social contexts. *Journal of Personality and Social Psychology*, 1979, *37*, 369–379.

Mettee, D. R., & Aronson, E. Affective reactions to appraisal from others. In T. Huston (Ed.), *Foundations of interpersonal attraction*. New York: Academic Press, 1974.

Mettee, D. R., & Wilkins, P. C. When similarity "hurts": The effects of perceived ability and a humorous blunder upon interpersonal attractiveness. *Journal of Personality and Social Psychology*, 1972, *22*, 246–258.

Meumann, E. Haus- und Schularbeit: Experimente an Kindern der Volkschule. *Die Deutsche Schule*, 1904, *8*, 278–303, 337–359, 416–431.

Meuwese, W., & Fiedler, F. E. *Leadership and group creativity under varying conditions of stress*. Urbana, Ill.: University of Illinois, Group Effectiveness Research Laboratory, 1965.

Michener, J. A. *Sports in America*. New York: Random House, 1976.

Middlemist, R. D., Knowles, E. S., & Matter, C. F. Personal space invasions in the lavatory: Suggestive evidence for arousal. *Journal of Personality and Social Psychology*, 1976, *33*, 541–546.

Milburn, T. W. The nature of threat. *Journal of Social Issues*, 1977, *33*(1), 126–139.

Miles, R. H. A comparison of the relative impacts of role perceptions of ambiguity and conflict by role. *Academy of Management Journal*, 1976, *19*, 25–35.

Milgram, S. Behavioral study of obedience. *Journal of Abnormal and Social Psychology*, 1963, *67*, 371–378.

Milgram, S. Issues in the study of obedience: A reply to Baumrind. *American Psychologist*, 1964, *19*, 848–852.

Milgram, S. Liberating effects of group pressure. *Journal of Personality and Social Psychology*, 1965, *1*, 127–134.

Milgram, S. The experience of living in cities. *Science*, 1970, *167*, 1461–1468.

Milgram, S. *Obedience to authority*. New York: Harper & Row, 1974.

Milgram, S. Subject reaction: The neglected factor in the ethics of experimentation. *Hastings Center Report*, October, 1977, 19–23.

Milgram, S., Bickman, L., & Berkowitz, L. Note on the drawing power of crowds of different size. *Journal of Personality and Social Psychology*, 1969, *13*, 79–82.

Milgram, S., & Toch, H. Collective behavior: Crowds and social movements. In G. Lindzey & E. Aronson (Eds.), *The handbook of social psychology* (Vol. 4, 2nd ed.). Reading, Mass.: Addison-Wesley, 1969.

Miller, C. E. A test of four theories of coalition formation: Effects of payoffs and resources. *Journal of Personality and Social Psychology*, 1980, *38*, 153–164. (a)

Miller, C. E. Coalition formation in characteristic function games: Competitive tests of three theories. *Journal of Experimental Social Psychology*, 1980, *16*, 61–76. (b)

Miller, C. E. Effects of payoffs on coalition formation: A test of three theories. *Social Psychology Quarterly*, 1980, *43*, 154–164. (c)

Miller, C. E., & Crandall, R. Experimental research on the social psychology of bargaining and coalition formation. In P. B. Paulus (Ed.), *Psychology of group influence*. Hillsdale, N.J.: Erlbaum, 1980.

Miller, D. T., & Holmes, J. G. The role of situational restrictiveness on self-fulfilling prophecies: A theoretical and empirical extension of Kelley and Stahelski's triangle hypothesis. *Journal of Personality and Social Psychology*, 1975, *31*, 661–673.

Miller, D. T., & Norman, S. A. Actor-observer differences in perceptions of effective control. *Journal of Personality and Social Psychology*, 1975, *31*, 503–515.

Miller, J. G. *Living systems*. New York: McGraw-Hill, 1978.

Miller, N. A questionnaire in search of a theory. In L. Berkowitz (Ed.), *Group processes*. New York: Academic Press, 1978.

Miller, R. L., Brickman, P., & Bolen, D. Attribution versus persuasion as a means of modifying behavior. *Journal of Personality and Social Psychology*, 1975, *31*, 430–441.

Millman, J., & Johnson, M., Jr. Relation of section variance to achievement gains in English and mathematics in grades 7 and 8. *American Educational Research Journal*, 1964, *1*, 47–51.

Mills, T. M. A sleeper variable in small groups research: The experimenter. *Pacific Sociological Review*, 1962, *5*, 21–28.

Mills, T. M. Review symposium on Bales (1970). *American Sociological Review*, 1971, *36*, 115–119.

Miner, J. B. The uncertain future of the leadership concept: An overview. In J. G. Hunt & L. Larson (Eds.), *Leadership frontiers*. Kent, Oh.: Kent State University Press, 1975.

Mobley, W. H., Griffeth, R. W., Hand, H. H., & Meglino, B. M. Review and conceptual analysis of employee turnover process. *Psychological Bulletin*, 1979, *86*, 493–522.

Moede, W. Die Richtlinien der Leistungs-Psychologie. *Industrielle Psychotechnik*, 1927, *4*, 193–207.

Moore, L. E. *The jury*. Cincinnati: W. H. Anderson, 1973.

Moos, R. H., & Humphrey, B. *Group environment scale, Form R*. Palo Alto, Calif.: Consulting Psychologists Press, 1974.

Moos, R. H., Insel, P. M., & Humphrey, B. *Preliminary manual for family environment scale, work environment scale, and group environment scale*. Palo Alto, Calif.: Consulting Psychologists Press, 1974.

Moreland, R. L., & Zajonc, R. B. Exposure effects may not depend on stimulus recognition. *Journal of Personality and Social Psychology*, 1979, *37*, 1084–1089.

Moreno, J. L. *Who shall survive?* (rev. ed.). Beacon, New York: Beacon House, 1953.

Moreno, J. L. (Ed.). *The sociometry reader*. Glencoe, New York: Free Press, 1960.

Moreno, J. L. The Viennese origins of the encounter movement, paving the way for existentialism, group psychotherapy, and psychodrama. *Group Psychotherapy*, 1970, *22*, 7–16.

Moriarty, T. Role of stigma in the experience of deviance. *Journal of Personality and Social Psychology*, 1974, *29*, 849–855.

Morris, W. N., & Miller, R. S. The effects of consensus-breaking and consensus-preempting partners on reduction of conformity. *Journal of Experimental Social Psychology*, 1975, *11*, 215–223. (a)

Morris, W. N., & Miller, R. S. Impressions of dissenters and conformers: An attributional analysis. *Sociometry*, 1975, *38*, 327–339. (b)

Morris, W. N., Worchel, S., Bois, J. L., Pearson, J. A., Rountree, C. A., Samaha, G. M., Wachtler, J., & Wright, S. L. Collective coping with stress: Group reactions to fear, anxiety, and ambiguity. *Journal of Personality and Social Psychology*, 1976, *33*, 674–679.

Morse, N. C., & Reimer, E. The experimental change of a major organizational variable. *Journal of Abnormal and Social Psychology*, 1956, *52*, 120–129.

Moscovici, S. *Social influence and social change*. London: Academic Press, 1976.

Moscovici, S., & Faucheux, C. Social influence, conformity bias, and the study of active minorities. In L. Berkowitz (Ed.), *Advances in experimental social psychology* (Vol. 6). New York: Academic Press, 1972.

Moscovici, S., & Lage, E. Studies in social influence. III. Majority versus minority influence in a group. *European Journal of Social Psychology*, 1976, *6*, 149–174.

Moscovici, S., & Personnaz, B. Studies in social influence. V. Minority influence and conversion behavior in a perceptual task. *Journal of Experimental Social Psychology*, 1980, *16*, 270–282.

Moscovici, S., & Zavalloni, M. The group as a polarizer of attitudes. *Journal of Personality and Social Psychology*, 1969, *12*, 125–135.

Moxley, R. L., & Moxley, N. F. Determining point centrality in uncontrived social networks. *Sociometry*, 1974, *37*, 122–130.

Mudd, S. A. Group sanction severity as a function of degree of behavior deviation and relevance of norm. *Journal of Personality and Social Psychology*, 1968, *8*, 258–260.

Mulder, M., & Stemerding, A. Threat, attraction to group, and need for strong leadership. *Human Relations*, 1963, *16*, 317–334.

Mulder, M., Van Kijk, R., Soutenkijk, S., Stelwagen, T., & Verhagen, J. Non-instrumental liking tendencies toward powerful group members. *Acta Psychologica*, 1964, *22*, 367–386.

Murnighan, J. K. Models of coalition formation: Game theoretic, social psychological, and political perspectives. *Psychological Bulletin*, 1978, *85*, 1130–1153.

Murnighan, J. K., Komorita, S. S., & Szwajkowski, E. Theories of coalition formation and the effects of reference groups. *Journal of Experimental Social Psychology*, 1977, *13*, 166–181.

Murray, H. A. *Explorations in personality*. New York: Oxford, 1938.

Myers, D. G. The polarizing effects of social comparison. *Journal of Experimental Social Psychology*, 1978, *14*, 554–563.

Myers, D. G. Polarizing effects of social interaction. In H. Brandstätter, J. H. Davis, & G. Stocker-Kreichgauer (Eds.), *Group decision making*. New York: Academic Press, 1982.

Myers, D. G., Bruggink, J. B., Kersting, R. C., & Schlosser, B. A. Does learning others' opinions change one's opinions? *Personality and Social Psychology Bulletin*, 1980, *6*, 253–260.

Myers, D. G., & Kaplan, M. F. Group induced polarization in simulated juries. *Personality and Social Psychology Bulletin*, 1976, *2*, 63–66.

Myers, D. G., & Lamm, H. The polarizing effect of group discussion. *American Scientist*, 1975, *63*, 297–303.

Myers, D. G., & Lamm, H. The group polarization phenomenon. *Psychological Bulletin*, 1976, *83*, 602–627.

Nachmias, D. Coalition politics in Israel. *Comparative Political Studies*, 1974, *7*, 316–333.

Nadler, L., & Nadler, Z. *The conference book*. New York: Gulf, 1980.

Napier, R. W., & Gershenfeld, M. K. *Groups: Theory and experience*. Boston: Houghton Mifflin, 1981.

NCSC (National Center for State Courts). *Facets of the jury system: A survey*. Denver, Co.: Research and Information Service, NCSC, 1976.

Nemeth, C., Endicott, J., & Wachtler, J. From the '50s to the '70s: Women in jury deliberations. *Sociometry*, 1976, *39*, 293–304.

Nemeth, C., & Wachtler, J. Creating the perceptions of consistency and confidence: A necessary condition for minority influence. *Sociometry*, 1974, *37*, 529–540.

Newcomb, T. M. *Personality and social change*. New York: Dryden, 1943.

Newcomb, T. M. The prediction of interpersonal attraction. *American Psychologist*, 1956, *11*, 575–586.

Newcomb, T. M. Varieties of interpersonal attraction. In D. Cartwright & A. Zander (Eds.), *Group dynamics: Research and theory* (2nd ed.). Evanston, Ill.: Row, Peterson, 1960.

Newcomb, T. M. *The acquaintance process*. New York: Holt, Rinehart & Winston, 1961.

Newcomb, T. M. Stabilities underlying changes in interpersonal attraction. *Journal of Abnormal and Social Psychology*, 1963, *66*, 376–386.

Newcomb, T. M. Individual and group. *American Behavioral Scientist*, 1978, *5*, 631–650.

Newcomb, T. M. Reciprocity of interpersonal attraction: A nonconfirmation of a plausible hypothesis. *Social Psychology Quarterly*, 1979, *42*, 299–306.

Newcomb, T. M. Heiderian balance as a group phenomenon. *Journal of Personality and Social Psychology*, 1981, *40*, 862–867.

Newcomb, T. M., Koenig, K., Flacks, R., & Warwick, D. *Persistence and change: Bennington College and its students after 25 years*. New York: Wiley, 1967.

Newton, J. W., & Mann, L. Crowd size as a factor in the persuasion process: A study of religious crusade meetings. *Journal of Personality and Social Psychology*, 1980, *39*, 874–883.

Nixon, H. L., II. *Sport and social organization*. Indianapolis: Bobbs-Merrill, 1976.

Nord, W. R. Social exchange theory: An integrative approach to social conformity. *Psychological Bulletin*, 1969, *71*, 174–208.

Nordholm, L. A. Effects of group size and stimulus ambiguity on conformity. *Journal of Social Psychology*, 1975, *97*, 123–130.

North, R. C., Brody, R. A., & Holsti, O. R. Some empirical data on the conflict spiral. *Peace Research Society International Papers*, 1964, *1*, 1–14.

Northway, M. L. *A primer of sociometry* (2nd ed.). Toronto: University of Toronto Press, 1967.

Ofshe, R., & Lee, M. T. Reply to Greenstein. *Social Psychology Quarterly*, 1981, *44*, 383–385.

Orcutt, J. D. Societal reaction and the response to deviation in small groups. *Social Forces*, 1973, *52*, 261–267.

Orne, M. T., & Evans, F. J. Social control in the psychological experiment: Antisocial behavior and hypnosis. *Journal of Personality and Social Psychology*, 1965, *1*, 189–200.

Orne, M. T., & Holland, C. H. On the ecological validity of laboratory deceptions. *International Journal of Psychiatry*, 1968, *6*, 282–293.

Orvis, B. B., Kelley, H. H., & Butler, D. Attributional conflict in young couples. In J. H. Harvey, W. J. Ickes, & R. E. Kidd (Eds.), *New directions in attribution research* (Vol. 1). Hillsdale, N.J.: Erlbaum, 1976.

Osborn, A. F. *Applied imagination*. New York: Scribner, 1957.

Osgood, C. E. GRIT for MBFR: A proposal for unfreezing force-level postures in Europe. *Peace Research Reviews*, 1979, *8*(2), 77–92.

Oskamp, S., & Hartry, A. A factor-analytic study of the double standard in attitudes toward U.S. and Russian actions. *Behavioral Science*, 1968, *13*, 178–188.

Padawer-Singer, A. M., Singer, A. N., Singer, R. L. J. An experimental study of twelve vs. six member juries under unanimous vs. nonunanimous decisions. In B. D. Sales (Ed.), *Psychology in the legal process*. New York: Spectrum, 1977.

Park, R. E., & Burgess, E. W. *Introduction to the science of sociology*. Chicago: University of Chicago Press, 1921.

Parkinson, C. N. *Parkinson's law and other studies in administration*. Boston: Houghton Mifflin, 1957.

Palmer, G. J. Task ability and effective leadership. *Psychological Reports*, 1962, *10*, 863–866.

Parloff, M. Can psychotherapy research guide the policy maker? *American Psychologist*, 1979, *34*, 296–306.

Parloff, M., & Dies, R. Group psychotherapy outcome research 1966–1975. *International Journal of Group Psychotherapy*, 1977, *27*, 281–319.

Parloff, M., & Dies, R. Group therapy outcome instrument: Guidelines for conducting research. *Small Group Behavior*, 1978, *9*, 243–285.

Parsons, H. M. Work environments. In I. Altman & J. Wohlwill (Eds.), *Human behavior and environment* (Vol. 1). New York: Plenum, 1976.

Parsons, T. On the concept of influence. *Public Opinion Quarterly*, 1962, *27*, 37–63.

Parsons, T., Bales, R. F., & Shils, E. *Working papers in the theory of action*. New York: Free Press, 1953.

Patten, S. C. Milgram's shocking experiments. *Philosophy*, 1977, *52*, 425–440.

Patterson, M. L. Compensation in nonverbal immediacy behaviors: A review. *Sociometry*, 1973, *36*, 237–252.

Patterson, M. L. Personal space—Time to burst the bubble? *Man-Environment Systems*, 1975, *5*, 67.

Patterson, M. L. An arousal model of interpersonal intimacy. *Psychological Review*, 1976, *83*, 235–245.

Patterson, M. L., Kelley, C. E., Kondracki, B. A., & Wulf, L. J. Effects of seating arrangement on small group behavior. *Social Psychology Quarterly*, 1979, *42*, 180–185.

Patterson, M. L., Roth, C. P., & Schenk, C. Seating arrangement, activity, and sex differences in small group crowding. *Personality and Social Psychology Bulletin*, 1979, *5*, 100–103.

Patterson, M. L., & Sechrest, L. B. Interpersonal distance and impression formation. *Journal of Personality*, 1970, *38*, 161–166.

Paulus, P. B. Crowding. In P. B. Paulus (Ed.), *Psychology of group influence*. Hillsdale, N.J.: Erlbaum, 1980.

Paulus, P. B., Annis, A. B., Seta, J. J., Schkade, J. K., & Matthews, R. W. Density does affect task performance. *Journal of Personality and Social Psychology*, 1976, *34*, 248–353.

Penrod, S., & Hastie, R. Models of jury decision making: A critical review. *Psychological Bulletin*, 1979, *86*, 462–492.

Penrod, S., & Hastie, R. A computer simulation of jury decision making. *Psychological Review*, 1980, *87*, 133–159.

Pepitone, A. Lessons from the history of social psychology. *American Psychologist*, 1981, *36*, 972–985.

Pepitone, A., & Kleiner, R. The effects of threat and frustration on group cohesiveness. *Journal of Abnormal and Social Psychology*, 1957, *54*, 192–199.

Pepitone, A., & Reichling, G. Group cohesiveness and the expression of hostility. *Human Relations*, 1955, *8*, 327–337.

Pepitone, A., & Wilpinski, C. Some consequences of experimental rejection. *Journal of Abnormal and Social Psychology*, 1960, *60*, 359–364.

Percival, L. *The coach from the athlete's viewpoint*. Toronto: Fitness Institute, 1971.

Perls, F. *Gestalt therapy verbatim*. Lafayette, Calif.: Real People Press, 1969.

Pessin, J. The comparative effects of social and mechanical stimulation on memorizing. *American Journal of Psychology*, 1933, *45*, 263–270.

Petty, R. E., Harkins, S. G., & Williams, K. D. The effects of group diffusion of cognitive effort on attitudes: An information-processing view. *Journal of Personality and Social Psychology*, 1980, *38*, 81–92.

Pfeffer, J. The ambiguity of leadership. *Academy of Management Review*, 1977, *2*, 104–112.

Philipsen, G., Mulac, A., & Dietrich, D. The effects of social interaction on group idea generation. *Communication Monographs*, 1979, *46*, 119–125.

Phillips, G. M. *Communication and the small group*. New York: Bobbs-Merrill, 1973.

Pigors, P. *Leadership or domination*. Boston: Houghton Mifflin, 1935.

Pinder, C. C. Concerning the application of human motivation theories in organizational settings. *Academy of Management Review*, 1977, *2*, 384–397.

Platt, J. Social traps. *American Psychologist*, 1973, *28*, 641–651.

Polivy, J., Hackett, R., & Bycio, P. The effect of perceived smoking status on attractiveness. *Personality and Social Psychology Bulletin*, 1979, *5*, 401–404.

Pollard, W. E., & Mitchell, T. R. A decision theory analysis of social power. *Psychological Bulletin*, 1973, *78*, 433–446.

Pollis, N. P., Montgomery, R. L., & Smith, T. G. Autokinetic paradigms: A reply to Alexander, Zucker, and Brody. *Sociometry*, 1975, *38*, 358–373.

Popham, W. J. The case for criterion-referenced measurements. *Review of Educational Research*, 1978, *48*, 6–10.

Porter, L. W., & Steers, R. M. Organizational, work, and personal factors in employee turnover and absenteeism. *Psychological Bulletin*, 1973, *80*, 151–176.

Potter, D., & Andersen, M. P. *Discussion in small groups: A guide to effective practice*. Belmont, Calif.: Wadsworth, 1976.

Prentice-Dunn, S., & Rogers, R. W. Effects of deindividuating situation cues and aggressive models on subjective deindividuation and aggression. *Journal of Personality and Social Psychology*, 1980, *39*, 104–113.

Prince, G. *The practice of creativity*. New York: Harper & Row, 1970.

Prince, G. The mind spring theory. *Journal of Creative Behavior*, 1975, *9*(3), 159–181.

Pruitt, D. G. Reciprocity and credit building in a laboratory dyad. *Journal of Personality and Social Psychology*, 1968, *8*, 143–147.

Pruitt, D. G. Choice shifts in group discussion: An introductory review. *Journal of Personality and Social Psychology*, 1971, *20*, 339–360. (a)

Pruitt, D. G. Conclusions: Toward an understanding of choice shifts in group discussion. *Journal of Personality and Social Psychology*, 1971, *20*, 495–510. (b)

Pruitt, D. G. *Negotiation behavior*. New York: Academic Press, 1981.

Pruitt, D. G., & Johnson, D. F. Mediation as an aid to face saving in negotiation. *Journal of Personality and Social Psychology*, 1970, *14*, 239–246.

Quadagno, J. S. Paradigms on evolutionary theory: The sociobiological model of natural selection. *American Sociological Review*, 1979, *44*, 100–109.

Quattrone, G. A., & Jones, E. E. The perception of variability within in-groups and out-groups: Implications for the law of small numbers. *Journal of Personality and Social Psychology*, 1980, *38*, 141–152.

Raven, B. H., & Kruglanski, A. W. Conflict and power. In P. Swingle (Ed.), *The structure of conflict*. New York: Academic Press, 1970.

Raven, B. H., & Rubin, J. Z. *Social psychology: People in groups*. New York: Wiley, 1976.

Read, P. P. *Alive*. New York: Avon, 1974.

Reckman, R. F., & Goethals, G. R. Deviancy and group orientation as determinants of group composition preferences. *Sociometry*, 1973, *36*, 419–423.

Redl, F. Group emotion and leaders. *Psychiatry*, 1942, *5*, 573–596.

Regan, D. T., & Totten, J. Empathy and attribution: Turning observers into actors. *Journal of Personality and Social Psychology*, 1975, *32*, 850–856.

Regan, J. W. Liking for evaluators: Consistency and self-esteem theories. *Journal of Experimental Social Psychology*, 1976, *12*, 159–169.

Reis, H. T., Earing, B., Kent, A., & Nezlek, J. The tyranny of numbers: Does group size affect petition

signing? *Journal of Applied Social Psychology*, 1976, *6*, 228–234.

Reynolds, P. D. *Ethical dilemmas and social science research*. San Francisco: Jossey-Bass, 1979.

Rice, O. K. *The Hatfields and the McCoys*. Lexington, Ky.: University Press of Kentucky, 1978.

Rice, R. W. Psychometric properties of the Esteem for Least Preferred Co-worker (LPC) Scale. *Academy of Management Review*, 1978, *3*, 106–118. (a)

Rice, R. W. Construct validity of the Least Preferred Co-worker (LPC) score. *Psychological Bulletin*, 1978, *85*, 1199–1237. (b)

Rice, R. W. Reliability and validity of the LPC scale: A reply. *Academy of Management Review*, 1979, *4*, 291–294.

Rich, A., & Schroeder, H. Research issues in assertiveness training. *Psychological Bulletin*, 1976, *83*, 1081–1096.

Rickards, T. *Problem solving through creative analysis*. London: Halsted Press, 1974.

Ridgeway, C. L. Conformity, group-oriented motivation, and status attainment in small groups. *Social Psychology*, 1978, *41*, 175–188.

Riess, M., Forsyth, D. R. Schlenker, B. R., & Freed, S. Opinion conformity as an impression management tactic following commitment to unpleasant behaviors. *Bulletin of the Psychonomic Society*, 1977, *9*, 211–213.

Riker, W. H. *The theory of political coalitions*. New Haven, Conn.: Yale University Press, 1962.

Rimm, D. C., & Masters, J. C. *Behavior therapy: Techniques and empirical findings*. New York: Academic Press, 1974.

Ringer, R. J. *Winning through intimidation*. Greenwich, Conn.: Fawcett, 1973.

Rodin, J. Crowding, perceived choice, and response to controllable and uncontrollable outcomes. *Journal of Experimental Social Psychology*, 1976, *12*, 564–578.

Rodin, J., & Baum, A. Crowding and helplessness: Potential consequences of density and loss of control. In A. Baum & Y. Epstein (Eds.), *Human responses to crowding*. Hillsdale, N.J.: Erlbaum, 1978.

Rodin, J., Solomon, S. K., & Metcalf, J. Role of control in mediating perceptions of density. *Journal of Personality and Social Psychology*, 1978, *36*, 988–999.

Roethlisberger, F. J., & Dickson, W. J. *Management and the worker*. Cambridge, Mass.: Harvard University Press, 1939.

Rogers, C. *Encounter groups*. New York: Harper & Row, 1970.

Rogers, W. R., & Prentice-Dunn, S. Deindividuation and anger-mediated interracial aggression: Unmasking regressive racism. *Journal of Personality and Social Psychology*, 1981, *41*, 63–73.

Roos, P. D. Jurisdiction: An ecological concept. *Human Relations*, 1968, *21*, 75–84.

Rose, S. *Group therapy: A behavioral approach.* Englewood Cliffs, N.J.: Prentice-Hall, 1977.

Rosenberg, S. W., & Wolfsfeld, G. International conflict and the problem of attribution. *Journal of Conflict Resolution*, 1977, *21*, 75–103.

Rosenthal, R., & Jacobson, L. *Pygmalion in the classroom.* New York: Holt, Rinehart, & Winston, 1968.

Ross, L. The intuitive psychologist and his shortcomings: Distortions in the attribution process. In L. Berkowitz (Ed.), *Advances in experimental social psychology* (Vol. 10). New York: Academic Press, 1977.

Ross, L., Bierbrauer, G., & Hoffman, S. The role of attribution processes in conformity and dissent: Revisiting the Asch situation. *American Psychologist*, 1976, *31*, 148–157.

Ross, M., Layton, B., Erickson, B., & Schopler, J. Affect, facial regard, and reactions to crowding. *Journal of Personality and Social Psychology*, 1973, *28*, 69–76.

Rothbart, M., Evans, M., & Fulero, S. Recall for confirming events: Memory processes and the maintenance of social stereotypes. *Journal of Experimental Social Psychology*, 1979, *15*, 343–355.

Rothbart, M., Fulero, S., Jensen, C., Howard, J., & Birrell, P. From individual to group impressions: Availability heuristics in stereotype formation. *Journal of Experimental Social Psychology*, 1978, *14*, 237–255.

Rotter, J. B. Trust and gullibility. *Psychology Today*, 1980, *14*(1), 35–36, 38, 40–41, 102.

Roy, D. F. "Banana time"—Job satisfaction and informal interaction. In W. G. Bennis, D. E. Berlew, E. H. Schein, & F. I. Steele (Eds.), *Interpersonal dynamics.* Homewood, Ill.: Dorsey Press, 1973.

Rubin, J. Z. Experimental research on third-party intervention in conflict: Toward some generalizations. *Psychological Bulletin*, 1980, *87*, 379–391.

Rubin, J. Z., & Brown, B. R. *The social psychology of bargaining and negotiation.* New York: Academic Press, 1975.

Rule, B. G., & Nesdale, A. R. Emotional arousal and aggressive behavior. *Psychological Bulletin*, 1976, *83*, 851–863.

Rush, M. C., Thomas, J. C., & Lord, R. G. Implicit leadership theory: A potential threat to the internal validity of the leader behavior questionnaires. *Organizational Behavior and Human Performance*, 1977, *20*, 93–110.

Russell, B. *Power.* London: George Allen & Unwyn, 1938.

Rutherford, W. L. *Team teaching—how do teachers use it?* Austin, Tex.: Research and Development Center for Teacher Education, University of Texas at Austin, 1975.

Ryans, D. G. A study of criterion data. *Educational and Psychological Measurement*, 1952, *12*, 333–344.

Ryen, A. H., & Kahn, A. Own-group bias: The effects of individual competence and group outcome. *Proceedings of the Iowa Academy of Science*, 1970, *77*, 302–307.

Ryen, A. H., & Kahn, A. The effects of intergroup orientation on group attitudes and proxemic behavior: A test of two models. *Journal of Personality and Social Psychology*, 1975, *31*, 302–310.

Sackman, H. *Delphi critique.* Lexington, Ma.: Lexington Books, 1975.

Saegart, S. High-density environments: Their personal and social consequences. In A. Baum & Y. M. Epstein (Eds.), *Human response to crowding.* Hillsdale, N.J.: Erlbaum, 1978.

Saegert, S., Swap, W., & Zajonc, R. B. Exposure, context, and interpersonal attraction. *Journal of Personality and Social Psychology*, 1973, *25*, 234–242.

Safer, M. A. Attributing evil to the subject, not the situation. *Personality and Social Psychology Bulletin*, 1980, *6*, 205–209.

Saks, M. J. *Jury verdicts.* Lexington, Ma.: D. C. Heath & Co., 1977.

Saks, M. J., & Hastie, R. *Social psychology in court.* New York: Van Nostrand Reinhold, 1978.

Sakurai, M. M. Small group cohesiveness and detrimental conformity. *Sociometry*, 1975, *38*, 340–357.

Salinger, P. *With Kennedy.* New York: Avon Books, 1966.

Sampson, E. E. *Social psychology and contemporary society.* New York: Wiley, 1971.

Sampson, E. E., & Brandon, A. C. The effects of role and opinion-deviation on small group behavior. *Sociometry*, 1964, *27*, 261–281.

Sampson, R. V. *Equality and power.* London: Heinemann, 1965.

Sanders, G. S. Driven by distraction: An integrative review of social facilitation theory and research. *Journal of Experimental Social Psychology*, 1981, *17*, 227–251. (a)

Sanders, G. S. Toward a comprehensive account of social facilitation: Distraction/conflict does not mean theoretical conflict. *Journal of Experimental Social Psychology*, 1981, *17*, 262–265. (b)

Sanders, G. S., & Baron, R. S. The motivating effects of distraction on task performance. *Journal of Personality and Social Psychology*, 1975, *32*, 956–963.

Sanders, G. S., & Baron, R. S. Is social comparison irrelevant for producing choice shifts? *Journal of Experimental Social Psychology*, 1977, *13*, 303–314.

Sanders, G. S., Baron, R. S., & Moore, D. L. Distraction and social comparison as mediators of social facilitation effects. *Journal of Experimental Social Psychology*, 1978, *14*, 291–303.

Sarbin, T. R., & Allen, V. L. Role theory. In G. Lindzey & E. Aronson (Eds.), *Handbook of social psychology* (Vol. 1, 2nd ed.). Reading, Ma.: Addison-Wesley, 1968.

Sarnoff, I., & Zimbardo, P. G. Anxiety, fear, and social affiliation. *Journal of Abnormal and Social Psychology*, 1961, *62*, 356–363.

Sasfy, J., & Okun, M. Form of evaluation and audience expertness as joint determinants of audience effects. *Journal of Experimental Social Psychology*, 1974, *10*, 461–467.

Schachter, S. Deviation, rejection, and communication. *Journal of Abnormal and Social Psychology*, 1951, *46*, 190–207.

Schachter, S. *The psychology of affiliation*. Palo Alto, Calif.: Stanford University Press, 1959.

Schachter, S., Ellertson, N., McBride, D., & Gregory, D. An experimental study of cohesiveness and productivity. *Human Relations*, 1951, *4*, 229–238.

Schachter, S., & Singer, J. Cognitive, social, and physiological determinants of emotional state. *Psychological Review*, 1962, *69*, 379–399.

Schachter, S., & Singer, J. E. Comments on the Maslach and Marshall-Zimbardo experiments. *Journal of Personality and Social Psychology*, 1980, *37*, 989–995.

Scheier, M. F., Carver, C. S., & Gibbons, F. X. Self-directed attention, awareness of bodily states, and suggestibility. *Journal of Personality and Social Psychology*, 1979, *37*, 1576–1588.

Schein, E. H. *Process consultation: Its role in organization development*. Reading, Mass.: Addison-Wesley, 1971.

Schellenberg, J. A. *Masters of social psychology*. New York: Oxford, 1978.

Schelling, T. C. *The strategy of conflict*. Cambridge, Mass.: Harvard University Press, 1960.

Schervish, P. The labeling perspective: Its bias and potential in the study of political deviance. *American Sociologist*, 1973, *8*, 47–57.

Schlenker, B. R. Liking for a group following an initiation: Impression management or dissonance reduction? *Sociometry*, 1975, *38*, 99–118.

Schlenker, B. R. *Impression management*. Monterey, Calif.: Brooks/Cole, 1980.

Schlenker, B. R., & Forsyth, D. R. On the ethics of psychological research. *Journal of Experimental Social Psychology*, 1977, *13*, 369–396.

Schlenker, B. R., & Goldman, H. J. Cooperators and competitors in conflict: A test of the "triangle model." *Journal of Conflict Resolution*, 1978, *22*, 393–410.

Schlenker, B. R., Nacci, P., Helm, B., & Tedeschi, J. T. Reactions to coercive and reward power: The effects of switching influence modes on target compliance. *Sociometry*, 1976, *39*, 316–323.

Schlesinger, A. M., Jr. *A thousand days*. Boston: Houghton Mifflin, 1965.

Schmidt, D. E., & Keating, J. P. Human crowding and personal control: An integration of the research. *Psychological Bulletin*, 1979, *86*, 680–700.

Schmitt, D. R. Performance under cooperation or competition. *American Behavioral Scientist*, 1981, *24*, 649–679.

Schmuck, R. A., & Schmuck, P. A. *Group process in the classroom* (3rd ed.). Dubuque, Iowa: William C. Brown, 1979.

Schneier, C. E. The contingency model of leadership: An extension to emergent leadership and leader's sex. *Organizational Behavior and Human Performance*, 1978, *21*, 220–239.

Schönbach, P. A category system for account phrases. *European Journal of Social Psychology*, 1980, *10*, 195–200.

Schriesheim, C. A., Bannister, B. D., & Money, W. H. Psychometric properties of the LPC Scale: An extension of Rice's review. *Academy of Management Review*, 1979, *4*, 287–290.

Schriesheim, C. A., & Kerr, S. Theories and measures of leadership: A critical appraisal of current and future directions. In J. G. Hunt and L. L. Larson (Eds.), *Leadership: The cutting edge*. Carbondale, Ill.: Southern Illinois University Press, 1977.

Schutz, W. C. *FIRO: A three-dimensional theory of interpersonal behavior*. New York: Rinehart & Co., Inc., 1958.

Schutz, W. C. *Joy: Expanding human awareness*. New York: Grove, 1967.

Schwartz, M. S., & Schwartz, C. G. Problems in participant observation. *American Journal of Sociology*, 1955, *60*, 343–354.

Scott, J. P. Biological and psychological bases of social attachment. In H. Kellerman (Ed.), *Group cohesion*. New York: Grune & Stratton, 1981.

Scott, J. W. Mating behavior of the sage grouse. *Auk*, 1942, *59*, 477–498.

Scott, M. B., & Lyman, S. M. Accounts. *American Sociological Review*, 1968, *33*, 46–61.

Scott, W. A., & Scott, R. Intercorrelations among structural properties of primary groups. *Journal of Personality and Social Psychology*, 1981, *41*, 279–292.

Seaman, D. F. *Working effectively with task-oriented groups*. New York: McGraw-Hill, 1981.

Seashore, S. E. *Group cohesiveness in the industrial work group*. Ann Arbor, Mich.: Institute for Social Research, 1954.

Seashore, S. E., & Bowers, D. G. The durability of organizational change. *American Psychologist*, 1970, *25*, 227–233.

Segal, M. W. Varieties of interpersonal attraction and their interrelationships in natural groups. *Social Psychology Quarterly*, 1979, *42*, 253–261.

Semmel, A. K. *Group dynamics and the foreign policy process: The choice-shift phenomenon.* Paper presented at the Annual Meetings of the Southern Political Science Association, 1976.

Sermat, V. Cooperative behavior in a mixed-motive game. *Journal of Social Psycholgoy*, 1964, *62*, 217–239.

Severy, L. J., Forsyth, D. R., & Wagner, P. J. A multimethod assessment of personal space development in female and male, black and white children. *Journal of Nonverbal Behavior*, 1979, *4*, 68–86.

Shaffer, J., & Galinsky, M. *Models of group therapy and sensitivity training.* Englewood Cliffs, N.J.: Prentice-Hall, 1974.

Shambaugh, P. W. The development of the small group. *Human Relations*, 1978, *31*, 283–295.

Shapley, L. S. A value for *n*-person games. In H. W. Kuhn & A. W. Tucker (Eds.), *Contributions to the theory of games* (Vol. 2). Princeton, N.J.: Princeton University Press, 1953.

Shaw, Marjorie E. A comparison of individuals and small groups in the rational solution of complex problems. *American Journal of Psychology*, 1932, *44*, 491–504.

Shaw, M. E. *Scaling group tasks: A method for dimensional analysis.* Technical Report No. 1, ONR contract NR 170–266, Nonr-580(11), July, 1963.

Shaw, M. E. Communication networks. In L. Berkowitz (Ed.), *Advances in experimental social psychology* (Vol. 1). New York: Academic Press, 1964.

Shaw, M. E. *Group dynamics: The psychology of small group behavior* (2nd ed.). McGraw-Hill, 1976.

Shaw, M. E. Communication networks fourteen years later. In L. Berkowitz (Ed.), *Group processes.* Academic Press, 1978.

Shaw, M. E. *Group dynamics: The psychology of small group behavior* (3rd ed.). McGraw-Hill, 1981.

Shaw, M. E., & Breed, G. R. Effects of attribution of responsibility for negative events on behavior in small groups. *Sociometry*, 1970, *33*, 382–393.

Shaw, M. E., & Gilchrist, J. C. Repetitive task failure and sociometric choice. *Journal of Abnormal and Social Psychology*, 1955, *50*, 29–32.

Shears, L. M. Patterns of coalition formation in two games played by male tetrads. *Behavioral Science*, 1967, *12*, 130–137.

Sheridan, C. L., & King, R. G., Jr. Obedience to authority with an authentic victim. *Proceedings of the 80th Annual Convention of the American Psychological Association*, 1972, *7*, 165–166.

Sherif, C. W. *Orientation in social psychology.* New York: Harper & Row, 1976.

Sherif, M. *The psychology of social norms.* New York: Harper & Row, 1936.

Sherif, M. *In common predicament: Social psychology of intergroup conflict and cooperation.* Boston: Houghton Mifflin, 1966.

Sherif, M., Harvey, O. J., White, B. J., Hood, W. R., & Sherif, C. W. *Intergroup conflict and cooperation. The Robbers Cave Experiment.* Norman, Ok.: Institute of Group Relations, 1961.

Sherif, M., & Sherif, C. W. *Groups in harmony and tension.* New York: Harper & Row, 1953.

Sherif, M., & Sherif, C. W. *An outline of social psychology* (rev. ed.). New York: Harper & Row, 1956.

Sherif, M., & Sherif, C. W. *Reference groups.* New York: Harper & Row, 1964.

Sherif, M., White, B. J., & Harvey, O. J. Status in experimentally produced groups. *American Journal of Sociology*, 1955, *60*, 370–379.

Sherrod, D. R., & Cohen, S. Density, personal control, and design. In J. R. Aiello & A. Baum (Eds.), *Residential crowding and design.* New York: Plenum, 1979.

Shiflett, S. Toward a general model of small group productivity. *Psychological Bulletin*, 1979, *86*, 67–79.

Shiflett, S. C. Group performance as a function of task difficulty and organizational interdependence. *Organizational Behavior and Human Performance*, 1972, *7*, 442–456.

Shiflett, S. C. The contingency model of leadership effectiveness: Some implications of its statistical and methodological properties. *Behavioral Science*, 1973, *18*, 429–440.

Shrauger, J. S. Responses to evaluation as a function of initial self-perceptions. *Psychological Bulletin*, 1975, *82*, 581–596.

Shure, G. H., & Meeker, J. R. A personality/attitude scale for use in experimental bargaining studies. *Journal of Psychology*, 1967, *65*, 233–252.

Shure, G. H., Rogers, M. S., Larsen, I. M., & Tassone, J. Group planning and task effectiveness. *Sociometry*, 1962, *25*, 263–282.

Sigall, H. Effects of competence and consensual validation on a communicator's liking for the audience. *Journal of Personality and Social Psychology*, 1970, *16*, 251–258.

Silver, M., & Geller, D. On the irrelevance of evil: The organization and individual actions. *Journal of Social Issues*, 1978, *34*(4), 125–135.

Simmel, G. *The sociology of Georg Simmel.* New York: Free Press, 1950.

Simmel, G. *Conflict.* Glencoe, Ill.: Free Press, 1955.

Simon, R. J. *The jury: Its role in American society.* Lexington, Mass.: D. C. Heath, 1980.

Simonton, D. K. Land battles, generals, and armies: Individual and social determinants of victory and casualties. *Journal of Personality and Social Psychology*, 1980, *38*, 110–119.

Singer, J. E. Sympathetic activation, drugs, and fear. *Journal of Comparative and Physiological Psychology*, 1963, *56*, 612–615.

Singer, J. E., Brush, C. A., & Lublin, S. C. Some aspects of deindividuation: Identification and conformity. *Journal of Experimental Social Psychology*, 1965, *1*, 356–378.

Sistrunk, F., & McDavid, J. W. Sex variable in conforming behavior. *Journal of Personality and Social Psychology*, 1971, *17*, 200–207.

Skolnick, P. Reactions to personal evaluations: A failure to replicate. *Journal of Personality and Social Psychology*, 1971, *18*, 62–67.

Slater, P. E. Role differentiation in small groups. *American Sociological Review*, 1955, *20*, 300–310.

Slavin, R. How student learning teams can integrate the desegregated classroom. *Integrated Education*, 1977, *15*, 56–58.

Sloan, L. R. The function and impact of sports for fans: A review of theory and contemporary research. In J. H. Goldstein (Ed.), *Sports, games, and play: Social and psychological viewpoints*. Hillsdale, N.J.: Erlbaum, 1979.

Smart, R. Social group membership, leadership, and birth order. *Journal of Social Psychology*, 1965, *67*, 221–225.

Smelser, N. J. *Theory of collective behavior*. New York: Free Press, 1962.

Smith, M. B. Is experimental social psychology advancing? *Journal of Experimental Social Psychology*, 1972, *8*, 86–96.

Smith, P. Controlled studies of the outcome of sensitivity training. *Psychological Bulletin*, 1975, *82*, 597–622.

Smith, W. P., & Anderson, A. J. Threats, communication, and bargaining. *Journal of Personality and Social Psychology*, 1975, *32*, 76–82.

Smoke, W. H., & Zajonc, R. B. On the reliability of group judgments and decisions. In J. H. Criswell, H. Solomon, & P. Suppes (Eds.), *Mathematical methods in small group processes*. Stanford, Calif.: Stanford University Press, 1962.

Snell, F. *How to win the meeting*. New York: Hawthorn Books, 1979.

Snyder, E. E. High school athletes and their coaches, educational plans, and advice. *Sociology of Education*, 1972, *45*, 313–325.

Snyder, M., & Swann, W. B., Jr. Behavioral confirmation in social interaction: From social perception to social reality. *Journal of Experimental Social Psychology*, 1978, *14*, 148–162.

Snyder, M., Tanke, E. D., & Berscheid, E. Social perception and interpersonal behavior: On the self-ful-

filling nature of social stereotypes. *Journal of Personality and Social Psychology*, 1977, *35*, 656–666.

Solomon, L. The influence of some types of power relationships and game strategies upon the development of interpersonal trust. *Journal of Abnormal and Social Psychology*, 1960, *61*, 223–230.

Sommer, R. Studies in personal space. *Sociometry*, 1959, *22*, 247–260.

Sommer, R. Small group ecology. *Psychological Bulletin*, 1967, *67*, 145–152.

Sommer, R. *Personal space*. Englewood Cliffs, N.J.: Prentice-Hall, 1969.

Sommer, R. *Design awareness*. San Francisco: Rinehart, 1972.

Sorensen, T. C. *Kennedy*. New York: Bantam, 1966.

Sorokin, P. A., & Lundin, W. A. *Power and morality: Who shall guard the guardians?* Boston, Mass.: Sargent, 1959.

Sorrentino, R. M., & Boutillier, R. G. The effect of quantity and quality of verbal interaction on ratings of leadership ability. *Journal of Experimental Social Psychology*, 1975, *11*, 403–411.

Sorrentino, R. M., King, G., & Leo, G. The influence of the minority on perception: A note on a possible alternative explanation. *Journal of Experimental Social Psychology*, 1980, *16*, 293–301.

Spence, K. W. *Behavior theory and conditioning*. New Haven, Conn.: Yale University Press, 1956.

Spitzer, C. E., & Davis, J. H. Mutual social influence in dynamic groups. *Social Psychology*, 1978, *41*, 24–33.

Stang, D. J. Group size effects on conformity. *Journal of Social Psychology*, 1976, *98*, 175–181.

Stanton & Poors. *Register of corporations, directors, and executives*. New York: Stanton & Poors, 1967.

Stasser, G., Kerr, N. L., & Davis, J. H. Influence processes in decision-making groups: A modeling approach. In P. B. Paulus (Ed.), *Psychology of group influence*. Hillsdale, N.J.: Erlbaum, 1980.

Steers, R. M. Antecedents and outcomes of organizational commitment. *Administrative Science Quarterly*, 1977, *22*, 46–56.

Steffensmeier, D. J., & Terry, R. M. Deviance and respectability: An observational study of reactions to shoplifting. *Social Forces*, 1973, *51*, 417–426.

Steffensmeier, D. J., & Terry, R. M. (Eds.). *Examining deviance experimentally*. Port Washington, N.Y.: Alfred Publishing Co., 1975.

Stein, R. T., & Heller, T. An empirical analysis of the correlations between leadership status and participation rates reported in the literature. *Journal of Personality and Social Psychology*, 1979, *37*, 1993–2002.

Steiner, I. D. Human interaction and interpersonal perception. *Sociometry*, 1959, *22*, 230–235.

Steiner, I. D. *Group process and productivity*. New York: Academic Press, 1972.

Steiner, I. D. Whatever happened to the group in social psychology? *Journal of Experimental Social Psychology*, 1974, *10*, 94–108.

Steiner, I. D. Task-performing groups. In J. W. Thibaut, J. T. Spence, & R. C. Carson (Eds.), *Contemporary topics in social psychology*. Morristown, N.J.: General Learning Press, 1976.

Steinzor, B. The development and evaluation of a measure of social interaction. *Human Relations*, 1949, *2*, 103–121, 319–347.

Steinzor, B. The spatial factor in face to face discussion groups. *Journal of Abnormal and Social Psychology*, 1950, *45*, 552–555.

Stiles, W. B. Verbal response modes and dimensions of interpersonal roles: A method of discourse analysis. *Journal of Personality and Social Psychology*, 1978, *36*, 693–703.

Stiles, W. B., Waszak, C. S., & Barton, L. R. Professorial presumptuousness in verbal interactions with university students. *Journal of Experimental Social Psychology*, 1979, *15*, 158–169.

Stock, D., & Thelen, H. A. *Emotional dynamics and group culture: Experimental studies of individual and group behavior*. New York: New York University Press, 1958.

Stogdill, R. M. Personal factors associated with leadership. *Journal of Psychology*, 1948, *23*, 35–71.

Stogdill, R. M. *Individual behavior and group achievement*. New York: Oxford, 1959.

Stogdill, R. M. *Handbook of leadership*. New York: Free Press, 1974.

Stokols, D. On the distinction between density and crowding: Some implications for future research. *Psychological Review*, 1972, *79*, 275–278.

Stokols, D. In defense of the crowding construct. In A. Baum, J. E. Singer, & S. Valins (Eds.), *Advances in environmental psychology* (Vol. 1). Hillsdale, N.J.: Erlbaum, 1978.

Stoner, J. A. F. *A comparison of individual and group decisions involving risk*. Unpublished master's thesis, Massachusetts Institute of Technology, 1961.

Strain, P. S. (Ed.). *The utilization of classroom peers as behavior change agents*. New York: Plenum, 1981.

Streufert, S., & Streufert, S. C. The development of international conflict. In W. G. Austin & S. Worchel (Eds.), *The social psychology of intergroup conflict*. Monterey, Calif.: Brooks/Cole, 1979.

Stricker, L. J., Messick, S., & Jackson, D. N. Conformity, anticonformity, and independence: Their dimensionality and generality. *Journal of Personality and Social Psychology*, 1970, *16*, 494–507.

Strickland, L. H. Surveillance and trust. *Journal of Personality*, 1958, *26*, 206–215.

Strickland, L. H., Barefoot, J. C., & Hockenstein, P. Monitoring behavior in the surveillance and trust paradigm. *Representative Research in Social Psychology*, 1976, *7*, 51–57.

Strodtbeck, F. L., & Hook, L. H. The social dimensions of a twelve-man jury table. *Sociometry*, 1961, *24*, 397–415.

Strodtbeck, F. L., James, R. M., & Hawkins, C. Social status in jury deliberations. *American Sociological Review*, 1957, *22*, 713–719.

Strodtbeck, F. L., & Mann, R. D. Sex role differentiation in jury deliberations. *Sociometry*, 1956, *19*, 3–11.

Strong, S., & Claiborn, C. *Change through interaction: Social psychological processes of counseling and psychotherapy*. New York: Wiley, 1982.

Strube, M. J., & Garcia, J. E. A meta-analytic investigation of Fiedler's contingency model of leadership effectiveness. *Psychological Bulletin*, 1981, *90*, 307–321.

Stryker, S. Developments in "two social psychologies": Toward an appreciation of mutual relevance. *Sociometry*, 1977, *40*, 145–160.

Stumpf, S. A., Freedman, R. D., & Zand, D. E. Judgmental decisions: A study of interactions among group members, group functioning, and the decision situation. *Academy of Management Journal*, 1979, *22*, 765–782.

Stumpf, S. A., Zand, D. E., & Freedman, R. D. Designing groups for judgmental decisions. *Academy of Management Review*, 1979, *4*, 589–600.

Sucov, E. W. European research. *Lighting Design and Application*, 1973, 39–43.

Suls, J. M., & Miller, R. L. (Eds.). *Social comparison processes*. Washington, D. C.: Hemisphere, 1977.

Sumner, W. G. *Folkways*. New York: Ginn, 1906.

Sundstrom, E. An experimental study of crowding: Effects of room size, intrusion, and goal-blocking on nonverbal behavior, self-disclosure, and self-reported stress. *Journal of Personality and Social Psychology*, 1975, *32*, 645–654.

Sundstrom, E., & Altman, I. Field study of dominance and territorial behavior. *Journal of Personality and Social Psychology*, 1974, *30*, 115–125.

Sundstrom, E., & Altman, I. Personal space and interpersonal relationships: Research review and theoretical model. *Human Ecology*, 1976, *4*, 47–67.

Swingle, P. G., & Santi, A. Communication in nonzero sum games. *Journal of Personality and Social Psychology*, 1972, *23*, 54–63.

Tajfel, H. Interindividual behavior and intergroup behavior. In H. Tajfel (Ed.), *Differentiation between social groups*. New York: Academic Press, 1978 (a).

Tajfel, H. Social categorization, social identity, and social comparison. In H. Tajfel (Ed.), *Differentiation between social groups*. New York: Academic Press, 1978 (b).

Tajfel, H. The achievement of group differentiation. In H. Tajfel (Ed.), *Differentiation between social groups*. New York: Academic Press, 1978. (c)

Tajfel, H., & Turner, J. An integrative theory of intergroup conflict. In W. G. Austin & S. Worchel (Eds.), *The social psychology of intergroup conflict*. Monterey, Calif.: Brooks/Cole, 1979.

Tarde, G. *The laws of imitation*. New York: Holt, 1903.

Taylor, D. W., Berry, P. C., & Block, C. H. Does group participation when using brainstorming facilitate or inhibit creative thinking? *Administrative Science Quarterly*, 1958, *3*, 23–47.

Taylor, F. W. *The principles of scientific management*. New York: Harper, 1923.

Taylor, H. F. *Balance in small groups*. New York: Van Nostrand Reinhold, 1970.

Taylor, R. B., & Stough, R. R. Territorial cognition: Assessing Altman's typology. *Journal of Personality and Social Psychology*, 1978, *36*, 418–423.

Tedeschi, J. T., Gaes, G. G., & Rivera, A. N. Aggression and the use of coercive power. *Journal of Social Issues*, 1977, *33*(1), 101–125.

Tedeschi, J. T., Schlenker, B. R., & Bonoma, T. V. *Conflict, power, and games*. Chicago: Aldine, 1973.

Tedeschi, J. T., Smith, R. B., III, & Brown, R. C. A reinterpretation of research on aggression. *Psychological Bulletin*, 1974, *81*, 540–563.

Teger, A. *Too much invested to quit*. New York: Pergamon, 1980.

Terborg, J. R., Castore, C., & DeNinno, J. A. A longitudinal field investigation of the impact of group composition on group performance and cohesion. *Journal of Personality and Social Psychology*, 1976, *34*, 782–790.

Terhune, K. W. The effects of personality in cooperation and conflict. In P. Swingle (Ed.), *The structure of conflict*. New York: Academic Press, 1970.

Tesser, A., & Rosen, S. The reluctance to transmit bad news. In L. Berkowitz (Ed.), *Advances in experimental social psychology* (Vol. 8). New York: Academic Press, 1975.

Tetlock, P. E. Identifying victims of groupthink from public statements of decision makers. *Journal of Personality and Social Psychology*, 1979, *37*, 1314–1324.

Thibaut, J. W. An experimental study of the cohesiveness of underprivileged groups. *Human Relations*, 1950, *3*, 251–278.

Thibaut, J. W., & Coules, J. The role of communication in the reduction of interpersonal hostility. *Journal of Abnormal and Social Psychology*, 1952, 47, 770–777.

Thibaut, J. W., & Kelley, H. H. *The social psychology of groups*. New York: Wiley, 1959.

Thibaut, J. W., & Strickland, L. H. Psychological set

and social conformity. *Journal of Personality*, 1956, *25*, 115–129.

Thomas, E. J., & Fink, C. F. Models of group problem solving. *Journal of Abnormal and Social Psychology*, 1961, *63*, 53–63.

Thorndike, R. L. The effect of discussion upon the correctness of group decisions, when the factor of majority influence is allowed for. *Journal of Social Psychology*, 1938, *9*, 343–362.

Thrasher, F. M. *The gang*. Chicago: University of Chicago Press, 1927.

Thurber, J. The day the dam broke. In *My life and hard times*. New York: Harper, 1933 (originally printed in *The New Yorker*).

Tiger, L. *Men in groups*. New York: Random House, 1969.

Tillman, R., Jr. Problems in review: Committees on trial. *Harvard Business Review*, 1960, *38*(2), 7–12, 162–172.

Tolstoy, L. *War and peace*. Chicago: Encyclopaedia Britannica, 1952 (originally published in 1869).

Torrance, E. P. The behavior of small groups under the stress of conditions of survival. *American Sociological Review*, 1954, *19*, 751–755.

Torrance, E. P. Group decision-making and disagreement. *Social Forces*, 1957, *35*, 314–318.

Torrance, E. P. *Education and the creative potential*. Minneapolis: University of Minnesota Press, 1963.

Torrance, E. P. *Rewarding creative behavior: Experiments in classroom creativity*. Englewood Cliffs, N.J.: Prentice-Hall, 1965.

Travis, L. E. The effect of a small audience upon eye-hand coordination. *Journal of Abnormal and Social Psychology*, 1925, *20*, 142–146.

Travis, L. E. The influence of the group upon the stutterer's speed in free association. *Journal of Abnormal and Social Psychology*, 1928, *23*, 45–51.

Triandis, H. C. *Interpersonal behavior*. Monterey, Calif.: Brooks/Cole, 1977.

Triandis, H. C. Some universals of social behavior. *Personality and Social Psychology Bulletin*, 1978, *4*, 1–16.

Triandis, H. C. Commentary. In W. G. Austin & S. Worchel (Eds.), *The social psychology of intergroup conflict*. Monterey, Calif.: Brooks/Cole, 1979.

Triplett, N. The dynamogenic factors in pacemaking and competition. *American Journal of Psychology*, 1897, *9*, 507–533.

Trow, W. C., Zander, A. F., Morse, W. C., & Jenkins, D. M. Psychology of group behavior: The class as a group. *Journal of Educational Psychology*, 1950, *41*, 322–338.

Tubbs, S. L. *A systems approach to small group interaction*. Reading, Mass.: Addison-Wesley, 1978.

Tucker, R. C. Personality and political leaders. *Political Science Quarterly*, 1977, *92*, 383–393.

Tuckman, B. W. Developmental sequences in small groups. *Psychological Bulletin*, 1965, *63*, 384–399.

Tuckman, B. W., & Jensen, M. A. C. Stages of small group development revisited. *Group and Organizational Studies*, 1977, *2*, 419–427.

Tuddenham, R. D. Correlates of yielding to a distorted group norm on individual judgment. *Journal of Psychology*, 1958, *46*, 227–241.

Tuddenham, R. D. Correlates of yielding to a distorted group norm. *Journal of Personality*, 1959, *27*, 272–284.

Turner, J. M. *The structure of sociological theory.* Homewood, Ill.: Dorsey, 1974.

Turner, R. H. Collective behavior. In R. E. L. Faris (Ed.), *Handbook of modern sociology.* Chicago: Rand McNally, 1964.

Turner, R. H., & Killian, L. M. *Collective behavior* (2nd ed.). Englewood Cliffs, N.J.: Prentice-Hall, 1972.

Turner, R. H., & Surace, S. J. Zoot-suiters and Mexicans: Symbols in crowd behavior. *The American Journal of Sociology*, 1956, *62*, 14–20.

Tuthill, D., & Forsyth, D. R. Sex differences in opinion conformity and dissent. *Journal of Social Psychology*, 1982, *116*, 205–210.

Tyler, T. R., & Sears, D. O. Coming to like obnoxious people when we must live with them. *Journal of Personality and Social Psychology*, 1977, *35*, 200–211.

Ulschak, F. L., Nathanson, L., & Gillan, P. G. *Small group problem solving.* Reading, Mass.: Addison-Wesley, 1981.

Upper, D., & Ross, S. M. (Eds.). *Behavioral group therapy, 1979: An annual review.* Champaign, Ill.: Research Press, 1980.

Uris, A. *Executive dissent: How to say no and win.* New York: AMACOM, 1978.

Van de Ven, A. H. *Group decision-making effectiveness.* Kent, Oh.: Kent State University Center for Business and Economic Research Press, 1974.

Van de Ven, A. H., & Delbecq, A. L. Nominal versus interacting group process for committee decision making effectiveness. *Academy of Management Journal*, 1971, *14*, 203–212.

Van Egeren, L. F. Cardiovascular changes during social competition in a mixed-motive game. *Journal of Personality and Social Psychology*, 1979, *37*, 858–864.

Van Sell, M., Brief, A. P., & Schuler, R. S. Role conflict and role ambiguity: Integration of the literature and directions for future research. *Human Relations*, 1981, *34*, 43–71.

Van Zelst, R. H. Sociometrically selected work teams increase production. *Personnel Psychology*, 1952, *5*, 175–185.

Varela, J. A. *Psychological solutions to social problems.* New York: Academic Press, 1971.

Varney, G. H. *Organization development for managers.* Reading, Mass.: Addison-Wesley, 1977.

Vecchio, R. P. An empirical examination of the validity of Fiedler's model of leadership effectiveness. *Organizational Behavior and Human Performance*, 1977, *19*, 180–206.

Verba, S. *Small groups and political behavior: A study of leadership.* Princeton, N.J.: Princeton University Press, 1961.

Vinacke, W. E. Negotiations and decisions in a politics game. In B. Lieberman (Ed.), *Social choice.* New York: Gordon & Breach, 1971.

Vinokur, A. A review and theoretical analysis of the effects of group processes upon individual and group decisions involving risk. *Psychological Bulletin*, 1971, *76*, 231–250.

Vinokur, A., & Burnstein, E. The effects of partially shared persuasive arguments on group-induced shifts: A group-problem-solving approach. *Journal of Personality and Social Psychology*, 1974, *29*, 305–315.

Vinokur, A., & Burnstein, E. Depolarization of attitudes in groups. *Journal of Personality and Social Psychology*, 1978, *36*, 872–885.

Vinsel, A., Brown, B. B., Altman, I., & Foss, C. Privacy regulation, territorial displays, and effectiveness of individual functioning. *Journal of Personality and Social Psychology*, 1980, *39*, 1104–1115.

Vollrath, D. A., & Davis, J. H. Jury size and decision rule. In R. J. Simon (Ed.), *The jury: Its role in American society.* Lexington, Mass.: Heath, 1980.

Vroom, V. H. A new look at managerial decision making. *Organizational Dynamics*, 1973, *1*, 66–80.

Vroom, V. H. Decision making and the leadership process. *Journal of Contemporary Business*, 1974, *3*, 47–64.

Vroom, V. H. Leadership. In M. D. Dunnette (Ed.), *Handbook of industrial and organizational psychology.* Chicago: Rand McNally, 1976.

Vroom, V. H., & Jago, A. G. On the validity of the Vroom/Yetton model. *Journal of Applied Psychology*, 1978, *63*, 151–162.

Vroom, V. H., & Mann, F. C. Leader authoritarianism and employee attitudes. *Personnel Psychology*, 1960, *13*, 125–140.

Vroom, V. H., & Yetton, P. W. *Leadership and decision making.* Pittsburgh, Penn.: University of Pittsburgh Press, 1973.

Wahrman, R., & Pugh, M. D. Competence and conformity: Another look at Hollander's study. *Sociometry*, 1972, *35*, 376–386.

Wahrman, R., & Pugh, M. D. Sex, nonconformity, and influence. *Sociometry*, 1974, *37*, 137–147.

Wallach, M. A., Kogan, N., & Bem, D. J. Group influence on individual risk taking. *Journal of Abnormal and Social Psychology*, 1962, *65*, 75–86.

Walster, E., Aronson, V., Abrahams, D., & Rottman,

L. Importance of physical attractiveness in dating behavior. *Journal of Personality and Social Psychology,* 1966, *5,* 508–516.

Walster, E., Walster, G. W., & Berscheid, E. *Equity: Theory and research.* London: Allyn & Bacon, 1978.

Wanous, J. P. A causal-correlational analysis of the job satisfaction and performance relationship. *Journal of Applied Psychology,* 1974, *59,* 139–144.

Warren, J. R. Birth order and social behavior. *Psychological Bulletin,* 1966, *65,* 38–49.

Warriner, C. H. Groups are real: A reaffirmation. *American Sociological Review,* 1956, *21,* 549–554.

Watson, R. I., Jr. Investigation into deindividuation using a cross-cultural survey technique. *Journal of Personality and Social Psychology,* 1973, *25,* 342–345.

Webb, N. M. A process-outcome analysis of learning in group and individual settings. *Educational Psychologist,* 1980, *15,* 69–83.

Weber, M. *The theory of social and economic organization.* New York: Oxford, 1947.

Webster, M., Jr., & Driskell, J. E., Jr. Status generalization: A review and some new data. *American Sociological Review,* 1978, *43,* 220–236.

Webster, N. *Webster's new twentieth century dictionary of the English language.* New York: Collins World, 1976.

Wegner, D. M., & Schaefer, D. The concentration of responsibility: An objective self-awareness analysis of group size effects in helping situations. *Journal of Personality and Social Psychology,* 1978, *36,* 147–155.

Weiler, D. J., & Castle, J. E. *The need for an open systems approach to naval ship habitability design.* Paper presented at the meetings of the Society of Naval Architects and Marine Engineers, New York: November, 1972.

Weiss, R. F., & Miller, F. G. The drive theory of social facilitation. *Psychology Review,* 1971, *78,* 44–57.

Wells, L. E. Theories of deviance and the self-concept. *Social Psychology,* 1978, *41,* 189–204.

Wertheimer, M. The general theoretical situation. In W. D. Ellis (Ed.), *A source book of Gestalt psychology.* New York: Harcourt, Brace, & World, 1938.

Weschler, I. R., Kahane, M., & Tannenbaum, R. Job satisfaction, productivity, and morale: A case study. *Occupational Psychology,* 1952, *26,* 1–14.

West, S. G., Gunn, S. P., & Chernicky, P. Ubiquitous Watergate: An attributional analysis. *Journal of Personality and Social Psychology,* 1975, *23,* 55–65.

Weston, S. B., & English, H. B. The influence of the group on psychological test scores. *American Journal of Psychology,* 1926, *37,* 600–601.

Weybrew, B. B. Psychological problems of prolonged marine submergence. In J. N. Burns, R. Chambers, & E. Hendler (Eds.), *Unusual environments and human behavior.* New York: Macmillan, 1963.

Wheeler, D. D., & Janis, I. L. *A practical guide for making decisions.* New York: Free Press, 1980.

Wheeler, L. Toward a theory of behavioral contagion. *Psychological Review,* 1966, *73,* 179–192.

Whitaker, D. S., & Thelen, H. A. Emotional dynamics and group culture. in M. Rosenbaum & M. M. Berger (Eds.), *Group psychotherapy and group function.* New York: Basic Books, 1975.

White, R. K. Misperception and the Vietnam war. *Journal of Social Issues,* 1966, *22*(3), 1–156.

White, R. K. Images in the context of international conflict. In H. Kelman (Ed.), *International behavior.* New York: Holt, Rinehart, & Winston, 1965.

White, R. K. Three not-so-obvious contributions of psychology to peace. *Journal of Social Issues,* 1969, *25*(4), 23–29.

White, R. K. *Nobody wanted war: Misperception in Vietnam and other wars* (rev. ed.). New York: Doubleday/Anchor, 1970.

White, R. K. Misperception in the Arab-Israeli conflict. *Journal of Social Issues,* 1977, *33*(1), 190–221.

White, R. K., & Lippitt, R. Leader behavior and member reaction in three "social climates." In D. Cartwright and A. Zander (Eds.), *Group dynamics: Research and theory* (3rd ed.). New York: Harper & Row, 1968.

Whyte, W. F. *Street corner society.* Chicago: University of Chicago Press, 1943.

Wicker, A. W. *An introduction to ecological psychology.* Monterey, Calif.: Brooks/Cole, 1979.

Wicker, A. W., Kermeyer, S. L., Hanson, L., & Alexander, D. Effects of manning levels on subjective experiences, performance, and verbal interaction in groups. *Organizational Behavior and Human Performance,* 1976, *17,* 251–274.

Wicklund, R. A. Group contact and self-focused attention. In P. B. Paulus (Ed.), *Psychology of group influence.* Hillsdale, N.J.: Erlbaum, 1980.

Wiesenthal, D. L., Endler, N. S., Coward, T. R., & Edwards, J. Reversibility of relative competence as a determinant of conformity across different perceptual tasks. *Representative Research in Social Psychology,* 1976, *7,* 35–43.

Wiggins, J. A., Dill, F., & Schwartz, R. D. On "status-liability." *Sociometry,* 1965, *28,* 197–209.

Wilder, D. A. Perception of groups, size of opposition, and social influence. *Journal of Experimental Social Psychology,* 1977, *13,* 253–268.

Wilder, D. A. Perceiving persons as a group: Effects of attributions of causality and beliefs. *Social Psychology,* 1978, *41,* 13–23. (a)

Wilder, D. A. Reduction of intergroup discrimination through individuation of the out-group. *Journal of Personality and Social Psychology,* 1978, *36,* 1361–1374. (b)

Wilder, D. A., & Thompson, J. E. Intergroup contact

with independent manipulations of in-group and out-group interaction. *Journal of Personality and Social Psychology*, 1980, *38*, 589–603.

Williams v. Florida, 399 U.S. 78 (1970).

Williams, K., Harkins, S., & Latané, B. Identifiability as a deterrent to social loafing: Two cheering experiments. *Journal of Personality and Social Psychology*, 1981, *40*, 303–311.

Willis, R. H. Two dimensions of conformity-nonconformity. *Sociometry*, 1963, *26*, 499–512.

Willis, R. H., & Hollander, E. P. An experimental study of three response modes in social influence situations. *Journal of Abnormal and Social Psychology*, 1964, *69*, 150–156.

Wills, T. A. Downward comparison principles in social psychology. *Psychological Bulletin*, 1981, *90*, 245–271.

Wilson, E. O. *Sociobiology: The new synthesis*. Cambridge, Mass.: Belknap Press, 1975.

Wilson, S. R. Some factors influencing instrumental and expressive ratings in task-oriented groups. *Pacific Sociological Review*, 1970, *13*, 127–131.

Wilson, W., & Miller, N. Shifts in evaluations of participants following intergroup competition. *Journal of Abnormal and Social Psychology*, 1961, *63*, 428–431.

Winter, D. G. *The power motive*. New York: Free Press, 1973.

Wish, M., Deutsch, M., & Kaplan, S. J. Perceived dimensions of interpersonal relations. *Journal of Personality and Social Psychology*, 1976, *33*, 409–420.

Wolber, G., & McGovern, T. A three component model for the evaluation of telephone counselor effectiveness. *Crisis Intervention*, 1977, *8*, 36–55.

Wolpe, J., & Lazarus, A. A. *Behavior therapy techniques*. Oxford: Pergamon Press, 1966.

Worchel, S. The experience of crowding: An attributional analysis. In A. Baum & Y. M. Epstein (Eds.), *Human response to crowding*. Hillsdale, N.J.: Erlbaum, 1978.

Worchel, S. Cooperation and the reduction of intergroup conflict: Some determining factors. In W. G. Austin & S. Worchel (Eds.), *The social psychology of intergroup conflict*. Monterey, Calif.: Brooks/Cole, 1979.

Worchel, S., Andreoli, V. A., & Folger, R. Intergroup cooperation and intergroup attraction: The effect of previous interaction and outcome of combined effort. *Journal of Experimental Social Psychology*, 1977, *13*, 131–140.

Worchel, S., & Brehm, J. W. Direct and implied social restoration of freedom. *Journal of Personality and Social Psychology*, 1971, *18*, 294–304.

Worchel, S., & Cooper, J. *Understanding social psy-

chology* (rev. ed.). Homewood, Ill: Dorsey Press, 1979.

Worchel, S., & Norvell, N. Effect of perceived environmental conditions during cooperation on intergroup attraction. *Journal of Personality and Social Psychology*, 1980, *38*, 764–772.

Worchel, S., & Teddlie, C. The experience of crowding: A two-factor theory. *Journal of Personality and Social Psychology*, 1976, *34*, 30–40.

Worchel, S., & Yohai, S. The role of attribution in the experience of crowding. *Journal of Experimental Social Psychology*, 1979, *15*, 91–104.

Wortman, C. B., & Linsenmeier, J. A. W. Interpersonal attraction and techniques of ingratiation in organizational settings. In B. M. Staw & G. R. Salancik (Eds.), *New directions in organizational behavior*. Chicago: St. Clair Press, 1977.

Wright, J. P. *On a clear day you can see General Motors*. New York: Avon, 1979.

Wrightsman, L. S. *Social psychology* (2nd ed.). Belmont, Calif.: Wadsworth, 1977.

Wrightsman, L. S. The American trial jury on trial: Empirical evidence and procedural modifications. *Journal of Social Issues*, 1978, *34*(4), 137–164.

Wrightsman, L. S., O'Connor, J., & Baker, N. J. (Eds.), *Cooperation and competition: Readings on mixed-motive games*. Belmont, Calif.: Wadsworth, 1972.

Wrong, D. H. *Power*. New York: Harper, 1979.

Yablonsky, L. The delinquent gang as a near group. *Social Problems*, 1959, *7*, 108–117.

Yablonsky, L. *The violent gang*. New York: Macmillan, 1962.

Yalom, I. *The theory and practice of group psychotherapy* (2nd ed.). New York: Basic Books, 1975.

Zajonc, R. B. Social facilitation. *Science*, 1965, *149*, 269–274.

Zajonc, R. B. Attitudinal effect of mere exposure. *Journal of Personality and Social Psychology*, Monograph Supplement, 1968, *9*, (2, part 2), 2–27.

Zajonc, R. B. Compresence. In P. B. Paulus (Ed.), *Psychology of group influence*. Hillsdale, N.J.: Erlbaum, 1980.

Zajonc, R. B., Heingartner, A., & Herman, E. M. Social enhancement and impairment of performance in the cockroach. *Journal of Personality and Social Psychology*, 1969, *13*, 83–92.

Zajonc, R. B., Markus, H., & Markus, G. B. The birth order puzzle. *Journal of Personality and Social Psychology*, 1979, *37*, 1325–1341.

Zaleznik, A. *Human dilemmas of leadership*. New York: Harper & Row, 1966.

Zander, A. Group aspirations. In D. Cartwright & A. Zander (Eds.), *Group dynamics: Research and theory* (3rd ed.). New York: Harper & Row, 1968.

Zander, A. *Motives and goals in groups*. New York: Academic Press, 1971.

Zander, A. Team spirit vs. the individual achiever. *Psychology Today*, 1974, *8*(6), 64–68.

Zander, A. Motivation and performance of sports groups. In D. M. Landers (Ed.), *Psychology of sport and motor behavior II*. University Park, Penn.: Pennsylvania State University, 1975.

Zander, A. *Groups at work*. San Francisco: Jossey-Bass, 1977.

Zander, A. The study of group behavior during four decades. *Journal of Applied Behavioral Science*, 1979, *15*, 272–282. (a)

Zander, A. The psychology of group processes. *Annual Review of Psychology*, 1979, *30*, 417–451. (b)

Zander, A., & Cohen, A. R. Attributed social power and group acceptance: A classroom experimental demonstration. *Journal of Abnormal and Social Psychology*, 1955, *51*, 490–492.

Zander, A., Cohen, A. R., & Stotland, E. Power and relations among the professions. In D. Cartwright (Ed.), *Studies in social power*. Ann Arbor, Mich.: Institute for Social Research, 1959.

Zander, A., & Medow, H. Individual and group levels of aspiration. *Human Relations*, 1963, *16*, 89–105.

Zander, A., Stotland, E., & Wolfe, D. Unity of group, identification with group, and self-esteem of members. *Journal of Personality*, 1960, *28*, 463–478.

Zanna, M. P., & Pack, S. J. On the self-fulfilling nature of apparent sex differences in behavior. *Journal of Experimental Social Psychology*, 1975, *11*, 583–591.

Zeisel, H., & Diamond, S. S. The jury selection in the Mitchell-Stans conspiracy trial. *American Bar Foundation Research Journal*, 1976, *1*, 151–174.

Ziller, R. C. Individuation and socialization: A theory of assimilation in large organizations. *Human Relations*, 1964, *17*, 341–360.

Ziller, R. C. Toward a theory of open and closed groups. *Psychological Bulletin*, 1965, *64*, 164–182.

Zillmann, D., Bryant, J., Cantor, J. R., & Day, K. D. Irrelevance of mitigating circumstances in retaliatory behavior at high levels of excitation. *Journal of Research in Personality*, 1975, *9*, 282–293.

Zillmann, D., & Cantor, J. R. Effect of timing of information about mitigating circumstances on emotional responses to provocation and retaliatory behavior. *Journal of Experimental Social Psychology*, 1976, *12*, 38–55.

Zillmann, D., Sapolsky, B. S., & Bryant, J. The enjoyment of watching sport contests. In J. H. Goldstein (Ed.), *Sports, games and play: Social and psychological viewpoints*. Hillsdale, N.J.: Erlbaum, 1979.

Zimbardo, P. G. The human choice: Individuation, reason, and order versus deindividuation, impulse, and chaos. In W. J. Arnold & D. Levine (Eds.), *Nebraska Symposium on Motivation, 1969*. Lincoln: University of Nebraska Press, 1969.

Zimbardo, P. G. Transforming experimental research into advocacy for social change. In M. Deutsch & H. A. Hornstein (Eds.), *Applying social psychology*. Hillsdale, N.J.: Erlbaum, 1975.

Zimbardo, P. G. *Psychology and life*. Glenview, Ill.: Scott, Foresman, 1977.

Zimbardo, P. G., Weisenberg, M., Firestone, I., & Levy, B. Communicator effectiveness in producing public conformity and private opinion change. *Journal of Personality*, 1965, *33*, 233–256.

Zubek, J. P. Behavioral and physiological effects of prolonged sensory and perceptual deprivation: A review. In J. E. Rasmussen (Ed.), *Man in isolation and confinement*. Chicago: Aldine, 1973.

Credits

Chapter 2

Chapter 3

Chapter 4

Chapter 5

Table 5-1, p. 114, from "Role Differentiation in Small Groups," by P.E. Slater. In *American Sociological Review,* 1955, *20,* 300. Copyright 1955 by The American Sociological Association. Reprinted by permission.

Table 5-2, p. 116, adapted from "Functional Roles of Group Members," by K.D. Benne and P. Sheats. In *Journal of Social Issues,* 1948, 4(2), 41. Copyright 1948 by Plenum Publishing Corporation. Reprinted by permission.

Figure 5-1, p. 117, reprinted with permission of Macmillan Publishing Co., from *SYMLOG: Case Study Kit,* by R.F. Bales. Copyright © 1980 by The Free Press, a Division of Macmillan Publishing Co., Inc.

Figure 5-2, p. 123, data from p. 102 in *The Psychology of Social Norms,* by Muzafer Sherif. Copyright © 1936 by Harper & Row, Publishers, Inc.; Renewed by Muzafer Sherif. Reprinted by permission of the publisher.

Figure 5-5, p. 132, from *Management and the Worker,* by F.J. Roethlisberger and W.J. Dickson. Copyright © 1939 by Harvard University Press. Reprinted by permission.

Figure 5-6, p. 135, from "Communication Networks," by M.E. Shaw. In L. Berkowitz (Ed.), *Advances in Experimental Psychology,* Vol. 1. Copyright © 1964 by Academic Press. Reprinted by permission.

Chapter 6

Table 6-1, p. 146, from "The Effect of Mere Presence on Social Facilitation: An Unobtrusive Test," by H. Markus. In *Journal of Experimental and Social Psychology,* 1978, *14,* 389. Copyright 1978 by Academic Press. Reprinted by permission.

Table 6-3, p. 153, from *Group Process and Productivity,* by I.D. Steiner. Copyright © 1972 by Academic Press. Reprinted by permission.

Figure 6-1, p. 154, from "Many Hands Make Light the Work: The Causes and Consequences of Social Loafing," by B. Latane, K. Williams, and S. Harkins. In *Journal of Personality and Social Psychology,* 1979, *37,* 822. Copyright 1979 by the American Psychological Association. Reprinted by permission.

Box, p. 155, from "Identifiability as a Deterrent to Social Loafing: Two Cheering Experiments," by K. Williams, S. Harkins, and B. Latane. In *Journal of Personality and Social Psychology,* 1981, *40,* 310. Copyright 1981 by the American Psychological Association. Reprinted by permission.

Chapter 7

Quotations, pp. 184–190, specified excerpts (pp. 19, 21, 23, 37, 68–69, 102) in *Obedience to Authority: An Experimental View* by Stanley Milgram. Copyright © 1974 by Stanley Milgram. Reprinted by permission of Harper & Row, Publishers, Inc.

Table 7-2, p. 182, adapted from "Multidimensional Scaling of Power Strategies," by T. Falbo. In *Journal of Personality and Social Psychology,* 1977, *35,* 537. Copyright 1977 by the American Psychological Association. Reprinted by permission.

Box, p. 184, from Figure 1 (p. 15) in *Obedience to Authority: An Experimental View* by Stanley Milgram. Copyright © 1974 by Stanley Milgram. Reprinted by permission of Harper & Row, Publishers, Inc.

Figure 7-1, p. 187, based on data from Figure 4 (p. 28), Table 1 (p. 29), Figure 5 (p. 30) and Table 2 (p. 35) in *Obedience to Authority: An Experimental View* by Stanley Milgram. Copyright © 1974 by Stanley Milgram. Reprinted by permission of Harper & Row, Publishers, Inc.

Box, p. 171, from "Ubiquitous Watergate: An Attributional Analysis," by S.G. West, S.P. Gunn, and P. Chernicky. In *Journal of Personality and Social Psychology,* 1975, *32,* 55. Copyright 1975 by the American Psychological Association. Reprinted by permission.

Chapter 8

Table 8-3, p. 219, from "Substitutes for Leadership: The Meaning and Measurement," by S. Kerr and J.M. Jermier. In *Organizational Behavior and Human Performance,* 1978, *22,* 375. Copyright © 1978 by Academic Press. Reprinted by permission.

Quotation, p. 221, from "The Contingency Model and the Dynamics of the Leadership Process," by F. Fiedler. In L. Berkowitz (Ed.), *Advances in Experimental Social Psychology (Vol. II).* Copyright © 1978 by Academic Press. Reprinted by permission.

Box, p. 222, adapted from "The Contingency Model and the Dynamics of the Leadership Process," by F. Fiedler. In L. Berkowitz (Ed.), *Advances in Experimental Social Psychology (Vol. II).* Copyright © 1978 by Academic Press. Reprinted by permission.

Table 8-4, p. 223, from *Leadership and Effective Management* by Fred E. Fiedler and Martin M. Chemers. Copyright © 1974 by Scott, Foresman and Company. Reprinted by permission.

Figure 8-1, p. 225, adapted from "The Contingency Model and the Dynamics of the Leadership Process," by F. Fiedler. In L. Berkowitz (Ed.), *Advances in Experimental Social Psychology (Vol. II)*. Copyright © 1978 by Academic Press. Reprinted by permission.

Figure 8-2, p. 232, adapted from Figure 1 in *Autocracy and Democracy* by Ralph K. White and Ronald Lippitt. Copyright © 1960 by Ralph K. White and Ronald Lippitt. Reprinted by permission of Harper & Row, Publishers, Inc.

Figure 8-3, (p. 234), Figure 8-4 (p. 236), and quotation (p. 235), reprinted from *Leadership and Decision-Making* by Victor H. Vroom and Philip W. Yetton by permission of the University of Pittsburgh Press. © 1973 by the University of Pittsburgh Press.

Chapter 9

Figure 9-1, p. 244, adapted from "An Experimental Investigation of Group Influence," by S.E. Asch. In *Symposium on Preventive and Social Psychiatry*, April 15–17, 1957, Walter Reed Army Institute of Research. Washington, D.C.: Government Printing Office.

Box, p. 247, from *Social Psychology* by L.S. Wrightsman. Copyright © 1977 by Wadsworth Publishing Co., Inc. Reprinted by permission of Brooks/Cole Publishing Co., Monterey, California.

Figure 9-3, p. 249, from "Opinions and Social Pressure," by S.E. Asch. In *Scientific American*, 1955, *198*, 31. Reprinted by permission. And from "Note on the Drawing Power of Crowds of Different Sizes," by S. Milgram, L. Bickman, and L. Berkowitz. In *Journal of Personality and Social Psychology*, 1971, *17*, 200. Copyright 1971 by the American Psychological Association. Reprinted by permission.

Table 9-2, p. 259, from "Deviance, Rejection, and Communication," by S. Schachter. In *Journal of Abnormal and Social Psychology*, 1951, *46*, 190. Copyright 1951 by the American Psychological Association.

Figure 9-5, p. 263, from "Reaction to Attitudinal Deviance: Impact of Deviate's Direction and Distance of Movement," by J.M. Levine, L. Saxe, H.J. Harris. In *Sociometry*, 1976, *36*, 97. Copyright 1976 by the American Sociological Association. Reprinted by permission.

Figure 9-6, p. 270, adapted from "Deviance and Sanctioning within a Small Group," by D.K. Dedrick. In *Social Psychology*, 1978, *41*, 94. Copyright 1978 by the American Sociological Association. Reprinted by permission.

Chapter 10

Quotation, pp. 277–278, reprinted from *Street Corner Society* by W.F. Whyte by permission of The University of Chicago Press. Copyright © 1943 by The University of Chicago Press.

Box, p. 280, from "Group Size and the Extension of Social Space Boundaries," by E.S. Knowles, B. Kreuser, S. Haas, M. Hyde, and G.E. Schuchart. In *Journal of Personality and Social Psychology*, 1976, *33*, 647. Copyright 1976 by the American Psychological Association. Reprinted by permission.

Table 10-1, p. 282, from "Privacy Regulation, Territorial Displays, and Effectiveness of Individual Functioning," by A. Vinsel, B.B. Brown, I. Altman, and C. Foss. In *Journal of Personality and Social Psychology*, 1980, *39*, 1104. Copyright 1980 by the American Psychological Association. Reprinted by permission.

Figure 10-2, p. 290, from "Compensatory Responses to Crowding: Effects of Personal Space Intrusion and Privacy Reduction," by C.I. Greenberg and I.J. Firestone. In *Journal of Personality and Social Psychology*, 1977, *35*, 644. Copyright 1977 by the American Psychological Association. Reprinted by permission.

Table 10-3, p. 294, from "The Role of Attribution in the Experience of Crowding," by S. Worchel and S.M.L. Yohai. In *Journal of Experimental Social Psychology*, 1979, *15*, 91. copyright © 1979 by Academic Press. Reprinted by permission.

Table 10-4, p. 296, from *An Introduction to Ecological Psychology*, by A.W. Wicker. Copyright © 1979 by Wadsworth, Inc. Reprinted by permission of the publisher, Brooks/Cole Publishing Co., Monterey, California.

Box, p. 298, from the *Richmond News Leader*, November 12, 1979, p. 14. Reprinted by permission.

Chapter 11

Box, p. 314, Copyright © 1933, 1961, by James Thurber. From *My Life and Hard Times,* published by Harper & Row. Reprinted by permission.

Table 11-1, p. 317, from "The Human Choice: Individuation, Reason and Order Versus Deindividuation, Impulse, and Chaos," by P.G. Zimbardo. In W.J. Arnold and D. Levine (Eds.), *Nebraska Symposium on Motivation*, 1969. Copyright © 1969 by the University of Nebraska Press. Reprinted by permission.

Chapter 12

Chapter 13

Chapter 14

Chapter 15

Name Index

Subject Index